# Frontispiece Map

Central Italy, 1494–1598

**Other books by Paul Oppenheimer**

*Before a Battle and Other Poems*
*Beyond the Furies: new poems*
*The Birth of the Modern Mind: Self, Consciousness and the
    Invention of the Sonnet*
*Blood Memoir, or The First Three Days of Creation* (fiction)
*Evil and the Demonic: A New Theory of Monstrous Behaviour*
*The Flame Charts: new poems*
*In Times of Danger* (poems)
*Infinite Desire: A Guide to Modern Guilt* (UK title: *An Intelligent Person's Guide
    to Modern Guilt*)
*Rubens: A Portrait* (biography)
*Till Eulenspiegel: His Adventures* (translation)

# Machiavelli

## *A Life Beyond Ideology*

Paul Oppenheimer

continuum

**Continuum International Publishing Group**

| | |
|---|---|
| The Tower Building | 80 Maiden Lane |
| 11 York Road | Suite 704 |
| London | New York |
| SE1 7NX | NY 10038 |

www.continuumbooks.com

First published 2011

British Library Cataloguing-in-Publication Data
A catalogue record for this book is available from the British Library.

ISBN: 978-1-8472-5221-0

Typeset by Fakenham Prepress Solutions, Fakenham, Norfolk NR21 8NN
Printed and bound in India

# Contents

## III. INTO A TUSCAN EXILE

## IV. EPILOGUE: THE HISTORICAL AFTERGLOW
### 293

# List of illustrations

**Map**

(Every reasonable effort has been made to credit properly the pictures and other reproductions. Errors should be understood as unintentional and on citation to be corrected in future editions).

# Preface

If the Renaissance marks a time when a novel fascination with change, motion and transformation begins to take hold among educated men and women across Europe, Machiavelli stands out as coolly interested in all three. Social transformation fills his pages. Metamorphosis dominates his view of history. War is unpredictable, strategy fragile, goals untenable.

Change can be a ruthless dictator. It trashes promises, reverses griefs and alters the certainty of facts. Theoreticians have their work cut out for them. This biography seeks to evoke the life and discoveries of one of the world's most mesmeric modern theoreticians, who was also a diplomat, philosopher, historian, playwright and poet, and who responded to change with courage, liveliness, enthusiasm and clarity.

It thus fits in with my earlier biography of Peter Paul Rubens, who roughly one hundred years later, in the seventeenth century, came to view beauty as a process. Machiavelli may rank among the first to view society in the same way. Where Rubens sought in his paintings to depict the universality of motion, and so anticipated the discovery of the laws of motion of his contemporary Galileo, whom he may have known, Machiavelli opened an important door on modernity by uncovering patterns of continuous, if not inevitable, social and historical restlessness. The work of the political and military thinker complements that of the artist. Each also owes a good deal to an emerging fashion in self-conscious expression coupled with silent reading. My somewhat earlier book, *The Birth of the Modern Mind: Self, Consciousness and the Invention of the Sonnet*, sought to describe its origins in the Italian *duecento*, or the thirteenth century.

Little if anything can be achieved without the generous contributions of others. Gifted scholars and writers have always been drawn to Machiavelli, and I am happy to acknowledge their assistance, both here and in the notes and bibliography. Theirs has been superb company to keep.

I have also been fortunate in my libraries, in New York with the research facilities of the New York Public Library, and at the City University of New York, especially City College and The Graduate Center, and elsewhere, at Princeton and Columbia Universities, and outstandingly in Florence, at the exquisite Biblioteca Nazionale Centrale and the Archivio di Stato di Firenze. Special thanks are due Pamela Gillespie, City College's Chief Librarian, who on occasion came up with all sorts of necessary rescues.

I am infinitely indebted to my editor-publisher Robin Baird-Smith. His astute and patient guidance has fundamentally improved these pages. My gratitude for his professionalism, sensitivity and expertise is great indeed. His assistant, Rhodri Mogford, has likewise proved inestimably helpful.

So have many colleagues and friends, among them Ed Breslin, with numerous suggestions; Fred Reynolds, former Dean of the Arts and Humanities at City College; his successor, Acting Dean Geraldine Murphy; and Josh Wilner, Mark Mirsky, Elizabeth Mazzola, Linsey Abrams, Renata Miller, Harold Veeser, Felicia Bonaparte, Barry Wallenstein, Jack Barschi, David Armstrong, Harry Rolnick, Stella Dong, Simon Sheridan, Anthony Rudolf, Lorenzo Clemente *e la sua moglie*. Federica K. Clementi came up with splendid insights into the diction of Machiavelli's early sonnets, Mariapaola Gritti, my research assistant, with useful information on Renaissance dress and culinary habits. A sabbatical leave, offering me the chance to do my own extended research in Italy and New York, made the work itself possible, and I am grateful to the City University of New York for providing it.

I remain more than grateful to Andras Hamori and William E. Coleman, of Princeton University and The Graduate Center of the City University, who read and checked the typescript, weeding out errors and proposing significant alterations. Their contributions have been of enormous importance, though I cheerfully lay claim to all defects. My son Ben, and his wife Alicia, and my daughter Julie, and her husband Dan, refreshed the months and years with their encouragement. Most of all, my wife Assia kept saving the day every day, reading and raising crucial questions through hours both dark and light, and insisting, when I had my doubts, that the push forward might be worth the candle. To her, as ever, my limitless gratitude, and more.

P.O.
New York, 2011

# Introduction: Modern Evil and The Sack of Rome

Machiavelli was the first philosopher to define politics as treachery. This is not to say that he approved of treachery, only that he wished to describe politics as various forms of it. That he set out to do so, however, is no doubt why for almost five hundred years the single most influential of all modern political thinkers, as this biography hopes to show, has himself been described as revolting, nauseating, unprincipled and evil.[1]

Many will no doubt have trouble admitting, or having it put to them, that the method according to which they are governed, whether in democracies, republics, monarchies, dictatorships, tribes, communes, bureaucracies or other systems of sovereignty, requires for its perpetuation an unavoidable mixture of hypocrisy and betrayal. Even more may deny that political stability depends on deceit, ambush, violence, murder and lies, or that this is as true of the most decent as of the most indecent governments, that none of them is exempt.

One can, to be sure, disagree with Machiavelli's premise, that all types of government require malfeasance, and utopians, idealists and moralizing others, who prefer to believe that ethics must now and then reign supreme, set out to do so. It is impossible to deny the fascination of the famous Florentine philosopher-playwright's insight, however, or of his piercing and steady attraction because of it. In fact Machiavelli expands on the subject by arguing that there is no reason to be hypocritical about hypocrisy, and so no point in denying the supple importance of ruthlessness, if not outright evil, in parsing the political relations of human beings: this if anything seems to have been the theme of his life.

It seems also to have formed the atmosphere gathering into the months surrounding his death, which looked to confirm his political convictions in a grotesque display of torture and carnage: the sack of Rome, commencing on 6 May 1527. A yellow fog, thick enough on the ground that morning to hide the movement of Spanish troops through an abandoned Roman house abutting the city's outer wall, camouflaged the footsteps of a horrifying assault. This was soon to obliterate the remnants of ancient Roman grandeur and the city's medieval magnificence, leaving behind mere ruins of the past and ruins of ruins, in bleak ways marking the end of the Italian Renaissance while ushering in the modern age, a major thrust of the pages to come.[2]

At the head of an army that appeared formidable even by today's standards, or some 22,000 men, including cavalry, the dashing and clever French Charles, Duc de Bourbon, sported his signature whites and a lush cream-coloured helmet-plume. He had advanced down the Italian peninsula from Milan towards Rome over five months, stirring up a stewpot of grief as he went.[3] Slaughter, pillage, the burning of towns and villages, mass rapes, estate-burnings – all accompanied by blackmail, theft, the humiliation of priests and local governments and kidnappings – had left a grisly trail behind his international mishmash of an army. Despite its initial discipline and official loyalty to the Holy Roman Emperor, the Spanish King Charles V, it consisted of competing factions from Germany, the Low Countries (then under Spanish rule), Spain itself, Italy and imperial France. Georg von Frundsberg, the adept and renowned fifty-four-year-old German commander, had contributed 12,000 of his *Landsknechte*, most of them Lutheran. Many were eager for revenge on a Roman papacy viewed as insulting to Christians everywhere for its out-of-control dissipation and corruption.[4]

The fog-beshrouded Roman *campagna*, stretching for miles round the cowering, half-oblivious city, and bathing its turrets in a reflected yellow glow, seemed no less hospitable to the 5,000 Spanish troops under the Marquis of Vasto, Alfonso de Avalos d'Aquino, or the 3,000 Italian under Gian d'Urbino, or the young Prince of Orange riding at the head of his 800 light cavalry, together with an additional 3,500 men bearing 700 lances between them.[5]

Still, no one expected that Rome's walls could be breached with ease, or breached at all. Bourbon himself, according to the contemporary historian Luigi Guicciardini, was by now in charge of a motley gang of soldiers ill-prepared for battle. He had 'arrived at Rome on the fifth of May, 1527, at 5 p.m., with his entire [force], but with such a severe shortage of supplies that he couldn't have lasted two days.' His mercenary soldiers were hungry, enraged at not having been paid and ragged.[6]

The Roman walls themselves, or with greater exactitude, the Aurelian Wall, continued as in ancient times to stretch in more or less good condition over some thirteen miles. It reached an average height of fifty feet, gathering an insolent twelve-foot-thick belt around the ancient rim of the old metropolis.

Until its fall in the fifth century, the city had housed some 2.2 million people. Since then it had seen its population shrink to a mere 53,000. Once all-mighty, but now no longer imposing from a military point of view, it remained in the sheltering luxuriance of the papacy an avaricious army's prize of prizes. Contracted sharply behind its wall, it gleamed with Renaissance churches, cathedrals, libraries, paintings, statuary and new villas for its Popes, as well as the unearthly radiance of the latest Renaissance art. The art included some of the most superb achievements of Michelangelo, Botticelli, Cellini and Raphael. It bespoke a legendary fame, glamour, delicacy and notoriety reminiscent of posh papal feasts on the one hand and orgiastic papal dinner parties on the other.[7]

The wall had just been ordered repaired by the latest Medici Pope, Clement VII, though work on various damaged areas was still unfinished. A domineering defensive structure, especially given the city's reduction in size, it encircled large grassed-over territories, and even villages, beneath which lay buried piles of unexamined treasures, among them parts of Nero's Golden Palace on the Palatine. Crammed in at various points behind the wall hummed a complex beehive of narrow, crowded streets and filthy alleys, though its bastions looked as trim as ever, with 353 hoary towers and 14 lofty, closed gates. Rome seemed as secure within its long-standing protections as amid the glittering robes of its spiritual officials.[8]

The modern viewer's attentiveness to that morning's assault, though, rapidly comes to focus on a single jagged corner of the crenellated battlement, and on just one house ravaged by its single man-high hole. This was swiftly widened by Spanish troops who began to climb and then scramble through it. Astonishment gave way to opportunity. In minutes there spread out before their eyes, untouched and available, if fogged-over and silent, the essence of the Western world's despised if adored, respected, admired and palpable heart.

If Rome's population seemed sizeable by sixteenth-century standards (that of London amounted to 100,000, of Venice 85,000), its available army consisted of a mere 30,000 Roman and foreign troops, plus 3,000 artisans recruited just a few days earlier, most of whom had little interest in fighting. On the other hand, the Spanish troops entering at the deserted house, and hoisting themselves over the wall at Porta Torrione, as von Frundsberg's lansquenets succeeded in doing with scaling ladders near the fort at Santo Spirito, had no notion of the weak forces opposing them.[9]

Fierce resistance sprang up anyway in the quarter known as the Borgo, where the Pope's remaining Swiss Guard held off imperial troops for over an hour.

Their object was to put up a solid defence at the fortress of Castel Sant'Angelo, within which Clement could be expected to take refuge in an emergency, and where, as news of the invasion spread, hundreds of priests, bishops and cardinals, their skirts and capes flapping, began to rush in desperation.[10]

Nor had the Spanish assault at Porta Torrione come without its massive shock. Eyewitnesses reported a tense pause, an ominous hesitation before the smudgy apparition of the wall – a bizarre halt in advance of their releasing a suppressed anger into what were to be some of the most outrageous events of the European sixteenth century.

A number of witnesses to what happened were both important in their own right and participants. The twenty-six-year-old Benvenuto Cellini, already recognized as a brilliant gold- and silversmith and sculptor, was in Rome that day. Regarding himself as much a swordsman and soldier as a sculptor, he had set out from Piero del Bene's palace, where he was staying, with Piero's son Alessandro, to reconnoitre the wall at Campo Santo, where Bourbon's army was attempting to break into the city with scores of ladders made of vine poles.

The fog along the path at the top of the wall reduced their visibility to less than six feet. As it cleared for a moment, Cellini, Alessandro and two other men who joined up with them came across the bodies of several soldiers shot dead by the invaders. Cellini suggested that they pull back as there was 'nothing to be done ... you see the enemies are mounting and our men are in flight.' When Alessandro panicked, however, and started to shout, Cellini changed his mind, at once intent on performing 'some action worthy of a man,' or at least inspiring his friend, and raised his arquebus, the primitive, single-round Renaissance musket usually incapable of much accuracy, telling the others to take aim as well.[11]

What followed, amid the flurry of the couple of shots each that they fired, remains a matter of dispute. It seems clear that the Duke of Bourbon, with his helmet and plume visible through the ranks of his men attempting to raise and climb the ladders, was hit at least once and fell back.

What is unclear is whether Cellini fired the crucial round. He himself makes no such claim, simply noting that 'one of our shots killed the Constable of Bourbon,' who remained alive for some seconds, or long enough to exhort his men with the selflessness and concern expected of a Renaissance nobleman: 'Cover me up, soldiers, so the enemy doesn't find out about my death, and get on with the battle, courageously. My death must not deprive you of so sure and hard-won a victory.'[12] Moved and thrilled, if grieving, those nearest him resumed the attack. In minutes, tens of thousands of soldiers swept cheering, shooting and slashing over the wall, and began to surge in a cascade through the streets beyond.

With Bourbon's leaderless army hot on their heels, Cellini and his friends raced into the Castel Sant'Angelo. There he was speedily placed under the command of Giuglio Ferrara, who had taken over the sole artillery battery. Cellini spent the day, and well into the night, helping to supervise and reload a battery of cannon while directing their angles of fire at the foreign troops attempting to establish a siege around the ancient Roman fortress, which soon drew over three thousand refugees behind its turrets. Pope Clement himself, as Cellini discovered, had made it in only with difficulty, puffing along the exposed gallery that connected the castle with the Vatican, as Cardinal Pompeo Colonna tossed a monsignore's violet cloak and cap over his bulk to hide him from the soldiers below, who would have shot him on sight.[13]

Meanwhile, out in the streets, a macabre spectacle presented itself: a terrified army pursued by gangs of killers, and with both surging among vivid new works of art depicting a bygone and obsolete heroism: scores of paintings of scenes extracted from ancient legends and Greek myths and over the previous couple of years painted onto the facades of the most expensive Roman mansions: Horatius Cocles and Mucius Scaevola saving Rome centuries earlier through deeds of soldierly defiance, Perseus turning his enemies to stone by flashing the decapitated head of Medusa into their eyes, Hercules strutting his muscular arrogance through his twelve labours: the ennobled past seemed devoid of meaning amid the wave of vulgar modern obliteration.[14]

The sack proper did not get underway till Tuesday, 7 May, even if on the first day some 8,000 people, or almost one sixth of the population, were murdered. The *tufo*, or orange-red stone, volcanic in origin, and forming the base of Rome's famed Seven Hills, picked up splashes of crimson as thirteen cardinals, one of them heaved up in a basket, scooted behind Ferrara's defensive artillery at the Castel Sant'Angelo.

Fires broke out in Rome's *piazze*. The great houses shook as their doors were torn off their hinges. The owners had fled. Within days, a pike had carved Luther's name into one of Raphael's frescoes at the Vatican. A city-wide smashing-up began, of bells, chalices, candlesticks, holy relics, clocks, religious paintings – with everything mangled, shredded, pulverized. The gem-studded vestments of the priests, found in the churches and pried free of their precious stones, were turned over to prostitutes for their daily use.[15]

The unrestrained soldiers raped scores of nuns, bartering for them with each other on rolls of dice. Soldiers took a humiliating pleasure in stripping the clerics, pummelling them into holding black masses, jeering at them for doing so and then chopping off their fingers for their rings. The poor were murdered because they had no money, the rich kidnapped and held for ransom. A helpless businessman, unable to cough up enough ready cash, was roped to a tree and tortured by ripping off one of his fingernails per day till he died.[16]

Amid the rioting, the stench of corpses left rotting in the streets and alleys, the smell of uncollected sewage, the defecation and urine, the frazzled clothes, knifed tapestries and broken furniture, and in days the deadly spreading of typhus and other diseases, the cries and lamentations, it seems doubtful that the killers, not to mention the Romans themselves, were aware of pouring through a glass membrane of history separating one era from another, of crossing a rare and significant boundary of the historical world.

Some, among them a few thoughtful artists such as Giuglio Clovio and Sebastiano del Polombo, who fled and survived but never painted in the same way again – either with their previous confidence in a world of secure relations, or even in the possibility of a compassionate community of people – may have divined the outline of a stark new shadow. It seemed to indicate the transition from one type of light, or illumination, to another, and the city's descent into a peculiar sort of darkness. A few Romans may have guessed.[17]

What seems clear enough is that prophecies, including at least one by Machiavelli himself, abounded, each foretelling a disaster that, as the English King Henry VIII wrote to one Cardinal Cibo a few weeks later, on 10 July, must be regarded as the world's most 'criminal' of acts: 'that those who had once been pledged to the Christian religion should exert themselves to destroy her.'

An eye-witness, Pierio Valeriano (1477–1558?), who knew Rome both before and after the sack, recalls in his bitter dialogue *il Contarenus sive de Litteratorum infelicitate* (*The Misfortunes of Writers*, published in 1529) how the droves of murders, and, over many days, suicides, blotted out the complex aspirations of the Renaissance. Not only artistic but literary life, along with multitudes of Roman authors, simply vanished into the slaughter and uproar.[18] Valeriano reports that though traces of literary culture survived, Latin never quite regained its previous prominence. The decline of classical Greek, already in progress despite the setting up of a Greek printing press in 1499 by Giovanni de'Medici, who was to become Pope Leo X, seemed guaranteed.

Luigi Guicciardini blamed the universal destruction on those venal 'ecclesiastical rulers' and other Italians who 'persist in effeminate and abominable vices,' by which he meant homosexual and other forms of illicit sex, on Rome's 'ignorance' of foreign malice growing without restraint over the previous thirty years, and on 'the wrath of God': 'Consider how small a number of foreigners fearlessly ranges through our miserable Italy every day, assaulting our cities, taking them with ease, sacking them without mercy and with little cost to themselves, then occupying them in happiness and security as long as it suits them. Certainly we should be ashamed of our cowardice and our failure to resist.'[19]

Whether incited by Roman helplessness or more selfish motives, a popular Sienese religious fanatic, Brandano, whose reddish skin, blowsy red hair and skeletal appearance lent him an aura of defiant doom, had confronted Clement VII before Saint Peter's on Holy Thursday, or 18 April.

Half-naked, but calling out to the crowd assembled to hear the Pope offer his traditional blessing, swinging from the statue of Saint Paul, Brandano had taunted Clement as the 'bastard of Sodom,' and proclaimed that 'for thy sins Rome shall be destroyed. Repent and turn thee! If thou wilt not believe me, in fourteen days thou shalt see it!'

Clement had ordered his arrest, but incarceration did nothing to stem the wave of hideous pronouncements that gushed out of his prison cell, or the spreading popular conviction that he must have foreknowledge of some impending and macabre Roman calamity. To Guicciardini and many Romans, the perilous atmosphere seemed confirmed by other portents: a mule that gave birth in the Cancelleria, the collapse of chunks of the Aurelian Wall connecting the papal palace with Castel Sant'Angelo, 'a lightning bolt [that lifted] the Infant from the arms of a highly revered statue of Our Lady in the Church of S. Maria in Trastevere,' with the result that the figure of the holy Child was broken and Mary's crown shattered, a Eucharistic wafer mysteriously 'thrown to the ground' in the pope's chapel – each of these, as the superstitious chronicler noted, 'strong signs that might reasonably frighten any Christian.'[20]

The persistence of omens and prophecies also remains revealing not merely as a guide to the general tenor of the times but as a modern spotlight exposing some of the chief struggles of Machiavelli's life. During the terror, as among the centuries before and after it, belief in omens, prophecies, witchcraft, demons, ghosts, magic, astrology, necromancy and miracles (or God's interference in nature) disturbed most European brains. Any trust in rational and empirical investigations, though common enough among merchants, architects, farmers, lawyers and weavers as they engaged in their trades, seemed abandoned once they turned their attention to politics, love, disease and war, or just about anything else.

In the twentieth century Adolf Hitler, an enthusiastic reader of Machiavelli, is reported to have consulted astrologers before launching his armies on *Blitzkrieg* invasions. If Napoleon cared little for prophecy, he too read Machiavelli, though perhaps as a rational nostrum, as did philosophers such as Hegel and Fichte, and Cardinal Richelieu, Queen Christina of Sweden, the leaders of the Italian *Risorgimento*, Frederick the Great, Bismarck, Mussolini, Clemenceau, Lenin and Stalin. Most Renaissance commanders sought out star-gazers as a matter of course: Bourbon huddled with his personal astrologers before cancelling his truce with Clement VII, on 28 March 1527, after which he decamped to the south to carry out his attack on Rome. Not much later, Clement remarked, 'I well deserve any calamity that might befall me.'[21]

In the German north, Martin Luther prophesied, on grounds of religious corruption, a savage end to what he viewed as Roman dissipation. In Florence, and later in other Italian cities to which he was sent as a diplomat after years of painful civic exile, Machiavelli provided a more restrained forecast. It seemed typical of his age-defying empirical style of analysis, though it was expressed in the conventional terms of religious prophecy, and had more to do with the possibility of a papal military defeat along the entire length of the Italian peninsula.

As early as November 1526, he found himself writing to Francesco Guicciardini, a well-known lawyer and future Italian historian, the papal governor of Piacenza and other towns, the brother of Luigi, and his own friend, that he

> remained in Modena for two days and talked with a prophet who maintained, with witnesses, that he had predicted the pope's flight and the [military] campaign's futility; and again he says that all the bad times are not yet over – both we and the [P]ope will suffer greatly during them.[22]

On 16 April 1527, he confided to his more intimate friend Francesco Vettori, this time during a stay in Forlì:

> I love my native city [Florence] more than my own soul; and I tell you as a result of the experience I have had over sixty years that I do not believe there were ever more

difficult problems than these [having to do with Bourbon's invading army], where peace is necessary and war cannot be renounced, and where we have a prince [Pope Clement VII] on our hands who can barely meet the needs of either peace by itself or war by itself.[23]

Actually, Machiavelli was not sixty but fifty-eight as he scribbled these apprehensive lines, perhaps exaggerating his age for effect as was sometimes his way, even if he seemed frailer than usual and may have been sinking into one of his miserable bouts with the recurring peritonitis for which he had been taking aloe pills over several months. The pills provided a pernicious medical treatment that, along with the illness itself, may have exhausted and killed him at home in his native city on 21 June, just six weeks after the tragedy in the south.

It may thus be understood that he cannot have been altogether surprised by the grim events in Rome. This probability seems likely, even if speculation is to be shunned in a biography intended to let him step forward into his own world on his own terms – or with his severe yet hardy presence pitted not so much into his times as against them, and with the contradictions of his life expressed as openly as the invasion racing through the Roman streets in early May.

In each of his books, and not just in his paradoxical if still unpublished masterpiece *The Prince*, he had predicted the downfall of any political state which lacked three crucial elements: a defensive army consisting of its own citizens rather than mercenaries, a leader more dreaded than loved, but above all respected, and a foundation in organized religion, or at least in spiritual values.

His premise throughout had been military, civil and spiritual reliability and not the unique qualities of the soldiers, leader or values. Nor had he argued for their flawlessness: soldiers, leaders and spirituality might each be wobbly, or as many as two of the three might be. If they were present, the state might still survive.

The sticking place had been that without some streak of naïve trust, the essential political instrument of treachery could not be brought into play. No survival at all without deceit, he had argued, drawing his conclusion from a heap of evidence both ancient and modern. No state could muddle through without its opportunities for betrayal.

*The Prince* itself, which was to appear in print only five years later, in 1532, well after his death, but whose circulation in manuscript copies had already established his reputation as an advocate of evil and murder for the sake of power, had itself been composed in a treacherous milieu of social anarchy. This point needs stressing because of a curious difference between the social worlds in which most political thinkers ever since have done their work and that in which he did so. Nearly all have beavered away amid fairly peaceful societies, while he was forced to seek out rare islands of contemplation amid a sea of blustery disorders.

Hume, Hobbes, Locke, Jefferson, the sixteenth-century Jean Bodin, Franklin, Hamilton, Acton, Burke, Danton, Robespierre, John Stuart Mill, Karl Marx, Engels, Jaurès (the eloquent French socialist leader, dying on the eve of the World War that he denied could take place because it would be contrary to the class interests of working people), along with lesser political (if enthralling psychological) thinkers such as Max Weber and Freud, had emerged from stable, and in the case of Karl Marx, well-policed environments. Often their insights saw the public light of day before their creators found themselves confronted by social and military catastrophes.

For Machiavelli the situation seemed reversed. His political reflections apparently coalesced only after he was dismissed from a long-held government advisory post. As he began writing *The Prince* in 1512, his social and political surroundings, once firm-seeming and richly appointed, descended into a shambles. Riots, battles, random killings, assassinations, sieges, abductions – all stormed almost at his elbow as he tried to make his way with his typical careful haste through the knotty strategic problems of princely power, as well as his *Discourses*, his *Art of War* and his *Florentine Histories*. If he concentrated on connections between politics and slaughter as he wrote, he did so not simply because they fascinated him but because he could see their relationship wherever he looked.

Italy itself, as he knew at first hand, was a land 'vanquished, despoiled, torn, devastated' – or sick and ailing, as he described it in his letters, an ill-compacted group of city states not so much impoverished as unceasingly plundered.[24] As a result, and from a grotesquely positive point of view, but one fundamental to the correctness of his insights because Italian society offered such cruel contrasts in education, wealth, poverty, security and depravity, his own culture seemed an ideal if unusual laboratory in which to study politics in the raw, so to speak, or politics without ideology.

But can such a condition have existed? An assumption of some historians is that any chance of a social and psychological breakdown so complete that people can lead lives, no matter how jumbled, without any ideology, or governing system of beliefs, is unimaginable. Politics, history and by extension the most delicate aspects of human behaviour are viewed as regulated by attitudes, or a mix of ideologies, or so-called 'unstable' ideologies, with the latter teetering towards breakdown and replacement because subject to batterings by conscious and unconscious social forces.[25]

But *no* ideologies? Everyone, it is argued, can no more escape the influence of at least implicit systems of ideas, or set-in-place ideological systems, than he or she can live outside societies governed by laws and rules: systems of belief and values reign everywhere over human lives, doing so with unerring determinism.[26]

In response, it should be noted that this claim seems to make no logical sense, or that it may as formulated have no meaning. The reason, as Karl Popper (*b*.1902) long ago demonstrated, is that no proposition can properly be understood as either meaningful or even comprehensible unless its opposite, or its falsifiability, is also conceivable. The assertion that ideologies are ubiquitous thus seems as self-contradictory as proposing that absolute truths cannot exist. It is equivalent to maintaining that sickness is universal, and so finding oneself unable to distinguish between sickness and health and unable to define either. While this sort of confusion may have gained acceptance in certain academic circles, it should be understood that, as will be seen, Machiavelli would have rejected it.[27]

Problems of trust, truth and reliability nonetheless remained challenges whose resolution he repeatedly sought. As a result, any new biography of him, beyond its attempt to paint his life in vital colours, and so to allow readers to see, feel, smell, taste and listen to his world as well as hear his voice with, it may be hoped, relatively fine tuning, ought to supply a comprehensive view of his intellectual adventures while relying on the superb work of earlier scholars. At a minimum it should promote an understanding of him as the first thinker to investigate incessant political change combined with political treachery. As he began to uncover the roles of each in the conduct of political states, and the influence of the irrational on both, his nuggety phrases, a bit like the chunks of some precious ore, began to shine forth as well, illuminating his conclusions.

Curiosity provoked style. Frustration invested awareness. Each induced his constant reconsideration of the irrational, together with its power to seduce, as keys to historical clarity. Each seemed abetted by encounters with his own contradictions, and this centuries before the Romantics and their successors in the social sciences began to move down parallel tracks.

In the meantime, in June 1527, Clement VII surrendered and was permitted to seek refuge in Citavecchia, though dozens of his prelates remained prisoners in the wrecked urban encampment that now surrounded the Castel Sant'Angelo, and in the darkness that had fallen inside the fortress itself, among whose disordered rooms hundreds lay sick and dying.[28]

In the company of Francesco Guicciardini, Machiavelli visited Orvieto, where he first learned of the circumstances of the sack and met frightened survivors, to whom he gave assistance. At the suggestion of Guicciardini, the Florentine city council sent him on to Citavecchia as well, by 22 May. The town had become the headquarters of Andrea Doria, the commander of the French fleet drawn up against the Spanish Charles V.[29]

The threat of Machiavelli's illness remained unknown to him, as did his future, which was not to provide him with more than a few additional weeks of life. He seems to have been unaware of his dilemma, however, as he returned home on horseback, assuming only that with Florence once again a republic, following on the flight of the Medici, he might be able to take up a position in the new government.

This was not to be. An appropriate post went to another former official, as had happened before and as his illness closed in.[30] If in late June he was buried in the Gothic Santa Croce church, where his pre-eminent mentor in poetry, if less so in political theory, Dante, was interred and where in 1564 his acquaintance Michelangelo would also be laid to rest, his last days were accompanied by the hushed drumbeat of the slight though definite renown that had come his way. It had little to do with politics. In the political world only his *Art of War* had brought him much real recognition. The wider notice had to do with his brilliant sex-comedy *Mandragola*, with which modern comedy if not modern theatre may be said to begin, and whose resonant theme is also treachery, if of the domestic type. His play had earned him an agreeable rush of applause, and run through a number of productions.

In the end he seems to have been amused by the paradox that while his ambition for political success had produced no genuine rewards, or so he wrongly guessed, his gamble on a career as a playwright had led to a muted glory.

In the end, too, the paradox seems appropriate to his appearance: his twisty nose, his gaunt, recessive cheeks, the hint of passionate mischief cast over his rumpled features and especially the smooth regard of his eyes. In the few nearly contemporary portraits that survive, a faint polish suffuses his tawny complexion: no hint of rawness, ruthlessness or injustice – just his remarkable precision, his wit, his often bawdy good humour and the gloss of a patient, triumphant irony.

I

*Machiavelli and the Changing Universe*

# Family and Growing Up

The mystery of his life begins in 1469, with his birth into a family of down-at-heels Florentine prominence, if not nobility. A yearning to belong to the nobility, or even to some decayed and irrelevant noble family, coupled with the likelihood that there may have existed genuine links between the Machiavelli family and the ruling lords of Montespertoli, a wisp of a hamlet 33 kilometres southwest of Florence. To satisfy it meant reaching back a few centuries, and it seems to have rippled with shabby eagerness through the Machiavellis' daily life. Powerlessness ached for extravagance. Respectability seemed to slip through their fingers.

Bernardo, Niccolò's father, and himself a lawyer, though oddly without any practice to speak of, took pride in tracing his family's lineage in Montespertoli back to 1120, with a definite glance farther back, to 1040. According to a fourteenth-century contested will, the Machiavelli line had mingled with that of the insignificant lords of Castellani, as they were called, on the death of Ciango d'Agnolo of the Castellani, in 1393.[1] Even earlier, and on the Machiavellis' side, or so Bernardo was convinced, the family's ancestry extended as far back as one Malchiavello, who had lived in Montespertoli in 1040. The Castellani, whose castle, together with their seigniorial rights in and around Montespertoli, came to be at issue with the Machiavelli during a court hearing over the will of Ciango's father, traced their own lineage back to one Dono Machiavelli and his son Buoninsegna, who could himself be traced to 1120.[2]

When, as followed on the Machiavelli winning their adjudication over Agniolo de Castellani's will in 1426–7, they assumed title to somewhat less than half the Castellani estates, they also assumed a part share of the rest of the Castellani legacy. The greater portion continued to be held by the Parte Guelpha, or, loosely, the Tuscan citizens bloc of the day. The Machiavellis' chief benefit from this adjudication seems to have been trivial: they were permitted to display their coat of arms, but only discreetly, on Montespertoli buildings, including churches and the local castle.

An appropriate inference is that the common descent of the Machiavelli and the lords of Castellani remains a shaky proposition, more so than Bernardo Machiavelli's enthusiasm for it. A strained aristocratic connection provided still less than before in the way of income and rights by the time Niccolò Machiavelli was born, with the latter consisting of the right to control the public scales and commercial measures in Montespertoli, plus an opportunity to exhibit the Machiavelli coat of arms over a well in the marketplace. The rest of the Castellani property, including the castle, had decades before been divided and dispersed among the rival branches of the two families. In the Machiavellis' case, at least, grasping at noble connections implied picking about among failed fantasies.[3]

Far surer, though not without its own implications of strain and even shadings of terror, was the Machiavelli link with Girolamo d'Agnolo Machiavelli (1415–60), one of Niccolò Machiavelli's more intimate ancestors: he belonged to the parallel Lorenzo branch of the family and was Bernardo's second cousin, a professor of both genuine renown and scandalous notoriety.

Girolamo had taught law at the University of Florence between 1435 and 1440, where it is to be supposed that Bernardo, Niccolò Machiavelli's father, had studied for his own law degree, possibly during the same years.

In the late 1450s, Girolamo began to profess defiant anti-Medici senti-ments precisely at a time when speaking out against Florence's leading, most powerful and often ruthless family could have lethal consequences. As a signif-icant member of an anti-Medici political group and known legal expert, and potentially dangerous to the government by virtue of his academic authority, Girolamo was arrested on 3 August 1458 and denounced for repudiating as corrupt several Medici economic policies as well as demanding the restoration of citizens' rights to criticize, or freedom of speech.

As was customary, he was at first tortured, and was then sentenced to banishment in Avignon for a period of ten years. It should probably be noted that for its disgrace alone, banishment in Renaissance Florence, as in ancient Athens, was regarded as a fate worse than death. His brothers, Piero and Francesco d'Agnolo, along with other members of the group, were likewise arrested and banished. Francesco was dispatched to Florence's feared municipal prison, built in 1299, and known as the Stinche, or dungeons, since 1302. He was beheaded at the Stinche in 1459. Girolamo fared little better. He tried to flee but was seized at Lunigiana, near the mouth of the River Magra, not far from Pisa.

Accused of forming a criminal conspiracy aimed at the Medici, he too was consigned to the Stinche, where he met his death, apparently by strangulation, in 1460 – leaving behind an extensive legal library, unusual for a period just prior to the introduction of the printing press in Florence, when purchasing even the least important manuscript books was expensive. The library, along with the rest of his property, was confiscated, depriving his wife and small son of a potentially substantial inheritance. His true legacy, however, may have been a ghostly influence on the life of the young Niccolò, with a suggestive effect on his future that today may only be surmised.[4]

On the other hand, Girolamo was by no means the only Machiavelli to attract much public attention, whether distasteful or estimable, in Florentine political circles. Several of his cousins, among them Alessandro Filippo Machiavelli, attained posts in city government, doing so despite Girolamo's abasement and ill repute, which could then have led to their rejection.

Notable along these lines was his cousin Paolo di Giovanni Machiavelli, elected to the ruling *balìa*, or municipal authority, in 1466, 1471 and 1480. Paolo was even elected *Gonfaloniere di giustizia*, or Standard-Bearer of Justice, or head of state, for two months in 1478, and accepted a top appointment in the Florentine navy (as a republican city state including many smaller cities and towns, Florence maintained a navy), serving as a *Capitano* in Pisa in 1483, and Livorno in 1488.

Not even these accomplishments added up to the family's whole political story, if only because it seems clear that suspect, rebellious influences shadowed Niccolò's early life from the start. In 1458, to cite a pertinent instance, his father, Bernardo, married into the Benizzi family, everywhere understood as anti-Medici. Girolamo's brother Piero had married into the same family, whose house was located more or less across the street from Bernardo's. He and three of his brothers were exiled with Girolamo in that ominous year for so many of them, 1458, or twelve years before Niccolò's birth.

Another Benizzi brother, Matteo di Piero, had also been sentenced to exile some twenty years earlier by the Medici on their return to Florence from their own period of exile in 1434. With Niccolò Machiavelli's mother, Bartholomea, a young (and recently widowed; she had been married before) sister-in-law of five brothers exiled for political reasons, residing in the house where he was born and grew up, it seems inconceivable, though little is rock-solid here, that Niccolò did not drink in giddy tales of defiant struggle, futility, torture and courage with, so to speak, his mother's milk.[5]

Even the Machiavelli house, it appears, reflected stifled yearnings after defeated prominence. Located in Florence at the equivalent of 16 Via Guicciardini (today the Via Romana), it was an imposing-looking if modest-sized four-storey affair, one of a group of linked buildings, and perhaps former towers, and so in the fashion of the day termed a *palazzo*, on the south bank of the Arno, almost at the entrance to the Ponte Vecchio, the oldest of the city's bridges, dating to 1345 and built with its neat rows of shops lining each side of a narrow crossing road: it resembled only superficially the messy exhilaration of silver- and goldsmiths' shops to be seen there today.

Just past the bridge and across from a small *piazza* called Santa Felicità, with its unassuming church free-standing in its bare elegance (minus its famous Vasari passageway, which would be erected only in the century to come), the Machiavellis' *palazzo* was politically positioned, it appears, in the Oltrarno neighborhood, where many Guelph families settled on returning from exile after their defeat by the Ghibellines in 1260. The families soon began to play vital roles in government, or as with the Machiavelli, to provide the city with over fifty government officials by the time Niccolò was born on 3 May 1469.[6]

Bernardo and his wife Bartholomea were about 42 and 31 respectively by then, Niccolò's two sisters, Primavera and Margherita, five and two; a brother, Totto, was born in 1475, when Niccolò was six. Surviving and revealing photographs of a destroyed, nineteenth-century model of a portion of one of the rooms of the house, most likely the large, ornate second-storey chamber used for dining and family amusements, are helpful, when compared, as here for the first time, with what is known about similar *palazzi*, in understanding the aspirations and domestic atmosphere in which Niccolò first came to know his world.

Two black and white pictures of the model (plate III), taken *c.*1898, show part of a wall, a ceiling and a door, each resplendent with an upper-class, sophisticated Florentine poshness. The wall, impressively, was frescoed by a Florentine master, Benozzo Gozzoli (1421/22–d. Pistoia 1497), most likely at the start of his career, which means that Niccolò would surely have known it in childhood. Benozzo was to collaborate with Fra Angelico on Pope Nicolas V's chapel in the Vatican, assist Ghiberti in the execution of the second door of his amazing baptistery, and later make spectacular contributions of other frescoes to the family chapel in the Medici palace.

Additional painting, of a frieze running above both door and wall, by an unknown artist, presents correspondingly extravagant work in the form of lush fruit trees. The lintels and the door jamb are done in the exquisite *pietra serena* style of gray sandstone indigenous to Tuscany. The door, in intarsia, an inlaid strips-of-wood method that arranges various hues side by side, complements the frieze. The ceiling's single beam (only one is shown) is delicately painted in repeated floral bunches. On the beam appears one of the three Machiavelli coats of arms: four long blue nails, each piercing a different central corner of a blue cross set into a white background.[7]

If little else is known about the interior of this one house of the several making up the Machiavelli *palazzo* – the house itself was deliberately destroyed by explosives in August 1944, during the German retreat north towards the end of the Second World War – the room's aura of Renaissance *élan*, interleaving an imaginative use of colour with a strong aesthetic sensibility and lingering hints of power and money, may be acknowledged as flattering their aristocratic ambience.

Its smart décor seems to elaborate the fact that both house and *palazzo*, or a siamese linking of buildings, had been owned by the Machiavelli family since the mid-fourteenth century, or for more than a hundred years by the time Niccolò was born. This was also the case with Bernardo's inherited small country estates and their steep farmland unfolding over fleecy, green-in-summer hills ten miles south of Florence, beyond the massive city gate today called the Porta Romana, though at the time the San Pietro Gattolino.[8]

If, as a boy wandering into the central room of the family's main house, Niccolò gazed up at the coat of arms, he no doubt understood, especially on growing older and beginning to wander through and explore his city, that his family's somewhat old-fashioned type of *palazzo* differed dramatically from the newer and more muscular ones being built or recently completed for far more powerful and wealthy families such as the Medici and Pitti.

Their city-block-sized, aggressive flaunting, combined with a placidity and a solid assertion of strapping financial and political dominance, outshone if not dismissed the medieval quaintness of the jumbled though not inconsiderable buildings in which he came to play, read and sleep. All of them harked back with a friendly collegiality to earlier, rural days in farming villages.

The house itself, for instance, still contained the old, rural, vaulted hall on its ground floor. Among urban families practising a trade – not the Machiavelli – this lower area would now have been used for work or as a shop. Casks of wine, as many as six fat standing ones of red alone, were kept there for coolness and easy access. They stood alongside bins and barrels for flax, olive oil, rye and wheat, perhaps meant as money-savers culled from Bernardo's two farms near his estate villa, or *albergaccio*, in Sant'Andrea in Percussina, the village among the hills south of the city. This villa was accessible on foot or by mule-drawn cart past the high Florentine walls with their gnarled battlements and the two enormous iron doors of each of the city gates, drawn shut at night and presided over by armed guards.

The second floor, containing the single room depicted in the destroyed model, would surely have been reserved for family life, or eating, bickering, washing up in traditional broad basins and relaxing. In similar houses this long room was often partitioned, as were the rooms in the upper storeys. The top storey was often set aside as the kitchen, allowing its fireplace and chimney, under the roof, to usher cooking smells and smoke into the street. As with similar houses, too, the windows were criss-crossed with stout bars against burglars, though mostly to keep the women from sneaking out.[9]

In his valuable if choppy and irregularly kept journal, or book of *ricordi* of memorable events, maintained from 1474, when Niccolò was five, to 1487, and which survives in the Florentine Biblioteca Riccardiana, Bernardo describes how his nephew-once-removed, Niccolò d'Alessandro, who headed another of the group of Machiavelli families residing at the *palazzo*, managed to squirm through the unbarred top-storey window next to the kitchen fireplace (*focolare di cucina*) to carry on with one of the servant girls: her own window, on a lower floor, had impassable bars.[10]

Along social and sexual lines as well, and for the sake of illuminating a bit of the bustle around the Machiavelli hearth and *palazzo*, it may be added that if local custom was followed, there would have been more than just a couple of servants: a serving woman, for instance, occupied a two-room apartment on the ground floor. The reason was that Florence was tricked out not only with servant women but slaves. It was ebulliently if miserably slave-garlanded, and some twelve to thirty per cent of all births registered in and around the city, even as far back as the fourteenth century, consisted of children born to slave mothers.

Slavery was legal, though it lacked all basis in race or religion, at least according to the official lists. The municipal legalization of slavery had begun in 1336, after the decimation of the servant as well as the general population following fierce outbreaks of the plague. Slaves were acquired from among the Tartars, Greeks, Russians, Turks, Circassians, Bosnians, Slavs, Cretans and even Moslems, though most were Christian. In Niccolò's day they were frequently imported. Younger slaves were deemed more valuable than older ones, girls more than boys.[11]

Slaves' clothing styles, as to a great extent the styles of others, were strictly controlled according to the prevailing sumptuary laws, vehemently but variously implemented straight across Europe. In Florence, these laws, whose purpose was to maintain class hierarchy by suppressing self-importance and arrogance through the purchase of luxurious, class-dismissive fashions, prevented female slaves as well as other servants from wearing *pianelle*, or high-heeled shoes of a flashy type then popular, or trains affixed to dresses or gowns, or bright, seductive colours.

While quite a few people, including indentured servants, sometimes flouted sumptuary laws, and with impunity, by, say, sporting a fur coat or gold earrings, slaves ran risks of beatings and imprisonment.[12]

Vicious beatings in any case, or slappings, kickings and punchings, together with buffeting spats and worse eruptions of violence, going as far as slaves poisoning their masters and vice versa, were not infrequent in Florence's crowded houses and *palazzi*, in which servants, slaves and groups of families such as the Machiavelli resided together in conjoined buildings.

Since ancient Roman and earlier Etruscan times, torture had been a built-in part of life. A not unfamiliar spectacle during Niccolò Machiavelli's boyhood was the public staging of city-authorized displays of drastic punishments, such as that which had taken place as long ago as 20 August 1379, of a female slave found guilty of poisoning her master with silver nitrate introduced into his enema. Sentenced to death, she was lugged through the streets in a cart as crowds looked on and as her skin was pried off with hot pincers, till arriving at the *piazza* designated for her execution, she was roasted alive.[13]

As Niccolò inspected the family coat of arms in the room lusciously frescoed by Benozzo Gozzoli, he may have found himself, like many other children and nearly everyone else, understanding quite a bit about the ambiguities and contradictions of domestic art and militaristic power, having seen them in action from a young age and witnessed their clashing and complementary absoluteness. As much was to be found in this not atypical specimen of fourteenth-century advice to housewives by one Fra Bernardino, a roving Sienese priest:

> If you don't get her used to doing all the work, she will become a little lump of flesh. Don't give her any time off, I tell you. As long as you keep her on the go, she won't waste her time leaning out of the window.[14]

If, as also happened, slaves were on occasion allowed to feel that they had become veritable members of their owners' families, among noble families or families with aristocratic pretensions their future remained unpredictable, though unpredictability could itself produce extraordinary compassion.

Alessandra Macinghis (?1407–71), from a family of successful merchants and marrying into the wealthy Strozzi, recorded with lugubrious commiseration the death of a slave alongside that of a neighbour, while describing the grim advance of Florentine poverty and plague in a letter of 2 November 1465, or just a few years before Niccolò's birth:

> It's been a hard year for poor men, and there's plague as well; several people have died of it in the last few days.... In Rimieri da Ricasoli's house his mother died of it, and then a slave and an illegitimate daughter.... So it is beginning, and it is winter. God help us.[15]

As Alessandra intimates, most of Florence's 45,000 people in the late fourteenth century, or throughout Niccolò's boyhood, even if they were not devout Christians and were perhaps persuaded of the dissipation and frivolity of their priests, saw their God as worried about slaves and others. They were convinced that divine justice existed for everyone.

Informed people – the majority – were also persuaded that they lived in an advanced republic. Though people today might not regard a slave society practising torture as progressive, governing committees and limited voting had long since been well established.

# 2

# Early Education

Niccolò's education, which started at the then usual age of seven, or perhaps the year before, and involved a series of tutors selected by his father, focused on politics, history, grammar and literary style. This approach was in no way eccentric. Among the more than one quarter of Florentine boys formally educated after the 1470s (unless girls came from noble families, they were unlikely to be taught outside the protection of their homes), most learned Latin, together with these and vocational subjects, such as accounting. For Latin they used a grammar book over a thousand years old, the *Donatello* (or as Bernardo termed it in his Tuscan dialect, the *Donadello*), *or Ars minor*, by Aelius Donatus.[1] Teaching, as elsewhere in Europe with this or a similar book, consisted of memorization through repetition, or for many, tedium leading into annoyance.

Here may be why, before considering any of the unquestionable advantages of Niccolò's way of learning, it seems necessary, especially if one wishes to understand its valuable influence on him, its strengths and even its beneficial intellectual and emotional results, to take account of two apparently unrelated phenomena: Florence's ivory and gold lights on his early tutorial mornings, which remain visible to this day, and the city's morning swallows, small, beautiful, unusual and also still to be seen.

Niccolò would have been sent off to school during the just-after-dawn hours (schools and schooling started early: his first tutorial visits began on 6 May 1476), as the sun bisected the claret-clear Florentine sky with its memorable, acute light. The rays shooting along the streets seemed brush strokes profiling the day. They matched in growing warmth his fascinated affection with the many passageways and high walls, and this with a mesmerized interest, it now seems evident, that must have increased over time. The city was a developing work of art, through whose cobblestoned *piazze*, with his noted irony perhaps flickering in his eyes even then, he moved in an awareness that he came from an old Florentine family whose history amid the scene spreading before him may have led into scepticism about his approaching schoolboy routine, possibly distracting him from any lasting commitment to scholarship.

For then as now the wild flocks of the city's swallows swarmed in their untidy and twisting bands, fluting, diving, soaring by their hundreds, unique to the place and even this part of central Italy. They looped at the centuries-old high watch towers, and at Giotto's *campanile*, which he had never seen finished beyond its second storey, with its ribbons of pink, green and white marble abutting Brunelleschi's *Duomo*, itself complete except for its entrance façade. The majestic eight-sided dome was just fifty years old and so relatively new. The swallows dashed through the morning's ivory lights. Their shifting dives curled past the Santa Felicità, just across from the windows of the family *palazzo*. They seemed to ignite the five o'clock dark and six o'clock shop-stirring, unless a rare summer rain had begun to fall.

By seven, though, and regardless of the weather, the Ponte Vecchio's shops would have opened, and the scattered *piazze*, fed by the night-freshened streets, began to breathe and whisper. Their activity mingled with his schooltime. They rose beside ground-in smells trundled in from the nearby farms, from the earth, from chunky troughs, from splintered hay.

Flocks of sheep and herds of cows, descending from the countryside, loafed across the terraced bridges over the Arno. Scores of mules appeared, gleaming, their sweaty backs and carts tipping now and then under the odd boar carcass. Other carts bent under boxes of vegetables whose greens and yellows, beneath fragile tomatoes turning misshapen amid an excess ripeness sucked out of the oozy Tuscan blend of hot sun and lava-enriched soil, shone against the granite and marble of the new palaces.

The richness of those mornings, especially at the Old Market (*Mercato Vecchio*), which was to be converted in the nineteenth century into the Piazza della Repubblica, poured through the poetry of Florence's town crier and bell-ringer of some decades earlier, Antonio Pucci (*c.*1310–88):

> Apothecaries and grocers put their wares on show;
> Traders in pots and pitchers can be found –
>
>       * * *
>
> Stalls elsewhere, though, deal in much fairer game
> And they are richly laden all the year
> With hares, wild boars and goats, fowl (wild and tame),

Partridges, pheasants and huge capons
Along with other birds for the gourmet's delight –
And if you want to hunt, buy hawks and falcons here.

* * *

Thus women from the farms as each new day succeeds
Bring fresh supplies in, and the good cook bears
Home again all that the kitchen needs.[2]

The sellers' pleasure in fiddling with their crops and animals, and smirking past each other, unfolded minutes from his path across the Ponte Vecchio, his most likely route. This took him along the river to the Ponte Trinità to meet his 'master of grammar' (according to Bernardo), probably Matteo della Rocca, or, if he went the other way, over the Ponte Trinità to Matteo's house at the foot of the bridge. Such practical mornings, with their swallows, lights and the nearby marketplace, were his familiars as he set out for his Latin. They came first, along with their inevitable crowds of hawkers, housewives, farmers and soldiers.

Bernardo paid Matteo five soldi, a trivial amount, probably because tutors were not permitted to accept more than an 'Easter tip' from their pupils, though it seems likely that he may on occasion have given Matteo somewhat more. Lessons with Niccolò's *maestro*, who taught the 'eight parts of [Latin] speech,' and who would have stressed the common medieval and Renaissance belief that grammar was the chiefest of the seven liberal arts (the others were logic, rhetoric, music, arithmetic, geometry and astronomy), and that Latin grammar, along with ancient Greek, opened the door to all important knowledge and thought, or to the world's greatest works of poetry, history and philosophy, seem to have lasted just a few months.[3]

Probably they did not end simply because Matteo saw fit to refer by way of insult to one of a number of Niccolò's disreputable ancestors, Giovanni d'Agnolo, or Agiolino, Machiavelli, the brother of Buoninsegna, a seedy criminal type from the thirteenth century, still glumly remembered, whose notoriety slipping into darkness credited him on the one hand with arranging a truce between warring Guelph and Ghibelline factions in 1279–80, and on the other with rape, pederasty, gambling, usury and murder (he had killed a priest and been suspiciously pardoned).

In Florence's prickly world, his tutor would more likely have mentioned another better-regarded ancestor, the respected Alessandro di Filippo. More recently, in 1438, in return for an annual donation of twelve florins to the

Benedictine convent at Santa Felicità, he had been granted proprietary rights to the church's San Gregorio chapel.

Alessandro had been rich enough to commission a fresco by Domenico Ghirlandaio of Christ's descent from the cross. With masterpiece in tow, he had adopted the San Gregorio as his personal place of worship even as he offered for all to see luxuriant proof of his commitment to the arts and to the Machiavellis' enduring honour (the fresco has since disappeared).[4]

Whatever Bernardo's reason for releasing Niccolò's first tutor, by 1477 his Latin was reassigned to a *maestro* Battista di Filippo da Poppi, a chaplain at the church of San Benedetto, just beyond the Old Market and hard by Brunelleschi's *Duomo*.

Bits of masonry belonging to this minor church can still be seen, together with its minuscule Piazza di San Benedetto, or enough to make it clear that as Niccolò returned home, perhaps for lunch and later dinner (as many school children did, though a few brought their lunches), he would have seen the colossal dome – it would have been hard to miss, just around the corner – and this every school day, with its staggeringly uplifting rouge roof that seemed to heave at heaven in an assertion of Earth-defying power, a candid display of its sphere as one of the architectural wonders of the world, before he recrossed one of the nearby bridges.

With Battista, Niccolò's instruction would have proceeded in a more businesslike way. If the usual formula was followed, his lessons entailed memorizing verses from a *salterio*, or collection of religious poems. The sort of humanist education sought for him by his father typically required up to five years of Latin, plus training in Italian (it is not clear how much).[5]

A few more aspects of his early schooling can be deduced, however, and even some of his father's interests, together with a whiff of the intellectual fragrance of his home-life, from an intriguing detail: a book-exchange between his father and his tutor, Battista. On Bernardo's side, this exchange consisted of his borrowing Battista's copy of Pliny's *Natural History*, on 8 April 1478, as Bernardo recalled it, or when Niccolò was almost ten. Bernardo owned a library of seventeen or so books – the number kept changing – in print and manuscript, a quantity small enough to indicate that while he was an avid reader, he had little money.[6]

His lack of funds scarcely kept him from borrowing and exchanging books frequently with several of his banker-, bookseller- and jurist-friends. The Pliny exchanged with Battista, for instance, was a fine copy, translated into Italian ('*uno*

*Plinio in volgare*'), leather-bound and shod with silver-plated brass corners, or 'shoes,' and published in Venice two years earlier. Bernardo seems to have returned it after six weeks, on 28 May, though not, one may assume, without having read it and even discussed it or some of it with his Latin-studying son.[7]

This likelihood is not only plausible but worth considering. Pliny the Elder, who managed through sheer curiosity about volcanoes to get himself killed during the eruption of one of them, Mount Vesuvius near Pompeii in 79 BCE, may not have ranked among the great stylists of ancient Roman literature, but his *Natural History* had remained a staple of scientific learning throughout the Middle Ages into the Renaissance. The reason was that in no sense was his book just a compilation of biological, geological and astronomical facts according to the ancient Romans, or a rehash of Aristotle, everyone's pundit in science, aesthetics and politics.

In a number of ways, none of them intended, Pliny's *Natural History* had come to seem a fairly radical book, slipping past the dour clerical gaze at a time when Church censorship or disapproval might be devastating. His willingness to take up questions that theologians such as St Augustine had urged Christians to ignore, but which had become hot subjects again, ever since the twelfth and thirteenth centuries, allowed his sole surviving major opus to act as a stick stirring a pot of controversies lately beginning to boil, as with his argument that nature was imperfect, even as Christian theology maintained the opposite, and that God had limitations:

> The chief consolations for nature's imperfection in the case of man are that not even for God are all things possible – for he cannot, even if he wishes, commit suicide, the supreme boon that he has bestowed on man among all the penalties of life, nor bestow eternity on mortals or recall the deceased, nor cause a man [who] has lived not to have lived or one [who] has held high office not to have held it – and that he has no power over the past save to forget it, and (to link our fellowship with God by means of frivolous arguments as well) that he cannot cause twice ten not to be twenty.[8]

Though pagan, Pliny showed no hesitation about acknowledging a supreme being, or God, as had Plato, even if his God seemed shockingly indifferent to human affairs:

> That the supreme being, whate'er it be, pays heed to man's affairs is a ridiculous notion. Can we believe that it would not be defiled by so gloomy and so multifarious a duty?[9]

He also argued, in passages that were to become supremely important to Bernardo's son Niccolò and the development of his own ideas about the world, for the enhanced powers of fickle fortune, or the goddess *Fortuna*, not traditionally regarded as of great importance by the ancient Romans. He approved of Chance, or a universe that he perceived as lacking in strict determinism and that must be tolerant of human choices. His was a universe in which randomness might reign as God:

> Everywhere in the whole world at every hour by all men's voices *Fortuna* alone is invoked and named, alone accused, alone impeached, alone pondered, alone applauded, alone rebuked and visited with reproaches; ... and we are so much at the mercy of chance that Chance herself, by whom God is proved uncertain, takes the place of God.[10]

Here – it could hardly be denied – might be a gateway, especially if one considered it as Bernardo may well have done in the light of other Greek and Roman books, such as Plato's *Timaeus,* then gaining a new appreciation, to an unchristian estimate of the world. At the very least, such passages promoted rebellious thoughts. It hardly mattered that the copy of Pliny belonged to a church chaplain who was his son's tutor. Christian humanism, peering over its own shoulder in astonishment at the intellectual freedom of the ancient Greek and Roman world, was untroubled by such risks.

Of equal importance to Niccolò's development, if with less influence on medieval and Renaissance thought, were the two books that Bernardo lent Battista by way of the exchange, his *Commentary on Scipio's Dream* and a *Saturnalia,* by the fifth-century Roman neo-Platonist Macrobius, who may or may not have been a Christian, but who moved easily between the Christian and pagan worlds somewhat before the collapse of the Roman empire.

Amazingly for his day, Macrobius had concerned himself with what is today called the unconscious. The admission key to it, he believed, must be allegory, and especially the type of allegory to be found in dreams. The sort of dream in which this could happen he called a *somnium*. He described it as presenting truth hidden by a bewildering story.

Allegorical dreams were to be distinguished from non-allegorical or practical ones, or *insomnia*, in which a dreamer might, for example, dream about food because the cupboard was bare. Beyond *insomnia* lay a more unsettling realm, that of *epialtes*, or nightmares, which he termed a third type (two further types he regarded as prophetic). *Epialtes* displayed diabolical beasts and frightening if senseless goblins. All these types helped to shape Niccolò's deepest attitudes towards both dreams and language, and towards how he would come to view the world.

During the Middle Ages Macrobius was seen as contributing to allegorism, or to how books, especially the Bible, ought to be read by Christians. A proper reading of a biblical or for that matter any text, he believed, led its reader into knowledge of the divine by laying bare the sacred implications behind the words' literal meanings, or within the words themselves, as well as in the outside universe. Over the previous two centuries, this method of reading, now often applied in the personal arena of dreaming alone, came to be understood as casting illuminating lights on the nature of the self. Its approach transformed an entire cultural atmosphere by awakening readers for the first time to the stages of their conscious and unconscious mental processes.[11]

An enthusiasm for spirituality, the ancient Greek and Roman world and history thus ran through all Bernardo's reading: it was reflected in the other books that Niccolò would have discovered in the small family library as he began to read on his own. They embodied the ideals of a growing class of Renaissance Christian humanists, and most of all perhaps those who might be deistic but not avowedly religious. It is surprising, for instance, that Bernardo owned no Bible (St Jerome's fourth-century Latin translation would not have been hard to get), though he mentions returning a borrowed copy of one to a Domenico Lippi on 13 March 1480. His books were mostly those of the admired ancient Greek and Roman philosophers and historians, as represented in Latin or Italian translations: Aristotle's *Nicomachean Ethics*; two volumes of Roman law, the *Codex Iustinianus* and *Digestum novum*, as might be expected of a lawyer; and Livy's *Three Decades*. The Livy is especially helpful in trying to understand him and something of the flavour of his relations to Niccolò.

The first-century Roman historian, only a few of whose 142 books on Roman history have survived, had been little read during the Middle Ages, but now attracted attention for his clarity of style, his insights into the formation of political states and his aphoristic insolence: 'Deceit in the conduct of a war is meritorious'; 'promises extracted by force need not be observed'; 'cunning and deceit will serve a man better than force to rise from a base condition to great fortune.'[12]

This particular copy was unbound, though printed, when Bernardo first came across it, in September 1475. It was offered to him by an obscure *maestro* Niccolò Tedesco (perhaps simply Niccolò the German), probably a scholar and maybe a printer, perhaps a cartographer, and maybe all three in one, who wanted him to make an index for it that would include each of its myriad place names.

Producing the index turned out to be a fairly arduous task, and Bernardo finished his work only by July 1476, when Niccolò was seven and beginning to learn Latin. Bernardo wrote it out on sixty sheets of twice-folded paper, and received in payment the copy used to make it. Immediately, it seems, he decided to have it bound: its print was elegant, and book-binding was one of those happy adventures on which he had embarked with other books, taking them off to the neighbourhood *cartolaio*, or stationer. Money for binding turned out to be lacking at the moment, though – binding was expensive – and so he let the matter drop, hoping to manage it in the future.[13]

# 3

## *The Cosmic Package*

Even more precious than his newly acquired Livy was the set of vital connections that it provided through his comprehensive index – remarkably, from a modern point of view – to the universe itself. If his law practice had never taken off, with the result that he had no established career because constant debts caused him to look a bit of a shambles or even a disgrace in the public eye, but not for any lack of charm and acuity – his friends hint that he had both in abundance – Bernardo understood that he was living in an age when important new questions were being raised about politics and the universe, and with startling answers proposed to some of them.

Certainly he understood that even a vague conception of the heavens' physical structure and their governance influenced anyone's life and choices. A sense of physical harmony propped up the idea of justice. An awareness of cosmic coherence lingered as a ghost behind the simplest business arrangement. Dream interpretation could be revealing. Even crossing a bridge for the sake of a Latin lesson might imply a hidden allegory.

Despite such self-evident facts, in Florence as well as right across Europe in his day, no one discussed the infinite. Everyone believed that the physical universe must be a sealed, limited affair, a bit like a round box: it was implacably finite. Centuries earlier, St Augustine had dismissed the tempting hypothesis of infinity as encroaching on Christian doctrine, and best left to God.[1] God was understood to inhabit the great gaps of eternity beyond space and time, which itself was conceived as abstract, absolute and independent of space. If God was pure Reason, or *ratio*, as seemed to everyone a sensible proposition, then logic accompanied by faith in His hidden essence ought to suffice for those in search of divine contact or heavenly knowledge.

Beyond these assurances, a long-accepted model of the physical universe seemed to take account of the known physical facts themselves. The Ptolemaic System represented outer space, as it is described today, in terms of a round compartment consisting of nine transparent spheres, each nesting within the next largest, and with this mobile-like arrangement ranging upward from the Earth and moon to the Empyrean, or the fiery abode of God in changeless eternity.

The second-century Alexandrian astronomer's drawings and discussions of a neatly tucked-in cosmos, based on earlier recorded observations of the skies by the ancient Babylonians, were also seen as complementing Augustinian spiritual postulates. Ptolemy's astronomical system thus agreed with Christian theology in offering an account of everyone's human address in the universe. This lay not at its centre, as modern scientists and others have often assumed, and even if that is how it appears, but at its bottom. An essential feature of medieval cosmic reality, it is described by Chaucer in Book V of his *Troilus and Criseyde* and by Dante in his *Commedia*, as well as in the accounts of scores of commentators. The universe's up-down nature may be better grasped as one realizes that medieval people refer to the Earth's location as 'wretched,' desolate and nearly abandoned by God's descending and hence weakening powers of Reason. The Earth is almost deserted in the lowest region of a cosmos understood as vertical, or as presenting permanent directions.

Of equal importance to understanding the fixed spatial design are two other facts. The first is that while the Earth was assumed to be round, or a globe, it was believed to be static. Its motionlessness meant that the sun literally rose, passed overhead and set. The sphere of the stars, or *stellatum*, the eighth sphere, below that of the Primum mobile, revolved in a measurable loftiness far above the Earth and those celestial bodies visible to the naked eye and located in their own revolving spheres: the moon, Mercury, Venus, the Sun, Mars, Jupiter and Saturn.

The second fact is that reality in an ultimate sense did not, as is now believed, consist in phenomena, or physical experiences, including physical events on Earth. Physics and the physical world were doomed. Over time, they would wear out, decay and vanish. Their importance was illusionary. Sense data themselves were seen as promoting delusions. Reality – or those elements that would endure and which could therefore be understood as superior to wear and tear – lay beyond the physical, and consisted in God and eternity, or, a bit like logic itself, in non-physical exceptions to decay.

The round Earth, placed at what looks like the centre of attention in the Ptolemaic but Christian-adapted and modified universal system, thus rested at the one point in it farthest from God, or reality, and so in the worst of positions from the standpoint of importance.[2] This wretchedness of the human location also rendered individual salvation far more problematic: if heaven shone high above everything, then damnation, as enacted in Hell, must be located below it, or below the universe, so to speak: Hell lay beneath the equator and oceans, or not too far from the sinners themselves, and so seemed more unpleasantly convenient than the distant blessings of paradise.

Despite these frosty if rationally organized beliefs, a spectral idea of infinity, or at least a suspicion that all might not be well with this broad account of space and time, had begun to gain ground during Bernardo's lifetime. The possibility of a revolution in ideas of perception and vision had long been taken seriously, and especially by painters, though even others indifferent to art could scarcely avoid seeing the changes in progress as they attended their nearest church – and almost everyone went to church more than a few times a year.

A powerful fad in depicting three-dimensional space according to naturalism, along with what it entailed – a drastic foreshortening of everything, from bent legs, arms, knees and horses' bodies to landscapes and lakes – had widely caught on. It was gaining a broad and growing support in the various community art centres, or the churches and homes of the middle and upper classes. Esteemed painters in Florence and other Italian cities found themselves competing to produce the most accurate naturalistic representations of a mundane rather than an eternal reality, or the complex, scruffy world in which people actually lived.

Rivalries over how to embrace a new naturalism with geometrical skill had been gaining momentum ever since Paolo Uccello (1396/7–1475) unveiled his startling *Annunciation* (perhaps in the 1440s: it is now lost) at the church of Santa Maria Maggiore. This was a painting that his near contemporary, the historian-artist Vasari, described as 'the first in good style showing artists how, with grace and proportion, lines can be made to recede to a vanishing point (*punto di fuga*), and how a small and restricted space on a flat surface may be extended so that it appears distant and large.... Artists achieving this effect ... deceive the eye so surely that the painting seems to be in actual relief.'[3]

The rabbit-out-of-a-hat evocation of a naturalistic illusion, or visual deception, even if others credited the same startling invention to the slightly earlier Masaccio (1401–?1428), seemed irresistible for its simplicity, though it might well have raised red flags among traditionalists. One reason was that any calculation of the geometrically sound vanishing point, or the spot, or *fuga*, or point of flight on a plane surface at which the viewer's intersecting lines of sight enabled the eye to experience a psychological and aesthetic lift-off, or, as it seemed, flight into an implied, invisible space that seemed to run on forever, provided a glimpse into infinity.

No one as yet considered infinity, but the implications of the aesthetic shift were understood as momentous. Far from merely supplying a clever new way to make paintings, the *punto di fuga* was rife with philosophical and religious implications. This became especially clear if the results of adopting it were compared to the near static basis of earlier art. Medieval paintings and frescoes, for instance, still on display in most churches, and so appearing directly beside the new naturalistic ones, emphasized a deliberate two-dimensional flatness, forcing the viewer to peer either up towards Heaven or down towards Hell. Hell might be grimly emblazoned with punishing demons, but it was in any event divorced from an Earth seen as isolated and wretched. Might the naturalistic style not induce a psychological and spiritual loosening of ties to the Ptolemaic System itself? Might it not invite a drastic expansion of empiricism, or even some trust in sense data as a standard superior to logic and metaphysics?

These questions seem even more apt when it is recognized that painting was not the only field, or even the first, in which attempts to represent physical space, or infinity in some definite sense, or to manipulate vision so as to imply and control distances, including those beyond the visible, had already led to controversial discoveries. Over a century earlier another Florentine, Salvino d'Armato (*d.?*1312), later to be buried in the same Santa Maggiore church as that in which Uccello exhibited his *Annunciation*, may have managed the world's first accurate grinding of lenses and shown how they might be used to make spectacles. For Salvino, the geometrical challenge, to come up with an instrument that might improve vision, was the same as that faced by Uccello and other painters interested in the vanishing point, even if it was expressed through a different medium: how to mould a transparent piece of glass so as to produce angles of sight converging evenly across a convex surface, and in the process engender focused magnification.[4]

From a practical point of view the consequences of Salvino's invention were widespread and important: an often well-educated Florentine population was becoming inured to new and hitherto dismissed insights into physical reality. Bernardo himself appears to have entertained some of them. Evidence indicating his enthusiasm, along with its influence on his son, Niccolò, is to be found in another coincidence: that as he began work on his index for Livy's history, he took on loan from a friend a copy of Ptolemy's *Cosmographia*.

Printed in Venice, this encyclopedia-like book, promoting medieval geographical ideas and still valuable as a reference tool in his own day, included many of the same place names as cropped up in the Livy. Bernardo seems to have kept it beside him while working on his index, regarding it as essential.[5]

That it was unquestionably useful, and that indices were then of far greater value than is today appreciated, is amply confirmed by the urgings of another Florentine, Giovanni Boccaccio (1313–75), famous during the Renaissance less for his *Decameron* and *Filostrato*, the love story that inspired Chaucer and became the source of his *Troilus and Criseyde*, than for his works of minor interest to modern readers but which his contemporaries regarded as exciting and *avant-garde*. These were his compilations of descriptive lists indicating relationships, among them his genealogies of the pagan gods and his tedious-seeming inventories of mountains, swamps, valleys, rivers, lakes and notable spots generally.

Boccaccio had been less medieval in outlook than his contemporary, Chaucer, and much more concerned to establish a modern and even alphabetically responsible order for his often geographically befuddled contemporaries: he set out to supply them with increasing quantities of the solid, clear details of their earthly human address. He also suggested that other authors ought to create their own lists and indices.[6]

By now the idea of doing so had come to complement yet another fad springing to life in Bernardo's fifteenth century: that gathering about maps, records of distant journeys, though not as yet of the unknown New World, and three-dimensional depictions in woodcuts and etchings, as if viewed from above or in flight, of the house-by-house appearances of cities.[7]

Bernardo's Livy contained none of these more imaginative types of illustrations, but his index, if published as part of a revised edition of Livy's book (it is unknown whether this was done), would have rendered his history more practical for readers consulting Ptolemy and other authors referring to the places that he cited.

All these subtle glimmerings of a prospective major change in old-fashioned attitudes, or of a cosmic shift, though nobody as yet knew how it would move forward, or whether it would, or in which direction it might propel human consciousness, blended into a passionate and strengthening fascination with the civilized ancient past.

Histories of Florence had now come into vogue. Flavio Biondo's *Deche* (Decades, 1441) presented a caustic view of the city's growth, leading into the Renaissance, following the fifth-century sack of Rome and tumultuous epochs of bloodshed. Bernardo borrowed Biondo's *Deche* in 1485, and his *Italia Illustrata*, a volume significant to the relatively new discipline of archeology, in 1477, from Bianco di Francesco da Casavecchia.[8]

A more comprehensive treatment of Florentine history, which would also intensely interest Niccolò as he grew older, Leonardo Bruni's humanist *History of the Florentine People* (1444) reached even further back, to the city's Etruscan founders, as well as forward into the fifteenth century. It amounted to a now celebrated attempt to reveal what that revered historian and government official had seen as the city's thousand-year-old quest for political stability and freedom.

Ancient Roman architecture had also begun to stimulate a novel curiosity. Roman ruins, visible in many of the city's *piazze*, were demolished to make way for new Renaissance buildings. Brunelleschi's *Duomo*, constructed to rival if not surpass the Roman Pantheon in size and beauty, expressed not simply admiration for the past but an unmistakable challenge to it. His design of the church of Santa Felicità, a remodelling across from the Machiavelli *palazzo*, offered an identical, complex challenge, as did his plans for a hospital and other secular buildings.

Everywhere architectural experimentation seemed to be gaining fluency through expanding ambitions. Narrow streets, long wrapped in semi-darkness, began to open to bands of light alongside clusters of medieval watchtowers, some soon to be torn down amid the new dust of chisel and hammer. Aesthetic questions and empirical awakenings poured forth on all sides, and Niccolò's Latin lessons seemed as much a gateway to a new stage of civilization as to the study of an old one.

# 4

# Poetry, Music and Militarism

At the same time, in the late 1470s, the grimmer likelihood of war seemed – as so often – on everyone's mind. Far more than a fortress, Florence was an educational, mercantile, artistic and banking centre. Despite the city's unending involvement in battles and sieges over the previous fifteen centuries, it lacked anything like a militaristic tradition, especially in comparison with rival city states, such as Venice, Genoa and Milan. For decades too it had flourished amid an authoritarian if prosperous peace. As battlefield successes once led to rejoicing, they had also induced military neglect.

To the population's educated ruling class – even Florentine bankers and merchants often busied themselves with studying classical Latin and Greek – the impervious calm seemed a condition that might only be improved.[1]

For years it had been pampered by Cosimo de'Medici the Elder, since his return from exile in 1434, to his death in 1464, and then for five years by his heir, his invalid son Piero. Piero's son, Lorenzo, sought to temper the quality of the peace by expanding a number of security pacts in 1474, to include such larger powers as Venice, Milan and the often bellicose papacy. Military interests continued to take second place to making money, staging ceremonial jousts and colourful sporting events, and more recently, for the government's legalistic and well-trained minds, speculating on the vanished glories of ancient Greece and Rome.[2]

In part because of their relative newness, the influence of classical studies, and their role in Bernardo and Niccolò's lives, cannot be overstressed. For one thing, they created a sense of legitimacy. The faded brilliance of ancient Athens, the beshrouded majesty of Homer's epic poems, sieved through poor Latin translations but which those who studied law and other subjects at the university of Florence-Pisa recognized as the dust-covered sources of their own civilization, had only just begun to be wiped off, polished and analysed in their originals by the end of the fourteenth century.

Recovered knowledge, imported from Athens across the Aegean, cast a fresh light on the imperial if in many ways gritty grandeur of the ancient Roman empire. Its flattering ruins everyone could glimpse in the nearest street, but they appeared a bit like the suggestive bones of incomprehensible dinosaurs, or the abandoned trinkets of a god who had been consumed in a mysterious conflagration.

A major reason for the growth of humanist or classical studies was cultural and historical ignorance. It left masses of people at sea in respect to their past while fostering a belief in their modern cultural inferiority. As the daunting conviction settled in that ancient times had been far grander than present ones, there also swung into play an infectious desire to slough off the ignorance itself.

A new hopefulness had emanated at first from a single compelling personality, astonishing as the idea may now seem, the poet Francesco Petrarca (1304–74), who had urged on everyone – and so not just on scholars – the inestimable value of the classics (he himself had acquired only a crude familiarity with ancient Greek). Petrarch's prodding complemented the unexpected arrival in Florence, if a bit late in the day, in 1397, of Italy's first real expert in ancient Greek literature, Manuel Chrysoloras, himself a Byzantine. His delivery before large audiences at the city's twin-branched university over the next several years of a series of spellbinding lectures on their heritage in ancient Greek poetry and philosophy caught the attention of the Florentine *literati*, a group that included future politicians and merchants.[3] It was now that the city began to head down a path to change, as it was later to change the world. In the end, Petrarch's impact on education, including reading and writing, seems as intriguing as the self-contradictory age in which Niccolò was growing up and learning Latin: on the one hand, gifted and daring: on the other, stubborn and superstitious.

A compelling if occasionally bombastic poet, Petrarch had enjoyed a widely lauded career as the most esteemed, laurel-crowned, Italian literary figure of the previous century. His reputation rested mostly on his scores of superb sonnets addressed to his beloved Laura, whose existence was always a matter of conjecture, but a more pertinent set of questions might have been raised about his favourite poetic form, the sonnet itself. Its unusual qualities had first been tested as an opportunity for patterns of poetic brilliance in Dante's *La vita nuova* (*c.*1292–1300), but they rapidly began to appeal to anyone who wanted to write poetry. As he grew older, they appealed in important ways to Niccolò himself.

The sonnet had been conceived or, more accurately, invented, by a *notaro*, or lawyer, Giacomo da Lentino, in 1225–30, probably in Sicily. Even in Niccolò's day, though, and from significant points of view, it remained an influential aesthetic novelty. Since the mid-1470s, or just a few years earlier, sonnets had begun to be set to music and sung. Petrarch himself had known the tricky, rhymed form, however, mostly as non-musical, or meditational. It seemed simply a one-stanza lyric of fourteen lines meant to be read aloud to oneself or another person or group of people, or sent off to someone in a sonnet-exchange, or *tenzone*.[4]

Even unsung, though, it was regarded almost from the moment of its invention as revolutionary, for the single compelling reason that since ancient Greek and Roman times it was the first poetic form to be incompatible with the by then universal requirement that all poems be set to music.

Silent reading was the sonnet's transforming and novel invitation, and it stimulated a new, spreading habit of reading in silence. Its built-in, unique feature, that the turn or *verso* after its eighth line rendered it at variance with the strictures of medieval music theory, according to which any twist or *verso* in the middle of a lopsided stanzaic structure made impossible the single unbroken melody demanded for the whole stanza, set it apart from other types of poetry. This quality also hinted from the start at the sonnet's potential power, that its intrinsic meditational nature might lead it to influence other branches of literature – that it might become a trend-setter.[5]

If writing in the new, non-music-oriented way were to catch on, as soon began to happen, might it not stimulate an abandonment of the performance requirement everywhere, and even dramatic changes in how nearly everyone read and wrote?

All this seems clear enough now because it is broadly recognized that prior to the invention of the sonnet, or throughout the High Middle Ages, readers would have encountered nearly all texts – and not only poems – audibly. In the fifth century Saint Augustine had noticed his mentor, Saint Ambrose, poring over a biblical page in silence, but his amazement had simply proved the rule. It seems apparent, in other words, that the practice of exclusively oral reading had been established throughout Europe as early as the fifth century, and that it had led to the performance or reading aloud of almost all poetry.

This had hardly been the case among the ancient Greeks and Romans, for whom silent reading apparently coexisted with public performance. Catullus's lyrics invited both meditation and recitation. Juvenal's satires might be read as well at home as theatrically in a tavern. Virgil's *Eclogues*, like Horace's odes, encouraged the intimacy of silent self-confrontation.

Eight hundred years after the fall of Rome, however, or during the first decades of the thirteenth century, a period later seen as the beginning of the Italian Renaissance, the stimulus for the invention of the sonnet had been the first complete translation into medieval Latin of Plato's suppressed and probably last work, his *Timaeus*. The translation itself was done at the court of the anti-papal, brilliant emperor Frederick II of Hohenstaufen. Shortly afterwards, the sonnet, invented and honed by Giacomo da Lentino, seems to have seen the light of day, most likely in Sicily, though Frederick's court tended to move quite a lot through his Italian-German empire. The invention itself, however, had come about because of yet another remarkable development.

In the *Timaeus* Plato had offered a description of the architecture of the heavens, alongside a set of mathematical ratios describing their structure, together with an argument that the same ratios also described the architecture of the human soul. By the fifteenth century these ratios had come to matter to Niccolò's understanding of the cosmos, as well as to that of Bernardo and anyone else in the know.[6]

The reason here was that Plato had viewed the soul as a microcosm or replica of the heavenly macrocosm. Each vibrated according to an 'inaudible' or magnificent music. This silent-seeming music (Aristotle had described it as 'celestial') was in part produced by the swishing through the universal ether (whose existence could be assumed, again following Aristotle) of the five known planets, and the moon, the sun and the *stellatum*, and partly by the ratios themselves, which Plato regarded as incorporating divine harmonies.

For Renaissance poets, or Niccolò's contemporaries, Plato's majestic conception of a universal if inaudible musical order was to become his most important if unacknowledged gift to poetry and literature. The reason in this case was that Giacomo da Lentino had adopted it as the mathematical basis of the structure of the sonnet. In a stroke of aesthetic brilliance, he had trans-ferred the principles of the Platonic music of the heavens and the human soul into a poetic form – or, from the Renaissance point of view, reproduced the architecture of the Ptolemaic System in a new, potentially silent poem whose unheard music consisted for everyone, including Niccolò, of the 'ditties of no tone,' as Keats would later describe celestial music in his 'Ode on a Grecian Urn.'

Plato's gift of design to what became the Western world's oldest poetic form still in prominent use (for so it continues today), together with its influence on Renaissance and later literature, via Dante, Petrarch and their successors, including in the years to come Niccolò and perhaps even his father, is thus of crucial importance to understanding their deeper conceptions of the universe and the human world.

Nor is even this the whole story. The sonnet's meditation-inducing lopsidedness, in which an octet precedes a sestet, or in which a problem, often in love, is depicted as a torment in its first part, with its resolution provided in its second, not only caught on but stimulated the development of a new literary expressiveness whose moorings were sunk in silent, self-conscious reading. As time passed, performance itself began to lose some of its seductiveness.

Inner frustrations, later described by Freud as the source of self-consciousness, began to become fashionable literary themes. Dante's *Commedia*, written in exile and in the wake of the new, silence-inducing form, is perhaps the world's first epic intended as much to present the silently endured conflicts between self and soul as to invite public performance. The *Commedia* is among the first works of modern literature to limn the protagonist's (possibly Dante's own) growth into an enlightened, spiritual and in his case Christian awareness as the result of inner conflicts.

The sonnet's curious commitment to logic, or rationality, or to resolving frustrations, also enabled it to act as a catalyst for the development of an inner-focused literature generally and to inspire new fashions in fiction. The attraction of these changes was to become pervasive throughout Niccolò's school years.

In belonging to the first generation to hear sonnets set to music and to listen to the new, unpredictable type of music composed for them, in the 1470s, he was becoming party to an extraordinary invitation. It offered not only a chance to resolve internal conflicts in an inventive way, or to ease his path as he wrote sonnets of his own along with (somewhat later) political-meditative poetry, but to grow along meditative-aesthetic lines as he engaged in the political-literary work of his life to come.

The age itself, or the period of his youth, was continuously caught up in a struggle with its own capacity for invention. As in any age, many inventions never got off the ground. Often, however, superstitions competed with innovation, along with a suspicion of machinery itself as 'unnatural.' Leonardo's war engines, for example, his submarine and armoured car, despite expectations by the early 1480s as in mid-1478 that momentous military violence was on its way in which both could provide an edge to one side or the other, were never built.

Petrarch himself, though a supporter of aesthetic novelties, remained throughout his life a fierce opponent of human dissection and autopsies for the sake of medical research, driven by an unshakeable conviction that the body was sacred.

Physicians, he argued, were 'godless.' The human body ought to be seen as a reincarnation of Christ's body, or even God. To dissect a corpse was to insult the divine, or to tamper with the sacred and inviolate order of things.

Many educated people, including aesthetically innovative poets and artists – with Leonardo a noted exception, slicing away at his stolen corpses in his candlelit studio in dead of night, poring over skeletons, veins, nerves and muscles in his quest for more accurate anatomical knowledge – agreed with Italy's foremost sonneteer while themselves carrying on experiments in paint, oil and perspective, and subscribing to turgid beliefs in witchcraft, astrology and the medieval doctrine, seldom questioned in public though it lacked empirical support, that the universe must be finite.

# 5

# *Murder in the* Duomo

In early 1478, the whisper of particularized hatred rippling along the streets seemed at first inaudible. Certainly Lorenzo de'Medici and his brother Giuliano, its targets, were oblivious to it. Had they caught wind of its grotesque energy, or learned of the strenuous and successful efforts to conceal its sinuosity, they might still not have reacted with alarm.

They and their supporters were convinced that they had provided far too much assistance to the city's population at large to provoke any serious hostility – and even in the end when this agreeable vanity blew up in their faces as an uproar whipping into assassinations, hangings and war itself, entertained the belief, and perhaps rightly, that most people empathized with the prevailing Florentine civil order so long and firmly under their control.[1] Their behind-the-scenes machinations had been much too sleight of hand, after all, amounting at most to a raised, discreet fist in the velvet glove, to be stimulating of seditious mistrust.

Yet the most vicious envy conducive to a dank sort of unguent scheming, and focused in Rome as well as Florence and Urbino, and boiling towards a calculated eruption in January or, when January seemed inopportune, in April 1478, seemed to lay bare for those in on it serious veins of treachery.

At the same time, and for reasons to be revealed later – it cannot help to leapfrog often over events to their effects – one may reasonably anticipate that the special terror of the bloodstained, taxing hours to come, and their suffocating aftermath, which would continue to unravel for decades, made the profoundest possible impression on Niccolò, and surely on his father. He had just borrowed Pliny's *Natural History* and might have been reading it at home with his son.

In this light, and for the sake of clarity, it is useful to begin with a single detail, the contrast between two libraries, and the naïve if often held belief that humanist values militate against violence and murder. The personalities involved, including those of the competitive Medici brothers, also deserve investigation.

As for the libraries, by 1492, or fourteen years later (but at the earliest moment for which a reliable list exists), Leonardo da Vinci's contained thirty-seven printed books, a quantity typical of none-too-well-off and self-educated people, though that of Bernardo, Niccolò's father, contained fewer. Leonardo's eclectic collection included the familiar humanist-leaning works by Aesop, Livy (his *Decades*, perhaps even the edition for which Bernardo had made his index), Ovid (his *Metamorphoses*, read in schools across Europe throughout the Middle Ages), Plutarch's *Lives*, John Mandeville (the popular travel writer, also liar, charmer and inventor of most of his adventures), the Bible, the Psalms, and books on mathematics, surgery, military strategy, weapons, music and law.[2]

By comparison, in 1478 the library of the organizing military commander committed to the Pazzi Conspiracy, as the groping hatred directed at the Medici brothers came to be known, the Duke Federico da Montefeltro of Urbino, one of the wealthiest men in Italy, contained over a thousand of the world's most exquisite and lushly illuminated manuscripts, many bound in creamy silver and leather, along with more than fifty early printed books, or incunabula, which with a trace of embarrassment he regarded as inferior to his manuscripts, despite his awareness that they ranked among the choicest products of the most important mechanical invention to date in human history: an imitative printing device more revolutionary than the wheel.[3]

A comparison between these libraries implies a good deal more than itself, and bits of it seem menacing as well as crucial to understanding the atmosphere and values, so different from modern ones, surrounding Niccolò's youth. If Federico's was one of the rarest collections of books not only in Italy but in the world, and if his court soon came to stand as a model of Renaissance courtly ideals in Baldesar Castiglione's *Book of the Courtier* (1516), his small city of Urbino was a paradigm of civilized perfection among the many remarkable cities of Renaissance Italy.

Some forty years later, Niccolò – or for a long time by then, Machiavelli – recalled these details, personalities and the events surrounding them, which he would now experience indirectly. Each affected the rest of his life. Their nuances would change his city, its history and his interests.

Florence had long seemed settled into a gap of serenity astride the opposed banks of the Arno and beneath the encircling crests of a set of rugged, soaring hills. Behind its walls, under its red-tiled roofs, and with the orb-like reddish *Duomo* at its centre, if considered from one of the hilltops it resembled nothing so much as a prize fruit, or intellectual strawberry. Urbino, by contrast and as Castiglione describes it, perched 'on the slopes of the Apennines towards the Adriatic ... among hills that are perhaps not as pleasant as those we see in many other places,' but 'still blessed by Heaven with a most fertile and bountiful countryside [causing it] beside the wholesomeness of the air [to] abound in all the necessities of life.'[4]

Chief among these necessities, as Castiglione admits, apart from the 'palace thought by many to be the most beautiful to be found anywhere in all Italy,' were the 'prudence, humanity, justice, generosity [and] undaunted spirit' of its ruler, the Duke himself. Castiglione makes no bones about Federico's selfishness, though, flipping the coin to take stock of his steelier if equally praiseworthy qualities, as they were then understood: 'his military prowess, signally attested to by his many victories, the capture of impregnable places, the sudden readiness of his expeditions, the many times when with but small forces he routed large and very powerful armies, and the fact that he never lost a single battle; so that not without reason we may compare him to many famous men among the ancients.'[5]

Witnesses remarked on Federico's periods of lordly calm, followed by grumbling, the gnarled *politesse* expressed in strict silences enforced in the precincts of his vast palace and his toleration of atrocities, especially if they yielded harvests of costly though pilfered books.

He had earned most of his money as Italy's most respected mercenary, or *condottiere*, doing so at a time when, amid constant shortages of Italian troops and experienced generals, together with unceasing armed struggles over the destiny of the Italian city-states, to be any sort of trusty gun for hire was to be counted heroic, no matter how nonchalant the throat-slitting.

On capturing Volterra in June 1472, for instance, while fulfilling a lucrative commission for Lorenzo de'Medici himself – the purpose was to restore Medici control over several Volterran-seized alum mines – the avuncular, strategic Federico had looked the other way as his men sacked and burned the city. He had apologized to the survivors, but what reveals more about his ethics was his failure to return an invaluable group of forty or more (the exact number is unknown) illuminated Hebrew manuscripts – rich loot for the ducal library – lifted from the shelves of the merchant-scholar Menahem ben Aharon Volterra.

No doubt the price of this addendum to his collection seemed less than steep. Menahem and hundreds of others, including women and children, were murdered by Federico's rampaging soldiers. Scores of women were raped. The city itself had been left a pile of filth-splattered ruins in flames, its devastation compounded by a coincidental storm that brought on an obliterating landslide.[6]

By 1478, and regardless of Federico's winking at the Volterran ghastliness, his library had become a touted extravagance, guided by his ambition to attain the heights of scholarly acquisition. At the start of his book-buying, some years earlier, when his relations with Lorenzo were more cordial, he had purchased his codices in Florence at the shop of the noted book dealer Vespasiano da Bisticci (c.1422–98), who also supplied the Medici and other wealthy humanist book-buyers throughout Italy. In those days he ordered fine batches of new manuscripts alongside the better esteemed older ones, with the plushest often the work of Vespasiano's own staff of copyists and illuminators. More recently, or by the mid-1470s, he had begun to shift his orders for new manuscripts into Urbino, enabling his duchy to swivel into prominence as a centre of manuscript production whose quality verged on exceeding that of Florence.

Along these lines it should be acknowledged that the invention of moveable type had scarcely impeded the respected arts of manuscript copying and illumination. On the contrary, as investments and items of unsurpassable beauty, the harder-to-make type of book had actually increased in value. Improvements in print technology stimulated greater demands than ever for illuminated Bibles, for example. A single superb biblical second volume, delivered to Federico just months after the Pazzi Conspiracy claimed its first victims, or a month or so past Niccolò's tenth birthday, elicited a letter of gratitude to Lorenzo, in June, 1478.[7]

Even more revealing of Federico's personality was a well-known double portrait of him with his son Guidobaldo, esteemed for more than its restrained grandiosity (plate IV). The painting was probably completed by 1475, when his son and heir was three or four, and is likely the work of Pedro Berruguete (d.1502). As many have suggested, it seems done from life, and shows the obese, placid, stumpy, palmy, roly-poly Duke in profile and from a poky angle that emphasizes his mountainous, hooked nose. He relaxes on a throne-like chair, clad in parade armour overlaid with a red tunic. An ermine boa, symbolic of nobility, is tossed about his neck. Tied at his left calf is the ribbon of the Order of the Garter.

Aside from these and other accoutrements of power and heredity – Guidobaldo, resplendent in goose-bumpy pride, stands at attention beside him, one arm resting on the paternal knee while the other grasps the imperial sceptre – what remains intriguing, though the fact has not so far been remarked, is the Duke's behaviour. He holds before him an open copy of his *Commentary on the Book of Job* by Pope Gregory I (590–604), or a manual on how to live the pious Christian life, but is shown reading with his lips closed, or in silence.[8]

Other contemporary paintings, to be sure, also show people with books: an *Annunciation*, for instance, by Alunno di Benozzi (also late fifteenth century?), in which Mary, the mother of Christ, appears with what is probably an open Bible. Almost none shows the sitter reading, though, and still fewer the sitter reading in silence (an exception is a cut-down portrait of Saint Ambrose by Giovanni di Paolo (*c.*1400–82): both paintings are at the Metropolitan Museum in New York).

That Federico da Montefeltro, thief, soldier, nobleman, bibliophile, despot, humanist and dedicated scholar, is depicted in a semi-official portrait as reading is only to be expected, given his passion for manuscripts. The comparatively rare act of reading in silence, however, suggests his conscious approval of the revolution in reading habits – that astonishing change from fashionable perfor-mance-reading to the newly fashionable reading in meditative privacy – now underway among educated people.

The Duke's *studiolo*, a private reading room which was to become the antecedent of the modern home library or den, and which he ordered custom-built at his palace in Urbino, also argues a commitment to the new spirit of individualism and cultivated solitude then beginning to assert itself in the arts and to a lesser extent in politics. The walls are set in vivid *trompe-l'oeil* intarsia depictions of books, plus more than twenty sensitive portraits culled from the medieval-Renaissance pantheon of philosophical luminaries, among them Plato, Aristotle, Ptolemy and Augustine.[9]

At the moment, as seems plain, the Duke was worried about matters less refined: organizing a deadly conspiracy. New evidence from a decoded letter sent by him on 14 February 1478 to Piero Felici and Agostino Staccoli, his emissaries in Rome, but meant to be delivered to Pope Sixtus IV, reveals that he had been hired by the seditious clique plotting the overthrow of the entire

Florentine leadership through ambush and assassination (the precise extent of his involvement has not until lately been established).

In the letter, Federico refers discreetly to the bristling plans by now afoot. He urges speed and decisiveness. He also promises to provide a small supporting body of soldiers from Siena. As matters fell out, his contribution amounted to about 550 armed men, plus fifty knights. He assures the Pope that on the day appointed 'for [the] main business' his troops will be formed up outside Florence, ready to march in and take over. In a section of the letter not in code, he again alludes to the conspirators' 'main business' – by implication the killing of Lorenzo and Giuliano – directing his Roman agents to thank Sixtus, whose involvement was soon to lead into war against Florence itself, for the gift to his son Guido of an expensive gold chain (his son appears wearing it in the double portrait with his father).[10] Federico might even have thanked the Pope, if a bit superfluously, for his own ennoblement some years earlier, in 1474.

In fact his prosperous military career owed a great deal to the manipulations of another major character in on the conspiracy, and with whom, at least indirectly, Niccolò was to have much to do, the sly, restlessly ambitious Francesco della Rovere (Pope from 1471 to 1484).

Sixtus IV's unabashed nepotism, which followed on his election as Pope, had swiftly led to the complementary elevation of six of his nephews to posh positions as cardinals (one may have been his own son), accompanied by scandal-provoking squabbles over medals, cameos, gold cups, marriages, palaces, pearls, tiaras and stacks of plate, in the midst of which spiritual values seemed to disappear.

Though records exist making mention of his laughter, and even scatterings of laughter in his presence, there survives none of its warmth. A chill hovers over the accounts of his magnificent feasts in the marbled halls of the Vatican. Guests recalled his squat papal fingers imprisoned in their crushes of gold and monstrous gems and his insistence on absolute loyalty, nourished by blackmail in Federico's case, through the marriage of one of Sixtus's opportunistic nephews, Giovanni della Rovere, to Federico's oldest daughter, thus snipping off all remaining ties between the Duke and Lorenzo de'Medici.

The Pope's gargantuan appetites by no means expressed his multiple talents, however, and in the end he shone forth as more acute than is suggested by his materialistic grasping. His efficient government, to cite one instance, reflected his thoroughly modern imagination. Having grown up in rustic poverty away from Roman extravagance – perhaps among Ligurian fishermen – he came up with daring programmes for widening and extending the clotted streets of his two-thousand-year-old metropolis. He cleared out slums, encouraged commerce and trade, established better hospitals and finally redesigned the Vatican, hiring for his project to transform the central mansion of the Christian world the most respected artists, among them Botticelli and Ghirlandaio, even as he ordered the construction of the new and eponymous Sistine Chapel.

Sixtus had been a distinguished scholar during his long-gone seminary days, when he also offered a piquant sketch of good looks. By now his passion for scholarship had not died, but in the late 1470s the good looks had tilted into a ballooning fatness, heaviness of jowl, shortness of breath, slithery toothlessness and an imperial stare.

His hatred of the Medici led to his support of the Pazzi Conspiracy, but only as long as no blood was shed (yet was not his innocent-seeming insistence on a bloodless coup just posturing?). His envy of the Medicis' banking acumen was intensified by his thwarted yen to secure one of their loans so he could purchase the picturesque town of Imola for his notorious nephew Girolamo Riario (perhaps his son), but which Lorenzo wanted for himself.

Sixtus next turned to the older banking family, the Pazzi, for his loan, and received it, but while with his customary canniness he retained the more influential Medici as his Vatican bankers, a nasty undercurrent of animosity persisted between the two men.[11]

These and murkier grudges became known only later. In the meantime, if better understood in banking circles, the resentments of the Pazzi themselves, or the more livid stars of the plot, festered and boiled – mostly those of Francesco, the family's dwarf-like, jittery, dyspeptic manager in Rome, and Jacopo, their acerbic overlord. His stinginess and snarling bouts of despair, often unleashed when he lost at cards, led him at first to dismiss the planned coup as too risky. In the end he embraced it with morbid excitement as he stomped about the corridors of the larger of his two Florentine palaces (after the conspiracy débacle, it was renamed the Palazzo Quaratesi).

His palace itself had been designed by Brunelleschi for his father, Andrea, but was built by him. Its sophisticated charms included a ground floor meant to imitate the rural graces of old farm houses. A tart elegance throughout, plus a Donatello-modelled escutcheon stationed in the courtyard, may have consoled his explosive temperament, which seemed ill-equipped to deal with frustrations.

The Pazzi themselves, who above all must be brought into any account of the violence to come, traced their lineage and claims on Florence to the First Crusade. In 1099, one Raniero had commanded a Tuscan regiment all the way to Jerusalem. He returned carrying a sacred flame supposedly lit at Christ's tomb. Raniero had also acquired what became the family name when he was dubbed *pazzo*, or the crazy one. In legend at least he had opted to ride the whole distance back to Florence seated the wrong way round on his horse, to shield his sacred flame from the wind. Ever since, in fact, on Saturday during Passion Week, a coal has been lit at the Carroccio to the Cantonata dei Pazzi to mark his devotion: its glowing ember is borne to the *Duomo* 'and, in both places, an artificial dove, symbolical of the Holy Spirit, by some mechanical contrivance is made to light a lamp before the sacred image at this corner, and on the high altar of the cathedral.'[12]

As may be inferred from these hints of Pazzi piety, Francesco's plan to assassinate Lorenzo and Giuliano would at first have been unconnected to killing them in the *Duomo's* nave – or across the *piazza* from the small church where Niccolò went for his Latin lessons. Nor were their assassinations scheduled for Easter Sunday, to avoid the possibility that Sixtus, along with the rest of the conspirators, might be accused of adding 'the crime of sacrilege to murder.' Nor were they to occur in Florence. Francesco's plan to murder the brothers in January, 1478, however, and not far out of town, either at Jacopo de'Pazzi's villa in Montughi, or at Lorenzo's in Fiesole, fell through when Giuliano failed to keep a dinner date at Montughi with the waiting assassins. He had injured his leg in a riding accident. The fact that he and Lorenzo were willing to show up at all, though, indicates their ignorance of the plotting against them.

Probably for these reasons the drama set for the *Duomo* on 26 April 1478 had already acquired, if just for its inventors, an aura of anticlimax. Despite the threat of public mayhem, a generous amount of overexposure and quarrelling may have drained it of any solid prospect of success, while from the start it seemed a shrunk, sleazy idea, or power-grabbing snagged on a cheap back-alley punch-up.

For others, though, the Pazzis' assault on politics and history would have seemed incalculably horrifying. The two victims, the hundreds of witnesses and thousands of indirect witnesses, among them Niccolò and his family, who were to learn the facts of the bloody affair almost at once – for reasons quickly to become clear – in reality faced what would have seemed a spewing terrorism pouring out of an obscure, nightmarish and possibly spiritual disorder.

Also figuring into the crowds at the great cathedral, and the dull, sallow light of its vast nave, was the anomaly that Giuliano was not eager to go out that morning. His injured leg still annoyed him. He might not have gone at all, except that two of the most enthusiastic potential assassins, Francesco de'Pazzi and Bernardo Bandini Baroncelli, a fortune-hunter who owed the Pazzi money, returned to the Medici Palace to get him. By then Lorenzo had left for the Easter services. He was accompanied by Raffaele Riario, the Pope's seventeen-year-old nephew and himself a newly appointed cardinal. It was agreed that the two brothers ought to be killed together to guarantee the coup's success.[13]

Francesco frisked Giuliano for concealed weapons as he limped along the street, disguising his treacherous inspection as an affectionate hug. As the two men reached the cathedral, which looked wan and sickly inside except for a few chandelier-lit areas, and was packed with Easter-worshippers, with Niccolò and his family probably among them, the divine service rising into the silvered semi-darkness, Francesco led Giuliano to a spot at the north flank of the choir. A nearby door opened onto the street: he had become attentive to his escape-route. Lorenzo stood far off, on the other side of the altar.

The assassins were to attack at eleven, at the sound of the sacristy bell. Two priests recruited into the conspiracy, Maffei and Stefano – Maffei was eager to avenge himself on Lorenzo for the massacre at his home city of Volterra – were to strike then as well. Even as these manoeuvres came off, however, none produced its proper effect.

The bell was to be their signal: it was to distract Lorenzo and Giuliano, who would be absorbed in their prayers. Once they had been killed, Archbishop Salviati, another conspirator, and yet another, Jacopo di Poggio Bracciolini, in charge of a cadre of armed men slipping their concealed swords and daggers from under their cloaks, would race to the Palazzo della Signoria. There, at the centre of government, they were to seize the actual reins of power.[14]

The well-known Jacopo di Poggio Bracciolini's role in what happened must still – after centuries – rankle as an enigma, and because of his influence on Niccolò, ought to be taken into account. The son of Poggio Bracciolini, a well-known scholar and the author of wildly obscene tales – his *Facezie* were to influence folk literature and other types of fiction straight across Europe, including in

Germany the hilarious, world-famous *Tales of Till Eulenspiegel* – Jacopo was an accomplished translator and had recently re-established good relations with Lorenzo after a dispute. It remains reasonable, though unproved, that he was attracted to the Pazzi Conspiracy by republican ideals. The poet Angelo Poliziano, a Medici supporter present in the cathedral during what immediately turned into a roaring brawl, dismissed this possibility with a disgusted shrug: Bracciolini was evil and would have done anything, even kill a friend, for advantage. Poliziano's contempt, however, seems even less convincing than the likelihood of Jacopo's duplicity, which contradicts any idealistic goals.[15]

Whatever twisted motives flickered through the *Duomo* as the sacristy bell rang out, their cruelty, along with the ugliness of the plan itself, went horribly awry.

Francesco de'Pazzi flung himself in a frenzy on Giuliano, stabbing him at least nineteen times, and in so ferocious an outburst of passion that he stabbed himself in the leg. The misaimed attack followed Baroncelli's 'Take that, traitor!' His dismal shriek followed a plunging of his dagger into Giuliano's head, with such vigour that it slammed through his skull.

Lorenzo did somewhat better as his brother fell sprawling, gasping and bleeding to death just past the altar. He fended off the two priests who took their swipes at him, acting with the same swiftness of calculation which had set him apart before that morning and would continue to do so throughout his life.[16]

Nine years earlier, on 3 December 1469, and then at the precocious age of twenty-one, on the death of his father Piero, and just as the poet-diplomat-partygoer prepared to assume control of the Medicis' financial and political empire, he had displayed a shrewdness whose subtlety astonished everyone, announcing that 'contrary to my age and involving great responsibilities and perils, I [take up my legacy] with great reluctance, and only to preserve our friends and possessions, for in Florence things can go badly for the rich if they don't run the state.'[17]

By now he seemed even more confident. Luca Landucci, a merchant and diarist, along with other eye-witnesses, records that while Lorenzo took a neck wound from one of his two ambushing assailants, he coolly unsheathed his sword, parried their weapons and managed to get away by racing into the sacristy.

Other bits of the fraying conspiracy now unravelled completely. Jacopo di Poggio's attempt to seize power at the Palazzo della Signoria failed when as he arrived the few officials on the spot became nervous and hastily locked themselves away in a secure room.

Once he heard that Lorenzo had escaped, Jacopo de'Pazzi's fumbling attempt to save the day by mounting his horse and galloping from one *piazza* to the next, shouting *'Popolo e libertà'*, and thus trying to rouse the people against the Medici, produced nothing except his unpleasant discovery that with nobody joining him he had better flee not only his *palazzo* but Florence itself.[18] Federico da Montefeltro's troops, waiting beyond the walls, were never brought in, and dispersed.

Each of these glimpses of failure, however, only pointed to the even more heartless drama to come. Landucci's diary entries reveal the spiralling dread, developing into mob violence, that now swept the streets and was likely to have been witnessed by Niccolò:

> The city was up in arms, in the *Piazza* and at Lorenzo de'Medici's house [to which he was brought]. And numbers of men on the side of the conspirators were killed in the *Piazza*; among others a priest of the bishop's …, his body … quartered and the head cut off, and … the head … stuck on the top of a lance, and carried about Florence the whole day, and one quarter of his body was carried on a spit all through the city, with the cry of: 'Death to the traitors!'[19]

Later, during the night, some of the dead themselves appeared in the high windows of the Palazzo della Signoria, whose panes overlooked the cobble-stoned square where *parlamenti* of qualified male citizens (or property owners) of the Florentine state were held on occasion. The larger windows seemed to glisten with a dance of corpses.

It had been choreographed to astonish the inhabitants still up and about and massed below, with a display of vengeful justice. It would unveil through its gruesomeness an undisturbed if threatened civil order, in a series of tableaux that everyone, even including boys and girls, was to remember for many years to come, if not for the rest of their lives:

> That evening they hanged Jacopo, son of Messer Poggio, from the windows of the *Palagio de' Signori*, and likewise the Bishop of Pisa, and Franceschino de' Pazzi, naked; and about twenty men besides, some at the *Palagio de' Signori*, and others at the *Palagio dei Podestà*, and at the *Casa del Capitano*, all at the windows,

in each case leaving the body dangling as per Florentine and European custom, its relaxing bag of flesh slapping against the walls and forecasting worse to come over the succeeding days, as when on

> [the 27th] they hanged Jacopo Salviati ... and the other Jacopo, also at the windows, and many others of the cardinal and the bishop. And the day after that (28 April 1478), Messer Jacopo de'Pazzi was captured at Belforte. And that evening of the 28th, about 23 in the Evening (7 p.m)., Messer Jacopo de'Pazzi and Renato de' Pazzi were hanged,

with the total of those put to death through the first week of public executions coming to at least ninety-one.[20]

Even more typical of the violent displays to which Niccolò and Florence as a whole, including other children, were systematically exposed, or about whose horrors they would have heard, were the savageries visited on the body of Jacopo de'Pazzi.

In its swinging about there seemed to emerge some of the more macabre shadows of the age itself, or the disconnection at times of the actors from any code of ethics – and this, paradoxically, as Lorenzo began to busy himself with reasserting his powers and dominance. Astonishingly, his greatest influence almost at once began to develop out of his ravishing commitment to aesthetics. As a fêted though secretly failed banker, he briskly promoted the careers of some of Italy's finest sculptors and painters, with the result that while the urban slaughter continued, he found himself trumpeted as 'il magnifico':

> 17th May. At about 20 in the evening [4 p.m.] some boys disinterred [Jacopo's body: it had first been buried in the cathedral of Santa Croce, then dug up and reburied close to the city wall] and dragged it through Florence by the piece of rope ... still round its neck; and when they came to the door of his house, they tied the rope to the door-bell, saying: 'Knock at the door!' ... And ... they went to the Ponte al Rubiconte and threw it into the river... . And as it floated down the river, always keeping above the surface [no doubt buoyed by its gases], the bridges were crowded with people to watch it pass. And another day ... the boys pulled it out ... and hung it on a willow, and ... beat it, and threw it back into the Arno.[21]

However many boys tossed Jacopo's body back into the river – or whether it was not thrown in by city officials out to get rid of it – scuffles over his body, as over the mangled bodies of other conspirators, ran on for months as they were hunted down and captured (several months later Leonardo was sketching the hanged body of Bernardo di Bandino).

In part as a response to the savagery, an enraged Pope Sixtus chose to launch a spluttering and eventually dangerous war against Lorenzo and Florence itself. The war aside, if only for the moment, it should be understood that among Florence's *polis* of 42,000, as the spate of hangings and other killings became daily more conspicuous, Niccolò was surely accumulating a cogent instruction in the basest aspects of governmental power, in the uses of symbolic brutality and in the slaughter that may seem congenial to sitting judges.[22]

Torture and execution might be boon companions. Advertising their connection might amount to sound governance. Openness alone might distinguish executions from mere murder, while all four – torture, execution, advertising and openness – might be understood as buttressing the legitimacy of the state.

# 6

# A Boyhood Excursion

One year later, during the summer of 1479, Bernardo dispatched his eldest son into a countryside colourful with flowers and farms, the district just north of Florence called the Mugello, chiefly to avoid the plague.

The scourge of Europe, as it was known since its epidemic Italian eruption at Genoa in 1348 – before that, it had raced through China, killing tens of millions – the usually deadly and always agonizing disease, whose origins many attributed to the wrath of God, saw entire populations of cities, towns and villages decimated or at least diminished by up to fifty per cent during its repeated outbreaks.

A recent outbreak, which had poured through Florence at the beginning of the fifteenth century, or a few decades before Niccolò's birth, had eliminated over half the 90,000-plus residents. By 1479, the city had scarcely recovered.

At its most infectious peak, Boccaccio had noted in his *Decameron* its catastrophic effects on Florentine society. These were even worse than the personal anguish of pain and death: 'the reverend authority of divine and human law had almost crumbled and fallen into decay, for its ministers and executors, like other men, had either died or sickened, or had been left so entirely without assistants that they were unable to attend to their duties. As a result everyone had licence to do as he saw fit.'[1]

The ushering in of a barbarism more rampant, unpredictable and grisly than the disease itself stood in contrast to the more familiar sorts of ugly social behaviour, which might, as many understood, be state-sponsored. It led thousands of citizens and others to flee as society itself seemed to disintegrate.

Boccaccio reported on women offering themselves to anyone, on boys to men, on thieves to their scavenging chances in the vacant manorial houses, on masters to servants. Acts of treachery achieved a morbid fascination in popular literature, as in Boccaccio's stories. Pathologies more vicious than the toxic expressions of greed, envy, poverty and murder became bizarrely interesting.

As many understood, the plague had no respect for class struggles – only for death, and it accosted both guilty and innocent with an incomprehensible, Jobian unfairness. Plunged into eddies of neglected laws, families, guilds and other social groups cracked and fell apart. Virtue turned into vice. Altruism seemed suicidal, selfishness philanthropic, rejection hygienic.

Substantial reductions of human contacts were seen from the start as valuable in reducing the contagion. Thousands understood that no matter what the mechanism of the spread of the disease – and nearly none grasped that its vampiristic appetite required strewing about the fleas borne by rats – any congress with the stricken, whether by touching, breathing, dressing, washing and kissing, might be one's last.

Suspicions flared against those who refused to flee, or to pile more logs and furniture on the useless, ubiquitous, smoke-pouring bonfires imagined as offering protection against 'plague-breezes' and 'plague-winds' (the word 'germ' was not used). Unscrupulous lawyers profited from taking down by dictation the wills of people detecting on their bodies the telltale swellings, which were followed in hours by black blotches, boils and terminal writhings.

As Boccaccio also reported and as occurred during subsequent outbreaks, the bodies of the middle class and rich were soon shovelled by their hundreds into mass-burial pits. The bodies of the poor lay scattered about the streets. Most priests were dead. The cemeteries were packed to overflowing.[2]

By 1479 a fear of new outbreaks which could prove even more appalling had lingered over the city for over half a century. The spectre of an earthly Inferno haunted the urban Renaissance brain, along with the ghosts of anarchy, violence and mistrust. To many, history had long come to seem a wicked jest, or an idea not uneasily propped up by Christian convictions.

Bernardo seems to have caught the disease himself and survived as one among the fortunate fifty per cent. On 30 June 1479, while returning to Florence from the family's farms at Sant'Andrea in Percussina, he fell ill. He began to worry that, as others about him were shivering with what looked like plague, he must have it himself.[3] Despite this likelihood, and aware that proper diagnoses were often unavailable and that many of those infected did not die, he realized that all hope ought not reasonably to be abandoned.

As per his practical habits in personal matters, he sketched out in his *libro di ricordi* the steps that he regarded as essential to dealing with his problem, along with arrangements to get three of his four children out of town. Niccolò, then ten, Totto, four, and Margherita, twelve, were sent to their uncle's country house in the Mugello hills (Primavera, Niccolò's elder sister, then fourteen, seems to have stayed behind with her parents).

Bernardo next hired several doctors at the extraordinary price of a single florin each. He provided the first with a testable urine sample, which his cousin, Buoninsegna, who kept his distance out in the street, received through one of the barred windows of the Machiavelli *palazzo*. He too was paid a florin.

Bernardo's physicians treated their lawyer-patient in the ordinary ignorant ways, with debilitating bleedings, plus helpful lancings of the abscessed boils. Syrups and honey-spiced drinks were mixed, herbal ointments rubbed into the excrescent sores. A barber, or *cerusico* (*chirurgo inetto*), who despite his title was given training in medical procedures, including surgery, dropped in with leeches. Their dainty blood-sucking possessed the unacknowledged virtue of sterility.

Over several weeks, or into July, as the doctors' efforts, or perhaps a natural recovery in Bernardo's case, seemed to work, other members of the Machiavelli clan fared far worse. Bernardo chronicles without comment the deaths of a number of his relatives, noting that these continued into August, when the epidemic tapered off.[4]

Interestingly, Bartolomea, Niccolò's mother, seems to have been unaffected. An unsubstantiated family legend credits her with piety, and even with composing religious songs or poems. No trace of them survives, or any hint of when they might have been written. A suggestion persists that they were kept in the family library into the nineteenth century. Bartolomea's strength of belief, however, and the role of her sacred poetry in appeasing what thousands took to be a divine judgement expressed through ferocious physical tortures, are unknown.

It should also be added that when she married Bernardo, as a woman in her thirties, she had already been married, possibly as early as eighteen, to an apothecary, Niccolò Girolamo di Niccolò di Benizzi. He had died in 1457, leaving her the mother of a daughter, Lionarda, who seems not to have survived.[5]

Despite Bartolomea's somewhat uneven background, it was to her brother Giovanni Nelli's safe-seeming estates in Montebuiano, in the Mugello hills, that Niccolò and Bernardo's other children were now sent. As Bernardo fondly recalled, Niccolò wore light summer clothes. He took along a coat and short tunic against the cooler nights.

Niccolò also preceded the other children, with Totto and Margherita following by mule a couple of days later. Totto rode wrapped in his father's bed and sheets, in a basket strapped to the flank of one of the mules.[6]

The glorious countryside around Montebuiano could not have been more agreeable. Its imposing hills spread out rumply, green and rough, as they do now, even if today they are more accessible by smoother roads.

Ample and comfortable vineyards, sporting hundreds of staked rows of strung and (in July) minuscule grapes, unrolled over many miles. They often seemed to run vertically, into a steepness twisted here and there among narrow dells that undulated below the perpetually blue-chambered sky.

In summer a gentle rain seldom fell among the hills' scorched parts. Wallows of plane trees, oaks, yews, beeches and white firs hung about like so many parasols and ushers. The olive trees seemed to have dawdled for centuries. At night, a lone wolf might lope by, foxes more often, trotting between the moonlit vines and hedges.

During summer, scattered flocks of sheep browsed among the truncated leas and tough hillocks, bearing the promise of the valuable wool trade through a taxing sunlight. Another promise, of cheese extracted from the freshest milk, was in preparation among the wandering goats and cattle. Cows were valued far more for dairy goods and leather than, as even in those days in parts of England, red meat.

To those aware of these age-old, agricultural circumstances – the majority – the countryside also yielded an intense, important hint of myth and magic. From ancient times the half-venerated earth had been transformed by the history and religion of its inhabitants, or its estate-owners, farmers, blacksmiths, cobblers, yeomen, wives, mothers, weavers, chandlers, children, ploughmen, priests, huntsmen and carpenters.

For aeons too, unlike other spots across the planet, the legend-nurtured hills had done a good deal more than to offer up a collection of soils, or greywacke scuffing through loam and rising through the occasional twist of summer dust. Over two-score centuries, these path-strewn dales, glens and rocky summits had been folded, pressed, seeded and nursed by a great many worshipful, fanta-sizing fingers.

Following the ancient subjugation of the Etruscans, who had introduced their schools of gods into this expansive, vertical-green theatre, the imperial and educated classes of the ancient Romans, adopting various Etruscan beliefs as their own, had settled in and coached, or so it seemed, their gods into joining them.

They too had admired the hills, but in their own way, through the verse of their epic rural poet, Virgil, who had hailed from not far off, near Mantua. His by now fourteen-centuries-old intimate *Georgics* mingled sound advice to farmers and bee-keepers with descriptions of the Italian farmland spreading out below the Mugello's brook-veined precipices.

In his *Georgics*, the chunky meadows opened southward. They bent toward the parapets and citadels of Rome, but in supple hexameters and through by now famous depictions of predictable, reassuring autumns, winters and springs, to be succeeded and elaborated by months of golden, crop-improving sunlight.

Virgil's phrases, sensible, philosophical and even celestial, as much juicy as admired, had everywhere been committed to memory, and not just by those who, as in ancient Roman times and for well over a thousand years by Niccolò's fifteenth century, might as schoolboys have immersed themselves in the discipline of a classical or humanist education.

Drawn to Latin himself, and hearkening to Virgil's speaking pictures, to cite the *simpatico* phrase of Sir Philip Sidney, who would himself not be born until the next century, Niccolò had probably not yet read Virgil's *Georgics*. He would have heard of them. Virgil's quartet of poems was set out according to a plan of one lengthy poem per season. Niccolò would have read snippets, and probably more, of the *Aeneid*, the Roman poet's stately, landscape-dominated epic centring on the violent invention of the ancient world's most politically suave empire.

He would thus have recognized about him, as if somehow intended to discover and rediscover this wild yet tamed and re-imagined countryside, the older, god-riddled world within it. Along with farming practices little changed since then, its mythic reality persisted. Niccolò had been encouraged by his teachers and his father to see wherever he went the still capable Roman ghosts amid the extant glimmerings of their lost yet somehow immortal culture:

> the ploughman hammers the hard tooth
> Of the blunt plough: one chap will fashion troughs from a tree-trunk,
> Another brand his cattle or number his sacks of grain.[7]

His growing knowledge of the fixed orb of the Earth on which he lived, with the heavens circling above it – these wrapped as much for him in a pagan Roman antiquity as in his Renaissance-Christian modernity – would have seemed richer, more intelligible when viewed through the poet's eyes:

> Wherefore the golden sun commands an orbit measured
> In fixed divisions through the twelve-fold signs of the universe.
> Five zones make up the heavens: one of them in the flaming
> Sun glows red forever, for ever seared by his fire:
> Round it to right and left the furthermost zones extend,
> Blue with cold, ice-bound, frozen with black blizzards:
> Between these and the middle one, weak mortals are given
> Two zones by the grace of God …
> Hence we foreknow the weather of the uncertain sky,
> The time to reap or sow,
> The time that's best for lashing the treacherous sea with oars,
> And launching an armed fleet.[8]

And during summer itself, doubling the ancient-Roman depth of the landscape, and close by in the hamlet of Cafaggiolo, there also remained, as if to appease his modern curiosity, a reminder of the new political world, the Villa Medicea.

Its *pièce de résistance* was its castle, restored in the fifteenth century and converted into a summer residence by Cosimo the Elder. It had been remodelled and was used as a summer getaway by Lorenzo de'Medici, and even more often after the recent attempt on his life.

Marsilio Ficino (1433–99), the mathematician and philosopher praised for his translations of Plato, including his *Timaeus*, was a frequent guest at the Medici villa. So too was the renowned logician Giovanni Pico della Mirandola (1463–94), Marcello's former student.[9] Both did more than earn their keep at the feasts arranged for relaxed summer evenings by adding to the sum of smart conversation. Everyone's Tuscan accents seemed to gain a new sheen from their debates on the meaning of history or the latest insights of natural philosophy, understood today as the hard sciences.

A broad enthusiasm for the history of ideas was at fever pitch among the educated, and despite both philosophers' odd meanderings into the obscure corners of medieval astrology and amulet reading, it was generally agreed that their conversation sparkled. For the most part, too, it consisted of rational

speculation, something less common among their gorgeously dressed, empiri-
cally oriented yet superstitious audiences of noblemen, noblewomen, politicians
and merchants.

If peace mingled with good sense at the Villa Medicea, the hemmed-in,
night-blackened villages not far off seemed as if dug into the countryside. They
were linked by scurfy roads, since Roman times stripped of their lead metalling.
Swathed in a virginal dark once the sun went down, away from the tapers lit at
Lorenzo's castle windows and at those of a few other houses in the evenings, the
isolation of the sylvan world admitted nearly no lights with the residents abed.

If in the hamlets and neighbourhoods of recent centuries the natural world's
separation from human inhabitants is harder to discover, it may be worth
recalling that in Niccolò's *quattrocento* mechanical or electronic sounds were
unknown, or as incomprehensible as plastic, tea, coffee, television screens,
aircraft engines, iPods and car alarms. The creak of steel, mechanical repetitions, oil-fuelled chinks or clangs, had not been heard, and were as unknown as
screens full of space-angled text messages.

By day and night the spice-packed air, bearing its weights of sage, mint and
rosemary, wherried by in a freshness as thick as that of the growing vegetables,
or as by daylight the sounds of the cabinet-makers, caners, potters, tailors,
spinners and dyers, perfecting their individual products, each different from
the next, as for instance those of the glass-blowers with their uneven bottles and
spidered, silvered mirrors sold to their better-off customers.

In an epoch prior to steam power and the Industrial Revolution, when the
universe seemed a finite affair, and even manageable according to *Fortuna*,
personal daring and divine influence, *manufatto* still retained the sense of
made by hand, and *prodotto manufatto* the actual impression of the craftsman's
thumb.

# 7

# The Lost Years

Niccolò flickers in and out of Bernardo's *ricordanza*, or his diary of domestic events important to him, until 1487, when for unknown reasons Bernardo stopped keeping it. At times Bernardo's entries reveal details of his son's childhood which seem essential to understanding his emerging confidence: a smattering of clues showing how at first the boy, and then the man, perhaps wandering into a room, or moving down a road, spent a solitary or a convivial day, or even a few minutes.

After the defeat of the Pazzi, the odour of corruption, unmentioned by Bernardo, perhaps because its implications of ethical collapse had no direct effect on him, his wife and his children, began to infiltrate the Florentine air. The near-total freedom of the rescued ruler, no matter how much in principle he might seem restrained by a revered constitution, knew no bounds. Lorenzo might do as he wished.

Still, the situation remained a paradox. If his greedy financial practices seemed largely unrestrained, any blame for the failure of just one foreign adventure – as for example a war – might be unlimited. The despot, more than the bureaucrat or elected official, no matter how well protected by testy sycophants, could rapidly attract a mass of public scorn, with all its attendant risks that he might be deposed.

An important problem in Lorenzo's case was that the Medici, who fancied themselves master-bankers, had begun to dissipate their resources in the expensive war unleashed by Sixtus and his allies. Chief among them remained King Ferrante of Naples.

Florence also languished under the restrictions of a papal injunction of excommunication for its republican defiance in seizing, torturing and executing treacherous priests and papal emissaries. Sixtus had 'flooded all Italy' with letters and whispered accusations. These mocked and denounced what he saw as the Florentine repudiation of God's legitimate representative on Earth.

Medici banks in Rome and Naples, ineptly run by Lorenzo in any case, were quickly forced to shut their doors. A dispute over Lorenzo's attempt to borrow money for his Florentine war chest from his bank managers elsewhere, which had been provoked by their refusal, led him in a fit of pique to shut down, quite on his own, the Medici banks in Bruges and Milan.

His blunder only intensified an equally self-defeating wish to pilfer tax revenues and other funds from Florence itself, to the tune of an impressive 75,000 florins over the next couple of years.[1]

A Medici legacy likewise fell prey to his avarice. As guardian of the two underage sons of his father's cousin, Pierfrancesco de'Medici, who had died in 1476, Lorenzo had access to their cash reserves. Between May and October, 1479, this amount, or nearly 55,000 florins, easily found its way into his pockets.[2]

The war meanwhile veered from bad to worse. Mercenary skirmishes evolved into fair-sized battles, hard on the heels of successive attempts at military intimidation. No one worried too much if paid-up soldiers flaunted rather than used their weapons, but it now seemed that familiar shilly-shallying mercenary tricks, ruses, feints and jabs had turned into an authentic conflict. Behind the menacing, clumsy artillery barrages, the residential populations of the cities and towns in the Florentine Republic found themselves increasingly drawn into the expectation of an immense assault, arousing fears for their independence and lives.

Indictments and humiliations also abounded. They seemed everywhere matched by suspicions spurring revenge-seeking. Demonizing poems, distributed as broadsides in the streets of Republican cities and towns, played a seditious role. If the mercenaries were driven by greed, slews of citizens surrendered to crazed passions.

What was increasingly clear was that in terms of anxiety and thoughtless responses, Florence's diverse groups, among them the Machiavelli, were becoming afraid and involved. As early as July 1478, when the war began, Landucci's diary cites battles in which citizens were killed and prisoners taken, both 'men and women of all classes.' By December, as the pillagings and burnings seesawed across a few thousand square miles of the Florentine territories – ranging as far east as Venice and as far west as Pisa – the fighting and slaughter had become inextricable from the latest eruptions of the plague, which as always was perceived as a type of divine vengeance directed at sinners ('the plague was … causing much mortality; it pleased God to chastise us').[3]

In the summer of 1479, Landucci himself fled Florence for a bit, more in fear of the disease than the war, as Niccolò was sent to the Mugello hills for the same reason.

By September, Bernardo, who in his quasi-diary often ignores military and political events, records the capture and wrecking of a Florentine fortress in southern Tuscany, anxious about its nearness to his family properties in Sant'Andrea in Percussina. He orders his *brigata*, or family-*cum*-workers, to return to Florence, getting them out of harm's way and making sure that his flocks of sheep are relocated to safety.[4]

A masterstroke seemed crucial to breaking what looked like an emerging military stalemate that might implode into a Florentine surrender. In December, 1479 Lorenzo set out to provide it.

To make matters clearer, it must be noted that daily life in the city had long since begun to be affected by rolling cannon, rusted armour and the leather of cavalry saddles drenched in mud. The treasury was bare. The wool trade, fundamental to the Republic's financial independence, seemed as impossible to keep up as to defend with unsuccessful sallies. The introduction of a startling new weapon, a primitive, inaccurate handgun, with 2,000 of some 8,000 Milanese foot soldiers using it in a single victorious battle, suggested by the autumn of 1479 that both sides might anticipate additional threats of an advanced, technological sort, despite the tenuous alliance between Milan and Florence.[5]

Even if a likely battlefield disaster failed to develop, the plague itself might wreak greater havoc than ever, bloated by the general malaise and economic hardships. In his customary flamboyant style, therefore, Lorenzo seized on a pre-Christmas moment to arrange a conciliatory meeting with King Ferrante of Naples, his primary enemy. Face to face negotiations might end the carnage, even if attempting them also meant risking his life. Rather than slipping off to a minor port on the Tuscan coast to take a discreet ship south to the Neapolitan capital, he consulted with his Milanese counterparts, as they did with theirs in Naples. The Neapolitan response was somewhat better than discouraging. He would be welcome, though his journey might run along improved lines if he embellished it with gifts: he ordered them at once.

From King Ferrante's point of view, the following two months of negotiations, after the Medici leader's majestic entrance into the old city, amid flocking, joyful crowds and grave flashings of steel and silk, had less to do with putting

an end to the war than with convincing everyone of a Florentine defeat. Tough
bargaining produced concessions. Money and slices of Republican territory
were cheerlessly given up. As Lorenzo acquiesced in his losses, his success at
home seemed to grew by the hour. It became clear that he had averted a far
worse military and political débacle.

A crucial moment came during the following August, when the Turks staged
an invasion by flotilla at Otranto. The Pope's hostility now abated. Like everyone
else, Sixtus understood the importance of setting aside intra-Italian quarrels
to confront a common 'infidel' enemy. The war faded away to an end, and by
December 1481, the Medici bank at Rome had reopened.[6]

A year earlier, in 1480, Niccolò Machiavelli, by then eleven, had begun learning
arithmetic and elementary business accounting (*l'abacho*) in a first venture into
the less poetic terrain of applied mathematics. These efforts complemented his
Latin studies. His younger brother, Totto, now five, had also started in on Latin,
though over the coming year both saw their education transferred to a third
tutor (for Niccolò), ser Pagolo Sasso da Ronciglione. Pagolo perhaps taught
Niccolò the rudiments of classical Greek, though he seems to have shown little
interest in it and no evidence survives of his retaining any.

By now, too, according to Bernardo, his twelve-year-old son had begun to
write brief Latin compositions and to translate into Latin from the Italian ('*fa
de' latini*'). He read the standard general children's history, Justinus's *Epitome*, in
a parchment manuscript version borrowed by his father from a neighbour, one
ser Piero, who according to his appellation 'ser' would have been a clergyman
or notary; 'messer' remained a title reserved for jurists, including judges, and
knights: Bernardo himself was usually addressed as 'messer'.[7]

Niccolò's new tutor, a priest, ser Pagolo [Paolo], ran his own school at the
*Duomo* and taught the clergy there, or at Santa Maria Reparata, as it was also
called. His *Duomo* pupils were often the sons of some of the most prominent
and influential families in Florence, including many well connected to the city's
government. Pagolo himself had been recognized for considerable intellectual
accomplishments. As a translator of Virgil, Lucretius, Ovid and Tibullus, he
assisted his students in parsing sessions, rhetorical analyses and the rote Latin
learning of the ancient Greek philosophers in translation and above all of
ancient historians and political writers such as Livy and Cicero.

The boys themselves, who ranged in age from twelve to about fifteen,
comprised an intellectually elite group: other boys their age were consigned to

what were designated as arithmetic-orientated schools. Among Pagolo's pupils were Pietro Crinito and Michele Verino, soon to achieve precocious renown as poets. Michele, who died at eighteen, in 1487, had already published in Latin his famous *disticha*, tidy, witty inventions comparable to the two-line epigrammatic verse of the Roman poet Martial. His death was mourned by the leading Florentine humanists, among them Cristoforo Landino, himself the author of an admired commentary on Dante's *Commedia*. Landino saw Michele as a noble spirit who had been cheated by *Fortuna* out of a brilliant literary career.[8]

Knowledge of Niccolò's comings and goings, of his doings, now begins to flicker, go dim and brighten over the next several years, especially as guesswork unsupported by data scarcely helps. He next crops up in Bernardo's *libro* in 1481, assigned to deliver more or less monthly payments in cash for his father (Bernardo paid in kind as well, with barrels of wine and bottles of vinegar: the expense was a big one for him) to a cloth-merchant for portions of his daughter Primavera's trousseau.[9]

Her wedding, to the twenty-three-year-old Francesco Vernacci – she was fifteen – was arranged in stages, as was usual, accompanied by inter-paternal negotiations over her dowry. In Primavera's case these stages, as was also usual, extended over a few years. The last followed the actual ceremony, scheduled for Sunday, 15 June 1483. It in turn was succeeded by the consummation of the marriage at her family's house after a celebratory wedding dinner that night. The final arrangements were capped on 6 July by her participation in the official bridal procession to her husband's home.

Primavera's bridal gown seems to have been luxurious and expensive. It consisted of a *cotta*, or elegant blue goat- or camel's hair undergarment, plus a *giachetta*, or blue silk outer garment. These ran her not-at-all-rich father well over 900 florins, to which, if one wishes to estimate the cost of the entire wedding, must be added linens and bedding, new clothes and two cradles, plus her portion of the accumulated *monte* (over 500 florins), or the bride's dowry money, invested by Bernardo over many years in a city-administered fund, a custom in practical-minded Florence, together with what he recalled as his modest outlay for the wedding dinner.[10]

Niccolò also reappears in his father's *libro* in an entry for 21 June 1486: at seventeen and with Bernardo off at Sant'Andrea in Percusina, he seems happy enough to deliver a payment of '3 bottles of red wine and a bottle of vinegar' to a local *cartolaio* for the binding – after eleven years – of Bernardo's copy of Livy's *3 Decades* ('*le Deche di Livio*'), given him for making his valuable index. Even after the long wait the binding turned out to be solid and elegant but hardly exceptional: wood boards half-covered in leather, with two clasps. Simplicity belied its preciousness.[11]

It is unclear whether Niccolò ever went to university, and if so, how or where, though he knew a great many who did, including a number of renowned scholars and professors. Even if he chose not to become a professional scholar, his admiration for textual and historical detective work shines out in ways that rapidly became evident, though his immediate educational path after his early school years remains baffling if not unclear.

Tantalizingly, Bernardo's *libro di ricordi* breaks off at just the moment, in 1487, when he may have started attending lectures at the financially run-down but vigorous *Studio*, Florence's first university, dating from 1321, with its *studio humaniora*, or well-trained faculty of scholars uncovering facets of humanist thought. He might even have attended the Republic's newer university of Pisa. This had been paid for by Lorenzo de'Medici since 1473, and had specialized schools in law, medicine and theology, though the odds in favour of his enthusiasm for these narrower concentrations seem long (the law school had appealed to his father).

At the *Studio*, from 1480 to 1481 on, he might have heard the respected poet Angelo Poliziano on the technical underpinnings of ancient Greek and Latin eloquence. He might also have listened to Cristoforo Landino on ancient rhetoric and *poesia*, or Marsilio Ficino on the nuances of Platonism. Here too he might first have met the already famous lecturer and scholar Marcello Virgilio Adriani. Marcello was nine years his senior, a noted Latinist and the translator of Dioscorides' *Materia medica*, a massive first-century pharmacopoeia, or standard physician's bible. While his translations were less than perfect, his more modern political ambition to join the Signoria might have surfaced in conversation and sounded attractive.[12]

A single remark of Paolo Giovio, a clerical author as dishonest as he was hostile, but who knew Niccolò during the early 1490s, is all that remains as evidence connecting him with university studies. In Paolo's *Maximus*, a collection of crisp, arch lives of contemporary celebrities, he claims that Niccolò 'plucked the flowers of Greek and Latin' under Adriani's tutelage, presumably at the *Studio*, though the claim is unsubstantiated and a suspicious twilight lingers over its author.[13]

What is clear is that at around this time, or within a few years, and most likely before 1494, and whether under a professor's guidance or not, Niccolò plunged into a scholarly enterprise of his own, copying out plays by the ancient Roman playwright Terence, as well as Lucretius's over 7,000-line poetic masterpiece, his *De rerum natura* (On the Nature of Things).[14]

These demanding efforts, which inevitably led into scholarly training, may be seen as banishing the educational shadows, not only because of what the act of copying must have taught him about style and fluency in Latin, and possibly Italian, or the skills essential to moving ahead in Florentine society in those days, and even into the city's political life, but also for the faascination of the works themselves.

In the light of Niccolò's 'disappearance' for almost ten of what have been described as his 'lost' years, roughly from 1487 on, more attention than usual needs to be paid to these copying efforts as keys to understanding his intellectual and artistic development.

Terence (*c.*185–*post* 160 BCE), as Niccolò came to know him, was the author of six surviving plays, among them *The Girl from Andros* and *The Self-Tormentor*. Influenced by earlier Greek drama, he was the first ancient Roman master of the bouncy rhetoric and banter of drawing-room comedy, or sexy, intimate, insulting, sleazy, entertaining foolishness. Lucretius (*c.*95–*c.*55 BCE) was the foremost ancient Roman master of philosophical empiricism, or the post-Platonic doctrine whose attractions he exhibited in a style both serene and brilliant, blending lucid, novel images with logic and plainness of phrasing.

Neither writer was much appreciated during his lifetime. Terence was derided as frivolously domestic by Julius Caesar, Lucretius dismissed by the anti-scientific Romans. Virgil had admired his breadth of vision in promoting the atomistic and genetic insights of the Greek philosopher Epicurus. Among them was the principle of inherited biological characteristics. Such radical notions placed Lucretius so far ahead of his time as to make him seem a buffoon.

Terence had long been known to humanist and medieval scholars, though the first printing of his plays had taken place in Strasbourg only in 1470. Lucretius by contrast was forgotten. The *De rerum natura* was rescued from centuries of ignorant darkness in 1417, or a bit over seven decades earlier, by the author-scholar whose son was later executed for joining the Pazzi Conspiracy, the unflappable yet tenacious hunter after ancient manuscripts (he also discovered lost works of Cicero and Quintilian), Poggio Bracciolini (1380–1459), apparently at a monastery in Fulda, in Germany.[15]

Both Roman authors would easily have appealed to Niccolò for their stylistic good taste, or humanistic liveliness, coupled with naturalism, an idea best understood in his day as an evidence-based approach to describing the physical world.

By the late fifteenth century, the influence of naturalism had been expanding for decades. This was especially the case among painters and sculptors, but the two ancient Roman poets (if a playwright as vivid as Terence is also considered a poet) had anticipated its basis of aesthetics and propositional truth in phenomenology, or the study of physical experiences, and this over sixteen hundred years earlier than almost anyone had thought possible.

Under their influence, Niccolò's humanist tendencies, or his education so far, began to veer down an interesting new path. Either that or his maturing inclination to depict and analyze the world from a naturalistic point of view received a powerful injection of intellectual vigour. As a copyist, he would have found compelling at least three among the scores of daring passages in Lucretius. These dealt with images, or the workings of the imagination, the foundations of political states and the plague.

Medieval attitudes toward the human imagination – or more precisely, mental images, or *imagines* – had been, and in his day remained, unflattering. All fantasies were considered self-delusions. They were ego-centred mirages rather than, as people today see them, whimsies, dreams, daydreams or attractive and exciting ways to reconfigure problems or experiences. Lucretius would have encouraged Niccolò to adopt a more modern understanding of images. It might prove a useful tool. His argument was that they induce vision, or what Newton in centuries to come would describe as a response of the optic nerve. As a result, they provoke perception. This becomes possible because both crude and refined *imagines* are shed by objects and enter the eye, enabling it to see. The more refined type of *imagines* in fact consists of

> flimsy films from the surface of objects flying about in a great many ways in all directions. When these encounter one another in the air, they easily amalgamate, like gossamer or gold leaf.... . These ... penetrate through the chinks of the body and set in motion the delicate substance of the mind within and there provoke sensation.

And the reason? It lies – and herein resides some of the originality of the

Epicurean account of the universe – in the nature of the mind, or its nimbleness. The mind has an elastic quality which allows it to be much more than a static organ: 'for the mind itself is delicate and marvellously mobile.'[16]

Put differently, from Lucretius's Epicurean standpoint the mind, like the body, is not a thing but a process. It not only represents but constitutes a superior form of alertness. Even when the body is asleep, the mind maintains its antenna-like trembling, or manner of action, as do the universe's atom-based, flighty particles and qualities, especially its most fundamental: those of emotional and sexual love. Love is to be understood as presiding over the welfare of living creatures. In combination with the underlying physical near-serenity of all phenomena, it sustains their renewal.

Despite his scorn of hedonism, therefore, his contempt of pleasure and his puritanical code of morality, Lucretius is unyielding in his conviction that Eros, conceived as a force, expresses a unifying process that often cannot help but triumph:

A woman deficient in beauty sometimes becomes the object of love. Often the woman herself, by humouring a man's fancies and keeping herself fresh and smart, makes it easy for him to share his life with her. Over and above this, love is built up bit by bit by mere usage.[17]

His view of nations and politics glides along similar lines: any society is a form of action rather than a settled institution. It expresses ceaseless flux. The rise of kings thus leads to an inflation of greed, which in turn incites regicide:

[And] so the kings were killed. Down in the dust lay the ancient majesty of thrones, the haughty sceptres. The illustrious emblem of the sovereign head, dabbled in gore and trampled under the fist of the rabble, mourned its high estate. What once was feared so much is now downtrodden. So the conduct of affairs sank back into the turbid depths of mob rule, with each man struggling to win dominance and supremacy for himself. Then some men showed how to form a constitution, based on fixed rights and recognized laws. Mankind, worn out by a life of violence, came naturally to a society in which every individual was ready to gratify his anger by a harsher vengeance than is now tolerated by equitable laws. Ever since then the enjoyment of life's prizes has been tempered by the fear of punishment. A man is enmeshed by his own violence and wrongdoing, which commonly recoil upon their author.[18]

And this condition too is seen as impermanent: only the serenity expressed by natural laws, or the deeper structure of the physical universe, aspires to permanence. More than this, no human being can separate him- or herself from his or her partly criminal nature, or the violence at the fringes of civilization:

> It is not easy for one who breaks by his acts the mutual compact of social peace to lead a peaceful and untroubled life. Even if he hides his guilt from gods and men, he must feel a secret misgiving that it will not rest hidden forever. He cannot forget those oft-told tales of men betraying themselves by words spoken in dreams or delirium that drag out long-buried crimes into the daylight.[19]

War is likewise seen as unavoidable:

> Mankind is perpetually the victim of a pointless and futile martyrdom, fretting life away in fruitless worries through failure to realize what limit is set to acquisition and to the growth of genuine pleasure. It is this discontent that has driven life steadily onward, out to the high seas, and has stirred up from the depths the surging tumultuous tides of war.[20]

And behind human fluctuations lie other more powerful waves, the stupendous, ruling and often grim adjustments of nature, as when, inevitably,

> some atmosphere that chances to be uncongenial to us is set in motion. The baleful air begins to creep. Like mist and cloud it glides, and wherever it comes, it sows disorder and change... . So, without warning, this new plague and pestilence falls upon the water or settles right in the growing wheat or on other human food or pasturage of animals; or else it remains suspended in the air itself so that, when we inhale the polluted atmosphere, we cannot help absorbing these foreign elements into our system.[21]

Astonishingly, given his belief in the ultimate prevalence of near-serenity, Lucretius concludes his epic description of creation, in which religion is dismissed as superstitious but necessary, with a detailed account of the horrors of the plague. These last moments of his grand and perhaps incomplete poem cannot but have impressed the young Machiavelli, who had recently seen or heard about similar horrors:

To no small extent the affliction was imported from the countryside into the city by the concentration there of the plague-stricken peasantry from every district, who crowded lanes and lodgings. Here, crammed within stifling walls, death piled high his heaps of victims... . Exposed in streets and public places you might see many a wasted frame, with limbs half lifeless, begrimed with filth and huddled under rags, dying in squalor with nothing to cover the bones or skin, well-nigh buried already in loathsome sores and dirt. Every hallowed shrine of the gods had been tenanted by death ... In this hour reverence and worship of the gods carried little weight: they were banished by the immediacy of suffering.[22]

And the suffering, like everything else in Lucretius's Epicurean world, remains a shifting process, a type of unrolling action.

In the light of Niccolò's copying out the epic, therefore, his own humanistic training would at least have experienced a challenge. As seems likely, it may have begun to shift from its earlier antiquarian if adventurous philology into a way of seeing the world and what lay beyond and within it as a series of intersecting, endless changes. Ovid, after all, had earlier suggested to him something of the sort in his *Metamorphoses*, which he had read during his school days.

# 8

# Poetry and the Medici

For the moment, though, his own poetry may have taken precedence. Two of his poems, or *canzoni*, have survived from his mid-twenties, and while terse and formulaic, they indicate in their implied apostrophes to Lorenzo de'Medici's son Giuliano that he and Niccolò were friends, and possibly close friends.

Both poems, which seem to date from 1492–94, and which are among the first surviving examples of his written voice, reveal him as before all else a literary man trained along humanist lines in the Latin classics, in Petrarch and Greek and Roman mythology. At the same time, an unexpected political fascination is implied, though not elaborated.

The two *canzoni* were gathered into a small volume that also included ten *canzoni* by Lorenzo de'Medici and one by Angelo Poliziano. Some pages were delightfully illustrated with sketches by Sandro Botticelli (1444–1510), among them at least one particularly apt sketch, given the pastoral genre of Niccolò's lines, of a nattily dressed shepherd seated on a sunlit rock and piping away before imperturbably foraging sheep.[1]

The seeming pastoral innocence is deceptive, however, even as it would be a mistake to see either of Niccolò's *canzoni*, or many in the age-old pastoral tradition that reaches back into ancient Greek and Roman times, as unctuous or naïve:

> O gift of so many gods, may you deign
> to accept me among your loyal subjects;
> may you not scorn to have me among your servants;
>    for my thoughts are meant
> to please you – such is my sole desire –
> I to obey, you to think of commanding me;
>    and though I stand surrounded by the throng
> of these uncouth shepherds, when thinking of you

I soar above the vulgar.
    You will see me soaring even higher once
I know that you accept my gift
which comes reciting your praises.
    Beyond all this, whatever I have I give you:
the herd that you see is yours, and more,
this poor sheep of yours is what I am.

The flattery and pastoral conventions here aside, of the sheep, the shepherds and service to someone somehow adored, what emerges is an unexpected roughness ('the vulgar' or 'rozi pastor') and an underlying acknowledgement – scarcely flattery – of the solid class differences between the two men.

In the rigidly hierarchical world of Florence and Europe itself, and despite Niccolò's likely descent from an obscure noble family, Giuliano, though only a citizen, would have assumed a decisive prominence of rank. This quality of difference is no doubt more than difficult to grasp on its own terms these days, after centuries of politically inspired, democratically inclined revolutions, the idea of which was then scarcely known. The modern mind is better acquainted with class cruelties, and more typically adverts to instances of class-inspired slavery.

Equally difficult is grasping the extent to which in Niccolò's day class distinctions remained powerful reminders of what was assumed to be the hierarchical structure of the universe itself. Masses of people believed that to dismiss class was to dismiss a celestial order, an idea as irrational as drastic, and in the end impossible. This belief was to endure as a justification of social and economic exploitation over several hundred years, and even amid yearnings for greater social and economic equality. What seems sheer flattery in Niccolò's poem, in other words, and despite his friendship with Giuliano, might better be accepted as a gesture of recognition. It amounts to an acknowledgement their social differences.

A similar implication appears in the opening lines of the second poem, in which paradox surfaces fashionably:

All the shepherds abiding in these forests,
no matter their youth,
confide in you their differences.
    You with your skilful and noble genius,

with your various methods and diverse strategies,
enable them to return happily to their fold.
    You are merciful: if one of them is made miserable
by adverse *Fortuna* or by love,
with your sweet speech you restore him to contentment.

The laudatory emotions here seem uncomplicated, yet on reflection one realizes that the nature of the contentment is odd. If 'sweet speech' (*dolce parlar*) suffices to restore a utopian condition, still its enemy is described not merely as *Fortuna*, which ought to be expected, but as 'amore', and in fact as positing a conflict inappropriate to the pastoral world: love conceived as an enemy belongs to a more ordinary, shabbier existence.

Similar mix-ups between a blissful pastoral world and a harsher real one tug at the poem's next tercets, which make up its central section and introduce its hero, Hyacinth, a stand-in for Giuliano de'Medici. In the ancient Greek myth, which Niccolò would have recalled from Ovid (*Metamorphoses* X, 162–219), the beautiful Spartan prince is depicted as beloved of Apollo. When he dies a far too early death, Apollo transforms his blood-droplets into his eponymous flower, on whose leaves there glistens with elegant ominousness the classical exclamation of despair, AI, AI:

Hyacinth, I remain one who celebrates your name
and to render it a memory for anyone alive
I carve it in every trunk, on every crag,
    for your excellent and noted beauties
and your high deeds remain fit to honour
those who speak and write about you.
    The heavens reveal their beneficial powers
by offering us so supreme a wonder,
by sharing such beauty with us;
    every brilliant star fades before this one:
first as it looks at that head worthy
of any crown and any diadem,
    next because the splendour governing that visage
and rippling through every aspect of itself
is Nature teaching us its worth and strength.
    The rest you see through a natural accommodation:

that you hear the sound of his graceful sermons
which can animate a piece of marble, a stone.

The smoothness of the poem's astral, royal and other comparisons – with tree trunks gleaming as they are carved in the name of the beloved, and stars fading as marble comes to life, Pygmalion-style, in response to Hyacinth's voice – may even suggest physical intimacy, at least to the modern reader. The political aspects of the poet's love seem to blend with the erotic. By implication, therefore, the lines seem to refer to a gay or homosexual love.

The Hyacinth myth itself appears to support some such reading, as do several commentators, though without sufficient additional evidence. In the story's Ovidian version, the hero is beloved not only of Apollo but of Zephyr, whom he rejects. Raging with jealousy, the god of the west wind induces one of Apollo's quoits, hurled during a sporting match, to fly wildly about and slam into Hyacinth's head, killing him.

No known circumstances suggest that Giuliano was passionately entangled in a similar or parallel way, or indicate that Niccolò sets out in this poem to echo the whole myth, rather than simply to allude to relevant parts of it. Indeed, his verses soon become a paean to Apollo, and make no reference, however slight, to what was even then regarded with self-conscious horror as 'the Florentine vice':

Helped so much by your grand worthiness,
O sacred Apollo, and by your power, I seek
to invest it in honouring your Hyacinth.

The emphasis here, as through to the end, lies not on sex, as seems plain, or even on an ancient Roman idea of noble friendship – *amicitia* – as much as on fame itself or, more narrowly, on a nod to the resuscitated Roman goddess Fama. Hyacinth's 'glory' becomes a recognizable spur to what Milton, a century and a half later, following in the Roman tradition revived during the Renaissance, would describe as 'That last infirmity of noble mind,/To scorn delights and seek laborious days':

Nor am I lacking in anything to grace
my natural desire to acquire such fame
as may establish your glory everywhere.

It is this challenge, to acquire fame, secured through poetry and an allegiance to the poet's influential and powerful citizen-friend, that becomes the governing theme. What is more, the refocusing makes sense. In the delicate, lush atmosphere of the *Palazzo Medici*, not far from the splendid chapel decorated with frescoes by Benozzo Gozzoli, who had earlier frescoed the walls of the Machiavellis' own *palazzo*, the Hyancinth allegory would have seemed agreeable and appropriate, as both *canzoni*, with their pastoral-political implications, pointed to a bright future for the poet himself.

Behind Niccolò's marvellous poetic trees and his crags carved in Hyacinth's name, and the stars that fade before Hyacinth's radiance, in the nearby Medici chapel Benozzo's mounted, stern-visaged Magi pressed ahead. They moved forever towards Bethlehem across the theatrical walls. They were accompanied by Lorenzo himself, by Pietro the Gouty (his father), his daughters, and even Benozzo's master, Fra Angelico. Groups of soldiers and their elegant servants, clad in rich blue and crimson tunics and cloaks, escorted them under an unnaturally pale, holy sky.

In the not so distant past as well, or ten years earlier, when Niccolò was fourteen, lay a complementary and matching moment of fame for his father Bernardo. This had also taken place in the Medici palace, and a glimmer of Bernardo's triumph persisted into the present as mute flattery of his son's success. It too had centred on a publication. Appearing to much acclaim in 1483, Bartolomeo Scala's *De Legibus et iudiciis dialogus* (Dialogue on Laws and Legal Judgements) represented Bernardo as a character in a dialogue, or as a lawyer-participant in a fictional debate with Scala over the tricky question of the requirements for ideal laws.[2]

Ought they to change according to the changing conditions of their societies, or remain fixed, much like the divinity understood as their source? In Scala's dialogue Bernardo is depicted as siding with the humanists, who saw ideal laws as unchanging. This turned out to be a liberal viewpoint because it shielded legal judgements from corruption, or the supposed arrogance and opportunism of lawyers themselves, despite the fact that in arguing his position Bernardo kept probing for common ground between himself and his amiable, important rival.

The witty Scala was Chancellor of Florence. A well-known historian and writer of fables, he was to continue as Chancellor until his death in 1497. In 1483, he dedicated his *Dialogus* to Lorenzo de'Medici, setting his debate with Bernardo in the luxurious atrium of his new *palazzo*, or not far from the *Palazzo Medici*, in Borgo Pinti.

In those days both he and Bernardo were warmly welcomed, or so the dedication of the *Dialogus* implies, into the Medicis' august literary circles. Ten years later, Bernardo's son, in shaping his two *canzoni* into an allegory of the life of Lorenzo's son Giuliano, was no doubt complimented on extending the relationship between their families.

# 9

# *The Religious Revolution*

Girolamo Savonarola seemed at first to emerge from nowhere. He loomed, people perhaps imagined, surprisingly and shockingly out of a wounded Christian landscape, even if by 1492 there had been subtle preparations for his appearance as a seductive revolutionary.[']

The preparations were both his own and those of the large number of Florentine congregations and leaders who responded to him with interest, contempt, devotion, fervour and, later, violence. At first, though, the preparations seemed nonexistent, or no more visible than, in the centuries ahead, those heralding the arrival on the world's stage of Napoleon, or Lenin or, as assaults on societies may issue from one end of the political and religious spectrum as much as the other and be as cheerful as malignant, Tom Paine, Jefferson, Mussolini, Adolf Hitler, Gandhi, Mao Tse-tung and Pol Pot.

As perhaps also seems self-evident, in politics revolutionaries often look forwards, in religion backwards. If a utopian or happier future awaits the Marxist or democrat, or even the Fascist and Nazi, the sacredness of a sacrificed yet divine past beckons to the priest or minister in search of a lost spiritual purity wrecked by earthly corruption.

No good cheer seemed apparent in Savonarola, in whose sermons irony sank into roaring accusations that rose as grim paradoxes: 'In the primitive Church the chalices were of wood, the prelates of gold; these days the Church has chalices of gold and prelates of wood'; 'O Florence, Florence, Florence, for your sins, for your cruelty, for your greed, for your lasciviousness, for your ambition, you have yet to suffer many adversities and much grief'; 'Bethink you well, O ye rich, for affliction shall smite ye'; 'This city shall no more be called Florence, but a den of thieves, of turpitude and bloodshed. Then shall ye all be poverty-stricken, all wretched, and your name, O priests, shall be changed into a terror ... Know that unheard-of times are at hand.'[1]

These pronouncements, together with many more on higher, intellectual planes of political theorizing, streamed forth from the wispy, acidic Dominican friar of Ferrara, whose sensual lips, looped nose and cadaverous body provoked feelings of revulsion, until he began to speak.

Then his cultivated, booming voice, which Michelangelo said he could never forget, together with his inspired gaze, and his fingers raised in blessings that cursed as much as pardoned, surged out at educated and uneducated alike, often in huge rapt crowds. His appeal was no accident. He had poured hours of rehearsal time into his quaverings of mood and volume, after in his apprentice years managing to hold the attention of 'only some simpletons and a few little women' for no more than a couple of exasperated minutes.

At the peak of his career, over thirteen thousand jammed the *Duomo* to listen to his charismatic, battering declarations of disaster and victory, among them, close to the end, Niccolò himself. By then, in the late 1490s, as Landucci, an early *Piagnono* (literally 'Weeper,' or one of Savonarola's fanatical supporters), observed, the tawny, gesticulating priest was 'held in such esteem that there were many men and women who, if he had said, *Entrate nel fuoco* (Step into the fire) would have actually obeyed him. He was considered by many to be a prophet, and he himself claimed to be one.'[2]

A major source of his success was coincidence. This took the form of super-stitious fears of the coming half-millennium in 1500. The dreaded milestone inflamed for many an end-of-the-world sense of doom. It was abetted by the threat of a French invasion, spreading poverty, religious mistrust and his own contradictions.

The latter elevated him above other crusading priests also offended by widespread churchly corruption and religious decline into a commanding position that attracted the attention of all Italy. His acuity and learning, which were considerable (they had a familial heritage: his grandfather had taught medicine at the university of Padua), weighed into the balance, along with heated single-mindedness, or monomania. These qualities he aimed not so much at power, as his critics assumed, as at the promotion of a genuine reformation of Florentine society. It was a goal that to some seemed repellant because if achieved it would have required a complete surrender of their wealth while dragooning them into altering their innermost natures.

Savonarola's first stay in Florence, which had lasted for five years in the 1480s, ended in failure from the standpoint of converting almost anyone to his cause.

When he returned in 1490–1, however, or by the time Niccolò was twenty-two, his now disciplined confidence, lashed by macabre dreams in which he saw himself reborn as a prophet gifted with what he called a 'terrifying' (*spaventoso*) style, blended into wooing the poor and overwhelmed his much larger audiences.[3]

'I said,' he scribbled in the margin of the published version of his Sermon 5, delivered on 20 February 1491, 'that the devil uses the great to oppress the poor so that they can't do any good.'[4]

By then two new political developments, which he appears with uncanny shrewdness to have anticipated, had begun to abet his attainment of broad religious goals: the sickness unto death of Lorenzo de'Medici, whose gouty body worsened with every passing day, and the likelihood that the French king, Charles VIII, would fulfil his longstanding ambition to seize Italian territory through an invasion pouring down from the north.

Lorenzo's decline, in April 1492 (when Niccolò was twenty-three), induced an embarrassing awkwardness. Savonarola had been invited to return to Florence by the Republic's de facto ruler, and he had responded not only by doing so but by denouncing his host from the pulpit in San Marco for frivolity, licentiousness and sponsoring the sexier productions of such artists as Botticelli, which he found disreputable. Unfazed or perhaps intrigued, Lorenzo sought Savonarola's deathbed absolution anyway, and he apparently administered it, though not, if tradition is credited, without harrumphing hesitations.[5]

Lorenzo's dying ushered in the revival of brutish, superstitious beliefs, together with an end to decades of expensive artistic patronage. Superstition had never fully died out, but now humanism and the spirit of liberal, empirical inquiry were shunted aside. The death scene itself ran along bumpy tracks.

Retiring in pain to his Villa Careggi in the hills just outside the city, the forty-three-year-old early promoter of Michelangelo bade farewell to his son Giovanni, who was about to leave for a new life in Rome. He accepted final visits from friends and his son Piero, who was to succeed him. Lorenzo offered Pierro the brusque advice that he be sure to get up early so as to deal with government business at his best: Piero's self-devoted, hazy grasp of administrative details, despite his hearty good looks, was less than reassuring.

The nursing home atmosphere at the Medici villa during those last days mingled recitations of Tuscan poetry by Lorenzo's miserable sympathizer, Angelo Ambrogini (who had taken the *nom de plume* Poliziano), with the dust of precious stones. On the advice of one of his more feckless physicians, several gems, along with pearls, had been crushed into a pointless medicinal brew, which the dying leader eyed sceptically, but then drank.

Ghastly portents abounded. Marsilio Ficino reported a nightmare vision of giants scuffling in his garden. Howling she-wolves tormented the dark. Queer flashes filled the pre-dawn Florentine sky. During the night of 5 April, or just before Lorenzo breathed his last on Sunday, 8 April, lightning smashed the lantern atop Brunelleschi's *Duomo*, shattering its marble balls and masonry and punching a cascade of blocks and bricks into the *piazza* below. On being informed that the cascade had fallen in the direction of his palace, Lorenzo's hopefulness collapsed and he remarked, 'I shall surely die.'[6]

Mourning for him, perhaps because many sensed an icy selfishness at the core of his aesthetically warm soul, was neither deep nor city-wide, despite a funeral laced with pomp, and the modest crowd attending his burial at San Lorenzo beside his brother Giuliano, who had been assassinated years ago. Nor in the months to come did Piero inspire trust in a Medici-ruled future. Savonarola kept up his vituperative exhortations, launched at his Sunday audiences, that the family come to the assistance of poor women, children and the sick. The new Medici autocrat seemed unaware of their plight.[7]

Piero favoured a regal splendour. His beribboned horses, his flowing locks and querulous eyes, which seemed to peer past people into vague stimulating glories, reacted with puzzlement to the Dominican friar's contemptuous barrage: 'You, you vile slaves, who dwell in filth, wallow as you will: let your bodies be full of wine, your loins loose in lechery, and your hands stained with the blood of the poor, for this is your [lot]. But know that your bodies and your souls are in my hands, and after a short time, your bodies will be scourged to a pulp.'

Charles VIII of France might provide a realization of these unpleasant visions, or so quite a few influential Florentines, along with Savonarola himself, began to believe, as the French King, in command of an army of over 30,000 smartly outfitted troops, and equipped with the latest in long-barrelled siege cannons, invaded Italy in September 1494.[8] What no one expected was that in an act of gushing cowardice Piero would collaborate in Charles's effort to humiliate his own city, or that his treachery might lead to a repudiation of the Medici themselves, followed by their expulsion from Florence and Savonarola's triumph.

In fact the youthful French king, who had succeeded to the throne at the age of fourteen in 1483, had for years been accustomed to thinking of himself along pampered, messianic lines. His claim to the Kingdom of Naples, which he planned to enforce through war and by arranging *en passant* treaties of surrender with Florence and Rome, was based not simply in a legal dispute but in his passionate Christian mission to cleanse and purify.

As far back as 1485, as he entered Rouen, an elaborate theatrical tableau showing him ensconced between allegorical representations of Justice, Prudence, Temperance, Peace and Sanctity, with each announcing that God spoke through his royal mind and body, had excited his sulky teenage intelligence. By autumn 1494 this sort of smarmy propaganda, appreciated by complaisant multitudes in France, had been extended into the idea that he had been born to promote a divine world-wide redemption.[9]

Inept, frightened, short of troops, needing a French alliance and the King's support against his embittered enemies at home, Piero granted him as he arrived in Italy the prominent Florentine seaports of Pisa and Livorno, together with fortresses along the Republic's frontier, in which each of the commanders seemed eager to lay down his weapons at the mere whisper of the Medici name, or, so to speak, its declining power. Piero also tossed in a promise to the King of 200,000 florins, no doubt hoping to render superfluous a French assault on the city itself.[10]

Informed of these manoeuvres, and following on Charles' gratuitous slaughter of troops defending the Florentine fortress at Fivizzano, a dire warning of what was to come if the Republic resisted him, the Signoria reacted with outrage. It rejected Piero's concessions to the scraggly-bearded King, and cobbled together to deal with his treachery a group of distinguished citizen-mediators, among them the now prominent Savonarola.

In the meantime, a catastrophe awaited Piero himself. Frazzled by the sneers of emboldened city officials on his return from meeting Charles at his encampment, where he was impressed by the blue silk flags of imperial triumph snapping in the October breeze and a gaudy display of camp followers, among them lounging cooks, gaggles of prostitutes and the soldiers' pretty wives, Piero tried to shrug off several humiliating incidents in which the gate at the Palazzo della Signoria was slammed shut against him.[11]

Advised by his few remaining friends to retreat into his own palace – at one point he was assailed by a mob of hooting citizens, then assaulted by thugs tossing boulders from the Signoria tower at his poorly armed escort – he did so, to no avail. Respect for him, for the Medici and their flagging régime seemed to fall apart in direct proportion to their previous repression of civil liberties.

As this demoralizing fact penetrated his fantasy world, he found himself that evening, together with his wife, his cousin Giulio and various retainers, fleeing in flustered desperation by coach and on horseback towards Venice, scrabbling at faint hopes of safety in the prayerful dark, amid the jingling of the family silver and other valuables that he and they had managed to snatch up at the last minute.

Within an hour, Charles's advance guard, sent ahead to the *Palazzo Medici* at Piero's invitation to arrange rooms for his visit, began looting the *palazzo* itself. The French officers were joined by crowds of citizens and others crashing in from the street. A senseless destruction of the priceless house, with its climax likely to be an act of enraged arson, was averted only by the Signoria's calling out troops to protect it.

Charles nonetheless proceeded as planned with his ceremonial entrance into the city on 17 November. He arrived on a bay charger and moving through the half-empty streets at a stately, authoritarian pace beneath a battle canopy and among over 10,000 men (he had divided his troops, sending the rest into other cities). At first he demanded that Piero's accustomed powers and prestige be turned over to him, and reacted with amazement when, as the leading member of the Signoria's delegation, Savonarola berated him with a contemptuous refusal.[12]

The moment seemed oddly to belong to the priest who had foretold the King's coming as the enemy of corruption in Italy and the Church. He showed scant shyness about seizing it himself, with his persuasive eloquence.

Over the next few minutes in fact there began to unfold a bizarre drama. It would spread about during the next several years, or until a bloodier theatre of excommunication, torture and executioners' flames foretold its end, a political-religious display that complemented an entire people's insulted, pious aspirations, and not just in Florence but in Italy and Europe itself.

To maintain, however, that Savonarola understood with any completeness the powerful historical energies coursing through the Medici palace as he met Charles that morning would be to nurse a hypothesis too fragile to be sustained by the evidence. At the same time, one misses the mark in assuming that he had no clues to the political implications of his ideas, or to the more daring ideas soon to succeed them, or to the remarkable, strategic role that he now began to play in what was to amount to an authentic religious-political revolution – with its dark-bright thrusts, its invasiveness both subtle and insolent into a European history not yet so much as written or conceived. The patterns of his life fitted coolly into his historical intuition and his apprehension of the tipping points of historical vulnerabilities.

Extracting from his pocket a silver crucifix and flaunting it before him while calling Charles the scourge and redeemer of Florence and Italy, Savonarola apparently threatened the King with God's wrath – and the King seems to have wept at the phrase – unless he at once reassembled his troops and departed with all good speed for Rome and Naples.[13]

Using a mix of flattery and cajolery, and coaxing Charles into agreeing and then into signing a treaty with the Signoria on 25 November, and next, as if prompted, into diverting his forces southward – actually into a quasi-defeat after his initially joyous reception and coronation at Naples – Savonarola found himself celebrated for having averted a Florentine Armageddon.

Whether this popular conviction was in any sense rational or simply an exaggeration, with the Medici out of the way he began to exult in his desire to take charge of the city's political life. His presence, he argued, was now essential to the future of the ancient Republic on the verge of its rebirth, and he repeatedly proclaimed his personal auspiciousness before government and church audiences alike. The city's future, he suggested, ought to march in step with his own: a dream, to which he had often alluded, of fateful crosses, one black and dangling over Rome and shedding lethal swords, and the other gold and soaring over Jerusalem, indicated Florence's disastrous and heaven-sent choices, and the citizens would have to make up their minds.[14]

This unexpected shift in tactics, abetted by his new immersion in actual power, seemed to many – and as later would seem apparent, to Niccolò too – both magnetic and justified. He declared himself ready to participate in designing a new law-based and socially progressive government. He also intended, or so he promised, to abstain from any hands-on role in running it. Popular loathing of the Medici would be dissipated by eliminating their deceptive governing committees. A façade of republicanism had only preserved their autocracy.

As a replacement he urged a far more representative Grand Council, consisting solely of citizens and arranged on Venetian lines, though without a Venetian-type Doge: he mistrusted the likely corruption of a single, dominant *capo*. Simultaneously, and here he insinuated a cause of supreme importance to him, the new-minted government would embody Christian ideals.[15]

Swept aside – and here too his popularity as the nominal saviour of the

Republic guaranteed an invitation to organize its constitutional mechanisms – would be any attempt by former officials to substitute a new government of their own. To most people their efforts seemed flimsily *popolano* in any case, or incompatible with the increasingly widespread desire to create a government administered on democratic principles.

Yet it was no genuine democracy that the priest-leader wished to establish, or a representational system responsive in class-neutral ways to the civil and material needs of ordinary people – one that might, for instance, as in various modern democracies, seek to safeguard minority rights. Crucially, his mind was biblical in its contempt of earthly riches and medieval in its adhering to a view of death as a gateway. Death offered vistas of Heaven and Hell, while politics could light a path to redemption.

Even helping the poor was less a goal than a ritual. Citizens and others must dedicate themselves to God's republican realm, or His semi-representative, divine kingdom on Earth. Indeed, Savonarola sought the establishment of a new Jerusalem: 'Blessed will you be, Florence, for you will soon become that celestial Jerusalem (*quella Jerusalem superna*)'.[16]

The reformed society would also, however, as soon became evident, be decked out in a number of the most rigid restraints of thought-control. Screws of intimidation, while themselves not new, would in novel combinations strangle any real opportunity for privacy and individuality: book-burnings; bonfires of the vanities, or the destruction of any item, especially any work of art, seen as conducive to pleasure; armies of children (*fanciulli*) thousands strong and trained to spy on their parents while raiding gambling dens; processions of Bible-thumping women (often directing their attention at a law banning sodomy, though only one 'sodomite' seems to have been executed); and throngs of sacramental wailers and shriekers.[17]

These hysterical clubs, or actually unleashed mobs, were to multiply in tandem with the growth of democracy as public behaviour was realigned with pious purposes. One outcome of his policies was that his divine utopia, in which politics bowed to religion, achieved more in the way of social paralysis than spiritual growth. Ultimately, it incited a storm of suspicion and terror.

For the time being, however, Savonarola's most dramatic innovations, harsh and pain-centred, lay months in the future. In late 1494, in a few philosophical sermons, any number of which, given their popularity, Niccolò is likely to have heard, he sketched out an apologia for what he regarded as the Aristotelian basis of his beliefs, seeking to soothe the aesthetic and humane anxieties of educated people, though the uneducated were not forgotten.[18] In essence, and before congregations of armed supporters consisting of segregated men and women, he maintained that the physical world was a deception. Christian philosophers such as Augustine and Aquinas, Aristotle's successors, had shown that faith sufficed to convey the soul into God's presence. Religious and other types of education were less consequential.[19]

As a good many of his listeners realized, the charm of this argument carried dangers of its own, including that of social disorder. In urging the desertion of knowledge for sincerity, which he put forth as the chief instrument of salvation, he seemed to authorize the liberation of violent passions. These he encouraged as long as they supported Christian tenets.

Marsilio Ficino, though envious of Savonarolla's mass following, took note of the suicidal trap in this promotion of emotions based on faith alone. Coupled with another subversive thesis, starting in 1495, that of denouncing the lax, militarist papacy, these passions might invite retaliation. In assailing both Church and clergy, Ficino maintained, the friar might license 'enemies that would not be stayed against him.'

Public purgations on a large scale also followed. These involved the burnings of paintings, tapestries, playing cards, gowns, fancy hats, sketches, mirrors and furniture in a set of fiery extravaganzas before the Palazzo della Signoria, in piles crowned by effigies of Satan (one of the first of these strange celebrations took place on Carnival Day, or 16 February 1496). Printed books and incunabula were incinerated, with each of these chant-accompanied, leaping, stomping conflagrations lauded as a bonfire of the vanities. They preceded by months, amid the menacing clouds surrounding his continual attacks on the Vatican, the publication of his excommunication in July 1497.

Botticelli, a devout supporter of Savonarola's campaign against 'impure' influences, whose studio, as gossip had it, was packed with 'loafers,' or hedonists and other dubious characters, hurled one of his canvases into the flames. Filippino Lippi did the same.[20]

Even if no evidence exists that Savonarola ordered the bonfires, his indignation certainly served as their catalyst. In a city aflame with religious fervour – pious plays were performed and new religious societies, or confraternities, sprang into being more or less weekly throughout the 1490s and beyond – acts of Christian affirmation and religious abuse were commonplace. Paranoid impulses ignited flagrant outbursts, including once or twice against the Jews.[21]

Nor, in tracing the patterns of these disturbances, ought their stimulation by the city's very streets, houses, towers and bridges, not to mention its network of churches, nunneries and abbeys, to be neglected. A religious aura, glorious if provocative and police-like, permeated an urban atmosphere full of the antique, incantatory hypnosis.

The glittering Christian world, plumped out in sacred images and icons, nestled in every mean, filthy, ancient and clean corner. Blessings and the grizzled shadows of torture, as well as shabby, bulking curses, squirmed among the lithest statues limping and lounging along the angel- and devil-saturated alleys.

Beyond the parapets of the palaces, or the amphitheatres created by the *piazze*, which served as staging sites for sacred mystery plays as well as 'profane' street theatre, and past the lovely bells up and down the cobblestoned streets, tolling the hours of worship by day and night, there arose amid chimings and ringings vast crowds of marble and painted saints in sheltering niches.

John the Baptist and St Thomas presided over open-air markets. Along the footpaths dragons awaited their saintly slayers. Sculpted martyrs vanished into granite flames. Redemptive crosses rose over the smithies, beside grocers' carts and taverns and at every scrubbed, worn threshold.

Provident cathedrals, with the lushest among them the *Duomo*, floated like instructional flowers over this intricate beehive of salvation, torment, sin and beauty. More modest churches caught the eye with supplications on the nearest lintel and its whittled demons, or hoary wooden doors overflowing with tales from Genesis, or Christ's passion or the punishments of sinners struggling amid the torments of Hell.

Through all the squares, Gothic *campanili*, flying buttresses and apses displayed their peaceful tentacles of rouge and green marble and glass. At intervals that resembled musical rests in the motet-singing, hymns and sacred chants, crowds of religious houses and hospitals bent and bowed, offering solace to any restless soul, or to men, women and children going about their daily business, or sinking to their knees in moments of despair before some sacred pillar, bereft of all but hope.

Nor, as may be imagined, within this urban oasis of music and sculpture, could the Vatican's apprehension of peril in the face of the Dominican priest's attacks, and nurtured by the Pope's fears and loathing, and anticipated by the insights of such as Marsilio Ficino, take long to assume some baleful form.

Months before the celebration of the new year, held as per custom on 25 March 1498, the Signoria sent off to Rome a new ambassador, messer Ricciardo

Becchi.[22] He would represent Florentine interests now understood as running counter to Savonarola's. The chances of the Republic's excommunication had awakened apprehension. If, as seemed likely, the impetuous friar continued to deliver his venomous sermons despite an injunction against them, the political, economic and military consequences could be severe.

In fact Savonarola delivered two of his most damning sermons at the *Duomo* on 2 and 3 March, with Niccolò among the thousands present to hear them. Nor were they his last. Many felt that his 'terrorizing' style had grown by leaps and bounds, and he kept up his defiance till April, relocating to another church, the San Marco. Alexander VI (Rodrigo Borgia, pope since 1492), hesitant, shrewd, orotund, deliberate, scornful and grouchy, vacillated between enforcing and ignoring his ban on a rebellious leader whose popularity might be on the wane.[23]

Machiavelli was now nearly twenty-nine. Bartolomea, his mother, had died a bit over a year earlier, on 11 October 1496.[24] Mourning for her had little to do with his attendance at the *Duomo*, however.

In his earliest-known political analysis, appearing as the third among his scores of astonishingly intimate and official letters, and addressed to the Signoria's new ambassador Becchi in Rome, he offered a scrupulous account of the friar's attitudes and style.

Beyond its personal impressions, his letter is important for its revealing his closeness to Florentine political and military power. Though he lacked any official standing with the Signoria, he clearly knew Becchi well. His letter's indication of their more than casual acquaintanceship – and this despite his use of the formal, conventional *voi* – affirms their cordiality if not collegiality. Becchi has sought out his views, which Niccolò is sending on to him 'in accordance with your wishes.' Equally striking is the letter's diction, its recipe of coolness and empathy. A ripening maturity, if not a spiky, thoughtful briskness, propels the clear, crisp argument, honing the brash conclusions beyond any needs of the assignment.

In permitting dispassionate observation, or the dictates of an on-the-spot journalism, to guide his pen while making no issue of himself, he lays bare a curiosity that amounts to a type of self-questioning. His judgements are sure-footed and prudent as he pins down the slippery details. In sentences allowing his personality to shine through sprightly chinks, he offers Becchi a mind at play with questions of power and how to manage it, implying that he has no aversion to managing it himself:

To give you [*voi*], in accordance with your wishes, a full account of matters here concerning the friar, you should first know that once the two sermons … were given … he said that if what he preached did not come from [God], [God] might [as well] display [some] sign of it. He did this, some say, … to unite his partisans and to strengthen their defence of him, fearing lest the new Signoria, already chosen but not made public, might be against him.[25]

Machiavelli at once focuses on Savonarola's fears for his own safety, and his bombastic method of rousing his supporters through evocations of outside threats:

Fearing greatly for himself and believing that the new Signoria would not be reluctant to injure him – and having decided that quite a few citizens [ought to] be brought down with him – he started in with great scenes of horror.[26]

At the same time, Machiavelli observes that his own eyewitness account will be solid and sceptical, adding that he has no desire to be taken in by 'explanations that [are] quite effective to those not examining them closely.'[27]

A sensitivity to deception leads him to minimize the drama in what follows, a nose-to-the-ground assumption that Savonarola may be out to bamboozle his audience. Suspiciousness runs through his ironic pretence to confusion over audience reactions ('as for what the common people are saying and what men hope or fear, I shall leave that up to you who are a judicious man to determine; you can determine these matters better than I can inasmuch as you are fully aware of our temperament, the nature of the times'[28]), which suggests the wariness evident in almost every line, as towards the end:

He seeks to set all of them [the Signoria and the people] at odds with the Supreme Pontiff, and turning towards him and his attacks, says of the [P]ope what could be said of the wickedest person you might imagine. Thus in my judgement he acts in accordance with the times and colours his lies accordingly.[29]

The word 'lies' bangs home a bit harshly, following on a summary of Savonarola's sermon and his reference to Moses killing the vicious slave-master of the ancient Jews in Egypt – the priest had compared himself to Moses and his rebellious heroism – as if someone were tumbling into a steam-room out of an ice-storm.

An odd frost suffuses the irony of Niccolò's request that Becchi 'not consider it too much trouble to tell me in your reply what judgement you make about the condition of the times and the people's minds concerning the condition of our affairs.' Both attitudes and affairs seem in his view threatened by the same icy winds: civilization may be loosening, the times pulling out of joint, the centre refusing to hold.

His phrases suggest harassed creatures wandering through eely shadows, eyes probing at virtues no longer apparent ('tell me ... what judgement you make about the condition of the times'). Strongly hinted at is his assumption that Savonarola's obstreperousness will provoke a reaction. This reaction, needless to say, might easily have provoked a counter-reaction. It might likewise have been both menacing and violent. Though no one could then have known it, it would eventually be set in motion by Martin Luther to the north, in Germany, and also 'would not be stayed.' Had anyone been granted a prophet's foresight, it might have seemed at least equally momentous.

11

*The World of War and Diplomacy*

# 10

# Executions and an Official Appointment

At the age of twenty-nine, therefore, Machiavelli began to move up in his world and for complementary and coinciding reasons: his family's slight prominence; his ambitions, connections and abilities as observer, political analyst and reporter; his tact, education and loyalty to Florence; the exile of the Medici; and Savonarola's revolution, along with his defiance, torture and eventual execution. The advancement of the priest's exact contemporary into a government position of narrow if prestigious importance filled an important gap.

This was a gap also created by a seismic shift in government itself, if not in Florentine society. Nurtured over the previous four Savonarolan-influenced years by chilly miseries, various morbid winds seemed to rise and coalesce in May 1498, or just months after Niccolò dispatched his report to Becchi. Among them must be counted the precipitious decline of the starving poor and serious outbreaks of syphilis, a disease probably imported by Charles's profligate troops.

The Republic was threatened by a papal injunction unless the friar was brought to heel, and on 8 May he was arrested. His seizure was accompanied by murderous scuffles among his thousands of devoted supporters and the contemptuous, violent, hissing, spitting factions demanding that he be executed, and which, had they been given a chance, would have killed him on the spot.

In streets packed with howling enemies, he found himself, hands tied behind his back, hustled off to the Palazzo della Signoria and imprisoned. In significant cases brought before the Signoria this was routine, or a test of the prisoner's soul and confession. Questioning and torture took place in a room at the top of Palazzo tower, the so-called *Alberghettino*, or 'little hotel,' a stony, skeletal place, whose grimness hinted for short-term residents at an unpleasant end.[1]

By now he was blamed by many but by no means all for masses of the city's problems. Prominent among them, along with the financial deterioration and the epidemic disease, was the inability of the Republic's mercenary soldiers to recapture Pisa, which had been ceded to King Charles by Piero de'Medici but which refused to end its resistance to the restoration of Florentine rule.

More pernicious was his claim that had covered him in adulation and ridicule: that he was a God-ordained prophet. His religious insolence, as it appeared, or heresy, no matter how strongly confirmed for his adherents by his symbolic dreams and his adroit handling of the French King, had led Marsilio Ficino not atypically to accuse him of 'tyrannical malignity' and practising 'a diabolical fraud.'

The power of these accusations was hardly diminished by the government's uncovering a substantial cache of small arms, including artillery pieces, smuggled into the church of San Marco, where he delivered his sermons, though he insisted on his ignorance of any plans for his defence or an uprising.[2]

His end proved as transfixing as prescient of his future unsettled reputation, whose fascination lingers with a special cryptic melancholy to this day. Together with two priest-followers, he accepted a challenge from the Franciscan friar Francesco da Puglia on 25 March to demonstrate the authenticity of his supposedly divine attributes in an ordeal by fire.[3]

This ghastliness required a public exhibition, not unknown if seldom successful, of his asserted miraculous connection to God by an exposure to deadly flames. Evidence indicates that before accepting Francesco's challenge Savonarola tried to wriggle out of it through hours of theological disputation, even if torture weeks later on the Signoria's *strappado*, which yanked his arms out of their shoulder-sockets, inducing indescribable pain, led him to confess that he had been a conman misleading everybody.

His forced confession he subsequently and unconvincingly recanted, though many, among them Landucci, remained persuaded to their horror that he had told the truth, even if he also in the end seems to have welcomed the fire-ordeal.[4] Abashed by pride and threats, as now seems likely, and faced with implacable hatred on all sides, he may simply have chosen to let matters take their course, especially as any hope of rescue or leniency no longer mitigated against the beauty of the martyr's unembarrassed sacrifice.

These ambiguities aside, his adherents, among them the future historian and Machiavelli's friend Francesco Guicciardini, continued to admire him long after his subsequent gruesome incineration under different circumstances. For decades Guicciardini argued that 'if he was good, we have seen a great prophet in our time; if bad, we have seen a very great man,' who 'knew how to feign in public so remarkable an enterprise [his religious-political revolution], without ever having been found in a falsehood.'[5]

A sudden April shower put paid to the fire-ordeal in any case – its cancellation by bad weather seemed to some a sign of his deliverance by God – though when on 8 May he found himself arrested by the Signoria and confronted with what amounted to his third trial for heresy, he also faced an alternate sort of fire test: execution by hanging followed by public cremation.[6]

The Signoria, packed with new members nominated and elected to replace others favourable to him, at first decided to burn him alive, in a perverse variation of the fire ordeal, but, as Landucci notes, on 22 (actually 23) May, a Wednesday morning, the eight hostile officials now in charge (the Eight, as they were termed) 'made the decision that [Savonarola and his two priest-followers] would be hanged and burnt.'[7]

In preparation for either possibility the previous evening had seen the construction of a scaffold walkway leading from the entrance of the Palazzo della Signoria into the middle of its fronting *piazza*, or the site previously chosen for the fire test. A circular platform was erected at the far end of the walkway. It was surmounted by a tall wooden cross, intended for the hanging and burning (the spot is today marked by an inscribed pink marble tablet set into the paving stones). When Savonarola's enemies objected to this unusual gallows that it looked as if 'they [were] going to crucify him,' chunks of its wooden arms were sawn off to avoid the indelicate suggestion of Christian martyrdom.[8]

A vast crowd composed of men only, citizens and others, with Niccolò likely among them – few, including the banished women, seemed to wish to miss out on the fateful occasion – assembled to watch what became a long divestiture ceremony for the three priests, consisting for the most part of an intricate ritual of degradation.

Francisco Remolins, the papal envoy, recounted their crimes against God and man. Tomasso Sardi, a Dominican conventual from the friary at Santa Maria Novella, relieved them of their priestly garments and other possessions, and perhaps even scripture, though each was allowed to wear a simple white robe. Once they had been turned over to the civil authorities for punishment, as was customary, and with the prearranged sentence of death passed on them, their heads and bodies were shaved and they were led along the walkway to the foot of the gallows.

Savonarola's priest-adherents preceded him into the hanging, chanting Christ's name as nooses were placed about their necks. Savonarola himself then stepped to the gallows, saying nothing that witnesses could hear, though his lips kept moving: he seems to have chosen to meet his death in a reverential silence reminiscent of Christ's on the cross.

Once all three were dead, or after a few minutes, the executioner set fire under them to a pile of logs, hay and gunpowder for their cremation, or, more accurately, the elimination of any proof of their existence. The gunpowder guaranteed speed and heat to the flames, which burned intensely for hours, or until their necks, which were strapped to the gallows by iron corselets to prop them up, and their torsos, arms, hands and legs, fell off, mixing with the acrid smell of sulphur and the stench of boiling organs, muscles and veins as these in turn dropped into the hot ashes.

The whole glowing mass was then scooped up and lugged off to the Arno. No trace of their body parts, which might have been seized on as relics, or which could at a minimum have attracted worshippers, was left to assuage the priest's thousands of *Piagnoni*: nothing.[9]

Yet each of these precautions failed, it should be noted, and within days a few women were spotted praying at the site. They were soon joined by others, and even now, at a distance of centuries, Savonarola's most powerful memorial, that of history, asserts its magnetic tugs and pulls.

Unresolved ambiguities seem to hover over his life and career, begging for resolution. The import of the pious, revolutionary adventurer shivers as an ambiguous image in the latest historical air – as dusky, attractive and daunting, to judge from Niccolò's letter, as it must then have seemed to him. The small, stiff, compassionate figure, affixed to the fiery scaffold that still somehow resembles a cross, teases out up-to-date dreams and fears as a type of bequeathed darkness, within which there stirs a terrible, perhaps holy and mysterious spot of light.

Machiavelli was appointed Second Chancellor of the Republic of Florence on 19 June 1498.[10] Savonarola had been dead for less than a month. Charles of France had also died, possibly of syphilis but nominally from cracking his head against a door in his castle at Amboise while rushing off with his queen to watch a tennis match the day before the priest's rained-out fire test. The twenty-nine-year-old novice Florentine official assumed another position as well, that of Secretary to a governmental committee called the Ten of War (*Dieci di Balìa*), sometimes referred to as the Ten of Liberty and Peace (*Dieci di Libertà e Pace*). Both positions offered civil service opportunities to influence policy at the highest levels. Each had required high-level nods of approval, with the first the result of a double election, by the Council of Eighty and the Grand Council, consisting of some 3,000 citizens.[11] Together the positions paid a decent salary of under 130 florins, if at a devalued rate.

To those in the know, Machiavelli's entrance into Florence's governing circles and his swift-seeming rise among them could scarcely have come as a surprise. Neither post had simply dropped into his lap, and one may justifiably speculate on the satisfaction that his arrival in the chambers of decision-making would have brought him. They had long been a familiar habitat for members of his family, and over several generations (one remembers the wealthy Alessandro Filippo Machiavelli, for instance, or the erstwhile *Gonfaloniere di giustizia,* Paolo di Giovanni Machiavelli). The morning boyhood walks across the Arno to his early Latin lessons had turned into more stimulating river crossings for the mature young man bound on state business to an office in the Palazzo della Signoria.

His office was located on the second floor of the today renovated and restored Palazzo Vecchio, as the Palazzo della Signoria is now called, that irregular, large yet elegant building at the centre of the city, more or less finished by 1313 and topped off with its over three-hundred-foot-high Etruscan-style tower.

In the Chancellery, where the narrow, high-ceilinged chamber reserved for his work was situated, his likely spot is indicated by a plaque and posthumous portrait by Santi di Tito (plate I), though the old, portly, stained desks, candles, papers and inkwells – his own and those of the other seven or so secretaries who would have served under him – are long gone.

Another speculation allows the modern eye to visualize his diminutive but vigorous and dark form, alert and in a bit of a rush – his letters often speak of haste and the press of responsibilities – moving across the *piazza* below as in the morning he approached the Palazzo's entrance.

Passing between its massive, iron-braced doors, sealed shut at night with hefty clasps and safety bolts, he would have noticed the graceful fountain by Michelozzo di Bartolomeo (*c.*1396–1472), stationed in the first courtyard. It sported a satirical winged *putto* by Verrocchio, toting a dolphin far too big for its childish arms: a characteristic self-mocking touch on the threshold of the Republic's political arena.

Extraordinary works of art, few of them satirical, would have surrounded him as he hurried through the building: an aesthetic brilliance, of which striking examples have survived, most of it smartened up, polished and installed according to a Florentine tradition reaching back over seventy years by then of urban magnificence (à la Lorenzo the Magnificent). An artificial assembly of painted eyes, fading colours, amorphous, brazen and monstrous limbs, released and restrained passions, epic battles and calming, mythical moments of dalliance, sensuality and religiosity mingled with idealized military victories.

The impressive vista seemed ubiquitous, and unrolled through a score of airy, sun-lit halls, corridors, conference rooms, clubby offices and apartments. Nor would it have seemed anything less than a political art gallery, or the delivery of superb propaganda out of an age of intense aesthetic devotion.

Conscious and unconscious influences, as he hurried past or paused among various gleaming presences, glancing at a picture here or at a piece of sculpture there in the course of his routines, or found himself attracted for seconds to some ruffle of stony liveliness, have not been much alluded to by the chroniclers. It may be surmised, though, that these instants of reckoning mattered a good deal to a sensibility in many ways consecrated to aesthetics and the rhetorical patterns of beauty, and that they remain essential to a more precise understanding of his temperament and even career.

The Palazzo's central rooms, for instance, formed the bureaucratic, diplomatic and negotiating centre of the Republic. They promoted the advantages of order, along with the risks of mess, war, honour, irrationality, love and even murder. In the mezzanine, the grand *Sala dei Dugento* (Ducento), where Council meetings still take place and which dates from 1472, with its coffered ceiling by Benedetto da Maiano (1442–97) and his brother Giuliano, brims as then with gorgeous fleur-de-lys and rosette patterns set in gold. Its frieze scrolls by amid repetitions of the Florentine coat of arms.

The *Sala di* (Pope) *Clement VII* retains its expensive original red and white floor tiles set in wheels and ovals. A decorative passageway leads into the elaborate *Sala dei Cinquecento*, built in *c.*1495 at the behest of Savonarola for his new, more representative Grand Council.[12] With its *invenzione*, or conception, by Simone di Tommaso del Pollaiuolo (*il Cronaca*; 1457–1508), the chamber spans over 170 by 77 feet, and has preserved its enticing laquearia. Even now it seems an *embarras de richesses* of marvellous allegorical scenes devoted to ancient battles, pacts, grotesques and legendary lovers.

The *Sala dell' Udienza*, the official receiving room for dignitaries, and built along the lines of an *invenzione* of Benedetto da Maiano, remains as rich and ornate as in Niccolò's salad days, with its gilt and coffered ceiling, its frieze of gold ropes and leaves. A tinge of artificiality in its colours conjures up clues to a mythical world beyond the ordinary one of government offices. It seems to hoist a more mundane reality into suggestive historical and spiritual dimensions.

Aesthetic luxuries augmented the pleasures of freedom. In a more liberal and developing political atmosphere, they imparted a fresh, negotiable air. Crucial choices might be swayed by the thrust of a painted limb, the calibration of a brushed-in eyelash, the swart clouds sweeping across painterly if adulterated skies, even some casually flirtatious exposure to celebratory gold.

Bartolomeo Scala, Bernardo Machiavelli's colleague and friend, had died in 1497, in a real sense dying out of the exhausted Medici government, whose Chancellor he had been for fifteen years, leaving a vacuum to be filled by other officials eager to establish their own directions for new policies. Almost the same might have been said of Alexandri Braccesi, who had not died but who as a pro-Savonarolan had been dismissed from his position as one of the 'due segretarii della Signoria,' following Savonarola's arrest, imprisonment and execution. Machiavelli now replaced him, serving out the second year of his two-year term, after which he would have to stand for election to a series of one-year terms, should he choose to do so.[13]

His titles and duties retained smatterings of bureaucratic confusions. Each had twice been redefined over the several years prior to his taking office, though modern investigations, coupled with re-readings of his and others' letters, have illuminated more about them and opened pathways to a better understanding of his work. Most importantly, the original meaning of 'secretary,' of significance to him and the Signoria, requires acknowledgement. Rather than acting as an assistant keeping the books or taking orders, minutes or dictation from higher-ups, a governmental secretary at Niccolò's level was far more a keeper of state secrets. He occupied a niche in which he was expected to examine the effects of the political past on the present.[14] A Chancellery secretary was in part recruited for his historical insights, which could easily involve secret military and political agreements. These might overshadow contemporary conflicts. The political landscape was always littered with the shards of broken treaties. It might be strewn with the ruins of ambitious yet failed policies.

Humanistically educated state secretaries, among them Machiavelli, were thus in demand to explore a paradox. Potentially violent disputes, either with the local nobility, as for example Caterina Sforza, or with Pisa, and into which, say, the French might be drawn following on the death of King Charles, or which might stimulate the lurking unscrupulousness of other Italian states such as Venice, required an historically astute approach if the Republic's future was to accommodate social and military challenges. Successful diplomacy, then as now, required the appointment of secretaries who might themselves be budding historians. At a minimum they would be sensitive to historical implications.

Machiavelli's job, more than that of his under-secretaries, also of necessity involved discussions, prudence, debates, travelling and correspondence, plus quasi-journalistic reports on the people and places that he might be ordered to visit.

A letter reached Rome in from three to six days, Venice and Milan in two to four, the on-the-move French court in almost a week. He began to produce a strong run of new official letters, and then a stream of them. His longer letters tended to be of the official rather than the personal variety, though his style in both reflected his confidence, care, sarcasm, apprehensive wit and enthusiasm.

Producing a letter to the Magistorato [*sic*] dei Dieci of 24 July 1499, for instance, which recounted an early mission to secure military support from the nearby ruler of Forlì, Caterina Sforza, found him scratching away in his typically severe, dark hand, with his emphatic yet sensitive nib-strokes, plus the prickly flourishes common to many fifteenth-century communiqués.[15]

His editing of his own official letters, as opposed to his personal ones, which as a rule he did not edit, he handled by chasing a line through the rejected words, avoiding any blottings out or hints of concealment, which in government (or 'public') documents might provoke distasteful suspicions of evasion. He quadruple-folded the official and most other letters, addressing them on the outside and sealing them with a waxed stamp for security according to a haphazard postal arrangement – it was scarcely a system – that might be tampered with. He could expect a reply within three days to a week or so, or often enough to establish some measure of efficient communication.

Often too, as in a July 1499 letter to the Ten of War, the ink shone or leaked through the thick sheets, making reading a chore. His pen, however, seldom abandoned its habitual speed and forward movement, even if, sometimes in haste, he now and then split a word down the middle, or left letters dangling, or made careless mistakes, as in a letter from Rome of 1503 (it has no firmer date) to 'uno principale cittadini di Firenze.'

Couriers were reliably to hand, and decently paid for transmissions of correspondence. The volume was always considerable, though members of the Signoria on occasion complained that he did not report in often enough.[16] In fact he soon began to dispatch at least two or three letters, each several pages long, more or less daily, spending hours at his writing desk and so working well into the night, poring over the squared sheets by flame-stumped candles. With *Fortuna* in the right mood, his couriers might arrive at their destinations *sans* robbery or assault by brigands, or vanishing: the postal air was full of alarms, and the loss of a letter, or even a delay, might affect not only policy but the outcome of a war.

# 11

# Caterina Sforza and the Crisis at Pisa

Many aspects of his new official life were put to the test in 1499 in two of his earliest missions, one to negotiate with Caterina Sforza at Forlì, where he was sent to bargain over weapons supplies and the future leadership of Florentine troops, another to help resolve the Pisa débacle. Neither proved less than tricky.

Everyone who knew Caterina described as extraordinary the young noble-woman and bastard daughter of the Duke of Milan, praising her sun-drenched blonde beauty, her roving – some said covetous, others uninhibited, sceptical or ravishing – eye, her brazen acts of military daring, and her impressive, quirky if sloppily educated intelligence (plate VII). She had rejected as much as possible of the classical tutoring which a high if illegitimate birth had conferred on her, preferring to focus her feral energy on mastering professional horsemanship and nurturing sensual pleasures.

Her book, *Experiments*, which grew into far more than a hobby, even if she seems to have compiled it only in stolen hours, consisted of catalogues of amulets and magical magnets. She believed them to contain special powers able to restore familial harmony, but added compilations of recipes and descriptions of exotic poisons, among them her pride, her *velano attermine*, which, she boasted, could provide 'perfect sleep.'

By the time Niccolò met her in mid-July, she had not only survived a few attempts on her life but triumphed over potent enemies. Her father, Galeazzo Maria, was assassinated in 1476. Her first husband, to whom she was betrothed at the age of fourteen in 1477, the Count Girolamo Riario, a dull, foul-tempered nephew of Pope Sixtus IV and a still-surviving member of the Pazzi Conspiracy, was stabbed to death, with his body tossed thumping into the street at Forlì, in April, 1488.

She reacted to his murder by ordering the capture and butchering of those involved, along with members of their families, and by slaughtering at random a group of other citizens to terrify everyone else. She was now thirty-six, and had seen a second husband, Giacomo Feo, killed as well (over two score citizens were slaughtered to avenge his death). A third husband, Giovanni de'Medici, the son of Piero Francesco, though from a branch of the family other than that of Lorenzo, died of natural causes in 1498, leaving her pregnant with the last of her eight children.[1]

Stories abounded of her sexual whims and aristocratic contempt. On one occasion she had sneered at a *condottiere* who confessed himself enthusiastic only about war, and thus unable to dance or enjoy music, or even love, telling him that he ought to be 'greased and stuck in a cupboard' to keep from becoming too 'rusty,' at least until he might be needed for combat.

She showed no hesitation about seizing command of her own troops, however, and a few months after meeting Machiavelli directed cannon fire from her Forlì palace-fortress into the streets at frightened citizens when Cesare Borgia, a still battle-green *condottiere* leading a small army of 8,000 troops into a town of about 7,000, laid siege to the fortress in what became a successful attempt to take her prisoner.[2]

At the moment her wish was to arrange a 15,000-florin payment from the sixty-kilometre-distant Florentine Signoria. This substantial amount, she proposed, would guarantee the continued participation in Florence's ongoing Pisan war of her son, himself a sometime *condottiere*, the twenty-year-old Count Ottaviano, plus one hundred armed infantry and one hundred armed light horse.

The Count had performed an identical service for Florence during the previous year, but the Signoria now sought a 5,000-florin reduction in his price, not only because Ottaviano seemed less than expert in military matters but also because the Signoria's entire object in retaining him in the first place had been to prop up good relations with his mother.

Forlì was advantageously placed between Venice and Rome, at a crucial intersection between the Republic's consistent enemies. Cultivating an alliance with Caterina's principality had long been understood as good policy (she had even been made an honorary Florentine citizen). Machiavelli was instructed to negotiate a one-third reduction for Ottaviano while setting up a major purchase of gunpowder and weapons from what everyone assumed to be Caterina's ample stocks of war matériel. If possible, he was to hire in Forlì up to five hundred infantrymen to be sent on to the Signoria's Pisan campaign.[3]

Ottaviano was unavailable, or at least out of town, but Machiavelli plunged into mutual compliments and a polite back and forth with his charming mother over more than a week. He noted that an agent of Ludovico 'Il Moro' Sforza, the Duke of Milan (Caterina was his illegitimate niece), was hanging about as well, and found himself exposed perhaps for the first time to the political negotiator's dithering with the invisible, or with unmentioned facts and motives that later reveal themselves as essential to a mission's success or failure.

Caterina's court resounded with odd clankings and bustlings, and the frustrated new official reported that between fifty and five hundred troops per day were assembling to ride or be marched off to Milan. Many were professional horsemen from other cities or the surrounding villages, plus infantrymen and crossbowmen, all of whom he and the Signoria would have welcomed in the struggle for Pisa, but that the Duke of Milan, a frank competitor with Florence for reinforcements of his own, also wanted: 'There was a review here yesterday of five hundred infantry, whom her Excellency sends to the Duke of Milan... . A couple of days ago there was also a muster of fifty mounted crossbowmen, equally destined for Milan. These will leave here within the next few days with one of the Duke's secretaries, who came here to enlist and pay them.'[4]

At home, his colleagues seemed unflustered by these practical problems. 'I have no doubt at all,' Biagio Buonaccorsi wrote him, trying to buck him up – he was one of the under-secretaries at the Chancellery in Florence, and also a sympathetic auditor and good friend from pre-Chancellery days – 'that Her Excellency is doing you as much honour, and is as happy to see you, as you write,' betraying a hint of envy over his colleague's mission to the palace of the glamorous Caterina.

A gossip as well as confidant, Buonaccorsi had found out that copies of Caterina's portrait were circulating at Forlì. He wanted one, if possible undamaged: 'I would like you to send me by return mail a portrait on a sheet of paper of Her Majesty's head, many of which have been done over there; and if you send it, roll it up so that the folds do not spoil it.'[5]

With Niccolò away, the Chancellery offices slipped into rancid moods amid jealous backbiting. Stationed near Machiavelli's desk were Luca Fecini and Agostino Vespucci (a close relation of Amerigo (1451–1512), the eponymous financier of Columbus's voyages to the New World) and Antonio della Valle, another under-secretary, who had helped to secure Machiavelli's appointment, and Buonaccorsi's some three months later, in August 1498, and who devoted himself to stirring up a hornet's nest of grievances that annoyed and rapidly offended everyone (Buonaccorsi wrote, 'I wish him bloody shit in his asshole'⁶).

Antonio's machinations often figured into Buonaccorsi's letters ('we were bawled out by our chiefs'), but Buonaccorsi himself had little respect for their chiefs in the Signoria, among whom office politics frequently overshadowed foreign policy, or many larger issues: 'I am pushed around ... by everyone, and I keep on begging and praying for you to come back.'

Relations at the Chancellery had turned more obnoxious ('since here no one else but him can be heard') and more ill-tempered by the day, though 'Marcello [has] heard your letters [his lengthy reports] being praised very highly.'⁷ Marcello was the Latin scholar Marcello Virgilio Adriani or di Adriani Berti (1464–1521), whom Niccolò may have known at university or through his likely contacts there, and who had headed up the First Chancellery since 1497. According to Buonaccorsi, the grave, reserved, purposeful, self-important Adriani was 'pushing' unceasingly for more troops to be dispatched to Pisa, or the military success of Niccolò's mission.

The Chancellery secretaries were nonetheless kept nose to the grindstone on the influx of reports of fresh wars breaking out not far away and seeming to confirm Dante's observation that northeast Italy was 'mai senza guerra' [never without war]: 'News is that the king [of France] has attacked Milan ... The Swiss and the Germans have come to blows during the last few days... . The Turkish fleet has issued forth from the strait, and it is thought it is going to strike Napoli di Romania; it is a great [formidable] thing ... And so [the] Signoria [of Venice] has made great preparations to defend itself and in addition has begun to give money to the men at arms it wants to use in Lombardy to attack Milan.'⁸

If the Republic's 'campaign in Pisa [was also] going better and better,' as Buonaccorsi informed him, by Machiavelli's lights his own mission seemed a failure. After receiving Caterina's consent to a 12,000-florin offer for the services of her son Ottaviano – he had originally proposed 10,000, as instructed, and then found himself teased ever higher – he watched icily as she reneged on her commitment a few days later. The reason, as she put it, was that since their bargain contained no guarantee that Florence would defend her principality, her son might as well not involve himself in the Pisan war at all. Machiavelli's irritation was scarcely eased by her telling him, even before turning down his offer, that in respect to her reputed supplies of ammunition and gunpowder, 'she had neither, and was herself greatly in need of them.'⁹

At that point, smoothly if without haste, he decided to leave, persuaded that his efforts had come to nothing. In his wanderings near Forlì, moreover, even before meeting Caterina, he had taken the trouble to interview a few of her subjects. As he told the Signoria, they attested to her and their other rulers' indifference to their welfare, or at least to their studied unconcern: 'It was only yesterday that a number of country people complained to me, saying, "Our lords have abandoned us; they have too many other things on their hands."'

In fact his mission had by no means been unsuccessful. The Signoria was happy enough with Caterina's vacillations, which only confirmed her need of a continuing alliance. It was also relieved to be excused from any obligation to the superfluous Ottaviano, and especially at no cost. From the Signoria's point of view as well, Machiavelli's previous mission, focused on Pisa, and undertaken back on 24 March, might also have been said to have produced better results than he realized.

He had not visited the city – to do so would have been dangerous – but, travelling on horseback, the town of Pontedera, at the confluence of the Era and the Arno, not far away, where he had dealt with the glib warlord-captain, Count Jacopo IV d'Appiano (1459–1510), governor of the seacoast town of Piombino as well as the islet of Montecristo and the ancient watery dominions of Elba and Pianosa, over which his family had for centuries exercised seigneurial rights. Appiano was one of the *condottieri* leading the Republic's Pisa forces.[10]

Before or after leaving Florence, but in his capacity as Secretary to the Ten of War, Machiavelli had also submitted to the Ten and the Signoria an evaluation, several paragraphs long, of the Pisan military situation. A terse, steely and even startling document, especially in view of his meagre experience to date in the area of military analysis, it may be his earliest surviving foray into strategy, tactics and the odds favouring battlefield success. It seems to have won him approval, if not admiration.

Described (perhaps by him or by someone else at the Chancellery, who might have added its title later) as *Discorso fatto al magistrate dei dieci sopra le cose di Pisa* (Discourse prepared for the Magistrates of the Ten on the issues having to do with Pisa), his analysis was apparently not intended for publication. On the contrary, it seems a fragment in which the author tackles his subject simply by sailing straight into it and without any preliminaries, indicating that it may have been intended for internal circulation among the officials in charge of the war.

He begins by arguing that the proper premise of any discussion of Pisa ought to be whether the city can be retaken ('riavere') by force or by diplomatic and

affectionate appeals ('o forza o l'amore'), 'whether it can be reoccupied by siege
or might yield in some voluntary way.' In dismissing the latter, he underscores
the persistent bitter feelings, amounting to outrage and firmly established by
then among many on both sides in the midst of what had become an erratic, if
protracted and bloody war.[11]

Bernardo Scala, in an essay published in 1496, *Defence against the Detractors
of Florence*, had vented a similar bitterness with respect to Pisa: 'What did we
not do to assist Pisa? What did they think of or demand that was not generously
given? Taxes were rescinded. Posts of honour and magistrates were allowed to
continue in place as if Pisa were free... . [Yet] the Pisans revolted, and just at a
moment when we needed their constancy and courage. They seized the chance
when our republic was struggling to maintain its liberty, and when they owed
us help in a crisis, they chose instead to take up arms and start a war.'[12]

Of note is his tone of agonised bafflement, or his suggestion that any
Florentine connivance at war had less to do with economic ambitions –
despite Pisa's wealth as the Republic's major port – than with humiliation. A
sacred trust had been broken. Philanthropy had been mocked. The modern
reader might imagine that Scala's sensitivity to these slights was a pretence
designed to mask Florentine pecuniary interests. No evidence to hand throws
his sincerity into doubt, however, or the comparable role played by bitterness
and other vindictive feelings, such as those produced by insults, not only in
the war over Pisa but in other Italian wars throughout this period – Sixtus's
Pazzi War comes readily to mind. In many of these conflicts, vanity seems
more likely to provoke a military response than money, even if money is to be
made as a result. A sense of outrage often trumps squalor as an inducement
to slaughter.

The rest of Machiavelli's analysis centres on how the battle for Pisa ought
to be organized, whether from two or three reinforced military encampments,
how many hundreds of men each might require, where they ought to be placed,
or on which strategic heights, together with the optimal quantity of cannon
necessary for any victorious siege or blockade. He has no doubt that the city's
resistance will be stiff, and also none that a Florentine triumph can be expected
as the massive outer wall is pierced by barrages and as assaults are pushed
through it. Bitterness has been converted into strategy.

These, at any rate, were his points of concentration, elaborated by an accumulating and to a large extent professional technical knowledge, as a few months

before visiting Caterina, in March, he rode out to meet the *condottiere* Jacopo d'Appiano. It seems evident, in other words, that he had already spent a good deal of time studying the methods of siege warfare, or discussing its tactics with returning soldiers and military supply experts.

Expertise by itself was always insufficient, though, and a more delicate question in respect to Appiano, whose camp had by then begun to bulge with soldiers, centred on his reliability. Not only had he fought on behalf of double-dealing noble families and other rival cities in the recent past, including Pisa itself, but he had now begun to demand – the immediate reason for Machiavelli's visit – an exorbitant additional payment for his services, or 5,000 florins (ducats) beyond the already agreed if breathtaking 22,400. His grounds were that one of Florence's other *condottieri*, Count Rinuccio da Marciano, had been granted the larger sum.

Machiavelli's instructions from the Ten of War took stock of their financial rivalry, plus the fact that from the start of his employment, in August 1498, Appiano had tried to alter others of his negotiated terms. He had put off showing up at the Florentine camp until February 1499: he had requested forty men beyond the 200 that he had agreed to provide (an infantryman could cost as much as fourteen lire, seven soldi: any substantial increase in their number was bound to strain the Republic's dwindling war-chest): and at the moment, or since his arrival in camp, and without warning, he had started pushing his request for a pay rise.

Machiavelli had been ordered to yield on none of these matters, or to equivocate and mislead Appiano in respect to all of them:

> You will … show our favourable disposition towards his Lordship, but you will do so
> in vague and general terms, so as not to commit us to any positive obligation whatever.

Among the hesitations of those back in Florence, or those managing the war, as surely with Machiavelli, lay an awareness of their vulnerability, that a capable mercenary officer might not fulfil the terms of his contract and so dissipate the chances of success: 'Above all you must have patience if he should threaten a rupture, and let him run on, and then reply, and also use your best efforts to induce him also to have patience.'[13]

The threat of a break in their strained relations, or of Appiano's walking out and taking his troops with him, and delaying or even cancelling the possibility of victory – or, worse, of his switching sides – could hardly be taken lightly.

It accounted for the peering-over-the-shoulder quality in the instructions themselves.

In the end, moreover, as seems apparent, the Ten's mistrust is also better understood as traceable to something more momentous. This too demands acknowledgement, if only because it guided and prodded the actors in the entire drama flickering about to Pisa. Not too surprisingly, perhaps, it reflected the shifting world of armies and politics at the moment, in which not much – not friends, enemies, allies and goals – seemed remotely clear or secure, in which military relations might be perceived as mere smeary fluctuations.

Wriggling through the Pisan conflict was an unfamiliar uncertainty that in fact seemed to be turning into the premise of a far larger aspect of human behaviour. Its result, as some had begun to realize, was the perverse promotion of uncertainty itself as a value. A major purpose of Machiavelli's mission, in other words, or of the negotiations on which he had been dispatched, was precisely to maintain a decent confusion.

Herein lay realism, or what might be understood as a newly fashionable realism. In nudging Appiano into accepting his agreed payment despite his sulking Achilles-like in his tent – a solution which Machiavelli achieved by referring to the minimal amounts of cash available – enough might be accomplished, or as much as could be expected, to allay for a while the commander's unacceptable insistence on more troops.

# 12

# *The Military Quandary*

A novel order of management, or as may today be conceded, a dramatic realignment of the mechanisms for administering armies, weapons and politics, had for some time been tilting into view. This development of an almost intangible condition of continuous political as well as military uncertainty seemed even to filter through the foundations of human hostilities. Armies, as always guides to the various mysteries of violence, themselves seemed to reflect new, unattached doubts. Novel shadows leapt and sank, along with cautiously examined fears. Nor is noting their strength meant to suggest that the new slipperiness had never existed before – it had – only that in fresh and ghostly forms it was now coalescing into the habitual.

Along these lines, the Ten's instructions to Machiavelli appear less as guides than political barometers. They attest to social and military fractures. Beyond them lay a novel and increasingly influential nervousness.

A pale hint of infinity – philosophy's great unmentionable during the Middle Ages – loomed as a glittering potential shadow on an advancing historical horizon. When at length, a century and a half later, its mesmerism had expanded, it would tempt many into less fanciful choices than those available in a static universe. Until then the new and fashionable state of unknowing would seem increasingly intense.

There was more. In a counter-reaction that may today appear natural, the growing status of instability had already begun to foster yearnings for its opposite, or absolute stability, often accompanied by a desire for military and even political absolutism.

Harsh, baffling acts, such as switching sides in a war, might imply an easy escape: an appeal to a charismatic, absolutist commander, one possessed of wealth as well as astuteness, a militaristic Savonarola, or panacea, a miracle- and victory-maker, able to redeem the virtues of the medieval past amid the military and political unease of the present. A dictator-type might rescue various weakening older values, if by ruthless means, and even at the cost of what might today be seen as political freedom.

The latest Florentine nights in any case seemed obscure enough to thousands of devoted *Piagnoni*, among whom the memory of Savonarola still provided a ceaseless inspiration. Not only had no Florentine leader emerged to replace him, but lawlessness invested the streets. As early as June 1498, or shortly after the friar's death, Landucci recorded a spate of unusual murders and feuds that rattled the nights. They seemed to be linked to the amusements of restless young men. Skeletal, violent, dancing figures wandered amid the shadows. 'Everyone,' he observed, was indulging in 'a vicious life, and at nighttime one saw halberds or naked swords all over the city, and men gambling by candle-light in the *Mercato Nuovo* [New Market] and everywhere without shame. Hell seemed open; and woe to him who should try to reprove vice.'[1]

Among these men, and perhaps better accounting for their behaviour than Landucci's assumption of a mere collapse in morals, there could also have been detected in the aftershock of Savonarola's death a new, shabby war-induced civil paralysis. As the demands of war rolled over everyone, and as the military uncertainties seemed to expand, near riots erupted over the taxes levied to pay for the unending battles, or to satisfy the hunger for soldiers, gunpowder and cannon.

The Ten of War were derided as spendthrifts. For a while the committee was in effect disbanded, or left with no elected replacements to its membership, though as a result Machiavelli's position as secretary became not only more secure but more prominent. Everywhere political squabbles hung on suspicions of the Republic's *condottieri*, or soldier-profiteers.[2]

Municipal wonders sprang up anyway, apparently offering moments of contact with the divine. As no epoch, even the most unstable, is probably without its ideas of marvels, shivers, quakes and calms, no message without strains, either tormented or lyrical, no whisper without echoes of grief, so on 10 June 1498 Landucci noted the miraculous-seeming appearance 'on the meadow of the *Servi* and the *Tiratoi* [the large open structures for drying and stretching cloth],' just downstream from the Ponte Vecchio, of golden caterpillars with human faces, or 'eyes and nose, [and] seeming to have a crown on their head, and round their face a diadem (a halo).'

Equipped with golden bodies and black tails, the never-before-seen creatures set about devouring all plant life: 'The sloe-bushes became white and peeled.'

Many believed that the caterpillar-like animals must be allegorical manifestations of Savonarola himself. They seemed to express a heaven-sent truth that his
life had been golden. In its aftermath the 'weeds [had to] be rooted out; and thus
the sloe, appearing to be the most useless and disagreeable, was to be consumed
by the [caterpillars'] tail[s], that is to say, by those who came after.'[3] The bizarre
beings vanished, but for a while they seemed to evoke an older, faith-inspired if
dying and medieval way of perceiving reality as a kind of tapestry of allegories.
In their wake the city's ancient precincts felt abandoned anew, as if a great belief
had sunk backwards.

Also in their wake, historical precedents extending back over a century,
but still as potent as threatening, seemed to anticipate uncertainties seeping
into many lives. Educated merchants, noblewomen and tradesmen, together
with people in government and the Church, recalled not only the executions following on the Pazzi Conspiracy but abetted by Leonardo Bruni's well
known *History of the Florentine People*, an early and often consulted bestseller,
the horrifying 'internal discord following immediately upon external peace'
in 1378, with its swarm of riots and its 'rashness of an aroused mob.'[4] Novel-
seeming terrors appeared to have been sparked by a devotion to violence for its
own sake, or to a newly fashionable, frightening yet plausible god of panic.

Arriving during one of the first class-inspired rebellions of modern times,
the panic-god had fostered a topsy-turvydom:

> [A] mob, growing in size plundered the palace of the podestà. Then, still gripped with
> fury, it went back to the Palace of the Priors. It compelled the priors to abdicate their
> magistracy and sent them home, reduced to the condition of private citizens ... . The
> mob itself [next] entered the Palace in victory ... . On the very same day an assembly
> of the people was called which passed numerous new laws regarding the governance
> of the state. The principal innovation was that the Standard-Bearer of Justice should in
> perpetuity be chosen from the lowest class.[5]

The surreal-seeming, surprising and primitive revolution had collapsed on
itself, crushed and stared down by the Republic's better-armed, better-trained
and more determined citizens. Yet its ghoulish demonstration of society
up-ended remained 'an eternal example and warning for the city's leading
citizens that they should not allow civil unrest and armed force to come down
to the whims of the mob. For it cannot be restrained once it begins to snatch the
reins and realizes that it is more powerful, being more numerous.'[6]

Murderous attacks by night reawakened disquieted souls to the same terrors, especially as by 1499 all the old mob-defying formulas seemed less effective. In a frightened social world, which in significant ways seemed unfamiliar to everyone, people seemed to be preparing for the worst.

Machiavelli returned from Forlì on 1 August 1499, just as news arrived that the Republic's mercenary army had advanced on Pisa. At least the war-situation was improving. This possibility was reinforced on 6 August, as a single thunderous artillery bombardment restored confidence in the entire campaign, even if the new optimism soon proved false. On the sixth, scores of cannon under the direction of Paolo Vitelli, the *condottiere* in charge, tore a forty-yard-long gash in Pisa's outer wall. Everyone now hourly expected that other reports would start pouring in, confirming that street fighting was in progress or announcing that the city had fallen.[7]

Vitelli had been appointed to his position in an elaborate ceremony on 1 June 1498, and was universally viewed as competent, energetic and cruel. As a lord of Città di Castello in Umbria, he harboured a well-nigh universal aristocratic prejudice against the use of personal fire-arms in battle, chiefly the musket-like, inaccurate arquebus, deeming any such weapons unsoldierly, though he did not oppose the use of more destructive cannon and mortars.

As recently as the battle of Buti, a year earlier in 1498, which he had won, he had ordered that the hands of any captured Venetian gunners, or *schioppettieri*, be chopped off, according to his belief that they had betrayed a military code of honour by resorting to guns brutal enough to eject an armoured knight from his saddle over some distance, and even kill him, without engaging in actual combat.[8] More worryingly, Vitelli was often accused of consorting with the Pisan enemy as well as with Piero de'Medici and other members of the Medici family, whose appetite for returning to power was widely seen as dangerous. Despite these problems, Vitelli's handling of the war seemed to produce solid results. His tactics propelled his troops forward, after delays and excuse-making, matched by what seemed their proper imperial strut.

Along with his brother, Vitellozzo, and a rival *condottiere*, Rimiccio da Marciano – and given that both brothers had been buoyed by a plan of action approved by Florence's Grand Council after a rancorous debate – he seemed to expect victory over Pisa after his impressive capture of Cascina. His mere appearance in a nearby field, accompanied by 200 heavily armed crossbowmen, had so frightened the Pisan commanders that they and their soldiers had cut and run. Their collapse had made possible his thrust at Pisa itself.

His preparations for the anticipated final assault were also complemented by his seizing the Rocco di Stampace, a major Pisan fortress, on 10 August. At exactly that moment, however, and without explanation, he had engaged in so humiliating a display of military cowardice, or incompetence, so it seemed, as to provoke suspicions of his loyalty, or at least his commitment to success. Worries about his behaviour infected the streams of rumours already circulating in the Florentine marketplaces. A riotous population, exasperated by previous military failures, was more interested in venting its frustrated rage than in fair play. No less disturbed seemed Machiavelli himself, who had developed the morbid conviction that Vitelli must be a traitor.

The chief reason was that he had enjoyed an insuperable advantage once he took Stampace and with heavy guns punched a gash in Pisa's outer defences. Inexplicably, it appeared, he had failed to seize his chance by ordering his troops to storm the city itself. Inexplicably, too, he had procrastinated, even turning back, and according to some accounts quarrelling with his men, who wanted to push on, rushing in among them to force their retreat.[9]

Whatever the motive for this carnivalesque behaviour, he continued to delay. To be sure, his success itself may have startled him, and the reason may not have been disloyalty. A batch of indignant letters from the Signoria exhorting him to get on with the job, however (these letters, referring to his 'shufflings' and 'deceit,' may have been written by Machiavelli), produced no change, and in the end nature, or *Natura*, or *Fortuna*, seemed to take the upper hand. An outbreak of malaria among his troops, spreading death left and right, including among his officers, forced his withdrawal on 14 September. Once more Pisa was left to the Pisans, who had recovered sufficient pluck to renew their struggle.

Vitelli's end now followed with frightening swiftness. Machiavelli was probably present at the secret Signorial discussions where it was decided to trick him into riding back to Cascina, there to arrange his arrest and return to Florence for quizzing and punishment. His brother and collaborator Vitellozzo, who was also a wanted man, sensed the danger and at the last minute managed to escape.

At 10:45 on the night of 29 September, the stern and proud Paolo Vitelli, surrounded by a squad of torch-bearing guards, found himself wrangled in chains into the Florentine grand *piazza*. Through the night and into the next day, he was tortured on the *strappado*, and afterwards hustled through a perfunctory trial.[10] During all this, he said nothing and admitted nothing. To most citizens, his silence, which in less disorderly circumstances might have seemed admirable, only confirmed his guilt. The new King of France, Louis XII, confirmed it too, accepting without hesitation reports of Vitelli's 'deceit.'

The trial itself smacked more of prejudgement and spite than judiciousness, even if Machiavelli urged a judicious approach. The diabolical situation was inflamed by a military catastrophe surrounding the breakup of the *condottiere's* camp at Pisa, during which ten packed barges, loaded with ammunition and artillery, sank in the Arno. They were later salvaged, but not before much of their cargo was stolen by the Pisans.

Less than a day after his forcible return to Florence, therefore, and on being found guilty of treason, Vitelli was beheaded in the Palazzo della Signoria, high up in the *ballatoio*, as Landucci reports, or the gallery behind the parapet, allowing the crowd below in the dark to catch a glimpse of his last moments: 'It was expected that his head would be thrown down into the Piazza; it was not thrown down ... but it was stuck on a spear and shown at the windows ..., with a lighted torch beside it, so that it could be seen by everyone. Then the people dispersed, considering that justice had been done, to the great honour of the city.'[11]

Machiavelli supported these acts and sentiments, taking what seems a self-righteous pleasure in the aristocratic soldier's beheading. When a few weeks later an unknown Chancellery Secretary in Lucca wrote disparagingly of the – as he saw it – precipitous, unethical treatment of the Republic's hired commander, Machiavelli answered him in a letter in which sarcasm, bitterness and petulance, perhaps for the first time in his correspondence, expose his pitiless condemnation. Accusing the official of 'mark[ing] so great a republic as ours with opprobrium,' he adds: 'I choose to ignore the maliciousness ... that your letter makes manifest.' He cites 'Vitelli's betrayal' and the 'countless troubles [that] have befallen our [military] campaign due to his culpability.' As Secretary of the Ten of War, he seems uninterested in questions having to do with the flimsy evidence presented at a hasty trial: 'Whether he committed one wrongdoing or the other or whether he committed them both, [he] deserves endless punishment.' Toleration of uncertainty had its limits.[12]

# 13

# On the Move with the French King

Machiavelli's father, Bernardo, died at about seventy on 10 May 1500 (he had been born *c*.1425–30).[1] His death left Niccolò, as one of his two surviving sons, and according to the terms of his father's will drawn up in 1483, the heir with his younger brother Totto to the family's several houses in Florence. By extension and custom, though they were not mentioned, he became heir as well, along with Totto, who was preparing for the priesthood, to the familial estates in Sant'Andrea in Percussina.[2] Provisions for their two sisters, in the event that they had remained unwed, had been made too, but Margherita, like Primavera, was by this time married, to one Bernardo Minerbetti.

While no record remains of Niccolò's mourning his father's death, it is worth recalling his strong boyhood relations with his affectionate first teacher, and his father's well-documented pride in his son's childhood achievements. Also worth citing is one of Niccolò's early lyric poems. Its date is uncertain, though it was probably written in his early to mid-twenties, and in the form of a jesting sonnet addressed to his father, then off at his farms and vineyards at Sant'Andrea. An odd piece of drollery, it consists of twenty lines, and is thus a *caudate* or 'tailed' sonnet in which a set of six added lines is by convention usually satirical. The poem brims with the flavours of feasts given and denied and family joshing.

Bernardo, apparently worried that his sons back in Florence, or just below the hills, might not be eating well enough, has sent Niccolò a goose. Niccolò responds with an exaggerated, if not absurd, description of their supposedly miserable city diet. The reference to Daniel in lines 10–11 is likely to a tradition, popular in those days and so familiar to many, that as the half-millennium approached confused the biblical prophet with recent books of the prophecies of Daniel, as they were called. These latter, which had been of interest to Savonarola, had to do with the reinvention and rejuvenation of the corrupt Church, the former with the Prophet Daniel's rejection (I, 5–16) of rabbinically unblessed food at the court of Nebuchadnezzar, King of Babylon, so that he might go on waxing healthy and (presumably) holy:

*Niccolò Machiavelli to M. Bernardo his father*
   *In the villa at San Cascano*
They've been living a month or more
   on nuts, figs, beans and dried meat
   so it's a positive evil and no joke
   to linger on here like this any longer.
Just as the Fiesolan ox, full of yearning, peers
   down at the Arno, thirsty, licking his lips,
   so they gaze at the peasant wife's eggs for sale
   and the butcher's mutton and beef.
But to make sure that even the maggots don't starve
   I must address a word to Daniel,
   who may already be reading something in our favour.
Because forced to eat bread with a knife [stale bread]
   we're now growing beaks as long as woodcocks'
   and cannot keep our eyes more than half open.
      Tell that brother of mine
   to drop by to triumph with me
   over that goose that you sent us last Thursday.
      If this game goes on,
   messer Bernardo, you'll keep buying
   ducks and geese but never get to eat them.[3]

Perhaps most pleasurable in these stanzas is the sly conversational mastery, influenced by Dante and Petrarch, of *terza rima* (9–14; not shown in translation), and the possibility that the poem may be part of a *tenzone*, in which the author awaits a lost reply in a sonnet game that Bernardo would have understood and would have enjoyed. The poem's earthy irony, combined with affection and technical ease, also gleams with an unsurprising empirical delight in experimental, vivid images, frankness, kindness and unlimited curiosity.

In mid-July 1500, a wide world to the north, spreading across the sophisticated and better organized kingdom of France, opened itself, and for the first time, to his curiosity as well. The court of Louis XII (1462–1515), later to become known as *Père de la France*, despite an untidy string of ham-fisted military defeats, was often on the move and, like that of his predecessor, Charles VIII, involved in Italy through French military adventurism. This had to do with Louis' claim to Milan, but not only to Milan: to Naples.[4]

From his reign's earliest days, the King had resented Charles's failure to hang on to the south-Italian kingdom, and the embarrassment of his near defeats as he retreated north into France. On the other hand, the French countryside, with its immense, lush and golden farms and vineyards, punctuated at intervals by elegant chateaux both ancient and modern, could boast during this period of the King's greatest good fortune both a peasantry and nobility mostly content, or at a minimum eating well, dressing better and unwilling to rebel against a royal government seen as compassionate.[5]

As with any interesting culture, rigid contradictions abounded within that of the French. Some of them attracted Machiavelli's eye as shortly after his father's death he set out on horseback, riding by post, or relays of horses, to present himself according to his latest orders as a diplomat-sojourner at Louis's court, then stopping in Lyons.

The French response to the late-medieval English invention of long bows, for instance, had been to increase the weight and strength of the bolt-and-plate armour still worn by their knights. The result was that French infantrymen were left exposed at a distance of roughly 200 metres to squadrons of English archer-enemies whose steel-tipped arrows showered forth in successive swarms of death.

Major advances in tapestry-making and other products of the large French looms, along with reinforcing the relative political freedom of the property-owning townspeople, improving the methods of iron manufacture and designing better ships, had not yet led to the efflorescence of art and literature that would announce the French Renaissance.[6]

The sonnet, perfected in Italy over the previous two-hundred years, was read in Italian or in French translations, including in their audiences Louis XII, who may have been among the first in France to enjoy Petrarch more as a poet than as a moralist, a sign of a shifting fashion. It failed, however, to attract home-grown imitations: no sonnets by French poets survive from before the 1540s.

The long-standing rivalry between French and Italian culture over literary and philosophical pre-eminence showed no signs of ebbing: French humanists regarded themselves as the direct 'heirs of the Athenians.' They bizarrely omitted from descriptions of their heritage all reference to ancient and medieval Rome, as well as to Italian accomplishments in the arts, philosophy and serious science, including pharmacology. Members of Louis's court usually imagined themselves cleverer than the ruling Italians, chiefly because none had as yet exhibited much enthusiasm for inventing a centralized government.[7]

Even the Roman Pope, Alexander VI, the former Roderigo Borgia (1431– 1503), seemed sympathetic to French fantasies of Italian submission. Scarcely missing a beat after Louis's lavish coronation, he had dispatched his virile, masterful son, Cesare, to meet the new King, assuring the French of his military cooperation in pursuing their claims to the Italian city states that caught their eye.

In October, 1498, Louis had welcomed Cesare to his elegant, peripatetic court, referring to him as Cesar, as the young, Spanish-born commander wished to be designated (and as he signed his name to documents), evoking the arrogance of the ancient, assassinated Roman Dictator. By then, through a tit-for-tat annulment of Louis's marriage, arranged by Cesare's father, he was able to negotiate for the hand (in May, 1499) of one of the King's nieces, the beautiful Carlotte d'Albret.

The principality of Valence was tossed into the matrimonial hopper as a wedding present. It was buttressed by annual revenues for Cesare's private use, plus a 2,000-strong French cavalry unit to complement his infantry and armed horsemen. The aim of this largesse was to guarantee his assistance in providing hoped-for French victories at Milan and Naples.[8]

As so often in Italy, anarchy prevailed over good sense. During the previous eight years, or since the death of Lorenzo de'Medici in 1492, Machiavelli had not only cultivated the contacts that now assisted his career but nurtured both amid the sickly atmosphere of the shattered Italian peace.

Abetting its collapse, or what Francesco Guicciardini was to describe as the elimination of Italian prosperity, geography itself, or the relative Italian isolation, as opposed to the general accessibility of France and other European countries, played a crucial role.

The long, mountainous peninsula, situated at the heart of Europe and containing remnants of the demolished Roman Empire, had not since the Middle Ages managed to come together as a lasting new empire or country. At present it looked unlikely to become either, though during the years under Lorenzo it had profited from the Italian League established by him between Florence and Naples.[9]

His death had quickly undermined the Republic's Naples relations. Competing passions of the more important militaristic noble families, among them the Este, the Aragona (of Naples) and the Sforza, which prompted their leaders in the past to form and dissolve bellicose alliances, or even to invite foreign armies, especially French, German and Spanish, to invade Italy to satify their infatuations with conquest, seemed once more free to do as they pleased. They began to stimulate a broad descent into unimagined depths of theft and murder.

Throughout most of this time, effective military tactics had depended not only on the peninsula's relative isolation but also on an almost natural, accomplice-like secrecy. Battles exploded among small rocky glens, dales, narrow valleys and mountain passes. They thrashed against the siege-nets thrown about towns and cities.

Since ancient Roman times, the most significant Italian military collisions had tossed back and forth at lighting speed. A dread of daylight- as well as night-attacks had led travellers to limit their excursions. Gangs of brigands lurking at the roads were more threatening to the forest wanderer, itinerant, artisan or diplomat, on the move by horse or walking, than most military flare-ups.

Hired soldiers often seemed indistinguishable from thieves and killers. Nationalism was unknown, though a good many soldiers, including soldiers for hire, espoused religious ideals. Loyalty to local noblemen, noblewomen or the Church might on occasion rise into a smothering of sadistic impulses.[10]

Machiavelli packed Caesar's *Gallic Wars* into his traveller's saddlebag in preparation for his first journey out of Italy, perhaps taking the slim volume for the pleasures of its lucid Latin prose, or even as a jokey antique tourist guide, though his instructions from the Signoria stipulated speed, as a war was underway, rather than reading. Did he have in mind some prospect of running into Cesare Borgia, either at Louis's court or en route – a vague possibility – or imagine that the war-memoirs of the long dead Roman Caesar would provide useful insights into his modern imitator?[11]

As ever, the Signoria's decisions about policies and manoeuvres hinged on Pisa. The Secretary of the Ten had in fact just returned from a recent, risky mission to the Florentine camp 'before Pisa' (not Vitelli's camp, which had been broken up), to which he was dispatched in June as an aide serving the Republic's commissioners, Giovanni Battista Ridolfi and Lucas degli Albizzi. There he had been ordered to oversee the deployment of 5,000 Swiss troops and 500 lancers.

These professional-looking reinforcements had been sent on loan from Louis XII. In line with Florence's gratitude for French military support, but coming at the expensive rate of 24,000 ducats per month, they were charged with propping up the Pisan siege, or carrying on where Vitelli had left off in his apparent self-defeat.

Even this sizeable contingent of troops, however, had begun to tack and feint in movements ranging from the embarrassing to the dangerous. The Swiss commanders had immediately launched a bombardment of the weakened Pisan walls, which had been repaired, and next, as if following Vitelli's lead and even echoing his incompetence or confusion, plunged into a retreat, amid shouting, riots, recriminations, stabbings and shootings.

The Florentines had not paid them, and their reaction was more violent than any animosity they might have tried but failed to direct at the Pisans. 'The commissioner [Lucas degli Albizzi] wrote you yesterday evening,' Machiavelli reported to the Signoria 'from the camp before Pisa' on 9 July, 'about the [terrible] condition of things in which we find ourselves here; and today at three o'clock there came about one hundred Swiss to his quarters and demanded pay, ... saying that they would not leave without being paid. The commissioner could not pacify them with words or promises, so that after much disputing they have carried him off prisoner.'[12]

The abduction of his superior officer, along with other Italian officers, and right before his eyes, left him shaken and in the dark about what to do, apart from requesting help: 'I have remained at the station of San Michele, so as to be able to give your Lordships this information, that you may take measures to prevent one of your citizens, with so many of his people, all your subjects, from being carried off, and by whom!'[13]

With enraged Swiss troops brandishing weapons about the commissioner's head, kidnapping him and threatening him with death for hours on end ('I know not,' he jotted down in terror, 'whether in the last hour of my life (which God grant may be soon!) I shall suffer one fourth of the pain and affliction which I feel at this time'), he had still maintained his level-headedness. Eventually in fact, he had arranged his own relief, as no other seemed possible, in the form of a signed ransom note stipulating his commitment to pay the mutinous soldiers over 1,300 ducats.[14]

The upshot of his concession to the rebellion, to which Machiavelli bore witness, was that the Swiss at once abandoned the Florentine camp and in their nattily dressed thousands began heading north toward Bologna. The prospects of any quick assault on Pisa had vanished into thin air.

The French had immediately blamed the Florentines for the mutiny and kidnapping, the Florentines the French for the indiscipline of their mercenaries. The King offered apologies: 'We have been informed only a few days since of the great disorders ... in the army engaged in the siege of Pisa, in consequence of the mutiny and quarrel of several ill-disciplined bodies of infantry ... which occurrence has caused us ... much regret.'[15]

He had promised extensive new backing for Florence in the war, but had then done nothing. The Pisans, meanwhile, began staging well-planned attacks of their own, capturing the town of Librafatta, along with a nearby fortress. For the first time, too, they had begun to receive supplies from neighbouring Lucca, and in part because of the resulting shift in their prospects – from hopeless to not so bad – a vicious circle of recriminations between the Signoria and the French court turned into squabbling as each side became more hostile and volatile by the day.[16]

Since Machiavelli had been present at the mutiny, his contribution to resolving the crisis affecting the fragile alliance seemed only appropriate. Along with Francesco della Casa, an experienced diplomat-replacement for the previous Florentine envoy to Louis's court, now recalled, he was ordered into France on a mission to smooth the severely ruffled French feathers. If possible, they were to re-establish good relations between their governments: 'The whole of this matter,' argued the Signoria, 'consists of two parts, viz.: first, to complain ... and second, to defend and exculpate.... It will ... be proper for you to speak of the capture of our commissioner, of the persons guilty of this outrage, and of [how] it was done, and of the outrages and insults we have had to bear.'[17] More than anything, the emissaries were to encourage solid French commitments to supporting Florence in any future assaults on Pisa itself.

From the start, though, as Machiavelli and della Casa set off on their more than 500-mile journey into the north, they faced an annoying problem: tracking down and locating the French court. The whole of French aristocracy appeared to disappear as King Louis and his aides reassembled for hunting and feasting expeditions, or without notice slipped off in unannounced directions, acceding to his command that they avoid any areas where epidemic disease, such as plague, might be in progress. Unintentionally but confusingly, the court and King kept days ahead of the Florentines, who over weeks spent trotting after them arrived too late in town after town, exhausted, sweating, poorer and vexed with the unending need to buy fresh horses.

Starting at Lyons, Machiavelli and della Casa straggled breathlessly into villages such as St Pierre le Moutier, only to be informed that the King had just left. From St Pierre, on 5 August, Machiavelli dashed off an early irate appeal to Florence for more money, an almost insolent message focusing on his frustration with traipsing about the French countryside and the hardships of day after day swinging back into the saddle, plus his dismay as his diplomatic hopes, not to mention his purse, flattened into floppy nothings: 'Your Lordships know what salary [twenty ducats per month] was assigned to me on our departure from Florence, and also the amount accorded to Francesco della Casa [much more]. Doubtless [it was set up in the] belief that in the natural course of things I would have occasion to spend less money than Francesco. Such however has not been the case: for not finding his Most Christian Majesty at Lyons, I had to provide myself with horses, servants and clothing, the same as he; and thus following the court has obliged me to incur the same expenses as Francesco.'[18]

His financial problems were formidable: 'I trust your Lordships will take such measures as will not ruin [me] and that at least I may be credited in Florence with the amounts for which I am compelled to become indebted here. For I pledge you my faith that up to the present moment I have [already] spent forty ducats of my own, and have requested my brother at Florence to make me an advance of seventy ducats more.'[19]

At Nevers on 6 August, Machiavelli and della Casa were finally received into the pausing if elusive royal cortège, although an audience with His Majesty, they were told, could not be announced for more than a day. Their first meeting with the King, on the other hand, proved almost as bewildering as the journey itself. Disregarding 'the fatigue and fear of sickness which prevails in this country,' the Florentine negotiators 'found [Louis] with a very small court, on account of the limited size of the place.'[20] They introduced themselves to his chief minister, Cardinal Georges d'Amboise of Rouen, who conducted them to a postprandial audience with the King, just awakening from his afternoon nap.

Everything appeared civil enough until Machiavelli, della Casa, Louis and the various officials settled into negotiations. These at once disintegrated into carping, blame-casting and bleak forecasts of a pointless military future in light of the failure at Pisa. An underlying sourness, barely concealed by everyone's good manners, came close to wrecking the chances of a resolution.

Nor were Machiavelli and della Casa able to prevent the serene firing off of sardonic accusations at the Signoria, or for that matter at what seemed to the French a Florentine ducking of their responsibility for what had happened, as expressed in their refusal to pay the Swiss with money transferred through the King's good offices. Machiavelli and his fellow emissary seem nonetheless to have avoided the development of even deeper fissures.

The tenth of August saw Louis's court once more slipping into its mazy migrations, this time on a beeline for Montagis, with the Florentine legates in pursuit, and from Montagis to Melun, where the fraying negotiations were resumed amid inflexible cross-purposes.

Not everything was a waste, though, at least from Machiavelli's point of view: by late August Biagio Buonaccorsi, his friend and colleague at the Palazzo, had written with news that some hoped-for financial assistance had at last, if only in part, been arranged by his brother Totto.

Andrea di Romolo, another secretary at the second-floor Chancellery desks in Florence, also hinted, in a postscript to Biagio's letter, at jolly parties and an attractive woman – she is not identified – who Machiavelli might be missing, as perhaps after a hard day at the office: 'Anyway, we often laugh in the First Chancellery, and we also have a few little parties at Biagio's house… . So get ready yourself, as soon as you [return], … for she is awaiting you with open figs [slang for sex], and Biagio and I saw her several evenings ago at her window like a hawk, you know who I'm talking about, *etc.*: *i.e.*, along the Arno by the Grazie.'[21]

Here at least was a touch of the human in the midst of his confusing French adventures, which despite their futility dragged on from September into October and then into November, with no money forthcoming from the Signoria after all, despite Totto's best efforts, and regardless of Biagio's and later his own assurance that it would be, and with little progress made towards arranging a Florentine-French *entente*.

Francesco della Casa now fell ill and left for Paris to recover. A replacement was supposedly *en route*, or so Machiavelli was informed, yet he was kept twiddling his thumbs at the French court without permission to return, and given almost no information about the future of his mission; only that, as before, he seemed to be missed most of all at the Chancellery.

'Return as soon as you can, I beg,' wrote Agostino Vespucci toward the end of October. 'Return posthaste, I pray; return as swiftly as possible, I beseech [you].' Vespucci was tormented by his old worry that his friend might lose his 'place in the palace,' though he insisted that everyone simply had a 'desire to see you': 'Your amusing, witty, and pleasant conversation, while it echoes about our ears, relieves, cheers, and refreshes us, who are spent and flagging from constant work.'

Machiavelli's gifts of entertainment had so far brought him scant comfort in a French diplomatic environment where not knowing much of the spoken language (though he could read it and was apparently able to translate letters into it), he found it necessary to conduct most conversations in Italian, weaving into them the odd Latin phrase, or even a couple of Latin sentences.

Vespucci kidded him about the legendary French prudery: 'Ripa [a mutual friend] added that there was no way you could stay in France, without grave danger, since sodomites and homosexuals are stringently prosecuted there. When we, who know your character is excellent and spotless, hesitated, and some asked what he meant, he muttered in reply that a horse had sodomized you and split your anus and buttocks (ah, what a crime!).'

Gratuitously, but no doubt because he knew that Machiavelli would be interested, he tossed into his letters dollops of economic and social news, about a nasty drop in grain prices and outbreaks of syphilis: 'One man has lost his genitals or penis, ... another's nose has fallen off, another has gone blind in one eye, another has become very much like Vulcan [lame].'

He allowed a note of pessimism to creep into his admiring, jittery remarks about Cesare Borgia, whom everyone referred to as the 'Duke of Valentino' in recognition of his acquisition of Valence as a gift from Louis XII. Cesare's military ambitions, at the moment projecting his forces into one prize chunk after the other of central Italian territory, had begun to inspire considerable if not universal dread: 'Valentino is accomplishing great marvels by himself along the Via Flaminia, and the rumour is spreading that when he has captured Faenza and Bologna, he will clear a path for Piero de'Medici to command ... a great state (a great crime).'[22]

Vespucci's reference to the Via Flaminia had to do with the superb highway, built during the régime of Gaius Flaminius, a Roman Censor in 220 BCE. Extending from Rome to Fani, it ran north along the Adriatic to Rimini. During Cesare's second major campaign, just then pushing ahead at full tilt, he had decided to follow this symbolically vital route, more or less, though not without meeting fierce resistance.

'May God,' wrote Vespucci, thinking of a possible Borgia-Medici threat to Florence itself, and that Cesare, who might launch his troops into some dizzy leap across the peninsula, might attempt to re-establish a Medici dictatorship, 'keep all evils from us, of which evils for (six years) we have had a great share.'

The brackets here, which are his own, allude to two lines in Virgil's *Aeneid* (II, 5–6) that Machiavelli would have recognized and which depict Aeneas recalling the devastation at the fall of Troy, when the Greeks had sacked the city, burning it to the ground.

# 14

# The Long French Patience

'This is the year of our misfortunes,' Totto wrote to his '*Honoured brother, etc.*' on 4 November. Machiavelli was still preoccupied with his efforts to resolve the uninterrupted silence surrounding his stay at the French court, as yet with no indication when he might be called back.

His sister, Primavera, he now discovered, had just died at the age of thirty five. Her son, Giovanni, aged thirteen, himself lay 'dying at death's door' of 'the same [unknown] disease.' Totto believed that her son might survive, or at least live to reach his fourteenth birthday and so be legally old enough to make a will: in the Machiavelli family worries about property frequently ran in tandem with close affections.[1]

By mid-November the French had relocated to Nantes, by late November to Tours. Machiavelli, who as before let Louis's court set the pace for him on some recently purchased horse, noted that the embassies of other governments and courts – the Turkish, German, Venetian, Milanese – seemed constantly dancing before the King as in an expensive ballet, and deluging him with pleas for help.

In the face of this brisk competition, what influence might a mere Florentine secretary hope to achieve? In early October, and as he put it, with thanks to God, he found himself at last able to welcome a report of the 're-establishment of the Ten,' or the unofficially disbanded committee of war: 'Let us expect much good from it; for from a better government we have the right to hope for happier results.'[2]

The Ten's new members might become the source of sounder policies in respect to Pisa, though all military decisions required debate and ratification by the less efficient, larger Council of Eighty. A War member's term lasted for six months, as opposed to two months for a member of the Signoria, who could nonetheless stand for re-election.

Like many Florentines, Machiavelli had serious worries by now about the possible French encouragement of Cesare Borgia, though Louis had written to him, making plain his hostility to any blackmailing excuses for invading the Republic. With growing reservations, Machiavelli had only minimal confidence that the new ambassadors now *en route* to relieve him and della Casa might revive the French interest in a strong military agreement between Florence and France. Its absence could risk the Republic's safety: 'If it does not very soon become known that your [the Signoria's] ambassadors are really coming, then his Majesty will be more inclined to believe the calumnies of [our] enemies than our justifications.'[3]

As Cesare's army mobilized at Faenza, and given the likelihood that after seizing it he would concentrate his attention on Florence, nurturing the French King's friendship had become more important than ever. Louis's influence on Cesare could be compelling, and perhaps most of all via his fickle papal father.

On 4 November in Nantes, Louis's minister, Cardinal d'Amboise, took Machiavelli aside, 'reflected a moment and said, "Preserve the friendship of the King, and then you will not need [him]; but if you lose his good graces, all the help [in the world] will not suffice you."'[4] Amid the skulking about at the nomadic French court, the Florentine Secretary's mere presence, or his 'becoming' manner, as he not immodestly put it in communiqués to the Signoria, might help to alleviate the unpleasant atmosphere of kingly denials. On the other hand, Louis would do nothing without being paid.

In the meantime, the chill autumn winds swept across the desolate French fields. They rustled through the royal tapestries rolled and unrolled for warmth and decoration on the monarch's perpetual journeys, often before glowing palace fireplaces that rarely supplied much heat. Outside, as November drifted into December, the latest crowded barn or tavern pitched its lights past scores of carousing soldiers.

François Villon (1431–63), the *déclassé* poet who had died to the north of this frozen country six years before Machiavelli's birth, had not celebrated nature or even the flocks of winter sheep to be glimpsed along the now almost deserted lanes, or the cows stranded among bursting icicles, only the salvations of sex, God and mead. His crazed rebelliousness had seemed resigned to Parisian gutters and alleys:

> our doom
> is, to be sifted by the wind,
>
> heaped up, smoothed down like silly sands.

We are less permanent than thought.
The Emperor with the Golden Hands
is still a word, a tint, a tone,
insubstantial, glorious,
when we ourselves are dead and gone
and the green grass growing over us.[5]

Amid the frustrations of Machiavelli's mission to France, Italy to the south appeared to pause and wait. For what? In Florence on 21 November, a superb snowstorm, the likes of which 'had never been seen [before],' according to Landucci, descended for hours. Snow froze 'without the roofs dripping,' and lasted for days. After the quiet settled in, many of the city's boys filled up the streets with prides of sculpted snow-lions.[6]

# 15

## Marriage and a Hint of Cesare Borgia

His permission to return, but only after informing the new ambassador, Pierfrancesco Tosinghi, who finally arrived, 'of all that you have done during your stay at court,' was signed by the Signoria and carried from Florence on 12 December.[1] Their letter took ages to reach him, as did his hundreds of miles ride home, and he was back in the familiar Florentine corridors and offices only on 14 January 1501.

Anxiety among the Signoria's officials about Cesare's no longer concealed intentions had stimulated an eagerness to settle up with the French, to the tune of an initial payment of 10,000 ducats. The Signoria promised that more would be sent without delay.

Machiavelli had now been gone for roughly five months. He returned to a slew of political and family problems, though with a bright spot among them: Giovanni, his nephew and the son of Primavera, had survived, as Totto had predicted, and was doing well. On the other hand, or so he had informed the Signoria as far back as 25 October, his personal life had fallen apart:

> As you are aware, my father died a month before my departure, and since then I have lost a sister; and my private affairs are so unsettled and without order, that my property is in every way actually going to waste. I hope, therefore, that your Lordships will kindly grant my request [to return], so that I may in some measure restore order to my own affairs. I should want to remain in Florence only one month, after which I am willing to come back to France, or to go to any other place where it may please your Lordships to send me.[2]

His request, with its air of melancholy, had been ignored at the time, even if months later it was granted. Nor, from the viewpoint of the larger political and military perspective over the past few months, had the Republic itself been able to do more than hold its own.

Cesare Borgia, Pope Alexander VI's favourite if illegitimate son since his elder son Juan's murder in a Roman back alley on 14 June 1497, and his mangled body's deposit in the Tiber (many suspected by Cesare himself), though dependent for success on his father's religious authority, had come a long way since defeating Caterina Sforza at Forlì less than a year earlier, in January 1500. In the apprentice days of his career, Caterina's defiance had kept his soldiers busy for three gory weeks. Impelled by her hostility to Louis XII as well as to him personally, she had blasted away with artillery at her own town from its castle, the Rocca di Ravaldino, which bent over it like a gnarled grim fist. Defiant even in defeat and capture, though perhaps willing to take a useless chance on his compassion, Caterina may have surrendered her body to her conqueror. More likely, she kept a discreet silence after he raped her.[3]

Whatever the pirouette of their arrangements at her surrender, she was bundled off to Rome. There Cesare displayed her as his trophy-beauty prisoner before his gloating father. He too had admired her and wanted her, but after she still refused to cede her seigniorial rights to Forlì, together with those of her children – her defiance returned as rapidly as it had collapsed – she failed to avoid Cesare's tossing her into a prison cell at the Castel Sant'Angelo.

As with Caterina, Cesare nearly always took delight in superfluous double-dealing. The measure of his malicious if not outright evil personality was *Schadenfreude*, or taking endless pleasure in others' experiences of ghastliness. Along these lines, it should be noted that he might have done better with what became his ghoulish, meteoric rise into notoriety had he yielded with somewhat less readiness to the opportunities for treachery that came his way. Restraint might have quelled the massive revulsion.

Certainly it would have provoked fewer quests for vengeance. Revealingly, his portraits (see plate VIII) show a face flat, inflexible and good-looking – some said beautiful – as well as nervous. A colossal arrogance seems buttressed by infinite self-adoration. Omitting his sense of personal injustice, which he nurtured constantly, his soldierly astuteness, humanist education, contempt for his enemies, wit, love of painting, scorn of his helpful father and viciousness, it was a face that in milder circumstances might even have been taken for that of a court jester – or at least of someone unlikely to attract the devotion of battle-hardened troops.

Devoid of its brashness, aura and religious lustre – his father had appointed him Bishop of Pamplona at the age of fifteen, though he showed no particular interest in religion – his *hauteur* might well have seemed naïve, despite its repertoire of unpleasant expressions.

Given his enjoyment of malignancy, his animosities might also, and just as relevantly, have been seen as demonic. Along with his limitless supply of pilfered money and the pride taken by his father in his military triumphs – he favoured capes, caps, gloves and doublets in clerical black to emphasize his authoritarian mystique – he seemed unquestionably magnetic. Those who met him remarked on his unwavering gaze, cleverness, impertinence and keenness of focus. He gleamed with charisma.

Another key to understanding him is that in a time of anarchy he proposed unity, if not peace. In the broader sense, therefore, his ferocity may not have mattered, at least to the humiliated populations that came under his metallic sway: any rivals, friends and enemies whom he traduced, enslaved, defeated and killed had already been well-schooled in ferocity by quite a few other *condottieri*.

During the years of his greatest influence on Italian politics, even ordinary people, had they been asked, and with few hesitations, might also have admitted to a wish for any unity at all, including that made available through violence, and at any cost, along with terror and murder. He himself preferred simple obedience.

During his theatrical entry into Rome, for instance, or midway through the elaborately staged semi-millennial celebrations of February 1500, his benign-seeming progress among the tens of thousands lining the bunting-decked streets to watch – many had walked hundreds of miles across Europe and Italy to be there – seemed more that of some streamlined ship gliding through unsettled waters than of a politician-soldier presiding casually over life and death.

A disorganized procession of priests, citizens and artisans seemed speared through by his disciplined, synchronized ranks of uniformed troops. His bodyguard of over a hundred grooms glittered in black velvet, black leather boots and new halberds. He rode at their centre, looking as always crisp, proud, clean, heaven-sent and invincible in his blacks on blacks. They winked with his single holy, gold medallion, as if proclaiming a new world order, or setting him off among surrounding craft that amounted to nothing.[4]

The year 1501 saw a flurry of insurrections throughout Republican territories. These Machiavelli and his colleagues made efforts to suppress. In several of them, Cesare was involved as a co-conspirator in search of advantages and gaining them. In each, moreover, his proximity if not actual involvement challenged Florentine diplomatic skills and the Signoria's flimsy preparations. A few months later they had still not much improved. The Florentines as always seemed to respond far more adequately to economic, artistic, political and literary opportunities than to military threats.

Machiavelli's eagerness to help maintain the Republic's territorial integrity nonetheless remained at a high pitch, and so his being sent for the third time that year, in mid-July, in a silk-drenching and mind-inflaming heat wave of a sweaty Florentine summer, to deal with the worst of these insurrections, at Pistoia, if only for a few days, remains intriguing. It may seem especially so because at home he had begun to prepare for a dramatic change in his way of life: his marriage to Marietta Corsini.[5]

Snippets of details, or chancy clues, linger about his wife-to-be, whom he must have courted and wooed as he turned thirty-two, or not long after the deaths of his father and sister. Marietta was the daughter of Ludovico (Luigi) Corsini. Along with her sister, and not unlike the Machiavelli, she came from a down-at-heels (*di origine popolana*) branch of a noble family able to trace its roots into Florentine history, or over hundreds of years, as well as forward into the elite merchant classes of the fourteenth century. The Corsini had also made their way into more recent government circles. In 1500, Marietta's brother-in-law, Piero del Nero, was elected to the Ten of War, the committee for which Machiavelli acted as Secretary.

The infrequent references to Marietta in his letters and those of his friends probably indicate more about their discretion than any indifference. Without exception they confirm a vivid impression of a woman warm-hearted, affectionate, thoughtful and devoted. Machiavelli himself seems scarcely lacking in sincere feelings toward his wife, at least at first, and perhaps not later, although marriages in Florence and the Europe of his day were often whimsical, representing merely the most practical arrangement for producing children to enhance a family's name and its financial interests. With Machiavelli the possibility remains real enough that another issue mattered as much and perhaps more, as seems reinforced by the timing of the ceremony. Hints of his isolation among the rooms of the almost deserted *palazzo* at Via Guicciardini, where he continued to live, haunt about his desire for domesticity. Grief may also have weighed in. As is likely, Totto had probably left to take up his priestly duties elsewhere.

Agostino Vespucci's letter to him from Rome in August, 1501, sent either weeks before or after his wedding, whose precise date is unknown, is hardly meant (as some have said) to offer marital advice. Most of it is about Alexander VI, and serves up the usual no-holds-barred jesting in much of the two friends' correspondence:

> And if His Beatitude the Pope should happen to [come up] there [to Florence], you and others who might want some dispensation, either to take or to leave your wives, will get it out of kindness of heart, *provided that your hand is loaded with money.*[6]

Vespucci here takes aim at Alexander's scrounging after cash and not at some imaginary annulment. His phrases sizzle with the ribaldry common between bachelor-comrades, one of whom has decided, perhaps cleverly and for the better, to alter the direction of his life.

# 16

## *Meeting the Captain-General*

At the same time, the insurrection at Pistoia, based on an ancient feud between the town's leading families, the Panciatichi and Cancellieri – it harked back to the Middle Ages – erupted and spilled into the countryside. In Rome, Michelangelo had just begun work on his magnificent *Pietà*. In Venice, Aldo Manuzio had just published the first book in Italian boasting his newly invented italic typeface. In Pistoia, house-burnings followed the flight of the Panciatichi themselves and scores of deaths.

In Florence, 'the plague [was] increasing rapidly' while in early April 'there came [to the city],' Landucci reports, 'ten citizens of Pistoia to explain to us their sad case.' A Florentine commissary, Niccolò di Tommaso Antinori, was dispatched to put down the disturbances.[1]

He 'hanged certain rioters' – the accepted method of restoring order – but ineffectually, as the murders and arson continued. By the end of April, Cesare had captured Faenza, after at first and to his surprise being repulsed and driven back at the city's walls. By July Vespucci, 'gasping from the great heat ... in Rome,' where he had been sent by the Signoria, was offering Machiavelli, still in Florence, his acid take on Roman religious life, as he saw it: 'Aside from the [P]ope, who has his own illicit flock ... at all times, every evening, from vespers to seven o'clock, twenty-five or more women are brought into the palace riding pillion with some people, to the point where the entire palace has evidently become the brothel of every obscenity.' The Pope's hedonism seemed a mirror-image of Cesare's violence.[2]

Machiavelli soon found himself enmeshed in a blur of decisions that could well involve Florence's survival as an independent state. Sent off himself to Pistoia, with its own plague-reduced population of about 8,000, he realized that in view of the town's military value his reports home would be anxiously anticipated, if only because the strategic and diplomatic situation in north-central Italy – a far bigger picture – was altering as well.

It seemed to shift dramatically just as he left, and he faced the need of dealing with a murky undertow of manoeuvres set in motion by Cesare Borgia. The Duke's territorial encroachments had abruptly coincided with an ongoing Florentine need to mollify the French. As ever, if Louis was to remain an active ally, he required the lubricant of additional payments. To date the Signoria had doled out over 30,000 ducats to him in compensation for the Swiss mutiny. Louis himself, as unrelenting as ever in his imperial ambitions, now ordered south into Italy, by land and sea, an invasion-army of 21,000 men. His goal was finally to lay claim to his coveted Kingdom of Naples, ruled by Frederic of Aragon. With a French army on the march and plunging through village after village, he might easily thrust aside or annihilate any trivial resistance thrown up against him.

The King posed no threat to Florence as long as the payments continued – on the contrary, his presence was reassuring – but Cesare, hurrying south at the head of his own smaller if considerable battle force, had for the moment chosen ease of access as an excuse for entering fringe areas of the Republic. He planned to eviscerate Florentine authority by claiming territory that he would later annex to his papal-established state of Romagna.

As they went, his troops sacked and burnt stretches of farmland. If nothing else, doing so made plain his usual strategy of spreading terror for the sake of promoting his influence. His soldiers were perhaps urged to rape as well as to rob and steal (Louis by contrast ordered his troops to refrain from criminal acts, and they appear to have done so). Cesare's sexual terrorism, however, was apparently directed indiscriminately at women in the frightened towns and hamlets raided by his soldiers. It rapidly assumed the character of an actual policy. The monstrous, moreover, preceded the humiliating. A sense of Republican defeat spread through and beyond a score of ruined and abandoned Florentine villages. It poured into major population centres. It seemed on the brink of precipitating a de facto Republican collapse.

Even a partial domination of Florentine soil by Cesare's army, if unresisted, might induce a paralysis of fear. Its influence could lead to the restoration in Florence of a dictatorship under Piero de'Medici. Lorenzo's heir, as despised as ever, was rumoured to be waiting in nearby Bologna, impatient and estimating his chances.

Machiavelli had been present at the French court months earlier when Louis promised that any such invasion by Cesare would not be tolerated: 'We have written in duplicate to our lieutenants in Italy that if the Duke ... should attempt anything against the Florentines or the Bolognese, they should instantly march against [him], so that upon this point you may rest in perfect security.'[3] By now, though, the influence of the royal guarantee had faded. Cesare seemed on the brink of realizing his dream of a takeover.

At Pistoia, Machiavelli took stock of these implications of the increasing civic disorder. To pacify the town, since 1351 under Florentine control, he recommended that the family of the exiled Panciaticchi, along with their supporters, be allowed to return. Reestablishing the previous civil society could well provide a natural barrier against a Cesare-led assault. A revival of the old arrangement also seemed appropriate, as both the Cancellieri and Panciatichi had for centuries represented rival but balancing factions engaged in a 'gara di uffici' (competition over offices) in running the government.[4]

As a result, after several days in which he ordered those in positions of power to abandon their prohibition against the Panciatichi, he seems to have felt certain enough to return to Florence. The tangled situation was, if not clarified, at least calmer. By October, though, he was back. The medicine had not taken, and robberies, threats, shootings and murders had started up again on a more devastating scale.[5]

It may be impossible to establish whether Machiavelli could have resolved the Pistoian *impasse*. Nor is guesswork likely to be as illuminating as recognizing that he was entrusted with the attempt. The point of trust measures his appeal, or that he could be called on at a delicate juncture. If nothing else, it draws attention to the growing pleasure taken in his resourcefulness.

All of which may be critical in making sense of his assignment soon afterwards as secretary to Francesco Soderini, the Archbishop of Volterra and brother of Piero. Francesco had just begun to achieve prominence in the Republic's political affairs. He would also (though he did not know it) be elected Gonfaloniere di giustizia for life. At this point, or during the inauspicious summer of 1502, he was sent off to meet and negotiate with Cesare himself. Machiavelli's skills and experience were now to be put to even fuller use as the Signoria tried once more to call a halt to his advances.

By now too, or as early as June, Arezzo had rebelled against the Republic. An important Tuscan city in the Valdichiana (Chiana Valley), as well as a bustling northern neighbour of Cesare's patched-together state of Romagna, it had been encouraged by the Florentine indecisiveness. Other towns and cities in the area, Cortona and Sansepolcro among them, at once joined in.

The rising at Arezzo was decisively if not unexpectedly supported by the treacherous brother of the executed Paolo Vitelli, Vitellozzo. He had already been recruited as one of Cesare's *condottieri* and had taken control of a fair-sized body of troops, though Cesare with his usual cool duplicity denied their military relations. In Florence it was reported that Vitellozzo had been accompanied into Arezzo by Piero de'Medici, but Vitellozzo's appearance alone served for many as a signal that Cesare was lurking behind a conspiracy to replace the Republic's government with his own, most likely led by Piero.[6]

The Florentine forebodings induced alarm. Threats of an uprising against members of the elite classes, or *ottimati*, widely though for the most part wrongly suspected of supporting Cesare and Piero, echoed in the streets. Calls poured forth for the *ottimati* to be arrested and their houses burnt to the ground.

The Signoria issued an emergency request to Louis of France to return with his army, lest he be taken unawares and driven out of Italy altogether. At the same time, Alamanno Salviati and other prominent Signoria members tried to raise money for troops to confront an expected invasion. It was assumed that the Duke's final assault would come after he seized territories close to the poorly defended city itself.

The reports of sexual terror practised by his soldiers, well-known for over a year, contributed strongly to the gathering fear. Much earlier, on 18 May 1501, Landucci had noted in his diary that 'the whole morning we heard of nothing but the iniquities of Valentino's troops; among other things they sacked Carmignano, and carried off all the girls that they found there, who were gathered in a church from all the country round.' Not atypically, a husband was forced to watch as Cesare's troops raped his wife.[7]

The result was that Machiavelli and Soderini's first meeting with Cesare was in no way easy, chatty or pleasant. It was arranged following a hasty trip on horseback and two hours after sunset (or at 'two o'clock at night,' according to the old style of telling the time by the bells rung for church services) on 24 June, in Urbino, at the famous ducal palace that with its magnificent library had long been 'thought by many to be the most beautiful to be found anywhere in all Italy.' Cesare had seized it the day before.[8]

The silvery sixty-year-old Duke of Montefeltro, who together with his brilliant second wife Battista Sforza (she had started her Latin studies at the age of three, and by fourteen, on her betrothal, was stunning audiences with her orations in Latin as well as her mastery of classical Greek, philosophy and mathematics) had put together one of the finest manuscript libraries in Europe, had by now been dead for over twenty years. His son, Guidobaldo, who as a child had posed with his father for their astonishing double portrait, was in his early thirties. He had become a *condottiere* himself, but had fled the great house with his family after Cesare deceived him into disarming his own city: Cesare had asked for a loan of artillery for a nearby campaign.

Neither Guidobaldo's naïve generosity, nor his loyalty to Cesare's father and the Borgias, nor his last minute pleas, had any effect on Cesare's treachery. In fact as Machiavelli and Francesco Soderini stood with the Borgian leader in the calm candlelit evening at the virtually deserted if well-guarded palace, they might have noticed, had they troubled to look, that his troops had already begun looting the famed library of a good many of its valuable, gem-encrusted, gold-trimmed manuscripts and incunabula.

Cesare's meeting with them had come about at his own request, though the Signoria, thoroughly afraid, was eager to answer his questions about their policy towards him. Their motive remained delay. They hoped that Louis XII might send troops to help them beat back the rebellions around Arezzo, if not to defeat Cesare altogether, at the moment an unrealistic idea. Cesare evinced little patience with his well-dressed and well-mannered guests, and even less with their insistence on Florentine friendship. A fantasy of Republican surrender alone seemed to stimulate his mind, though he apparently hoped that he might manage it by negotiation rather than invasion.

Machiavelli's report on their discussions, which ran on through that evening and into the next, and which he describes in a single long letter, with minute gaps in the writing, or omissions indicating haste, reveals the edginess of the three men, and even an uneasy white heat as he cites Cesare's exact words: 'I don't like this [Florentine] government, and I can't trust it. You [Florentines] must change it and offer guarantees of the observance of what you promise me.... . If you don't want me as a friend, you'll find out what it's like to have me as an enemy.'[9]

According to Machiavelli (in the account that he put together and wrote up, but that was signed by Soderini), the Florentines felt perhaps foolishly unimpressed by the aggressive tone of the Captain-General of the papal armies, as his father had designated him. They observed that their 'city had the best government it was able to devise and that, since the city was itself quite satisfied with its government, its friends ought also to be satisfied with it.'[10]

Their unbending manner seems to have produced no effect. Cesare simply announced his military aims, or that he would insist on the Signoria's acquiescence, amounting to a complete surrender, along the whole of the Republic's lengthy border with Romagna: 'I desire to have explicit assurances [on this matter] since too well I know that your city is not well-minded toward me, but would abandon me like an assassin, and has already sought to plunge me [into] terrible conflicts with the Pope and King of France.'[11] Incredibly, if glibly, he remarked that he planned to demonstrate his good intentions towards Florence by forcing the pig-headed Vitelli into retreating from Arezzo.

So far, at least as indicated by his report, Machiavelli exhibits only a minimal awareness, though he is sensitive enough to Cesare's contempt, that he might be dealing and negotiating with the most significant political leader of the age, or a commander whom he might come to see as emblematic of political and military trends over decades if not centuries to come.

In the competition of the moment, political reflections may have been diverted by their mutual hostility. Nor does Machiavelli show much interest in admitting to Cesare that he might have been more or less right about the Florentine government. Debates were just then in progress over its constitution. Only as a compromise would Piero Soderini be granted the unprecedented honour of being chosen as *Gonfaloniere di giustizia* for life, out of a field of 236 candidates. This would occur on 22 September, amid a mixture of jealousy, envy, a broad if inaccurate sense of yielding to corruption, generally insincere congratulations and, in the face of Cesare's continuing menaces, relief.[12]

Even in these strained circumstances, though, Machiavelli appears to have drawn a number of solid conclusions about his host's character, or enough to announce, albeit frighteningly in reference to a political adventurer several years younger than himself, but who was scarcely a novice: 'This lord styles himself quite splendid and magnificent, and so strong that there seems no enterprise in war so great that to him it will not seem trivial. In adding to his domains and glory he acknowledges neither exhaustion nor danger. He arrives in a new place before people realize that he has set out from an old one. His troops admire him, and he has gathered round him the best men in Italy – all of which facts, plus his perpetual good fortune [*una perpetua fortuna*, a phrase that preserves its ghostly implication of destiny], leave him victorious and formidable.'[13]

To which he might also have added: uncompromising. The first meeting with Cesare having abruptly ended in collisions, the Florentine representatives left to write up their notes (or to allow Machiavelli to do so), only to be confronted the next day by Cesare's confederates, the Orsini. They too demanded a Florentine capitulation, while dishonestly hinting that Louis of France might switch sides and team up with Cesare.

Beyond one twist lay another. That evening, as Machiavelli and Soderini met Cesare for the second time, they were told that the diplomatic situation had changed. They were now confronted with an ultimatum, though perhaps its rudeness seemed unsurprising in a leader whom Machiavelli had already described as smooth enough to be able to 'install himself in someone else's house before he so much as notices it.'[14] Within four days the Signoria would either accede to his intentions in respect to Florence or, as he intimated, he would deploy his forces, comprising some 25,000 troops, in such ways as he might deem appropriate.

If the danger seemed greater, Cesare's citing a figure of 25,000, while meant to seem impressive, must have seemed a careless or strategic mistake. On enquiring discreetly here and there, Machiavelli had discovered that the *Capitano's* nearest military camps, some three miles off, along with others in Tuscany, held far fewer soldiers than he claimed, or no more than 16,500, including cavalry.[15]

This lower number still represented a threat. Certainly it seemed high enough to induce both Florentines, a bit later that evening, to agree that while Soderini ought to stay behind, pursuing such negotiations with the Duke as might still be possible, and perhaps even arranging a delay, Machiavelli ought to return to Florence as fast as he could.

He accordingly set off on horseback early the next morning (26 June), in effect chasing his own dispatched report. The idea was to reach the Signoria with a personal description of Cesare's ultimatum, or in time to give his Florentine colleagues the best opportunity to evaluate their options.

It may have been now that fate, or *Fortuna*, at least in one of the Renaissance senses of the term, put in her oar. *Fortuna* had little to do with luck. Ordinary men and women strapped themselves to the goddess's turning wheel, on which she whipped them mercilessly, and where their circumstances constantly altered between good and evil, because their brains were ruled by irrational passions: this in contrast to saints, who might overcome their passions through prayer and contemplation.

Cesare had already proposed that Florence offer him a *condotta*, or a formal alliance setting him up as a well-paid overseer of the Republic's military affairs, including its soldiers. His request, which he delivered more or less as a demand, had been rejected.

The swift advance northward of a body of Louis's French troops through the Arno valley towards Arezzo – an intervention of *Fortuna*? – now seemed to blow a good deal of wind out of his sails. Days passed and, puzzled, he insisted on reopening negotiations for the rejected *condotta*. His insistence was received in silence. The Signoria had begun to rejoice in a possible rescue by the French. Recognizing his difficulty, Cesare lapsed into a silence of his own.

Machiavelli almost at once found himself sent off on important missions at mid-to-late-summer intervals, this time in the direction of Arezzo, which he visited twice in August and once in September. His presence was intended to accelerate its French-assisted restoration to Florentine rule. Each of his stays was brief, lasting no more than a day or two – he apparently popped in and out – and may testify less to his negotiating skills than his equestrian stamina. The initial resistance of the French commanders to surrendering their hold on the city, which had more or less fallen into their lap as they marched in, and stubborn problems with Arezzo's citizens over abandoning their rebellion against Florence, required mediation.[16]

This Machiavelli was prepared to offer, and with another helpful diplomatic success under his belt he returned to his office in the Palazzo della Signoria, to his friends and his wife, who had just become a young mother: a daughter, Primerana, had been born to them in early summer.

Domesticity seldom held him in check. By early October he was off on another assignment, and again at the shifting headquarters of Cesare Borgia. Its purpose now was to protect Florentine interests in the face of his latest attempts to undermine them, or once more to divert Cesare's ambitions to stage-manage a takeover of the Republic.

These he had never abandoned. In fact he had only just slipped back among his own troops from a secret meeting with the French King in Milan. There he had promised Louis vital military support against the Spanish in his campaign to seize Naples. Cesare's ultimate goal, however, was to drain off the French support of Florence itself. In a sign that all might not be well, or that he might have worries of his own, his trip had not been easy. In travelling back and forth from Urbino to Milan, he had had to sneak in and out of both places, doing so in disguise.

# 17

# *Investigating the Sources of Power*

The paradox of Machiavelli's latest assignment to Cesare's headquarters, now relocated to Imola from the picturesque double-peaked mountain of Urbino, was that it came about chiefly because of a decades-in-the-making Florentine constitutional crisis. The crisis had developed out of the contradiction inherent in the workings of almost all democracies and republics. On the one hand, it has to do with most people's suspicion of authority, and on the other, with a need of authority if a government is to function at all.

For decades the Florentine method of dealing with this problem had erred on the side of suspicion. Sour experiences at the hands of Piero de'Medici, and Lorenzo before him, had reinforced a powerful majority in favour of restricting by institutional means all concentrations of power. Extremely close supervision, however, rendered almost impossible the sort of rapid decision-making desirable in a crisis.

In these circumstances, even policy-making became a slippery ideal. A too generous tolerance of personal freedom might also promote military laxness. The Florentine cynicism in respect to authority had exhibited itself in a careful layering of the committees required to elect the Republic's officials, and even more in the brevity of their terms of office. The central purpose of these restraints was to suppress any authoritarian inclination.

At the same time, an insistence on committee control everywhere strengthened a bureaucratic paralysis. An upper level civil servant, such as Machiavelli, found himself forced to stand for election as Second Chancellor once a year. Members of the Signoria were pushed into so many elections for their shorter two-month terms that they scarcely had time to catch their breath. As fast as they came in, they went out, and even when a few achieved an occasional re-election, the chances of frequent or semi-permanent office-holding generally lay beyond their grasp, as did the amassing of practical, extended government experience.

More than other economic or social classes, the *ottimati* had opposed the Florentine system as a quicksand. At first their antagonism had hardly mattered, as proposals to increase the tenure of members of the Signoria to between three and five years failed to win sufficient support in the Grand Council, with its 3,000 disputatious citizens.

An alternative proposal, to create a post of lifetime *Gonfaloniere di giustizia*, was at first rejected, but then, in August 1502, surprisingly found acceptable. The reason was that it had begun to appear enticing to many citizens, if not the *ottimati* themselves, who recognized the need for change but who felt even more worried about the potential power of entire groups of officials offered the boon of lengthy terms. The upshot was that in September Piero Soderini was elected for life.[1]

This plum of enhanced political power, if still regarded by many with mistrust, was widely believed to have fallen to the distinguished, honest, if by no means brilliant yet hard worker on the Republic's behalf, a pragmatic, eloquent, educated man, for three reasons. These were his canniness as a negotiator, his assumed secret deals with the *ottimati* and other factions (an idea that turned out to have little basis in fact) and his having remained aloof, or taken no sides, during the violent struggles over Savonarola.

Machiavelli and Piero Soderini now became warm and soon fast friends. As Machiavelli's close relations with his brother Francesco already seemed solid, his career advanced smartly enough.

Piero had himself done a stint as an emissary to Cesare Borgia. This had occurred the year before, and the experience had allowed him to familiarize himself with the Duke's fear-provoking tactics. He now sought out the services of a sympathetic colleague with a background resembling his own.

The new, burly, sensitive standard-bearer of the Republic, as the surviving likenesses show (among them a probable life-mask terracotta bust of the type issued for many local leaders, sold by the dozen and meant for display in private homes), seemed to mellow behind his brooding eyes and his sensitive glance that suggested a personality as passionate about art as politics. From the start, he addressed Machiavelli in his letters not simply as 'Notable man' but 'very dear friend.'

Revealingly, Piero sent him (at Cesare's headquarters) his first brief note to anyone following his election as *Gonfaloniere*. Also revealingly, it had to do with a team of stolen mules:

I ... write to you on behalf of some people from whom six mules were taken during the past months at Castel Durante by some of His Excellency's [Cesare's] men [a mule train carrying goods for two Florentine merchants had been abducted to a castle occupied by Cesare's secretary-treasurer, Alessandro Spannocchi]. ... I would like you to be so kind as to speak in my name to His Most Illustrious Lordship; first of all, you will offer my respects to him; thereafter you will come with His Excellency to the specific case of the six mules that were taken, which it may please him to have returned, for my sake, to ... our carters; you will beseech him for this *over and over again*.[2]

Soderini's mulish gesture – it looks at first glance merely petulant – seems actually to have been meant to serve as a basis for his conception of firmly grounded diplomacy. It underscored his practical habits. The trivial might offer a clue to those who had to deal with him, or set in place a foundation from which they might sensibly approach more abstract questions and problems.

The new Florentine leader's shrewdness, in other words, was no more to be overestimated than Machiavelli's, and from the start the two worked well as a team. Amid war, treachery and crippling political miscalculations, teamwork counted for a lot, as did Machiavelli's adroitness in resuming his relations with Cesare:

Finding myself not well on horseback at my departure from Florence [he reported back promptly on 7 October] and believing that my commission required all speed, I took the post at Scarperia [*i.e.*, exchanged his slow horses for faster relays] and came here without loss of time, arriving today at about the eleventh hour. Having left my horses and servants behind, I presented myself at once, in my travelling costume, to his Excellency, who received me most graciously.[3]

In the face of mounting threats, no time was to be lost by the now seasoned official: even a change of clothes might be ignored at the risk of appearing a mass of wrinkles, or washing up after a sweaty ride. More than ever, the hours leaked their plots, rumours and gossip.

From the start, therefore, he made every effort to ingratiate himself with Cesare, and perhaps most felicitously by disclosing what he knew about those conspiring to destroy him: 'I [right away] ... spoke of the defection of the [powerful] Orsini [family], of their meeting with their adherents [or those most committed among the several known plotters], how they had cunningly endeavored to induce your Lordships [the Signoria] to unite with all of them,' or to join in fomenting an uprising to cripple the Duke's military ambitions throughout central Italy, and perhaps even provoke his assassination.[4]

At the moment there seemed little doubt that a major conspiracy had been developing for weeks among the leaders of the major military families and some of Cesare's trusted aides, *condottieri* and civil confederates. Machiavelli thus assumed that improved relations might be achieved by feigning if not feeling some concern for his welfare.

Over a glass or two of the sour local wine and chunks of the coarse local bread – each reputed to possess qualities beneficial to the exhausted traveller – he seated himself in the receiving room of the quadrangular fortress built for her protection by the recently imprisoned Caterina Sforza. With its fifteen-foot-thick walls and forty-foot-deep moat, the castle provided a solid defence against the latest artillery, or an optimal place for informing Cesare of the Signoria's having rejected the invitations of two of the three Orsini brothers and other conspirators. Among them was the embittered Vitellozzo Vitelli; Cesare described Vitellozzo as having 'thrown himself at his feet, weeping,' begging him to invade Florence. All had urged the unwilling Florentines to join in luring him into a battlefield disaster.[5]

Despite its sincerity, Machiavelli's gambit seems to have made only a superficial impression. Equipped with spies of his own, Cesare was already apprised of the plot. He had a list of those involved: Giampaolo Baglioni (known as 'the tyrant of Perugia'), Antonio da Venafro (a roving emissary of Pandolfo Petrucci, ruler of Siena), Oliverotto da Fermo, Vitelli himself and Cardinal Giambattista Orsini, now living in Rome, along with his brothers, Paolo and Francesco.

Probably as a result, the Duke allowed himself a mere nod and a trace of frowning dismissiveness, casually pledging his gratitude and devotion to the Signoria and the Florentine people. Machiavelli nonetheless imagined that his time had not been wasted, or that their hasty meeting, intended to reintroduce him to the Duke's court, was not without its value. This was because a pattern of mutual reassurance had been established which might prove useful. Having gained a measure of Cesare's trust, or as much of it as in his chary lifetime he allotted to anyone except his beautiful, well-read and perhaps incestuous sister Lucrezia, Machiavelli might even expect to become the beneficiary of one of the Duke's subtler quirks. It appeared at odd moments – but might it not simply be the eccentricity of the expert liar? – his almost desperate need, and especially on occasions demanding secrecy, to exchange confidences.

Cesare had acted in a quite similar way a few months earlier, in July and August, if with someone better known, Machiavelli's neighbour, Leonardo da Vinci. Leonardo's Florentine studio was located a few streets over from the Machiavelli *palazzo*. It is uncertain whether the Second Chancellor got to know the fifty-year-old artist-inventor before his arrival in Imola. It seems likely that they had known each other, however, and even that Machiavelli and Piero Soderini were instrumental in promoting Leonardo's abilities with the Duke as a military engineer and architect, or as capable and versatile enough to assist him in his ideas of territorial expansion.[6]

No doubt for the sake of hagiography, Leonardo is even today often admired as placid, soft-bearded, spiritual and oracular, when at fifty he was bristly, bustling with plans and self-promotional. The serenity of the sage had not yet replaced the brashness of the autodidact.

In the autumn of 1502, Leonardo found himself at Imola, and not simply at the same moment as Machiavelli but also as the Duke's prized guest. In a small town overflowing with slapdash, hired soldiers, the artist had been ordered to make elaborate sketches of the layout of Caterina's fortress, taking measurements of its lofty walls, moat, parapets, corridors and windows, and amassing the mathematical and military data essential to his new responsibilities as Cesare's military engineer.

His presence there had segued out of a tour during the summer just past, also paid for by Cesare, which led him into the fertile nearby provinces and included trips to Urbino, Pesara, Rimini and Cesena. As he moved about, he made notes not only on architectural issues pertinent to his professional curiosity but also on his reactions to the fussier habits of the peasantry, such as their preference for carts with absurdly small front wheels, which rendered them hard to push and apt when loaded to fall apart or tip over.

At Pavia in August, Cesare had recognized his gifts by granting an unlimited passport-licence to 'our most excellent and well-beloved architect and general engineer Leonardo Vinci, who by our commission is to survey the places and fortresses of our states.'[7] Leonardo was rapidly put to military uses. Accompanying Cesare in early October into a swampy battle at Fossombrone, he had improvised a wooden bridge, enabling the Duke's army to cross a river and suppress a rebellion. Elsewhere, Leonardo examined tower defences and proposed improvements. He investigated optimal artillery and mortar positions, military escape routes, harbours, assembly points for soldiers and the soft spots of castles. He drafted a map of Imola and modified old maps of the

Valdichiana to indicate prominent landscape contours, which remain accurate to this day. He displayed over them the valley's extensive, intricate waterways with precision, creating an atlas of its lakes, ponds, streams and rivers.[8]

Much of his cartographical work he clarified in contrasting colours. It is not known whether he and Machiavelli discussed while at Imola the perennial Florentine challenge of defeating Pisa, or turned their attention to a daring scheme to cut the city off from the sea and leave it open to a land invasion by diverting the Arno. In his reports to the Signoria, Machiavelli makes no mention of Leonardo or the plan, and it seems plausible that had he done so, given the chance that his reports might have been read by Cesare's censors, he could have run some risk to his safety. Within months, however, the plan was to appeal to both men, and it may then have been discussed.

As on earlier missions, Machiavelli's reports rolled out in waves, if with a frequency and length that indicated his absorption in the commercial, diplomatic, amorous, military and secret comings and goings at what had become Cesare's headquarters. They overflowed with descriptions of his ability to bob and weave, to throw his enemies off guard, to assuage blind hatred, to mollify critics with lies and ultimately to commit ferocious acts of treachery while persuading his victims of his undying respect.

From another point of view, Machiavelli's reports, some of which are a few thousand words long, should also be understood as only-to-be-expected expressions of his efficiency. On 20, 22, 26, 28 and 29 November, not to mention 6 and 18 December, he wrote and dispatched by courier more than seven voluminous, information-packed communiqués.[9] Most were written during long stints stretching late into the night. When else at Cesare's nerve-centre of military planning, or his crossroads for repairing and distributing weapons (including new armour and shields), training exercises and negotiations, could the Ten of War's Secretary have found the time?

Often his crammed pages reflect an anxiety about the Republic ('on taking my leave of his Excellency he reminded me again to recall to your Lordships that if you remained undecided you would certainly lose, while by uniting with him you might be victorious'[10]), and the odd flicker of danger ('we see all his enemies armed and ready at any moment to light a general conflagration'[11]).

Several reports focus on Cesare's efforts to increase his always inadequate, often declining number of troops. A couple allude to his practice, still fairly radical in those days, of recruiting entire regiments of soldiers from Romagna and others of the conquered territories, rather than continuing to rely exclusively on mercenaries: 'Five days ago he mustered six thousand infantry into his own service from his own states, and which he can have together in two days.'[12]

Though ease of recruitment retained a perpetual attraction, Cesare's purpose was not so much to enlarge his army, always in search of untested, ready troops, as to gain the edge granted by the loyalty of soldiers convinced that they were fighting for house and home as well as profit (which for the ordinary soldier remained mostly a delusion): 'As to men-at-arms and light cavalry, he has caused it to be published that he will take into his pay all ... as are within his own states, and they are at once to report themselves to him.'[13]

For Cesare – or, to cite a similar European example of some centuries later, Napoleon, and especially as the French Emperor advanced east across Europe into Russia, with his progress following the enactment of the world's first national conscription laws – the push into a peninsula-long Italian victory would most smoothly come about through a new military equation. This would combine superior strategic abilities with those of native-born soldiers and their interest in self-defence, plus lightning-fast shifts between attacks, retreats, counter-attacks and ambushes. The whole package might best come wrapped in the deliberately terrifying and treacherous.

# 18

# *Retribution and Dominance*

At the same time, Machiavelli was hardly proving a reliable husband. 'Madonna Marietta wrote me via her brother,' scribbled his friend Biagio Buonaccorsi in red-faced haste just after his arrival at Imola in October, 'asking when you will be back.'

As far as Marietta was concerned, as a result of her husband's demanding diplomatic activities, once he had left home and Florence he seemed simply to vanish. At first she was astonished, and then became stubborn and angry:

> 'She says she does not want to write, and she is making a big fuss, and she is hurt because you had promised her you would stay eight days and no more. So come back, in the name of the devil, so the womb [or their sex life, though Biagio's remark is meant in jest rather than earnest] doesn't suffer.'[1]

The devil lay in the details of his sense of urgency. His diplomatic work might have allayed it, but it would no more be quashed by wifely remonstrances than sluggish horses, or even complaints about a stylish black cloak that he wanted to buy and that he had ordered sent out to him over Marietta's objections. 'Madonna Marietta has learned of this mantle [that you've ordered through me] and is [once more] making a big fuss,' wrote Biagio on 21 October. Just before Machiavelli's departure, her annoyance was soothed by his arranging the marriage of one of her servants, and doing it 'well,' though she still wanted information about the woman's dowry, which he seems to have paid.

His cloak, on the other hand, with its new hat to match, he asked to be made up in a plush black damask – expense was no object – or decently enough to flatter him as a representative of the Signoria, though he was no ambassador. One Lorenzo, the merchant providing the material, was afraid to approach Marietta for payment and entered it into a private account of Machiavelli's: 'I do not know whether I shall have [your new] mantle this evening,' noted Biagio. 'If

I do, I shall send it; if not, I shall not fail to by the first messenger.... . Be patient, since I have to be.'[2] In the meantime, and perhaps irked, Marietta went to stay for a few days at the house of her brother-in-law, Piero del Neri.

These petty-seeming issues of clothing and marital neglect are probably easier to understand in the light of the constant threats of conspiracy and invasion, not to mention the political unease, despite Soderini's election as *Gonfaloniere*. In Florence spats also erupted more often than usual over the meagre salaries of many in government. As during his first year in office, Machiavelli's remained fixed at 128 gold florins. For months, the military quagmire mesmerized the population. Might the French King not change his mind and cut off assistance to the Republic? Landucci reports that, as early as June, five of the city's tall gates, the San Giorgio, San Miniato, la Giustizia, Pinti and Porticciuola al Prato, were ordered shut against incursions which might be tried by night and hostile 'people and [subversive] letters [that might be] brought in' by day. Homeowners along the Arno were warned not to leave ladders in the water. Borgo had rebelled, and Anghiari surrendered, to Cesare's satisfaction.

Florence itself began to look dishevelled, or 'wounded to death,' as Landucci describes it, and a target of popular ridicule. Two hundred troops were mustered by the Signoria, a bare minimum. Morale-boosting sermons in their support could be heard daily in the pulpits of the churches. Graffiti of hanged men and waiting gallows – sneers of contempt – were smeared on the outer walls of the houses of government employees and officials, among them that of Soderini. The malaise lifted a little on the politically historic Tuesday (1 November) when 'Soderini, [now officially proclaimed] *Gonfaloniere* for life, entered the *Palagio* with [a] new *Signoria*. All Florence was in the Piazza, as this was a new thing never done before in our city. Everyone seemed to have hopes of living in comfort.'[3]

Perversely, the best hopes of Florentine comfort, at least for the present, depended on Cesare defeating the plots directed at him. His own idea of peace, or a thug's peace, might be peace as well. At Soderini's prodding, therefore, and because he needed the most reliable information on Cesare as rapidly as possible, Machiavelli extended his stay in Imola through November into December, if in a half-hearted manner. His enthusiasm subsided further as he fell ill. In late November he wrote that he was running a 'violent fever.'[4] In early December he added that if the illness persisted he might be brought home 'in a box.'[5] His enigmatic illness may have been more ploy than reality. He recovered quickly enough: all references to illness are omitted from his subsequent letters.

As on his previous mission to Cesare, he may have concluded that keeping tabs on the Duke's unpredictable tacking about had lost any practical value. A Florentine official might better be employed in Florence (on 14 December he remarked, 'My remaining here is of no further use'[6]). His sense of futility seems emphasized by the sheer whimsy of his personal letters during those autumn months. Bartolomeo Ruffini, a friend and co-worker at the Chancellery, describes them as 'most welcome … and the jokes and witticisms you write … make everyone split [their] sides laughing and give great pleasure.'[7]

Praise for his official reports continued to pour in, accompanied by requests that he make them longer. His gift of conjuring up a convincing atmosphere through details, of letting his readers feel present at Cesare's thrust-and-parry encampment as he trained his troops and issued his barrages of orders, struck Machiavelli's employers as vital to grasping their own predicament.

In describing Cesare's enemies, the Orsini, who succeeded only ineptly in concealing their motives, Machiavelli had noted that the Duke termed them a 'gang of bankrupts', arguing in his defence that 'the reason … they had no wish to declare themselves openly against me was that they were raking in my cash.' As long as his father the Pope and the French King supported him, he jeered, only a 'fool' would risk opposing him. His allies 'had kindled so great a fire in his favour that all the water the Orsini might command could not quench it.'[8]

Yet at just that moment, or during the last weeks of autumn, as Machiavelli realized, and after biding his time, Cesare came up with a plan to eliminate the conspiracy altogether. This was to reach beyond the immediate threat to his success. It would rid him of the malign neighbours and false friends who had, by his lights and when push came to shove, revealed themselves as agents of 'treachery.' As he ordered Machiavelli to inform the Signoria: 'I have no lack of true friends [the French King and his father], amongst whom I would be glad to count your Signori, providing they promptly let me understand as much. If they do not, I shall ignore them to the extent that even if I find myself in water up to my throat I will never again allude to any friendship between us, though I might always regret having a neighbour to whom I could not render any friendly service, or receive any from him.'[9]

Disarmingly in its early phases, his plan consisted of a generous enough gesture, or an invitation to his enemies to set aside their differences for the sake of harmony, conquest and money. It seemed an offer too good to be refused. At any rate, their refusal might easily run the risk, or so the conspirators assumed, of provoking him into dangerous retaliations. In retrospect, their suspicions seem to have been unrealistic, though they offer lingering testimony to Cesare's charisma. By late September 1502, not only was he in command of far weaker forces than they knew, but their own situation had substantially improved.

After seizing Urbino and reinstalling Guidobaldo, Duke of Montefeltro, as its ruler, they had concentrated their efforts on occupying nearby villages. Their victories sounded alarm bells in Cesare's mind, but he managed to forestall any damage with his offer of peace. Those defying him, he said, could simply keep what they had taken. He insisted on ruling in name only. With this concession, he enticed into carelessness those eager to see him destroyed. By early October Paolo Orsini had been assigned to meet him in negotiations intended to end all hostilities.

From the start, though, and deliberately on Cesare's part, these negotiations, or what turned into tedious disputes, bogged down among wheedling, dithering over boundaries, complicated treaty-clauses and problems of administration. At the same time, in Imola and others of his encampments, as Machiavelli noticed and informed the Signoria, there began to pour in a hefty stream of French lancers – some 400, accompanied by yeoman-aides, or about 2,500 men altogether – along with hundreds of troops (Cesare had been allocated money by his father to pay them, and within weeks accepted 'six loads of silver coin from the French King' to pay the lancers[10]).

To everyone's confusion, his offers of peace seemed to mark the start of preparations for war. On 20 November, influenced by a perhaps naïve trust in Cesare's good faith, Machiavelli reported that 'no one knows what to make of the warlike preparations of the Duke in the midst of all these peace negotiations,' conceding that 'companies of infantry are also returning here ... [even if] it is not believed that [Cesare] will fail of his word where he has once given it.'[11]

Two days later, though, Machiavelli found his trust slipping a bit: 'I think I know his character pretty well,' he assured the Signoria, remarking that he found it senseless 'to exasperate rather than to soothe' the Duke with questions concerning his motives: it would be better to 'wait until I am spoken to in relation to these matters... . I do not know whether it will be easy for me to obtain [a new audience with him], for he lives only to advance his own interests, or what seem to him such, and without placing confidence in anyone else.'[12]

Despite these mystifications, everyone expected that Cesare and his army would rapidly move out of Imola. He intimated as much, acknowledging that relocating his forces was essential to quelling the anxieties about his plans. The army's departure came quietly, however, on the morning of 10 December, amid a smothered clattering of wagons, boots, carts, mules, baggage and horses. The units moved at a leisurely pace, undulating in a snowstorm along the road toward Forlì.

Machiavelli planned to follow the next day, though he had just seven ducats in his pocket. These would soon be gone, and he would have to petition the Duke and his officers for food and a place to stay, and even a blanket against the cold, at least until the Signoria sent him money in an appropriation that they were proving slow to make. The consequence of his immediate poverty was that when the not entirely unexpected bloodbath started, or about two weeks later, Machiavelli found himself in the company of Cesare's troops, though his presence hardly signified an enthusiastic acceptance of what they were about.

By 14 December, writing from Cesena, the effective capital of Cesare's state of Romagna ('I myself, who heard him, and noted his very words and the terms which his Excellency employed, ... and observed the gesticulations with which he accompanied them, can scarcely believe it'), he was troubled by the Duke's establishing his latest military base in overwhelming numbers along the town's main streets.

On 23 December, also writing from Cesena, Machiavelli noted in a letter that went astray, but for which he wrote a replacement, that Ramiro Lorqua, Cesare's governor in the Romagna since 1500, a sly, lumbering *condottiere* dreaded by everyone for the torture-driven methods by which he shored up the Duke's power, but who had himself been exposed as part of the conspiracy, had been arrested and 'confined at the bottom of the tower': 'It is feared that he will be sacrificed to the populace, who are eager that he should be.'[13]

Expressions of joy at Ramiro's arrest formed an overture to his execution a few hours later. Even his manner of dying held terrible implications: '[The governor] was found [at dawn] today cut into two pieces in the public square, and his body still remains there, so that the whole population has been able to see it. The [reason for] his death is not precisely known, other than that it was the pleasure of his Excellency thus to show that he has the power to make and unmake men at his will, and according to their merits.'[14]

As many sensed, with the evidence of Cesare's power left on public display, a new policy of repression, involving a gorier handling of Cesena than under Ramiro, had been set in motion. Through calculated acts of terror, Cesare seemed to be expunging all hints of dissent from his increasingly absolutist rule.

The sacking of Senigallia, a small port city on the Adriatic at the mouth of the Misa, which had been sacked by Pompey in 82 BCE and by Alaric in 408, came next on his agenda. Here, as in other towns, the conspirators had gathered to greet him to celebrate their just-arranged peace. Their own arrest, however, and the disarming, killing or absorption into his army of their soldiers, a price extracted in a vicious surprise attack that soaked the urban snow for over ten hours – sackings required hard work, along with arson, rape and murder – were witnessed by Machiavelli, though he was not present at the executions. A few of the conspirators guessed what might be in store. They decided to meet Cesare anyway, though, as if placing their heads in the lion's mouth.

In an incontestably religious world, consecrated as ever to an inculcation of ancient guilt and spiritual, religious concepts of personal worthlessness, treachery remained the basest and most self-contradictory of criminal acts. It exceeded even the shabby acts of kidnapping and assassination, with its primary disgraced exemplar the deformed though once heavenly seraph Lucifer. His banishment from heaven into the nethermost, icy, boggy region of Dante's Hell, had never been completely forgotten, even by the indifferently religious.

Knowledge of one's own acts of betrayal, or one's treacherous, oath-breaking guilt in respect to deeds buried in the past, or the treasonous behaviour of one's family and associates, exercised a merciless hypnosis. Many judges might be guilty of equally hideous crimes. A corrupt death sentence often retained its whispers of redemption.

Vitellozzo bade an eerie farewell to his soldiers that morning, riding out to greet Cesare in the snowy brightness on his peace-implying mule, unarmed, polite, even doffing his hat. Cesare had decided to meet him *en route* from Fano to Senigallia. He had divided his troops, concealing half of them a few leagues off to avoid any hint of an ambush. Along with the Orsini brothers and their soldiers, but buoyed by his assumption of the Duke's standard, Vitellozzo had already laid claim to Senigallia as a prospective gift. Cesare seemed ready to receive it with his always charming expressions of gratitude.

The Orsini had assisted Vitellozzo when he claimed Senigallia. Along with their allies and Oliverotto da Fermo, but only after, at Cesare's request, stationing their troops outside the city walls, he joined the two commanders. The schedule called for them to enter the city together, although Oliverotto, a *condottiere* whose suspicions had become implacable, had to be prodded before he consented to ride with them at all. This dispute continued into the morning of 31 December as all five soldiers proceeded to an elegant town-house set aside for their celebratory feast. Traces of Cesare's innocent-seeming smiles attended their hopeful glances on the wintry air.

The city itself looked white and brimming with expectation, the weather, as can be deduced from Machiavelli's reports and his subsequent description, cold but agreeable. He had not yet, it seems, received an encouraging letter of 23 December from Alamanno Salviati, expressing certainty of a positive outcome for him of his approaching annual election as Second Chancellor ('I do not believe that your being absent is going to reduce your chances for reconfirmation, especially since your activities are well known, and are of such a nature that you are the one to be begged, rather than begging others; all the more [so] since you are abroad on public business').[15]

Like many letters, Salviati's was probably delayed as Machiavelli moved from town to town. For the same reason he seems also not to have heard about Marietta's most recent outburst, alluded to in a letter written by Biagio on 21 December. She no longer felt as miserable over his ignoring her as being cheated. After more than a year as his wife, she had still not received the dowry promised at their wedding: 'Madonna Marietta is cursing God, and … feels she has thrown away … her body and her possessions. For your own sake, arrange for her to have her dowry like other women, otherwise we won't hear the end of it.'[16]

That morning, though, along with the eyes and ears of Senigallia, Machiavelli's attention was fixed on Cesare and his fellow *condottieri*'s arrival in the icy streets, and then on the squad of soldiers surrounding the small group of men. Like Vitellozzo, they had defied the Duke's leadership and now rode beside him in what seemed a civilized reconciliation.

Machiavelli was apparently as enthralled as they by the silky tableau, and so as shocked by what next occurred without warning: '[As] soon as [Cesare] had entered the place with them at his side, he suddenly turned to his guard and ordered them to seize these men; and having thus made them all prisoners, the place was given up to pillage.'[17]

Astonishment plunging into fright, and then into a flourishing of swords, axes and daggers, followed by ghostly crunchings with the slaughter of the troops waiting at the gate, and a wholesale slaughter bunching into the murder of the citizen-witnesses just inside the gate, and then the murder of those in the houses close by as the neighbourhood more or less blossomed with arquebuses and lances unleashing violence – maimings, shootings, choppings, gushings, pitched against a crackling of armour, horses falling, the crisp snapping of bones: 'It is now the twenty-third hour, and the greatest turmoil prevails, so that I really do not know whether I shall be able to dispatch this letter, having no one whom I can send. I shall write more fully in my next, but according to my judgement the prisoners will not be alive tomorrow.'[18]

Most were not, though for days afterwards Cesare held off killing them all. With the capture of two of the Orsini brothers and Vitellozzo, and after their soldiers had been seized, with many killed as they surrendered, or in some instances, often among soldiers posted to nearby castles, drawn into bloody skirmishes in which they were killed after agreeing to surrender, broadsides flooded the streets, proclaiming that 'the Traitors are captured,' intended to stir up sympathy for Cesare.

Machiavelli's report on the betrayal, written up after his more detailed account again failed to get through, also makes it clear that the conspirators' arrest took place not at the city gate, as he at first surmised amid the panicked jumble of men, mules and horses, but inside the *appartamento*, or the house reserved for their feast. There Vitellozzo tried uselessly to defend himself with a knife while Cesare's plan went off like clockwork: 'At two o'clock in the night [a couple of hours after sunset] [Cesare] had me [summoned] and with the most serene air in the world expressed to me his delight in his success.'[19]

By then Vitellozzo and Oliverotto had been strangled, though Cesare continued to hold prisoner two of the three Orsini brothers. His plan was to eliminate them only after his papal father in Rome had let the third brother, Cardinal Giambattista, learn of the sack at Senigallia. At that point the most influential and potentially most dangerous of the three might be expected to ride to the Vatican to offer Alexander spurious, fearful congratulations on his son's victory. Giambattista could then (as happened) be arrested and locked up at the Castel Sant'Angelo, also according to plan, where, as it turned out, he would be left to die in the dark after a few more days, a likely victim of poisoning.

Only afterwards, or with the elimination of the Orsini as a threat, and certain of a complete round-up of the rest of the conspirators, did Cesare plan to go ahead with the executions, also by strangulation, of the brothers now in his custody (as occurred on 18 January).

Even now, though, he understood that his reputation must be growing by leaps and bounds. Notoriety would be developing into fame, fame into legend. Even if the legend seemed tarnished, still it would shine darkly: the dingiest historical fable might be expected to exercise a useful influence. Over the next few weeks, as he guessed, the ingenuity with which he had seduced and eliminated his enemies would be granted its gossip-embellished admiration in Florence and elsewhere, or among tens of thousands of citizens from Venice to Milan to Rome. Superior cunning at the princely level could always be counted on to assume some sheen for its efficiency, much like the professional staging of a play. The model of the successful ruler was always the gifted actor.

As a result, in the heady aftermath of the first executions and amid the triumphant lights gathering about the ravishing of Senigallia, he could risk preening himself before Machiavelli, larding his skill with self-righteous praise and in the end proffering the *coup de grâce* announcement that his true purpose in destroying the conspiracy had been unselfish. Throughout, he avowed, he had attempted only to ensure the well-being of Florence, to remove 'the chief enemies of the King of France, of himself and the Florentine Republic, … [and so eliminate the] seeds of trouble and dissension calculated to ruin Italy, for which [as Machiavelli reported] your Lordships [the Signoria] ought to be under great obligations to him.'[20]

An apparent quest of revenge, Cesare remarked, had only masked his devotion to fostering a climate of political and military improvement. Republican freedoms had concerned him rather than ratcheting up victories. He ought therefore to be congratulated, and seen less as conqueror than liberator, or at least as a reluctant warrior. Unmentioned if inescapable amid these declarations, lay the suggestion, noted by Machiavelli and later the Signoria, that his success could also be construed as assisting him in finally achieving his long-sought goal of dominating if not conquering Florence.

In the meantime, and also during those chancy hours, the plight of hundreds trapped in the ruins of Senigallia, among them his own soldiers, slipped from the sickly into the desperate into the deathly desperate. Flames, mangled limbs, broken furniture, torn-up streets, smashed glass, along with crowds of the dying, suffering and wounded, with many huddling amid the freezing winter winds and rains, left Machiavelli breathless: 'You would not believe it were I to describe the condition of the army and its followers; [any] man [able to] sleep under [any] cover [at all] is deemed fortunate.'[21]

# 19

# Plans to Change the Arno

Peering through the semi-wreckage of Senigallia, early 1503 (though the new year was celebrated on 25 March) showed Cesare consolidating his achievements. January added to the districts succumbing to his charisma, as a string of Umbrian towns, among them Gualdo to the east, and the Etruscan-built city of Perugia to the west and west of the Tiber, mounted on its famous, pregnant hill, surrendered at his bidding, or without a struggle. In some towns frightened, dazed citizens flooded the streets, shouting 'Cesare, Cesare!' and '*Duca, duca!*' The end of the conspiracy had come to mean more than the collapse of resistance to his rule, even if it released waves of terror, rebellions against civil order and contagious criminality.

Machiavelli watched a familiar loosening and falling away of social restraints with estranged helplessness: 'Your Lordships … will excuse the delay if my letters are behind time. For the peasants conceal themselves; no soldier is willing to absent himself, not wanting to forego his chances of plunder; and my own domestics are unwilling to separate themselves from me for fear of being robbed.'[1]

By now the mob of disorderly, shunned soldier-supporters of the Orsini and Vitellozzo, on the prowl for loot and safety, had begun to bash and brawl their way towards Siena. Spreading into the inhabited valleys and glens, they terrorized the countryside. Peasants hid in the many abandoned houses, and at Siena itself, virtual centre of the conspiracy, but still controlled by Pandolfo Petrucci, who seemed intimidated, the riotous soldiers met with a chilly embrace. Other towns and villages fought them to a standstill. At Torciano and Assisi they were routed, at Chiusi turned away.

Cesare's army behaved no better – in fact much worse. At Santa Quirica, which his soldiers seized after strolling into Pienza and Sarteano, the population fled, leaving behind dead horses, cattle rotting in the streets and nine old women and two old men. The soldiers strung the women up by their arms, lit fires under their feet and tortured them for money. None had any, but they were left to die in the flames. The soldiers then ransacked the town, stealing what they could, cracked open casks of wine, which they spilled in the street, and set the houses on fire. In Acquapendente, Montefiascone and Viterbo, they raped the women and razed the houses.[2]

On 8 January in Assisi, Machiavelli, still following the Duke's army, finally found a place to stay, paying for it with money sent him by the Signoria, which had at last arrived. As early as the sixth, however, when entering Gualdo amid Cesare's soldiers, he realized that he had changed his mind about the apparently invincible young commander, or that it might be appropriate to register a less contemptuous view of what was becoming his unstoppable string of victories: 'People here wonder that you [the Signoria] have not written, or in some way sent your congratulations to him upon what he has lately done for your advantage; for he is persuaded that our whole Republic should feel under great obligations to him. He says that the killing of Vitellozzo and the destruction of the Orsinis' power would have cost you 200,000 ducats [had you tried to organize their defeat on your own], and, moreover, that you would never have [managed it as smoothly] yourselves as … [has been] done by him.'[3]

Entering Assisi, south of Perugia, where the medieval houses and streets still seemed to kneel before their majestic castle perched on its swaggering mountain, or moving forward on the momentum of Cesare's troops, who had begun stepping out in a swagger of their own, Machiavelli may have surprised himself by launching into an appreciation of Cesare's success. He went too far, it was thought back in Florence, lauding his 'unheard of good fortune, with [his] courage and [a] confidence almost superhuman, … [he believes] himself capable of accomplishing whatever he undertakes.'[4]

To Machiavelli it seemed that Fortune's wheel had turned, or that the political weather had shifted. A new wind was blowing down the valleys. A cruel if intelligent sun had risen. It might bestow harmonious, militarized beams throughout the peninsula. Everyone, including members of the Signoria, could do worse than take stock of its apparent glory.

This conviction did not last, as would probably have been unlikely, and one reason lay in Cesare's modest military strength. His army at this point consisted of 'five hundred men at arms, eight hundred light cavalry and about six thousand infantry.' It thus formed a scarcely unchallengeable force, though it might be taken more seriously if supplemented by the *condottiere* messer

Giovanni Bentivogli's generosity to the tune of an additional hundred men at arms and two hundred light cavalry. These Bentivogli felt 'bound to furnish', even if tossing them into the mix still left Cesare too weak to seize Siena, at the moment under the protection of the French, whose ally, the *condottiere* Pandolfo, had fled in fear of his life.

With one eye as always on the main chance, Cesare now decided to test Pandolfo's gullibility by luring him into a trap. This time, however, his usual scheming, lubricated by flattery, failed to entice his quarry from an escape hole and went badly wrong. The soldiers springing the trap were blocked by a wary Florentine commander, and Cesare forced both to abandon his attempt and the risk of trying to seize Siena.

In terms of Machiavelli's estimate of him, however, his change in plans seems to have made no difference. An almost supernatural aura surrounded Cesare's accomplishments. It would not easily be dissipated, and especially not in the atmosphere of military romance gathering about his leadership and hallowing the fantasies of friends and foes alike. Colourful descriptions of his exploits, ruses, betrayals and victories began to decorate his reputation. Over time they would enhance a new Christian-oriented history.

It was to unfold among the latest epic poems, such as Ariosto's *Orlando Furioso* (1532), and many of the adventure stories, love lyrics and heroic novels of France, England, Italy, Spain and Germany, and by such as Dumas *père et fils*, Friedrich Schiller and Walter Scott. A sanguinary culture of derring-do had been born. It was laced with dash, ruthlessness and a heady dose of grandeur. A fair-minded observer might even have concluded with Machiavelli that a few raw circumstances, or some twist of Fortune's wheel, which neither slowed nor stopped, and which had now permitted a few shadows to fall across Cesare's frustration with a single enemy, was of little consequence. Flickers of opposition seemed only to intensify the brilliance of his destiny.[5]

Its brilliance helped to shift Machiavelli's focus over the coming months, as with Cesare's it settled on Rome, and for other reasons too, as his attention also returned to Pisa and Leonardo and the scheme for diverting the Arno. As always, questions about the Republic's safety seemed more stimulating than the challenges of family life, though the spring of the following year found Marietta pregnant with their second child.

For decades, the military edge to be gained by diverting Florence's commercially essential river had seemed self-evident. A new channel to the

Mediterranean would deprive the Pisans of any opportunity to interfere with Florentine exports. Pisa itself might be left high and dry. The Republic's appeal to the French and other allies could be enhanced. Republican independence thus rested to some extent either on retaking the port city, or, should doing so prove too difficult, dodging around it. Given a few innovative engineering techniques, including an as yet unbuilt massive digging machine, a dodge seemed feasible. Were it handled by Leonardo, regarded by many as the most imaginative among the available engineers, a diversionary channel might tip the scales towards winning the Pisan war.

By 23 January, and perhaps wearing his expensive new cloak and hat against the cold, Machiavelli found himself back in Florence after his months-long stay at Cesare's court and among his troops. Here he realized that the question of financing a project as bold as redirecting the river – never mind the more pressing need to recruit a Republican army capable of defying Cesare – was becoming increasingly dubious. Vehement debates stormed back and forth between citizen-members of governmental committees over whether to levy a new war tax, whether to tax the *ottimati* more than everyone else and whether local priests and the rest of the Florentine clergy ought also to be taxed, with the additional revenue slotted into payments for an expanded army. Support for the clerical tax would have required the consent of the Pope and seemed a direct slap in the face of his son Cesare. It led Soderini for the first time into becoming the target of insults.[6]

Machiavelli inserted himself into these quarrels on his friend's behalf, mostly in favour of his proposal for the war tax, defending it in a shrewd political analysis that he wrote up as a speech. It may have been delivered by Soderini, or some other sympathetic colleague, and even before the Grand Council. What is striking is its impatient tone, or a linking of logic, politics, history, journalistic conciseness and a half-disguised aggressiveness, all of which suggest that, though undated, he would have written it now rather than months or a decade later, as a few have suggested. Packed with intimate references to the military conflicts over the past few years, mostly at Arezzo, and despite his calling it mere 'rhetoric', it stresses the urgency of the moment, and his audience's understandable angst.

Under the title 'Words [or *Concione*, a belittling term, with humorous hints of bombast] to be spoken on the Law for Appropriating Money, After Giving a little Introduction and Excuse', he starts off with a sweeping statement framed as an historical principle. 'Force and prudence,' he announces, echoing his humanist education, '[create] the might of all the governments that ever have been or will be in the world.'[7] His key phrase is 'ever have been.' It pegs an understanding of the sources of military and political power to the past as teacher of the present. His premise thus implies the worthlessness of any argument about modern problems that is unsupported by historical knowledge. By insinuating that history is an ingredient of all knowledge, he also implies that it may be the most significant source of thinking.

His audience of humanist-trained scholars, politicians and businessmen would probably not have found his declaration in any way unfamiliar. Among his peers, the past seemed always a pressure and a pleasure. What would have seemed controversial was his steely insistence. It cuts as might the thrust of a sword, or as does his absolutism. An historical law is adduced. It permits no refutation. It begs no exception. Even more controversial would have seemed his support of the idea with strictly modern evidence, plus his modernistic appeal to psychology: 'Let us not deceive ourselves; let us examine a bit, if you will, our situation; and let us begin by looking within.'[8] 'Looking within,' or so his sense runs, suggests that the Republic needs to take stock of its inability to protect its citizens. The humiliating result has been that 'Pistoia, Romagna, Bargo [are] places that have become nests and refuges for every sort of thief.'

Just a short time ago, he recalls, the Republic's neglect of its interests had left it 'in danger of losing Arezzo,' a city whose problems he knew at first hand (it may be assumed that many in his audience would have been aware of his diplomatic experiences there). He then broadens the argument to indicate that his admiration of Cesare's tactics in no way contradicts his hostility to their despotic aims. He urges his audience to consider 'all Italy: you see her controlled by the King of France, the Venetians, the Pope and Valentino.'

One effect of switching perspective is to transform the speech into a kind of manifesto. A plea for new taxation becomes a demonstration of the need for a dramatic alteration of Florentine political life, and especially the Republic's indifference to maintaining a large enough army. His style also emerges as a combination of provocations, accusations and bits of hope, and this as he evokes a surprising vision of idealized republicanism.

Any republican system, he argues, requires a rooting in precisely the type of self-examination that he has been advocating: 'Other people often grow wise through the dangers of their neighbours; you do not grow wise through your own, you put no faith in yourselves, and you do not see the time that you are losing and that you have lost.' A republican political life requires real stewardship of its freedoms: 'You are free Florentines and … in your own hands rests your liberty. For that liberty I believe you will have such regard as they always have had who are born free and hope to live free.'[9]

If his idealism seems a bit forced, perhaps mostly in the context of a plea for new taxation, still it offers a reply to those who have argued that he harboured only the haziest interest in the Republic's democratic future. His interest, at least for the moment, seems to have been driven by a genuine passion.

It was no doubt a passion stimulated by his encounters with Cesare's treachery. In confirmation of this idea it may be noted that he had begun to revisit the hideous consequences of the Duke's betrayal at Senigallia, including his sacking of much of the city.

What seems clear is that Machiavelli had now decided to write up a far more detailed account of the tragedy than had appeared in his on-the-spot letters. Nor was his reason terribly obscure. As he reconsidered his sketchy reports, patched together in the heat of battle or the days just afterwards, he seems to have realized that a fleshed-out description, in which he arranged the events in a more plausible sequence, could allow the insights of art to illuminate an original tangle of horrors. A literary-historical approach might expose the order within the confusion. The issue of confusion aside, what he produced was one of the world's first if not most exquisite examples of the modern war correspondent at work.

A tactile atmosphere is probably not everything in the work of the war correspondent, but it inevitably matters greatly. Physical details point up patterns or their absence. These details rarely figure into the battle accounts of Machiavelli's close and exact contemporaries, Leonardo Bruni and Francesco Guicciardini, but he seems now to have set out to provide a mass of them, as in his description of the sites of Cesare's ambushes and their impact on the fighting, plus his speculations on the inner lives of the participants, each of which is presented as he sets the scene:

> Whoever approaches Senigallia has on his right the mountains, with foothills that come so close to the sea that there is often only a narrow strip of land between them and the waves…
> . Senigallia lies a bow's shot from these foothills, and less than a mile away from the shore.[10]

Against these background strokes, but in a paragraph that requires a more or less full citation to show his close-up lens at work, Cesare's cunning leaps out with all its sinuosity:

Duke Valentino approached Senigallia. When the vanguard of his cavalry arrived at the bridge, it did not cross, but stopped and formed two lines, one along the river, the other along the open country, leaving a path in the middle for the foot soldiers, who then marched straight into the town. Vitellozzo, Pagolo and Duke Orsini of Gravina rode towards Duke Valentino on mules, accompanied by a handful of horsemen. Vitellozzo, unarmed and wearing a cape lined in green, seemed quite afflicted, as if he were aware of his impending death, which, in view of the prowess of the man and his former fortune, caused some amazement. And it is said that when he parted from his soldiers to go to Senigallia to meet the Duke, it was as if he was saying a final farewell. He told his generals that he had left his house and its fortunes in their hands.[11]

The eruption of orchestrated violence ('had [Cesare] not put a stop to [his troops'] audacity in putting many of them to death they would have looted the town entirely'), including the first executions, is intimately handled:

When night came and the turmoil stopped, the Duke felt that the time had come to kill Vitellozzo and Liverotto. He had them taken to a place together and strangled. Neither … uttered any words worthy of their previous life: Vitellozzo begged that he might throw himself on the Pope's mercy, … while Liverotto heaped all the blame for the harm done … on Vitellozzo.

The restraint here paradoxically emphasizes the Duke's barbarity by focusing on his victims' begging and blaming and not on the manner of their deaths. It is accompanied by psychological curiosity and leads into a matter-of-fact, chilling conclusion:

The Duke left Paolo Orsini and Duke Orsini of Gravina alive until he heard from Rome that the Pope had seized Cardinal Orsino, Archbishop of Florence, and messer Iacopo da Santa Croce. At this news, on the eighteenth of January 1502 [1503], they too were strangled … at the Castle of Pieve.[12]

Only now, perhaps, does the reader take in Machiavelli's larger purpose: to provide an almost tactile accuracy. He rejects the monstrous. Exaggeration gives way to irony. It haunts his style, stressing his practicality.

All of which perhaps indicates why he and Leonardo now set about pursuing their project to alter the course of the Arno with a refreshed intensity: if nothing else, it also seemed practical.

For Leonardo, a meticulous sense of what worked had sharpened his worship of clarity ever since childhood. At this point he was as much a fanatic about strict accounting methods for saving money as a devotee of empirical data, performing his late-night autopsies to expose the veiny, muscular secrets of the human body. His *Mona Lisa* was as much a graph of emotional ambiguity as a portrait done on commission. His *Lady with an Ermine* was as much an investigation of fashions as a depiction of the sceptical beauty of Cecilia Gallerani.

From his point of view, painting without 'science', or rational knowledge, had always seemed an absurdity. Since the 1480s, but perhaps as early as his apprenticeship in Verrocchio's studio, where he may for the first time have read Archimedes on hydraulics, he had trained himself to sketch the chameleon-like changes of water under pressure, or water-power. His drawings of stream-driven screws, turbines, drills and propellers appear to date from as far back as the turn of the century. His designs of dredges may be traced to just after 1501.

He had never regarded himself as a fully modern scientist, however, in the sense that empiricism seems never to have been his only guide to experience: throughout his career he wrestled with the medieval belief that the universe must be animate, as often adopting as questioning the common view.[13] For him and everyone else the planets kept to their circular dance according to a divine choreography, each fixed in its revolving sphere. Outer space and the idea of complete darkness, or some concept of a near-perfect vacuum, lay beyond his or anyone's comprehension: 'Water is that which serves the vital humour of the arid earth; it is poured within it, and flowing with unceasing vigour through the spreading veins it replenishes all the parts that depend of necessity on this humour.'[14] His hundreds of observations of water currents had led him to understand their strengths in canals, locks, rivers and brooks as well as their military and commercial value for espionage and shipping.

On 21 June 1503, he arrived at the fortress of La Vernucca on a hill overlooking the lower reaches of the Arno, with their flatlands, not far from Pisa. The whole area had just been seized by Florentine troops. His assignment was to examine the fortifications for weaknesses, deciding whether they needed strengthening against counterattacks. He stayed just two days, but in mid to late July, and escorted in a coach-and-six driven by Giovanni di Andrea Cellini, or *il Piffero*, as he was called (because he was one of the pipers for the Signoria), the father of Benvenuto Cellini, he came back to sketch the river as it meandered on to Pisa.

His proposal to redirect the river had by now attracted military interest. The Florentine Captain, Francesco Guiducci, reported, 'We studied [his] plan, and … concluded that the project was very much to our purpose, and if the Arno can really be turned or channelled at this point, this would at least prevent the hills from being attacked by the enemy.'[15] At least at first, the primary purpose of any diversion was therefore defensive. Machiavelli was not present at these discussions: in April he was sent to Siena to negotiate, uselessly, with Pandolfo Petrucci, who had now returned. There seems little doubt, however, given his more than ninety references to Leonardo's proposal for diverting the Arno in his reports to the Signoria, that he and Soderini were enthusiastic supporters.[16]

Leonardo stipulated a twelve-mile-long rechannelling, starting just before the river's descent to Pisa. A single immense excavation – or perhaps two – consisting of a ditch (or two) some 32 feet deep, would force the currents south toward Livorno, into a marshy area called the Stagno, and then past it to the sea.[17] Several of Leonardo's sketches – including a detailed, almost-to-scale rendering of the rechannelling – have survived. Their details and measurements suggest a tentative commitment of Florentine officials to the project.

Despite these preparations, over the following months Leonardo devoted himself to other matters, and perhaps even to painting the *Mona Lisa*. Among these projects was a different sort of artistic challenge, as he produced his first sketches for a vast war-historical mural, the *Battle of Anghiari*, also commissioned by the Signoria. From the standpoint of the Arno idea, however, his time was not wasted. He spent some of it on calculating the costs and engineering requirements of the excavations.

Machiavelli himself had already taken note of the military value of eliminating Pisa's fresh water supply, extracted from the Arno, by means of a rechannelling (in July he urged Livorno to refuse to help Pisa with as much as a single drop of water). Leonardo concurred, and pointed to other advantages justifying the monumentality of the project, among them that the new channel would reduce the distance from Florence to the sea by over twelve business-profitable miles, and that 'guiding the Arno' would offer farmers new and sought after acreage for irrigation. The extra farmland ought to prove an agricultural 'treasure.'

About the project's monumentality there should have been little question, though its complexity must have accounted for some of the delay. Leonardo estimated the cost at 750 ducats per mile over twenty-five miles, based on the assumption that the great density of river water would require a channel twenty *braccie* wide at the 32-foot depth and that, if properly built, it would need a service road twenty *braccie* across (3,000 *braccie* equalled one mile) running beside it. Two thousand workers would have to be hired.[18]

Late winter would be the best time to start, or even early spring, when the earth was still pliant. Little digging, with or without his as yet unbuilt machine designed to rotate numerous cogs and pails for scooping and lifting out large volumes of rock and soil, would be possible during the hot months of July and August.

That summer, at any event, with its anxious political, military and religious dilemmas, raised doubts about every project. On 18 August, Alexander VI, whose papacy and son had for years frightened many millions, died at Rome, sunk into a pasty, probably malarial fever and staggerings, as remonstrances flickered through his crowds of thirsty servants bobbing about the sweaty corridors of the Vatican, their cunning hushes accompanied by quicksilver thefts, not least of his personal property, down to the rings on his thinning fingers, which swelled in death.[19]

His generally welcome end, which brought Machiavelli to the ancient capital for the first time, as instabilities shivered through the bureaucratic foundations of an apprehensive Christian world, incited anxiety out of all proportion to the whispered last minutes on the papal bed. Like other officials, including the cardinals expected to assemble to elect a new Pope, Machiavelli seemed for a moment thrown off his stride, though not off his sense of the Republic's opportunities. The Pope's death was scarcely a surprise.

Cesare had always known about the mortal shadow looming back at him from his future. He had attempted to guard against his vulnerability once deprived of access to his father's money and the pride taken in his conquests. He had failed to anticipate his own brief, crushing illness, however, or that it might overwhelm him at the same time, or to imagine that it might stop him in his tracks. This illness, bearing down as his father slipped into unconsciousness, prompted a swift erosion of his influence and intimated ruin.

For the Borgias, including Lucrezia, who arranged to spend the rest of her irritable, perfumed life as a pious recluse wrapped in spiritual devotion, Fortune's wheel had simply rolled on. This time it seemed to leave the triumphant defeated, the powerful abashed.

In the first weeks of August, however, these possibilities had still seemed unlikely. Two months earlier Cesare's forces had seized Camerino. Before that, he had threatened Urbino. Yielding to his fondness for treachery, he had seized it as well, expelling his and Alexander's ally, the duke Guidobaldo, who fled to Mantua. News of Camerino's fall reached Rome on 23 July. When it was followed by reports that the town had surrendered without a fight, or on the strength of Cesare's reputation for vicious retribution, Alexander ordered a 'great salute' fired from the Castel Sant'Angelo, celebratory bonfires lighted, rockets shot off and a 'magnificent feast held at the Piazza di San Pietro.'[20]

Throughout central Italy, the success of the papal states seemed more or less guaranteed. The father-son experiment in power-sharing ought to endure. Their political adventurism, based on murder, money, bribes, theft and a superficial religious devotion, should prove self-sustaining. The Vatican world itself, battered by Alexander's acquisitiveness, trembling before his and Cesare's changeable passions, might bustle on for years, or according to the whims of their authoritarianism.

# 20

# The First Journey to Rome

A somewhat complementary development in the arts might now have seemed only appropriate. In Florence that summer, and into the autumn, Leonardo, followed a year later, in August 1504, by Michelangelo, who had begun his marble *David* in 1501 (it was to be unveiled to universal applause in 1504), was lauded for his abilities and then hired to paint a magnificent, fanciful fresco of victory in battle, eight metres high by twenty long. It would be intended as a theatre of political propaganda proclaiming the Republic's pride and freedom.[1]

Both artists were offered contracts for one such massive fresco each. While these were abandoned long before they were finished, the two men would leave behind them at the Palazzo della Signoria, where the frescoes were meant to complement each other and to occupy equal-sized, opposed walls in the Grand Council chamber, some of the world's finest monumental cartoons. Lavishly detailed, and in parts fully worked out, their respective *invenzioni* would involve extensive depictions of weapons, battles, horses and soldiers far beyond what audiences for artistic displays had ever seen. Though no one might then have guessed it, the historical uncertainty in Rome would also be matched by the momentous artistic uncertainty in Florence.

By late October Machiavelli would have learned all about Leonardo's fresco preparations simply through keeping up his normal routines at the Palazzo. From the start he had been involved in negotiating Leonardo's salary and work schedule. He may even have been instrumental in securing the artist's commission, his first major one in his native city. An original if lost contract, dating to October, 1503, provided him with an advance of thirty-five florins, to be supplemented by fifteen florins per month till the job was done. Machiavelli also prepared a second contract, which superseded the first and was dated 4 May 1504. This reveals the Signoria's exasperation with Leonardo's constant delays – procrastination haunted his entire career – and stipulated a new deadline, for February 1505, but now with no excuses.[2]

Machiavelli's involvement in what soon became a testy rivalry between the two artists could also have been anticipated, as might his assignment to Rome after the death of Alexander. The papal fever seemed to incite realignments of art, diplomacy, propaganda, politics, war and religion. Machiavelli, Leonardo and Michelangelo might even have been seen as somehow blending their complementary passions and interests.

The theme alone of Leonardo's fresco – that of legendary violence leading into victory – and the space allotted for his preliminary work on it at the relatively new church of Santa Maria Novella, seemed appropriate to the changes presently afoot. Leonardo had watched this church built not thirty years earlier. He was now given its rectory as his studio, the Sala del Papa. The Signoria arranged repairs to its roof to keep the rain from splashing in, and it accommodated his immense cartoons. He picked up a refectory key on 24 October, on the same day as Machiavelli left for Rome, or as both entered a new political atmosphere.

Over the next few months Leonardo poured himself into realizing his unparalleled heroic vision. Large and small sheets of flax-rag paper acquired clots of clashing men and horses, or passionate, glittering groups, which he then blended into a scene-by-scene depiction of the Battle of Anghiari. The actual battle, fought in 1440, had been insignificant. No more than a skirmish, it had seen a contingent of Florentine soldiers driving off Milanese units commanded by Niccolò Piccinino. Sixty-three years later, though, in the cleared out, sunlit studio-area at the Santa Maria Novella, Leonardo's rolls of inky flesh seemed traumatized by their own exhibitions of unexamined rage, madness and callousness. Historical unimportance was transformed into a penumbra of artist-conceived, drenching ferocity.

Commentators on Leonardo's sketches have noted their deliberately blurred lines and sequences of dusky whirls, but the blurring itself seems an aspect of a novel investigation of motion, as if it were endless and feisty, and continuous in the universe. Reality itself, and not merely some long past battle reality, is understood as a series of undulations and processes, as flux and transformation, as an ancient Ovidian tumbling, or even shocking displays of metamorphosis.

His sketches seemed to flow forth as torn and ghastly meditations on life, death, victories and defeat, while pointing to shattered muscles, faces, eyes and cheeks. If the battle at Anghiari had been little more than an historical footnote – only one soldier had been killed, and this because someone's horse fell on him – Leonardo's renderings (guided in part by a written-up, exaggerated description mentioning thousands of troops and provided to help him out by

Machiavelli's office-mate Agostino Vespucci at Machiavelli's request) ushered into the world an anthology of battles and, more disturbingly, of wounds and change as divine judgements (plate IX).[3]

An evocation of war at its most horrific – even to suggesting its bleakness amid mud, shrieks, showers of lymph and its withering stench – seemed designed to carry the viewer through fearful episodes into an hallucinated Florentine triumph as sheer brutishness foamed against clouds of artillery smoke ('You must show the smoke of the artillery,' he had urged his fellow artists in a note, "How to represent a battle," many years earlier, 'mingling in the air with the dust thrown up by the movement of horses and soldiers'[4]).

A diorama of pain seemed to dally with honour, as had been requested, yet in the end to pay homage to incompleteness itself, or a frustrating lack of colour – he had not yet painted it – perhaps because the idea of finishing a triptych devoted to infinite violence might have seemed a contradiction. Nor, perhaps, would its incompleteness matter. His sketches alone formed a diagnosis of violence, including an understanding of the universe that promoted it.

One week before Leonardo's first Anghiari sketches saw the public light of day, on 22 September, Machiavelli missed out on the election of the new Pope. The aura of incompleteness now began to surround other events. Less than two months after his election, the old-new Francesco Todeschini Piccolomini, who had taken the name Pius III, became ill and died. White-haired, hunch-backed, learned, compassionate to the point of gullibility ('I have been deceived,' he said, as he berated himself for underestimating Cesare's deceit), learned, gouty, constantly smiling, he had been a compromise between noble and religious factions.[5]

His election, and the choice of his successor, were prepared and inspected like a hawk, though from the sidelines in his resentful weakness, by Cesare Borgia. The stouter, much friskier, sixty-year-old Giuliano della Rovere (1443–1513), a devotee of hunting, painting, the nursing of grudges, sculpture and soldiering, became Julius II as the votes for him in a nearly unanimous first ballot piled up according to the thousands that he spent on his own election.

Twisting in the helplessness of his probably malarial sheets in Rome after his father's death, Cesare saw his cobbled-together empire begin to crumble and fall apart. '[The Pope's] face … changed to the colour of mulberry and was covered with blue-black spots,' recalled the papal secretary Burchard in respect to Alexander's rapid decay in the August heat. The frightened Vatican carpenters, in their hurry making his coffin too short, had to 'pummel' his body into it, apparently breaking his legs.[6]

Ordering a confederate, Michelotto, to loot the papal treasury of 100,000 ducats might stave off the coming fragmentation, but not for long. No amount of money could suppress the appetite for vengeance among those – the Orsini and Colonna especially, but also the Vitelli and other leading families of the cities of the Romagna – whose estates and other possessions Cesare and his father had confiscated and whose seigniorial rights they had treated with contempt.[7]

As he recovered, he tried to terrorize the papal conclave about to elect Pius III. He would either force Pius's election, or that of a Pope even friendlier to him, by seizing the Castel Sant'Angelo. This was a place that he knew, though not as the virtual prisoner among its barn-lofty halls that he now became. Bernardo di Betto (or Pinturicchio, 1454–1513), the Pope's court artist, had painted quite a number of rooms at the Castello, mostly *a grotesche*, to satisfy Alexander's pleasure-tormented tastes.[8]

For the garden below the tower, he had supplied various portraits of members of the Borgia family, among them those of Cesare and his sister Lucrezia, plus a group of ludicrously dishonest scenes elaborating an officially triumphal version of Alexander's life. These misrepresented the French invasion of Italy under Charles VIII, and showed the King prostrating himself before the rotund, beaming Pope, and even holding his stirrup for him (these paintings are now lost).

Familiarity also abetted helplessness. Cesare's efforts to use the castle as a kind of bludgeon with which to intimidate the enclave, as Rome steadied itself among masses of troops edging into riots, failed entirely. The commander at Sant'Angelo seemed unimpressed by his money, and refused to blink at his tantrums. His illness had cost him the initiative, and every effort to regain it foundered in the face of resentments levelled at him from all sides. As a mild embarrassment coughing his way among his paternal paintings, Cesare agreed in September to be trundled out of Rome on a velvet-covered stretcher – his recovery remained incomplete – to a nearby Borgia-loyal town protected by the French King.

At the same time, the short reign of Pius III offered Machiavelli and officials such as Cardinal Francesco Soderini, brother of Piero, who was to participate in the vote for the new Pope, an ideal moment to be sent to the Vatican. Between Pius's death and the election on 1 November of Julius II, he might supervise Florentine interests dependent on good relations with Rome. Oddly, Machiavelli now found himself in a position superior to that of Cesare. If he wished (but he did not), he might even have lorded it over the commander whom he had served as a liaison, and who had mesmerized the Signoria and his own early insights into the mechanisms of autocracy.

More immediately, the fantastical ancient capital of one of the world's oldest and most influential empires would have captured and held his attention. Despite his usual haste when on assignment ('You will proceed with all diligence to Rome,' the Signoria instructed him on 24 October, '[and] present yourself … in our name, [now that we have] heard of the death of Pope Pius III, which has greatly afflicted our whole city'[9]), Machiavelli would have spotted and appreciated compelling elements of his own history amid an autumnal Roman atmosphere of cooling ruins.

At the Forum, the shaggy-looking pagan temples, unimproved by restorations, jutted into pockets of brown grass and staring sheep. What Nathaniel Hawthorne as late as the nineteenth century would call 'the bad odours of our fallen natures' freighted all the winds and breezes. As in many southern European cities, the houses of rich and poor languished amid effluvia and sweetening, suppressive scents. Poor families, less worried about public appearances, slouched *en masse* at their stoops in the cleaner if dreary outdoor air, chattering, napping, dicing. Horses, cats and pigeons rummaged in mounds of trash. Carriages whisked past in the gassy mud.

The recent Renaissance architecture, inserted among tatty, huge remnants of eviscerated ancient buildings, rose over the plushly robed figures of cardinals and bishops hurrying by, or the silks of the ambassadors (among them secretaries such as Machiavelli), and the tunics, striped hats and capes of thieves, jesters, brigands, slaves, actors and prostitutes lolling in the squares and alleys.

Rome seemed an ecstasy of decay tottering among its noble families and billeted foreign troops, mostly French and Spanish, who lounged at the palace entrances.

The daytime moonlight discoloured the stones and the youthful as well as constricted faces, commenting on their Etruscan, African and Roman complexions. It paused over an infinite loss amid the gabbled hawking that tumbled from doorway to doorway, mostly about the odds on the latest candidates for Pope.

Ramshackle markets teemed with fruit, flesh and fowl beneath cages holding criminals for a month or two of punishment. Spikes lined the bridges, displaying the impaled heads of convicted murderers left out as warnings. 'It is not safe ... to go out at night,' Machiavelli remarked in a letter detailing his contacts with cardinals and others working on the election of the second Pope in less than two months; '[at] night I can neither send nor go myself to enquire whether anyone ... is dispatching a courier to Florence, [as] it is not safe.'[10] Information came to him via messengers surrounded by armed guards. A Roman population of under 50,000 fretted over its fourteen or so murders per day. If kidnapping was rare, theft was commonplace, and safety as elusive as political stability.

Cesare shuttled in and out of the wary Roman neighbourhoods in September and October in a useless quest for allies and influence. His army had shrunk by ninety per cent, to under 650. On 15 October, after a failed attempt to escape to Orvieto – his way was blocked by hostile troops – he barely made it back to the Castel Sant'Angelo. With his two young sons, he raced along a secret passage from the Borgo, where the Orsini had already started breaking into his house.

The death of Pius III provided some letup in the violence. It may have saved his life. He threw the last residues of his prestige – embodied in an appeal to the Spanish cardinals – into supporting the papal election of Giuliano della Rovere. This was a desperate gamble on behalf of an implacable enemy, or so Machiavelli thought, sceptical of the rashness of Cesare's judgement: his father Alexander had driven Giuliano into exile in France, a contemptuous act not easily forgotten. In fairness it may be added that Cesare perhaps had little choice: the prince who had once inspired dread seemed reduced to stimulating jitters.[11]

Machiavelli's duties in relation to him emphasized their reversed roles while stressing the Signoria's friendliness to the new Pope, whoever he turned out to be. He had arrived in Rome on 27 October, or a few days before the second papal conclave, and took stock of Giuliano's good-politician promises to everyone, including Cesare, who was led to believe that he would see his cities in the Romagna restored to him.

After his election, though, the now Pope Julius exposed an obsession with righting family wrongs and his conviction that the needs of the Church ought to come before all other considerations. This seemed especially true of his pre-election promises, which he dismissed out of hand as he stomped in and out of explosive deliberations with his advisors. As a consequence, Cesare was almost at once forced to prepare to move on. By contrast, Machiavelli seemed gratified by Giuliano's election, writing to the Signoria on 1 November, 'Under favour of God, I inform your Lordships [in a memorandum delayed, as so often] that the Cardinal di San Pietro in Vincola was this morning proclaimed Pope [Julius II]. May Heaven make him a useful pastor for all Christendom! *Valete!*'[12]

Cesare's leave-taking, encouraged by Julius, prompted rumours of his death and a fear that, whether dead or alive, he might come back: his reputation for astonishing supernatural acts seemed as lively as ever. In calling attention to the 'great celebrations' mounted in Florence on the election of the Pope, Landucci reported (on 28 November) that 'Valentino [has been] captured at Ostia, and [has] been beheaded,' then corrected himself according to the next reports: 'It [is] not true, however, that he [is] dead.'

The French army was eager to protect him but, mired in a retreat from Naples and abandoned by its own King, had lapsed into anarchy. In Rome, where French soldiers ran into a cold snap, they smashed their way into the nearest houses, fighting with the owners determined to keep them out. A new French reputation for theft and rape in southern Italy had preceded them, and in a demented quest for warmth, they snuggled into the city's dung-heaps. Over five-hundred died in the filth as others froze in the *piazze*.

On 9 November, Machiavelli's relative Battista wrote to him that Marietta had just given birth to a son, Bernardo, 'a fine, bouncing boy' named after his father. Battista looked forward to becoming one of the boy's godfathers, along with 'a fine gang' of others, or so Biagio Buonaccorsi informed Machiavelli on the seventeenth. Among the four others was Biagio himself.[13]

# 21

# Cesare's Downfall and the First Decennale

Cesare had vacillated before leaving, and after being forced back to Rome by Julius, this time under temporary arrest for defying papal authority, he turned to desperate schemes that Machiavelli observed with a cold, bewildered interest: 'We see that the Duke's sins have little by little brought him to expiation. May God guide things for the best'. In Florence the proximity of the two men, pushed into repeated contact over several days, raised questions about Machiavelli's loyalty.

'[Giuliano della Rovere] will have enough to do to fulfil all the promises he has made,' Machiavelli informed his colleagues in Florence on 1 November, before it became clear that as Pope Julius he would keep few or none of them, 'but he is Pope now, and we shall soon see which course he is going to take.'

In less than a week Machiavelli was reporting back on 'the Pope's hatred of [Cesare],' which 'is notorious. And it is not to be supposed that [Julius] will have forgotten the ten years of exile which he had to endure under Alexander VI.' Julius's ruthlessness had already led him into barking and scoffing at officials and military commanders alike. His stentorian tone was beginning to make itself felt.[1]

The general military stalemate in northern and central Italy was also upset by Venetian forces attempting to seize parts if not all of Cesare's rebellious Romagna. While this turn of events was in itself nothing new, as important Venetian banking and other commercial interests had often posed a threat to Florentine control throughout the region, the latest Venetian aggressiveness reinforced Cesare's hopes of being assigned command of the Pope's armies and regaining his prominence.

Unexpectedly, any such prospect was denied him by the apprehensive though not now overtly hostile Julius, and in compensation Cesare applied for a *condotta* from the Signoria. This would have allowed him to cross Florentine territories with the small number of troops, comprising a mere 'seven hundred horse' and five hundred infantry, according to Machiavelli, that he had so far put together, paying for them with money stolen from his father's treasury.

The *condotta*, however, was also denied: the vaguest hint that his forces might parade across the Florentine Republic inspired more apprehension among the Signoria than any dangers posed by the Venetians. The Signoria felt reassured in one respect, however. As Machiavelli was aware, Cesare's rages seemed no longer to exhibit their previous theatrical grandeur. His moods had become 'irresolute, suspicious and unstable,' perhaps because 'of his natural character, or because the blows of fortune, which he is not accustomed to bear, have stunned and confounded him.'[2]

From Cesare's point of view, in fact, the future looked ominous, though neither he nor anyone imagined that the upshot of his vulnerability could be political after-effects rippling across the spreading Italian disunity over decades, or for that matter hundreds of years. The fickle twists of *Fortuna*, the dreadful wheel, combined with passion-dominated human choices, always seemed to most people governed by inevitable pulsations, or unaffected by social forces. Their mere existence, had anyone conceived of them, would have seemed incomprehensible.

Incensed by the Signoria's denial of the *condotta*, on 10 November Cesare did an about-face. He told Machiavelli that despite not having a commission he would launch his troops across republican territories anyway. He would tackle the Venetians on his own, or possibly with the Pope's tacit blessing. This dramatic stroke, he argued, would bolster his claim as an Italian and military leader still to be reckoned with.[3]

Perhaps unsurprisingly, he also seized on a chance for blackmail, announcing that 'if [the Signoria] hesitated or dealt unfairly with him, which would become manifest within four or five days, the time necessary for his envoy to come to Florence and write [back], he would make terms with the Venetians and with the Devil himself; or he would go and join the Pisans, and would devote all his money, his power and what allies remained to him to injuring our republic.' Even amid his diminished resources, his fascination with treachery, humiliation and abuse seemed to continue unabated.

These tactics, however, quickly proved useless. The *condottiere* Michelotto, who had helped him loot the papal treasury and his father's Vatican apartment, where troops under his command filched silver and plate worth hundreds of thousands of ducats, granting Cesare a temporary financial independence, headed into Tuscany with most of their hired troops. Cesare left for Ostia, where he sought out a complementary route by sea to Spezzia, chartering five ships to ferry north his five hundred remaining infantry.

At Ostia, however, he ran into a lack of essential good weather for sailing, and had to wait, and part of his grand plan fell apart. In a test of his loyalty, Julius had ordered two cardinals to catch him up. They demanded that he turn over to the Vatican a couple of his castles in the Romagna.[4] To their astonishment, he refused. Nor was he to be won over by Julius's promise that the castles would be returned once either the Venetian threat was eliminated or the Venetians defeated.

Arrogance may have addled him, or he may simply have blundered. Whatever the reason, his refusal proved his undoing. As the Venetians moved through the Romagna after seizing Faenza and Rimini, and their progress followed a declaration that their purpose was to rid the Romagna of the Borgias altogether, Julius, who lacked enough troops of his own, became frightened of what looked like the impending loss of the papal states. As a safeguard, he ordered Cesare's immediate re-arrest – a squad of armed men quashed a last-minute attempt at escape – and his forcible return to Rome. There he was locked up at the Vatican's *Torre Borgia*.[5] The Pope's advisors argued for his execution, but Julius bided his time: Cesare's diminishing influence might still win over the hearts of thousands in the Romagna. It could even prove helpful should his own position *vis-à-vis* Venice deteriorate further: Machiavelli had by now come to view Julius, whom he met often, with guarded respect, or as guided by a 'choleric temper and [an] honourable character', a mix of vitriol and reason.[6]

From a practical standpoint too, forbearance might prove useful in reducing Cesare to the role of a pawn in the competition between Venice and the Vatican while anxious members of the Signoria looked on amid their secret diplomatic reports, Machiavelli's among them. The outcome of all this squirming about could after all still be a Venetian invasion of the Republic.

Less reassuringly, Machiavelli's reports, delivered at his customary efficient pace, combined descriptions of Cesare's problems with demands that he be paid for his mailing costs and complaints about his (as he saw it) meagre salary ('if my salary cannot be increased, at least have me reimbursed for the postage'[7]). His reports had become harder to get through, despite specially hired couriers. The roads were 'wretched.' Military shifts were also outstripping his analyses at such a clip that it had become hard to keep up.

Plague had broken out in Rome and parts of the Romagna. By the end of November news of it reached Marietta in Florence. The news was followed by an outbreak in the city itself and over 800 deaths: 'You know very well how happy I am when you are not down there,' she wrote, 'and all the more so now that I have been told that there is so much disease.'[8] For some days she was ill herself, though not with plague, and unable to write. On recovering, she dared to hope for more than the three letters that she had received from him. Bernardo, their son, 'seems beautiful to me,' she noted, reproaching her husband's absence with affection, because 'he looks like you,' 'white as snow' and with a head 'like black velvet' and 'hairy.'

For Cesare, the future had turned bleak, though he kept trying to squirm ahead of it. On 30 November Michelotto was captured and his troops disarmed by 'the inhabitants of Castiglione and Cortona,' acting on behalf of the Pope and for the *condottiere* Gianpaolo Baglione and his own troops. His arrest amounted to an almost complete erasure of Cesare's military abilities, and Machiavelli told the Signoria that, to emphasize his debasement, the Duke was 'this morning [1 December] ... brought to the palace ... [and confined] in the chamber of the treasurer.'[9]

His dignity had collapsed amid a flurry of shouts, the cracking of whips, saddles and expensive shoes and furious raspings of iron and steel helmets, or the casual ticking of a cheeky doomsday clock in a post-chivalrous Renaissance world. Stripped of soldiers and officers, cursing his father, begging forgiveness of those he had harmed, while delivering a questionable outpouring of tears – or more likely some irritation of rationality – he had surrendered his castles in the Romagna, as requested.

Afraid of even more trouble, his friends deserted him and Rome. Machiavelli saw him 'slipping little by little into his grave.' Though everything seemed not quite lost, by mid-December 1503 Cesare's influence on affairs of state, not to mention military matters, had become a phantom of thinning speculations.

In contrast to his downfall, the early days of the following April found Michelangelo Buonarroti (1475–1564) busier than ever in Florence – for which Machiavelli himself finally set out on 18 December, 1503 – and dealing with his vastly improved artistic chances.

His 'almost finished' *David*, as would now be determined by a government committee including Leonardo, was to be accorded a place of honour and symbolic guardianship of the city beside the tall, buckle-bound doors of the Palazzo della Signoria. Leonardo had wanted to shunt Michelangelo's carved 'giant' off to one side, or into the Loggia, a spot less prestigious, but in disregarding his wishes the committee may have been trying to paper over a well-known huffy rivalry between the two artists.

This had already found expression in a public exchange – which may also have occurred later – when, according to Anonimo Gaddiano, Leonardo was left 'red-faced' in a city street among a crowd of people, as on challenging Michelangelo to explain a passage in Dante's *Commedia*, he had replied, 'Explain it yourself – you who designed a horse to [be] cast in bronze, and couldn't cast it, and abandoned it out of shame.' His allusion was to Leonardo's huge bronze statue, known as the Sforza Horse, which he had failed to finish.[10]

There had perhaps been other acrimonious exchanges between the two, which together spurred the Signoria into taking advantage of their mutual envy – it was more fiery on Michelangelo's part – to stimulate their hostility for the benefit of the Republic. Such at any rate followed the bulky installation of Michelangelo's finished *David* in August, with over forty men tugging and yanking the ponderous statue along fourteen greased and reshuffled pole-like beams over four days. He was granted a studio space suitable for his large cartoons, and comparable to Leonardo's, in the *Sala grande* at the Ospedale di Sant'Onofrio. Here in late October – his contract was broached only in September – he set to work on his own war fresco, meant to outshine that of his rival, a triptych representation of the Battle of Cascina, according to an arrangement that stipulated payments in lire commensurate with what Leonardo was to receive.

The battle itself had taken place in July 1364. It had witnessed a rout of Pisan by Florentine troops, and so offered a theme juicy enough to satisfy members of the Grand Council and the Signoria. As with Leonardo's *Battle of Anghiari*, and perhaps in a fit of Michelangelo's notorious pique, it was to be left unfinished when he abruptly left for Rome and more lucrative commissions offered him by Pope Julius.[11]

War as a stimulant to civilization, the terror of bloodshed and murder as horrible yet heroic premises of human improvement: these intractable historical impulses, as they then seemed, influenced the *invenzione* guiding Michelangelo's preliminary work on his fresco, as they had Leonardo's sketches, though Michelangelo's approach to illustrating them was his own. Few if any of his contemporaries were likely to question the premises themselves. Machiavelli seems to have drawn even darker conclusions about the same ideas ever since his childhood experiences during the slaughterous aftermath of the murders at the *Duomo*.

Had everything gone as planned, the effect of the two frescoes would therefore have amounted to a triumph of realism: as members of the Republic's Grand Council engaged in deliberations, these two huge works of art would have provided roving eyes – and the opportunity to avoid them would have been more or less denied – with a feast of extravagant, rampant dishes of fanta-sized, persuasive slaughter.

Only one cartoon illustrative of Michelangelo's *invenzione* has survived, in the form of a grisaille-on-panel copy made much later, in 1542, and attributed to Aristotile da San Gallo: *Soldiers Bathing*. Startlingly, in the light of its military theme, this sketch (76.2 x 132.1 cm; plate X) offers up no violence at all, only twenty-one young men, if one takes as the twenty-first the two hands rising from the water at the bottom of the picture, who may be soldiers, and who are seen wrestling, heaving, gliding into tunics and tights, fondling their weapons, flexing well-toned muscles, gazing, pointing and lurching about naked or in stages of undress beside a pond or lake where they have been washing and relaxing. On either side of what seems to have been the centrepiece sketch, there would have been located, to the left, a cavalry scene showing some of the horsier preparations for battle, and to the right, a depiction of the battle itself.

In making sense of Michelangelo's unprecedented cartoon, or what at first appears a colossal jumble of faces and bodies, and for which he began to paste together outsized sheets of paper in anticipation of a public exhibition in the autumn of 1504, it may be useful to recall that he had always seen himself as much a poet, albeit an unpublished one, as a sculptor and painter, and that – a relevant fact in an era in which the medieval *canzone* still retained its popularity – he seems to have spent much of his time composing sonnets.

The still novel form, whose blend of compression with an invitation to meditation, including a compelling invitation to silent reading, resulting in a mix of rational argument and explosive self-confrontation, or a cunning provocation of intense self-conscious states, repeatedly attracted the sculptor of the Republic's *David*. Among Michelangelo's scores of surviving poems and fragments of poems, at least 64 are sonnets, and at least one, that beginning *Quand'il servo il signor d'aspra catena* [When the master binds his slave in the harshest shackles], a *caudato*, or twenty-lined, tailed specimen. His first-known efforts in the form appear to date from around 1504, or just as he finished his *David* and started work on *Soldiers Bathing*.[12]

These coincidences seem significant, not only because they mattered to Michelangelo himself, but also because his war cartoon presents a frozen emergency of self-consciousness. External motion has been halted to allow the viewer to contemplate the inner tensions affecting the faces and muscles of a group of young men who are almost certainly preparing for combat. If Leonardo's sketches were intended to investigate motion sweeping across a battlefield, Michelangelo had settled on an investigation of the transforming conflicts within the bodies and souls of a group of Florentine soldiers.

Motion is thus treated as kinetic, or as a barely suppressed muscular energy on the verge of its stormy release. The twenty faces and bodies, superbly individualized as the warriors fling themselves up in alarm, fright, rage, scorn, suspicion, bloodlust and self-possession, are captured in a doubtful, thrilled response to the news that just over a nearby hill, unseen by them and the viewer, a battle has broken out.

Michelangelo's rendering of this decisive moment, comprising a knotty yet controlled unravelling of minds and bodies preparing to erupt into struggle, despair and an unknown but anticipated victory, is itself, or so one may finally come to accept, a type of visual, tailed sonnet: the twenty bodies, which may be understood as equivalent to the *caudate*'s twenty lines of verse, are delivered before the viewing audience by the two hands emerging from the water below, which seem to show them off as catalysts in a military-political upheaval.

Partly as a result, compression counts for everything in Michelangelo's sketch, or so it seems, and this aspect is unusual for its captivating suggestion of a sound, or even a voice, expressed as silence. The announcement of a battle in progress, or about to begin, must be understood as washing over the sultry logic of the warriors' bodies pausing and petrified in dread, but for the viewer any sense of immediacy, or self-conscious emergency, is established by a warning, which has not been heard and cannot be heard.

The outcome is that the picture's dramatic success depends on an eerie absence, as the viewer strains to listen to an inaudible or soundless alarm raised in exasperation. The effect of this silence is extended by a strange isolation, the futile, wild staring about, as into some private space, of the soldiers themselves. Only two of them, at the centre, appear joined in a furious, comradely gaze. It serves as a beam balancing the exiled anxieties of the rest.

Machiavelli had himself been spending time straining to listen to almost inaudible warnings, as it were, or quiet alarms over a hill, and on occasion with success. The political and military twilight had intensified across Italy. Towards the end of 1504, during a concentrated two-week period in November, he began to describe what he had heard, and for the first time for publication, though its appearance would not come until over a year later. His description took the form of a chronicle poem conceived along the lines of Dante's account of Roman history in the sixth canto of his *Paradiso*. Machiavelli's *Decennale Primo* [First Decennale] amounted to an ambitious reconstruction, or a quasi-objective memoir, of 'the vexations of Italy over [the previous] ten years.'[13]

The challenge lay in rendering recent Italian and more specifically Florentine history in 550 lively *terza rima* lines. As planned, his poem would reach back to the French King Charles' invasion of Italy in 1494, and forward into the seedy military and cultural 'miseries' of the present.

Abetting his commitment to writing it were probably two frustrating missions from which he had just returned, plus a technological-military fiasco in which he had participated and which had cost the Republic much in lives and money, to the tune of about 7,000 ducats. Contributory too may have been the insulted reactions to his controversial proposal, placed before the Signoria and members of the Grand Council back in May, to create a new type of state-sponsored citizen militia.

As conceived, this unusual army, whose inspiration is traceable into precedents reaching back to thirteenth-century Florentine history, and methods that he had seen Cesare Borgia sometimes adopt, would have replaced nearly all the Republic's mercenary soldiers with local volunteers. The mere thought of any such innovation, however, chiefly because the recruits would be deployed defensively, had stirred outrage among Council members. They insisted that under no circumstances could some ramshackle collection of amateurs be turned into soldiers capable of ensuring the Republic's safety. Far from doing so, and possibly at the behest of the *ottimati* or even Piero Soderini, they might simply take over the city.[14]

It remains uncertain that this or any of his missions now inspired him to take a stab at epic-historical verse, though all four exercises, including an attempt, at first with Leonardo and then with others, at last to have a go at diverting the Arno – which produced the technological fiasco – returned him to familiar situations.

They had all changed, as had the people involved in them, or as for that matter had Cesare, a soldier whose prestige seemed for the moment consigned to the dust heap of fantasy and legend. Early January 1504, for instance, or the first of his missions, had seen him once more in France, but not to mend fences, as a few years earlier. A new Spanish threat was emerging in well-equipped attacks and supported by a flotilla disgorging an invasion force not far from Naples. It ignited wild battles over the city, and seemed about to lead to the loss of a large chunk of Italian territory in the south, and possibly even into distracting the French from protecting Florence in the north.[15]

A defeat of the French would allow the Spanish a relatively complete domination of central Italy. As the Spanish victories piled up and the French appeared headed into withdrawals – King Louis had already relocated his headquarters to Lyons – the risks rose high enough to nudge Machiavelli into offering the Signoria a bet that he could handle a relief-seeking trip into the north to the French court, by horse and via Milan, in just six days, no easy task over the hundreds of hilly miles.

Omitting the two days that he set aside for talks with King Louis's minister Charles D'Amboise, himself then in Milan, and who flippantly denied the importance of the Spanish menace, Machiavelli won his bet and by mid-January was in Lyons. The hoped for negotiations, however, to be undertaken with the Florentine ambassador, his friend Niccolò Valori, and intended to induce the French, despite their evident embarrassment, to deliver military aid to the Republic, inched forward at only a snail's pace, if not without results.

His near failure in Lyons was succeeded on 2 April by his mission to Piombino, just south of Pisa. Here telltale signs of war, focused on the districts around Siena, had attracted the attention of the Signoria. Jacopo d'Appiano, with whom Machiavelli had bickered over salary demands in March 1499, now seemed eager to swing his forces into backing the Pisans. Machiavelli was sent off to evaluate Jacopo's war-preparations.[16]

He harboured no illusions about the strategic value of either mission except as a stopgap in the face of Spanish encroachments. Italy seemed on its way to becoming a feeding trough for imperial Iberian appetites. Their indulgence looked likely to be arranged by their elegantly dressed and astute commander, Grand Captain Gonzalvo Fernández da Córdoba, even as the French kowtowed before a superior Spanish military dazzle.

Machiavelli had recorded his distaste of the French in a prickly memorandum, *De natura Gallorum*, following his first visit to France in 1500. This document echoed prejudices that they might well have reciprocated: '[They] are so intent on immediate advantage or injury that they have little memory of past wrongs or benefits, and little care for future good or evil;' 'While they may not be able to do you a good turn, this does not hinder them from promising to do so;' 'They are miserly rather than cautious.'[17]

Weighed against an increasing French battle-squeamishness, as he saw it, his own efforts to stimulate Louis into taking the field against the Spanish might easily – as almost happened – prove worthess. Despite his hurried trip into the north, therefore, he was hardly surprised at failing to win a warm or fast audience with the French King. Louis, it was whispered, had been rendered speechless by the news of his latest military reverses in the south.[18]

These difficulties aside, Machiavelli's missions seem subtly to have contributed to a fragile peace that by late 1504 began to settle across Italy, the outcome of a surprising three-year truce concluded in late March between the French and Spanish monarchs. A tranquil moment, understood as unlikely to last, may as much as his almost useless diplomacy have allowed him to feel free to devote fifteen days to his *First Decennale*.

As early as April, he could in any case have been found writing poetry, though of another sort and meant to be set to music as a now lost love song. He sent it off to Francesco Soderini, who was still acting as the Republic's ambassador in Rome, and who was glad to get it: 'I was pleased by the verses you say you wrote.... . We shall save them for when we can sing them and accompany them on the rebec.'[19]

None of this should be construed as implying that the collapse of his Arno project had not proved equally disastrous. For one thing, Leonardo had withdrawn his participation. For another, his replacement, a hydraulics expert, Maestro d'acque [*sic*; Master of water] Columbino, had turned out to be incompetent. Renewed enthusiasm for pushing ahead with the diversion had emerged only because of the military paralysis resulting from a setback at Pisa in the summer of 1504. On the Florentine side, and lasting through July, the prospects at Pisa had at first looked promising. Even the Pisans acknowledged that near-siege conditions established by Florentine mercenary troops rendered 'it [impossible] for a man to leave ... without running great danger.' Francesco Soderini had written optimistically to Machiavelli that 'you are not [now] going to have such obstacles that, if you are willing to do quickly what is required, you cannot take Pisa by force.'[20] Within weeks, however, several reversals turned the whole undertaking into an abject failure.

Leonardo's withdrawal should perhaps have aroused forebodings. In July his father, ser Piero da Vinci, had died at the age of eighty. Leonardo's relations with him had been cool, though his grief seems to have been genuine. Among his two sisters and nine brothers, his father left him alone nothing in his will.[21] The neglect may or may not have affected him. By August, however, he was at Piombino, taking up a new position as military advisor (it had perhaps been arranged by Machiavelli). To Piombino's minor prince and ruler, Jacopo d'Appiano, Leonardo presented a novel idea to level only the upper portions of the outer Pisan walls with cannon, as preparation for an invasion to pour into the city straight over them rather than through the conventional bottom and central gaps laid open by indiscriminate artillery fire.

His idea was never tested. Reports of well-trained Pisan reinforcements, detected by the Republic's spies in the city streets, as many as two thousand infantry, mostly smuggled-in Spanish troops, and other armed men, discouraged Florence's already nervous mercenaries. With Machiavelli's support, therefore, thousands of ducats and gangs of hired workers were recruited, combined and pressed into implementing a variation of Leonardo's original scheme for the Arno, but this time directed by Columbino.

An aloof if sloppy engineer, he seems to have misunderstood his predecessor's calculations for the adequate design of ditches roomy enough to accommodate a river diversion, crucially forgetting to make them several fathoms deep. As the late-summer rains poured in, slashing through the dug-up swamplands, over eighty workers drowned or were buried in floods and mudslides.

All the remaining teams of diggers and the troops guarding them were ordered out. The project itself was abandoned amid slovenliness and horrified chagrin ('The work of turning the Arno to Livorno was set in hand,' noted Landucci on 22 August, 'but it was not continued'; 'It gave us great pain,' Francesco Sodernini complained in a letter of 26 October to Machiavelli, 'that so great an error should have been made in those waters that it seems impossible ... that it should not have been ... the fault of those engineers, who went so far wrong. Perhaps it also pleases God'[22]).

The diversion's gruesome finale perhaps served as the tipping point for Machiavelli to switch into the more appealing task of writing his *First Decennale*, a poem which remains impressive not only for its imaginative aspects but for clarifying his insights so far into history, or indicating how he believed it ought to be written by the committed poet-investigator.

He dedicated his poem to the prominent (Machiavelli calls him, in Latin, 'pre-eminent') Alamanno Salviati, the former leader of the Signoria, at whose invitation, he announces, conventionally if somewhat improbably, he has composed it, in Italian.

He notes that his aim is to present a history that will be selective, not just for the sake of conciseness, or even for illuminating recent events, but for describing an Italian and specifically Florentine tragedy, which he terms a 'misery.' Florence, if not Italy, he argues, has been almost destroyed by French and other invaders. The Republic's prosperity has been wrecked, its culture assaulted. In despair, he has taken up his chronicler's pen to reveal how the sabotage began, rose to a crisis and finally reaped the whirlwind.

He also implies another, more majestic purpose. In composing his history in the *terza rima* form that educated people would recognize as having achieved its sensuous perfection at the hands of the most sublime of Italian poets, Dante, and having soared to heights of expressiveness with Petrarch in his sonnets, he indicates his desire to discover amid the horrid events that he plans to cite, and despite their blood-stained barbarity, the healing strength of aesthetics. His lines will be ennobled with a famous linguistic music and metaphorical beauty. They will exhibit amid their tones and keys a calamity more dramatic than that of mere misery: an ethical collapse, or even tragedy, but wedded to the hope of finding amid its chaos a terrified redemption.

A measure of his success lies in the fact that, to his consternation and that of his friends, the *Decennale* was almost immediately stolen. A pirated edition appeared in early 1506, within weeks of its first publication.

The poem's aesthetic qualities also attracted quite a bit of attention. 'A few days ago,' Ercole Bentivoglio, Captain General of the [Florentine] Army, wrote to him on 25 February, 'I received … your poem, a brief history of the past ten years. Seeing with how much elegance you have discussed in it all the things that have occurred in that time, I cannot help but admire and praise profoundly what you have accomplished.'[23]

Overwhelmed by the poem's evocation of a depressing past, however, Bentivoglio seems to have missed Machiavelli's point about the future. Following a vivid description of Charles' invasion of Italy, his retreat and an account of King Louis's invasion and his own retreat, and between them a summary of the seesawing battles that Cesare Borgia had launched across Tuscany and other provinces, the *Decennale* in its final lines turns its full attention to an 'unexpected road to salvation.'

This lies, so Machiavelli indicates, in the Republic's setting up his citizen militia: 'We trust in the skilful steersman [an allegorical reference to Piero Soderini], in the oars, in the sails, in the cordage; but the voyage would be easy and short if you [Florence] would open the temple of Mars.'[24]

Salvation lies at hand, but only for those willing to open the gates of Mars, or war, and release into combat the Republic's own soldiers. The *Decennale* gains a tragic power as the reader comes to understand that Machiavelli has pitched his appeal backwards into the Republic's misery, viewing Florence less as the victim of outside rapacity than its own passivity, as yearning for rescue instead of summoning up its considerable if neglected assets:

> All Tuscany was in confusion; so you lost Pisa and those states the Medici family gave to the French.// Thus you could not rejoice as you should have done at being taken from under the yoke that for sixty years had been crushing you,// because you saw your state laid waste; you saw your city in great peril, and in the French arrogance and pride.[25]

The tercets seem to glow almost atrociously through his description of French cruelties under Charles, the nephew of the king from whom over the past few weeks he has been seeking military assistance:

> So with his conquering army he moved upon the kingdom like a falcon that swoops or a bird of swifter flight,[26]

and his history glimmers with betrayed terror as he cites the sufferings of ordinary people:

> Long would it take to tell all the injuries, all the deceits encountered in that siege, and all the citizens dead from fever.[27]

In its last stanzas Machiavelli's memoir of the Republic's destitution seems actually to delight in its fantastical and willowy dreadfulness ('Of how many mountain paths, of how many swamps must I tell, full of blood and the dead through the vicissitudes of splendid kingdoms and states'[28]), and a painful, commiserating wit ('Thus my spirit is all on fire, overwhelmed now with hope, now with fear, so much that it wastes to nothing drop by drop'[29]).

Radiating an exhausted melancholy, the lines nonetheless rejoice in their insistence, which Machiavelli shared with his contemporaries, that history always has a meaning, even if a cruel one. So pervasive is his conviction that the reader may overlook various misstatements (Louis XII, it may be recalled, rescued rather than assaulted Florence: in Machiavelli's favour, however, his picture of Cesare tricking his nominal allies into entering Senigallia – he calls the Duke a 'whistling basilisk'[30] – seems apropos). The poem may linger longest in memory as a paean to a sacrificed form of civilized order, if not to a travestied population that, he believes, has lost its way.

# 22

# Anarchy and the Citizen Militia

Yet it was just afterwards, and in the Republic's small towns rather than in Florence, as new forms of disorder spread into rural and urban worlds alike, soon giving way to new bouts of mayhem, that he managed to take advantage of the belatedly granted permission to recruit citizen-soldiers for his new militia, doing so by their dozens, hundreds and thousands. How would they behave if trained, equipped and flung into battle against an enemy? Would they flee, or stand and fight, behaviour rare enough among mercenaries?

Cesare had cut and run, it seemed, from his own recent opportunities, and at last surrendered. As Pope Julius's agent, Cardinal Maximilian Carvajal, took possession of his two castles at Casena and Bertinoro, and because Julius incorrectly expected that the Duke's other castles would be turned over to him, he was set free at Ostia in April 1504.

He quickly fled by ship to Naples, there to be welcomed by his uncle, Cardinal Luis Borgia. He was treated to a far chillier greeting by the Spanish commander, Gonzalo. His plans remained unchanged: to hire troops (he assumed with Spanish help), to sweep back into the north, to reclaim his lost territories in the Romagna and to resume his previous unquestioned authority.

The Spanish King, Ferdinand II of Aragon (1452–1516), felt completely out of sympathy with these (as they seemed to him) personal fantasies. It scarcely mattered that Cesare was a fellow countrymen, and he responded with treachery of his own. More anxious to curry favour with the Pope than to support his nephew's recovery of territory, on 27 May 1504 he ordered Cesare's arrest.[1]

Deprived of his castles, soldiers, weapons and money, reduced to the humiliations of poverty and even the unclean clothes on his back, he found himself brusquely shipped off to Spain as the King's prisoner, where on his arrival he was locked up in the royal fortress at Chincilla. A bit later, when Ferdinand became anxious that the fortress might not hold him – Cesare's sympathizers, or those still enchanted with the legend, tried one getaway ploy after another

– Ferdinand had him transferred to a more secure castle at Medina del Campo, where he was better watched and well treated.

No evidence in Machiavelli's career and life to date suggests a parallel experience of isolation. He knew even less of exile, though it may be emphasized that either punishment, whether in politics or private life, would have differed in its meaning and effects from its modern versions. If in his day ostracism bore an acrid odour of darkness, substantiality and silence, still it seemed psychologically milder than the brutal invasiveness of modern tortures of the mind: sense-deprivation experiments, maimings by drugs, needles and electrodes and the assaults on personality unleashed by brain-washing.

In a semi-Christian universe, the punishment of exile, while swathed in disgrace, implied its alternative of rescue. It might glisten with vague possibilities of mercy, and even hints of the divine. While appalling the body, it could preserve and even nourish the spirit. Some recognition of the singular unpleasantness of the sixteenth-century Florentine punishment of ostracism or exile can thus be more than helpful in contemplating Machiavelli's possible sensations as for the first time he faced the likelihood of his expulsion by a majority on the Grand Council. Its more conservative members had turned hostile to his presence in government, or alarmed at what seemed his seditious intentions, born of his advocacy, starting in 1504 and running into the succeeding months and years, of a citizen militia. His goal of Florentine military success had provoked strong suspicions of his possible disloyalty.

It may also seem unsurprising that a helpful way to understand the experience of exile in his day seems to lie in wandering among illicit Florentine pleasures after dark, as well as recalling the universal belief in the Ptolemaic-Christian cosmic world.

Festive occasions, judicial decisions (executions and wrenchings on the *strappado* usually proceeded at night), crimes (smuggling at the city gates, robberies, murders, mostly after-dark affairs as well), drinking sprees and outlawed sexual pursuits: all sought out the unique, hedonistic and isolating nightfall reaching among the city's taper-lit streets and alleys. Alchemy and magic, the casually blessed amulet or figurine, the magician's or witch's cauldron, the garbled incantation, saturnine masks, star-studded hats and quavering spell-castings – each for the sake of better friendships, finances, children and love-making – could have been bought at the nearest street corner, or discreetly during a post-sunset rendezvous with an alchemist, witch or magician.

*Gioventù*, or the love of boys, retained an enticing, *sub rosa* popularity, despite ferocious laws requiring the execution or banishment of anyone caught engaging in it. The Via dei Pellicciai was a haunt of male prostitutes. Two taverns, the Buco, near the Ponte Vecchio, located in an alley that still bears its name, and the Sant'Andrea or del Lino, near the Old Market, supported a trade in adolescent boys, who might have been spotted as well in the *piazza* at the *Duomo*, at least until a few years later when they were chased off. Still other taverns accommodated heterosexual pleasures: the Bertuccie, Chiassolino, Fico, Malvagia, Panico, Porco [the Monkey-Pussy-Ugly Whore, Little Whorehouse-Little Confusion-Little Outhouse, Fig-Cunt, Wicked Woman, Panic, Pig].[2]

Many of these cheerless establishments, poorly lit to hide the identities of customers and vendors from a roving constabulary, and fitted out with squat, lithe shadows, woody wine casks and musicians grinding away at polished rebecs as they ministered to the eager, exhausted, cynical, naïve, wretched and lonely, rattled on not far from the Palazzo della Signoria, where Machiavelli and his colleagues laboured into the evening, decoding dispatches, considering state expenses, writing up their reports. Sleazy escapes awaited them down the street, should their interest in work flag a bit.

Close by too arose a more awe-inspiring escape, equally available by night, an untouchable display of the unveiled stars, planets and angels, or Heaven as most people conceived it. As they also believed, the stars offered a glimpse into the very brains of God. Their proximity, soaring above the cobblestoned dark with its incivilities, and disputing earthly pleasures, could no more be dismissed than sin itself. Even the poor street lighting rendered clearer the rivalry between hired sex and spiritual freedoms.

Those wandering the streets – and never mind the others pent into the darker countryside – thus knew a good deal about the miracles lying beyond the transparent blackness sailing between the Earth and the sphere of the stars, or the *stellatum*. Since ancient times, Western peoples had understood the minute stars to be God's far off intelligence shining through tumescent, ancient holes, more than a little like divine pinpricks puncturing the sphere itself. If Heaven lay far off and high above, its relative closeness, with the idea of infinite space unknown, remained reassuring. Salvation lay past the measurable expanse that might be traversed by virtuous acts.

The crucial choices of life, or so everyone felt, lay either at one's feet or over one's head. The idea of uncertainty had just begun to become fashionable, and for most the dark retained its vitality. It seemed no mere absence of light, as

Leonardo, who lacked many religious and other superstitions, had long since begun to see it.

Machiavelli's world therefore encouraged few of the tormenting doubts that some decades later would be articulated by Hamlet, Macbeth, Don Quixote and Juliet: angst-provoking enquiries into being and not being, or the lonelier, amputated, more modern human condition. The terrors of conscience failure seemed manageable rather than irrational. The void was unknown. Even physical pain seemed less threatening if more voluptuous, perhaps because everywhere there seemed to shine wild streaks of doom and glory.

'Do not leave off,' Francesco Soderini urged him on 29 May 1504, as he drifted into what seems to have been disillusionment, after a first debate on his proposal for a citizen militia. 'Perhaps the favour that is not given one day will be given another.' Throughout the controversy, Machiavelli looked to the Cardinal, the brother of Piero Soderini, as his trusted ally: 'The argument against the militia is not good in a thing so necessary and so sound: and they cannot be suspicious of the force, which will not be raised for private, but for public, convenience.'[3]

Yet suspicious many remained, even into late 1505. By then, Piero had arranged to bring the matter to a vote in the smaller Council of Eighty. He was assisted by a lengthy description of how the militia ought to be designed and run, which had been written up for the Council of Ten by Machiavelli. In winning the smaller council's approval to recruit Republican soldiers, however, Soderini appeared to quite a few only to have boxed the opposition into a sullen silence.

The new vote, before January 1506, gave Machiavelli the licence he sought, and took him into the Republic's rural districts – to the Mugello, for example, the hilly region undulating amid its farms and villages, where years ago he had spent a few childhood summer months at the house of his uncle Giovanni, his mother's brother.[4]

He rode eastward as well, into Casentino and other villages, consulting the tax records, or *catasti*, for help and then ordering all prospective soldiers between the ages of fifteen and forty to report to him.

Their age range was probably determined by his knowledge of ancient Roman methods of organizing legions. The Romans had deployed the age groups in tandem, with combat squares of older veterans placed behind those younger and less experienced. The younger bore the brunt of the attacks while the veterans were employed as tested reinforcements.[5]

Importantly, Machiavelli's permission to recruit seemed unaffected by his never having served in an army. Even his political enemies recognized that his administrative and battle experience was extensive. He knew the rhythms of sieges, the design and manufacture of weapons, the logistics of attacks, military supply problems and how to schedule the necessary financing of troop formations. Of great value was his having spent years poring over ancient Greek (in translation) and Roman military histories, with their accounts of the patterns of successful battles, along with other books that offered tips on tactics and how wars in the republican and imperial Roman periods had most effectively been fought – by Livy (running back through his boyhood readings with his father), Xenophon, Plutarch, Tacitus, Polybius, Frontinus and Vegetius, and recent accounts by such authorities such as Leonardo Bruni.

Nor was this to be his first experience in recruiting native soldiers. The collapse of the Republic's mercenary army at Pisa, just prior to the futile attempt to divert the Arno, had seen the service of over two thousand conscripts, all native-born and recruited by him, a desultory lot, ragged, ill-mannered, ill-trained, yet fielded as part of an expedition that, even though in the end it accomplished little, had carried some of the Ten's highest hopes. No Florentine soldiers had fought at Pisa, but many had answered the call.

The prospect of enlisting much larger numbers, though, or as many as 10,000, the announced goal, presented special problems. If the members of the Grand Council had worried about the possibility of citizen-soldiers seizing the capital, any recruiter of rural soldiers, chosen precisely for their unthreatening distance from the city, had to contend with the animosities of their towns and villages, or their jealousies, rivalries and allegiances which often ran back centuries.

'Two causes have contributed to give me the greatest trouble in this matter [of conscription],' Machiavelli wrote to the Signoria on 5 February. 'The one is the inveterate habit of disobedience of these people, and the other is the enmity existing between the populations [for instance] of Petrognano and Campana,' who occupied opposite sides of a mountain.[6]

Conscripts often objected to joining unless guaranteed service under their village or clan leaders. Still others would do so only if at liberty to report at certain times of the year, usually exclusive of the harvest and planting seasons. Most were indifferent to the reality that war paid no attention to convenience, or that an army's usefulness lay in its reliability. Over the next few snowbound weeks, Machiavelli interviewed hundreds of candidates, winnowing them accordingly (an attraction for new soldiers, in addition to minimal pay, was that the Republic promised to forgive their debts). In one district, a typical case, he accepted only 'about seven hundred choice men' out of twice the number.

His newly recruited units also needed constables to supervise them, and weapons, such as pikes and short swords. These had to be delivered from Florence. Most were dispatched by 5 March, along with identifying banners, emblems and standards. Snow delayed the arrival of everything.

Essential as well was hiring an overall commander. Everyone agreed that for reasons of civil mistrust (the commander might himself conspire to take over the city) he ought not to be a Florentine. Because the troops lacked experience, he should also be a *condottiere*. Machiavelli's first choice, made on returning to Florence in February, was Cesare Borgia's captured, knowledgeable henchman, Michelotto. He had just been let out of prison by Pope Julius. Michelotto's reputation for viciousness, however – he often preferred strangling his enemies for no apparent reason – had led to his being hated and shunned. He won only lukewarm approval from the Council of Eighty, amid the reservations of influential citizens such as Piero Guicciardini, a brother of Francesco. Piero worried that Michelotto's sadistic temperament could easily render him uncontrollable and likely to turn on his employers. On 19 April, however, he was hired anyway, and over the following summer, true to form, directed 150 of the new troops on raids against Pisan farms. He torched houses and slaughtered livestock. Within a year he had predictably been removed from office. A bit later he was killed in a battle.

On 15 February, though, Landucci was anxious to record his impression of Machiavelli's recruits. About four hundred of them, summoned by the *Gonfaloniere* Piero Soderini, were assembled in the *piazza* before the Palazzo della Signoria. City officials had provided these 'Florentine peasants' with a sort of uniform, 'a white waistcoat, a pair of stockings, half red and half white, a white cap, shoes, and an iron breastplate and lances, and to some of them [arquebuses]. [The units] were called battalions; and they were given a constable [astutely, from a district other than their own] who would lead them, and teach them how to use their arms. They were soldiers, but [remained] at their own houses, being obliged to appear when needed.'

Landucci reflected the by now growing public enthusiasm for the future of the citizen army: 'It was ordered that many thousand[s] [of these soldiers] should be [recruited] in this way all through the country, so that we should not need to have any foreigners. This was thought the finest thing that had ever been arranged for Florence.'⁷ Whether finest or simply practical, Machiavelli's battalions retained a flavour of originality, if not quite as Landucci had assumed. Armies made up in part of citizen-soldiers had for decades been deployed by France, Germany and Spain. As was the case since the military reforms of Charles VII of France in 1445, however, they were organized by kings, and consisted of soldiers answerable to them or an occasionally treacherous nobility.⁸ Machiavelli's innovation lay in the principle (his friend Biagio termed it his 'invention') of an army of citizen-soldiers answerable to other citizens as well as to citizen institutions.

The difference implied a shift in the relations between war and politics. It promised, if retained, other important changes. Bellicose greed, paralysing instabilities, poisonous hatreds and the cunning of military profiteers, all masked by lies about motives, might be suppressed to a great extent by military arrangements made among citizens acting in concert with other citizens. At a minimum, various grisly impulses would be reduced. A distant but significant antecedent of this shift, as Machiavelli knew, was to be found in the armies of Cicero's Roman Republic. The danger in Cicero's day lay in the option granted to Roman soldiers, mostly for reasons of morale, to swear allegiance to their commanders instead of the state. Ultimately, the arrogating of personal loyalties over patriotism contributed to the fall of the Republic. It was a mistake that Machiavelli was determined to avoid.

A law setting up the new militia, but grounded in his earlier description of it, his *Discorso dell'ordinare lo stato di Firenze alle armi* [Discourse on the military organization of the State of Florence], was granted broad legislative approval in December 1506. It stipulated that during times of peace the militia would be administered by a civilian committee, or board of Nine, and during times of war by the Ten of War, or Dieci, on which Machiavelli continued as Secretary.⁹

The first board of Nine was elected on 10 January 1507, with him appointed as its first chancellor. The appointment more than satisfied him, even as it implied a considerable amount of work yet to be done to improve the new army. On becoming the Nine's chancellor, moreover, he seemed in the eyes of many to have redeemed his devotion to government service, and on a more elevated level and with greater opportunities to influence policy than before.

Throughout the Republic, it should be understood, the atmosphere of violence also boosted support for the citizen militia. Not all of this violence, which reached back into the years before 1500, was visited on the peasantry and citizens by invading armies. Ruffians, thugs and murderers, often acting in gangs, spread their own terrors and stimulated a general desire for a military authority operating more or less at will among the Republic's towns and villages, no matter how risky to personal freedoms they might be.

Historians such as Francesco Guicciardini took note of the scores of citizens killed in their beds for their money and other property, of the quantities of blood gratuitously spilt, of the casual stabbings, the vendettas and robberies carried out in the remote lanes, alleys and forests.

Most of these crimes could not have been prevented by the new militia acting alone. On the other hand, its presence might provide comfort, lightening as well as policing the urban and rural shadows.

Exactly this happened in spring 1506, under the crude leadership of Michelotto, who meted out arbitrary punishments requested by the Signoria with a swaggering contempt. A more welcome form of relief, just as violent but mitigated by prayers and good humour, was to be seen in the unexpected military campaigns of Pope Julius II.

Immediately on assuming his papal office, Julius, soon to be dubbed 'the warrior Pope,' revealed his determination to make use of the tenuous peace between the kings of France and Spain. Quiescence might let him seize the Romagna while taking control of important adjacent territories. Venice might be humbled.

A taste for battle induced him to launch an invasion. At night on 25–26 August 1506, in the wake of Machiavelli's recruitment successes, the Signoria ordered him to bring a message to Julius, indicating the Republic's approval of his contemplated forays against the rebellious cities of Perugia and Bologna.[10] Machiavelli joined Julius's progress, already underway and glittering in armour, tuneful pipes and pomp across the countryside, at Nepi, some twenty-five miles northeast of Rome. He gained an audience with the Pope at Civita Castellana, and there delivered a speech full of eloquent phrases in 'praise of [his] good and holy intent.'

Machiavelli had been instructed to accompany him, while also urging restraint in his deployment of his 400 men-at-arms, with their 'two crossbowmen for each lance.'[11] These were complemented by a contingent of musicians, a costumed choir, chefs and twenty-four none too happy cardinals, most of whom exhibited no enthusiasm for going to war.

To everyone's amazement, however, and especially in consideration of his comparative military weakness, Julius declared his purpose to be the reestablishment of papal authority throughout the recognized papal states. Machiavelli assured him that not only would the Signoria support his efforts but that he could expect a safe-conduct through republican territories, and even extra troops, should he require them.

About the troops Machiavelli need not have worried. Julius boasted that 'his pockets were full of soldiers.' He indicated that he could stare down any conceivable opposition: he had received ample pledges of troops from several nobles. His campaign was planned to last several months, or into autumn, but as Machiavelli remarked in a letter from Forlì on 9 October, the Signoria might as well realize that if Julius handled it well it might 'lead the King of France, on whom [he] mainly relies, [to] be at liberty to defend the Church and to protect Italy against those who would devour her.'

With Florence's representative in tow, Julius's itinerary now led him from Perugia, on 27 September, through Fratta, Gubbio, Cesena, Forlì, Palazzolo and Imola. Earlier, and without a shot fired, he and his retinue had tramped their way into the lofty, ancient city of Perugia itself. Machiavelli was astonished as its gloomy, established ruler, Giampaolo Baglioni, a parricide and mass-murderer who enjoyed leaving piles of his enemies' bodies lying about in the streets, a one-time confederate of Cesare Borgia, thief and opportunistic slitter of throats, whose family had lorded it over the city's precincts for more than a century, surrendered his government and placed his castles, fortresses and hostages in papal hands. 'If he does no harm to the man who has come to take away his state,' Machiavelli reported, 'it will only be out of kindness and humanity.'[12]

Kindness had little to do with it. Julius's tempestuous person, lavish rhetorical skills and an uncanny ability to reconstruct lapsed alliances, plus the reviving majesty of the papacy, rapidly loosed apoplectic fears more than sufficient to permit him to achieve many of his goals. At the same time, Machiavelli's belief in an Italy assailed, or 'devoured,' rippling through his *First Decennale*, began to permeate his latest reports to the Signoria. Often a despairing outlook combined with gloomy convictions about the decisive role of *Fortuna* in human affairs.

In the days from 13 to 21 or perhaps 27 September, but at any rate during his stay in the city, he wrote a more than one-thousand-word-long disquisition (or *Ghiribizzi*, as it came to be called, or fantasies in the manner of speculations) on *Fortuna*, adapting several of his crystallizing ideas into the form of a letter that in the end he may not have sent. During this time he seems also have written a 192-line poem, the *Capitolo/di Fortuna*. The letter was addressed to Giovan

Battista Soderini (1484–1528), Piero's nephew. The poem, arranged in the *terza rima* manner that had by now become more or less his favourite in verse, he also dedicated to the twenty-two-year-old Giovan Battista.

The letter is remarkable for its resolution of an enigma – what after all is *Fortuna*? – in simple yet comprehensive terms, the poem for its rational vigour buttressed by techniques retooled from other authors. The series of allegorical, history-oriented paintings described in its last lines, for instance, owes much to Boccaccio's *Teseida*, the popular Arthurian and neo-classical Romance of knighthood, chivalry and courtly love on which Geoffrey Chaucer (1349–?1400) had based his celebrated 'Knight's Tale.'

The influence of the ancient Roman poet Statius (Publius Papinius, *c.*45–96) and the Spanish poet-philosopher Boethius can also be detected, if palely, in Machiavelli's animated images. Both the letter and poem, were, it seems, the result of intense personal disappointments. Indeed, he seems to have conceived them against a Perugian backdrop of dour, inspiring Etruscan stone ruins full of smooth blacks on blacks, and among delicious modern paintings that he probably would have seen in the government buildings and churches: Perugino's frescoes of the Transfiguration, the Adoration of the Shepherds and the Six Heroes of Antiquity had for some years been on display in one of the two Halls of the Merchants, just past the Palazzo Pubblico.

'My fate,' he writes in his letter to Gian Battista, but in a sceptical vein that by now begins to feel familiar, '[shows] me so many and such varied things that I am forced rarely to be surprised or to admit that I have not savoured, either through reading or through experience, the actions of men and their ways of doing things.'[13] Citing two ancient generals, Hannibal and Scipio, the one 'cruel' and 'treacherous,' the other 'pious' and 'loyal,' he argues that they achieved 'identical results' among their hard-to-tame respective populations of Spain and Rome. Differing qualities seem to have made no difference to their accomplishments. The same might also be seen among the best and worst of men. Ethics, character and intelligence must count for nothing, he now remarks, a paradox that he finds excruciating, but that leads him to examine the controversial nature of *Fortuna* herself.

The fiercest of goddesses, as Machiavelli sees her, who presides over all human affairs, those of saints aside, should be understood as consisting of nothing but circumstances and people. These constantly change. They are also unpredictable. The human failure to keep up with the changes, however, or to adapt to them, which he sees as tricky in the short run and impossible in the long – how can anyone constantly alter both his personality and methods? – produces human defeats and victories. One result is that the defeats and victories are not merely unpredictable but inevitable: 'Because times and affairs often change, both in general and in particular, and because men change neither their imaginations nor their ways of doing things accordingly, it turns out that a man has good fortune at one time and bad fortune at another.'[14] Beyond this fixity of human methods and habits, people are also 'shortsighted' and naïve, or 'unwilling to master their own natures': 'it follows that [*Fortuna* seems] fickle, controlling men and keeping them under her yoke,' when it is only shifting circumstances that sabotage human endeavours.

Despite this situation, from a political point of view all may not be lost: 'cruelty, treachery and impiety are effective in providing a new ruler with prestige in that region where human kindness, loyalty and piety have long been common practice.' The opposite will also apply to new rulers in areas where cruelty, treachery and impiety have reigned before. In the face of the relentless alterations of circumstances and people, political success can be achieved, but only by means of contradictory policies. Their success will have nothing to do with ethical considerations, however, as ethics are always irrelevant to success.[15]

His poem about *Fortuna* reveals a similar stress on facts. *Fortuna* 'rules with fury' [regni impetuosamente] and 'often keeps the good beneath her feet; the wicked she raises up; and if ever she promises you anything, never does she keep her promise.' *Fortuna* inhabits the bleakest of palaces. In its rooms, all greatness of spirit, or every humane impulse [Liberalità], 'stands ragged and torn' [stracciata e rotta] while Fraud and Usury gambol and disport themselves.[16] Only the person capable of leaping from wheel to wheel among *Fortuna's* changing events can hope to escape her tyranny, and even he or she will seldom be able do so 'because while you are whirled about by the rim of a wheel that is lucky and good, [*Fortuna*] is wont to reverse its course in mid-circle.'[17]

Thus it is that the secret force [occulta virtù] that rules us manages to defeat our greatest need, which is for flexibility, and so it also happens that *Fortuna's* palace is everywhere decorated 'with [historical] paintings of those triumphs from which she gets most honour,' or works of art that recount the enslavement of the world's peoples by hordes of grim oppressors: the Egyptians, Assyrians, Medes, Persians, Greeks and others. Only he or she lucky enough to die before *Fortuna's* wheel whips round again, plunging him or her to the bottom, may appear to have beaten her at her savage game.

Scribbling away among Julius's military-religious entourage at Perugia, Machiavelli was surely aware of a familiar figure to whom many of his strictures about *Fortuna* might easily have applied: the charming, intelligent thirty-one-year-old Cardinal Giovanni de'Medici, brother of Giuliano, to whom he had addressed a few deferential poems in his mid-twenties, which Lorenzo de'Medici, now long dead, had collected in a book. Lorenzo's son Piero, who as a refugee had fled Florence with the Medici family, had died five years before, in December 1503, drowned in a boating accident on the river Garigliano while fighting for the French against the Spanish.[18] Giovanni was now the custodian of the Medici legacy, along with their hostility to the Florentine Republic, and their desire, of which Machiavelli was also aware, someday to overthrow it and replace it with a government of their own.

# 23

# *The German Enigma*

Among the competing German duchies, as to a lesser extent in France, militarism and culture seemed constantly at war. Their peculiar feud fired the personality of the loosely acknowledged ruler, in Germany's case that of the Holy Roman Emperor-to-Be, who had so far not been elected and whose empire seemed only invisibly to exist, King Maximilian I (1459–1519). It fired as well his fantasy of conquering Italy.

The famous portrait by Albrecht Dürer (plate XI) shows Maximilian about ten years later, or long after Machiavelli had been sent to Germany to meet and negotiate with him, greying amid shoulder-length locks, abstracted, attentive, dollops of melancholy probing his bony Roman nose. Maximilian was delicate and strong, or adrift between paradoxes. Speechless till the age of nine, he became the master of seven languages, among them French, English, Italian, Spanish and Latin. Crazy about hunting, he kept up the hunt long after his exhausted companions and the animals themselves tired of it and fled the forest. A light eater, he died after devouring a mass of melons.

A military innovator *à la* Machiavelli, who established the *Landsknechte*, or the first regular German infantry, in the Netherlands, he was often defeated in battle because of miscalculations of enemy troop strengths. Sympathetic to a fault, he was often poor and spent a lot of time borrowing money. A good marksman, he often ran away from his enemies (Machiavelli reports on his cowardice before the Venetians[1]).

Stories about Maximilian's evasive, aggressive, cash-strapped behaviour helped shape the Faust legend, and even the *Faustbuch* (1587), source of Christopher Marlowe's Elizabethan play. Indecisive, as when he set out to invade Italy and then changed his mind, he vacillated on other occasions, as when he allowed the French Charles VIII to abduct his intended bride, Anne of Brittany, and marry her himself.[2] From early 1507, the nine members of the

Florentine Signoria had (perhaps therefore) grown increasingly worried about Maximilian's plans for Italy.

The French-German rivalry kept yanking the Republic in opposite directions. Leading members of government fretted lest a French incursion in April, which had involved seizing Genoa, might not intensify Maximilian's desire to force the French, Florence's frequent protector, out of Italy altogether. This move might assist his sought-after election as Holy Roman Emperor. It could unite the vast, diffuse Holy Roman Empire. Florentine apprehensions increased as Maximilian convened a diet in Constance, where he pressurized numerous German princes into supplying money and troops for an Italian invasion making a beeline for Rome.[3]

The Florentine quandary – what to do about the German danger – at first led Soderini to propose sending Machiavelli, as ever his own man, to Maximilian's court to evaluate the King's intentions and military capabilities. In the process he would gather intelligence on German resources. These remained unknown. Soderini's proposal was rejected by members of the Signoria, however, and others on the Grand Council, jealous of Machaivelli's, or a mere secretary's, influence as well as suspicious of Soderini himself.

A compromise was agreed – the Ten would have preferred sending Alamanno Salviati and Piero Guicciardini – with the selection as ambassador of Francesco Vettori (1474–1539). His *ottimati* family, with its imposing *palazzo* in the Santo Spirito district not far from the Machiavelli and the Guicciardini *palazzi*, and his family's commitment to a humanist education of their sons, had the right credentials for delicate diplomatic assignments. Vettori set out in June 1507, at the same time as a meeting of the French and Spanish Kings at Savona, not far from French-controlled Genoa. Each King was eager to proclaim his friendship for the other in the face of the German threat.

Machiavelli eventually found himself also put to use, but in August, as Soderini dispatched him to Siena. Here his assignment was to confer with the Pope's legate, Cardinal Bernadino Carvajal of Santa Croce, who was likewise making his uncertain way towards Maximilian's court in the wake of disturbing news that some of the princes attending his diet in Constance had accepted his plans for an Italian invasion.

Every possible manoeuvre would now be set in motion to deter the King, including promoting an arrangement whereby he could be crowned Holy Roman Emperor in Germany instead of Italy, and flattery, with the designation of the Pope's 'Legate [as Machiavelli wrote back] [having the task of distracting] the Emperor with the assurances of the high opinion which his Holiness the Pope entertains of his Majesty.'

The Sienese, who were themselves apprehensive of Germany, showered Julius' emissary with presents for his journey, their hopes rising on the slightest indication of papal support: 'two skinned and dressed calves, six skinned and dressed sheep, 13 sacks of grain, … 12 barrels of wine, nine barrels of fowls (six pairs each), four barrels of young geese (six pairs each), … 14 dishes of seafish, 12 pairs of white wax torches, … [and] 24 marchpanes [or fruit-cakes].' Luxuries complemented their dreams of German restraint.[4] It is unknown whether these gifts eased the Cardinal's rocky, snowy path into the Swiss-German north. As it became evident that his exertions would be insufficient to forestall an invasion, Machiavelli was also sent on to Germany, on 25 December. Riding via Constance in a last ditch effort to see whether mere money, or a 50,000-ducat bribe – actually a payoff – might settle the fears of the Signoria, he spent two isolated weeks hurrying through forests whose darkness seemed unrelieved.

The long ride was taxing, and the point of it questionable, as often since the start of his diplomatic career. By the time he arrived in Botzen in the Tyrolean Alps on 11 January, he had already spent the 110 ducats allotted for his trip by the Signoria. To his relief, he found Vettori living in luxury at the German court.

Beyond this attractive fact, and because some princes had refused to commit themselves to the King's Italian campaign, and with the Swiss unhappy about going to war with France (they eventually dispatched 6,000 troops to assist the French), the prospect of avoiding an invasion seemed at least alive. 'You want to [find out] in two hours,' Machiavelli was told over dinner by one Monsignore de Disviri, an ambassador of the Duke of Savoy, 'what I have not been able to learn in many months.' Disviri noted the Emperor's obsession with keeping his invasion cards close to his chest: 'This nation is very discreet, and the Emperor observes the greatest secrecy in everything he does; if he but changes his lodgings, he sends his cook only after he has himself been for an hour on the way, so that no one may know where he is going.'[5]

The fluid situation might still have its advantages as it offered Machiavelli time to delve into the habits of the Swiss and the Germans. Some bits of what he learned were military ('there must be some four thousand infantry and a thousand horse fit for service'), others diplomatic, still others cultural and political. He entertained the Signoria with his detailed account of the political organization of the Swiss into cantons, a distributive system of shared power not readily understood in more reserved Italian political circles. He transmitted his discoveries in long communiqués, whose writing he shared with Vettori, even to alternating paragraphs as the two began to become friends.

His sweeping insights into Germany-*cum*-Austria, moreover, indicated a growing, almost encyclopedic desire to analyse unfamiliar societies. He stayed at Maximilian's court for over six months, or until mid-June. After returning to Florence, he wrote up a 'Second Report on the Affairs of Germany.' Its aim was to offer his colleagues a reliable summary of the attitudes and customs typical of their likely northern enemies:

> The Germans are rich … because they live as if they were poor; for they neither build, nor dress, nor furnish their houses expensively. It is enough for them to have plenty of bread and meat, and to have a stove behind which they take refuge from the cold… . Everyone lives according to his rank … . No money leaves their country, as the people are content with what their country produces; and thus they enjoy their rough and free life, and will not enlist to go to war, unless they are overpaid.[6]

By now he had also picked up a great deal on the 'great wealth' of the Germans, or the sort of information important to evaluating their military efficiency, and on Maximilian's personal wealth, which he felt 'free to use as he pleases,' as in going to war: 'The power of Germany cannot be doubted by anyone, for she has abundant population, wealth and armies.' German frugality, he observed, if combined with the country's abundant stocks of weapons and formidable quantities of troops regularly trained and exercised, must keep the King's readiness for battle at a high pitch. A significant number of so-called German 'free cities,' however, could confront the King with a tactical problem. They might offer tacit support to Florence's desire for peace: the ambitions of the German free cities centred less on conquest than on preserving commercial relations, which yielded them sizeable profits from their trade with Italy.[7]

Remarkably, Machiavelli produced each of his reports on the basis of the skimpiest acquaintanceship with German-speaking peoples. At most he had visited a few Swiss and German towns. His claims seem entirely sound, however, a quality probably due to his having read, if not pored over, Caesar and Tacitus, whose historical and social accounts, acting as models, even to influencing his style, lay in providing him with a suave, almost surgical manner of arriving at tenable social generalizations by showing him how to cut away everything superfluous. The Roman approach he naturally combined with his own intuitions, tested against meetings with diplomats, other officials and non-government people, and his trained empirical principles. Together, they let him obtain a thorough cultural understanding, often on the basis of mere shreds of evidence.

Nor, as the German invasion clouds closed in, could it fairly have been said that his and Vettori's bargaining with Maximilian was useless. At first, their negotiations served as a bare bones means of delaying the execution of the King's plans. Later, once these plans were abandoned, the Florentines might have been seen as instrumental in their scuttling.

Machiavelli was authorized to appease Maximilian's territorial appetites with 50,000 ducats. These were to be paid in installments starting at 30,000, though the Signoria later raised the sum to 60,000.[8] Ever evasive, however, the Emperor at first rejected the amount as trivial, but ran into problems as he failed to attract the strong German support that he needed from his diet at Constance. Worse, his poorly organized invasion – typical of his indecisiveness – led to victories, defeats and routs by the Venetians. In March 1508, for instance, lured into a valley 'in hopes of plunder,' some 'thirteen hundred of [his German] infantry, under [the] command of a reckless captain,' were attacked from above by a local population hurling stones, and next surrounded by 6,000 Venetian cavalry and infantry, who killed over a thousand of them.[9]

The King's military competence thus seemed scarcely a harbinger of success. Certainly it would never match the nimble brilliance of Cesare Borgia, who, as Machiavelli knew, had himself met with catastrophe just a year earlier. Cesare had skidded from freedom into disaster. After a few Castilian noblemen finally abetted his escape from Medina del Campo in 1506, he rushed off to Navarre. There he appeared to many who recalled his ruthlessness as 'the devil' incarnate. He had nourished hopes of reclaiming his privileges under Louis XII, but now discovered that his French estates had been expropriated and that his stolen money, invested with Genoese bankers, had itself been stolen at the behest of Pope Julius.

As was his wont, he overreached himself, though Machiavelli's admiration of his insights into the duplicity of princely life remained unaffected. Galloping ahead of a body of troops handed over to him on 11 March 1507, he seized the town of Larraga and then dashed into a follow-up battle before the castle at Viana, which he tried to seize as well. Here he found himself isolated in a ravine. A couple of enemy cavalrymen, whom he had been pursuing, swung back on him, flung him from his horse and killed him. Extracted from his armour and clothes, and castrated, his naked body was left bleeding under a rock. News of Cesare's death threw his sister Lucrezia into an insane grief. She 'tortur[ed] herself with calling his name night and day.' Her life seemed, if not over, at least ruined, perhaps mostly because whatever her brother's misjudgements, and as if in a horrible contradiction of his amazing abilities, at the time of his death he was just thirty-one.[10]

Maximilian's Italian campaign, by comparison, ended at least for the moment on a purely embarrassing note: a three-year truce that he felt forced into signing with the Venetians, in June 1508. For Machiavelli the German reversal, which proved temporary, had come none too soon. In May, according to Vettori, he 'met with an accident [to his health].' It seemed 'serious' and may have been gallstones, though in the terminology of the day, as Vettori observed, it was described as 'gross humours in the blood.' Machiavelli's 'malady,' as he himself put it, forced his return to Florence for medical treatment.[11]

I. Santi di Tito (1536–1603): Portrait of Machiavelli (author's photo)

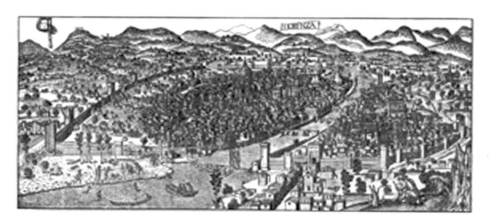

II. Florence c.1480–90 (author's photo collection)

III. Inside image (1896; neg.
19122) of a room in the Machiavelli
palazzo (©V&A Images/Victoria
and Albert Museum, London)

IV. Duke Federico da Montefeltro and his Son
Guido (Bridgeman Art Library)

V. The Excution of Savonarola (Bridgeman Art Library)

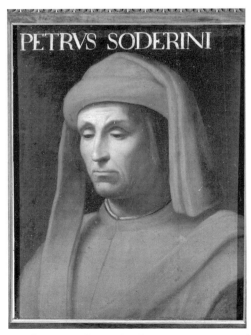

VI. Portrait of Piero Soderini (Scala/Art Resource NY)

VII.  Portrait of Caterina Sforza
(Scala/Art Resource NY)

VIII.  Portrait of Cesare Borgia
(Bridgeman Art Library)

IX.  After Leonardo da Vinci (Peter Paul Rubens):
The Battle of Anghiari (Bridgeman Art Library)

X.  After Michelangelo (Aristotile da Sangallo): The Battle of Cascina, or Soldiers
Bathing (©Collection of the Earl of Leicester; Bridgeman Art Library)

Imperator Caefar Diuus Maximilianus
Pius Felix Augustus

XI.  Albrecht Dürer: The Emperor Maximilian (author's photo)

XII. Sant'Andrea in Percussina (author's photo)

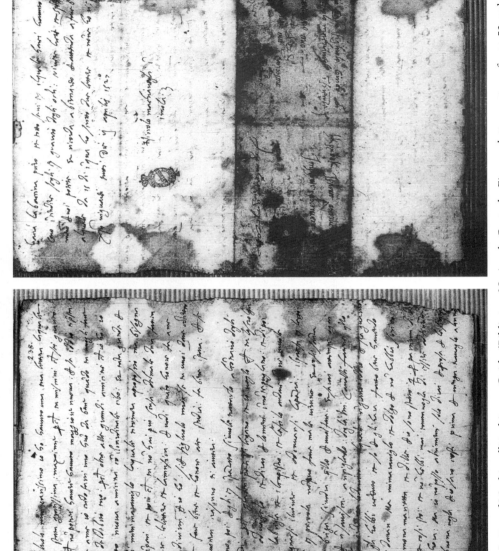

XIII. Letter of Machiavelli to his son Guido (Biblioteca Nazionale Centrale, Firenze; lettera autografa, no.53, vol. 1) (See pp.288–9.)

# 24

# *Victory at Pisa*

The deep winter of the next year, or just nine months later, discovered him on the verge of what looked like his greatest professional triumph. At first it did not seem that way. Now fully recovered and acting as chancellor of the Nine, he had been asked to take command of the citizen militia during the previous summer. He had deftly used it in attacks on Pisan farms, houses and soldiers, right up to the damaged walls of Pisa itself. These new assaults had the blessing of the Signoria and a Florentine population eager as never before to put an end to the long rebellion and its draining of the Republic's wealth. His campaign had begun on 21 August, as he mustered out battalions of enlisted men from San Miniato and Pescia.

He had showed no hesitation about accompanying his men on their daily raids, in setting up ambushes and even joining the fighting, as indicated by a curt note of 20 February from his encampment beside a mill at Quosi, on the Arno just below Pisa: 'We are here ... to watch whether any new convoy of boats is attempting to come in [to relieve the city], and to prevent it, as we have done the others.'[1]

His strategy was deliberately provocative. Its aim was further to isolate the tower-dominated city by cutting it off from efforts by ship to break what was becoming a vice-like Florentine siege. This involved hundreds of troops, and hammering into the river-bed brass-joined, brass-supported wooden piles to form a palisade. The plan moved efficiently ahead, and its success was decisive. If the King of France objected to so harsh a method, as he saw it, of carrying on the war, or openly attempting to starve the Pisans into submission, they themselves soon perceived the pointlessness in continuing.

Acts of barbarism implicated the populations on both sides. On 20 January, Florence signed a three-year pact with Lucca, denying Pisa any assistance. In April, the Republic's troops captured sixty horses, along with a group of men attempting to smuggle Luccan corn at the Pisan gates. Sixty were killed, but fifty-four, taken prisoner and bound by a rope, were dragged back to Florence and paraded before a rejoicing crowd.[2]

In April also, a false Pisan peace offer led to an ambush of Republican soldiers at the city walls. A score or more were slaughtered by cannon fire. Captured Pisan troops held in Florence's *Stinche* prison were shown off in the public stocks 'because we heard the Pisans had done the same to ours.' Pisan protests of peaceful intentions, and repeated proposals to negotiate, were met with suspicion.

In March, Machiavelli immersed himself in this back-and-forth war-peace routine as the Pisans applied to Jacopo d'Appiano of Piombino, his acquaintance from early negotiating days, to represent them. The blockade was already producing dire effects. Ever dubious, the Ten of War ordered Machiavelli out of his camp at Pisa to Piombino to meet Jacopo and other Pisan representatives, but with discouraging results: 'I left ... camp on Monday, and arrived here at Piombino yesterday, ... and half an hour later I called upon his Lordship.' Jacopo introduced him to the Pisans, but Machiavelli soon realized that their idea of a settlement was no more than a joke: '[The Signoria, they proposed,] should leave them all within the walls of Pisa, and take for [them]selves all the remainder of their dominion; ... they [said that they] considered it a great gift for [the Signoria] to obtain a just title to so much as [they] had never possessed before.'

He found their announcement an insulting waste of his time. He told them so, told Jacopo that he was being made fun of ('It must be evident to your Lordship that these gentlemen are merely laughing at you') and returned to his camp and men, or to what in some ways had become a personal war.[3] In April the Signoria expressed anxiety about his safety. They tried to convince him to accept reassignment, but he replied, 'I am aware that [a] post [at Cascina] would expose me to less danger and fatigue, but if I wanted to avoid danger and fatigue I should not have left Florence.'

His eagerness to see the war through had become unshakable: 'Here I can make myself useful, but [there] I should not be good for anything, and should die of sheer desperation.'[4] His reply was sent from the camp at Mezzana, but the needs of command now saw him shift from camp to camp – there were three – each crowded and open to the winds, if made lively at night by soldiers singing among their tent-lined alleys. He organized the arrival of new troops in their hundreds, called strategy sessions, prepared counter-attacks against skirmishes and did his best to pay the men on time and resupply them, mostly via 'the [local] government shops' controlling the 'sale of bread.' Shortages provoked riots. Loaves came from the nearby commune of Val di Nievole, but as he told the Signoria in May, 'I have myself experienced the way these communes act, sending large [quantities] one day and nothing the next.'

On 20 May, however, an improvement seemed to drop out of the blue. Four Pisan emissaries, who seemed earnest enough about peace, rode into the camp at Val Serchio. Their arrival led the three Commissioners General there to report that 'our discussion was pretty long, and … it may well be that, whether they come here or proceed to Florence to settle the details, a satisfactory result will be reached.' The fifteen-year-old war, with its unpredictable battles, might be tilting towards an end after all, and in a manner welcome to the Republic. A few days later, on 1 June, the 'country people,' or farmers living near the city, also sued for peace: 'We learn,' wrote the Commissioners, 'that they really cannot hold out any longer, and if the hope of peace were extinguished, one half of the inhabitants of Pisa would die of hunger.'[5]

A truce now seemed likely, and travelling with a few Pisan representatives, as he was bidden, and under guard, Machiavelli left for Florence. On 4 June he joined an assembly of officials for the signing of Pisan articles of surrender, placing his name just below that of the Republic's First Secretary, Marcello Virgilio. As he did so, and in the presence of the Republic's Ten of War, a dove, at once taken by many as prophetic of better days to come, flew in through an open door of the Palazzo della Signoria, where everyone had gathered. It fluttered about their heads.

This happened at ten in the morning, and 'as if by a miracle,' or so Landucci recalled, it frisked 'all round the [interior] court … and dashing against the wall, fell at [their] feet.… . [Their] *Proposto* [foreman] picked it up but could not hold it, only some feathers remaining in his hand. [It] was thought a good omen, especially as it was at this hour that the Pisans had ratified the agreement – a sign that it was reality, and that an end had been put to so much evil.'[6]

The dove might have been taken as miraculous for another reason, that it reminded them of the mechanical doves, 'symbolic of the Holy Spirit,' which on the Saturday of Passion Week and ever since the twelfth century had flown on wires running across the Carroccio to the Cantonata dei Pazzi and at the *Duomo*. Anyone aware of how Florence celebrated Easter might well have thought that the city had entered a blessed moment.

On that Friday too, or 8 June, in the company of the three Florentine commissioners, plus a thousand men selected from his own battalions, Machiavelli watched as the Pisan gates were flung open, and actually entered the city. The war was over. The previous days had in fact seen it dissolve into the topsy-turvy confusion not unusual at the end of many wars. Sides seemed switched about as the defeated pushed into the camps of their conquerors, seeking relief from their hunger and offering the hand of friendship.

Along the streets, work on rebuilding the bombarded walls, houses, *piazze* and towers had already begun. Shops reopened. In Florence, even if he was not present and not officially lauded, Machiavelli was congratulated, along with other leaders, on what everyone took to be a solid military success:

> It is not possible to express how much delight, how much jubilation and joy [Agostino Vespucci wrote him on 8 June], all the people here have taken in the news of the recovery of that city of Pisa; in some measure every man has gone mad with exultation; there are bonfires all over the city, though it is not yet three in the afternoon.... . *If I did not think it would make you too proud, I should dare say that you with your battalions accomplished so much good work that, not by delaying but by speeding up, you restored the affairs of Florence.*[7]

Unofficial appreciations of Machiavelli's part in the Pisan victory were touted everywhere. As one of the commissioners at Pisa, Filippo Casavecchia, a friend and colleague, wrote to him on 17 June, 'I wish you a thousand benefits from the acquisition of that noble city [Pisa], for truly it can be said that your person was cause of it to a very great extent.' Filippo had been one of the first to appreciate the importance to the victory of Machiavelli's citizen militia: 'Every day I discover you to be a greater prophet than the Hebrews or any other nation ever had.' He added that his own time might now best be spent in a spot of fishing near his home in Barga: 'I am saving you a ditch full of trout and a wine [such as] you never tasted.... . [A] fishing party is arranged for the end of the month, more or less, whenever you come.' Filippo's insistence on a country vacation coupled with fishing surely caught Machiavelli's eye: 'Please, Niccolò, come quickly and send me or rather write me a couple of lines about where you are.'[8]

Apparently he did so, and over the next five months, or till 10 November, when he was again sent out on a mission, but now to Mantua with 10,000 ducats to pay Maximilian for abandoning any temptation to interfere in the Pisan surrender, he stayed in Florence, where he returned to more mundane office work. Perhaps it was now, or as the hush of peace descended on an optimistic diplomatic moment, and as the Venetians languished in semi-idle weakness, that he turned to a more frivolous pursuit. It is not known just when he produced his satirical piece of fluff, 'Rules for an Elegant Social Circle.' It is likely that he wrote it during these months (a reference in it to Michelangelo's *David* sets its composition to at least after 1504).

What also seems clear is that even as momentous battles erupted across northern Italy, in some broad sense the international mood had grown more receptive to satire. Across prosperous stretches of western, northern and central Europe – and detectably so in Italy – a fresh stew of scepticism, mischief and jokiness, of punning and even publishing catalogues of ironic obscenities, was coming to a boil. One inspiration for this shift in taste lay in the career of the humanist Italian scholar-writer Poggio Bracciolini, discoverer of Lucretius' *De rerum natura*. Some thirty years earlier, in 1474, he had brought out a scruffy, scatological prose collection, the *Facetiae*, a gaggle of rollicking tales and anecdotes that he had turned into a jest book.

The *Facetiae* was widely imitated. It influenced the unknown author of the tales of Till Eulenspiegel [or Owlglass], the unprincipled, free-seeming German rogue whose wanderings and adventures were compiled in 1500 at the liberal press of Johannes Grüninger of Strasbourg. Their appearance, perhaps in 1508, in a book packed with woodcuts by Hans Baldung-Grien, one of Albrecht Dürer's most brilliant pupils, and other good artists, led Eulenspiegel to begin to establish himself in his amazing career as Germany's most famous (or notorious) folk anti-hero, a success which continues into the present century through almost four hundred editions in dozens of languages.[9]

In France, François Rabelais (1490–1553) was then twenty; in England, Thomas More (1478–1535) thirty-one. Neither had yet delighted his world with the uproarious pages that would soon make his reputation. As Machiavelli's 'Rules' with its wry insults implies, however, a novel satirical spirit of defiance and social criticism had begun to wash over a number of European societies. The 'Rules' nonetheless scarcely represents Machiavelli's best work: delicate, cagey and experimental, it is perhaps most accurately understood as exposing the hypocrisy of an upper-crust Florentine world along with the cruelties twisting beneath it.

As he also implies, the 'Rules' is pure entertainment: 'A circle of ladies and gentlemen' (he starts off) '[gathers] for soirées where they often [do] amusing things, but often dull things as well.' The 'elegant' circle's passion for pleasure

requires discipline, if not regulation, which a single 'quick-witted' member –
Machiavelli himself – plans to provide.[10]

Anyone disobeying his rules will pay the piper, or so his modest proposal
intimates, while the rules themselves were meant to expose the dishonesty of
the circle, to wit: 'Any gentleman or lady who does not within a day broadcast
everything said or done at one of the soirées will be punished in the following
manner: A lady transgressor will have her slippers nailed in a prominent place
for all to see, with a note bearing her name [and presumably revealing her foot-
stains]; a gentleman transgressor will find his hose hung prominently inside
out for all to see.' The hint at excremental stains instances an early literary use
of excrement as a satirical weapon, a device later deployed in the 'shittier' tales
of Till Eulenspiegel, and later still in Swift's *Gulliver's Travels* and his *Wonderful
Wonder of Wonders, or An Accurate Description of the Birth, Education, Manner
of Living, Religion, Politics, Learning, etc. of Mine A-se* (1720).

As with any satire worth its salt, the 'Rules' pulls no punches. It moves tartly
from irony into ridicule into contempt amid dashes of excrement and nausea.
What is unclear, and probably should not be assumed, is that the author saw his
larger social world as moving along the same path.

# 25

# A Government Overthrown

Seldom had the fortunes of Soderini, Machiavelli and the Republic looked so prosperous. Pisa's reabsorption into Republican territory stimulated public confidence. The defeat of Venice back in May by the League of Cambrai, which had been formed in the spring of 1509 between the French King and the German Maximilian, and later, reluctantly, the Vatican, bolstered a broad conviction, at least in the Grand Council (Soderini almost alone remained sceptical), that any threat to the Republic's security could for the moment be dismissed.[1]

Florence still counted on Louis XII for protection. Relations between the French King and the Pope, as between Florence and the Pope, continued amiable. If Maximilian, a late-comer to the Venetian-Pisan defeat, had to be paid off at the insistence of the nervous French to the tune of an extravagant 40,000 ducats, the second installment of which, or some 10,000, would come due in Mantua in November, Machiavelli could deliver it himself. He could also use the journey, which the Signoria asked him to extend to Verona, as an opportunity to gather intelligence on the ability of the Venetians to restart the war.

The Venetian chances seemed minimal, or at least uncertain. From the Florentine point of view they felt unthreatening. Few in Florence seem to have paid much attention to another uncertainty, which might have seemed less inconsequential: the ambition of Giovanni de'Medici to overthrow Soderini and the Republican government and restore his family to power. Ever the playboy in cardinal's robes, despite his respectable classical education, he had perfected the reckless manners, sly aggressiveness and corpulence of a fop indifferent to power. Often he allowed himself to appear interested mostly in food, sex, jokes and clothes. His conspiratorial intentions, however, humming a bit like the malarial mosquitoes of Tuscany in his peaceful-seeming brain, might still have been worth noticing.

In late November Machiavelli delivered the Republic's ducats intended as
a payment to Maximilian's agent in Mantua. By the twenty-second, he had
reached Verona,[2] where he took note of the hostility of citizens astonished at the
Venetian defeat: 'the citizens and the populace are altogether [pro-]Venetian'.
He submitted a report on Verona's garrison and additional troops ('the garrison
consists of German infantry' – not more than a thousand men – as well as
Spanish, Italian, Burgundian and French cavalry and foot-soldiers), and picked
up information on Venetian units roaming and pillaging not far from the city:
'[their] soldiers ... are occupying themselves with plundering and ravaging
the country around, and we see and hear daily of the most unexampled and
extraordinary things, so that the minds of the country people are filled with a
desire for death and vengeance'.[3]

These professional duties completed, he whiled away his autumn hours
'dream[ing] up diatribes that I write to the Ten' and 'having a good time.' Often
he seemed to drift into nonsense: 'I have no letter to the [E]mperor, so ... I
might be arrested as a spy.' By 8 December he had begun to make up nonsense,
or to compose and send off to Francesco Guicciardini's brother, Luigi (1478–
1551), the future politician and historian, a fantasy letter amounting to a minor
satirical masterpiece. Certainly it seemed a foray in prose far more complex
than his earlier 'Rules.' On the surface, it describes his encounter in Verona with
a prostitute a few days before, or so he says. An impression of ulterior motives,
however, hovers over the letter from its first disarming phrases: 'Hell's bells,
Luigi, see how Fortune hands out to mankind different results under similar
circumstances.'[4] This idea sounds familiar, if not identical to the theme of his
earlier letter on *Fortuna* to Soderini's nephew, though he is writing in response
to a playful note (since lost) of Luigi's, in which he revels in his enthusiasm
for 'fucking' again a woman whom he has just 'fucked': 'Why you had hardly
finished fucking your woman before you wanted another fuck, and you wanted
to take another turn at it.'

Machiavelli's response to Luigi's challenge veers off unexpectedly, however,
into a plot, characters (including himself) and a journalistically sensational or
at least questionable story, combined with scoops of rich, suspicious atmos-
pherics and exaggerated language. The implication is that some preposterous,
teasing game must be afoot:

> But as for me, why I had been here three days, losing my determination because of
> conjugal famine, when I came across an old woman who launders my shirts; the house

she lives in is more than half underground; the only light you see in it enters through the door.[5]

Implausibly, or so he hints, he was led into what seemed a shabby, cave-like stage set – what else could this odd place be? – where his 'laundress' offered to show him a shirt that she hoped he would buy:

So, naïve prick that I am, I believed her and went in; once inside, I made out in the gloom a woman cowering in a corner affecting modesty with a towel half over her head and face. The old slut took me by the hand and led me over to her, saying, 'This is the shirt that I wanted to sell you, but I'd like you to try it on first and pay me afterwards.'

His reaction to her brazen invitation, especially as the 'old bawd' quickly abandoned him, was one of 'terror.' He plunged in anyway, though, or forged lustily ahead, even as he found the 'shirt's' 'thighs flabby and her cunt damp … her breath stank a bit.' Frustration rankled against his awareness of the night-marish circumstances and the dinginess of the encounter. Any reader half as alert as the educated Luigi, moreover, will surely have sensed by this time a developing tone of self-mockery.

If it seems a bit too early to spot the parody implicit in the underground room's darkness, in which the 'only light' came in at the door, which was closed, a fine mist of eeriness and the enforced urgency suffusing his startled feelings may signal the meaning of an absurd-seeming mystery in which he found himself having sex with an unknown, invisible woman: that in some unclear if allegorical way he had stumbled into a perverse sexual version of Plato's philosophical cave, in which what is real cannot be seen except as a set of shadows reflected on a wall.

Here too may be why, once he was done with her, he at once seized the initiative, though his grim-hollow mood, or silent jeering – but at whom, or what? – enveloped his as well as the reader's descent into what may by now be understood as an ironic, fulsome horror:

Feeling like taking a look at the merchandise, I took a piece of burning wood and lit a lamp that was above it; but the light was hardly lit before it almost fell out of my hands. Ugh! I nearly dropped dead on the spot, that woman was so ugly.[6]

Too ugly to be real, one may well imagine, except as a quasi-literary figure ladled out of some soupy myth or folktale: too ugly as well, amid the torrent of

sordid details that he now dishes out about her, to be less than satirically nauseating: 'a tuft of hair, part white, part black, ... although the crown of her head
was bald (thanks to the baldness one could make out a few lice promenading
about)'; 'in the centre of her tiny, wrinkled head ... a fiery scar'; 'at the end of
each eyebrow ... a nosegay of nits'; 'one eye looked up, the other down, and one
was larger than the other.'

She had 'no eyelashes,' and a 'turned-up nose stuck low down on her head' –
in the style, one notices, of some *papier mâché* jester's face leering through the
crowd on a Florentine festival day, or some Pinocchio-type slaloming past at a
masquerade ball – even as 'one of her nostrils was sliced open and full of snot.'

His excursion into a realm of exaggeration and grotesque parody seems
more than a little accented by the group of well-known folktale motifs that
cluster about her and the roles she plays: that of the old lover taken for young,
of the deceptive seductress and (though the wrong way round) of the loathly
hag transformed, as in Chaucer's 'Wife of Bath's Tale'. Even his story-telling
technique, with its obscene reversals, imitates Poggio in his *Facetiae*, Boccaccio
in the *Decameron* and Apuleius in his *Metamorphoses* (or *The Golden Ass*), and
perhaps most tellingly Apuleius's recasting of an ancient Roman folktale in
which an old witch is taken for a young wife.[7]

Echoes of Juvenal's second-century Roman satires, linking sex with vomit,
ripple through what follows as he builds to an hilarious, horrible dénouement:

> Her mouth resembled Lorenzo de'Medici's [he seems unable to resist political caricature
> amid the sexual frippery], but it was twisted to one side, and from that side drool was
> oozing, because, since she was toothless, she could not hold back her saliva.... As soon
> as she opened her mouth, she exuded such a stench on her breath that my eyes and
> nose, twin portals to the most delicate of the senses, felt assaulted by this stench and
> my stomach became so indignant that it was unable to tolerate this outrage: it started
> to rebel, then it did rebel, so that I threw up all over her.[8]

His hapless gushing, or perhaps taunted baptismal dousing, completes what, it
may by now be agreed, becomes a voluptuous tour de force, even as it reveals
that the whole disease-shot story, which at first seems aimed at Luigi, is directed
past his friend and at himself.

Few doubts may seem to persist, in other words, that the target of all his
vituperative nonsense is not some disfigured female effigy, or fictional 'shirt,' or
even a Pandora's box chamber of Platonic darkness, but his own propensity for

sexual self-delusion, and beyond it, the glamorizing ruin of fantasies that often accompany all sorts of sexual appetites. A frivolous fuss in a false Platonic cave demolishes both his egotism and self-flattery.

Satire here also becomes something new. In the strong sense, Machiavelli reinvents its methods, redesigning it not so much as a super-enlarged imitation of life as an indictment of the monstrous tendencies of self-deceptive, frustrated passions. These are allowed to shade into each other, and to rise into a soufflé of distortions unimpeded by actual experience, or into slapstick comedy based on inner terrors and compulsions. At the same time, the tale swivels under its slew of classical motifs. It acquires stature and impressiveness. His letter seems larded with a dark, mad grandeur. All these qualities may already have begun to recommend themselves as novel aids in the invention of literature, or the release of intense, modern self-consciousness.

Perhaps for this reason – that he has been watching himself call his own bluff – he feels entitled to round off the cheeky parable by remarking, 'I shall stake my birth in heaven that as long as I am in Lombardy I'll be damned if I think I shall get horny again,' and 'I no longer need fear experiencing so much disgust.'

Perhaps too it was no coincidence that his life itself now seemed rife with scandal. Over the previous several days, envy and ambition, whether focused on him and deflected, or nurtured in secret and brushed aside, had begun to worry some of his closest friends, who were zealous to protect him. A week or two before his adventure with the prostitute of darkness, or his invention of it, damaging rumours had begun to circulate about him in Florence. He had just composed and sent off to Luigi another scathing satirical piece, or as he self-deprecatingly describes it, a bit of 'doggerel' (*cantafavola*), a poem in terza rima of 187 lines (it has an extra line), *Dell'Ambizione* (On Ambition).

To consider this exciting if unfunny poem first, because it sets the stage for the more slanderous weather to come: it seems meant as a companion-piece to his poem *On Fortuna*. If the earlier poem (they are also similar in length) explores how changing people and circumstances may become a source of human failure and success, his *Dell'Ambizione* digs into a similar conundrum of rise and fall, but inwardly, or as a problem of the soul, and masterfully, with the drama more intimately framed:

Oh how many times, while the father holds his son tight in his arms, a single stab pierces the breasts of both!//Another abandons his ancestral home, accusing the cruel and ungrateful gods, and with his children overwhelmed by sorrow.//Oh, strange events such as have never happened before in the world! Every day so many children are born by sword cuts to the womb.//To her daughter, trumped by sorrow, the mother says, 'For what miserable marriage, for what a cruel husband have I kept you!'//Filthy with blood are the ditches and streams, packed with heads, legs, arms, and other members gashed and severed.//Birds of prey, wild beasts, dogs have now become their family tombs – Oh tombs repulsive, terrible and unnatural! (ll 136–53)[9]

The odd springiness amid the tormented images enables them to leap beyond themselves into ghastly stylistic pleasures, or past morbidity into a poetry of shock. The pain described may be great, but its language streams with a serene control, or an accuracy untrammelled by abhorrence. Crimes are rendered not less horrible but more literary, which is to say more comprehensible amid accurate if disturbing metaphors.

Ambition itself is laid bare not so much as a personal drive as a force in the universe. It may be as old as Eden, the rebellion of Adam and Eve and the first murder – 'When man was born into the world, [Ambition and Avarice were born too]' – but it has been relocated to the human mind and heart.[10] Minds, hearts and souls are seen as containing the protean, elemental powers of destruction and creation: they have become darkness and light, Shiva-like pulsations of angels and demons. Some can resist their seductions, but none their temptations. Even the holiest men and women may aspire to holiness, and so any aspiration, even to holiness, can be seen as secreting the poison of ambition and infecting the thoughts of the pious. Human desires are betrayed if not corroded from within.

As he worked on this poem, an unidentified masked man accompanied by 'two witnesses' visited the home of a notary of 'the Protectors of the Law,' or so Biagio Buonaccorsi wrote him from Florence on 28 December.[11] The man declared that as Machiavelli's father Bernardo had been disreputable – his offence was not specified – 'you can in no way exercise the office that you hold.' Bernardo's crime had perhaps been indebtedness – that he had been *a specchio* – a serious problem in the Republic: it would indeed have denied his son any chance to hold a civil appointment: whether inherited or not, indebtedness ranked as a disgrace in the eyes of the law.

Biagio was worried, though he seems to have been a jittery type anyway ('do not go off and assume that I am making the worst of things'). He guessed that

Machiavelli might laugh the whole thing off ('do not make fun of it and do not neglect it'). He was already trying to mitigate the possible legal consequences for his friend, and by association himself. 'The law is as favourable as can be,' he agreed, but 'the nature of the times' and the 'great number' of people gossiping about 'your case' ('your adversaries are numerous and will stop at nothing') proved that the whole shabby business had already become common public knowledge, and 'everywhere, even in the whorehouses.'

Faced with their possible 'ruin,' Biagio added, the best thing for the moment would be that he remain in Verona, 'and not return here for anything': the winds of libel were more likely to blow over 'if you are not here than if you are.'[12] In fact they blew over quickly, or at least Machiavelli was back in Florence by 2 January. The incident nonetheless reveals an aspect of his vulnerability just then, in which a wounded ghost from his past could tangle viciously with jealous hatred. Omens might have been divined in the unpleasant drama – Biagio thought he had spotted them – though they were to some extent glossed over.

Machiavelli had begun to stay away for months at a time in any case, at first on assignment to recruit new troops, including cavalry, and later to promote Florentine interests in France as a fresh spill of political darkness blotted the shifting military horizon.

At the moment, the most worrisome manipulator of armies, hostilities, pent-up ambitions and power was Julius II. His actions threatened the Republic's quasi-democratic future. Alliances subsided into betrayals. Anxiety displaced opportunities for organized policies. Despite his devotion to art, as exemplified by his encouraging Michelangelo and commissioning the Sistine Chapel, he remained adamant about satisfying the two ambitions dearest to him from his earliest days as Pope: the elimination of foreign troops from Italian soil, and an expansion of Church power.

The defeat of Venice, which he had taken in hand with Louis XII and Maximilian, seemed to provide a crowbar by which to gratify his yearnings: the Venetians themselves. With their strengths now adjustable to his touch – if cultivated, they might support his interests in decisive ways – he conceived a strategy which might enable him to pry loose from Italy both of his erstwhile allies, the French under Louis and the Germans under Maximilian, though inklings of his intentions would inevitably cause unease among the Florentines.

As ever, the Republic looked to a strong French presence in Italy as a safeguard against outside threats. As before too, the Signoria hoped that money and flattery would prop up the flimsiest military arrangements. Machiavelli's third mission to the French court, therefore, which had by now moved back to Lyons and was set to move on to the cliff-high royal castle at Blois, had as its purpose the protection of the venerable Florentine-French connection. His journey to France in June 1510 was organized to reinforce it, preferably without weakening the Republic's equally important papal relationship.

Ominously, however, a pro-Medici faction in Florence, comprised of *ottimati* and other disaffected citizens, was becoming more restive. A group of semi-opportunists, they and their followers had never been exiled, only repressed. A quest of vengeance, reaching back to the Savonarolan revolution of more than a decade earlier and the expulsion of Piero de'Medici and his family, coincided with Julius's intentions. The upshot was that, within the city and without, sensitive political and military sore spots had become more tender. Irritating this condition, as Francesco Guicciardini was to observe a few years later, were the idiosyncrasies of the rulers themselves. If Maximilian seemed 'perplexed,' Julius seemed 'possessed of jealousy,' or embittered over the possibility that the German Emperor might manage to become 'Lord of Verona.'

Julius's best bet seemed to lie in stimulating the tacit hostility between the French and English under Henry VIII. To push his intentions forward, he invited the leading officials of Venice, including their ambassador, to the Vatican. In these holiest of surroundings he welcomed their prostration before him 'in [his] pontifical Chair near the Brazen Gate, ... [among] the Body of Cardinals and a great number of Prelates.' He absolved them of venal sins, lifted an interdict which had secured his triumph over them several months earlier, herded them back into the Church, and so ushered the entire Venetian governing class into abetting his power-seizing plans for northern Italy.[13]

By default Machiavelli became the Signoria's only representative in France. Given these complicated Vatican pirouettes, he could do little but watch as his mission turned into a juggling act of evasiveness and promises of Florentine financial assistance. It seemed doubtful whether the Republic could buy or fight its way out of this latest threat to its independence. A rumour had also begun to circulate that Julius was eager to return Giovanni de'Medici to Florence, thereby lopping off French support for the Republic. A pro-Medici, pro-Vatican faction within the city could prove more useful to his ambitions than a military assault.

Machiavelli arrived in Lyons on 7 July, in the wake of the death on 25 May of Cardinal Amboise, Archbishop of Rouen, who had been his sympathetic contact in France during his previous missions. He called on the Cardinal's presumptive successor, General Florimond de Robertet, secretary to Kings Charles VIII and Louis and treasurer of France. He approached Robertet 'with all the ceremony and politeness due to so good a friend of our republic.'

Almost at once, too, Machiavelli met with the King, who expressed a need to 'know who are my friends and who are my enemies.' Persuading him of the Signoria's friendship lay at the heart his mission, but given the King's dread of Julius's anti-French motives, and his awareness of the Republic's desire to maintain good relations with Rome, he craved 'more positive assurance.' This over the next few days, and with the assistance of his colleagues in Florence, Machiavelli set out to provide. Nonetheless Louis's doubts remained unallayed. 'The Pope has struck a blow at me,' he reflected in early August, 'but I will bear all except the loss of honour and state.' Morosely, he added that 'if the Pope makes any demonstration of affection towards me, be it only the thickness of my fingernail, I will go the length of my arm to meet him.'[14]

Machiavelli had long believed that 'the character of the French is naturally suspicious' and that 'it is this that [has given] rise to their request [for assurance]': 'If war breaks out between the Pope and the Majesty of France,' he advised the Signoria, 'you will not be able to avoid declaring yourself in favour of one of the parties.' Louis, on the other hand, saw himself as a man of principle: 'The Emperor [Maximilian] … urged me to divide Italy with him, but I have always refused …; now, however, the Pope [may have obliged] me to do it.'

On 8 August Machiavelli rode into the countryside with Robertet, mulling over the prospects of war. He seems to have been aware that his personal life was increasingly, if sometimes reassuringly, infringing on his duties. An unknown correspondent in Florence, perhaps a copyist for Marcello Virgilio di Adriano Berti, kept him abreast of family news. Towards the end of August the correspondent wrote that 'your wife is here, and she is alive; your children are getting along, each in his own way.'

Machiavelli would have felt less happy about 'the meagre harvest at [his farm in Sant'Andrea in] Percussina,' and disappointed with the inept efforts by Florentine officials to recruit additional troops. He was surely put out by his correspondent's low estimate of the Republic's future: 'As for me, I think that in any case it will happen with the Pope and the Church as it happened with Venice, which pushed so hard that it got [into war and defeat].'[15]

On 24 August negotiations over Louis's 'assurances' were interrupted when he caught the flu-like ailment 'prevalent throughout the country.' Machiavelli

caught it himself, and also ran out of cash, for which he issued an immediate
appeal. During those weeks, Julius's forces were constantly being strengthened,
to this point with hundreds of lancers. He had decided to devote his attention
to stirring up hostility between the French and the Spanish Kings. Machiavelli's
interests pulled him in several directions, though his private life managed the
odd sparkle here and there. He learned, for example, that his brother Totto was
in Lecce, south of Brindisi, trading oil paintings for bolts of cloth, or making
money. In Lyons he had also taken up with a courtesan, Jeanne, whom he knew
from earlier missions. According to Giovanni Girolami, a friend and the agent
of Francesco Soderini, her company was bound to ease any loneliness, as she
was 'devoted to [him].'[16]

Throughout these months, scandal also seemed seldom to be a stranger. On
27 May, or two months earlier, he had become the victim of an anonymous
accusation of sodomy. He was supposed to have engaged in it with a 'Curly-
Haired Woman,' Lucrezia, or La Riccia, as she was called, a courtesan-friend
over many years, perhaps from before his marriage.[17] In the end the charge
was dropped, but the merest hint of sexual illegality could well be dangerous.
Throughout Europe what was notoriously referred to as 'the Florentine vice,'
though understood as mostly involving young boys, merited the harshest
punishment.

By January 1511, Julius's increasing appetite for conquest was crashing about
in bizarre directions. Decorum meant little, safety less, recklessness all. The
ignominy gathering about the leader of the Christian Church was as insignificant to him personally as it seemed shocking to everyone else. He regarded his
insulted dignity as of no consequence, while scaling the walls of besieged towns
with his troops, scrambling for lodgings amid artillery fire and laying plans for
sieges, or snorting at the scud of a cannonball flying across the kitchen of the
house where he was staying, just missing him. Battles seemed less important
than whispers of his licentious behaviour with boys back in Rome. Martin
Luther, who may have visited the city in 1510–11, bore questionable witness
to his semi-secret sexual antics, which seven years later helped to inspire the
Reformation.[18]

Machiavelli got back to Florence in October 1510. In France he had been
replaced by Roberto Acciaiuoli, the Signoria's accredited ambassador. Both
the Republic and the Pope now became helpless onlookers as the succeeding

months rose and crumpled into a tumult of councils, futile negotiations, duplicitous grins and violence. A conspiracy between Louis and Maximilian to replace Julius was humiliated by the Vatican armies. The forces of the Venetians and the Spanish chimed in. Most informed people realized that the Republic would inevitably be caught up in a war between the Pope and the French King.

The desperate need, far greater than before, for loyal Republican troops, along with better defences, was finally being recognized in Florence. During January and February 1511, Soderini dispatched Machiavelli to Pisa, Arezzo and Poggio Imperiale to recommend improvements to their fortifications. He spent part of March in the Valdichiana, where he recruited light if untrained cavalry units. In early spring he led them on parade at the Palazzo della Signoria.[19] For Soderini himself, if not for the administration of the Republic, the political and military situation continued to drift and sink. He seemed to pay little attention to the several constricting shadows.

Whether from overconfidence or insensitivity, the lifetime standard bearer, or *Gonfaloniere*, had also become recklessly indifferent to the decline of his own popularity. This problem reached back over several years and matched a renewed esteem for the Medici, and especially for Cardinal Giovanni, who 'nourished and enhanced his reputation with great cunning.'

By August 1512, the frustrating combination of papal advances and retreats, French advances and retreats, and a build-up of Spanish troops allied with Julius and poised to take on the French by invading the Republic, had sapped Soderini's influence and inflamed an already unsettled atmosphere. Hostile troop movements centred about the town of Prato, only twelve miles from Florence. For some they intimated a strong possibility of changes in the Republic's constitutional governance. For others they seemed divinely inspired.

The role of bad weather as well as war ought probably not to be dismissed in evaluating the conditions of societies threatened by foreign troops and in conflict with themselves. Now as well as over the next few months, at any rate, a batch of frightful thunder- and hailstorms triggered alarms among the superstitious residents of Florence and Rome. For Landucci and others, these ominous celestial tea leaves had started settling at least since 24 August 1511, or just before and after the papal notice of excommunication issued against Florence by Pope Julius on 22 September, which prohibited so much as the holding of masses: 'We heard that there had been a terrible hailstorm at Crema in Lombardy, with meteoric stones of the weight of 150 pounds each, so that roofs were broken and many men and beasts killed... . At this time [4 September] great fires were seen in the air, in the evening, at the castle of Carpi... . On the night following this date [4 November], two thunderbolts fell in Florence in the middle of the night,' twisting 'a certain bronze band which was at the base of [Michelangelo's] "David".'[20]

The natural disturbances – there were others – seemed to many to be linked to the 'cruelties' committed in or near the Republic by Spanish, French and papal soldiers: in Ravenna, which was sacked, in Volterra, which was also sacked ('a short time after a ... horned human monster had been born there') and in the Romagna, where the Spanish were 'plundered' by the French. In August 1512 a hailstorm shedding ice balls 'as large as eggs' thudded across Rome, turning day to night, killing livestock and shattering holy statues.

By now too the peasant population in the neighbourhood of Prato had been forced to flee before the Spanish advance. The roads and the 'whole of the plain' were choked with lines of refugee-carts 'more than a mile long,' in search of safety past the outer gates. 'Poor women and children,' Landucci wrote, could be seen 'laden with their scanty possessions; anyone who saw them could not help feeling moved and forced to weep.'[21]

It seems unlikely that in August 1512 Soderini delivered the dramatic speech to the Grand Council that Guicciardini later attributed to him. Inventing the right speech had long been a prerogative of historians. It also seems clear that he must have said something like it. Pleading that the Spanish demand for him to give up his office hardly represented their true intentions, that he was of no importance and that the Republic was threatened, he argued (according to Guicciardini) that 'I have always been prepared to risk my life for your benefit [or that of the several thousand in his audience], and that it would be much easier to renounce the magistracy which you have given me, and so free myself from the troubles and dangers of war.' He urged his fellow citizens to 'deliberate wisely' and 'attend to the preservation and defence of [their] liberty.'[22] However he may actually have phrased it, his appeal led to an agreement among a majority, passionate about preserving popular government, that he stay on. It was combined with a compromise resolution inviting the Medici back, but only 'as private citizens.'

Encouragingly, and with Machiavelli's assistance, Florence had by now raised over 17,000 local troops. Three to four thousand were posted to Prato, the objective of the local Spanish commander, Raimondo da Cardona. The Viceroy, so-called, had at his own disposal just five thousand infantry and two small cannon. The Florentine hope was that since his army was operating at near starvation levels, and with its ineffectual artillery unlikely to let it force its way into Prato's crowded, well-armed, walled-in streets – the town was an elegant place, renowned as the birthplace of Fra Lippo Lippi – a truce would be concluded, with scores of lives saved.

This might well have happened – most people expected it as sensible – had Soderini not acted with a self-wounding irrationality. Responding with what Guicciardini terms his customary 'timidity', or some belief that the Spanish would pull back in the face of more or less equal numbers, he did nothing. His inaction, on the early afternoon of 29 August, with both sides expecting a signal to negotiate, provoked the Spanish into an attack against all odds on Prato itself.

Moving his cannon to higher, commanding ground, and despite one of them blowing apart on his first volley, Raimondo punched a hole twelve cubits wide through the wall and close to a turret. Through this opening and using scaling ladders, his soldiers climbed and then dashed into Prato's streets, killing the two men left on guard at the turret. Their deaths, which seemed even more terrifying because no one anticipated them, wiped out every shred of morale among the defending troops, who in their inexperience simply took fright and ran off. What followed was a grisly triumph of hunger and brutality over cowardice – greatly to the astonishment of the Spanish – and with tragic consequences for the Republic.

The extent of the carnage that ensued is still unclear: in a letter of 16 September to an unknown noblewoman, possibly Isabella d'Este, Machiavelli put it at four thousand dead, Landucci at five thousand, Bartolomeo Cerretani (a contemporary historian) at 4,500. The horrors certainly exceeded the numbers.

As the Republic's volunteers threw down their weapons and bolted for the nearby houses, two thousand women and children rushed into the cathedral. There they would surely have been hacked and beaten to death by the Spanish pikes, axes, short swords and knives, had not Cardinal de'Medici, who came riding in with Raimondo's army, ordered his own troops to guard the various church entrances and so saved them. Thousands of others, mostly men, were nonetheless cut down in the streets. A barbaric impulse had clearly been unleashed. The rich were kidnapped and held for ransom. The poor were murdered and dismembered. The desolate region round about Prato's walls rang out at night with the shrieks of the doomed as their trashed and fired homes brightened the echoing sky.[23]

The effects of the massacre on the citizens of Florence were deep and conclusive. Landucci saw the town's immolation as the result of 'our sins.' Ambassadors were quickly sent out to bargain with Raimondo, and accepted his demand for a 60,000-ducat ransom, plus Soderini's removal from office, followed by his house arrest, and the return of the Medici. A smothering terror, immobilising and silencing a Florentine population unused to taking responsibility for its own defence, or even to putting up a struggle on its own behalf, left many citizens and others the 'easy prey of anyone who wished to oppress them.' The Republic's leaders themselves seemed paralysed.

Over the next few days Machiavelli spent pointless hours with Soderini, trying to arrive at a face-saving solution, but despite their efforts papers surrendering the city were signed on 30 August. The Florentine soldiers protecting the Palazzo della Signoria were withdrawn, and scores of prisoners loyal to the Medici were released from the Stinche prison, located on what is today the site of the modern Teatro Verdi, between the Via del Fosso and the Via Ghibellina. Crowds of Medici supporters, swarming in 'a tumultuous uprising all over,' found weapons and seized the Palazzo.

Soderini, surprised and trapped in his spacious offices, dispatched Machiavelli to Francesco Vettori, still in charge of the Republic's forces, to arrange his escape. This was arranged, and after the pro-Medici crowd had been persuaded not to attack him, but hemmed in by enraged enemies anyway, he hurried over to Vettori's house. After sunset, accompanied by Vettori and 'a large escort' – Machiavelli stayed behind – the leader of the Florentine Republic departed in disgrace. At first he headed towards Siena, but soon altered his course towards Ragusa, or modern Dubrovnik.[24]

With his desertion of the city in its most desperate hour, though amid threats to his life, the arrival of Giovanni de'Medici was understood as imminent. More than a few people thought that they could detect a cooling of the body of the Republic. Above them, the unknown hand of an unfamiliar ruler seemed to descend with a no longer obscure inevitability.

III

*Into a Tuscan Exile*

# 26

# The Aftermath of Freedom

Rarely perhaps has torture been so smoothly converted into literature. Rarely has suffering so efficiently blended into the invention of a guide to political thought that has outlasted centuries. For weeks after Soderini's departure, over the next couple of months, Machiavelli held on to his position as Second Chancellor, or was allowed to keep it. This in no way implies that all was easy, or even that bloodshed was entirely avoided, only that the occasional riots and slaughter failed to affect the general peace or the more elegant rooms of the Palazzo. The unfinished frescoes by Michelangelo and Leonardo continued undisturbed on the walls of the Grand Council chamber.

As early as 1 September, Giovanni de'Medici's brother Giuliano staged his arrival in the city. Shaved, and wearing his street clothes, he did a walkabout with friends, peering at and admiring his surroundings. The imprisonment of Prato's wealthier citizens, still held for ransom, continued. Giovanni had set himself up, at first in the *piazza* at the doors to the Palazzo della Signoria and then inside it, accompanied by a Signoria of his own, along with squads of troops and armed citizens.

During the early days of the momentous political change, triumphant Spanish soldiers continued to stream into Florence, attempting to sell off the loot they had collected during the sack. Hated everywhere, they were often lured into ambushes and murdered by the incensed and frustrated citizens.[1]

Giovanni himself handled his seizure of power with reasonable sophistication and care. He clearly understood that more would be needed to prevent a Florentine uprising than a merely arbitrary proclamation and the enforcement of his wishes. Above all, he understood that he needed legitimacy. From the start, therefore, he reassured citizens and others that his return to his native city, officially proclaimed on 14 September in the company of 200 cavalrymen and a pre-arranged crowd of followers, should not be viewed as a reversion to the pleasure-despising, repressive government of Savonarola. Pleasures would be allowed. Businesses, festivals and education could go on. No magnanimity, however, kept his supporters from arranging a pro-Medici demonstration in the *piazza* before the Palazzo. It at once led into a contrived demand for a complete Medici restoration, along with, as Machiavelli put it, 'the honours and dignities of their ancestors.'

On 16 September Melchiore Ramazotti, a Medici commander, 'together with his soldiers' and 'other men, [raced into] the Palazzo, shouting "Palle, palle" [Balls, balls: a reference to the Medici family crest, and the Medici rallying cry]. The ... city was suddenly up in arms, and [the Medici] name was echoing everywhere.'[2] This outburst seemed impressive enough, but it failed to tamp down the persisting hostility. As Giovanni realized, melodrama could scarcely overcome long-simmering suspicions of his family's obsession with power, and more convincing measures would be necessary.

The seizure of the Palazzo was thus allowed to merge with his summoning a *parlamento*, or an all-inclusive assembly of citizens. Supervised by Spanish soldiers who surrounded them in the *piazza*, they compliantly voted to abolish Savonarola's Grand Council. They also created Medici-agreeable replacement committees and reduced the *Gonfaloniere's* term of office from Soderini's lifetime length to fourteen months.[3] The office itself was turned over to Giovanbattista Ridolfi, a well known member of the *frateschi*, or the followers of Savonarola, a faction that for years had drawn Soderini's wealthier enemies into its ranks. Ridolfi insisted that he had no plans to remain *Gonfaloniere* for longer than two months.

At this point Giovanni de'Medici allowed himself to be 'persuaded' to organize a *Balìa*, or administrative group. Its powers were extensive, and it could intrude at will into all the towns, villages and valleys of the Republic. He limited membership in the *Balìa* to forty-six, cannily appointing a number of Soderini supporters, among them Piero Alamanni, Jacopo Salviati and Piero Guicciardini. Their prominence, together with the *Balìa's* suggestion of some sort of continuity of representative government, as opposed to being simply an arena for Medici whims, attracted smatterings of citizen support. Meanwhile the Republican secretariat, including Machiavelli and his colleagues, continued at the Palazzo, working on as before.

Each of these configurations may indicate why Machiavelli from the start felt less uneasy about remaining at his desk. They may shed light on his effort to work with the new régime, which at first he seems to have managed with no lack of interest. The changes may also point up the oddity of his being sacked on 7 November. Without warning, the Signoria announced that it had 'dismissed, deprived and totally removed him' (*cassaverunt, privaverunt et totaliter amoverunt*). Only one of his fellow secretaries was also sacked, his friend Biagio Buonaccorsi.

The dismissal seems even stranger when set against a conciliatory letter that he had written to Giuliano, to whom Machiavelli's youthful poems had once been addressed, on 29 September. Still acting as Second Chancellor, he had offered his estimate of how the Medici might succeed in 'win[ning] friends over to your side and not turn[ing] them away,' or what amounted to a crafty psychological analysis of a delicate political situation. He no doubt hoped that the Medici would welcome it: 'I ... should see to it that [after a discussion in the *Balìa*] ... it would be decided that you should have from the Commune of Florence ... four or five thousand ducats per year as an imbursement to your house.' A public pay-off could be arranged, in effect blessing the new adminis-tration with the Florentine imprimatur.[4]

A second letter supporting them, his 'Caution to the Medici Faction' [*Ai Palleschi*], which he wrote during this confused time, was probably likewise meant to add fuel to his dimming fires. In September his position as head of the Nine in charge of the Republic's militia had also been abolished. The militia itself, mauled during the sack of Prato but regarded by the Medici as a poten-tially seditious force, had been disbanded. 'I wish to caution you,' he had then urged the two brothers, but especially, as may be surmised, Giovanni, 'against the counsel of those who argue that you would benefit by exposing Piero Soderini's shortcomings.'

Little could be achieved, he had maintained, from slandering the exiled Florentine leader: as far as the Medici were concerned, any effort to advance themselves through insult could backfire: 'By exposing [him they could] destroy his reputation but not in any way strengthen [their] own position, only that of ... individuals who were his enemies.... These enemies would then have more influence with the populace [than they themselves].'[5]

Admittedly, Machiavelli's motives in producing these documents may have been disingenuous: after writing to him from Ragusa, and at some risk to his safety, Soderini had been grateful for his reply: 'I know you and the guiding compass of your navigation; and if it could be condemned, which it cannot, I would not condemn it.'

As all Machiavelli's defensive moves came to nothing – or at least no record exists of their success – what followed three days later in November can only have seemed laced with viciousness. At a minimum, it indicated that Giovanni and Giuliano saw him merely as an unrepentant Soderini loyalist. How else explain his sentencing by the new Signoria on 10 November to a year's confinement to Florentine territories, amounting to an intra-state term of imprisonment? How else understand their order banning him from entering the Palazzo, and another requiring him to pay a deposit, or type of bail bond, of a thousand gold florins, a huge sum that he did not have but that friends such as Francesco Vettori cobbled together for him? What sense could be made of the Signoria's summary dismissal of one of the Republic's most valued civil servants?[6]

Worse was coming. The bitterness directed at him had probably been shaping up ever since a distasteful incident on 3 January 1511, when Piero Soderini issued a proclamation of treason against anyone residing at Cardinal Giovanni's house or that of his brother, or having anything to do with them. Filippo Strozzi, one of the Republic's most prosperous men, had soon afterwards uncovered a conspiracy against Piero. It was apparently organized by Giovanni in revenge for the blocks placed on his promoting the marriage of Piero de'Medici's daughter Clarice to Filippo. The marriage would have guaranteed a strong Medici influence over the Republic. Machiavelli's role in deterring the marriage, along with his support of Soderini's proclamation, had not been forgotten. Were a plot now uncovered against Giovanni, suspicions might reasonably settle on him as a co-conspirator.

Precisely this occurred in February 1513, though in less tempestuous times the discovery might have been ignored as unimportant. A conspiracy in progress, or so it seemed, and aimed at both Medici brothers, was exposed, ironically as their attitudes toward Machiavelli had begun to improve. His expulsion from the Palazzo, where he had sweated away over the previous fourteen years, had just been rescinded for a week or two as he was called in for quizzing about possible irregularities in his payments to the defunct citizen militia. He had showed up – Giovanni was busy there too, ordering several of the halls stripped of their woodwork to allow their remodelling into quarters for his troops – answered their accusations and been acquitted of misconduct.[7]

Such was not the case when his name was found inscribed as seventh on a scribbled list of eighteen to twenty likely plotters against Giovanni. The list had dropped out of the pocket of Piero Antoni Boscoli, who along with an idealistic accomplice, Agostino Capponi – they seem to have thought of themselves as a modern Brutus and Cassius team, or as liberators of Florence from the new Medici-Caesar – had drawn up a sketchy plan to assassinate Giovanni and perhaps his brother. Few of the other collaborators seem to have known of Boscoli's list, and not Machiavelli, or so he swore on being arrested. His claim to innocence, which may have been genuine despite his avowed scepticism of the Medici, made no difference. He was hustled off to the Stinche for interrogation and torture. Boscoli and Capponi were sentenced to death.[8]

In the darkness of the small, befouled prison with its cells for about forty inmates, the Republic seemed conclusively to collapse. Threats of torture, pain and death confirmed a gloomy prophecy embodied in one of the strangest artistic displays ever mounted in the city just two years earlier, during the Carnival of 1511. The *Carro della Morte*, so called, had been designed and built in secret, in the Hall of the Pope, by Piero di Cosimo (1461/2–1521).

For the rest of their lives, or so the story went, those who saw it were unable to forget what they had seen. At the time, opinions differed over the meaning of Piero's triumphal Chariot of Death, drawn by stately black-dyed buffaloes, each painted with phosphorescent human bones scattered over alabaster crosses, above which sat a colossal, anthropomorphic shape bearing a fearsome scythe.

Crowds gazed in apprehension at the series of tombs built into the chariot. As its wheels creaked past, pausing here and there amidst a 'chanting,' or ghostly, windy music, the various tombs had opened and black figures decked out in other painted bones crept out of their mouths, greeted by weak-sounding horns and a muffled solemnity. Encircling the chariot, as Vasari reports, corpse-like figures rode by on black, bony horses. The hideous display had set a standard of imaginative terror for years in the carnivals to come, as did a quavering chant that rose over it in a rendition of a psalm of David, his *Miserere*. People whispered that Piero's float with its skeletal horses was intended to evoke the exiled Medici and their restoration. As if resurrected, they would soon return to inflict horrors on the city.[9]

This fate, or so it seemed, or something like it, had befallen Machiavelli in his cell at the Stinche, and on the *strappado*, as for Savonarola years earlier the expression of state power had earned the same reward. With his hands tied behind his back, in a room full of racks, iron torture shoes, thumb-screws and funnels, or out in the open street, where tortures were put on public display, he seems to have submitted to six drops or wrenchings by the wrist (*tratta di corde*), if his testimony is accepted. Each was ferocious enough to dislocate the shoulders.[10]

By any standards the punishment was horrific. Even after its application, though, as also seems credible on the evidence, plus what may be understood of his nature and resourcefulness, he appears astonishingly and almost at once to have turned to writing poetry. Resorting to his favourite form, that of the tailed sonnet, he produced a candid account and indictment of what had just happened to him. He addressed his poem to Giuliano de'Medici, and its purpose was to wring clemency from apparently rigid fingers. In fact the resort to poetry, and his dispatch of a poem to Giuliano, the Medici brother to whom he had years ago addressed poems of praise, and who was himself a cultivated man, may have seemed both last-ditch and appropriate – or in the end not as unusual a manoeuvre as sending a poem to his father about a goose. The crucial difference lay in the circumstances, which were evil as well as alarming.

Just before writing his sonnet, on 23 February 1513, or at about an hour before dawn (the hour mentioned in lines 10–12), he had heard intoned outside his cell the phrase *Pro eis ora* (Pray for them). This was the customary incantation for the procession of black-hooded monks trained in the *ars moriendi* manner of leading the condemned to their deaths. Boscoli and Capponi were being taken away to be beheaded.[11]

If some modern readers remain sceptical that Machiavelli could have written poetry in these frightful circumstances, not to mention his own pain, and, more, come up with a polished sonnet full of complex images, controlled hyperboles and an ironic matter-of-fact tone, it may be recalled that just this type of surrender to literature, and against the odds, made practical sense – and when else might he have written it? For decades he had been schooled in writing poems of just this sort, or fashioning at speed the rhetorical flourishes that he knew might captivate and mollify if not win over his Medici audience:

Giuliano, I've got a set of shackles on my legs and six yanks of the cord across my shoulders: my other miseries I omit, since this is simply how they treat poets here.// The broken walls loom with lice as big and fat as butterflies, nor was there ever such a stench in Roncevalles [the bloody battlefield described in the French epic *La Chanson de Roland*] or Sardinia, among those groves,//as in this posh inn of mine. Amid a clatter resounding as if Jove and all Mongibello [Mount Etna]//were tossing thunderbolts about, the one prisoner is chained up and the other unchained, with his locks, keys and bolts dashing together: another screams, 'I'm too high off the floor!' – //What terrifies me most is that toward dawn, sleeping, I began to hear, 'Pray for them!'//Well, let them go, I pray, as long as your mercy turns to me, and so surpasses the good name of your father and grandfather.

Some profit may lie in taking stock of the political situation here. Certainly he was not the first quasi-modern author to be snatched out of a life of relative comfort and unjustly imprisoned. Nor was he the first to face the possibility of execution. His contemporary, the biblical translator William Tyndale (1494–1536), and Dostoyevski centuries later, and Osip Mandelstam later still, come readily to mind. Yet he may have been among the first to meet the terror of political execution by depicting its vulgarity, incompetence and stupidity. He may also have been the first to do so at once, as might a modern journalist, or poet-journalist.

His grim, jesting sonnet, in which he acknowledges the executions of others while understandably praying for rescue, seems in addition unable to escape its modern atmosphere of unrelieved emergency. Put differently, it preserves a special coolness that sets its lines apart from Dante's or Michelangelo's, as it plunges relentlessly ahead.

Strikingly, it manages to do so in the absence of any reference to ceremony. The odd omission – of some nod to religion, say – draws attention to itself, not so much because it testifies to unbelief, which it may not, as because religion seems irrelevant. At a minimum, it seems to be discarded as a membrane capable of shielding sanity from agony and madness. Another type of membrane may be wanted. In the meantime, the poem's grim sense of humour suffices, or its jesting – and perhaps because his sonnet received no response, a few days later he seems have sent another, and now one in which he depicts himself as faintly ridiculous:

Last night, pleading that the muses, with their sweet zither and sweet songs, would, to console me, visit Your Magnificence and make my excuses,//one appeared who embarrassed me by saying, 'Who are you, who dares summon me?' I told her my name, and she, to torture me, slapped me across the face and shut my mouth//saying, 'You're not Niccolò but Dazzo [the well known Andrea Dazzi, a follower of Marcello Adriani and secretary of the First Chancellery], since your legs and heels are tied up and you're sitting here in chains like a madman.'//I tried making a rational reply, but she answered, 'Get on like the fool you are in your comedy of rags.'//So give her some proof, Magnificent Giuliano, that I'm not Dazzo, but me.[12]

In the end Giuliano's acceptance of Machiavelli's sonnets, if it occurred, would not have mattered as much as the mortal intercession that now helped him out. In Rome, on 21 February, at the age of sixty-nine, turning feverish while laying out his plans for his next military campaign, Julius II began to weaken. During the last days of January, as recorded by the Venetian ambassador, his body failed and sank. His mind remained lucid, however, and the papal warrior who by his own reckoning had never been able to sit still, and who might even have had a promising career as an art critic, realized that death was imminent. He tried eight types of wine to see whether any could restore his health. None did. He next summoned the College of Cardinals to his bedside to instruct them in the virtues of self-sacrifice. The most important was the rejection of simony. Some objected.

His daughter Felice asked for the restoration of her papal privileges. Julius refused her, and soon a large, adoring crowd, among whom pressed hundreds trying to kiss his exposed toes, followed his scented, bejewelled, befurred body to its burial place near his uncle Sixtus IV in the floor of the Vatican. Alongside his vigour, intelligence and piety, his familiar titanic eruptions, evident since the start of his papacy, seemed less disturbing.[13] Unaware of his altered position in the Christian world, his successor-to-be, Giovanni de'Medici, just thirty-seven and also ailing, as well as sweaty, jolly, anxious and, as many were aware, flatulent, was trundled south from Florence on a fast-moving, bumpy litter.

Machiavelli's efforts to regain his freedom by appealing to him through their mutual friends, among them Francesco Vettori, seemed superfluous in the light of the amnesty, granted to all prisoners, even to forgiving their fines, that followed Giovanni's unanimous election on 11 March as Pope Leo X. The smoke of burning ballots at the Vatican ignited expressions of joy in Florence. Favours, including liberal dispensations, might follow.

Landucci reported that amid the thunder of 'cannon and continual cries of *Palle! Papa Lione!*' nearly all the wood in the city, ripped from its roofs, gates, parapets, doors, galleries and malmsey butts (once the wine had been drunk) was set afire in celebratory blazes before hundreds of houses by thousands of happy, oblivious citizens.[14]

'I got out of prison amid this city's universal rejoicing,' Machiavelli told Francesco Vettori on 13 March after returning home from watching the three-day-long street parties. Vettori, away in Rome, was now the Florentine Ambassador to the new Pope (he had first been sent to Rome as Ambassador to Julius).[15]

Uncertain of his future, especially in regard to money, Machiavelli had a wife and five children to support: Bernardo, Primerana, Lodovico, Bartolomea and Guido (though records regarding his children remain unclear).[16] With another child on the way, he had certainly not forgotten the good words, no matter how useless they seemed at the time, that Francesco and his brother Paolo had tried and failed to put in on his behalf with the new Pope, 'for which I thank you.'

He remained acid about his imprisonment ('I shall not repeat the long story of my disgrace, but merely say that Fate has done everything to cause me this abuse'), relieved ('thank God it is over'), anxious to assist his brother Totto in securing a post in the new Vatican administration ('I implore both your favour and Paolo's for him') and eager for a job himself ('if it should be possible [that] either [the Pope] or his family might start engaging my services in some way').

He was agreeably impressed by his ability to deal with pain: 'I should like you to get this pleasure from these troubles of mine, that I have borne them so straightforwardly that I am proud of myself for it and consider myself more of a man than I believed I was.' If it was true that 'all that is left to me of my life I owe to the Magnificent Giuliano [which suggests that Giuliano may have received his prison-sonnets] and your Paolo [Vettori, who had also offered his assistance],' but having almost no money and confined to Republican territory for another nine months, he could at most look forward to scraping by.

Nonetheless, he remarked, 'I shall act in such a way that [everyone] will have reason to be proud of me.' Misleadingly, he recalled his childhood full of anxiety about his father's indebtedness, even if his family had never in a desperate peasant sense been poor: 'I was born in poverty and at an early age learned how to scrimp rather than to thrive.'

Scrimping might not be quite the unpleasant necessity that it seemed, as he admitted to the probably puzzled Francesco, who knew him. 'The whole gang [of his former co-workers] sends you [their] regards,' he wrote, and then offered a reassuring hats off some recent sexual adventures, which had been voluptuous and welcome: 'Every day we visit the house of some girl' – a previous girlfriend perhaps, or a prostitute in his good books – 'to recover our vigour.' Pleasure was not all, however, and an odd wistfulness had begun to circumscribe his thoughts, as if he had caught himself glancing into a mystery: 'And so we go on marking time … enjoying the remainder of this life, so that it seems to me that I am making it all up.'[17]

# 27

# Making History at Sant'Andrea

With the accession of the new Pope, the political leadership of Florence subsided into dour confusion. Machiavelli and his family decided to stay briefly at their large family house on the south bank of the Arno, between the Ponte Santa Trinità and the Ponte alla Carraia, near the corner of the Via del Santo Spirito and the narrow Via dei Coverelli, at numbers 5–7, or just behind the church.[1]

From there it would have been a short walk, which he could no longer make with his old confidence, over one of the bridges to the Palazzo della Signoria, which remained closed to him. Nor did he do so. Over the next eight months he spent less than three weeks, either alone or with his family, in the city. Instead he retreated with them to the modest estate inherited from his father in the hills at Sant'Andrea in Percussina, nine winding miles south of the city gates, amid its vineyards, the summer heat, local farmers, birding, letter-writing – this often at considerable length – and reflections, mostly now on history and politics.

Giovanni's departure for Rome and his coronation in early April saw the elevation of his cousin Giulio to the position of Archbishop of Florence 'amid great rejoicings.' As before, wild celebrations led to a singular opportunity for happy if accidental moments of incineration, this time of 'the houses at the back of the Archbishop's palace.'[2]

Francesco Vettori, who seems often to have undervalued himself, or at least to have viewed his ambassador's role as of slight importance, had begun to prove too modest to advance Machiavelli's interests with the new Pope ('I am sorry to be able to offer you so little,' he wrote him on 30 March). Giuliano, Giovanni's brother, who had also moved to Rome, had been made a Roman patrician and commander of the Vatican's ecclesiastical troops. He exhibited only a mild interest in wielding administrative power in Florence itself. In August 1513, Giovanni appointed a newcomer to politics, his twenty-year-old nephew, Lorenzo de'Medici (1492–1519), nominal governor of the city, but with the understanding that he would accept papal advice. Given Lorenzo's meagre experience, however, and his autocratic, excitable temperament full of smirks, quibbles and affectations, this appointment met with unease.

The election of the new Pope also opened a vacuum at the centre of power in Italy. It rapidly became an invitation to the players on the Italian military stage, the French, Germans, Venetians and Spanish, to stake out dramatic claims to wealth and influence. Over the following seven months, or from March through September, familiar foreign armies, fielded by one or another of the competing military powers, joined and fought, or retreated and fought, or bickered while licking their wounds, or withdrew in bloodied chagrin as Henry VIII of England maintained his soldierly pressure on what became their cascade of collisions.

Machiavelli heard of these clashes through Vettori's letters, sent on to him for advice in the quiet of his sanctuary at Sant'Andrea. On occasion he responded with estimates of the military and diplomatic options. 'If I could talk to you,' he wrote on 9 April, 'I could not help but fill your head with castles in the air [or speculations], because *Fortuna* has seen to it that since I do not know how to talk about either the silk or the wool trade, or profits or losses, I have to talk about politics.'[3]

His own career spent on pacifing the Italian countryside, or curbing the very assaults that once more began to overwhelm many Italian cities, his diplomatic and military struggles over the previous ten years, seemed to evaporate before his eyes. Florence looked adrift amid the new Pope's opportunities. Lorenzo, himself a Roman by upbringing, quickly disregarded the advice given him. He began to run Florence for himself, diverting the city's money to pay his soldiers. These soldiers would soon be put to use on the battlefield, or according to grandiose dreams of conquest.

In the meantime Machiavelli paused amid his political if not philosophical isolation in a tiny hilltop hamlet with its single, ribbony, sweltering street or, as one sees it today, its single *Alimentari* selling cheese, bread and groceries. The latter stands amid a row of stone houses, some showy and smart-looking, which curl along the old Roman post road towards San Casciano. As then, too, Sant'Andrea overlooks glorious, grapevined slopes, ancient olive groves, cypresses, oaks and pink, blue and lavender blossoms that preside over copse-green valleys. In summer, the single through road and the surrounding fields echo to the strident chirping of cicadas. The scents are full and sleepy.

Never perhaps had a self-designed exile seemed so calm, flexible and lush –
not Ovid's, whose *Metamorphoses* Machiavelli knew, but who was banished by
Augustus to a village on the Black Sea at the edge of the empire, where he had
managed to do well despite the primitive conditions, and not Dante's, following
his expulsion from Florence in the *trecento* to a roving, mazelike homelessness.
Nor, with Sant'Andrea's lone, tower-topped church mounted on a rise behind
its one street, and with the lovely, post-republican city situated far below its few
houses, could his isolation have seemed better suited from a strategic point of
view to admonishing his urban-haunted soul.

With church above and city below, the blue summer air swept between
run-down stone buildings, cracked and rebuilt even then with old millstones,
and in need of repair amid their rough-hewn windows. All this had now
became his home. A short walk along the road to its tilt toward Florence, miles
away, brought a glimpse of the *Duomo*. It seemed to shine like a pale rouge gem
amid the distant trees, plump and tantalizing.

He owned a well and three buildings at Sant'Andrea, among them the *Albergaccio*,
or *casa da signore*, so called (it meant 'wretched inn') after the *albergo* just behind
it. There he and his family slept, rose and ate. The *albergo* had long served as a
crude tavern and stopover place for workers in the fields. Travellers stopped in
en route to Florence, Siena or San Casciano, with its weekly farmers' market, two
miles away. Across the road – or former *Strada regia romana* – stood a thick stone
building where the family's coat of arms could, and still can, be seen carved over the
fireplace, with its oil press, wine press and stables. A vegetable garden just behind
sat over earth-immured cellar vaults for wine storage (plate XII).

If the scenery was rustic, reassuring and even beautiful, luxuries were
few. Machiavelli had inherited a commercial farm with a vineyard and some
scattered additional acres. What now seemed important, if perhaps unsurprising, was his unselfpitying adaptation to his new circumstances. Diplomacy
had quickly surrendered to crops and fence-mending. Military analysis had not,
though, or not always.

On 6 June Louis XII and his Venetian allies were defeated by the Spanish
and Milanese in the Battle of Novara. In a letter to Vettori, Machiavelli wrote
of the resulting military turmoil, that 'considering the current state of affairs, I
should be as afraid of a new treaty as a new war.'[4] Louis suffered another defeat
in July, inflicted by the armies of Henry VIII. It prompted the French King's
abandonment of all plans for future operations in Italy. By now the Florentine
ex-Secretary was no more than concerned. His daytime hours were spent in

tending his vines, hunting (mostly thrushes) and, at night, reading, thinking about history and, in four-hour stints by candle-light, writing up his at first disjointed reflections on Livy. He had to hand the Roman author's ancient history and other books. He had requisitioned them from friends and his own library and brought them to Sant'Andrea by donkey.

History had always somehow been at the forefront of his thoughts, as indicated by his letters, for instance to Vettori on 10 August 1513: 'I beg you to reflect upon human affairs as they should be given credence and upon the powers of the world – and particularly of republics – how they develop: you will realize how at first men are satisfied with being able to defend themselves and with not being dominated by others; from this point they move on to attacking others physically and seeking to dominate them.'[5]

Just now history seemed to offer greater consolations than usual, or greater at least since finishing his *First Decennale*. If he harboured some idea of extending his account of the Florentine 'tragedy' beyond 1509 into a *Second Decennale*, though, he had so far made no attempt to do so.

Instead he directed his attention elsewhere, to the energetic, lugubrious first-century Roman historian, about whom so little was known. The conundrum of the Roman Empire, with its dizzy vastness, success and failure, attracted him as never before, along with its intriguing relations to the messy present. To some extent, to be sure, the empire had remained a humanist fascination absorbing him since childhood and his father's preparation of an index for the 1476 edition of Livy's history, when he was seven.

Did he turn to Bernardo's old copy of Livy's history, of which only 35 books of 142 had survived? The chances are great that he did, and that he might even have experienced a type of vindication on engaging with the Roman historian's work at the country estate that had meant so much to his debt-stricken father. Bernardo's index, mapping out the ancient political world, might now be joined with his own response to Roman and modern history. It could provide the impetus for an extension of the family's contribution to a deeper political investigation – or a new brand of *scientia* – and in an original way.

The idea of originality had itself always seemed crucial to him, and perhaps never more so than now. He was to insist on it in an introduction written later to what was about to become his first book in prose, the *Discorsi sopra la prima deca di Tito Livio* (Discourses on the First Decade [or first ten books] of Livy). Originality meant risk-taking. It might even be as adventurous, or so he was later to argue, as the storms and voyages into the unknown experienced by the explorers among his contemporaries 'seek[ing] out new lands and seas [in the Americas].' These risks deserved recognition, if only because any author who sought 'to bring a common benefit to everyone' with originality, and so 'establish new systems and institutions,' was bound to attract 'trouble and hardship.' A majority would be 'more eager to blame than to praise the actions of others.' At the start of his most daring sally so far into literature, therefore, among the hills of Sant'Andrea, he had already begun to take note of the potential new dangers to his already battered reputation. The road to innovation could easily be marred by unexpected pitfalls of disgrace.[6]

But why Livy in any case? The connections with his father and his childhood aside, other Roman historians, among them Tacitus, Florus and Suetonius, whose accounts Vettori recommended 'to while away the time' in a letter from Rome on 23 November, might just as easily have aroused his interest. Even earlier historians, such as Sallust (86–34 BCE) and Polybius (c.205-c.123 BCE), in the end influenced several of the more elegant or almost truffle-like sections of his *Discorsi*.

Yet the irresistible appeal of Livy seemed to lie in a coincidence of their temperaments, backgrounds and attitudes toward the past. Above all, they seemed to agree on how change, perhaps the most important ingredient of any history, came about in the world. For Livy, as for Machiavelli, the essential sources of change lay in the personalities of the actors who dominated the historical stage, the vagaries of *Fortuna* – or other people and circumstances – and *virtú*, or the strength and skills of the actors. Neither strength nor skills had anything to do with ethics, which both viewed as irrelevant to political achievements.

Beyond these similarities lay the two historians' almost parallel relations to public life, or the fact that Livy in Rome, like his successor in Florence, had to some extent played the role of outsider. Livy had known but not gained the complete confidence and trust of the important leaders of his day, in his own case that of Augustus. Both seem also to have shared the conviction that their civilizations, even in their moments of triumph, were failures: 'I would have [my reader,' writes Livy] 'trace the process of our moral decline, to watch, first, the sinking of the foundations of morality as the old teaching was allowed to lapse, then the rapidly increasing disintegration, then the final collapse of the whole edifice, and the dark dawning of our modern day when we can neither endure our vices nor face the remedies needed to cure them.' For Livy, as for

Machiavelli a millennium and a half later, history remained 'the best medicine for a sick mind … [in which] you can find for yourself and your country both examples and warnings; fine things to take as models, base things, rotten through and through, to avoid.'[7]

Machiavelli's organizing principle from the start was to write 142 short chapters of commentary that would correspond to the number of Livy's known historical books. If many had been lost, lists of the events described in all but two of the lost books had survived. Machiavelli's larger plan was to account for the growth of political institutions, states and empires from their beginnings to their rise and fall, but not systematically. His method, as his title makes plain, would be discursive, or rambling and even informal. For reasons never explained he would concentrate on Livy's first ten books, and these only loosely. His style was to be ruminative, his approach allusive. It would be capacious enough to allow for the occasional reference to Ovid, Virgil and other poets with relevant insights.

Aristotle, Plato and utopian thinkers of recent times, such as Savonarola, had produced accounts of the past modelled on their political goals, or what ought to be – human happiness, for instance, in the case of Aristotle: 'every state … is established with a view to some good'. Machiavelli planned to limit his commentaries to what had actually happened. Prescription, while not eliminated, would be restricted. In this manner, a new kind of political knowledge could be coaxed into existence. Its basis would be empirical in that its premises would meet elementary tests of evidence. Conclusions about the present would be measured against patterns and events recovered from the past. His reasons never appeared less than commonsensical: if people did not change over time – a major premise – then the discovery of patterns between past and present must be as inevitable as illuminating. History might not be cyclical, but it would present similar phenomena in various guises.

During the summer of 1513, his developing *Discorsi* seemed to slot into still another pattern, a division into three books. The first was to deal with how states acquired their forms, citizens and institutions; the second with how they matured, including descriptions of their types of conquests; and the third with how they expanded until decay set in, often as the result of conspiracies, as they fell apart.[8] Here too the design would be left open. Sections might overlap. Digressions would be tolerated, personal reminiscences encouraged. The point was to ignore nothing politically significant, or to let as few fish as possible escape his net. It was also to reject false combinations of the facts and resist facile conclusions. In more modern terms, there was to be no encouragement, either consciously or unconsciously, of ideals, popular causes or ideological systems.

The *Discorsi's* structure would also render impossible the advocacy of any position as correct in all circumstances. Ethical principles, for example, might on occasion prove destructive to a state's political health. They might even be subversive. Machiavelli's method would serve as a corrective to such instances, and even to his own natural desires to impose meanings. In no sense could his work ever be regarded as finished – or no more so than the essays of Montaigne (1533–92), to which it would often be compared.

Here might be originality indeed, though during the summer of 1513 his so far assembled commentaries may have seemed a mere mishmash. What he foresaw, as his introduction was later to make plain, was that his method and results would act as a challenge to any reader who expected the sort of artificial neatness to be found in most other histories. A gauntlet would be thrown down before writers and readers, and before those competent historical accounts, such as Bruni's, which to their credit had also relied on evidence and research. The conventions of story-telling, with cherry-picked beginnings, middles and endings, were to be avoided. The aim was to be as revealing of the disorder among the facts as possible.

By mid-July he had finished a major part of the first section, or Book I, though it is likely that bits had been written earlier and were now altered and reshuffled.

The chief evolving theme, stringing together his to this point combined facts and reflections, was and remained change, and this of the social, political and military varieties. It seemed in no way belied by his parallel assertion of the fundamentally unchanging nature of human beings. Perhaps for the first time too, the principle of change was viewed as governed by two causes. The first was human irrationality and its consequences, an anti-medieval idea. The second, surprisingly (for who else had considered it?), was boredom:

> As all human things are kept in a perpetual movement, and can never remain stable, states naturally either rise or decline, and necessity compels them to many acts to which reason will not influence them…. [If] Heaven favours [that a particular state] … never … be involved in war, [its] continued tranquillity would enervate [it], or provoke

internal dissensions, which together, or either of them separately, will be apt to prove [its] ruin.[9]

Wars might as easily be started out of a need for amusement, it seemed, or as an alternative to inertia, as for seemingly profound reasons. This hypothesis was bolstered by his view of governments as generally desperate affairs, constantly threatened by emotions.

The history of republics showed that only a citizen's right to accuse, combined with the rule of law, might act as a counterweight to the power of emotions run riot: 'Nothing ... renders a republic more firm and stable than to organize it in such a way that the excitement of ill-humours ... may have a way prescribed by law for venting itself': it is 'necessary for a republic to have laws that afford ... the masses the opportunity of giving vent to the hatred they may have conceived against any citizen.'[10]

Of great importance, though it may seem peculiar to those who wish to see him as unapologetically anti-Christian, anti-clerical, anti-papal or anti-religious, was the role that he imputed to religion in maintaining the state, and in particular any republic: 'Whoever reads Roman history attentively will see in how great a degree religion served in the command of the armies, in uniting the people and keeping them well conducted'; 'religion [is] the most necessary and assured support of any civil society' – though nothing here sheds light on his own attitudes towards God and the Church.[11]

This may not have been necessary. As he makes plain, he had long since come to see human beings as mixtures of good and evil, rather than the one or the other, and to re-examine his earlier beliefs about mass murderers such as Giampaolo Baglioni, whose surrender to Julius II, unexpected in view of his military superiority, he had witnessed at Perugia in 1505. Changing one's mind might be as rational as it was practical. Memory might best be understood as an instrument of a revising intelligence. Where he had earlier been convinced that Baglioni was simply overwhelmed by Julius's rhetorical abilities, he now conceded that the Perugian ruler's emotional complexity, despite his viciousness, could have been greater than had once seemed conceivable.[12]

Machiavelli changed his mind as well about other significant figures out of his immediate past, such as Cesare Borgia and Louis XII. He seemed willing to ascribe their achievements less to extraordinary abilities than to Florentine fears, glibness and foolishness: 'It is the worst fault of feeble republics to be

irresolute, so that whatever part they take is dictated by force ... Their weakness
never allows them to resolve upon anything where there is a doubt.'[13]

As Book I of the *Discorsi* grew and expanded, he also began to place a greater
emphasis on princes and princely types, such as kings and popes, than on semi-
democratic republics. The focus of his attention had begun to shift, at least for
the moment, to autocrats and principalities, or dominions. Republics might
not be suitable for everyone: 'Let [them] be established where equality exists,
and on the contrary, principalities where great inequality prevails.' To establish
a stable republic it might be advisable to eliminate the gentility, or the idle rich,
either by expulsion, taxation or murder.[14]

By mid-summer he had set up a stable routine to accommodate both his
farm life and his wish to write, or a schedule which in itself indicated that as
the lights of his interest altered from going on with the *Discorsi* to possibly
producing a quite different book – and this by the end of July – he had already
begun to groom himself for the effort. His new book might emerge from his
commentaries but it would centre more completely on princes. Farm life was
prompting originality along unexpected lines.

At about this time Marietta gave birth to a girl who died after three days,
though she herself survived. Machiavelli felt physically well 'but ill in every
other respect.' He was 'grateful' that God had 'not [so far] abandoned me.'[15]

His devotion to clarity, so vital to the *Discorsi* and crucial to any new book,
poured out in a letter to his nephew, friend and confidant Giovanni Vernacci
on 4 August: 'I urge you to use a clear style ... so that whenever [people read
a letter by you] they think, because your way of writing is so detailed, that you
are there.' The journalist, historian and poet of his better days seemed not only
in accord with each other, but in rehearsal for a new undertaking.[16]

November found him well into it. The book seemed to fit awkwardly among
others in the medieval moral tradition of the so-called 'mirrors of princes' and
others on the subject of governing, by Majo (*d.*1493) and Diomede Carafa
(1406–87), *De regis et boni principis officio* (On the office of king and the good
prince). In fact its novelty was soon to exceed that of the *Discorsi*.

Vettori teased him about his unusual silence. He sent his friend a description
of his own typical day as Florentine ambassador to Rome, mostly to prompt
him into describing his life at Sant'Andrea. At Rome Vettori was doing well by
spending more than he could afford on 'a nice house [with] many small rooms'
not far from Saint Peter's Square. He was up by ten and off to the Vatican. There
he exchanged twenty words with the Pope, ten with Giulio de'Medici, six with

Giuliano de'Medici and fewer with the petty officials from whose whispers he deduced the day's gossip and political news.

His diplomatic duties over, he hurried home to lunch with his household and guests, played a few games of cards, took a late afternoon horseback ride beyond the city gates (he kept seven horses plus a staff of nine, including a chaplain) and spent the evening reading Roman historians such as Livy, Florus, Sallust, Tacitus, Suetonius 'and those others who write about the emperors' such as Herodian and Procopius: 'With them I pass the time; and I consider the emperors that this poor Rome, which once made the world tremble, has put up with.'[17]

On 10 December, Machiavelli took Vettori's bait and replied with a letter of his own – it was to become his most famous – in which he sketched out his day at Sant'Andrea while letting his friend know that a new writing scheme was in place and was distracting him. He might send along his results for Vettori's approval. He felt anxious about them, though, seeing himself as a bit like the proverbial fox when confronted with a lion, or so he had referred to himself in a letter back in August. He might surrender to apprehension, 'almost die of fright' and 'hid[e] … behind a clump of bushes to [peer out].' Nonetheless, 'having collected [his] wits,' he would try to answer his friend's request for information as best he could:

> I get up in the morning with the sun and go into one of my woods that I am having cut down; there I spend a couple of hours inspecting the work of the previous day and kill some time with the woodsmen who always have some dispute on their hands either among themselves or with their neighbours. I could tell you a thousand stories about these woods and my experiences with them.[18]

He refrains from doing so, however, and instead speaks of wandering off to hang out his 'bird-nets' for thrushes. He totes 'a book under my arm: Dante, Petrarch or one of the minor poets like Tibullus, Ovid, or some such. I read about their amorous passions and their loves, remember my own, and these reflections make me happy for a while.'

After lunch, which he takes at home, he heads over to the inn behind his house, and there through the afternoon does a sort of slumming with the innkeeper, a butcher, a miller and kiln-workers. He squabbles and shouts his way through backgammon games, which 'get the mould out of my brain and let the malice out of my fate.' Evening brings him home again, or round the corner, but now to enter his study. Here during the next few hours his writing and a leap in his very existence seem to tumble out of the evening air: 'On the threshold I take off my workday clothes, covered with mud and dirt, and put on the garments of court and palace.'[19]

These would have included his *Lucco*, or the ample toga-like red cloth, a symbol of Florentine citizenship. Given his father's indebtedness, he would have been prevented from wearing it until at the age of nineteen in 1488 he became a citizen himself. Most Florentines considered the *Lucco* as valuable as an ancient Roman senatorial toga, and the city saw itself as the daughter of Rome. His desire to wear it thus seems more than poignant. Despite ostracism, arrest, torture and dismissal, as he donned his citizen's cloth, or decked himself out according to a revered tradition, he might slip back into the civilized ancient world, move among its thinkers, and wander through ancient as well as modern history[20]: 'Fitted out appropriately, I step inside the venerable courts of the ancients, where, solicitously received by them, I nourish myself on that food that *alone* is mine and for which I was born; where I am unashamed to converse with them and to question them about their motives, ... and they, out of their human kindness, answer me.'

Here, then, might be the polished circumstances, including an appropriate rural isolation, in which *The Prince* could be written: 'Dante says that no one understands anything unless he retains what he has understood, [and so] I have jotted down what I have profited from in their conversation, and composed a short study, *De principatibus* (On Principalities, or usually *The Prince*), in which I delve as deeply as I can into the ideas concerning this topic, discussing the definition of a princedom [or any established territory: it might have little or nothing to do with an hereditary prince], the categories of princedoms, how they are acquired, how they are retained, and why they are lost.'[21] The overriding problem, to be sure, to which he had devoted a great deal of attention over many years, was why they were lost.

# 28

## *Power and Memory*

The rapidly emerging book, though no more than a fifth the length of what the *Discorsi* would later become, turned out above all to be an act of recollection. What he remembered blended with deductions from his humanist principles.

A few telling aspects stand out at once. Strikingly, and despite his frequent references to ancient history and Roman historians, what he recalls seems mostly to be his personal past, or his experiences among the princes and other rulers whom he has seen in action. *The Prince* is a fiercely contemporary book. Second, as in the *Discorsi* so far, he often alters his views of his past. The Cesare Borgia of his legations and letters, for instance, differs somewhat from the Cesare who appears in these pages. Third, his diction and style are unusual in ways that set them apart from those of other political books. These continue to influence even now how his ideas are understood.

The literary shift has little to do with the length of his sentences and their rhetorical structure, which retain the eely coils recognizable in the work of other Italian authors, if without their 'rounded periods or big, impressive words.' It has much more to do with the flame-like intimacy running through his personal letters, or his vivacity and insolence. If the clarity is sublime, his candour comes as a splash of ice water. His focus throughout is also well nigh perfect. If, as has often been noted, *The Prince* explores a fenced-in realm of political power while offering a manual on how to acquire and keep it, power remains its only theme.

His twenty-six short chapters thus pay scant attention to ethics, the pleasures of power and even cruelty, except in the last chapter, which he may have added later, in which he pleads for the rescue of Italy from foreign invaders: 'Italy, left almost lifeless, waits for a leader who will heal her wounds.' Subsequent attempts, whether out of embarrassment, distaste, compassion or mistrust, to pretend that the book is about something other than power, such as suppressed republicanism, seem doomed to frustration and self-contradiction.

Almost immediately the book homes in on treachery as a crucial aspect of power, and its scope and methods, or how to practise it, refine it, restrict its consequences so as to get away with it while improving on it and perfecting it. Deceitful tactics are seldom viewed in a favourable light, however. They are never presented as attractive in themselves. Nor are they viewed as guiding principles. Instead, painted with as menacing a reddish hue as Darwin's legendary tooth and claw, they are treated as essential to improving the aptness of princely or any other politics, much as a surgeon might require both a scalpel and bloodshed to save a patient's life.

Readers with little enthusiasm for seeing his book along these often disturbing lines, which he regards as realistic, may reject it out of hand, or even disgust, nausea, bitterness, bafflement and disbelief. They may shrug it off or dismiss the author as a cynic. In fact he seems not even to be a pessimist. As later becomes clear, though, he wishes above all to be seen as a diagnostician of an intractable difficulty: how to handle political negotiations and military conflicts while retaining political power. He also assumes that if he elucidates this problem as clearly as possible he may win honour for himself and find a decent job.

Finding a job by writing a good book seemed of enormous importance, even if nothing was to come of it. Machiavelli introduces his interest in future employment almost at once, in his book's dedication to Giuliano de'Medici, though after Giuliano's death in 1516, he rededicated it to the more sympathetic Lorenzo, as if what he had written was itself a brilliant résumé or job application – brilliant because it might show his prospective employer how to keep his own job: 'If you read it and consider it diligently, you will discover in it my wish that you reach that eminence that fortune and your other qualities promise you.'[1]

This was not to be. Either Giuliano never saw the book, perhaps because Vettori, who may have had his own reservations about the violence of his friend's ideas, never showed it to him (Vettori nonetheless wrote to him on 18 January 1513 [14], 'I have seen the chapters of your work, and I like them immeasurably, but since I do not have the entire work, I do not want to make a definitive judgement'[2]), or because Giuliano saw it and frowned, possibly over its advocacy of appalling methods.

Machiavelli seems also not to have attempted to see his book through the press, though he fiddled with several of its chapters at least into 1514. Instead, he allowed it to be copied and shown about. The result was that at the beginning of its nonpareil literary career, which continues among the most influential of any books analysing political power, *The Prince* acquired a reputation for evil based on a meagre first-hand knowledge of its contents, as if a lit fuse sizzled away in the dark.

This lost opportunity seems the more surprising because the entire book is both frank and practical. After disposing in his early chapters of basic questions, such as the types of principalities – whether inherited or bestowed, or purchased, acquired by theft, slaughter and assassination – Machiavelli takes up the thorny question of any principality's military needs. Here, as might be expected, he urges the establishment of a citizen militia not dissimilar to what Cesare and he had earlier set up, if without mercenaries. Law and order now become a leitmotif, though Machiavelli insists that order alone may suffice for the prince who knows his business.[3]

The next sections deal with the psychology of power, or with how a prince or other ruler may sensibly manage his subjects. These are more controversial than the rest because in them he comes down heavily in favour of lying, playing people false, including allies, and oath-breaking for the sake of defeating any opposition. His premise is that humanity under pressure is dishonest, flaccid and untrustworthy:

> One can make this generalization about men: they are ungrateful, fickle, liars and deceivers, they shun danger and are greedy for profit; while you treat them well, they are yours. They would shed their blood for you, risk their property, their lives, their sons, so long … as danger is remote; but when you are in danger, they turn away.[4]

As against human insincerity, any confident prince, both remarkably and alone among everyone else in his realm or under his sway, will come to see his ambitions as flourishing in a type of private realm of their own. They will seem beyond the reach of others, or at least beyond ideology. With survival and power remaining for him and his supporters their only worry, all other values or systems of belief will appear of less consequence than the disobedience of a pet dog, or as requiring only punishment, reproof and restraint. The physical demands of power, and the acts of treachery needed to sustain it, will overshadow all abstract principles.

Machiavelli argues that as people 'are a sad lot, and keep no faith with you, you in your turn are under no obligation to keep it with them.' He reverts to an image that he has previously found useful. He proposes that a clever prince ought to 'pick for imitation the fox and the lion,' vacillating between cunning

and brutality, as the situation may warrant. He should 'be ready to enter on
evil if he has to,' and have no compunction about becoming 'a great liar and
hypocrite' – phrases which leave little doubt that he believes in evil as an
acceptable policy.[5]

The unavoidable yet major problem of *Fortuna*, which has to do with a prince's
need to adapt to changing circumstances and a possible inability to do so, he
deals with only at the end. Here he maintains that while *Fortuna* may be an
implacable foe of human success, she can often be tamed – and he now makes
plain his belief in the limited effectiveness of human free will – but only by
force, or as one might deal with a stubborn woman: 'It is better to be rash than
timid, for [*Fortuna*] is a woman, and the man who wants to hold her down must
beat and bully her.'[6]

In this shadowy arena may be discovered Cesare Borgia's fatal mistake.
Always ready to react with force no matter what the circumstances, and thus
rarely drawn down the quieter paths of calculated retreat, he used the same
tactics over and over again, or predictably at the wrong times, as when he was
killed by knights whom he had rashly pursued but who turned on him, or even
earlier when he fell ill while his father lay dying and so allowed his influence to
be dissipated: 'Though one man recently showed certain gleams, such as made
us think that he was ordained by God for our salvation, still we saw how at the
very zenith of his career, he was deserted by [*Fortuna*].'[7]

It is here that the most telling connections between *The Prince*, the *Discorsi* and
the other major artistic achievements of the day seem most fully on display.
The conspicuous themes of the book are its uncompromising naturalism and
its empirical approach to reality, which dovetail with those of the contemporary painting and sculpture. Both reveal an insistence on reality as ceaseless
motion and change. Both implicitly look ahead to the weakening of European
confidence in the staid repetitions of the Ptolemaic System, or with how over
the previous thousand and more years everyone had understood the physical
universe to be operating.

Beyond these points of comparison, there shine out in Machiavelli's style
traces of the growing fashion, permeating literature ever since the invention
of the sonnet, for expressing self-conscious conflicts. Put in another way, the
aesthetic naturalism of his political insights has not perhaps received as much
attention as it deserves, even if the influences on his childhood and adulthood

of world-changing artists such as Benozzo Gozzoli, Michelangelo and Leonardo remain deeply suggestive.

The rhythms and muscularity of Michelangelo's human figures expose transformations unfamiliar to artists of a century earlier. Leonardo's sketches for his *Battle of Anghiari*, like his attempt to divert the Arno, and Gozzoli's depiction in the Medici chapel of the journey of the Magi, with its parade of *cavalieri* mounted on powerfully muscular horses, parse motion in novel and exact ways, doing so decades before Galileo proposed his mathematical description of the universe as a theatre of shifting changes and a field for the permutation of star-packed gravitational forces.

As much might have been said of a third tailed sonnet which Machiavelli sent to Giuliano in early 1514. The poem deals with a gift of trapped thrushes, but is impressive for their deft insertion into an unfolding drama that shows the poet under siege by his enemies, even as he ekes out a private victory:

I send you, Giuliano, some thrushes, not because this gift is good or fine, but so that for a moment Your Magnificence may remember your poor Machiavelli.//And if nearby you find somebody who likes biting, you can hit him in the teeth with it, so that as he eats the bird[s] he may forget about biting others.//'But,' you say, 'perhaps they will not have the effect you speak of, because they are neither good nor fat: backbiters will not eat them.' I answer any such words to the effect that I too am thin, me too, as my enemies well know, and yet they get some hearty mouthfuls off me.//Won't Your Magnificence at last give up your [poor] opinion [of me], and feel and touch, and judge by the hands [or investigate] and not just by what you see?[8]

What was to be seen was his exclusion from the treacherous political worlds of Florence and Rome, whose vigour his witty Tuscan Italian hints at in crisp phrases (*ch'io son maghero anch'io, come lor sano*: I am thin, me too, as my enemies well know). The sonnet's earthy intimacy seems of a piece with change itself, or with adaptation, though its pliancy is anticipated by poems of Villon, whom Machiavelli had not read, and Dante, whom he had.

Appropriately, he also seems to have written and left unfinished at about this time a short essay on Tuscan and its sinewy superiority to other Italian dialects, a *Discorso o dialogo intorno alla nostra lingua* (Discourse or dialogue concerning our language). The essay is unexpectedly if devastatingly critical of Dante, who had been among the first to whip Tuscan into a literary language but who Machiavelli sees as a slavish imitator of classical poets such as Virgil.

Despite his greatness as a poet, Dante exercised an unhealthy influence on the political development of Italy and the West.[9] His mistake lay in his acceptance of imperial rule and his insufficient appreciation of the inevitability of treachery in politics. These were blunders resulting from self-delusions. An annihilation of self-delusion was one of the chief goals of *The Prince*.

Even in the scientific sense of his own day, none of these views, including those of Dante, might in fairness have been regarded as terribly gloomy. Laying bare the role of treachery in politics, or seeing politics as provoking treacherous acts, amounted to accepting that one inhabited a universe whose basis was mutation. In such a universe, ethical issues necessarily took second or third place, despite the purported goodness of God and the fact that the universe itself was governed by physical, emotional and spiritual laws. The uncertainty of the political world required a constant frustration of ethical ambitions. Even the gifted prince must find his opportunities bitterly circumscribed.

# 29

# The Ambush of Love

'While living in the country I have met a creature so gracious, so refined, so noble – both in nature and in circumstance – that never could my praise or my love for her be as much as she deserves.' Thus one of his letters to Vettori on 3 August 1514.

He was writing from Florence, to which he had begun regularly to return. That his 'creature' was a country woman whom he saw on the sly, probably the unnamed widowed sister of one Niccolò Tafani, seemed as seductive as his enchantment: 'Suffice it to say that although I am approaching my fiftieth year [he was forty five], neither does the heat of the sun distress me, nor do rough roads wear me out, nor do the dark hours of the night terrify me: I adapt to her every whim … [and] even though I may now seem to have entered into great travail, I nevertheless feel so great a sweetness in it that not for anything in the world would I desire my freedom.'

He had fallen for another sort of freedom, though. Whether because Vettori had been able to read the whole of *The Prince*, and found it unacceptable, or because he had abandoned his own high hopes for it, he had freed himself at least for the moment from his 'delight in reading about the deeds of the ancients or in discussing those of the moderns.' 'Everything has been transformed into tender thoughts,' he wrote, or his enthusiasms newly revealed, and even to himself.[1]

Whoever she was as she captured him in her graceful 'nets of gold woven by Venus,' she was not at all like the saucier *La Riccia*, who complained that he made a nuisance of himself by hanging about her house: 'she calls me her "House Pest."'[2] Nor had she been discovered in his familiar circle of Florentine prostitutes. They might, for instance, enjoy seeing an acquaintance tricked into paying for some stranger having sex with a sly teenage boy up a dark alley, a *Decameron*-like escapade that, on hearing about it, he found hilarious. Neither, however, was she apt to refuse a gift of 'blue woollen yarn for a pair of hose', which he asked Vettori to send him in early December 1514.

By 31 January 1515 he had begun to complain that 'you will realize to what extent that little thief, Love, has gone in order to bind me with his fetters.' He wove another ironic and moving sonnet into this letter, portraying love as a 'youthful archer' who has often 'tried/to wound me in the breast with his arrows.' He has finally 'let one fly' with such force 'that I still feel its painful wound.'

Still, his personal contradictions amused him: 'Anyone who might see our letters, honourable *compare,*' he told Vettori, 'and see their variety, would be greatly astonished, because at first it would seem that we were serious men completely directed towards weighty matters and that no thought could cascade through our heads that did not have within it probity and magnitude. But later, upon turning the page, it would seem to the reader that we – still the very same selves – were petty, fickle, lascivious, and were directed toward chimerical matters.'

Their shifts were only natural, however: 'If to some this behaviour seems contemptible, to me it seems laudable because we are imitating nature.' Nature, like *Fortuna*, is always 'changeable, [and] whoever imitates nature cannot be censured.'[3] To prove the point, he at once changes the subject, or shifts away from love to his usual exasperated quest for work, either with the Medici or the Pope, or Vettori's brother Paolo. Paolo had lately been visiting Lorenzo de'Medici in Florence.

Despite himself, too, he scarcely ignored political and military questions in any ultimate sense. His value as an analyst remained in demand. Francesco Vettori was discreetly asked by Cardinal Giuliano de'Medici (as was revealed to Machiavelli only that December) to obtain his estimate of a contemplated Vatican alliance with Spain as opposed to France, or with either as opposed to remaining neutral. Machiavelli's lengthy and unpaid-for examination of the alternatives ran to several thousand words. It concluded with his describing neutrality as the least attractive of the three, and repeating in his aphoristic way a few of his ideas advanced in *The Prince*: 'A league of many leaders against one is hard to achieve and, once achieved, is hard to preserve'; 'There is nothing more necessary for a prince when interacting with his subjects, his allies or his neighbours than not to be hated or despised by them'; 'Pope Julius II never gave any heed to being hated, provided that he was feared and respected'; and 'It is better to lose everything gallantly than to lose a part ignominiously.' To choose and join, he argued, would always prove more useful than to stand aside, or to speculate and hope.[4]

It may have been at this time too, or in 1514, that he turned once more to his unfinished *terza rima* history of modern Florence. He worked up parts of his *Decennale Secondo*, or some 216 lines, prolonging his chronicle of the Republic's 'tragic' drift towards failure from where he had left off in 1504. It now took him into 'the lofty … and insane actions that in ten succeeding years have occurred since, falling silent, I laid down my pen.' The defeat of Pisa ('a stubborn enemy, yet by necessity compelled and conquered') was now permitted to anticipate Pope Julius's assault on Faenza. 'The King of the Christians'' capture of Lombardy was allowed to incite the Emperor Maximilian's devastation of weak, defensive armies at Padua and Treviso.

Here again, though, or on reaching the year 1509, his poetic account faded into silence, just when it seemed to be slouching towards the disaster that would overwhelm the Florentine Republic in 1512.[5] The reason may have been twofold. On the one hand, he had returned to his more ambitious *Discorsi*. On the other, and assisting him, was a refreshing improvement of his professional life. He had for some time been welcomed as a respected and popular member of regular and remarkable gatherings of a major part of the Florentine literary intelligentsia.

Their meetings took place in the sprawling, practically suburban estate of Cosimo Rucellai (*d.*1519), remnants of which can still be found along the eponymous street named for his father, the bookish Bernardo, or at a decent stroll from the Palazzo della Signoria. Sliced up and truncated at number eight, or opposite the American Church built in 1911 by J.P. Morgan, the plush Rucellai gardens, then termed the Orti Oricellari, were enchanting for their tall, exotic, ancient trees, and already well known for the Pantheon degli Accademici Neoplatonici, a recently disbanded Platonic-Aristotelian discussion group that seems to have been located in the airy palace built here along neo-Albertian lines, if not by Alberti himself, in 1482. In the gardens of the Rucellai some of the most advanced political ideas of the day, among them questions about Lorenzo de'Medici's increasingly absolutist government, were hotly if unobtrusively taken up and debated.[6]

In these exclusive, green precincts too, Machiavelli began to test his insights for Books Two and Three of his commentaries on Livy. He read them out before an audience that would have included, in addition to the sickly, cheerful, rich Cosimo, whose servants lugged him about in a cradle-like chair, other friends of the Medici, no matter that they yearned for political liberty, such as the young Zanobi Buondelmonti, to whom later, along with Cosimo, the *Discorsi* would be

dedicated, and Piero Alamanni, a poet with a naïve desire to write in the style
of Virgil's *Georgics*.

Machiavelli's commentaries followed, as before, out of his premise, often
restated, that 'all affairs of this world are in motion and will not remain fixed.'
They stressed his view of politics, history and the universe as continuous
processes: 'Human affairs are always in motion and will consequently either
rise or fall'; 'Human appetites are insatiable because nature gives us the ability
and will to desire everything, while *Fortuna* gives us the ability to acquire only
a little,' with the result a 'continuous discontent in the minds of men, and dis-
satisfaction with the things that they possess.'[7]

Social and religious issues were hardly ignored: 'If the world seems to have
become effeminate, and heaven disarmed, this doubtless arises more from the
cowardice of men who have interpreted our religion [Christianity] through the
prism of indolence, and not through that of skill [*virtú*] and valour [as had been
the case in pagan Rome]'; 'The liberality with which the Romans used to grant
the privileges of citizenship to strangers ... [led them] ... to exercise so great an
influence in the elections that it sensibly changed the government, and caused
... Quintilian Fabius, who was Censor at that time ... [to confine them] to such
narrow limits [that] they should not corrupt all Rome' – his purpose being to
allow these 'strangers' or outsiders to be absorbed into the state and to remain
even as the state was in the end 'sensibly' changed.[8]

The calm of the gardens contrasted with the busy city beyond their walls. In
June 1514, in the Piazza della Signoria, Machiavelli might have witnessed a
staged hunt involving lions, bears, leopards, bulls, buffaloes, stags, other wild
game and horses. Platforms and corrals were erected at enormous expense in
the *piazza* to accommodate the crowds and animals.

In the audience six masked cardinals from Rome, among them the Pope's
nephew, Cibo, who had sneaked off to Florence for a few days, paid as much
for their tickets as did forty thousand others. Many had walked from as far as
Milan and Venice. Jousts took place at the Piazza di Santa Croce, with sixteen
armed riders tilting for two prizes, or *pali*, in gold and silver brocade. One was
thrust through, fell off his horse and died. At the *piazza*, lions were co-mingled
with bears in a large wooden box, and to everyone's surprise refused to fight. A
female lion defended a bear when a male lion attacked it.[9]

Other signs of vitality were abundant: on 30 November 1515, Pope Leo X
arrived in Florence on an official triumph. The jaunty rich among the citizens,

dressed in purple silk softened with miniver collars, carrying small silver lances and followed by a gilt supporting cast on horseback, stepped out to meet him. Leo drew up before one of the embellished city gates with scores of his German infantry wielding double-bladed, French-style axes, mounted bowmen and squares of musketeers. Arrayed beneath a lavish canopy, or *baldacchino*, he was hoisted off to the *Duomo*, surrounded by lit torches lining the streets as far as the entrance and inside up to the High Altar.

An even better impression of his power and wealth could have been had from noting the aesthetic energy poured into the whirlwind of decorations made for his visit. Triumphal arches and silvered-over columns adorned the streets, their pilasters, statues, cornices, bannerettes and painted porticos conceived and executed by the best, and best paid, local artists, among them some echoing designs of Filippo Brunelleschi, with air-borne aureoles displaying saints and goddesses amid cherubs and clouds.

Leo responded to this joyful welcome with his own largesse, tossing money into the crowds packing the public spaces and hailing and blessing them.[10]

Not everyone was thrilled, though, and from another point of view it could have been observed that the quasi-rebellious if subdued atmosphere of the Rucellai gardens reflected Machiavelli's disillusionment in failing to find employment with Lorenzo de'Medici. Even if he seemed no longer to nurture the family's previous hostility towards the former Second Secretary, it seemed impossible to win more than a nod of recognition from his mighty, ennobled, sacred, fatty and rich uncle, the Pope, who had till now ignored his appeals.

# 30

# Literary Adventures

Over the next few months, silences gathered between his letters. '*Fortuna* has left me nothing but my family and my friends,' he wrote from Florence on 19 November 1515 to his cousin Giovanni Vernacci, who had become a close confidant, 'and I make capital out of them.' His situation had scarcely improved by 15 February of the following year, or as he informed Vernacci, 'I have become useless to myself, to my family and to my friends because my doleful fate has willed it to be so.... All I have left is my own good health and that of my family.'

This was not quite true, though his sense of desolation had perhaps deepened. By now he had switched much of his energy into writing, with a good deal of it concentrated on treachery and related themes – pretence, dishonesty, deception and the mocking tones of satire – as might perhaps have been expected.

He had also become touchy about the indifference sometimes shown him by more prominent authors. On 17 December 1517 he enquired of Ludovico Alamanni about his famous friend Ludovico Ariosto and his *Orlando*. Its first edition was published in Ferrara in April 1516, and Machiavelli may have met the poet in Rome during his visit there some years earlier, or in Florence: Ariosto had arrived in the city on the day of his own release from prison. He now added, 'Lately I have been reading Ariosto's *Orlando Furioso*; the entire poem is really fine and many passages are marvellous. If he is [in Rome] with you, give him my regards and tell him that my only complaint is that in his mention of so many poets he has left me out like some prick, and that he has done to me in his *Orlando* what I shall not do to him in my *Ass*.'[1]

In fact he sought no revenge in his *Ass*, and the absence of Machiavelli's name from Ariosto's list in his *Orlando* of a number of highly regarded if today neglected Italian Renaissance poets was not reciprocated in the perhaps unfinished, more than one-thousand-line-long *Dell'Asino* (The Ass; an erroneous retitling of it as 'The Golden Ass' came about later), on which he may just then have been working. A fascinating, lengthy poem, which in his lifetime was to remain unpublished, *The Ass* delivers up a schizophrenic-seeming story that sails off in several directions at once. This may be why it leaves the impression among many readers of never having been finished, though he may have considered it done, and may even have shown it about or read it at one of the banquets held in the Rucellai gardens.

Tenderness, affection and a lush sensuality, each streaming through a magical love story influenced by Dante, alternate here with satirical scenes based on Apuleius – specifically, his second-century *Transformations* (or *The Metamorphoses* or *The Golden Ass*) *of Lucius Apuleius* – as when the narrator announces in the first few lines that he has endured much 'grief' while living as an ass, but then fails to fill us in, as promised, on how his dramatic alteration came about.

Vistas displaying gloomy assemblies of large, dilapidated animals, among them a mass of tired and rug-like lions, who seem post-human, or not at all like the alert horses and pigs of George Orwell's *Animal Farm*, lumber past, immersed in an existentialist, Circean twilight and hinting at a fulfilled wish, or so the poem implies, to revert to their original beast-like condition, even if Machiavelli's hirsute specimens seem somewhat tongue-tied. In Chapter 8, this zoo-like enigma is resolved by a philosophical if undemonstrative hog. He winds up Machiavelli's mock epic, or as much of it as exists, by revelling in his rejection of his former humanity. He avers that he is better off than any human being 'because in this mud I live more happily;/here without anxiety I bathe and roll about.'[2]

It should be noted, however, that Apuleius' *Golden Ass* (the 'golden' refers to the author's orotund, professional Latin style and not to the precious metal) seems deliberately diffuse in its organization, images and meanings. It evokes a plethora of confused implications. The question arises whether Machiavelli has not also aimed at producing a puzzle; whether in fabricating a poem whose theme is escape from human conflicts he has not invented a clear mirror of some of the most common human perplexities.

During this period he seems as well to have written some now lost *gesta*, or entertaining, moralistic tales. The modern short story, while loosely descended from their medieval and Renaissance prototype, differs greatly from the *gesta* in plot, psychology and characterization. To judge from Machiavelli's sole surviving example, however, his own *gesta* or *favole* cannot have been moral in any conventional way.

*Belfagor*, often referred to as *Il demonio che prese moglie* (The devil who took a wife), seems a product of these years, or between 1515 and 1519. It only barely resembles Boccaccio's tales in *The Decameron*, and is surely not a novella, or not in the modern sense, but edges closer to its more florid medieval forebears. Populated with stock characters – frightened and frightening devils who seem as pagan as Christian, an obnoxious wife, a tricky, opportunistic peasant – it also cannot be understood as autobiographical, or as implicating Machiavelli's marriage, as some readers have suggested. Despite a few blips here and there, his marriage apparently continued amid expressions of affection on both sides.

In *Belfagor*, Pluto, the ruler of the underworld, decides to investigate a claim that most of the souls of men condemned to the flames of Hell have been driven to sinning by their insatiable wives. An arch-devil, Belfagor, is fitted out with money, princely good looks and a trip to Florence to find out the truth. He is told to locate a suitable woman, marry her and live with her for ten years. He adopts the name Roderigo, disguises himself as a merchant and succeeds in marrying Onestà, whose beauty is undeniable. Because of her incessant demands, which he feels unable to refuse, he is soon plunged into monumental debt and faces bankruptcy.

In flight from enraged creditors, he is hidden in a dung-heap by a peasant, Gianmatteo, to whom he promises money in exchange for protection. When Gianmatteo asks him to keep his word, however, Roderigo tells him that he will do so by entering someone's body – he quickly takes possession of another man's wife – and arranging that Gianmatteo handle her exorcism for a fee. This he does, and money is made. Roderigo's next target is the daughter of the King of Naples. Her exorcism brings in 50,000 ducats. This is more than enough for Gianmatteo, who by now wants only to go home and spend what he has earned.

He has not, however, reckoned on Roderigo's enjoyment of these acts of possession, and is horrified to learn that the daughter of King Louis VII of France is now also possessed. With his reputation for exorcism growing by leaps and bounds, Gianmatteo is expected to rescue her too, or face execution. Terrified, he agrees, but then sets about tricking the trickster-devil. On a platform before Notre Dame in Paris he arranges a ceremonial exorcism for the King's daughter. At a pre-arranged moment he orders a crowd of nobles and musicians to make crunching and crashing sounds on musical instruments. Roderigo wonders what all the noise can be about, but Gianmatteo says that it announces the imminent arrival of his wife. Aghast, Roderigo races back to hell, and there '[bears] witness to the ills that wives [bring] on a house, while

Gianmatteo, who [has] outwitted the devil, [travels] back home a cheerful man.'[3]

Machiavelli's story has spawned a number of dramatic and literary adaptations: Respighi turned it into an opera, Pirandello into a modernistic poem. It is also nothing new. The sexist plot is traceable to a venerable Indian story collection, the *Sukasaptati*, probably introduced into Europe by the invading Mongols under Genghis Khan (*c.*1162–1227), or long before Machiavelli transposed it to Florence.

The tale's interest thus lies not in some indictment of marriage – an absurdity suggested only by Belfagor, even if his wife turns out to be no bargain – but in a reenactment of the age-old jest type, found in many *favole* and *fabliaux*, which shows a peasant traducing the devil. A greater attraction lies in the smoothness of Machiavelli's style.

A contradiction between the disreputable passions on display and Machiavelli's softening of them through civilized phrases creates many delicious echoes. The retold folktale invokes a euphoria of antiquity. An Indian afternoon turns into a Florentine evening as modern connections dispute with the temporal fixations of history: 'A miraculous change came upon Roderigo when he heard the word "wife." The change was so momentous that he gave no thought to whether it was even possible or a reasonable assumption that his wife could have come, and without another word, he fled in terror, releasing the young princess.'[4]

By 1518 too, if not perhaps several years before, Machiavelli had also committed himself to playwriting, and with success. In retrospect this alternative career seems natural enough to him, though at first it may have amounted only to a diversion. Like other Italian and European Renaissance cities, Florence had no professional acting troupes. It had no buildings intended as theatres (Palladio's Olympia in Vicenza, probably the first, dates from 1565) and only mysterious Roman ruins to remind the curious of an ancient theatrical history that few knew much about.

Many, however, enjoyed their memories of sacred, biblically based medieval plays, which were often revived. Theatrical experiments, too, whether read or acted out in religious or noble houses, or in academic settings, stimulated an avid popular interest in drama.

Pope Leo's glittering welcome might easiest have been understood as complementing the established tradition of court masques. The rediscovered plays of Seneca nurtured a modern interest in tragedy, though their soaring heroics seemed alien to the tastes of ordinary audiences.

The obscene plays of Plautus and Terence, however, dug into the customs of taverns, whorehouses, streets and the tradesman's life. Their stock characters – the cheating servant, the ridiculous aged husband, the love-crazed youth, to cite Machiavelli's descriptions of them – fed a more general pleasure taken in comedy. Terence had concentrated on comedies of manners. Plautus had taken as his realm Rome's swashbuckling brothels.

Machiavelli had copied out plays of Terence in his mid-twenties, and so knew them well. In his recent discourse on language he had announced his theatrical intentions. A comedy ought to hold up 'a mirror to domestic life … with a certain urbanity and with expressions which excite laughter, so that the [people] who come eagerly to enjoy themselves taste afterwards the useful lesson that lay underneath.'[5]

His *The Woman of Andros*, an adaptation of Terence's *Andria*, may date from as late as 1517. In rewriting the ancient Roman drama of baffled young love, he was working against a well-known academic current of Latin humanist comedies. Termed *commedie erudite*, their popularity spanned the fifteenth century and included such plays as Pier Paolo Vergerio's *Paolus* (c.1390), *Chrysis* (1444) by Aeneas Silvius Piccolomini, who later became Pope Pius II, and Tommaso Medio's *Epirota* (1483).[6]

Machiavelli was thus already a playwright of some repute by the time, most likely in 1518, he produced his single indubitable masterpiece, which would act as a catalyst in the development of modern drama, *La Mandragola* (The Mandrake). As now seems evident, his lost *Eunuchus*, another adaptation of Terence, his *Aululia*, a recasting of a comedy by Plautus, and yet another lost play, *Le Maschere* (The Masks, an original satire in which he supposedly raked familiar public figures over some fairly hot coals), all praised by those who saw them, may have been written and put on as many as ten or more years earlier.

But put on how? If not a lot is known about his or anyone else's early productions, it seems clear that by 1518 major artists had become as fascinated with the idea of creating theatrical illusions as were the actors and playwrights. The earliest-known revolving stage was invented by Leonardo in 1490. It offered audiences a puffy *papier-maché* mountain that split and shivered apart to reveal the play in progress.[7] Important artists such as Bastiano da San Gallo and Andrea del Sarto painted sets for early performances of Machiavelli's

*Mandragola*, with backdrops showing three-dimensional illusions of streets and interiors.

Costumes, which had seemed plain and inconsequential at the academic readings held in universities, were now enhanced. Masks and disguises all at once became as *de rigueur* as illusion itself (what, after all, was real?). Acting styles shed their bombastic lumps and exaggerated tics for naturalistic gestures: a duel might actually resemble a fight to the death.

An old theatrical war-horse, windy declamation, or inflated phrases and pompous outbursts, subsided into the more convincing succulence of everyday speech. A significant shift along these lines, at which Machiavelli excelled, involved dialogue. In his hands, it not only sounded like the real thing but became pitch perfect.

Other innovations, if not his own but improved by him over what was on tap in plays by such as Ariosto, had to do with characterization and theme. Stock characters were retained, but Machiavelli enriched them with contradictions. Triteness was endowed with the complexities of living people.

Other devices of ancient Roman comedy, such as sprinkling tricks, japes and ironies with puns and lies, gathered into a more credible atmosphere of unceasing betrayal and treachery. *The Mandragola* was among the first of what may be termed the modern comedies of treachery. Loops of deceit, which left no one innocent, emerged as risible and charming rather than humiliating and menacing. Their final effect was one of paradoxical happiness, in which an audience might discover the pleasures of self-recognition.

In *The Mandragola*, these innovations are flattered by a sassy wit. Nicia, the beautiful Lucrezia's oafish husband, who yearns for an heir, is presented not simply as a typical lecher whose age renders him an apt and satisfying target for catcalls, but also as a lawyer capable of social commentary: 'These damned doctors couldn't find your gizzard if you dangled it before their eyes'; 'In Florence if you're not in with the ruling party, you can't even get a dog to bark at you.'[8]

The Friar, a well-known type usually depicted as all flab and corruption, is here spruced up as a greedy apologist for clerical weakness: 'It's not our fault! We've not done a good job of keeping the church's reputation going.'[9]

Callimaco, Lucrezia's lust-driven lover, an example of the moonstruck idiot-type, is allowed shrewdness and a chance to anticipate his own confusion: 'I have been seized by such a desire to be with her that I shall go mad.'[10]

Lucrezia, to whom another corrupt priest has proposed that drinking a pointless potion of mandrake juice will allow her to become pregnant, is suspicious of everyone: 'Of all the things we have tried, this seems to me the strangest.'[11]

Ligurio, a retired matchmaker and a recognizable image of duplicity, coolly observes that 'men in love have quicksilver feet,' but is then permitted to comment on the growing climate of betrayal and camouflage in which fool is tricked by fool: 'We'll all be in disguise.'[12]

As Nicia is duped into assisting at the bedding of Callimaco and his own wife, going so far as to lock the door on them at night and offer them the key the next day, Machiavelli's ironic final scenes perpetuate the marital treachery while converting it into a delight that embraces Nicia himself. Lucrezia may rationalize her ethically dubious joy with her new lover as 'Heaven's will,' but what the play ultimately makes fun of – and audiences more than warmed to the idea – is the futility of applying strict ethical formulas to human behaviour. Life and experience are likely to make nonsense of them.

Machiavelli himself offered no apologies for his play's veritable gush of paradoxes. In his Prologue he candidly alludes to his, or, as he puts it, the Author's, hardships as he speaks of wanting to come up with a comedy which would 'lighten his misery, for he has nowhere else to turn, barred as he is from demonstrating his skills and abilities through worthier tasks, his labour no longer prized.'[13]

One act of treachery may deserve another, it seems, or at least a stunning play showing how treachery operates on the domestic level. As a bonus, it may also demonstrate how on occasion treachery may work for the common good.

# 31

# *Reflecting on the Craft of War*

A series of coincidental deaths among his military-minded acquaintances, friends and enemies during those years spurred his reflections on the *arte*, or more accurately, the craft, of war.

Louis XII of France died of dysentery on 1 January 1515. He was succeeded by Francis I. The Holy Roman Emperor Maximilian died at Wels (not Linz, as Guicciardini thought[1]) in early 1519, 'intent,' as the Florentine historian reliably puts it, on 'hunting wild beasts,' as was his habit. Closer to home, Cosimo Rucellai, the benefactor of Machiavelli's conversations at the Orti Oricellari and just twenty seven, also died in 1519. A respected nobleman and *condottiere*, Fabrizio Colonna, a visitor at the Rucellai gardens, where Machiavelli probably came to know him, died in 1520.

Lorenzo de'Medici, the egotistical twenty-five-year-old ruler of Florence, died of tuberculosis worsened by syphilis in April 1519. This was a few days after the death following childbirth of his French wife.[2] Though few mourned his death, and despite Machiavelli's rededicating *The Prince* to him after the death of his uncle, Giuliano, it paved the way for revisions of the city's constitution, or a more sensitive leadership under Cardinal Giulio de'Medici. He had arrived in Florence and taken charge of affairs before news of Lorenzo's death was bruited about, thus ensuring that 'there was no unrest.'

The quasi-original conception of *L'Arte della Guerra* (usually translated as The Art of War) apparently occurred to Machiavelli in 1520, after the deaths of his two friends, Cosimo Rucellai, 'whom I never remember without tears in my eyes,' and Fabrizio Colonna.[3] The book presents a fictional dialogue between them in what remained the fashionable manner for investigating philosophical subjects, such as free will, though Machiavelli-*cum*-Colonna here deals with the problems of war and militarism from a good many practical angles.

The dialogue is set in the Rucellai gardens during a single afternoon back in 1516, or well before his friends' deaths. Fabrizio has just returned 'from

Lombardy, where he has commanded his Catholic Majesty's [or the new Spanish Emperor Charles V's] forces' – this bit is no fiction – and is invited to show off his expertise on matters military before reporting to the Pope in Rome. Cosimo has 'long wished to hear [these matters] thoroughly discussed,' as have a number of his 'intimate friends,' among them Machiavelli.[4]

Even now *The Art of War* exerts a considerable influence on the history of ideas, and not simply because it is the only one of Machiavelli's major works to be published in his lifetime, in 1521. Its several minor deficiencies, or the not really crippling errors scattered among its seven chapters, are also easily identified. They seem attributable to the skewed conclusions that he may have arrived at as a result of his still somewhat limited war experience, though he cites the fact that he has never served as a soldier as providing him with independence of judgement.

He seems too flippantly dismissive, for instance, of the use of small arms or arquebuses in battle. He is equally dismissive of the advantages of cavalry, no doubt because he had seen almost nothing of massive cavalry attacks, though he knew quite a bit about the relative helplessness of small cavalry units sent out against disciplined infantry armed with pikes and swords. Some of the book's blemishes may also be due to changing military conditions, as when Colonna (or Machiavelli) pronounces himself unable to find much to praise in concentrated artillery fire. Artillery was just then coming into its own in a new way as commanders learned how to apply it against infantry in the field rather than only against town and castle walls. In each of these cases, however, rapid technical improvements, leading to increases in the numbers of weapons and more and better trained mounted men, would soon prove crucial to victories straight across the Continent.

It also goes without saying that Machiavelli and his contemporaries understood war almost entirely from the infantry's point of view. Colonna makes no mention of naval battles, for instance, which may have seemed irrelevant. Nonetheless, and while misjudging artillery, he displays a certain flexibility as he concedes that the pre-artillery battlefield methods of the ancient Roman general Scipio would be inadequate in the face of the reloading and refiring of heavy modern weapons.

The ghosts of ancient Roman soldiers, strategists and engineers haunt *The Art of War*, as might be expected, given Machiavelli's humanist values. A more telling reason for their presiding over the various chapters, though, lies in his implacable persuasion of Roman military greatness, or the streak of Roman victories running through the Republican period and continuing into that of the Caesars and their successors (Augustus had seized much of central and northern Europe: Vespasian had added vast territories in England and Germany). It made no difference that corruption and selfish passions had by then eroded many naturally generous motives and moulted into dictatorial ambitions.

Roman and Greek ideas of war had a lot to teach the modern soldier, or so he felt, and not only by comparison. The diverse sections are thus peppered with ancient military data, together with diagrams, and focus on such topics as Greek and Roman as well as recent arms and armour, battle formations, the size of armies, marching styles, choosing camp sites, pitching tents, managing 'military' women, restricting gambling, the quantities of troops necessary for engagements, fortifying towns, obtaining horses and preparing ambushes.

His primary source is the fourth-century *De re militari* (On the Military Question) of Vegetius, though he resorts to other authorities such as Polybius. He copies out chapter and verse as he needs them. While much of this material retains a fascination on antiquarian grounds, it would be a mistake to ignore the forest for the trees, or to scant his book's original features. These dominate everything else and consist in his grasp, in advance of other analysts, of the inevitable relationship between politics and war, his insights into the value of militias to the survival of the state, as opposed to standing armies, and his realization of the importance of military discipline to the political as well as the military education of entire populations.[5]

In respect to these issues alone, *The Art of War* may be said to continue to affect if not actually alter history, as is evidenced by the continuing attention focused on the book in military academies, and the strategic dreams – or nightmares – of significant political-military leaders of recent decades, among them Napoleon, Hitler, Mussolini and Stalin, along with democratically elected ministers and presidents.

Unexpectedly perhaps, Machiavelli almost at once voices his opposition to the militarization of society. He insists on the greater need of a well-grounded civilian government. Any army, he believes, ought to be the servant of its state. Dangerous to the state's survival, moreover, is some division between its political and military leaders, as will occur when its army is led by professional soldiers who view soldiering and war as occupations or businesses.[6]

The result, as witnessed in the more despairing annals of ancient history, or for that matter those of Italy in recent times, will be political weakness keeling over into collapse. War, he argues, as would Karl von Clausewitz (1780–1831), himself an avid reader of his *Art of War* some centuries later, is without exception politics expressed by other means. Even the most pointless-seeming violence, if protracted, assumes the patterns of a political policy.[7]

Machiavelli's uncovering the relations between political and military tugs and pulls should also be understood as pointing to the superiority of militias over standing armies. In pressing home this idea he ironically shows himself in sympathy with those who suspected him of disloyalty to the Florentine Republic when years earlier he had urged the establishment of a citizen militia, and who worried lest an armed citizenry should stage (in the modern sense) a *Putsch*.

A *Putsch* or *coup d'état*, he (or Colonna) suggests, is far more likely to emanate from a standing army than from native-born troops holding jobs or careers apart from soldiering, and who will be apt to be sent home after their battles and wars. The *ad hoc* nature of a citizen militia guarantees its commitment to peaceful politics as opposed to *putschist* treachery.

In teasing out this conviction Machiavelli seems in important ways to antic-ipate the military policies of modern democracies, whose armies may consist of both small standing and large militia-type units, but the vast majority of whose soldiers are conscripted for limited tours of duty. Again he here insists on the superiority of the civilian to any military government: 'A well-ordered kingdom must avoid the soldierly profession ... since those men corrupt the king [or any other type of ruler] and are the ministers of tyranny.'[8]

A major theme, already sounded in *The Prince* and the *Discorsi*, is that any healthy state ought to arrange its politics and soldiering so that they flow back and forth into each other in complementary currents. The life of the soldier and that of the citizen should blend and merge for the sake of the tranquil preser-vation of both.

These arguments lead into his somewhat surprising conclusion that military discipline is fundamental not only to the success of any army but to the education of the non-military surrounding population of citizens. His reason here is that military-style discipline, if exported into the outside social world, can provide an essential paradigm of education in civil courage and social responsibility.[9]

Such a policy may stimulate patriotism (or, somewhat later, nationalism), while any failure to nurture patriotic sentiments is likely to lead to a social implosion and military defeat. The social uses of military discipline, however, should not be confused with the military domination of society, which is to be avoided.

To illustrate these principles, he recalls that 'the dreadful alarms, the disgraceful defeats and the astonishing losses ... sustained [by Italian forces] in 1494' 'resulted from the [poor quality] of their military discipline.' An 'ancient discipline [ought now to] be reintroduced among raw, honest men' by princes who refuse to debase their armies' morale and confidence by spending 'their time in wanton dalliance and lascivious pleasures, [maintaining] a haughty kind of state, [humiliating] their subjects ... [and disposing] of their military honours and preferments to pimps and parasites.'[10]

Probably the most innovative of his ideas lies in his promotion of a quantificational approach to setting up military organizations. The proper arrangements of troops, armies, battles, ammunition and weapons are or should be reducible to numbers, equations, designs (as of military units) and statistics. The challenge of training and deploying an army, he implies, can be converted into an exact science, or form of engineering. Any calculation of an army's supplies, for instance, should be based on an estimate of available social resources. Military calculations can thus help to ensure the survival of civil politics.

He refrains from applying the quantificational approach himself, however, with the exception of his introduction of it into a few camp designs and battlefield suggestions.[11] Instead, and despite his stress on discipline and a view of armies as marvellously efficient because perfectly organized machines, he is apparently willing to leave to others the development of military science. His interest in it seems to be satisfied by his establishing the principle of quantification. It unquestionably enhanced his book's popularity. A second edition appeared in 1529, with translations into Spanish, French and English following over the next forty years.

He may also have been exceedingly busy. He addressed his Preface to *The Art of War* to Lorenzo di Filippo Strozzi (1482–1549), a wealthy young nobleman whom he may have met at the Rucellai gatherings, and who had done him some unspecified favours and was acquainted with Giulio de'Medici. The contact could not have been more helpful. Where until now various official doors had been shut they seemed to fly open. As early as 21 April 1520, Battista della Palla, a friend and Rucellai regular, a dialogue-participant in *The Art of War* and an intermediary of sorts between Giulio and the Pope, wrote that he had 'found [the Pope] very well disposed towards you.'

The popularity of *La Mandragola*, with its promise of sexy pleasures, had appealed to Leo's hedonistic temperament. Despite his myopia and billowy stoutness, he remained an ardent playgoer and voluptuary, if a mediocre writer. In view of Machiavelli's historical and literary achievements, it seemed that Leo might be interested in 'commissioning [him] to do some writing,' and here may be a first reference to what would become a valuable invitation: he might be asked to take on the challenge of doing a new history of Florence. After years of neglect and indifference, he might even begin to enjoy a measure of official approval.

His play, especially, seems to have worked as a catalyst. Its cheering Florentine reception had led Leo to order a separate Roman production, arranged by Battista. Leo's idea was to make himself better acquainted with what Battista called 'your intelligence and judgement' ('I spoke of your comedy, telling him that it is all ready'), or at least to learn more about his potential historian.[12]

Machiavelli was now busy in another way as well, and it too may have caught Leo's eye. To make money, he accepted commissions taking him into nearby cities such as Genoa to settle bankruptcy and other financial claims, chiefly on behalf of people whom he knew. His abilities as a negotiator had thus begun to prove modestly lucrative. The summer of 1520 found him in Lucca, nudging away for the Salviati at a bankruptcy problem involving Michele Guinigi. This too meant assisting a member of the Pope's family.

His Lucca commission lasted for several months, or into early September. It left him with time on his hands, and he at once set about turning it into a literary-historical opportunity which might also have brought him closer to the Pope and the Medici: the chance to produce a several-thousand-word-long sketch of the life of the medieval Luccan commander Castruccio Castracani (1281–1328), a well-known military hero who had once soundly defeated Florence while ravaging the Florentine countryside.[13]

It is fair to say that for sheer strangeness and beauty, and despite some uneven patches, Machiavelli's account of Castruccio's life has few equals in the history of biographical propaganda. And how else except as propaganda to understand his extravagant treatment of Castruccio's life? On the one hand, Machiavelli idealizes an historically remote soldier, whose rise from squalor seems as abrupt as his lapse into an excruciating death. On the other, he takes care, even to the point of wild inventions, to make the right impression on his possible employer in Rome. Following on from a quasi-mythical opening, his fantasy consists of a utopian cameo-history of the hero and his era. A good deal of both seems intended to provide some surprising ethical lessons along a rocky road.

A more appropriate way to see his *Life*, however, may lie in accepting as more than a coincidence the fact that he produced it and sent it off to his friends within a few years of the publication of Thomas More's *Utopia* (1516, in Latin). More's book, which also came out in Florence in 1519, was most likely known to him. The time in any case continued to be receptive to utopias and satires, as had been the case with the tales of Till Eulenspiegel. Machiavelli's life of Castruccio is no satire, but its utopian features may easily lead the modern reader into discovering in him the portrait of an ideal, heroic, controversial prince, *à la* Cesare Borgia. Here, however, a problem emerges: his biographer's heroic values differ from almost any recent ones. The modern reader quickly runs into trouble, for instance, over the seeming contradiction that while the *Life* deplores militarism, it appears to endorse military violence, and even huge gobs of it.

Castruccio starts off a bit like Moses, as a foundling 'wrapped in leaves.' He is raised in Lucca by a priest and his childless sister. He acquires his military training from their friend, 'a fine gentleman of the Guinigi family' (a detail that falsely connects him to the Medici). His instructor notices that Castruccio's martial skills far surpass those of other boys.[14] At eighteen, or during his first military campaign, he exhibits 'so much prudence and courage' that he becomes famous through 'all of Lombardy.' The death of Guinigi, however, who has named him his estate manager and guardian of his thirteen-year-old son, provokes slanderous attacks on Castruccio by influential and jealous men who believe that he has his 'mind set on tyranny.'

A slew of battles, leading to victories, ambushes, defeats and additional victories, swirls about him through the next exhausting stages of his life. A pattern is established in which he is betrayed, taken prisoner, liberated, returned as a 'prince of Lucca' and again betrayed, imprisoned and released. Routs, maimings, shrieks, kidnappings, explosions and shootings accompany the deaths of up to 'ten thousand men' per day. The elephantine numbers of deaths plump out a stew of implausible adventures.

Throughout all these disturbances, too – and herein may lie the modern rub – Castruccio betrays his own men (and women) right and left. The innocent are sacrificed with the guilty, allies as casually as enemies. An odour of sanctimonious slaughter is unmistakable, as is his indifference to human values.[15]

Can anyone so monstrous be a hero? In Machiavelli's implied affirmative answer to this question is to be found a dramatic masterstroke. It redeems by contrast what has come before, and even projects his biography beyond the limitations of taste of his day. As Castruccio lies dying – *Fortuna* strikes him down with an illness (also *à la* Cesare Borgia?) at the age of forty-four – he makes his confession, but in it takes note not so much of his evil acts, which are well known, as his guilt in committing them. He does so, moreover, not from some idea of religious convenience but in a spirit of complete contrition.

As he bares his soul, the reader's sympathy may be oddly startled. The sense of a divine power guiding the hand of justice, as if – amazingly – amid a flight of angels, is strangely awakened. To Pagolo Guinigi, whose guardian Castruccio has remained and to whom he leaves his conquered cities – or Lucca, Pisa and Pistoia (in this fictional account) – he bequeaths the plausible reflection that 'in this world it is vital to know oneself.'

# 32

# The Dream of History

Machiavelli's contract for the new Florentine history, officially for Cardinal Giulio de'Medici, came through in the autumn of 1520. He had proposed his own terms, and these were sent on to the university or *Studio* officials in Florence. The Pope was the *Studio's* head and Francesco del Nero, his own brother-in-law, its chief administrator.

His fee, which he did not specify, turned out to be not much, '*100 fiorini di studio*,' slightly over half what he had been paid when he served in the chancellery; eventually, in 1525, it was doubled, to '*100 ducati d'oro*'. The deadline was set for two years hence (though it was later extended to four), and his job was to write, as he put it, 'the annals or else the history of the things done by the state and city of Florence.' His historical starting point as well as his choice of language, 'either Tuscan or Latin,' was left up to him.[1]

From the beginning, he appears to have known that he would write in Tuscan, but he may initially have chosen to deal only with the Republic's preceding seventy or so years. Leonardo Bruni's history, as well as that of Poggio Bracciolini, who had been Chancellor of Florence from 1453 to 1459, had ended in the 1430s. There seemed little point in repeating what they had done.

A major problem, however, with their own and others' histories, as Machiavelli observes in his Preface, was that while these earlier writers dealt competently enough with foreign affairs, they skimmed over 'civil disorders and internal enmities.' They also omitted the reasons for most domestic problems, or the currents of 'hatreds and divisions' that had driven the Republic to act as it did. From Machiavelli's point of view, they had thus omitted a good deal of the history.[2]

He was aware too of an irony built into his own situation: that a Medici Pope had chosen a political enemy to recount the history of his city, or someone who had devoted years of his life to toiling away on behalf of the politically opposed Florentine Republic. Precisely their opposed attitudes, however, may have prodded Machiavelli to begin his new history more or less at the city's founding, or with a majestic overview of Italy from ancient Roman times. The contrast between the pagan older world and the Christian new one could illuminate his passionate desire to expose the long struggle into maturity of Florentine republican tendencies. After an initially broad description in fact he might concentrate on the major events between 1440 and the present. If he focused on the rivalry between republicanism and despotism, he might make a valuable and original contribution.

He planned to do most of the work at his farm in Sant'Andrea, but except for the first few months found it hard to get away. Praise for his life of Castruccio poured in from friends such as Zanobi Buondelmonti, who found it 'as dear ... as anything in the world.' Some had reservations about an anthology of often lame witticisms, falsely attributed to the hero, which Machiavelli had tacked on at the end (for example: 'Castruccio [actually Diogenes Laertius (*2nd c.*)] used to say that the path to hell was easy, since you went downward with your eyes shut').[3] Zanobi urged him to drop his anthology and get on with the history 'because you rise higher in your style [in writing that sort of thing] than you do elsewhere, just as the material requires.'

As always, though, money mattered. He was briefly intrigued by, if led to reject, an offer to become a government secretary in Ragusa. This had come his way through Piero Soderini. His friend and employer was now thriving across the Adriatic. The secretarial position would have paid a handsome 200 gold ducats, plus expenses, but Machiavelli's just-accepted historian's position required him to stay put or risk a likely confiscation of his property.[4]

Another opportunity, somewhat more amusing and paradoxical, cropped up in May 1521. The government committee acting in place of his old one at the Palazzo della Signoria, but now called the *l'Otto di Pratica* (the Eight in Charge of Affairs), reaffirmed his momentary good standing in Florentine political circles, mostly because they had decided to send him on a minor official mission, his first since the fall of the Republic. The mission seemed little more than absurd, as perhaps it must have to anyone with his anti-clerical and sceptical religious attitudes. It may, however, have been offered as a partial test of his loyalty.

He was ordered to attend a Chapter General meeting at Carpi, a few score miles to the north, of the recently established group of Minorite Friars. The purpose was to urge them to sever their connections with other Tuscan Franciscans. Since 1517, when the Minorites had declared themselves in rebellion against their own monastic order, they had pursued a devoutly reformist path. In practice this meant leading lives of prudish scorn and pomposity. As Machiavelli himself put it, they had become a 'Republic of Clogs.' Self-righteousness in sexual matters, though, had hardly prevented them from devoting themselves to luxuries, such as fine food and comfortable beds.

They represented as well a mild threat to papal control over their other Franciscan brethren, who were more renowned for cheating and fornication. To someone with Machiavelli's whorehouse-oriented cast of mind, his potential holier-than-thou Minorite hosts could merit only a sardonically raised eyebrow.

His journey to Carpi took him to Modena, giving him a chance to catch up on his friendship with Francesco Guicciardini, governor of the town. Though conservative, standoffish and often icy, he remained generally *simpatico*, taking pleasure in Machiavelli's playwriting success and sharing his dim view of the Minorites.[5]

The deeper context of this mission, however, was the spreading Reformation movement to the north, or off in a Germany that looked increasingly tempestuous. 'Lutheranism,' with its threatening emphasis on individual salvation, Bible reading in private – which perhaps more than any other force for revolutionary change was to abet the relatively new fashion in silent reading straight across Europe – and scathing denunciations of Church materialism, was resented throughout much of Italy. Its appeal had been sapped, at least for the moment, by the diversity of Italian religious life, particularly as reflected in splinter groups such as the Minorites.[6]

The Vatican, in other words, remained anxious. Harbingers of religious violence were seen everywhere, though all the important clashes had so far occurred only in Germany and farther north, in the Netherlands and Antwerp. Precautions seemed essential. The twenty-one-year-old Spanish Holy Roman Emperor Charles V, himself born in Ghent, had just attended his first bloody *auto-da-fé* in Louvain in May, or at about the time when Machiavelli arrived in Carpi.

The Reformation seems to have made no impression on him, however, and he saw the friars as simply fussy and foolish. On arriving, he discovered that they were unable to agree or disagree with his request – or the Signoria's (really the Pope's, through Cardinal Giulio de'Medici) – that they cut off contacts with other Franciscans.

As promised, his accommodations were superb. A request from the leaders of the Florentine Wool Guild, reaching him on 14 May, that he invite a popular

Minorite friar, a rousing preacher nicknamed Rovaio ('the north wind'), to deliver a sermon at the *Duomo* in Florence during Lent, fell on deaf ears as Rovaio showed no interest.

Guicciardini urged Machiavelli to wrap up the mission quickly, and wondered whether he might not be risking his honour among 'these holy friars' who could 'pass some of their hypocrisy on to you.' It could be embarrassing 'if at this age you started to think about your soul... . Since you have always lived in a contrary belief, it would be attributed rather to senility than to goodness.'

He need not have worried. Whatever Machiavelli's convictions about the soul, his honour among friars seemed in no danger: 'I was sitting on the toilet when your messenger arrived [with your letter], and just at that moment ... mulling over the absurdities of this world,' among them the rejected invitation to Fra Rovaio: '[The Wool Guild] would like a preacher who would teach them the way to paradise... . I should like to find one who would teach them the way to go to the Devil.'[7] He felt not above playing a practical joke on his hosts, and asked Guicciardini to send out a few unctuous, phony messengers to bow and scrape in his presence to let him appear more impressive. This gambit produced the desired effect, but he realized that he could keep it up only in dread of being found out and exiled to some nearby ramshackle inn ('I am scared shitless' [of that]), where he would be without the 'solid meals, splendid beds and the like in which I have been recovering my strength for three days now.'[8] In the end, he packed up and left anyway, though only after having absorbed as much as he could about Minorite regulations, information which might come in handy for his history.

At home in Florence in September, he was delighted with a letter that amounted to a rave review of his *Art of War*. The book had been brought out a month earlier, by the heirs of the well-known printer of classical texts, Filippo di Giunta, and the review was by Cardinal Giovanni Salviati, a prominent figure in Florentine political circles. His mother was Lucrezia de'Medici, the daughter of Lorenzo the Magnificent. 'You have coupled,' he wrote, 'to the most perfect manner of warfare in antiquity everything that is good in modern warfare and compounded an invincible army.'[9]

The scope of his *Istorie Fiorentine* (Florentine Histories) would be no less ambitious, and he now set seriously to work, probably at Sant'Andrea. He had with him as sources not only editions of Bruni, Poggio and Livy, but also of Piero Minerbetti (his *Cronica fiorentina*), Flavio Biondo (his *Decennali*, purchased by his father back in 1485), Giovanni Villani (his *Cronica*), Gino Capponi and Marchionne di Coppo Stefani (for their apparently eye-witness accounts of the riots of 1378, which had led to the Medici's assumption of power) and Giovanni Cavalcanti: his own *Istorie fiorentine*, which started off in 1420, was to prove so trustworthy a guide to later events that Machiavelli more or less copied out whole chunks of it.[10]

His choice of Tuscan as the language in which to write would probably have struck his contemporaries as unusual for an enterprise as formal as a history. It would also have seemed exciting, as it affirmed a growing acceptance of the vernacular. A good deal more, however, seems to have been involved in his choice than catering to trendy developments. Apart from a few Florentine chronicles, which basically supplied listings of dates and events, there existed few thorough-going histories of the city. The best, by Bruni and Poggio, had been written in a stuffy, scholastic Latin, no matter how clear their style. The choice of Tuscan would thus have seemed original on historical, cultural and literary grounds.

In a remarkable passage in Book I, Machiavelli indicates that his choice also coincides with an important theme of the history itself, or with the momentous shift in language from Latin to Italian following the sack of Rome in the fifth century – this amid the reeling into collapse of the Roman empire:

> One can easily imagine what Italy and the Roman dependencies must have suffered in those troublous times, in which not only the government changed, but the laws, customs, ways of living, religion, language, dress, and even names: such vicissitudes – or even any one of them singly ... – are enough to terrify the strongest and most constant soul. From these changes there arose the foundation and growth of many cities, and also the destruction of many.... . Amid these troubles and changes of population there arose a new language, as is evident from the speech now prevailing in Italy or in France, and in Spain, caused by the native tongue of the new population mingling with that of the ancient Romans. Moreover the names were changed, not only of the provinces and countries, but of the lakes, rivers and seas, and also of the men themselves, for Italy and France and Spain were full of new names, and all the ancient ones were altered.[11]

The new language had fostered the new history as much as the new history had shaped the new language. To understand the history, one would need to trace out the new culture's linguistic development, or the growing flexibility that had enabled the new language to accommodate the most sensitive and ambitious literary expressiveness.

Dante's Italian had shaped the present as much as it had been shaped by Virgil and the past. Machiavelli's humanism required an acceptance of modern Italian culture to permit its blending with classical brilliance. Both his style and training had prepared him for the challenge. His committed empiricism, always intolerant of superfluous abstractions ('if anything in a history delights and instructs, it is that which is described in detail'[12]), might enable him to indicate the most important historical change of all: how coming along after the fall of Rome 'the strife between the customs of the ancient faith and the miracles of the new caused the greatest tumults among men,' together with the most crucial result: that *en masse* 'men living among so many persecutions began at last to carry written in their very looks the terror of their souls.'[13]

The point would be to acknowledge and take stock of the momentous modern terror. It had provoked both psychological calamities and spiritual marvels, and even new forms of compassion and ruthlessness, together with the novel Judeo-Christian brands of suffering, if not torment.

In charting the great historical change, he would also describe another phenomenon which had not been dealt with by others: the Italian fragmentation, or how 'of the many wars waged in Italy by the barbarians almost all were caused by the Popes, as it was by them that the barbarians who inundated Italy were called in, and this state of things has lasted down to our times and has kept Italy disunited and still keeps her weak.'[14]

So much for his approach: the modern reader may still find the history defective. Often he seems to wander, perhaps because in his haste to assemble so complex a work whose eight books describe whole centuries, as well as their battles and political conflicts, up to 1492, he often neglects to compare his sources.

Over the many pages, however, this problem ceases to matter. It becomes clear that he is embarked on an exciting investigation of an even larger theme: that of a bizarre human restlessness which, he maintains, sprang into being with the fall of Rome. It is this restlessness that was to stimulate the yearning for republican freedoms. Throughout the *Florentine Histories*, as this unusual phenomenon is revealed rising into violence, flourishing and subsiding, only to rise again, it appears both powerful and irresistible.

Only gradually, as Machiavelli concentrates on its various manifestations, does the reader begin to realize that this strange restlessness was apparently unknown to the ancient Romans. Thus Corso Donati, an influential Florentine who died in 1308 and who 'deserves to be enumerated among our choicest citizens', is described as having 'a restless mind [that] caused his country and his party to forget the obligations they owed him, and in the end his restlessness brought upon his country an infinity of evils and to himself death'; Castruccio is recalled as inflicting great damage 'upon the Florentines in pillage, captivity, desolation and fire'; and fourteenth-century Florence is referred to as possessed of 'innumerable tumults.'[15]

Again, it seems not to be the upheavals that attract his attention, or their barbarity, as much as their emotional, psychological and spiritual powers of transformation. These are seen as disturbing and altering the entire post-Roman atmosphere. Around and through this atmosphere, moreover, as if amid the spasmodic gleams of a sort of occluded moonlight, his own balanced and symmetrical style casts its magical, softening, aesthetic glow. More transparently than in the stiffer Latin of Bruni and Poggio, it allows the succession of catastrophes to be glimpsed and witnessed through a moderating aura.

Nowhere is the contrast between these restless events and Machiavelli's style more serenely apparent than in his descriptions of the Pazzi Conspiracy of 1478 and the death of Lorenzo (the Magnificent) de'Medici in 1492:

Francesco and Bernardo [two of the Conspiracy's murderers] were inspired by such feelings of hatred [for the Medici] and the lust of murder, and pursued their object with such callousness and resolution, that as they led Giuliano [de'Medici] to the church, and even within it, they amused him with droll and jovial stories.... . Francesco covered him with wounds whilst he lay there; indeed with such rage did he strike that he wounded himself seriously in the thigh.... . In the midst of these terrible deeds it seemed as if the church would fall in upon the people; the cardinal [Lorenzo] clung to the altar, and with difficulty was saved by the priests; when the tumult was appeased he was taken by the signori to the palace where he remained until his liberation.[16]

To see him [Lorenzo the Magnificent] at one time in his grave moments and at another in his gay was to see in him two personalities, joined as it were with invisible bonds. During his last days he suffered great agony owing to the malady with which he was afflicted – oppressed by some deadly stomach trouble – which terminated fatally in April 1492. There had never died in Florence, nor yet in Italy, one for whom his country mourned so much or who left behind him so wide a reputation for wisdom.

Heaven gave many signs that ruin would follow his decease; among such signs was the destruction of the highest pinnacle of San Reparata [the *Duomo*] by lightning.[17]

Yet Lorenzo's death, with which Machiavelli chooses to end the Florentine history, serves only as an augury of further disasters, including 'the downfall of Italy, and which, none knowing how to [prevent], will perpetuate her ruin.' The restlessness, or a constant modern uncertainty, seems to have been selected to provide both the theme and a type of spyglass on the work itself.

# 33

# Lights before the Storm

He wrote these final lines in early or mid-1525. He had spent the previous couple of years, mostly at Sant'Andrea, on little apart from writing his history, and with few distractions aside from birding and tending to his farm.

Pope Leo X, who had hired him, did not live to see the results. He died soon after the contract was signed, in December 1521, of a sudden 'violent chill,' though full of dreams, among them that his armies, united with the forces of Charles V of Spain, would drive the French out of Italy. In exchange, the Emperor had promised to deal with the excommunicated and troublesome Martin Luther, by putting him on trial and having him executed.

Leo had been succeeded by a timorous, scholarly, Flemish stopgap Pope, Adrian VI. He had been unanimously elected in January 1522, mostly to prevent the election of Cardinal Giulio de'Medici, whose name seemed to frighten the rest of the cardinals. Adrian had known Charles since the future Emperor was seven, when he was hired as his tutor. He shared both his trust and his hostility to Luther. He was unable, however, to institute Church reforms or bring about Luther's prosecution for heresy before falling ill and dying in 1523.

Unimpeded, Giulio de'Medici was now able to step into the breach among happy if soon to be deflated hopes for his future. It was to him as Pope Clement VII in Rome that Machiavelli presented the finished or nearly finished *Florentine Histories*, in May 1525.[1] Clement had already expressed his positive feelings about his historian to Francesco Vettori on 8 March: 'He ought to come [to the Vatican with his work], and I feel for certain that his books [the multiple volumes of the *Histories*] are going to give pleasure.'[2]

In July, presumably after having browsed through what Machiavelli had written, Clement confirmed his approval in the finest way, by doubling what he was to be paid. Further confirmation lay in his sending Machiavelli to Faenza to mull over with Guicciardini the advisability of raising a citizen militia in

Romagna. Its purpose, as had suddenly and surprisingly become plain, would be to take on the armies of Charles V.

Amid every Pope's constant switching and realigning of his unreliable, often betrayed, dwindling and collapsing alliances simply to guarantee his survival, as between France and Spain, Charles had once again become a likely menace. Guicciardini remained opposed, as always, to the recruitment of native-born, unprofessional troops, even if he and Machiavelli got on famously despite their tactical disagreements, as when he wrote to Machiavelli, now back in Florence, in a more personal vein on 25 July: 'I understand that after your departure Mariscotta,' a courtesan with whom Machiavelli spent some time in Faenza while awaiting Clement's eventually negative decision on recruiting the citizen militia, 'spoke of you very flatteringly and greatly praised your manners and conversation. That warms my heart.'[3] It certainly warmed Machiavelli's ('I glory in this [news] more than in anything I have in the world[:] I shall be pleased if you would give her my regards'), perhaps because over the past few years, the favourable reception of his history aside, much of the rest of his life had gone badly enough.

His brother Totto – priest, occasional art-dealer and businessman, whose affection mattered greatly – had died in his late forties in June 1522, probably during an outbreak of plague in Florence. In April 1523 Francesco Vettori had worried with him over their both growing older and a bit 'finicky.' They ought to reflect more honestly on what they had been like when young. What troubled him at the moment was the problematic behaviour, at least for those days, of Machiavelli's by now adult son Lodovico: 'He has a boy with him, he plays with him, sports with him, walks about with him, whispers in his ear; they sleep in the same bed. What about it? Perhaps even beneath these things there is nothing wrong.'

Remembering his hedonistic youth, and Machiavelli's, Vettori voiced some solid regrets: 'My father, if he had known my ways and character, would never have tied me down to a wife, since nature had meant me for games and sport, not sighing after profit, scarcely concerned for family matters. But a wife and daughters have forced me to change.'[4]

Or both of them to do so, and this with other miseries pouring in. Piero Soderini had died on 13 June 1522, soon after a new conspiracy aimed at the Medici, or at least at Cardinal Giulio, had been discovered, though it was swiftly crushed. On this occasion an anti-Medici-planned ambush had not involved Machiavelli, even if he and Soderini may have sympathized with the idea.

Its discovery, however, put an efficient end to the convivial gatherings at the Rucellai gardens which had kept up his intellectual spirits over some years. The assassination plan had been entirely amateurish, and fumbled preparations to murder Cardinal Giulio saw Machiavelli's close friends Zanobi Buondelmonte and Luigi Alamanni accused and forced to flee, though on their later return from France they were captured and released. Two other conspirators were arrested, tried and beheaded.[5]

It was probably now as well, or a little earlier, that Machiavelli composed (in a document surviving in his own hand) a set of modest reforms for governing Florence (*Discursus florentinarum rerum post mortem iunioris Laurentii Medicis*). Written shortly after the death of Leo X, who had requested it, and appearing to support a restoration of the Republic while evaluating political improvements that might seem practical only under a continuation of Medici rule, Machiavelli argues that 'unless [the government] is inclusive in such a way that it will become a well-ordered republic, its inclusiveness is likely to make it fall more rapidly,' and that as long as the city has 'institutions that can ... stand firm [because] ... everyone has a hand in them ... no class of citizen ... will need to desire revolution' (*innovazione*).[6]

Perhaps as early as 1523, though possibly as late as 1524, and despite his work on his *Florentine Histories*, his trips to Florence led him into a new love affair which rapidly came to mean far more than any of his others. It rolled on, flared up, waned and seemed to burn with a spellbinding intensity over the next few years, or according to his passionate opportunities with the popular, beautiful actress-madrigalist Barbera Raffacani Salutati.

Widely known as Barbera Fiorentina, she was a well-educated woman who belonged to the class of performers termed *cortigiane oneste*, or 'gentle' courtesans, or those of 'noble' character. In her case the phrase implied musical accomplishments more than sufficient to inspire him to compose *canzoni* or *intermedii* for her, which were to be inserted into new productions of *The Mandragola*. It seems likely as well that another of his plays, *Clizia*, which owes its plot to Plautus's *Casinia* – parts of Machiavelli's play are almost word-for-word translations of Plautus's Latin – and which he may have finished before 1525, was actually written for her, and even dashed off at speed, as if intended for a party or a gala performance.

He had probably met her at one of the lavish feast-entertainments, organized around music, dance and often a play, at the house of Jacopo di Filippo

Falconetti, nicknamed *il Fornaciaio* (the owner of a furnace) after the profitable brick-making kiln located on his farm with its famous estate-garden, just past the San Frediano gate in Santa Maria in Verzaia.[7]

Jacopo's evenings drew large audiences from the cream of the city's commercial and show-business families, along with less fashionable citizens and even craftspeople. His delicately, elegantly perfumed and costumed guests rode, walked or were taxied by carriage from the centre of the city to his garden and banqueting tables. Even in those warlike times they would have moved through taper-lit streets and alleys lined with the devices of the declining but still extensive wool and cotton industry.

Sheep pens and wool racks bulged along the Arno: the brittle scent of ammonia, essential for cleansing the fabrics, including the silks, lent an onion-like zing to the night air. The outer walls of many houses, as if quilted with iron clasps for drying and fixing the dyes, flaunted bold banners of cotton that flapped colourfully in the smoky dark.

At night, too, the streets boasted groups of musicians: Florentines had always been eager for the latest love song, especially as printed sheet music had begun to become available after 1500: Leo himself had once hired a lutanist at 300 florins per year, an astounding sum, and ennobled him: another musician had been granted an archbishopric.

Rich, but in no sense a nobleman, Jacopo had decided to present the première, complete with *entr'acte* music by Philippe Verdelot and a stage set painted by Bastiano da San Gallo, of Machiavelli's full-length *Clizia* on 13 January 1525. His real purpose, however, was to announce the end of his own five-year term of banishment: once a member of the Signoria, he had been dismissed from office and exiled to his house. With his term of exile now at an end, he pinned his hopes of resuming his former social prominence on a theatrical extravaganza meant to outshine the widely praised staging of Machiavelli's *Mandragola* in Florence a few months earlier.

'The fame of your revelries has spread,' Filippo de'Nerli wrote to him in February, or just weeks later, with what seems a touch of exaggeration. 'I know about the garden levelled off to make it into a stage for your comedy. I know about the invitations not only to the first and most noble patricians of the city but also to the middle class and after them to the plebeians.... The fame of your comedy has flown all over.'[8]

As well it might have, given the city's appetites for paradox, wit and sex-comedies. In Machiavelli's five-act play a father and son fall in love with the same woman, who also happens to be the eponymous heroine, the father's seventeen-year-old adopted daughter and his son's adoptive sister.

In a less confident age, perhaps the twentieth century of Eugene O'Neill, Tennessee Williams or Harold Pinter, this unbalanced domestic situation might have provoked violence, drunkenness, poetry, divorce, murder and foul language. Plautus and Machiavelli treated it as an opportunity for silly marital manoeuvrings combined with slapstick deceptions.

Flippancy aside, however, it would be a mistake to imagine that Machiavelli's Florence was more amenable to father-son sex competitions than other cities or ages. Also mistaken would be the naïve assumption, made by some on the basis of skimpy evidence, that Nicomaco (a contraction of Niccolò Machiavelli), the spry, lusty, foolish and hopeful father-lover, is some sort of literal stand-in for Machiavelli himself – an unflattering if not pointless idea.

What seems to have mattered to Machiavelli, as may be deduced from the liveliness of the plot, is the sheer entertainment value of the love triangle, or that the play presents a set of plausible psychological relations. These ricochet between father, son, Clizia and everyone else. Their mostly imaginary sex lives seem in fact to be rendered with an even shrewder authenticity than by Machiavelli's Roman predecessor.

A remarkable touch in both the Latin and Italian versions is that the heroine never shows up. Her unexplained absence, together with the audience's frustrated expectation that she had better show up somehow, shifts the focus from who beds whom to who marries whom. Her proxy father's oafish effort to marry her off to a proxy servant-husband willing to accept another man's making love to his own wife, and his son's less oafish efforts to marry Clizia himself, are each appropriately frustrated and rewarded.

At the core of Machiavelli's adoptive comedy, or his fiddling with each of his characters' delicate marionette strings, is the manipulative, bewitching Sofronia, Nicomaco's prankster-wife and the mother of the lovesick Cleandro. Her son's crazed passion for his at first reluctant foster-sister is rendered even more absurd by his childish gullibility.

The play thus thrives not simply on mad reversals but on reversals of reversals. At one point Nicomaco is tricked into going to bed with his manservant and, believing him to be Clizia, sexually assaulting him, to his criminal embarrassment. The play battens on treachery betrayed, which in the end is presented as a nostrum for the tangled ambitions of an uproarious household.

Machiavelli's Prologue is surprising and original along these lines, and given its subsequent influence on other playwrights, such as Goethe in *Faust* and Pirandello in *Six Characters in Search of an Author*, of significance to the history of drama. 'Come on out, all of you,' the Author (or Machiavelli) calls to his actors as the play gets underway, and then turns to the audience: 'It's a good idea ... to meet the characters, so that you will know them when you see them on the stage.'[9]

This self-conscious ploy, which allows the actors to be seen with their make-up half on and their costumes unlaced and rumpled, heightens rather than lessens the sense of audience-participation in the illusion-making to come. The playgoers become a source of the theatrical magic, while the actors are perceived neither as the only role-players nor as ordinary people but as sliding back and forth between the two on a type of aesthetic-psychological shuttle.

Mingling the theatrical with their ordinary lives, or what Shakespeare was to describe as their lives as poor, bare, fork'd animals, they spark fascination in another way as well. They become alert to their role-playing in the theatre of life itself, if only, as the author insists, because the world must be a stage.

Machiavelli seemed to switch about more than usual between his own roles over the next few months. At one point he played estate agent for Francesco Guicciardini, scouting and reporting on run-down farms which he visited and that his friend bought sight unseen but which could be treated as investments.

In August he played the father amazed at the histrionics of his son, Ludovico, whose paranoid letters overflowed with menaces: 'I shall punish that scoundrel,' 'I feel like ... revenge.' Ludovico had frequently run afoul of the law, and Machiavelli now decided not to honour his debts.

In September (1525) he reverted to the role of active Florentine citizen, learning to his relief that the *accopiatori*, or magistrates, had finally pronounced him *imborsato*, or eligible for public office (should he join the Signoria, or stand for *Gonfaloniere*?).

In August again, he took a fling at playing the amateur chemist, supplying Guicciardini with a recipe for headache and constipation pills: he should mix various quantities of aloe, saffron, myrrh, betony, Armenian bole, germander and pimpernel.

In October he resumed the role of busy father, this time tending his son Bernardo, 'sick with a double tertian fever' in Sant'Andrea. In October too he discovered that he had become a much heralded man of the theatre, plunging into preparations for a new production of the *Mandragola*: 'I have been dining with Barbera these last few evenings [he told Guicciardini] and discussing the play; ... she has offered to come with her singers and sing the songs between the acts. I have offered to write lyrics consistent with the action, and [Luigi Alamanni] has offered to provide her and her singers with lodging.'

Ironically by mid-October, and in view of each of his roles probably only half in jest, he had begun signing his letters 'Historian, Comic Author and Tragic Author.'[10]

# 34

# The Assault on Rome and a Fatal Illness

Ever since the election of Clement VII, diverse if ominous military pressures, magnified by his incompetence and folly, had been building across northern Italy. 'We are all walking in the shadows,' Guicciardini had remarked in August 1525 when he considered the political-military signals bunching to the north and then rippling south as they began to affect the whole peninsula, 'but with our hands tied behind our backs, so that we cannot avoid bumps.'[1]

Reflecting on the unmistakable military aspects of their dilemma, and in the light of an abortive attempt, betrayed by Ferrante Francesco de Avalos (1489–1525), the Marquis of Pescara, to drive Charles V out of Italy altogether – even if he had since died – Machiavelli wrote to Guicciardini in December that 'this gang [of leaders here in Florence] will never do anything honourable and bold worth living and dying for; I observe so much fear in the citizens of Florence, and such disinclination to offer any opposition to whoever is preparing to devour us.'[2]

Despite his pessimistic outlook, he decided to take on a measure of responsibility for the city's defences. Over the next few weeks, he actually seemed yanked in opposite directions. On the one hand, he felt inclined to continue with his playwright's career. On the other, he felt the importance of advising Florentine and Roman leaders on how to protect themselves against what he regarded as an inevitable foreign invasion. In Rome he had acquired a quasi-friend and partisan in the person of the Pope. Since the publication of *The Art of War*, the former Giulio de'Medici had viewed him as an expert on military matters and so worth dispatching to trouble spots as a defence consultant. As tensions between France, Spain and the Vatican became more potentially violent, Machiavelli's playwriting ambitions surrendered to a concentration on war itself.

This shift stimulated reapplications of energy and his analytical abilities, seconded by travel and his submission of speedy reports. As both had been aspects of his earlier diplomatic life, he seemed in significant ways to have returned to his former routines.

Three events, including one just past, now also proved crucial to the uncertain Florentine future as well as to a horror that shortly unfolded to the south, in Rome, and, to the north, in and near Florence, and to him personally. These were the capture on 24 February 1525 of the French King Francis I by the Spanish, led by the Marquis of Pavia (who later died); the formation on 22 May 1526 of the anti-imperial, anti-Spanish League of Cognac, a defensive alliance of mutually suspicious leaders whose interests clashed senselessly from the start; and his accepting an assignment to investigate, together with a senior Spanish military officer, such improvements as might be essential to the defensive walls surrounding Florence.

Of the three, the defeat and kidnapping of the French King was to become most instrumental in unleashing a wave of menacing popular disapproval against the Pope. It would be succeeded within less than two years by a military storm, or the opportunity for the unthinkable to become thinkable in the form of an assault on the capital, and this on a scale more atrocious than almost any let loose against any civilized community.

In the revised edition of his *Orlando*, Ariosto shows himself grimly impressed by the defeat of the French King. Though his capture and months-long imprisonment were brought to an end by an agreement signed by Charles V – an event unexpected by Machiavelli, who saw no reason for Charles to cede his advantage – the papacy itself now seemed in danger.[3] The King was granted his freedom in exchange for handing over his young sons as hostages, but doing so hardly helped as the French weakness had become perceptible to everyone. Matters looked worse when set against the Spanish and German advances into Italy. As Ariosto saw it, the King's humiliation seemed most portentous because it had developed out of self-deception:

> Fortune treats us like the dust that the wind catches up and swirls about, wafting it skywards and the next moment blowing it back to the ground from which it came; and she has the [K]ing believe that he has concentrated a hundred thousand troops round Pavia, for he looks only at his outlay in wages, not at whether his forces have in fact increased or dwindled./The fault lies with his own skinflint ministers, and with his own indulgence in having trusted them.[4]

Yet trust them he had, and the result was that 'the flower of French nobility [lay] obliterated in the field,' to the tune of 8,000 killed or wounded. Cornered in a park strewn with the bodies of immense numbers of his officers, he had surrendered to 'five soldiers who did not know who he was; but the Viceroy happening to come, he made himself known to him, who kissing his hand with great reverence, took him prisoner in the name of the Emperor.' His arrest seemed the worse for Charles's deferential treatment of him, as if he no longer mattered.[5]

He no longer did, or not then, except that his outrage led to the formation of the League of Cognac. His resentments combined with those of the Pope, who had been his supporter (news of their alliance was published as early as 5 January 1525), of Henry VIII of England (who later snubbed them), of Venice, whose rulers feared losing their colonies to the Emperor, and of Francesco Maria Sforza (b.1492), the Duke of Milan, who attempted to provoke Pescara into rebelling against Charles and was deposed for his trouble. From the start, though, the whole flimsy alliance seemed to reflect more in the way of wishful thinking than military agility. During its brief existence it was guided by vengeance rather than strategy, and later by defeat rather than practical hopes of success.[6]

Guicciardini had reluctantly abandoned his desire to sponsor a production of Machiavelli's *Mandragola* in Faenza. This happy event had been planned for the carnival season of February 1526, but in the newly toxic military climate, which required his participation as the papal-appointed negotiator assigned to patch up the League of Cognac, he had no time to stage-manage a play.

Machiavelli might in any case take comfort from his already solid dramatic triumphs. Twice published in Venice in 1522, including once by the renowned printer Alessandro Bidoni in a small, elegant edition as *Comedia di Callimaco & di Lucretia*, the *Mandragola* had met with a Venetian reception so boisterous that the first of its two scheduled performances had to be cancelled because a delirious demonstration by a mob of spectators had become chaotic.

In February 1526, Venetian performers staging a revival of Plautus's *Menaechmi* (in translation), on 'seeing [your play, which was done at the same time, or so Giovanni Manetti, who served as the production's prompter, reported to him] …, praised it so much more highly …[that] spurred on by shame, they requested your play's company … to be so kind as to perform it in their house.'[7] As its popularity increased, merchants living in the Florentine colony at Venice begged Machiavelli to send them any new plays he might write, and his life all at once seemed transformed. If his political ambitions had failed to win him a coveted government position, the theatrical adulation might compensate.

In contrast, too, his attempts to deal with a likely war over Florence and other Italian cities were hamstrung by widespread hesitations. Every measure essential to preventing an invasion, or the city's possible sacking by imperial troops, hung fire. For the most part, indeed, the lack of preparedness seemed attributable to Medici squabbling. As an official investigation following a bitter but short-lived 1527 Florentine uprising against the Medici was later to make clear, even when confronted by threats to their survival, leading members of the family kept up their scrambling after money, pilfering where they could, and scavenging after power. It made no difference that both were rapidly becoming elusive.

The election of Giulio as Pope had left Florence and its territories still under his indirect rule, but they were now also under the chillier supervision of Cardinal Silvio Passerini (1459–1529), who represented the ambitions of two Medici bastard offspring, Ippolito and Alessandro. They were the sons, it was said, of Giuliano and Lorenzo.[8] Their claims clashed with those of Clarice, the daughter of Piero de'Medici, whose interests in turn defied the ambitions of a formidable young Medici soldier, already glowing with victories achieved elsewhere in Italy, Giovanni de'Medici (1498–1526), known as Giovanni delle Bande Nere, or Giovanni of the Black Bands, after the black stripes which he ordered stitched across the armour and clothing of his private army in a gesture of mourning for Leo X.

The entire family's interference in the social, military and economic life of Rome and Florence led them to nurture and throttle if not strangle it. As a group, they ignored the urgency either to prepare for war or to risk the loss of the Medici papacy and their political dominance. In these messy circumstances, on 25 November 1526, or just as Giovanni and his two thousand soldiers had achieved a critical importance for the defence of Rome, he met with a horrid, absurd death. It took place precisely as his units stormed into battle against an imperial army consisting of German *Landsknechte*, or well-trained Lutheran Protestants heading south under Georg von Frundsberg.

If historical changes may reasonably be attributed to incidents or tipping points, one such might well have been the incompetent behaviour of the army surgeon summoned that evening to treat the wound inflicted on his right leg by a falconet-ball. Extracted from the battlefield where he had been directing his troops in a so far winning effort to prevent von Frundsberg's army from crossing the Po and plunging south toward Florence and Rome, he held up a torch to let the surgeon see where to amputate his leg – an instance perhaps of his typical bravado – but then watched helplessly as the skidding medical blade maimed him to death (he died on 30 November), together with, as Guicciardini put it, 'so much courage.'[9]

Machiavelli had known and admired him, and their admiration had been mutual. A rough-and-tumble, sophisticated soldier, Giovanni thought highly of his *Art of War*, and back in July had made Machiavelli his guest at the headquarters of the League of Cognac in the Badia a Casaretto near Milan. There he had issued a friendly challenge to him to put the 3,000 troops then at his disposal through a military drill according to the methods described in his book. To his astonishment, he had noted Machiavelli's inability, after two frustrating hours spent shouting orders at them in a sweltering sun, to form them into much more than a tumbling, swarming mess. Matteo Bandello (1480–1562), a Dominican priest and author, whose plays were later to become the sources of Shakespeare's *Romeo and Juliet* and *Twelfth Night*, and who was present, reports that Giovanni finally managed to array the troops on his own, but adds that Machiavelli redeemed himself at dinner with some salacious and witty tale-telling.[10]

Nor were his abilities as a military analyst any less than professional. In Florence three months earlier, in April 1526, he had been asked by an anxious Pope to accompany the respected military engineer and refugee from imperial Spain, Count Pietro Navarra, on a tour of inspection of the city's ramparts and walls. Machiavelli submitted a report arguing for an aggressive re-design of nearly all of them: 'Some of the walls ... on the far side of the Arno ought to be torn down, some ought to be extended, and some ought to be contracted... . Count Pietro will be here tomorrow and the next day, and we shall do our best to pick his brains as much as possible.'

Nor had he been shy about offering Guicciardini, then serving as lieutenant-general or overall commander of the Pope's forces, some sharp criticism of Clement's unquestionably garbled war aims: 'For the love of God, let us not lose this opportunity [to see that] the Spaniards are somehow pulled out of Lombardy so that they cannot return.'

He doled out the occasional smidgeon of congratulations on his own behalf: 'If the fortifications proceed, people here believe that I am to be given the position of supervisor and secretary, that I am to be given one of my sons [Bernardo] as an assistant.'[11] He and Bernardo received the appointment, but while the next months still found him 'in the field,' and even if by September Milan looked likely to fall to one of the League's assaults, all chances of victory over the Emperor abruptly vanished on 23 September.

Reports now poured in that Rome had simply surrendered to the Colonna faction, based in Naples and involved in a conspiracy with Don Ugo da Moncada, the Emperor's captain and military representative. The shock of this capitulation was overwhelming. After reducing his forces because of assurances he had received of Charles's peaceful intentions, Clement was ambushed in dead of night by 500 troops. Threatened with capture or death, he had fled to the Castel Sant'Angelo, where he had begun to attempt negotiations.

For Machiavelli, away from Florence (or 'in the field'), a more or less strategic balance seemed to have collapsed in hysterical confusion. Clement himself created the impression of surrendering not only to the Colonna but to irrationality. Grasping at straws, he at once signed an agreement with his enemies. This allowed him to return to the Vatican, but also let the Emperor conclude that the war had been settled in his favour. Clement next sabotaged what he had signed, and the result was an uproar. Bourbon's army, joining with Spanish units capable of fielding 18,000 additional troops, swept forward in a more determined than ever advance on Florence and Rome.[12]

Beliefs and values frayed amid these frantic pressures. Fresh waves of violence produced acts of betrayal with an eerie reliability. Atrocities followed. In Florence an insurrection aimed at the Medici, on 26 April 1527, the 'Friday rising,' as it was called, was undertaken just as the Pope's reserves were lethally depleted. Despite its brief success, in the end it provided neither the city nor Machiavelli himself with any real gains.

Over the next few weeks, as would have seemed natural enough, he sought out a position with the new government. He soon discovered that where the Medici had rejected him because he had served the Republic, the new Signoria rejected him because he had served the Medici. In addition, as he learned of the violence accompanying the rebels' takeover, he realized that his loyalty would probably have lain with his government friends Francesco Vettori and Bartolomeo Cavalcanti. Both had been trapped in the Palazzo della Signoria as 1500 pro-republican troops surged momentously at its entrances. His joy in a republican restoration might well have expired in his anxiety over their safety and that of the hundreds of fleeing citizens.[13]

And with good reason: the countryside surrounding Florence, as far as the Mugello and up to Sant'Andrea in Percussina, and later even straight down into the city streets, saw the League's returning soldiers – the army under Francesco Guicciardini, ordered back as a defence against Bourbon's expected attack – jostling, lurching and threatening everywhere.

A dread of the *Landsknechte* in Tuscany had preceded their reputation for cruelty and rape. Where months earlier Machiavelli had fretted over Barbera's devotion – 'She told me she would like you to write every week,' Jacopo di Filippi (*il Fornaciaio*) let him know in August 1526 – his fears now raced along lines best indicated by Francesco Vettori: 'Men have come here [to Florence] from both Milan and Cremona who have told such tales about the imperial troops, the Spanish as well as the Germans, that there is no one who would not prefer to have the devil rather than them.'[14]

Of greater importance was the fact that in bringing the League's forces into Florence, Guicciardini had altered the entire military picture. Their redeployment persuaded Bourbon, a soldier experienced in the frustrations of sieges, that he would be better off as the commander of hungry, unpaid men if he bypassed the city and made for the jugular, so to speak, or for Rome. This he did, and Guicciardini, who also switched strategies, set off in uneasy pursuit of his long columns, which had already moved to within twenty-five miles of the Florentine gates. As the local danger abated, Guicciardini decided to offer the Pope whatever assistance he could manage. Like everyone, though, he remained convinced that Rome would prove sturdy enough, with its ancient towers, tunnels and redoubts, to survive all attacks, and so was in no hurry.

As Guicciardini moved south, Machiavelli seems to have gone with him, so the evidence suggests. If not, he soon followed on horseback, and if not as far as Rome, then over much of the way.

Elements of mystery now begin to intrude on what were to become his final weeks. The intervals themselves seemed somehow protracted by his growing illness – peritonitis most likely, or a long-standing complaint of the bowels and intestines – which may well have affected his ease in travelling.

In early April at Imola, to which he was sent by Guicciardini to arrange for billeting the League's soldiers heading back to Florence, he wrote about his forebodings to his school-age favourite son Guido, who was later to become a priest, in a letter ostensibly about family matters (a mule had gone 'crazy'; it ought to be turned loose; Guido should devote himself to his studies; like

his father before him, he had begun learning Ovid's *Metamorphoses*): 'Greet
Madonna Marietta for me and tell her I have been expecting – and still do – to
leave here any day. I have never longed so much to return to Florence as I do
now, but there is nothing else I can do. Simply tell her that whatever she hears,
she should be of good cheer, since I shall be there before any danger comes'
(plate XIII).[15] He tried to keep his word, but later in April, as Guicciardini
sent him to Forlì, he let Vettori know about his deeper doubts. At that point
Bourbon's push on Rome was still to come. The threat to Florence was blowing
hot and cold, and most options seemed unappealing.

He offered up a soupçon of affection for 'Messer Francesco Guicciardini' and
Florence itself, which he 'loved more than my own soul,' and then observed
that 'Despair often discovers remedies that choice could not.' He suggested that
a 'reckless' assault on Bourbon's forces might be necessary to save his beloved
city. Despair and recklessness were rare enough terms for him, though they may
only have reflected his sense of an unusual emergency.[16]

To be sure, what came next, or the sack of Rome, proved far worse, with its more
than 10,000 dead, its hundreds of homes and monuments wrecked and burned, the
tens of thousands injured, wounded, starving and dying, than what he or anyone
might have imagined. He first heard of the sack from witnesses and through written
reports reaching him after most of the damage had been done, in mid-May. This
was at another stopping-off place on his Guicciardini-directed journeys, Orvieto,
where he was able to provide minimal financial assistance to survivors.

On 6 May, as he now learned, Bourbon's troops had managed to pour
through an opening in the Roman walls, and then into the dishevelled, lovely,
half-unprotected city itself. Bourbon had been killed in the initial assault, but
his rampaging army had driven the Pope, Cardinals, nuns, scores of other
prelates and crowds of citizen-refugees back into the dismal safety of the Castel
Sant'Angelo. Outside, a shabby, atrocious battle had erupted, leading to the
Pope's defeat amid ghoulish acts of carnage.

The battle's symbolism could only have impressed him in the worst way
possible. The numbers of dead, the shadowy ruins and desecration, clearly
meant much more than themselves, and more than anyone could yet understand. A grotesque tragedy had occurred. A frightening, murderous impulse
had squirmed out of the dark. A spectre of cultural annihilation, perhaps
hoisting itself out of a barbarous past, seemed to have surfaced and wreaked
havoc.

Surely it had emerged from the fifth century and the earlier sack. Surely its animosity was directed at history itself. Surely as *Fortuna's* wheel turned, the historic previous fall, entailing the collapse of the Roman Empire, had now, after a thousand years, been somehow reenacted.[17] As a humanist spending a good deal of his life attempting to make sense of history, he recognized familiar ingredients: the cataclysm and slaughter, followed by inarticulate shock – signals that the world was bearing witness to no mere act of vandalism or murder, but to an ancient drama strangely boiled over, as if the modern world shifted among inklings of an end.

He could not have known that the sack preceded by weeks the end of his life, though other endings were also on their way. Guicciardini sent him to the port of Citavecchia, perhaps to assist the Pope as a refugee. Clement and his hangers-on might be helped by the French warships gathered there under the command of the Genoese naval officer Andrea Doria (1468–1560). At Citavecchia Machiavelli would have learned fresh details about the uprising in Florence, whose new government was to last just three years. The hope was awakened that if he returned he might be offered a post in the reborn republic, perhaps even his old one. Not only was this not to be, however, as he soon realized, but the idea itself put paid to his or anyone's belief in republics as necessarily linked with tolerance and justice.

Administered from the start by a cadre of surviving Savonarolan sympathizers, or religious fanatics, the revived Florentine Grand Council ordered all Jews, by means of an anti-semitic edict that was unevenly enforced, to close up shop, and especially their money-lending businesses, and leave town. A new citizens council rushed through sumptuary laws. It larded them with draconian regulations of dowries, blasphemy, prostitution, sodomy, gambling and discussions of religion, which priests were authorized to prohibit. In the Savonarolan manner, political discussions were banned, publications censored and books of which the Church disapproved destroyed. The new republic would be oriented to 'the health of the soul,' as its officials coolly announced, or 'the good life.'

In this repressive atmosphere it scarcely surprised him in the end to see the post of Second Secretary awarded on 10 June to Francesco Tarugi. He had served on a Medici committee designated The Eight in Charge of Affairs (*l'Otto di Pratica*). Machiavelli's frustration at failing to obtain the post seems nonetheless to have affected him intensely. He had submitted letters of recommendation from influential friends, among them Zanubi Buondelmonti and

Luigi Alamanni, but they appear to have been airily dismissed.[18] Whether in response to the rejection or because his disease was running its course, on 20 June he became more seriously ill. At the family *palazzo* in Florence, with friends gathered about him, he took doses of the aloe concoction which he had prescribed for Guicciardini. They probably made him worse.

Five of his six living children were on hand: Ludovico, who as recently as 22 May had been off near Ancona, whence he had written his father about a horse that he wanted help in selling; Bernardo, his eldest son; Guido; Piero, just thirteen; and Bartolomea, also known as Baccina, who would later marry his literary executor. Totto, his infant son, named for his father's dead brother, who would not survive his first few years, was off with a wet nurse. Marietta was present.

To judge from the warm-hearted letter sent him by Guido on 17 April, when he was at Forlì, family feelings ran as ever strong and true: 'We learn from your letter to Madonna Marietta that you have bought such a beautiful chain for Baccina, who does nothing but think of [it] and pray God for you, that He should make you come back soon.' Machiavelli had always urged him to 'take pains to learn [literature] and music, for you are aware how much distinction is given me for what little ability I possess.'[19]

Death came on 21 May. He took confession, as was usual for everyone, regardless of his hostility to the Church.[20] His interment at Santa Croce followed the next day, though it is uncertain where in the basilica he was buried as his monument dates from centuries later. If his life had now come to an end, his new career in a wider world, which would attract the attention of millions, most of them as yet unborn, had scarcely begun.

I V

*Epilogue: The Historical Afterglow*

No one sets out to become an eponymist, not the Marquis de Sade, who may be reckoned among the mildest of men, with the exception of the occasion when he heaved a rival through a whorehouse window, not the Baron Sacher-Masoch, who took no pleasure in pain, not Peter Paul Rubens, whose women were as often svelte as Rubenesque, and not Machiavelli, who throughout his life was admired as a poet, historian, dramatist, diplomatist, lover, father, husband, satirist, politician and philosopher. In his own day it would have seemed inconceivable that he might be seen as Machiavellian along the frigid lines of subsequent ages.

These have to do with evil and the machinations essential to promoting it. Alongside them runs the assumption of dreadful calculation, as evil can scarcely be an accident. Machiavelli nonetheless hardly evades all responsibility for the diabolical views that were soon to be attributed to him. If 'evil' refers to acts of massive destruction reaching beyond the merely criminal, no matter how 'criminal' is defined, and if it takes place in an environment conducive to diabolical behaviour, his own preoccupation with its devastations remains undeniable. In devoting so much of his life to investigating political and military leaders engaged in evil, and to exposing their methods as well as immersing himself though hesitantly in their careers, he may fairly be said to exhibit much more than a passing interest in what is later seen as 'Machiavellian.'[1]

Such at any rate was the consensus as after his death his reputation began to pick up its unjustifiably evil mystique. Even his name became a sticking place for tantalizing, demonic tales suggestive of the 'Machiavellian.' Some of them may have been true. The tales themselves eased the conversion of his life into a legend. A significant example centres on a dream which he may have recounted as he lay dying. In it he saw two groups of men strolling past, the first charming, pagan and doomed to Hell, the second boring, Christian and awaiting salvation. Asked whose company he preferred, he smiled and said, 'The pagan': their liveliness would be more entertaining than the moralizing certainties of those in some state of bliss.

The story may be false. It seems raffishly tailor-made. He may have invented it for the pleasure of providing his friends with some final macabre jest. It was also attributed to him decades later, by an acquaintance who claimed to have seen him during his last hours. Like his books and other paradoxical stories, however, it seems to capture fundamental aspects of his character.[2]

The chief source of his notoriety was *The Prince*, known to the ruling circles of Florence and much of the rest of Italy as well as elsewhere, either in

manuscript or as an item of malicious, ignorant gossip, years before its publication in 1532. Here his political realism was taken to indicate the corruption
of the author. His analysis of treachery was seen as approving it.

The Prince was first translated into French in 1553, into Latin in 1560, and
into English by Edward Dacres in 1640. The lack of an English translation
scarcely prevented the term 'Machiavel' from becoming common in Enlgish as
early as 1570. By then, or starting in 1559, his entire corpus of work had been
banned as seditious by the Holy Inquisition in Rome. Renewals of the Church
ban were issued periodically. The Prince and most of his other books were
available anyway, though, especially with not hard to obtain clerical dispensations. Several of his books, including The Prince, were also kept on tap for
lawyers doing research into the paradoxes of power.

The Church likewise lost no time in denouncing The Prince as an incitement
to Protestantism. Protestants themselves saw it as a menace to their existence:
the St Bartholomew's Day massacre of thousands of Huguenots, in Paris
and elsewhere in France, in 1572, was widely attributed to a 'Machiavellian'
influence.

In England both author and book fared little better. As early as 1590, poets
and playwrights, among them Marlowe, Shakespeare, Ben Jonson, Robert
Greene and John Donne, began to cite Machiavelli and The Prince, which was
available in Latin, as the source of anything 'subtle,' sly, unscrupulous and
malevolent. Machiavelli's now nefarious person shows up in Marlowe's The Jew
of Malta, where 'Machiavel' as Prologue introduces the action, in Shakespeare's
The Merry Wives of Windsor ('Am I subtle? Am I a Machiavel?'), in Henry VI, 1
('that notorious Machiavel!') and in The Tragedy of Richard III, whose anti-hero
is often taken to be an incarnation of the 'Machiavellian.' A 'Machiavel' as a
stock figure influences Jonson's Volpone and Donne's Ignatius his Conclave,
which presents the Jesuit Ignatius of Loyola as engaged in a debate with
Machiavelli before Lucifer.[3]

Piled-on centuries of calumnies diverted if not obscured any broad public, if
not scholarly, consideration of the deeper themes of The Prince, The Discourses
and the Florentine Histories. These consist in politics as continuous change,
treachery as inevitable amid continuous change and the universe itself as a
series of processes in which little if anything, apart from change, can be viewed
as permanent. Machiavelli's modernism has often if not always been scanted
and his historical foresight ignored. Insufficient attention, for instance, has

been paid to the fact that the inevitability of treachery renders inevitable an invalidation of all ideologies. Leaving aside any purely subjective viewpoint, the truth of religion can no more be seen as certain than the truth of communism, capitalism or fascism. Truth may be available, but in an ideological sense it remains elusive.

In modern times, surprisingly, the ideas of the political revolutionist Thomas Paine (1737–1809), who contributed to the development of democracy in America and France, match up in revealing ways with Machiavelli's. A new tradition has developed in an unexpected place, perhaps because both men had professional experience with the actual operations of political power. Though neither knew the work of the other, and though Paine never mentions Machiavelli, their enthusiasm for republican democracy and limitless empiricism, or what may work for a society in a practical sense, for religious scepticism and for unmasking hypocrisy, often at the expense of sacred beliefs, is uncannily similar. Paine's insights become a lens through which to focus on Machiavelli's, or to clarify strands of his political philosophy.

Both Machiavelli and Paine are above all linguistic purists, or authors to whom plain speech is not only preferable to jargon, *Newspeak*, misleading hipness, cant and academic mumbo-jumbo, but a kind of deity. For Paine as for Machiavelli, a humane government can only be founded amid a general cleansing of ordinary speech. Though times and issues may change, the simple phrase will always be superior to some complicated simplicity. Cleverness remains concreteness. Details remain the soul of argument. Language ought to sweat with vigour. Societies may collapse because of poor diction, bad grammar and meaningless expressions, rather than collapsing economies. Military failures are often the result of muddy sentences.[4]

Paine's *Common Sense* (1775) is common in the best sense because it represents the unadorned thinking of a disinterested, passionate person talking to people much like himself ('I shall therefore avoid every literary ornament'[5]), rather than the effusion of a bureaucrat eager to smother vitality with dullness. Machiavelli, who also refuses to adorn his sentences, had learned from Dante and Petrarch how lucid phrases may induce the magnetism of aesthetics. A combination of lucidity and aesthetics may expose the power of the universe itself, or God, if one believes in God, as the implicit logic of the sonnet and the meditational aspects of silent reading may induce self-consciousness and self-examination.

Savonarola and Cesare Borgia had taught him not merely ruthlessness but the medicinal surgery of candour. Since childhood, Ovid had shown him the universality of change. An acceptance of change as a ruling principle in every circumstance was essential to uncovering any truth at all.

Astonishingly, if hard to accept, neither Machiavelli nor Paine, as the author of *The Rights of Man* (1791), believed in democracy as the sole prescription for all political situations. Autocracy might be needed if the state were threatened. In overcoming invasion from without and the viciousness of squabbling nobles from within, Napoleon might prove more capable than Jefferson, Cesare Borgia more adept than Piero Soderini. Power was not for the squeamish.[6]

Both Machiavelli and Paine viewed autocracy as an interim remedy, however, even if neither paid much attention to how to remove it once it had been established. Change, or mutability, or what Machiavelli describes in his *Histories of Florence* as a modern 'restlessness' leading into a struggle for democracy, might resolve the contradiction of simultaneously needing and abhorring a tyrannical leader.

For Machiavelli, contradiction had always been as important as change. It contained the deeper senses of *Fortuna*. It supplied the richness of the characters in his plays and best poems, while encouraging a pliant approach to diplomacy. Its mystery lay at the heart of his early modern or Renaissance spirit. It allowed for the brilliant Renaissance mingling of nature with art, as when the morning flocks of Florentine swallows out of his childhood flashed about Brunelleschi's *Duomo*, or when as a result and as an adult he experienced time and again the revelation of the universe as perpetual surprise.

# Notes

Abbreviations

| | |
|---|---|
| *Correspondence* | James B. Atkinson, David Sices eds, *Machiavelli and His Friends: Their Personal Correspondence*. DeKalb, Ill., 1996. |
| Hook | Judith Hook, *The Sack of Rome*. London, 1972. |
| *Life* | Roberto Ridolfi, *The Life of Niccolò Machiavelli*. Cecil Grayson trans. Chicago, 1963. |
| *Diary* | Catherine Atkinson, *Debts, Dowries, Donkeys: The Diary of Niccolò Machiavelli's Father, Messer Bernardo, in Quattrocento Florence*. Frankfurt am Main, 2002. |
| Villari | Pasquale Villari, *The Life and Times of Niccolò Machiavelli*. Linda Villari trans., 1899. |
| *Society* | Gene Brucker ed., *The Society of Renaissance Florence: A Documentary Study*. Toronto, 1998. |
| *Florence* | Harold Acton intro., Edward Chaney ed. *A Traveller's Companion to Florence*. New York, (rpt) 2002. |
| Landucci | Luca Landucci, *A Florentine Diary from 1450 to 1516*. Alice de Rosen Jervis trans. New York, (rpt) 1969. |
| *CM* | John M. Najemy ed. *The Cambridge Companion to Machiavelli*. Cambridge, 2010. |
| *History* | John M. Najemy, *A History of Florence, 1200–1575*. Chichester, 2008. |
| *DW* | *Historical, Political and Diplomatic Writings of Niccolò Machiavelli*. 4 vols. Detmold trans. Boston, 1882. |
| Gilbert | *Machiavelli: The Chief Works and Others*. Allan Gilbert trans. Vols I–III. Durham, 1965. |

## Introduction

1 Good summaries may be found in Caferro, p.176; *CM*, p.6f; Leo Strauss in Adams ed., *The Prince*, pp.180–5; and Sheldon S. Wolin, *ibid.*, pp.185–94; also *ibid.*, pp.227–38.

2 Luigi Guicciardini, *Sack*, p.89f; Hook, *Sack*, pp.162–3. Cf. also Francesco Guicciardini, *History*, p.382.

3 Hook, p.146f; L. Guicciardini, p.19; F. Guicciardini, pp.380–1; Hibbert, *House of Medici*, p.241f.

4 Hook, pp.144–5, pp.70–1; Najemy, *History*, pp.447–8; Chastel, p.157.

5 L. Guicciardini, p.32, pp.49–50; p.80; Hook, pp.172–4.

6 L. Guicciardini, p.77.

7 Hook, p.177. On population estimates, see also Mee, *Daily Life*, p.10; Cowell (on citizens only), p.48.

8 Hook, pp.159–61.

9 L. Guicciardini, pp.83–4; Hook, pp.159–61.

10 *Ibid.*, p.183.

11 Cellini, p.81f.

12 L. Guicciardini, p.90.

13 Cellini, 83–4.

14 Chastel, p.127.

15 Hook, p.183–4.

16 L. Guicciardini, pp.96–100; pp.106–8.

17 *Ibid.*, p.3.

18 Chastel, p.217; Hook, p.289.

19 L. Guicciardini, p.62.

20 *Ibid.*, pp.85–6.

21 Hook, p.141–2.

22 *Correspondence*, p.408.

23 *Ibid.*, p.416.

24 Cited in Chabod, p.146. See also *Correspondence*, pp. xxvii and 249–50, with his often expressed views that 'we cannot hope for anything but ill,' and 'there will never be any union in Italy that will do any good.'

25 See useful accounts of the modern history of the term in Lichtheim and Plamenatz.

26 On Marx's well known dismissal of the notion that ideas can be autonomous, rather than socially determined, see his *The German Ideology* (first pub. 1927) and Karl Mannheim's *Ideology and Utopia* (1929). Pertinent refutations are still to be found in Russell, pp.787–90, and A.J. Ayer, pp.44–5 and 88f.

27 On Popper's notions of tentative verification and falsifiability, see his *Logic of Scientific Discovery* (1934; trans. 1959), in which it is maintained that hypotheses become testable, or meaningful, only when the conditions of their possible falsification have been established.

28 Hook, p.183.

29 *Life*, p.247. *Correspondence*, p.412.

30 *Correspondence*, pp.412, 561, 565. *Life*, pp.248–50.

*I. Machiavelli and the Changing Universe*

*Notes to Chapter 1: Family and Growing Up*

1. *Diary*, pp.35–8.
2. *Ibid.*, p.36; *Life*, pp.2–3.
3. *Diary*, p.38. Villari, pp.218–19.
4. *Diary*, pp.38–40; *Life*, p.2.
5. *Diary*, p.40; Villari, p.220; *Life*, p.2.
6. *Diary*, pp.40–4; Rubenstein, 'The beginnings of Niccolò Machiavelli's career in the Florentine Chancery', pp.72–91.
7. Cf. *List of Works of Art acquired by the South Kensington Museum during the year 1892*: inv. no. 600–1892, p.79. Painting executed by W.H. Allen. H. 2 ft 7in., W. 24.5 in., Depth 11.75 in. See also Fiona Leslie, p.174.
8. *Diary*, pp.43–4.
9. *Ibid.*, pp.56–7.
10. *Ibid.*, p.57.
11. '106. Slavery Legalized', *Society*; pp.222–8.
12. '83. Sumptuary Legislation', *Society*; pp.179–83.
13. Edward Chaney ed., pp.283–5; also 107f.
14. Hibbert, *Medici*, p.23. See also *Florence*, p.285.
15. *Selected Letters of Alessandra Strozzi*, p.173.

*Notes to Chapter 2: Early Education*

1. *Diary*, pp.50–1; *Life*, p.3; Grendler, p.43; Black, 'New Light on Machiavelli's Education', in Marchand ed., *Niccolò Machiavelli, politico, storico, letterato*, pp.391–8.
2. *Florence*, pp.89–91.
3. Armando Verde, pp.535–7.
4. *Diary*, pp.34, 40.
5. Verde, *op. cit.*
6. *Diary*, pp.68, 137–41.
7. *Ibid.*, pp.138, 167–71.
8. *Pliny: Natural History*, p.187.
9. *Ibid.*, p.183.
10. *Ibid.*, pp.183, 185.
11. Lewis, pp.60–9. See also *Diary*, p.139.
12. Lerner intro., *The Prince and The Discourses*, pp.526, 528, 318.
13. *Diary*, 142–4.

## Notes to Chapter 3: The Cosmic Package

1. Henry Paolucci ed., St Augustine, *The Enchiridion on Faith, Hope, and Love*, pp.9–10.
2. On the Ptolemaic-Christian model of the universe see also Lewis, *op. cit.*, pp.92–121. On the difficulty of refuting Aristotle even at this time, see Crombie, pp.43–7, 80–4.
3. Vasari, *Lives of the Artists*, vol. I, p.97.
4. While there seems little question that spectacles were invented in Florence, and possibly as early as 1284, doubts persist about Salvino as their inventor. See E. Rosen, pp.183–218; also V. Ilardi.
5. *Diary*, pp.144–5.
6. As in his *De montibus, silvis, fontibus, stagnis seu paludibus et de nominibus maris*; also *Diary*, p.146.
7. *Ibid.*, p.147 and n.
8. *Ibid.*

## Notes to Chapter 4: Poetry, Music and Militarism

1. *History*, pp.210–18, 222f.
2. F. Guicciardini, *History of Italy*, pp.3–4; Najemy, *ibid.*, pp.291–306; Hibbert, *op. cit.*, pp.107–27.
3. On Chrysoloras see Leonardo Bruni, *History of the Florentine People* (vol. 3), *Memoirs*, p.321f.
4. Mönch, pp.82–3.
5. Oppenheimer, *Birth of the Modern Mind*, pp.175–90.
6. On the ratios, see Wittkower, p.30; also Oppenheimer, *op. cit.*, pp.189, 20–5.

## Notes to Chapter 5: Murder in the Duomo

1. Martines, *April Blood*, pp.111–12.
2. Charles Nicholl, p.215.
3. Peruzzi, pp.27–39. *History,* pp.348–52.
4. Castiglione, p.13.
5. *Ibid.*
6. Hibbert, *op. cit.*, pp.126–7. Proverbio, in Simonetta, *op. cit.* Smith, in J.H. Plumb, *The Italian Renaissance*, p.275f.
7. Smith, *ibid.*; Peruzzi, *op. cit.*; Martelli, in Simonetta, *op. cit.*, pp.41–9.
8. See Simonetta, *op. cit.*, pp.102–6.
9. Cf. Fenucci, in Simonetta, *op. cit.*, pp.88–99.
10. Simonetta, *op. cit.*, pp.185–8.
11. Martines, *op. cit.*, pp.97–9, 107, 152, 158–61, 163–4, 175–6, 209; Plumb, *op. cit.*, pp.93–8. Pastor, pp.198–296.
12. Martines, *op. cit.*, pp.62–82, 93–6; *History*, pp.352–6; Hare, Baddeley, p.63.

12. Martines, *op. cit.*, pp.112–16; Najemy, *op. cit.*, pp.156–7; *Diary*, p.83.
13. Hibbert, *op. cit.* pp.137–40; Martines, *op. cit.*, pp.117–22.
14. *History*, p.356; also on Poliziano, see Watkins, pp.171–83.
15. Martines, *op. cit.*, pp.117–18.
16. Hibbert, *op. cit.*, p.123.
17. Landucci, pp.15–16.
18. *Ibid.*, p.16.
19. *Ibid.*, p.17.
20. *Ibid.*, p.19.
21. Martines's estimate of population, *op. cit.*, p.111.

## Notes to Chapter 6: A Boyhood Excursion

1. Frances Winwar trans. Boccaccio, *Decameron*, p. xxvi.
2. *Ibid.*, p. xxviii.
3. *Diary*, pp.63–4.
4. *Ibid.*, pp.49–50.
5. *Ibid.*, pp.47–8.
6. *Ibid.*, p.49; *Life*, p.3.
7. C. Day Lewis trans. *The Georgics of Virgil*, p.11.
8. *Ibid.*, pp.10–11.
9. Hibbert, *op. cit.*, pp.164–5.

## Notes to Chapter 7: The Lost Years

1. Hibbert, *op. cit.*, p.159.
2. *Ibid.*
3. Landucci, pp.21, 26.
4. *Diary*, p.124.
5. Mee, *op. cit.*, p.47.
6. *History*, pp.359–61; Landucci, pp.28, 29, 31.
7. Verde, *op. cit.*, p.526; *Diary*, pp.141, 146, 147; *Life*, p.4.
8. *Diary*, p.51; Gilbert, p.321.
9. *Diary*, p.120.
10. *Ibid.*, pp.52, 119f, 172.
11. *Ibid.*, pp.168–9.
12. Goodman, pp.3–4; Brown, in *CM*, p.160; Verde, *op. cit.*, p.537; *History*, p.367.
13. Cf. F.A. Gregg trans. Paulus Iovius, p.124.
14. Cf. Bertelli (1961), pp.544–57; (1964); pp.774–92.
15. Gordon ed.and trans. *Two Renaissance Book Hunters: The Letters of Poggio Bracciolini to Nicolaus de Niccolis*, p.296. Also Goodman, *op. cit.*, p.149.
16. R.E. Latham trans. Lucretius, *On the Nature of the Universe*, pp.152–3.

17. *Ibid.*, p.170.
18. *Ibid.*, p.206.
19. *Ibid.*
20. *Ibid.*, p.215.
21. *Ibid.*, p.251.
22. *Ibid.*, p.255–6.

### Notes to Chapter 8: Poetry and the Medici

1. On dating, publication and texts, cf. Martelli (1971), pp.377–405.
2. Cf. Brown intro., Renée Neu Watkins trans., Scala, pp. xi-xii, 158–231. *Diary*, pp.149–52.

### Notes to Chapter 9: The Religious Revolution

1. Mee, *op. cit,* p.113. Weinstein, p.139; Erlanger, p.48; *History*, pp.390–400; Martines, *Savonarola*, pp.8–28.
2. Landucci, p.89.
3. Savonarola, *Selected Writings*, p. xx; Landucci (on crowds), p.89.
4. *Ibid.*
5. Weinstein, pp.212–13; Erlanger, p.51f.
6. Erlanger, pp.57–60; Hibbert, p.181; Martines, *Savonarola*, pp.28–30; Savonarola, *Selected Writings*, p. xxi.
7. Martines, *Savonarola*, p.29–30.
8. Baumgartner, pp.19–21.
9. R. Strong, pp.9–10.
10. Martines, p.35.
11. *Ibid.*, pp.37–8; Hibbert, pp.186–8; Erlanger, p.95.
12. Martines, *Savonarola*, 43f; Villari, p.204.
13. *Erlanger, p.108.*
14. Savonarola, *Selected Writings*, p.69f.
15. *Ibid.*, p. xxvii.
16. Martines, *Savonarola*, p.103.
17. *Ibid.*, pp.115–18; Savonarola, *Selected Writings*, p. xxviiif.
18. Martines, *Savonarola*, p.90.
19. On segregated crowds, Landucci, p.88; .
20. Martines, *Savonarola*, pp.114, 286; on excommunication, Erlanger, pp.188f.
21. *Ibid.*, pp.287–9.
22. *Correspondence*, p.4f.
23. *Ibid.*, pp.3–6.
24. *Diary*, p.48.
25. *Correspondence*, p.8.
26. *Ibid.*

27. *Ibid.*
28. *Ibid.*, p.10.
29. *Ibid.*


## II. *The World of War and Diplomacy*

### Notes to Chapter 10: *Executions and an Official Appointment*

1. Martines, *Savonarola*, p.263; Erlanger, p.266.
2. *Ibid.*, p.267.
3. *Ibid.*, p.264.
4. Martines, *Savonarola.*, p.220f; Erlanger, p.241f.
5. Cited in Martines, *Savonarola*, p.244.
6. Landucci, pp.138–9; cf. also pp.135–6.
7. *Ibid.*, p.142.
8. *Ibid.*
9. *Ibid.*, pp.142–3; Martines, *Savonarola*, pp.274–6.
10. Rubenstein, *op. cit.*, p.82f.
11. *Ibid.*, pp.84, 85; *Life*, p.15.
12. Landucci, pp.92f, describes the rapid construction of this chamber ('it will be magnificent').
13. *Correspondence*, pp.4, 6.
14. Cf. Simonetta, *Rinascimento segreto. Il mondo del Segretario da Petrarca a Machiavelli.* Milan, 2004.
15. On the pre-publication history of Machiavelli's letters and other works, see Gerber, esp. Part One, *Die Handschriften* (Part Two: *Die Ausgaben*), with its 147 facsimile-reproductions. Gerber wishes to establish (p.100) grounds for crediting Machiavelli's authorship.
16. On couriers, see *Correspondence*, #89 (p.101); on payments, #121 (p.402); on intercepted mail, #7 (p.17), #17 (p.30).


### Notes to Chapter 11: *Caterina Sforza and the Crisis at Pisa*

1. *Life*, pp.26–7; Johnson, pp.187–8, 150–2.
2. Plumb, *op. cit.*, pp.142–3.
3. *Life*, *op. cit.*
4. Villari, pp.237–8; Bertelli ed., Machiavelli, *Legazione e commissarie*, vol. I, pp.30–1.
5. *Correspondence*, p.19.
6. *Ibid.*
7. *Ibid.*, pp.20–1.
8. *Ibid.*
9. *Life*, p.27.
10. *Ibid.*, pp.25–6; Villari, p.233.
11. Bertelli ed., Machiavelli, *Arte della Guerra e scritti politici minori*, pp.13–17; see also abbreviated translation in Constantine, pp.349–50.

12. Scala, pp.243–5.
13. *DW*, vol. 3, pp.3–4. Bertelli, *Legazione*, vol. I, pp.11–12.


*Notes to Chapter 12: The Military Quandary*

1. Landucci, p.146.
2. *Life*, p.28.
3. Landucci, pp.144–5.
4. Bruni, *History of the Florentine People*, vol. 3, p.9.
5. *Ibid.*, p.7.
6. *Ibid.*, p.9.
7. *Life*, p.28; Landucci, p.159.
8. Johnson, *op. cit.*, p.106.
9. Villari, p.241.
10. *Ibid.*, pp.242–4; Landucci, p.162.
11. *Ibid.*
12. *Correspondence*, pp.22–3.


*Notes to Chapter 13: On the Move with the French King*

1. *Diary*, p.160.
2. *Ibid.*, pp.46, 164–5.
3. Cf. Italian in Villari, pp.540–1.
4. *Life*, p.28; *Correspondence*, p.24.
5. Baumgartner, p.65f; Parker, pp.42–5.
6. Baumgartner, pp.55–6, 68–9, 269–70.
7. Simone, *French Renaissance*, pp.93–4 (on the sonnet); Baumgartner, pp.200–7.
8. Johnson, pp.138–41; Bradford, pp.77–9.
9. F. Guicciardini, pp.3–8.
10. On nationalism, cf. Cowan, pp.4–5.
11. *Life*, p.15.
12. *DW*, vol. 3, p.30.
13. *Ibid.*, p.30.
14. *Ibid.*, p.32.
15. *Ibid.*, p.37–8.
16. Villari, p.255.
17. *DW*, *op. cit.*, p.41.
18. *Ibid.*, p.55.
19. *Ibid.*
20. *Ibid.*, pp.56, 57.
21. *Correspondence*, pp.26–8.
22. *Ibid.*, pp.31, 32–3.

*Notes to Chapter 14: The Long French Patience*

1. *Ibid.*, p.33.
2. *DW, op. cit.*, p.110.
3. *Ibid.*, p.111.
4. *Ibid.*, p.126.
5. Basil Bunting trans.
6. Landucci, p.174.

*Notes to Chapter 15: Marriage and a Hint of Cesare Borgia*

1. *DW, op. cit.*, p.140.
2. *Ibid.*, p.125.
3. Johnson, p.152.
4. *Ibid.*, pp.152–5; Bradford, pp.83–5.
5. *Diary*, p.162; *Correspondence*, p.450; *Life*, p.46.
6. *Correspondence*, p.42.

*Notes to Chapter 16: Meeting the Captain-General*

1. Landucci, pp.177–8.
2. *Correspondence*, p.38.
3. *DW, op. cit.* p.135.
4. Herlihy, p.203.
5. Villari, pp.263–4; *Life*, pp.44–5.
6. *DW, op. cit.*, summarized on pp.145–6.
7. Landucci, p.181f.
8. *Correspondence*, p.45f.
9. Bertelli, *op. cit.*, pp.262–3.
10. *Ibid.*, p.263.
11. *Ibid.*, p.262.
12. *History*, pp.406–7.
13. Bertelli, *op. cit.*, pp.267–8.
14. *Life*, p.49.
15. Bertelli, *op. cit.*, p.267.
16. *Life*, p.51.

*Notes to Chapter 17: Investigating the Sources of Power*

1. Cf. also *History*, p.407, which emphasizes the ambiguous influences surrounding his election.

2. *Correspondence*, p.58.
3. *DW, op. cit.*, p.144.
4. *Ibid.*
5. *Ibid.*, pp.144–5.
6. Nicholl, p.344f.
7. *Ibid.*, p.347.
8. *Ibid.*, p.348; Masters, p.87f.
9. *DW, op. cit.*, letters XXVI, p.215f.
10. *Ibid.*, p.151.
11. *Ibid.*, p.153.
12. *Ibid.*
13. *Ibid.*

*Notes to Chapter 18: Retribution and Dominance*

1. *Correspondence*, p.52.
2. *Ibid.*, p.55.
3. Landucci, pp.196–7, 201.
4. *DW, op. cit.*, p.223.
5. *Ibid.*, p.239.
6. *Ibid.*, p.245.
7. *Correspondence*, p.59.
8. *DW, op. cit.*, p.146.
9. *Ibid.*, p.150.
10. *Ibid.*, p.242.
11. *Ibid.*, p.220.
12. *Ibid.*, p.222.
13. *Ibid.*, p.257.
14. *Ibid.*, p.259.
15. *Correspondence*, p.79.
16. *Ibid.*, p.78.
17. *DW, op. cit.*, p.259.
18. *Ibid.*, pp.259–60.
19. *Ibid.*, p.261.
20. *Ibid.*
21. *Ibid.*, p.263.

*Notes to Chapter 19: Plans to Change the Arno*

1. *Ibid.*
2. Burchard, p.216.
3. *DW*, p.268.

4. *Ibid.*, p.269.
5. *Ibid.*, p.280.
6. *Life*, pp.65f.
7. Bertelli ed., *Arte della guerra e scritte politici minori*, pp.57f; Gilbert trans., vol. 3, pp.1439f.
8. *Ibid.*, p.1440.
9. *Ibid.*, p.1443.
10. Constantine trans., p.370.
11. *Ibid.*
12. *Ibid.*, p.371–2.
13. Nicholl, p.417.
14. Leonardo, *Notebooks*, vol. II; p.388.
15. Nicholl, pp.357–8.
16. Masters, p.101.
17. Nicholl, p.358f.
18. *Ibid.*, pp.358–9; *Notebooks*, *op. cit.*, p.438.
19. Burchard, pp.220f.
20. *Ibid.*, p.211.

*Notes to Chapter 20: The First Journey to Rome*

1. Nicholl, p.371; Bull, pp.58–9.
2. Nicholl, *op. cit.*; Bull, p.59.
3. Nicholl, p.373.
4. *Notebooks*, vol. III, p.45.
5. Johnson, pp.180–1.
6. Burchard, pp.225–6.
7. *Ibid.*, p.221.
8. Vasari, vol. II, p.83; Gregorovius, pp.132f.
9. *DW*, *op. cit.*, p.284.
10. *Ibid.*, p.296.
11. Johnson, p.181; Bradford, p.209.
12. *DW*, *op. cit.*, p.296.
13. *Correspondence*, p.86.

*Notes to Chapter 21: Cesare's Downfall and the First Decennale*

1. *DW*, *op. cit.*, p.300.
2. *Ibid.*, pp.326–7, 320.
3. *Ibid.*, p.309.
4. *Ibid.*, pp.336, 338.
5. *Ibid.*, p.345.
6. *Ibid.*, p.334.

7. *Ibid.*, p.342.
8. *Correspondence*, p.93.
9. *DW, op. cit.* p.364.
10. Nicholl, p.379.
11. Bull, pp.58–60.
12. *Rime*, G.R. Ceriello ed., p.139.
13. Gilbert, III, p.1444.
14. *History*, pp.410–11; *Life*, pp.79–80.
15. *DW, op. cit.*, p.389.
16. *Life*, p.79.
17. Constantine trans., pp.355–6.
18. *DW, op. cit.*, pp.396–7.
19. *Correspondence*, p.101.
20. *Ibid.*, p.102.
21. Nicholl, pp.384–5.
22. *Correspondence*, pp.106–7.
23. *Ibid.*, p.118.
24. Gilbert, *op. cit.*, p.1457.
25. *Ibid.*, p.1445.
26. *Ibid.*, p.1446.
27. *Ibid.*, p.1450.
28. *Ibid.*, p.1445.
29. *Ibid.*, p.1457.
30. *Ibid.*, p.1454.

*Notes to Chapter 22: Anarchy and the Citizen Militia*

1. Johnson, p.184; Bradford, 236.
2. Ruggiero, in Crum and Paoletti eds, *Renaissance Florence: A Social History*, pp.304–7.
3. *Correspondence*, p.102.
4. *Life*, p.87; *History*, p.411.
5. Cowell, p.37.
6. *DW*, IV, pp.4, and see also p.3.
7. Landucci, p.218.
8. Baumgartner, p.55.
9. *Correspondence*, p.116.
10. *DW, op. cit.*, pp.10–11.
11. *Ibid.*, p.20.
12. *Ibid.*, p.36.
13. *Correspondence*, p.134.
14. *Ibid.*, p.135.
15. *Ibid.*, pp.135–6.
16. Gilbert, II, pp.745–9.

17. *Ibid.*, p.747.
18. Hibbert, p.202.


*Notes to Chapter 23: The German Enigma*

1. *DW, op. cit.*, pp.126f.
2. Cf. especially Waas, pp.23–72, 87f.
3. *Ibid.*, pp.101–2.
4. *DW, op. cit.*, p.82.
5. *Ibid.*, p.87.
6. *Ibid.*, pp.396–7.
7. *Ibid.*, p.398f.
8. *Ibid.*, p.89.
9. *Ibid.*, p.126.
10. Bradford, p.270; Johnson, p.186.
11. *DW, op. cit.*, pp.148, 153.


*Notes to Chapter 24: Victory at Pisa*

1. *Ibid.*, p.156.
2. Landucci, p.231.
3. *DW, op. cit.*, pp.165f.
4. *Ibid.*, p.178.
5. *Ibid.*, p.184.
6. Landucci, p.234.
7. *Correspondence*, p.180.
8. *Ibid.*, pp.182, 183.
9. See discussion of Poggio's *Facetiae* in Oppenheimer trans., *Eulenspiegel*, p. liii.
10. Constantine trans., pp.381–5.


*Notes to Chapter 25: A Government Overthrown*

1. *History*, p.413.
2. On the twentieth he wrote, 'I shall mount my horse and proceed … to Verona, … where all lies originate, or rather where it rains lies' (*DW, op. cit.* p.202).
3. *Ibid.*, pp.203–4.
4. *Correspondence*, p.190; *Lettere*, pp.321–3.
5. *Ibid.*
6. *Ibid.*
7. *Metamorphoses*, I, 7, pp.16–19. Cf. Thompson, pp.193, 203f., 259, 282 on the folktale motifs.

8. *Correspondence*, p.191.
9. Gilbert, II, p.738.
10. *Ibid.*, p.735.
11. *Correspondence*, p.192.
12. *Ibid.*, p.193.
13. F. Guicciardini, p.208; *DW*, *op. cit.*, p.220.
14. *Ibid.*, pp.243–4.
15. *Correspondence*, pp.204–5.
16. *Ibid.*, p.208.
17. *Ibid.*
18. F. Guicciardini, pp.212–15.
19. *Correspondence*, p.195; *Life*, pp.121f.
20. Landucci, pp.247–8.
21. *Ibid.*, p.255.
22. F. Guicciardini, pp.259–60.
23. *Ibid.*, pp.262–3; Landucci, pp.256–7.
24. *History*, p.421; F. Guicciardini, pp.263–4.

## III. Into a Tuscan Exile

### Notes to Chapter 26: The Aftermath of Freedom

1. Landucci, pp.258–9.
2. *Ibid.*, p.261; *History*, pp.424–5; see also Machiavelli's description of the disaster at Prato and subsequent events in *Correspondence*, pp.214–17.
3. F. Guicciardini, p.266.
4. *Correspondence*, p.424.
5. Bertelli ed., *op. cit.*, pp.219–27.
6. Devonshire Jones, *Vettori*, p.104; Butters, 'Machiavelli and the Medici,' in *CM*, pp.65–6.
7. On the remodelling, see Landucci, pp.264–5.
8. Butters, p.67; *Life*, p.135; *History*, pp.426–7.
9. Vasari, vol. II, pp.109–10.
10. *Correspondence*, p.497.
11. Landucci, p.266.
12. The Dazzo referred to is apparently a second-rate writer apprenticed to Marcello Virgilio. Both sonnets, discovered only in 1828, remain controversial, though their authenticity is not disputed. Cf. *Life*, pp.136–8; Gilbert, II, pp.1013–14; Ascoli and Capodivacca in *CM*, p.203; Villari, vol. II, pp.36–7, 541.
13. F. Guicciardini, pp.272–3.
14. Landucci, pp.267–8.
15. *Correspondence*, p.221.
16. See *Diary*, p.162.
17. *Correspondence*, pp.222–3.

## Notes to Chapter 27: Making History at Sant'Andrea

1. Hare, *Florence*, p.233.
2. Landucci, p.269.
3. *Correspondence*, p.225.
4. *Ibid.*, p.237.
5. *Ibid.*, p.249.
6. Constantine trans., p.105.
7. Ogilvie intro., *Livy*, pp.8, 9–10.
8. Villari, II, pp.97–9; but see also Najemy in *CM*, pp.96–9.
9. Lerner, *op. cit.*, p.129.
10. *Ibid.*, p.131.
11. *Ibid.*, pp.147, 146.
12. *Ibid.*, pp.185–6.
13. *Ibid.*, p.215.
14. *Ibid.*, pp.256, 257.
15. *Correspondence*, p.244.
16. *Ibid.*
17. *Ibid.*, pp.260–1.
18. *Ibid.*, p.263.
19. *Ibid.*, p.264.
20. Clough, pp.13–14.
21. *Correspondence, op. cit.*

## Notes to Chapter 28: Power and Memory

1. Bull trans., p.32.
2. *Correspondence*, p.276.
3. Adams trans., p.35.
4. *Ibid.*, p.48.
5. *Ibid.*, p.50.
6. *Ibid.*, p.72.
7. *Ibid.*, p.73.
8. See Gilbert, II, p.1015; *Life*, p.140.
9. *CM*, pp.194, 208; *Life*, pp.174–5; Shell in Sullivan ed., *Comedy and Tragedy of Machiavelli*, pp.80f.

## Notes to Chapter 29: The Ambush of Love

1. *Correspondence*, p.293.
2. *Ibid.*, p.278.
3. *Ibid.*, pp.311–12.

4. *Ibid.*, p.301.
5. Gilbert, III, pp.1457–62.
6. *Life*, p.168; *Correspondence*, pp.309, 318.
7. Constantine trans., pp.222, 223.
8. *Ibid.*, p.232; Lerner, *op. cit.*, p.540.
9. Landucci, pp.274–6.
10. *Ibid.*, pp.279–85; Symonds, *Shakespeare's Predecessors*, p.325.

## Notes to Chapter 30: Literary Adventures

1. *Correspondence*, pp.314, 315, 318.
2. Gilbert, II, p.772; cf. Ascoli and Capodivacca, *op. cit.*, pp.198–204; also Harvey in Sullivan ed., *op. cit.*, pp.120–37.
3. Constantine trans., p.401.
4. *Ibid.*
5. Hale trans., p.188; also cited by Saxonhouse in Sullivan ed., *op. cit.*, p.58.
6. *Ibid.*, p.57; see also Duerr, *Acting*, pp.89f.
7. Leonardo, *Notebooks*, III, p.179; Nicholl, p.258.
8. Constantine trans., pp.441, 447.
9. *Ibid.*, p.475.
10. *Ibid.*, p.438.
11. *Ibid.*, p.461.
12. *Ibid.*, p.465, 467.
13. *Ibid.*, p.436.

## Notes to Chapter 31: Reflecting on the Craft of War

1. Waas, *op. cit.*, p.87f.
2. Hibbert, p.235.
3. Farnworth trans., Neal Wood rev., p.7.
4. *Ibid.*, p.10.
5. *Ibid.*, xx.
6. *Ibid.*, pp.17–20.
7. *Ibid.*, pp. xlv-li.
8. *Ibid.*, p.19.
9. *Ibid.*, p.40 and n.
10. *Ibid.*, p.210.
11. *Ibid.*, p. xxxv.
12. *Correspondence*, p.325.
13. On the historical Castruccio, see *History*, pp.121–3.
14. Constantine trans., pp.406–7.
15. *Ibid.*, pp.418–22.

## Notes to Chapter 32: The Dream of History

1. *Correspondence*, pp.329, 534–5.
2. Constantine trans., pp.317–18.
3. *Correspondence*, p.328; Constantine trans., p.428.
4. *Correspondence*, pp.331–2, 334.
5. *Ibid.*, p.332; *Life*, pp.186f.
6. On private reading, see Cameron in Pettegree ed., *Early Reformation*, p.196; on Italy, see *ibid.*, pp.188f.
7. *Correspondence*, pp.335, 336.
8. *Ibid.*, p.341.
9. *Ibid.*, p.342.
10. Cf. also *Life*, p.197.; Cabrini in *CM*, pp.133–4.
11. Marriott trans., *Florentine History*, p.7.
12. Constantine trans., p.318.
13. Marriott trans., *op. cit.*, p.8.
14. *Ibid.*, pp.13–14.
15. *Ibid.*, p.78, 85, 131.
16. *Ibid.*, pp.370–1.
17. *Ibid.*, p.416.

## Notes to Chapter 33: Lights before the Storm

1. F. Guicciardini, pp.327–38; Hibbert, pp.236–8.
2. *Correspondence*, p.355.
3. *Ibid.*, p.357.
4. *Ibid.*, pp.339, 345, 539, 349.
5. *Ibid.*, p.345; *Life*, p.203.
6. Gilbert, I, pp.106, 115; Bertelli ed., *Arte della guerra e scritti politici minori*, I, p.277.
7. *Correspondence*, p.351; *Life*, pp.207–8.
8. *Correspondence*, p.354.
9. Evans trans., p.25; on the theatrical tradition, see also Faulkner in Sullivan ed., p.39.
10. *Correspondence*, pp.358, 363, 364–5, 367, 368.

## Notes to Chapter 34: The Assault on Rome and a Fatal Illness

1. *Ibid.*, p.360.
2. *Ibid.*, p.372.
3. *Ibid.*, p.378.
4. Waldman trans., *Orlando Furioso*, p.402.
5. F. Guicciardini, p.345.
6. *History*, p.447.

7. *Life*, pp.224–5; *Correspondence*, pp.379, 551.
8. Hibbert, p.248.
9. *Ibid.*, p.242; *Life*, p.234; for Machiavelli's view of him, cf. *Correspondence*, p.382.
10. *Life*, pp.230–1, 323n.
11. *Correspondence*, pp.385–6, 386–7.
12. *Ibid.*, pp.376–7; F. Guicciardini, pp.373–5.
13. *History*, pp.448–9.
14. *Correspondence*, pp.393, 395.
15. *Ibid.*, pp.413–14.
16. *Ibid.*, p.416.
17. For contemporary thinking along these apocalyptic lines, see F. Guicciardini, pp.376, 385–6, 389.
18. *History*, p.452; *Life*, p.248; Villari, II, p.503.
19. *Correspondence*, pp.561, 417.
20. *Ibid.*, p.425.

## IV. Epilogue

1. On evil conceived in this way, see Oppenheimer, *Evil and the Demonic*, pp. ix-x, 1–11.
2. Villari, *op. cit.*, p.505; *Life*, pp.249–50.
3. Adams trans., pp.227–38.
4. Keane, *Paine*, p.97.
5. *Ibid.*, p.295.
6. *Ibid.*, pp.435f.

# Bibliography

Machiavelli has always attracted considerable scholarly and critical attention. Silvia Ruffo-Fiore reports on more than 3,000 books and articles devoted to his life and works in modern times alone. Since 1988, when her list breaks off (see below: it begins in 1935) at least 1,500 more may confidently be said to have been added to the total. Like their predecessors, many are fascinating and original. The list presented here thus includes a mere fraction of the scholarly-critical enterprise to date, or those books and articles which have seemed essential to the present effort.

Acton, Harold. *The Pazzi Conspiracy*. London: 1979.

—, intro., and Edward Chaney ed. *A Traveller's Companion to Florence*. (rpt). New York: 2002.

Apuleius. J. Arthur Hanson ed. and trans. *Metamorphoses*. Vol. I. Cambridge, Mass.: 1989.

Ariosto, Ludovico. Guido Waldman trans. *Orlando Furioso*. Oxford: 1974.

—. Alexander Sheers, David Quint trans. David Quint intro. *Cinque Canti/ Five Cantos*. Bilingual ed. Berkeley: 1996.

Ascoli, Albert Russell, and Angela Matilde Capodivacca. 'Machiavelli and poetry.' See Najemy, *Cambridge Companion to Machiavelli*, pp.190–205.

Atkinson, Catherine. *Debts, Dowries, Donkeys: The Diary of Niccolò Machiavelli's Father, Messer Bernardo, in Quattrocento Florence*. Frankfurt am Main: 2002.

Atkinson, James B., and David Sices trans. and eds. *Machiavelli and his Friends: Their Personal Correspondence*. DeKalb: 1996.

Augustine. Henry Paolucci ed. and trans. Adolph von Harnack crit. appraisal. *The Enchiridion on Faith, Hope and Love*. Chicago: 1961.

Ayer, A. J. *Language, Truth and Logic*. London: 1956.

Bartlett, R. *Trial by Fire and Water*. Oxford: 1986.

Baumgartner, Frederic J. *France in the Sixteenth Century.* New York: 1995.

Bayer, Andrea, ed. *Art and Love in Renaissance Italy.* Exhibition catalogue: Metropolitan Museum of Art, New York. New Haven: 2008.

Benner, Erica. *Machiavelli's Ethics.* Princeton: 2009.

Berlin, Isaiah. Henry Hardy, Roger Hausheer eds. Noel Annan forward. *The Proper Study of Mankind: An Anthology of Essays.* New York: 2000.

Bertelli, Sergio. 'Noterelle Machiavelliane: Un Codice di Lucrezio e di Terenzio.' *Revista Storica Italiana.* Vol. 73 (1961): pp.544–57.

—. 'Noterelle Machiavelliane: Ancora su Lucrezio e Machiavelli.' *Revista Storica Italiana.* Vol. 76 (1964): pp.774–92.

Black, Robert. 'New Light on Machiavelli's Education.' See under Jean-Jacques Marchand ed. Pp.391–8.

Boccaccio, Giovanni. *Il Decamerone.* 2 vols. Bari: 1966.

—. Frances Winwar trans. (rpt). New York: 1955.

Bradford, Sarah. *Lucrezia Borgia: Life, Love and Death in Renaissance Italy.* London: 2005.

Brown, Alison. *Bartolomeo Scala, Chancellor of Florence, 1430–1497: The Humanist as Bureaucrat.* Princeton: 1979.

—. 'Philosophy and religion in Machiavelli.' See Najemy, *Cambridge Machiavelli.* Pp.157–72.

—. Intro.; see under Bartolomeo Scala.

Brown, Patricia Fortini. *Private Lives in Renaissance Venice: Art, Architecture and the Family.* New Haven: 2004.

Brucker, Gene, ed. *The Society of Renaissance Florence: A Documentary Study.* Toronto: 1998.

Bruni, Leonardo. James Hankins ed. and trans., with D.J.W. Bradley. *History of the Florentine People. Vol. 3: Books IX-XII, Memoirs.* Cambridge, Mass.: 2007.

Bull, George. *Michelangelo: A Biography.* London: 1996.

Bullock, Allan. *The Humanist Tradition in the West.* New York: 1985.

Bunting, Basil. *The Complete Poems.* Oxford: 1978.

Burchard, Johann. Geoffrey Parker ed. and trans. *At the Court of the Borgia: being an Account of the Reign of Pope Alexander VI written by his Master of Ceremonies.* London: 1963.

Burckhardt, Jacob. *Die Kultur der Renaissance in Italien.* 2nd ed. Wien: (n.d.).

Burke, Peter. *The Italian Renaissance: Culture and Society in Italy.* Princeton: 1987.

Butters, H. C. *Governors and Government in Early Sixteenth-Century Florence: 1502–1519.* Oxford: 1985.

—. 'Machiavelli and the Medici.' See Najemy ed., *Cambridge Companion to Machiavelli*, pp.64–79.

Cabrini, Anna Maria. 'Machiavelli's *Florentine Histories.*' See Najemy ed., *Cambridge Companion to Machiavelli*, pp.128–43.

Caferro, William. *Contesting the Renaissance (Contesting the Past).* Oxford: 2011.

Calamandrei, E. Polidori. *Le vesti delle donne fiorentine nel quattrocento.* (ltd. ed). Florence: 1924.

Cameron, Euan. 'Italy.' See Pettegree, pp.188–214.

Castiglione, Baldesar. *The Book of the Courtier.* Charles S. Singleton trans. New York: 1959.

Cellini, Benvenuto. Ettore Camesasca ed. *Vita.* Milan: 1954.

—. *Autobiography of Benvenuto Cellini.* John Addington Symonds trans. (rpt). New York: 1961.

Chabod, Federico. David Moore trans. A.P. D'Entrèves intro. *Machiavelli and the Renaissance.* (rpt). New York: 1965.

Chastel, André. Beth Archer trans. *The Sack of Rome, 1527.* Princeton: 1983.

Cianchi, Marco. *Leonardo's Machines.* Carlo Pedretti intro. Lisa Goldenberg Stoppato trans. Florence: 1984.

Clough, Cecil. 'Machiavelli's "Epistolario" and again what did he wear in the country.' *Bulletin for the Society of Renaissance Studies.* Vol. 1, no. 3 (Oct. 1983), pp.7–18.

—. 'Yet again Machiavelli's *Prince.*' *Annali, Sezione Romanza* (Istituto Universitario Orientale). Vol. 2 (Iuglio 1963), pp.201–26. [Offprint with author's Corrections.]

Cochrane, Eric. *Florence in the Forgotten Centuries, 1527–1800.* Chicago and London: 1973.

Cohn, Samuel K., Jr. *Creating the Florentine State: Peasants and Rebellion, 1348–1434.* Cambridge, Eng.: 1999.

Colish, Marcia L. 'Machiavelli's *Art of War*: A Reconsideration.' *Renaissance Quarterly*, 51 (Dec. 1998), pp.1151–68.

Conti, Elio. *I Catasti agrari della repubblica fiorentina e il catasto particellare toscano (secoli XIV-XIX).* Rome: 1966.

Cowan, Robert. *The Indo-German Identification: Reconciling South Asian Origins and European Destinies, 1765–1885.* Rochester: 2010.

Cowell, F. R. *Cicero and the Roman Republic.* New York: 1948.

Crombie, A. C. *Medieval and Early Modern Science. Volume II: Science in the Later Middle Ages and Early Modern Times: XIII-XVII Centuries.* (rev. 2$^{nd}$ ed). New York: 1959.

Crum, Roger J., and John T. Paoletti eds. *Renaissance Florence: A Social History.* Cambridge, Eng.: 2006.

Devonshire Jones, Rosemary. *Francesco Vettori: Florentine Citizen and Medici Servant.* London: 1972.

Dionisotti, Carlo. 'Appunti sui capitoli di Machiavelli.' Giovanni Aquilecchia, Stephen N. Christea, Sheila Ralphs eds. *Collected Essays on Italian Language and Literature, Presented to Kathleen Spaight.* Pp.55–71.

Duerr, Edwin. *The Length and Depth of Acting.* New York: 1962.

Erlanger, Rachel. *The Unarmed Prophet: Savonarola in Florence.* New York: 1988.

Farrell, Joseph, and Paolo Puppa, eds. *A History of Italian Theatre.* Cambridge: 2006.

Faulkner, Robert. '*Clizia* and the Enlightenment of Private Life.' See Sullivan, pp.30–56.

Feldman, Martha, and Bonnie Gordon eds. *The Courtesan's Arts: Cross-Cultural Perspectives.* Oxford: 2006.

Fenucci, Fabrizio, and Marcello Simonetta. 'The Studiolo of Urbino: A Visual Guide.' See Simonetta, *Federico da Montefeltro*, pp.88–99.

Fido, Franco. 'Machiavelli in his Time and Ours.' *Italian Quarterly*, 13 (1970), pp.3–21.

Field, Arthur. *The Origins of the Platonic Academy of Florence.* Princeton: 1988.

Frick, Carole Collier. *Dressing Renaissance Florence: Families, Fortunes and Fine Clothing.* Baltimore: 2002.

Fronsini, Giovanna. *Il cibo e i signori: La mensa dei priori di Firenze nel quinto decennio del sec. XIV.* Firenze: 1993.

Gerber, Adolph. *Niccolò Machiavelli. Die Handschriften, Ausgaben und Uebersetzungen seiner Werke im 16. und 17. Jahrhundert. Eine Kritisch-Bibliographische Untersuchung. Erster Teil: die Handschriften. Zweiter Teil: die Ausgaben.* Gotha: 1912, 1913. Rpt: Turin: 1962.

Gilbert, Felix. 'The Concept of Nationalism in Machiavelli's *Prince*.' *Studies in the Renaissance*, 1 (1954): pp.38–48.

—. *Machiavelli and Guicciardini: Politics and History in Sixteenth-Century Florence.* Princeton: 1965.

Goldthwaite, Richard A. *The Building of Renaissance Florence: An Economic and Social History*. Baltimore: 1980.

Goodman, Peter. *From Poliziano to Machiavelli: Florentine Humanism in the High Renaissance*. Princeton: 1998.

Gordon, D. J., Stephen Orgel eds. *The Renaissance Imagination*. Berkeley and London: 1975.

Gordon, Phyllis Walter Goodhart, ed. and trans. *Two Renaissance Book Hunters: The Letters of Poggio Bracciolini to Nicolaus de Niccolis*. New York: 1991.

Gregorovius, Ferdinand. John Leslie Garner trans. *Lucrezia Borgia, According to Original Documents and Correspondence of her Day*. New York: 1903.

Grendler, Paul F. *Books and Schools in the Italian Renaissance*. Norfolk, Eng.: 1995.

Gouwens, Kenneth. *The Italian Renaissance: The Essential Sources*. Oxford: 2004.

Guicciardini, Francesco. *The History of Italy*. Sidney Alexander trans. New York: 1969.

Guicciardini, Luigi. *The Sack of Rome*. James H. Mc Gregor trans. and ed. New York: 1993.

Hale, J. R. *Florence and the Medici: the Pattern of Control*. London: 1977.

—, and Michael Edward Mallett. *The Military Organization of a Renaissance State: Venice, c. 1400*. Cambridge, Eng.: 1984.

Hare, Augustus J. C., and St. Clair Baddeley. *Florence*. 6th ed. London: 1904.

Harvey, Michael. 'Lost in the Wilderness: Love and Longing in *L'Asino*.' See Sullivan, pp.120–37.

Herlihy, David. *Medieval and Renaissance Pistoia: The Social History of an Italian Town*. New Haven: 1967.

Hibbert, Christopher. *The House of Medici, its Rise and Fall*. (rpt). New York: 2003.

Hörnqvist, Mikael. *Machiavelli and Empire*. Cambridge, Eng.: 2004.

Hoeges, D. *Niccolò Machiavelli: die Macht und der Schein*. Munich: 2000.

Hollingsworth, Mary. *Patronage in Sixteenth-Century Italy*. London: 1996.

Hook, Judith. *The Sack of Rome*. London: 1972.

Ilardi, V. *Renaissance Vision from Spectacles to Telescopes*. Philadelphia: 2007.

Iovius, Paulus. F. A. Gregg trans. *An Italian Portrait Gallery*. Boston: 1935.

*Italian Wall Decorations of the 15th and 16th Centuries: A Handbook to the models, illustrating the interiors of Italian buildings in the Victoria and Albert Museum, South Kensington*. London: 1901.

Jardine, Lisa. *Worldly Goods: A New History of the Renaissance*. London: 1996.

Johnson, Marion. *The Borgias*. London: 1981.

Keane, John. *Tom Paine: A Political Life*. London: 1996.

Kennedy, William J. *The Site of Petrarchism: Early Modern National Sentiment in Italy, France and England*. Baltimore: 2003.

Kirkbride, Robert. *Architecture and Memory: The Renaissance Studioli of Federico da Montefeltro*. New York: 2008.

Landucci, Luca. Alice de Rosen Jervis trans. *A Florentine Diary from 1450 to 1516*. (rpt). New York: 1969.

Larivaille, Paul. *La vie quotidienne en Italie au temps de Machiavel*. Florence, Rome: 1979.

Leonardo da Vinci. Edward MacCurdy trans. Ladislao Reti additional trans. Charles Nicholl intro. *The Notebooks*. 3 vols. London: 2009.

Leoni, M. *Opinioni sul Principe di Niccolò Machiavelli*. Parma: 1822.

Leslie, Fiona. 'Inside Outside: Changing Attitudes Towards Architectural Models in the Museums at South Kensington.' *Architectural History*, 47 (2004): pp.159–99.

Lewis, C. S. *The Discarded Image*. Cambridge, Eng.: 1965.

Lichtheim, George. *The Concept of Ideology and Other Essays*. New York: 1967.

Livy, Titus. Aubrey de Sélincourt trans., R.M. Ogilvie intro. *The Early History of Rome*. Books I-V of *The History of Rome from its Foundation*. (rpt). Harmondsworth: 1973.

—. B. O. Foster trans. *History of Rome*. Books I-II. Bilingual ed. (rpt). Cambridge, Mass.: 1998.

Luchinat, Cristina Acidini, ed. *Renaissance Florence: The Age of Lorenzo de' Medici*. Exhibition catalogue. Florence: 1993.

Lucretius (Titus Lucretius Carus). R. E. Latham trans. *On the Nature of the Universe*. (rpt). London: 1988.

MacFaul, Tom. *Male Friendship in Shakespeare and his Contemporaries*. Cambridge: 2007.

Machiavelli, Bernardo. Cesare Olschki ed. *Libro di Ricordi*. Florence: 1954.

Machiavelli, Niccolò. *Opere*. Mario Bonfantini ed. Milano-Napoli: 1954.

—. Mario Martelli ed. *Opere*. Florence: 1971.

—. Fredi Chiapelli ed. *Legazione, commissarie, scritti di governo*. 2 vols. Roma-Bari: 1971, 1973.

—. Sergio Bertelli ed. *Legazione e commissarie*. Vol. I. Milan: 1964.

—. Sergio Bertelli ed. *Arte della Guerra e scritti politici minori*. Milan: 1961.

—. Allan Gilbert trans. *The Chief Works and Others*. 3 vols. Durham and London: 1989.

—. David Sices, James B. Atkinson eds. and trans. *The Comedies of Machiavelli*. Bilingual ed. Hannover: 1985.

—. *The First Decennale*. A facsimile of the 1st ed. of Feb. 1506. Cambridge, Mass.: 1969.

—. Angela Guidotti intro. and notes. *Delle cose di Lucca: testi e documenti*. [Lucca?] M. Pacini Fazzi: 1992.

—. Genaro Sasso intro. Giorgio Inglese nota. *La Mandragola*. 23rd ed. Milan: 2002.

—. Max Lerner intro. *The Prince and The Discourses*. New York: 1950.

—. Robert M. Adams ed. *The Prince*. New York: 1977.

—. George Bull trans and intro. Tim Parks pref. *The Prince*. 3rd ed. rev. London: 2006.

—. Harvey C. Mansfield trans. and intro. 2nd ed. *The Prince*. Chicago: 1998.

—. Peter Bondanella trans and ed. *The Prince*. Oxford: 2005.

—. Andrew Brown trans. *Life of Castruccio Castracani*. London: 2004.

—. Peter Constantine ed. and trans. *The Essential Writings*. Albert Russell Ascoli intro. New York: 2007.

—. Christian E. Detmold trans. *The Historical, Political, and Diplomatic Writings of Niccolò Machiavelli*. 4 vols. Boston: 1882.

—. Ellis Farnsworth trans. Neal Wood rev. and intro. *The Art of War*. New York: 1965.

—. W. K. Marriott trans. John Lotherington intro. *Florentine History*. New York: 2004.

—. Corrado Vivanti ed. *Discorsi sopra la prima deca di Tito Livio, seguiti dalle Considerazioni intorno ai Discorsi del Machiavelli di Francesco Guicciardini*. Torino: 2000.

—. Oliver Evans trans. and intro. *Clizia*. New York: 1962.

Mannheim, Karl. *Ideologie und Utopie*. Frankfurt am Main: 1969.

Mansfield, Harvey C. *Machiavelli's Virtue*. Chicago: 1966.

Mantovani, Sergio. '*Ad Honore del Signore Vostro Patre et Satisfactione Nostra*': *Ferrante d'Este Condottiero di Venezia*. Modena-Ferrara: 2005.

Marchand, Jean-Jacques, ed. *Niccolò Machiavelli: Politico, storico, letterato*. Rome: 1996.

Martelli, Cecilia. 'The Production of Illuminated Manuscripts in Florence and Urbino.' See Simonetta, *Federico da Montefeltro*, pp.41–9.

Martelli, Mario. 'Preistoria (Medicea) di Machiavelli.' *Studi di filologia italiana.* Vol. 29 (1971): pp.377–405.

Martines, Lauro. *Lawyers and Statecraft in Renaissance Florence.* Princeton: 1968.

—. *April Blood: Florence and the Plot against the Medici.* London and New York: 2003.

—. *Scourge and Fire: Savonarola and Renaissance Italy.* London: 2007.

—. *Strong Words: Writing and Social Strain in the Italian Renaissance.* Baltimore: 2001.

Marx, Karl, and Frederick Engels. *The German Ideology.* Moscow: 1976.

Masters, Roger D. *Fortune Is a River: Leonardo da Vinci and Niccolò Machiavelli's Magnificent Dream to Change the Course of Florentine History.* New York: 1998.

Mee, Charles L., Jr. *Daily Life in Renaissance Italy.* New York: 1975.

Michelangelo Buonarroti. G. R. Ceriello ed. *Rime.* Milan: 1954.

Mönch, Walter. *Das Sonett: Gestalt und Geschichte.* Heidelberg: 1955.

More, Thomas. Robert M. Adams trans. and ed. *Utopia.* 2nd ed. New York and London: 1975.

Nagemy, John M. ed. *The Cambridge Companion to Machiavelli.* Cambridge, Eng.: 2010.

—. *Between Friends: Discourses of Power and Desire in the Machiavelli-Vettori Letters of 1513–1515.* Princeton: 1993.

—. *A History of Florence, 1200–1575.* Chichester: 2008.

Nicholl, Charles. *Leonardo da Vinci: Flights of the Mind.* New York and London: 2004.

Oman, Charles. *A History of the Art of War in the Sixteenth Century.* London: 1937.

Oppenheimer, Paul. *The Birth of the Modern Mind: Self, Consciousness and the Invention of the Sonnet.* Oxford: 1989.

—. *Evil and the Demonic: A New Theory of Monstrous Behaviour.* London and New York: 1996.

—. *Rubens: A Portrait.* London and New York: 1999, 2002.

—, ed. and trans. *Till Eulenspiegel: His Adventures.* 4th rev. ed. New York: 2001.

Orme, Nicholas. *Medieval Schools from Roman Britain to Renaissance England.* New Haven: 2006.

Parel, Anthony. *The Machiavellian Cosmos.* New Haven: 1992.

Parker, Geoffrey. *Europe in Crisis: 1598–1648.* London: 1990.

Parks, Tim. *Medici Money: Banking, Metaphysics, and Art in Fifteenth-Century Florence*. London: 2005.

Pastor, Ludwig. *The History of the Popes*. Vol. IV. London: 1949.

Peruzzi, Marcella. 'The Library of Glorious Memory: History of the Montefeltro Collection.' See Simonetta, *Federico da Montefeltro*, pp.27–39.

Pettegree, Andrew. *The Early Reformation in Europe*. (rpt). Cambridge, Eng.: 1994.

Petrarca, Francesco. Monsignor Bembo ed. *Il Petrarca. Con dichiarationi non piu stampate … Annotationi. (Canzoni, sonetti)*. Venice: 1573.

Piper, Ernst. *Der Aufstand der Ciompi: Ueber den 'Tumult' den die Wollarbeiter im Florenz der Frührenaissance anzettelten*. (rpt). Berlin: 1990.

Pirrotta, Nino, and Elena Povoledo. *Music and Theatre from Poliziano to Monteverdi*. Cambridge, Eng.: 1982.

Plamenatz, John Petrov. *Ideology*. New York: 1970.

Pliny the Elder (Gaius Plinius Secundus). G.P. Goold ed. H. Rackham trans. *Natural History*. I (Praefatio, Libri I, II). (rpt). Cambridge, Mass.: 1979.

Plumb, J.H. *The Italian Renaissance*. Boston: 1987.

Pocock, J.G.A. *The Machiavellian Moment: Florentine Political Thought and the Atlantic Republican Tradition*. Princeton: 1975.

Poggio. *Facezie di Poggio Fiorentino*. Rome: 1885.

Poggius Bracciolini. Riccardo Fubini pref. *Opera omnia*. Torino: 1964.

Popper, Karl. *The Logic of Scientific Discovery*. New York: 1968.

Prezzolini, Giuseppe. Gioconda Savini trans. *Machiavelli*. New York: 1967.

Proverbio, Delio. 'Notes on the Diaspora of the Hebrew Manuscripts: From Volterra to Urbino.' See Simonetta, *Federico da Montefeltro*, pp.50–61.

Raimondi, Ezio. 'Machiavelli and the Rhetoric of the Warrior.' *Modern Language Notes*, 92 (1977), pp.1–16.

Rebhorn, Wayne A. *Foxes and Lions: Machiavelli's Confidence Men*. Ithaca and London: 1988.

Richardson, Brian. 'The Structure of Machiavelli's *Discorsi*.' *Italica*, 49 (1972): pp.460–71.

Ridolfi, Roberto. *Gli archive delle famiglie fiorentine*. Florence: 1934.

—. Cecil Grayson trans. *The Life of Niccolò Machiavelli*. Chicago: 1963.

—. Cecil Grayson trans. *The Life of Girolamo Savonarola*. London: 1959.

Rocke, Michael. *Forbidden Friendships: Homosexuality and Male Culture in Renaissance Florence*. Oxford: 1966.

Romby, Giuseppina Carla, and Massimo Tarassi eds. *Vivere nel contado al tempo di Lorenzo*. Firenze: 1992.

Rosen, E. 'The Invention of Eyeglasses.' *Journal of the History of Medicine and Allied Sciences*. Vol. 11 (1956), pp.183–218.

Rowland, Ingrid D. *The Culture of the High Renaissance: Ancients and Moderns in Sixteenth-Century Rome*. Cambridge: 1998.

Rubenstein, Nicolai. 'The Beginnings of Niccolò Machiavelli's Career in the Florentine Chancery.' *Italian Studies*, 11 (1956): pp.72–91.

—. 'Lay Patronage and Observant Reform in Fifteenth-Century Florence.' See Verdon and Henderson, pp.63–82.

—. *The Palazzo Vecchio, 1298–1532: Government, Architecture and Imagery in the Civic Palace of the Florentine Republic*. Oxford: 1995.

Ruffo-Fiore, Silvia. *Niccolò Machiavelli: an annotated bibliography of modern criticism and scholarship*. New York: 1990.

Russell, Bertrand. *A History of Western Philosophy*. New York: 1945.

Savonarola, Girolamo. *Selected Writings: religion and Politics, 1490–1498*. Anne Borelli, Maria Pastore Passaro trans. and eds. Donald Beebe exec. ed. Alison Brown intro. Guiseppe Mazzotta foreword. New Haven: 2006.

Saxonhouse, Arlene W. 'Comedy, Machiavelli's Letters, and His Imaginary Republics.' See Sullivan, pp.57–77.

Scala, Bartolomeo. Renée Neu Watkins ed. Alison Brown intro. *Essays and Dialogues*. Cambridge, Mass.: 2008.

Schevill, Ferdinand. *History of Florence from the Founding of the City through the Renaissance*. (rpt). New York: 1961.

Schiaparelli, Attilio. *La casa fiorentina e i suoi arredi nel secoli XIV e XV*. 2 vols. Florence: 1908; (rpt. 1983).

Shaw, Christine. *Julius II: The Warrior Pope*. Oxford and Cambridge, Mass.: 1993.

Shell, Susan Meld. 'Machiavelli's Discourse on Language.' See Sullivan, pp.78–101.

Simone, Franco. H. Gaston Hall trans. *The French Renaissance: Medieval Tradition and Italian Influence in Shaping the Renaissance in France*. London: 1969.

Simonetta, Marcello. *Rinascimento segreto: il mondo del Segretario da Petrarca a Machiavelli*. Milan: 2004.

—, ed. *Federico da Montefeltro and his Library*. Jonathan J.G. Alexander pref. Morgan Library exhibition catalogue: June 8-Sept. 30, 2007. Milan: 2007.

Skinner, Quentin. *Machiavelli and Republicanism*. Cambridge (Eng.): 1990.

Smith, Denis Mack. 'Federigo da Montefeltro.' See Plumb, pp.268–83.

Soll, Jacob. *Publishing "The Prince": History, Reading and the Birth of Political Criticism*. Ann Arbor: 2005.

Steinitz, Kate. 'A Reconstruction of Leonardo da Vinci's Revolving Stage.' *The Art Quarterly*, XII (1949), pp.325–38.

Strauss, Leo. '[Machiavelli the Immoralist].' Adams ed. *The Prince*, pp.180–5.

—. *Thoughts on Machiavelli*. Chicago: 1978.

Strong, Roy. *Art and Power: Renaissance Festivals, 1450–1650*. (rpt). Woodbridge: 1995.

Strozzi, Alessandra. *Selected Letters*. Heather Gregory trans. and intro. Bilingual ed. Berkeley: 1997.

Sullivan, Vickie B., ed. *The Comedy and Tragedy of Machiavelli: Essays on the Literary Works*. New Haven and London: 2000.

Symonds, John Addington. *The Renaissance in Italy: Italian Literature*. Vol. 1 of 2. London: 1875.

—. *Shakespeare's Predecessors in the English Drama*. London: 1884.

Thompson, Stith. *The Folktale*. New York: 1946.

Vasari, Giorgio. George Bull trans. *Lives of the Artists*. 2 vols. London: 1987.

Verde, Armando. *Lo studio fiorentino, 1473–1503: Ricerche e Documenti*. 5 vols. Firenze e Pistoia: 1973–1994.

Verdon, T. and J. Henderson eds. *Christianity and the Renaissance: Image and Religious Imagination in the Quattrocento*. Syracuse: 1990.

[Vergerio, Pier Paolo; Alberti; Pisani; Piccolomini; Mezzo.] Gary R. Grund ed. and trans. *Humanist Comedies*. Cambridge, Mass.: 2005.

Villari, Pasquale. Linda Villari trans. *The Life and Times of Niccolò Machiavelli*. London: 1899.

—. *La storia di Girolamo Savonarola e de' suoi tempi*. (rev. ed.). Florence: 1930.

Virgil (Publius Vergilius Maro). C. Day Lewis trans. *The Georgics*. New York: 1947.

Viroli, Maurizio. *Machiavelli*. Oxford: 1998.

Waas, Glenn Elwood. *The Legendary Character of Kaiser Maximilian*. New York: 1966.

Watkins, Renée Neu. *Humanism and Liberty: Writings on Freedom from Fifteenth-Century Florence*. New York: 1978.

—. *Bartolomeo Scala: Essays and Dialogues*. Cambridge, Mass.: 2008.

Weinstein, Donald. *Savonarola and Florence: Prophecy and Patriotism in the Renaissance*. Princeton: 1970.

Witt, R. 'What did Giovannino Read and Write?' *I Tatti Studies*, 6 (1995): pp.83–114.

Wittkower, Rudolf. *Architectural Principles in the Age of Humanism*. New York: 1971.

Wolin, Sheldon S. '[The Economy of Violence].' Adams ed. *The Prince*, pp.185–94.

# Index

# THE SCIENCE OF SPORT

# Rugby

## Edited by Kevin Till and Ben Jones

### Forewords by Sir Ian McGeechan, OBE,
### Kevin Sinfield, MBE, and Jamie Peacock, MBE

THE CROWOOD PRESS

First published in 2015 by
The Crowood Press Ltd
Ramsbury, Marlborough
Wiltshire SN8 2HR

**www.crowood.com**

**British Library Cataloguing-in-Publication Data**
A catalogue record for this book is available from the British Library.

ISBN 978 1 78500 106 2

Typeset by Servis Filmsetting Ltd, Stockport, Cheshire

Printed and bound in India by Replika Press Pvt Ltd

# CONTENTS

# ABOUT THE EDITORS

**Kevin Till** is a senior lecturer in sports coaching at Leeds Beckett University. He completed his PhD on talent identification and development in rugby league. He has published numerous academic articles on his research within rugby. Recently, his research interests have revolved around player development within youth rugby, where he now co-leads the Carnegie Adolescent Rugby Research (CARR) project. Kevin is also currently working as a strength and conditioning coach at Leeds Rhinos RLFC and Yorkshire Carnegie RUFC.

**Ben Jones** is a senior lecturer in sport and exercise physiology at Leeds Beckett University. His PhD explored fluid and sodium homeostasis in rugby players, but more recently he has undertaken and published numerous research articles around adolescent rugby performance and development. Ben also co-leads the Carnegie Adolescent Rugby Research (CARR) project and is head of academy athletic development at Leeds Rhinos RLFC and Yorkshire Carnegie RUFC, overseeing strength and conditioning and sports science provisions to academy players. You can follow Ben on Twitter @23Benjones.

# AUTHOR BIOGRAPHIES

**Andy Abraham** is principal lecturer and academic group lead for sports coaching at Leeds Beckett University. He has been engaged in research and teaching in sports coaching since 1997. His principal interests are in coach and coach educator practice, expertise and development. He is a voluntary coach in youth rugby union.

**Damien Austin** has worked in all three major football codes in Australia, as a high performance coach for the Sydney Swans football club, Sydney Roosters rugby league and Queensland Reds rugby union teams, plus New South Wales Swifts netball side. Damien has completed a PhD specializing in high-intensity activity profiles in professional rugby codes, having previously completed a masters and bachelor's degree. He has also authored numerous articles in peer-reviewed international journals and presented at a variety of conferences and seminars in strength and conditioning and sports science.

**Warren Bradley** is a performance nutritionist working with professional athletes at an elite level while concurrently conducting PhD research in sport nutrition. His research is focused on the energy expenditures and intakes of elite rugby players during the pre-season and competitive season, and assessing the metabolic demands of a competitive rugby game while manipulating energy intake. Warren has provided nutritional guidance for professional athletes as a performance nutritionist with Munster Rugby and England Rugby.

**Amy Brightmore** is currently undertaking research for a PhD in the evaluation of movement and physiological demands of rugby league referees and is a lecturer in sport and exercise physiology at Leeds Beckett University. She is an experienced applied sports scientist, having worked with amateur and professional athletes across a range of sports disciplines. Amy has provided sports science support to the Rugby Football League referees for many years and has worked as the sports scientist for a Premiership rugby union club.

**Graeme Close** is a reader in applied physiology and sports nutrition at Liverpool John Moores University, where he is the programme lead for the MSc in sports nutrition. His research is focused on the effects of vitamin D deficiencies in athletic performance, the role of antioxidants in the recovery of muscle function, applied nutrition in elite sport and the etiology of age-related loss of muscle mass. Graeme is an accredited strength and conditioning coach (UKSCA), an accredited physiologist (BASES) and on the Sport and Exercise Nutrition register (SENr) as well as being on the SENr board. Graeme is currently the expert nutrition consultant to England Rugby and the lead nutritionist for British Ski and Snowboard as well as working with European and US tour golfers and professional jockeys.

**Stephen Cobley** received his PhD in developmental and sport psychology from Leeds Metropolitan University in 2009. He is currently a senior lecturer in motor control and skill acquisition and sport and exercise psychology within the Faculty of Health Sciences at the University of Sydney in Australia. His research interests examine developmental factors that constrain learning and performance. This research and applied work has led to the evaluation, modification and writing of athlete and coaching programmes and policy for sport governing bodies and associated organizations. Stephen has co-edited *Talent identification and development: International perspectives*.

**Paul Comfort** is the programme leader for the MSc in strength and conditioning at the University of Salford. Paul is an accredited strength and conditioning coach and has combined lecturing with work and research in applied environments across a range of sports including rugby league, rugby union and football for more than a decade.

**Balin Cupples** is a PhD candidate at the University of Sydney currently exploring contributing factors in successful talent development environments and pathways in rugby league. Balin works full time as head of athlete development with an Australian National Rugby

League (NRL) club. In this role, he oversees all aspects of athlete physical preparation from the NRL through to the elite youth performance pathway. Balin is a former professional player who has coached at various levels within rugby league and lectured in sport coaching and administration.

**Stacey Emmonds** is currently undertaking research for a PhD in the physiological and movement demands of professional rugby league referees and the implications for decision-making. She is a senior lecturer in PE and sports pedagogy at Leeds Beckett University, head of strength and conditioning for the England Women's rugby league team and head of academy sports science and medicine at Leeds United football club.

**Tim Gabbett** has twenty years' experience working as an applied sport scientist with athletes and coaches from a wide range of sports. He holds a PhD in human physiology (2000) and has completed a second PhD in the applied science of professional rugby league (2011), with special reference to the physical demands, injury prevention and skill acquisition in this sport. He has worked with elite international athletes over several Commonwealth (2002 and 2006) and Olympic (2000, 2004 and 2008) Games cycles. He continues to work as a sport science consultant and advisor for several high performance teams around the world. Tim has published more than 150 peer-reviewed articles and has presented at more than 100 national and international conferences.

**Sharief Hendricks** is a research fellow at the University of Cape Town, Department of Human Biology, Exercise Science and Sports Medicine Division. His research interests include technical and tactical skill development, sport participation, injury prevention, science communication, strength and conditioning, concussion and performance analysis. You can follow him on Twitter @Sharief_H.

**Jamie Highton** is currently a lecturer in exercise physiology at the University of Chester, where he completed his PhD examining the effects of nutritional supplementation on performance and recovery associated with multiple-sprint sport exercise. Jamie has provided consultation for elite rugby league teams and governing bodies in nutrition, physiology and testing. He has also published several empirical and review articles on monitoring fatigue, recovery, movement demands and pacing strategies in team sports.

**David Joyce** is one of the first people in the world to lecture on and hold postgraduate masters degrees in sports science and sports medicine. He has trained, rehabilitated and maintained multiple World and Olympic champions along with more than 100 national champions and 300 national representatives. He is currently head of athletic performance at GWS Giants Australian Football League team and the co-editor of *High-Performance Training for Sports*.

**Paul Larkin** holds a research position in the Faculty of Education and Social Work at the University of Sydney. He received his PhD in 2013 from the University of Ballarat, Australia, focusing on the decision-making performance of Australian football umpires. Paul conducts applied research in many football codes, with specific interest in talent identification, player development and perceptual-cognitive performance. In his current position Paul is working on an Australian Research Council-funded project in collaboration with Football Federation Australia.

**Gareth Morgan** is youth coach educator for the Football Association, having previously been a senior lecturer and MSc sport coaching programme leader at Leeds Beckett University. His research and teaching interests include the areas of talent development, annual/longer-term planning and the development of psycho-behavioural skills through coaching.

**David Morley** is professor of physical education and youth sport at Liverpool John Moores University. He has led large-scale national evaluations in the fields of talent development, physical literacy and inclusion for a range of national governing bodies (NGBs) of sport and national organizations such as the Youth Sport Trust. He advises and offers consultancy and research support for NGBs of sport and professional sport clubs on establishing developmentally appropriate pathways for children and young people and has previously been seconded to the RFL as head of player performance services.

**Bob Muir** is a senior lecturer in sports coaching at Leeds Beckett University. His teaching, research and consultancy interests focus on coaching pedagogy and practice, coach education, learning and professional development. He is a highly experienced coach and has consulted for the Rugby Football League as well as British hockey and sailing.

**Donna O'Connor** is an associate professor and the course co-ordinator of the postgraduate programme in sports coaching at the University of Sydney. A former strength and conditioning coach, Donna publishes and presents on her research interests which focus on sports expertise, and athlete and coach development. Her current project focuses on the development of decision-making skills in players. Donna has worked with a number of teams and coaches in the various football codes in translating theory into practice. She is currently a member of the National Rugby League research board and the World Congress Science and Football Steering Committee.

**John O'Hara** is currently a reader in sport and exercise physiology at Leeds Beckett University, as well as an accredited sport and exercise physiologist (scientific support) with the British Association of Sport and Exercise Sciences (BASES). He has overseen the delivery of sport science support for the European Super League referees for many years. He is also the lead researcher at Leeds Beckett University for assessing the movement and physiological demands of European Super League referees. He has published numerous journal articles on sport and exercise physiology, including articles related to rugby refereeing.

**Daniel Owens** attained an honours degree from Liverpool John Moores University before working as a laboratory assistant, researching redox biology and ageing. He is now a doctoral researcher at Liverpool John Moores University investigating the role of Vitamin D in skeletal muscle health. Daniel is also a performance nutritionist for England Rugby Union age-grade teams and has previously worked with British Ski and Snowboard, Thai Boxing Women's European Champion, Premiership rugby teams and amateur boxers.

**Emidio Pacceca** is a sports physiotherapist who has graduated with a BSc and a masters in sports physiotherapy at Curtin University in Perth, Australia. He has worked as team physio for a variety of sports including Australian rules football and cricket and is currently the head physiotherapist at Western Force Rugby Union. Prior to his current role, he was a sports physiotherapist/medical coordinator at the Australian Institute of Sport European Training Centre in Italy. Emidio has also been involved with course development and lecturing at Edith Cowan University as well as presenting on courses for the Australian Physiotherapy Association and Sports Medicine Australia.

**Colin Sanctuary** currently works as the performance director for the Newcastle Knights National Rugby League team in Australia. Previously he was the performance director for the Newcastle Knights High Performance Unit, head of sports science support for Wakefield Trinity Wildcats and head of sports science support with Durham County Cricket Club. He has also worked as a lecturer at York St John University. Colin successfully attained his PhD in 2007, which examined 'Factors required for success in professional cricket'. He is an accredited strength and conditioning coach. He has also co-supervised postgraduate students from the UK and Australia and has published articles based on his applied work in professional rugby league and cricket.

**Craig Twist** is a reader in applied sports physiology at the University of Chester. His primary research interests revolve around the applied physiology of rugby league and recovery after fatiguing exercise. Craig is an accredited sport and exercise scientist with the British Association of Sport and Exercise Sciences and also serves as a consultant to the Rugby Football League and several elite sports teams.

# INTRODUCTION

Over the last twenty years the professionalization of both codes of rugby has led to increasing demands on players and a greater spectacle for the supporter. Science has played a large part in this development. Professional rugby clubs around the world now employ a number of scientific staff with the aim of optimizing players' performance and this practice will only continue to increase over the coming years as coaches and players look for that extra edge to their performance.

Having worked in both professional rugby league and union for the past decade, it is clear how the ever-evolving science has influenced (and continues to influence) our practice. The need to provide coaches and players with cutting-edge information is key to the success and longevity of a practitioner. Alongside the increasing application of science within practice, the interest and development of research within rugby has also increased dramatically in recent years. Owing to their research, each of the contributing authors in this book has had a significant impact on the development of the game. A number of groups around the world undertake and publish research, continually updating the body of knowledge of how performance can be improved in rugby. This research aims to provide an evidence base to help practitioners understand the most effective ways of improving player performance.

The challenge for the practitioner across all levels of the game is to use this research evidence base effectively in practice with their players on a daily basis. This book aims to bridge the gap between theory, research and practical application of science within rugby. The book's chapters not only provide an overview of the latest cutting-edge research for specific disciplines within rugby but also provide a case study of how this research is applied or recommendations for how it can be applied in practice. Consequently, this book is essential reading for anyone within the sport, from high-level international practitioners to students wanting to learn more about sport science and its application within rugby.

*Kevin Till and Ben Jones*

# FOREWORDS

## Sir Ian McGeechan, OBE

There is no doubt that rugby in the last decade has become more intense and more physically and mentally demanding for the players. Because of this evolvement of the sport, coaches and players now need the best knowledge and information to make meaningful decisions to help them perform at the top of their game. Hence, understanding how science can now help to determine the best results for match and training performance is vital for all involved in the sport.

As a coach, it is now critical to measure the playing demands, and understand the differences between individuals and positions in order to be able to plan monthly and weekly training to create the most effective and repeatable outcomes. Once a coach has this knowledge it is important that it can be shared and acted upon by all the support staff involved in the programme. Player's bodies need continuous conditioning and nutritional interventions to support training activity and recovery. In addition, medical staff need to analyze player injury management and rehab to ensure a healthy player. As a coach, using

information from sports science and analysis allows a clear picture of the strengths and weaknesses of the skills to be targeted or interpretations in controlling contact. The better this becomes the more impact a player will have on a game. From this clarity comes confidence to play with a positional mental approach. Psychologically we, as coaches, are producing stronger players.

As an ex-schoolmaster, I am also conscious we must map and plan the programmes for young developing players. We must understand the physical and mental requirements of players developing in the game from fifteen to adulthood. Science now allows us to plan that progress better than ever and give young players the best pathway for success. Whether delivering rugby as a coach, playing it or developing through it, or indeed as part of the essential support service behind it, I believe it is now so important for everyone to have the complete picture, which books such as this provide.

If we do this together, then the sport is in good hands.

*Sir Ian McGeechan OBE*

## Kevin Sinfield MBE and Jamie Peacock MBE

Having both played at the top level of rugby league for more than a decade, as well as both captaining our country, we understand the importance of science for rugby. Since starting playing professionally almost twenty years ago, the development of the science within the game has been fundamental to maintaining and developing our performances over our careers. Collectively, this has led to us winning fourteen Super League Grand Finals, four Challenge Cup Finals and seven World Club Challenges, while making more than 950 Super League and eighty-eight international appearances. During our playing careers, the intensity of the competition has increased significantly. As a result of this, our preparations for a season and for each game is a detailed plan, preparing us to perform optimally week in, week out.

Our preparations now include looking carefully at the demands of training and playing through wearing GPS technology. We are regularly fitness tested and have individual recovery and nutritional programmes to support our recovery and training. Strength and conditioning, injury management and rehab are a major part of our training week, alongside developing the technical and decision-making aspects of our rugby. Also, we have seen the detail that coaches go into when planning and delivering our training and match preparation. The development of youth players is now a major focus in preparing them for Super League competition. All these areas are covered in this book, which shows the level of detail that science now plays in the preparation of a Super League player.

The current research in rugby is also impressive but the exciting part within the sport is seeing that research being used in clubs by practitioners and coaches. As such, it is important that all coaches, old and young, keep up to date with the latest research and apply it to their practice. This book should therefore act as a key resource for students entering into rugby and coaches who have worked in the game as long as we have played.

We both recommend this as the practitioner's handbook and look forward to seeing how science continues to progress the sport over the next two decades.

*Kevin Sinfield MBE and Jamie Peacock MBE*

# CHAPTER 1

# THE MOVEMENT AND PHYSIOLOGICAL DEMANDS OF RUGBY

## *Damien Austin and Tim Gabbett*

## INTRODUCTION

Rugby is a sport that involves skill, ball play, tackling, kicking, team work, positional specific play and the ability to read the opposition. Based on this, rugby has large technical, tactical and physical demands. There are two codes of rugby: rugby league and rugby union. Both rugby codes are international field sports that involve competitions across various levels and age groups, from amateur to elite. Although the objectives of both codes are the same, there are fundamental differences that impact upon the two sports.

### Rugby League

Rugby league consists of two teams of thirteen players (and four interchange players) who compete for two halves of forty minutes (modified for junior competitions based on age), separated by a ten or fifteen-minute half-time recovery. The laws of the game dictate that a team has a set of six tackles to progress the ball over the opposition's try line and score a try. A player is considered tackled when he is in possession of the ball and either held stationary or put to the ground by the opposing team. The attacker then plays the ball between their feet to progress to the next phase of play; the same team is then allowed to pass (only backwards), run or kick the ball until the next tackle. Up to two players from the opposing team are permitted to stand in front of the tackled player, known as markers, while the rest of the team must retreat 10m. Possession of the ball is relinquished either after the sixth tackle is completed, the opposing team kicks, makes a mistake or a law of the game is infringed (i.e. a penalty). Points are scored via grounding the ball over the opposition's try line through conversions, penalties or drop kicks. The successive interchange of ball possession means players are required to attack and defend throughout the game (Gabbett, 2005).

The thirteen players are split across nine different playing positions in a team and with each position there are different playing demands (Austin and Kelly, 2013, Austin and Kelly, 2014, Gabbett, 2005). Player numbers and positions are shown in Figure 1.1. Positions are generally classified based on role similarities; forwards (two props, one hooker, two second row and one loose forward)

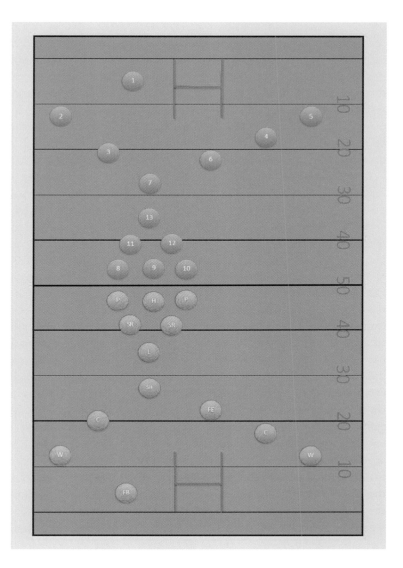

**Fig. 1.1: Rugby league playing position structure. The red team represents the playing positions (P – prop, H – hooker, SR – second row, L – loose forward, SH – scrum half, FE – five-eight, C – centres, W – wings and FB – fullback). The blue team represents the numbers worn by each of the individual playing positions.**

and backs (one scrum half, one stand-off/ five-eighth, two centres, two wingers and one fullback) or further classified as hit-up forwards (inclusive of front row forwards), wide-running forwards (second row and loose forward), adjustables (hooker, scrum half, stand-off/five-eight) and outside backs (centres, wings and fullback).

## Rugby Union

Rugby union consists of two teams of fifteen players (and up to seven interchange players) who also compete for two halves of forty minutes (modified for junior competitions based on age), separated by a ten or fifteen-minute half-time recovery. Rugby union is a territorial game in which the aim is to progress the ball over the opposition's try line by running with the ball, kicking the ball and/or passing the ball by hand (only backwards) to another team member. The team in possession of the ball has an unlimited tackle count and may lose possession through an error (e.g. dropping the ball, losing possession in a ruck), penalty infringement or through kicking the ball. Points can be made through scoring tries, penalty kicks, drop goals or conversions.

Rugby union matches can be restarted via scrums, line-outs, kicks or a tap, depending on the infringement or how possession was conceded. A breakdown occurs when the defending side stops the player with the ball, either by bringing them to ground (a tackle, which is frequently followed by a ruck) or by contesting possession with the ball carrier on their feet (a maul). In a maul the ball handler remains on his feet and once any combination of at least three players have bound a maul has been set. A ruck is similar to the maul but the ball has gone to ground with at least three attacking players binding themselves on the ground to secure the ball. Should the ball leave either side boundary of the field, a line-out is awarded against the team that last touched the ball. Forward players from each team line up a metre apart, perpendicular to the touchline and between 5m and 15m from the touchline, while the hooker of the team that didn't play the ball last throws the ball from the sideline, down the centre of the two forward lines. The exception to this is when the ball went out from a penalty, in which case the side that gained the penalty throws the ball in.

The fifteen rugby union players are split across ten playing positions with player numbers and positions shown in Fig. 1.2. Positions are generally classified, based on role similarities, into forwards and backs. Forwards are classified as either front row forwards

(inclusive of two props and one hooker) or back row forwards (two second row, two flankers and one lock), while backs are classified as inside backs (one scrum half, one fly half) and outside backs (two centres, two wingers and one fullback).

Both rugby codes are characterized by intermittent, high-intensity exercise in which players are expected to frequently run at high speeds and engage in physical contact with opposing players (e.g. scrums, rucks, mauls and tackles) (Austin et al., 2011a, Austin et al., 2011c). Due to the game demands, physical performance is very important and therefore players require high levels of strength, power, speed, agility and endurance (Baker and Newton, 2006, Gabbett et al., 2007). The impact of professionalism and rule changes over the last two decades have resulted in more intense matches and, at the elite levels of the game, players are now quicker, stronger and possess greater endurance than elite players who competed before the game turned professional (Duthie et al., 2003b).

Understanding the differences in physical qualities and the match demands of players throughout different levels of competition are vital for coaches in the planning of training and player development. The first aim of this chapter is to detail the physical characteristics of players competing at different levels that are considered important to rugby performance, such as anthropometry, speed, muscular strength, power and aerobic capacity. The second aim is to then outline and compare the movement (such as distance covered, high-intensity efforts) and physiological (for example, heart rate) match demands of rugby league and rugby union. The chapter then uses a practical applications section to show how this information can be used by coaches working within rugby.

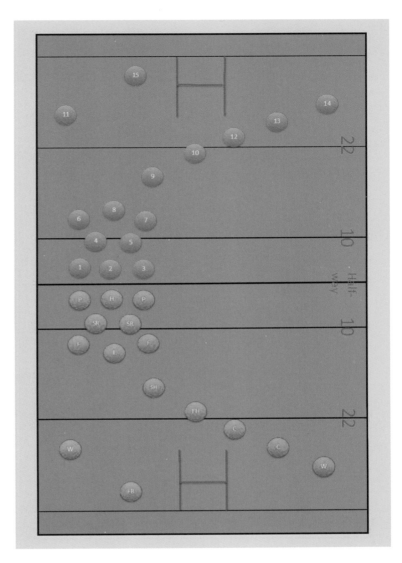

Fig. 1.2: Rugby union playing position structure. The red team represents the playing positions (P – props, H – hooker, SR – second row, L – lock, F – flanker, SH – scrum half, FH – fly half, C – centres, W – wings and FB – fullback). The blue team represents the numbers worn by each of the individual playing positions.

# RESEARCH OVERVIEW

## Physical Characteristics

Table 1.1 (rugby league) and 1.2 (rugby union) provide an overview of the physical characteristics of rugby players across various ages (junior and senior) and playing levels (amateur to elite).

ANTHROPOMETRY

Owing to the physical demands (movement and collision) placed on rugby players, they tend to have a physical stature related to their playing level and playing position (Atkins, 2006, Gabbett, 2014b). Although not always consistent, as the playing level increases players are taller and heavier, with a reduced sum of skinfolds (Quarrie et al., 1996, Smart et al., 2013). Forward positions commonly have higher

| Table 1.1: Physical Qualities of Rugby League Players over Differing Playing Standards | | | | | | |
|---|---|---|---|---|---|---|
| Playing Standard | | Elite | Sub-Elite | Junior Elite | Sub-Elite Junior | Amateur |
| (Age, Years) | | (23–25) | (23–24) | (18–20) | (16–18) | (20–21) |
| Body Comp | Height (cm) | 184–188 | 178–186 | 178–185 | 175–176 | 178–181 |
| | Body mass (kg) | 94–100 | 82–96 | 78–95 | 73–76 | 83–88 |
| Speed | 10m sprint (s) | 1.61–1.71 | 1.60–1.90 | 1.65–1.99 | 1.67–2.01 | 2.00–2.67 |
| | 20m sprint (s) | 2.83–2.95 | 3.21–3.48 | 2.83–3.36 | 2.83–3.68 | 3.22–3.57 |
| | 40m sprint (s) | 5.19–5.32 | 5.13–5.96 | 5.15–5.83 | 5.52–6.39 | 5.64–6.89 |
| Strength | Squat 1RM (kg) | 165–200 | 111–150 | 60–180 | N/A | N/A |
| | Bench press 1RM (kg) | 125–143 | 111–144 | 111–142.5 | 70–147.5 | N/A |
| Power | CMJ (cm) | 36.9–64.7 | 42.1–60.6 | 33.7–65.5 | 33.1–65.5 | 33.7–46.5 |
| Aerobic | Est VO$_2$ max (ml.kg$^{-1}$.min$^{-1}$) | 54.9–55.9 | 45.8–53.2 | 42.0–57.1 | 40.3–54.5 | 35.4–48.5 |

(Austin and Kelly, 2013, Austin and Kelly, 2014, Baker and Nance, 1999, Baker, 2001a, Baker, 2001b, Comfort et al., 2011, Gabbett, 2000, Gabbett, 2002b, Gabbett, 2002a, Gabbett et al., 2007, Gabbett et al., 2011c, Till et al., 2014d).

body mass than backs, which is largely due to the repetitive nature of the position using mass and force in individual ball carries to a defensive line (Gabbett et al., 2010, Waldron et al., 2013).

SPEED
In both rugby codes, the ability to accelerate over short distances (up to 20m) is very important. Running speed has generally been shown to increase with age and playing level. In relation to playing position, backs will generally have a greater running speed than forwards, especially at longer distances (approximately 40m). This is due to their increased opportunity to be involved in broken play, which can allow open field space and hence use their ability to use maximum running velocity over distances greater than 40m (Comfort et al., 2011). Forwards have a greater emphasis on tackling and ball carrying involving efforts at distances of approximately 10–15m.

| Playing Standard | | Elite | Sub-Elite | Junior Elite | Sub-Elite Junior | Amateur |
|---|---|---|---|---|---|---|
| **(Age, Years)** | | **(24–26)** | **(20–24)** | **(16–18)** | **(14–18)** | **(18–22)** |
| Body Comp | Height (cm) | 182–193 | 181–190 | 178–182 | 172–184 | 176–182 |
| | Body mass (kg) | 91–111 | 89–109 | 74–84 | 72–96 | 81–98 |
| Speed | 10m sprint (s) | 1.91 | 2.04 | 1.80–2.00 | 1.70–2.00 | 1.90–1.98 |
| | 20m sprint (s) | 2.89–3.21 | 2.93–3.00 | N/A | N/A | 3.18–3.34 |
| | 40m sprint (s) | 5.18 | 5.81–6.26 | 5.30–5.90 | 5.30–5.80 | 6.05–6.45 |
| Strength | Squat 1RM (kg) | 150–194 | 95–182 | 151 | 100 | N/A |
| | Bench press 1RM (kg) | 138–147 | 85–160 | 82–115 | 63–98 | N/A |
| Power | CMJ (cm) | 43.9–46.0 | 28.0–31.3 | N/A | N/A | 50.6–51.8 |
| Aerobic | Est VO$_2$ max (ml.kg$^{-1}$.min$^{-1}$) | 43–56.3 | 53.3–57.7 | 49 | 51 | 54.7–55.2 |

Table 1.2: Physical Qualities of Rugby Union Players over Differing Playing Standards

(Appleby *et al.*, 2011, Argus *et al.*, 2009, Argus *et al.*, 2010, Argus *et al.*, 2011, Argus *et al.*, 2012, Austin *et al.*, 2013, Cunniffe *et al.*, 2009, Durandt *et al.*, 2009, Fletcher and Jones, 2004, Green *et al.*, 2011a, Hansen *et al.*, 2011b, Hansen *et al.*, 2011a, McMaster *et al.*, 2013a, McMaster *et al.*, 2013b, Pienaar and Coetzee, 2013, Smart *et al.*, 2013, Tobin and Delahunt, 2014).

MUSCULAR STRENGTH AND POWER

Strength and power are important for both rugby codes due to the collision nature of the sport. Strength and power have been shown to increase with age and playing level. The most common tests of strength used in rugby are the back squat (lower body) and bench press (upper body), with the vertical jump the most common test for power. Forwards generally have greater absolute strength than backs.

AEROBIC CAPACITY

Due to the eighty-minute duration of rugby matches, the distance covered at low intensity and the intermittent involvement in high intensity activities, such as sprinting, tackling and scrummaging, means aerobic capacity is essential to performance. The aerobic capacity of elite athletes has been shown to be greater than lower playing standards. The only exception to this is for rugby union forwards, in

| | Rugby League | | Rugby Union | |
|---|---|---|---|---|
| | Forwards | Backs | Forwards | Backs |
| Total playing time (min) | 40–80 | 70–90 | 40–80 | 80–95 |
| Total distance (m) | 4,000–8,500 | 5,000–8,000 | 4,500–6,500 | 5,000–7,500 |
| Relative distance (m/min) | 74–101 | 74–120 | 55–65 | 65–75 |
| HI running distance (m) | 220–550 | 500–900 | 400–650 | 500–900 |
| Mean HI running distance (m) | 14–18 | 16–18 | 10–20 | 10–25 |
| HI running frequency (no.) | 34–120 | 18–74 | 36–109 | 58–116 |
| Collisions (tackles) | 38 | 25 | 23 | 23 |

**Table 1.3: Summary of the Movement Demands of Rugby League and Rugby Union**

(Austin and Kelly, 2014, Austin and Kelly, 2013, Cahill *et al.*, 2013, Cunniffe *et al.*, 2009, Deutsch *et al.*, 2007, Duthie *et al.*, 2003a, Duthie *et al.*, 2006, Gabbett, 2012, McLellan *et al.*, 2013, Roberts *et al.*, 2008).

particular front row forwards, who have been shown to have a lower aerobic capacity than other positions across different playing standards. This is most likely due to their increased body mass.

## Movement and Physiological Demands

Understanding the movement and physiological demands of any sport is integral to developing training programmes to advance a player's ability in order to meet or exceed the demands of the game. The understanding of match demands has been achieved through the use of time-motion analysis, previously through video analysis and, more recently, with Global Positioning Systems (GPS) worn by individual players in matches and training sessions. Players wear an individual GPS unit positioned between the scapulae inside a vest. The GPS units have been shown to be a valid and reliable measure of distances and speeds

at low to high-intensity running (Austin and Kelly, 2013, Austin and Kelly, 2014). Players' GPS data can be downloaded via specific software for future and in-depth analysis of a player's or a team's movement demands.

The awareness of the distinct differences in the types, duration and frequency of high-intensity activities, such as sprinting, tackling or repeated high-intensity efforts, is essential to understanding the demands of rugby (Duthie *et al.*, 2003a, Duthie *et al.*, 2005). The ability to develop and analyze skill drills and conditioning programmes allows coaches to monitor closely the physical demands and movement patterns specific to rugby.

## Rugby League

### PLAYING TIME
Throughout the eighty minutes, backs will generally play all the match unless injured or replaced for tactical reasons, while the forwards are generally interchanged with

replacement players and can play between forty and eighty minutes. The differences in playing time occurs due to forwards generally having a higher involvement in collision events and their greater physical size impacting on fatigue throughout the match (Austin and Kelly, 2014). During a match, the total time the ball is in play at an elite standard was fifty-five minutes, while junior elite was fifty minutes (Gabbett, 2012). This ball-in-play time impacts on the physical demands placed on players, as the greater duration of ball-in-play means increased absolute running and collision demands (Gabbett, 2014a).

## TOTAL AND RELATIVE DISTANCE

Total or absolute distance is the distance achieved over the completed period of time, while relative distance refers to distance covered divided by the total playing time, represented as metres per minute (m/min). While similar relative distances (m/min) are performed, differences have been found between positions for absolute distances covered. The greatest distance (5,500–8,000m) is covered by outside backs, followed by adjustables (6,000–7,000m), and hit-up forwards (3,500–6,000m [Austin and Kelly, 2014, Gabbett, 2012, Gabbett and Seibold, 2013]). Sub-elite players cover 4,000–7,500m per match, while junior elite players cover substantially less total distance (4,000–5,000m [Gabbett and Seibold, 2013, McLellan et al., 2013]). Amateur rugby league players have also been found to cover 5,000–6,000m in a match (Duffield et al., 2012).

## HIGH-INTENSITY RUNNING

High-intensity running is generally defined as speeds >18km.h$^{-1}$ and is considered integral to the game, and these high-intensity efforts occur at critical times during match play (Austin et al., 2011c, Gabbett, 2014b). It has been shown that high-intensity running accounts for 300–450m for props, 300–550m for wide-running forwards, 450–700m for adjustables and 650–950m for outside backs of the total distance achieved during a match (Austin and Kelly, 2013). There is a greater frequency of high-intensity running in backs compared to forwards. The differences in high-intensity running in backs covering greater distances can be due to various reasons, such as more space for backs to run before contact with the opposition, chasing a kick, line breaks or because of the greater playing time experienced by backs (Austin and Kelly, 2014, Gabbett, 2012).

## REPEATED HIGH-INTENSITY EXERCISE

A repeated high-intensity exercise (RHIE) bout was defined as three or more sprints and/or tackles with fewer than twenty-one seconds recovery between each high-intensity effort (Austin et al., 2011c). The ability of players to perform RHIE is recognized as being central to elite performance in rugby league. They occur at critical phases of a match (Austin et al. 2011b) and diminish a player's ability to perform high-intensity running in the period after a RHIE bout (Gabbett, 2014b, Johnston et al., 2014a, Johnston et al., 2014b). Hit-up forwards, wide running forwards, adjustables and outside backs have been shown to perform 8–17, 10–12, 2–14 and 3–15 RHIE bouts, respectively (Austin et al., 2011c, Gabbett et al., 2012b, Gabbett, 2014b). Elite junior players have been shown to perform slightly fewer RHIE bouts to elite players (9.7 vs. 13.1 bouts), while amateur players (9.8) also perform fewer RHIE bouts (Duffield et al., 2012, Gabbett, 2014b).

## TEMPORAL CHANGES AND PACING

Due to the repetition of high-intensity exercise and the collision nature of rugby league, players experience deteriorates in most physical performance measures during the second half of match play (Austin and Kelly,

| Table 1.4: Repeated High-Intensity Efforts (RHIE) of Rugby League and Rugby Union | | | | |
|---|---|---|---|---|
| | Rugby League | | Rugby Union | |
| | Forwards | Backs | Forwards | Backs |
| Frequency of RHIE bouts (No.) | 6–17 | 2–15 | 15–17 | 7–16 |
| Mean duration of bouts (s) | 53 | 37 | 52 | 28 |
| Max duration of bouts (s) | 64 | 64 | 165 | 64 |
| Mean time between bouts (s) | 376 | 631 | 294 | 415 |
| Minimum time between bouts (s) | 42 | 55 | 25 | 26 |

(Austin et al., 2011b, Austin et al., 2011c, Gabbett et al., 2012b, Gabbett, 2014b)

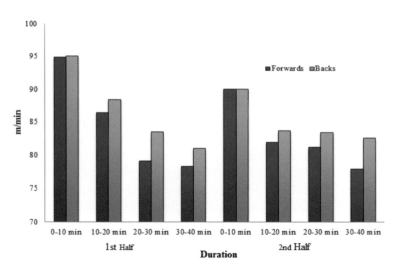

Fig. 1.3: Mean metres per minute per ten minutes of match play in rugby league. (Austin et al. 2013a)

2013). During each half, the first ten minutes have been shown to be the more physically demanding, when compared to the final ten minutes of play (Austin and Kelly, 2013). Players have also been shown to 'pace' themselves by reducing low-intensity activities in order to maintain their involvement in high-intensity activities (Black and Gabbett, 2014). The decrement in physical performance over time has been shown to coincide with a reduction in the player's ability to perform skill and technical-related tasks in the final stages of match play (Kempton et al., 2013). Therefore, it is the teams that can maintain intensity and skill level that generally win the matches (Black and Gabbett, 2014).

CONTACT/COLLISIONS
During the course of match play, collisions occur frequently as part of attack and

defence (Gabbett et al., 2011d, Gissane et al., 2001). Defensive collisions, involving completed, missed or ineffective tackles are more common than attacking collisions, such as tackled in possession, broken tackles, tackles with offloads, support runs or decoy runs (on average nineteen and thirteen respectively [Gabbett et al., 2011d]). Forwards have been shown to have a higher incidence of defensive collisions per match than backs (on average thirty-eight and twenty-five per game, respectively), with no difference in playing position for attacking collisions (on average thirteen per game for each position [Gabbett et al., 2011d]).

## Physiological Demands

### HEART RATE

Heart rate is used as an indicator of intensity during physical activity in relationship to work rate (Coutts et al., 2003). During elite rugby league matches, the average percentage of maximum heart rate has been shown to occur at 84 per cent for forwards, 82 per cent for adjustables and 84 per cent for backs. The heart rate demands are also consistent between the first and second half of a match (Waldron et al., 2011). Sub-elite, junior elite and amateur rugby league players have been shown to have mean heart rates of 84, 93 and 78 per cent of maximal heart rate respectively (Coutts et al., 2003, Gabbett, 2005).

### BLOOD LACTATE CONCENTRATION

Blood lactate concentration has been used as an index of exercise intensity (Coutts et al., 2003). It has been suggested players in higher standard competitions experience greater anaerobic demands during rugby league match play, as evidenced from the progressive increase in blood lactate concentrations of amateur (5.2 mmol.l$^{-1}$), sub-elite (7.2 mmol.l$^{-1}$)

and elite (9.1 mmol.l$^{-1}$) levels, respectively (Gabbett, 2005). Blood lactate concentrations have also been shown to be higher in the first half of match play, as opposed to the second half (8.4 and 5.9 mmol.l$^{-1}$ respectively [Coutts et al., 2003]). Given that players need to perform high-intensity efforts repeatedly, the anaerobic system is highly taxed during match play, while the aerobic system is important to facilitate recovery during low-intensity activities.

## Rugby Union

### PLAYING TIME

Since the evolution of rugby union from amateur to professional status, the time the ball is in play has increased significantly (31 per cent of time in 1991 to 44 per cent in 2011 [IRB, 2011]). This increase in ball-in-play time has aided the spectacle of the match but also has implications for the physical fitness of players, as there are a greater number of player involvements with the ball. Playing time for rugby union is relatively similar across playing positions due to the substitution rule; once a player is substituted for tactical or for injury (other than blood control) purposes they cannot return to the field. Although, rugby union match play is usually eighty minutes, matches can last up to ninety-five minutes due to stoppages. Forward positions are generally substituted earlier than backs due to the higher physical collision rate of forwards involved in tackling and scrummaging events (McLellan et al., 2013).

### TOTAL DISTANCE

There is generally no difference in the total distance covered based on playing standard, unless the playing duration is less than eighty minutes for the standard of competition (Duthie et al., 2003a). Backs will generally cover greater distance than forwards, due to them moving greater distances at lower intensities when realigning themselves for attacking and defensive positions, plus the increased need for them to carry out high-intensity running, due to positional requirements, such as cover defence. Forwards will generally also cover less distance due to the likelihood of substitution and increased fatigue related to collision events, such as tackles, rucks, mauls and duration of time spent in static exertion such as scrums (Cunniffe et al., 2009, Duthie et al., 2005, Roberts et al., 2008).

## HIGH-INTENSITY RUNNING

High-intensity running, as in rugby league, is generally classified as speeds >18km.h$^{-1}$ (Cunniffe et al., 2009, McLellan et al., 2013, Roberts et al., 2008). The differences between forwards and backs are primarily a result of the different roles in competition, as backs have been shown to sprint longer and more frequently than forwards, who spend greater time in static exertion activities (Austin et al., 2011a, McLellan et al., 2013). There is a need for backs to be able to beat the opposition in open play, requiring a high maximum running velocity and agility (Holway and Garavaglia, 2009, Quarrie et al., 1996).

## REPEATED HIGH-INTENSITY EXERCISE (RHIE)

RHIE for rugby union includes the high-intensity running and tackling (as per rugby league). However, these bouts also include static exertion, such as scrums, rucks and mauls, which are considered highly exertive physical activities. Forwards engage in the greatest number of RHIE for the longest durations, while backs are involved in the lowest number of RHIE bouts and for the shortest periods of time (Austin et al. 2011a). In particular, scrums, rucks, and mauls are responsible for the relatively high number of repeated high-intensity

exercise bouts recorded, particularly for the forwards.

## TEMPORAL CHANGES AND PACING

The intermittent nature of high-intensity activity interspersed with long durations of low-intensity activity, allows rugby union players to maintain running intensity throughout a match. Comparing first and second half match play, there is an ability of players to maintain relative match play intensity without deterioration in distance or high-intensity running (McLellan et al., 2013). This is also true for ten-minute time periods throughout the match, where there is no significant difference in high-intensity running or volume, nor static high-intensity activities, such as tackling, scrums, rucks or mauls. Although there is a greater total distance travelled in the first ten minutes of play compared to the last ten minutes of a match, this change is in low-intensity running (Roberts et al., 2008). The amount of time the ball is out of play may allow players to recover from intermittent bursts of high-intensity activities and also ensure that players are likely to maintain high-intensity running while limiting lower intensity activities for recovery (Duthie et al., 2005, Roberts et al., 2008).

## CONTACT/COLLISIONS

Rugby union has numerous contact and collision events throughout a match, in the form of tackles, scrums, rucks and mauls. These collisions have been shown to reach more than 450 instances recorded for a team in a single match (Fuller et al., 2007). Tackles, followed by rucks have the highest occurrence in match play occurring 221 and 143 times respectively, while scrums and mauls are substantially less at twenty-nine and nineteen occurrences, respectively (Fuller et al., 2007). Tackles are made in rugby union when the ball carrier is brought to ground, however the ball carrier can be held up to form a maul, offload the ball while on their feet or break the tackle. Approximately 90 per cent of tackling events involved one or two tacklers (McIntosh et al., 2010). With an unlimited tackle count in rugby union, collision events such as tackles and mauls, can happen numerous times in phases of play. Forwards are involved in more collision occurrences than backs due to their higher contribution in defensive situations involving tackling, scrums and mauls (McLellan et al., 2013).

## Physiological Demands

### HEART RATE

Heart rates of professional rugby union players during match play have been shown to average 172 beats.min$^{-1}$ and reach up to 200 beats.min$^{-1}$ (Cunniffe et al., 2009). Forwards, due to the higher frequency and duration in bouts of static exertion, such as scrums, rucks and mauls, have been found to spend a greater proportion of match play at >90 per cent of maximum heart rate than backs (51.1 and 41.4 per cent of time respectively [Cunniffe et al., 2009]). However, it was also shown that backs spend a higher duration in moderate heart rate zones (70–90 per cent of max. heart rate) than forwards (56.1 and 43.4 per cent of time respectively). Rugby union requires the anaerobic system to meet those high demands in the match and aerobic system to aid in the recovery and maintain low-intensity activities (Duthie et al., 2003a).

### BLOOD LACTATE CONCENTRATION

Similar to rugby league, higher standard of competitions have been shown to have higher blood lactate concentrations, with elite, sub-elite and junior elite recording blood lactate concentrations of 6.6, 5.4 and 2.8 mmol.l$^{-1}$ respectively (Deutsch et al., 1998, Docherty et al., 1988, McLean, 1992). Forwards have been reported to have higher blood lactate concentrations than backs, possibly due to the high frequency and intense nature of static exertion activities (Deutsch et al., 1998). Players with higher aerobic capacity have also been shown to have lower blood lactate concentration following high-intensity activity (Deutsch et al., 1998). Given forwards in rugby union have much lower aerobic capacity than backs, their ability to recover from high-intensity activities may be inferior.

# PRACTICAL APPLICATION

The previous sections discuss the movement and physiological demands of rugby league and union players across a range of competition levels. However, it is the application of this information to develop training and recovery protocols based on individual and positional needs, level of competition and match play demands that a coach or sport scientist must recognize to influence practice. This section will detail how GPS data has been assessed and used from match play and training, within either a professional rugby league or union club.

## GPS Analysis

The monitoring of match play using GPS can give coaches an understanding of what movement demands have been performed and can aid the planning of training progression, recovery period and individual training requirements. Fig. 1.4 demonstrates the variance that can occur between matches throughout a season in both total distance and distance achieved at high-intensity (>18km.h$^{-1}$)

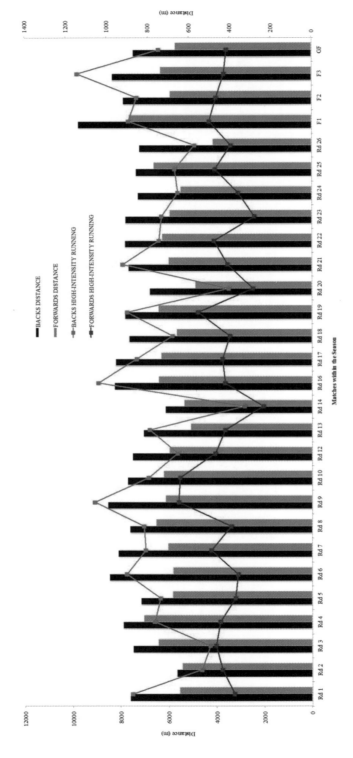

**Fig. 1.4: GPS analysis, measuring total distance and distance in high-intensity running (>18 km.h⁻¹) for a rugby league season. Rd = round, F1 – finals and GF – Grand Final.**

| GPS VARIABLE | | Time / Distance | | | SPEED (m) | | | | | | High-intensity Running | | | | | | Repeated High-Intensity Exercise | | | |
|---|---|---|---|---|---|---|---|---|---|---|---|---|---|---|---|---|---|---|---|---|
| POSITION | PLAYER | Total Duration | Total Distance (m) | M/min | Walk | Jog | Stride | HI running | Very HI running | Sprinting | Distance (m) | Percentage | M/min | Entries | Entries per min | Avg Distance (m) | Frequency | Min Recovery (s) | Max Duration (s) | Avg Duration (s) |
| BACKS | Player 1 | 01:27:32 | 7935 | 91 | 3619 | 2512 | 937 | 481 | 344 | 37 | 862 | 11% | 10 | 176 | 2.0 | 22 | 12 | 34 | 53 | 34 |
| | Player 2 | 01:08:18 | 6497 | 96 | 2774 | 1977 | 928 | 298 | 355 | 158 | 811 | 12% | 12 | 148 | 2.2 | 16 | 3 | 268 | 28 | 22 |
| | Player 3 | 01:27:32 | 7350 | 84 | 3486 | 2186 | 928 | 434 | 243 | 66 | 743 | 10% | 9 | 143 | 1.6 | 20 | 6 | 158 | 33 | 18 |
| | Player 4 | 01:27:32 | 7120 | 82 | 3458 | 2156 | 950 | 397 | 154 | 2 | 553 | 8% | 6 | 96 | 1.1 | 15 | 8 | 55 | 44 | 32 |
| | Player 5 | 01:27:32 | 8285 | 95 | 3371 | 2709 | 1148 | 555 | 411 | 86 | 1052 | 13% | 12 | 175 | 2.0 | 16 | 4 | 92 | 54 | 28 |
| | Player 6 | 01:27:32 | 8594 | 99 | 3732 | 3173 | 1190 | 282 | 175 | 36 | 493 | 6% | 6 | 95 | 1.1 | 17 | 8 | 32 | 40 | 20 |
| | Player 7 | 01:27:32 | 9143 | 105 | 3334 | 3266 | 1700 | 510 | 230 | 97 | 837 | 9% | 10 | 148 | 1.7 | 18 | 11 | 44 | 47 | 33 |
| FORWARDS | Player 8 | 00:53:47 | 4954 | 94 | 2242 | 1629 | 740 | 249 | 81 | 9 | 339 | 7% | 6 | 76 | 1.4 | 17 | 7 | 52 | 44 | 36 |
| | Player 9 | 01:03:08 | 5879 | 94 | 1958 | 2655 | 938 | 245 | 78 | 0 | 323 | 5% | 5 | 73 | 1.2 | 17 | 10 | 44 | 37 | 28 |
| | Player 10 | 01:27:32 | 7364 | 84 | 3605 | 2424 | 1058 | 218 | 55 | 0 | 273 | 4% | 3 | 66 | 0.8 | 18 | 17 | 22 | 39 | 33 |
| | Player 11 | 01:27:32 | 7409 | 85 | 3575 | 2447 | 829 | 349 | 196 | 7 | 552 | 7% | 6 | 93 | 1.1 | 20 | 10 | 78 | 55 | 38 |
| | Player 12 | 01:27:32 | 7722 | 89 | 3379 | 2553 | 1075 | 427 | 280 | 2 | 709 | 9% | 8 | 140 | 1.6 | 14 | 15 | 64 | 48 | 35 |
| | Player 13 | 01:02:51 | 5484 | 89 | 2262 | 1999 | 711 | 275 | 222 | 7 | 504 | 9% | 8 | 103 | 1.6 | 16 | 9 | 124 | 33 | 21 |
| SUBS | Player 14 | 00:33:45 | 3012 | 89 | 1318 | 996 | 419 | 167 | 109 | 1 | 277 | 9% | 8 | 56 | 1.7 | 16 | 3 | 222 | 27 | 18 |
| | Player 15 | 00:24:24 | 2543 | 104 | 1228 | 837 | 365 | 75 | 19 | 15 | 110 | 4% | 4 | 36 | 1.5 | 14 | 4 | 33 | 32 | 22 |
| | Player 16 | 00:19:14 | 1765 | 92 | 857 | 534 | 235 | 98 | 38 | 0 | 137 | 8% | 7 | 30 | 1.6 | 15 | 1 | - | 15 | 15 |
| | Player 17 | 00:24:41 | 2194 | 89 | 1059 | 725 | 245 | 103 | 58 | 2 | 163 | 7% | 7 | 38 | 1.5 | 16 | 3 | 56 | 32 | 28 |
| SUMMARY — Backs | Average | 01:23:41 | 7846 | 90 | 3342 | 2308 | 978 | 433 | 301 | 70 | 804 | 11% | 10 | 148 | 1.8 | 18 | 7 | 98 | 42 | 27 |
| | SD | 00:08:36 | 700 | 6 | 329 | 296 | 95 | 96 | 102 | 59 | 181 | 2% | 2 | 33 | 0.4 | 3 | 4 | 87 | 12 | 7 |
| | Max | 01:27:32 | 8285 | 96 | 3619 | 2709 | 1148 | 555 | 411 | 158 | 1052 | 13% | 12 | 176 | 2.2 | 22 | 12 | 268 | 54 | 34 |
| | Min | 01:08:18 | 6497 | 82 | 2774 | 1977 | 928 | 298 | 154 | 2 | 553 | 8% | 6 | 96 | 1.1 | 15 | 3 | 32 | 28 | 18 |
| SUMMARY — Forwards | Average | 01:17:43 | 6772 | 88 | 2956 | 2416 | 922 | 303 | 166 | 3 | 472 | 7% | 6 | 95 | 1.2 | 17 | 12 | 66 | 42 | 31 |
| | SD | 00:13:27 | 1014 | 4 | 784 | 250 | 154 | 85 | 96 | 4 | 177 | 2% | 2 | 29 | 0.4 | 2 | 4 | 39 | 9 | 7 |
| | Max | 01:27:32 | 7722 | 94 | 3605 | 2655 | 1075 | 427 | 280 | 7 | 709 | 9% | 8 | 140 | 1.6 | 20 | 17 | 124 | 55 | 38 |
| | Min | 01:02:51 | 5484 | 84 | 1958 | 1999 | 711 | 218 | 55 | 0 | 273 | 4% | 3 | 66 | 0.8 | 14 | 9 | 22 | 33 | 21 |

Fig. 1.5: A sample GPS report of a rugby league match, with emphasis on high-intensity running and RHIE.

speeds. The graph shows backs and forwards do not necessarily follow a similar path in demands from game to game (i.e. high-intensity running distance may be low for forwards but high for backs). However, what the graph does not show is the collision or contact events (tackles) the forwards or backs may have undertaken. This highlights the coach's requirement to interpret individual match demands on a week-to-week basis. Greater high-intensity running demands may suggest extra duration in post-match recovery or modified training sessions, such as shorter sessions or reduction in training load, throughout the week preceding the next match.

## Sample GPS Match Report

Fig. 1.5 is a sample GPS summary report for the movement demand of a rugby league match. The summary focuses on the high-intensity movement demands and repeated high-intensity exercise. This summary can be used to evaluate each player's work rate throughout the match to be compared to previous and future matches. Greater high-intensity work rate, such as involvement in RHIE or high-intensity running percentage, can be compared to a player's normal or average rate or frequency, which can be used by coaches to manipulate training and recovery protocols, but in the same respect can be manipulated if a player's lower work rate is demonstrated.

## GPS Velocity Graph

A GPS match report can be aligned with match statistics of coaches' key performance indicators (e.g. hit-ups, tackles, line breaks and so on) to give insight to player performance and what constitutes a high standard of team,

positional or individual match play. In the same respect, the alignment of GPS to match vision allows coaches and sports scientists to distinguish work rates, movement patterns and match involvement throughout a match or at particular parts of play, such as patterns to tries scored, maximum duration RHIE undertaken or work rate while defending repeated sets of play. This can also be an important educational tool for younger players to demonstrate higher level playing demands but also what impacts the player to influence their decision making. Fig. 1.6 shows an example of an instance in match play, along with a player's GPS velocity graph over a five-minute time period prior to the opposition scoring a try, with efforts above $18km.h^{-1}$ highlighted. Coaches can use this information and similar examples to develop comparable scenarios through their drills, with emphasis on how to overcome the opposition scoring and the entailing workload requirements of players to ensure a positive result.

## Monitoring Training

In order for players to be capable of achieving a high standard of skills and intermittent high-intensity running, coaches need to accommodate a progressive development in training to meet the match demands players will encounter. Through GPS monitoring of players' training, just as match play, the progression of the movement demands of training (i.e. total distance, high-intensity running distance) can be used by coaches retrospectively and for planning future training loads. Fig. 1.7 demonstrates a progression of total and high-intensity running distance, throughout a five-week pre-season training phase. The figure demonstrates a gradual increase in the movement demands of training that allows coaches to monitor and progress the physical

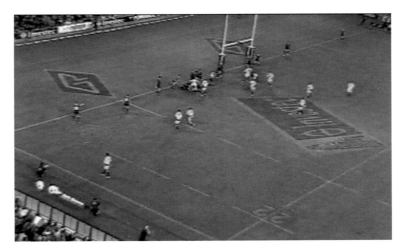

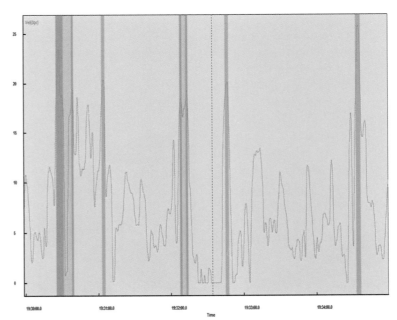

**Fig. 1.6: a) A still shot of a rugby team defending their try line that relates to: b) A screenshot of GPS time and velocity graph of a rugby union player over a five-minute time period. The red line indicates running speed (km.h–1), while the green sections highlight when the player was required to go above 18km.h–1.**

demands placed upon players through the appropriate planning of training duration, skill or conditioning drill selection and increasing the specificity to match play demands. Planning and progressing specific movement variables, such as high-intensity running, can aid in minimizing injury rates and ensuring appropriate physical development.

The ability for coaches to analyze training should not only include the movement demands the players undertake but what skills are being developed. Fig. 1.8 represents the percentage of time a rugby league team spent on various aspects of training during the pre-season period. The categorization of drills to certain skill components or training modalities using GPS analysis allows coaches and sport scientists alike to assess how their

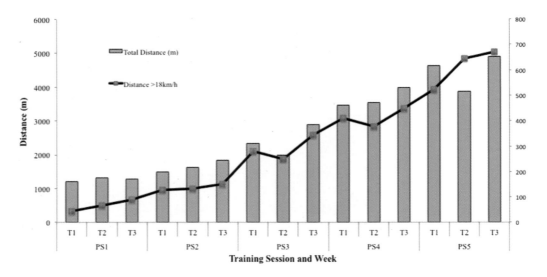

**Fig. 1.7: Progression of the movement demands of pre-season training sessions over a five-week period; total distance, high-intensity running (>18km.h⁻¹) distance. PS = pre-season week; T = training session of that week.**

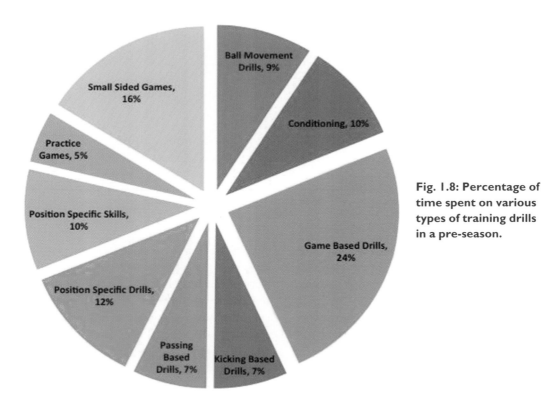

Fig. 1.8: Percentage of time spent on various types of training drills in a pre-season.

programme time is spent. Fig 1.8 shows game-based drills and small-sided games represent a major portion of training. Sport scientists can use this information to determine if there are relationships with the skill acquisition and time spent on skill specific drills, improvements in physical capacities and whether these activities were conducive to the development of players to meet or exceed match play demands.

## IMPLICATIONS AND RECOMMENDATIONS FOR PRACTICE

- Understanding the physical qualities (i.e. speed, strength and so on) of players and the position specific movement and physiological demands of match play are important considerations for coaches in developing training interventions for players.
- GPS can be used to analyze both absolute and relative distances, with particular attention to high-intensity running (> 18km.h$^{-1}$) to monitor daily, weekly and seasonal training loads.
- Practitioners should also consider monitoring the number and magnitude of contacts and collisions within training and match play.

- Forwards should be conditioned to accommodate greater frequency of collision events, such as tackling, while backs should be conditioned for greater higher-intensity running demands over a variety of distances.
- The interpretation of RHIE bouts has the potential to assist in the preparation of rugby players for competition. It is the maximum periods of activity coupled with the minimum periods of recovery (rather than average values) that should be used to develop position-specific tests.

# CHAPTER 2

# FITNESS TESTING FOR RUGBY

## *Kevin Till and Ben Jones*

## INTRODUCTION

Fitness testing is essential to monitor and evaluate the physical capacities of rugby players. Although, the game demands of both codes of rugby require players to have well developed physical qualities (see Chapter 1), these capacities can often vary between individuals, playing positions and playing levels (Smart et al., 2013, Till et al., 2014d). Recent research in rugby (Gabbett et al., 2011e, Gabbett and Seibold, 2013) has identified correlations between physical qualities and game performance, demonstrating the importance of the development of these qualities for both codes of rugby. Therefore, practitioners working within rugby including coaches, strength and conditioners, sport scientists and physiotherapists should aim to obtain objective information about a player's physical capabilities to optimize player development and game performance. This fitness assessment information can then be used for profiling players' strengths and weaknesses, talent identification and selection processes, evaluating training interventions and monitoring progress, prescribing training, providing feedback and educating players and coaches (Pyne et al., 2014).

Based on the importance of fitness assessment and evaluation for rugby performance, the aim of this chapter is to detail several field and laboratory-based fitness assessments, including anthropometry, speed, agility, strength, power, aerobic capacity and high speed running ability, which are all deemed important for rugby performance. The content will reflect some of the most commonly used fitness assessments as it is not possible to summarize all protocols used by practitioners and sports scientists. In addition, the chapter provides a case study of the application of a fitness testing battery and the evaluation processes used within a club to demonstrate how fitness testing data can be collected and used within the field.

## RESEARCH OVERVIEW

Field-based fitness testing protocols involve assessing capacities under 'real-world' conditions (e.g. 'on the field'). Such protocols have the advantage of increasing the specificity of the assessment to rugby, require minimal equipment and can be conducted with relative ease. However, field based assessments may provide less accurate measurements,

## Table 2.1: Commonly Used Field and Laboratory Fitness Assessments

|  | Field | Laboratory |
|---|---|---|
| Anthropometry | Stature<br>Body mass<br>Sum of skinfolds (4–9 sites) | Dual energy X-Ray absorptiometry (DXA) |
| Speed | Sprint tests | Sprint tests |
| Agility | Agility 505<br>Illinois agility test<br>L-Run<br>Reactive agility (Human) | Reactive agility (Video) |
| Strength | Repetition Max. (e.g. 1–RM) | Isometric strength<br>Isokinetic strength |
| Power | Vertical jump<br>Medicine ball throws | Force plate assessments<br>Wingate test |
| Aerobic capacity and high speed running ability | Multi-stage fitness test<br>Yo-Yo test<br>Repeated sprint ability | Direct assessment of lactate threshold |

which can be controlled by ensuring consistent conditions (e.g. surface, time of day, environmental conditions, etc. [Pyne et al., 2014]) to increase the reliability of the results. Reliability refers to the ability to reproduce the same results on different occasions. Laboratory-based assessments are performed in a controlled environment and generally provide more accurate and reliable results (Drust and Gregson, 2013). However, the access, cost and time constraints of using laboratory-based measures are often high, resulting in their reduced use in the practical application of fitness assessment within rugby. However, it is vital practitioners understand the importance of such measures and therefore the field and laboratory-based fitness assessments are detailed below for anthropometry, speed, agility, strength, power, aerobic capacity and high speed running ability.

## Anthropometry

Stature, body mass and body composition are the most common assessments of anthropometry used within rugby. The aim for players is to develop functional mass through the development of lean muscle with a reduction in fat mass (Johnston et al., 2014c). Body mass and body fat percentage have shown to differentiate between playing positions and playing level. Body composition should be assessed regularly to optimize physical performance as increased body fat percentage is negatively correlated with fitness performance (e.g. speed, estimated $VO_2max$ [Till et al., 2010a]).

*Body Mass:* Body mass should be measured using calibrated scales and with the participant wearing only shorts. Scales should be calibrated using a known standard mass to ensure the reliability and validity of data. Measurements are typically taken to the nearest 0.1kg.

| Patient: | | | | Referring Physician: | |
|---|---|---|---|---|---|
| Birth Date: | | Age: | 16 years 7 months | Patient ID: | PRECISION |
| Height: | 179.5 cm | Weight: | 81.7 kg | Measured: | 17/03/2014 16:18:58 (15 [SP 1]) |
| Sex: | Male | Ethnicity: | White | Analyzed: | 19/03/2014 09:05:41 (15 [SP 1]) |

Total Body Tissue Quantitation

**Composition (Enhanced Analysis)**

| Region | Tissue (%Fat) | Z-score | Total Mass (kg) | Fat (g) | Lean (g) | BMC (g) |
|---|---|---|---|---|---|---|
| Arms | 19.0 | - | 10.05 | 1,821 | 7,778 | 452.3 |
| Legs | 20.7 | - | 26.96 | 5,333 | 20,377 | 1,247.9 |
| Trunk | 17.2 | - | 40.17 | 6,719 | 32,293 | 1,162.6 |
| Android | 15.2 | - | 5.23 | 787 | 4,376 | 68.7 |
| Gynoid | 17.6 | - | 13.99 | 2,395 | 11,221 | 376.0 |
| TBLH | 18.7 | - | 77.18 | 13,873 | 60,447 | 2,862.7 |

**UK Reference Chart: No reference data for Total Body [TBLH] region.
UK Reference Population did not support Pediatric Total Body Composition.**

**Total Body: TBLH**

Fat (g) [Black]    Fat Free (g) [Magenta]

**UK Trend: TBLH (Enhanced Analysis)**

| Measured Date | Age (years) | Tissue (%Fat) | Z-score | Total Mass (kg) | Tissue (g) | Fat (g) | Lean (g) | BMC (g) | Fat Free (g) |
|---|---|---|---|---|---|---|---|---|---|
| 17/03/2014 | 16.6 | 18.7 | - | 77.18 | 74,320 | 13,873 | 60,447 | 2,862.7 | 63,310 |
| 02/12/2013 | 16.3 | 20.2 | - | 75.65 | 72,825 | 14,696 | 58,130 | 2,823.6 | 60,953 |
| 02/12/2013 | 16.3 | 19.8 | - | 75.78 | 72,981 | 14,417 | 58,564 | 2,802.5 | 61,366 |

Image not for diagnosis

**Fig. 2.1: DXA report for a rugby player.**

*Body Composition:* Dual energy X-ray absorptiometry (DXA) is the gold standard assessment of body composition when undertaken in standardized conditions (i.e. euhydrated) and has recently been used in research within rugby league (Harley et al., 2011) and rugby union (Delahunt et al., 2013). DXA scans provide both total values of fat mass, lean mass and bone mineral content, which allows more accurate and reliable evaluations of body composition in athletes. A DXA scan will also show the regional (right and left arms, legs and trunk) body composition. Although this assessment method is the most accurate and would be recommended as ideal, the cost, exposure to radiation and availability of DXA limit the use of such assessments. Fig. 2.1 shows an example DXA report.

In the field, a commonly used measure of body composition is the sum of skinfolds using Harpenden skinfold callipers. Sum of skinfolds are assessed by pinching the skin and subcutaneous tissue and applying the calipers at a range of sites around the body. Guidelines for skinfold assessments have been recommended by the American College of Sports Medicine (ACSM et al., 2006). Within rugby research, skinfold measures have included assessments at four-site (biceps, triceps, subscapular and suprailiac; (Jarvis et al., 2009)), seven-site (biceps, triceps, subscapular, suprailiac, abdomen, thigh and calf; (Gabbett et al., 2011d)) and nine-site (triceps, subscapular, biceps, iliac crest, supraspinale, abdominal, thigh, calf and mid-axilla; [Morgan and Callister, 2011]). The use of sum of skinfolds should, therefore, be considered by practitioners for assessing body composition due to its use as a simple indicator of fatness. However, where possible an International Society of

Advancement of Kinanthropometry (ISAK) accredited individual should undertake skinfold assessments to increase the reliability and accuracy of such measures.

## Speed

The ability to move fast in attack and defence is another important physical capacity required for rugby, with a large number of sprints observed during match play in both codes (Duthie et al., 2003a, Johnston et al., 2014c). Common sprint distances have been reported to be between 10–20m and last approximately three seconds (Cunniffe et al., 2009, Duthie et al., 2003a). Therefore the assessment of sprint speed, especially acceleration due to the shorter distances covered during match play are important variables to assess for the practitioner.

A range of research studies (Barr et al., 2014, Gabbett et al., 2008, Till et al., 2011) have assessed acceleration and maximum speed at distances of 5m, 10m, 20m, 30m, 40m and 60m within rugby. The use of short and longer distances allows acceleration and maximum speed to be considered, with split times used to differentiate between the two. One important consideration in the assessment of speed is the available equipment. Electronic timing gates are the most reliable and accurate method of assessing speed if distances are marked out accurately. The use of timing gates is usually essential for practitioners to have any confidence in the accuracy and reliability of such scores (Brown et al., 2004). Handheld devices, such as stopwatches, may be inaccurate and should only be used at longer distances (30m plus) with results used only as a guide. In addition, practitioners should consider the surface, environmental conditions and previous activity of players when implementing assessments of speed.

Due to the collision and contact nature of both rugby codes, practitioners should also consider the combination of speed and body mass in their assessments, known as speed momentum. As it is recommended for players to develop lean body mass, evaluating speed momentum may be more important for rugby performance than just speed alone. Research studies in rugby league and union have recently shown speed momentum to differentiate between playing level (Baker and Newton, 2008), correlate with ball carrying ability (Waldron et al., 2014b) and be more trainable (Barr et al., 2014, Till et al., 2014c). It therefore seems that speed momentum should be an important variable to measure in rugby. It is recommended to assess momentum at shorter distances (e.g. 10m) due to the common distances sprinted when carrying the ball.

Momentum Calculation:
Momentum $(kg.s^{-1})$ = velocity $(m.s^{-1})$ × body mass (kg).

## Agility

Agility is a complex action and has been defined as 'a rapid, whole-body, change of direction or speed in response to a sport-specific stimulus' (Sheppard and Young, 2006). Therefore, agility can include pre-planned changes of direction or changes of direction in response to a stimulus. Rugby performance includes both elements of agility through the large number of changes of direction and decision making processes that occur during match play. Therefore, the assessment of agility is important for the practitioner to consider but the current research literature is contradictory in terms of the types of test that have been applied. A range of research studies have assessed agility using change of direction tests including the agility 505 (Till et al., 2011) and the agility L-Run (Gabbett, 2006). Recent studies have begun to explore reactive agility, including reaction to a stimulus (Gabbett et al., 2008, Serpell et al., 2010, Green et al., 2011).

CHANGE OF DIRECTION TESTS

- Agility 505 – This test involves assessing a 180–degree turn off one foot. Timing gates are positioned 5m from a turning point and participants start 15m from the turning point (i.e. 10m from the timing gates). Participants accelerate as fast as possible from the starting point, turn on the 15m line and run as quickly as possible back through the timing gates.
- L-Run – This test involves assessing 180-degree turns off one foot along with 90-degree changes of three cones are placed 5m apart in the shape of an L. Timing gates are placed at the start and participants perform a 5m forward acceleration, a 90-degree turn, then a 180-turn and another 90-degree turn before sprinting through the start/finish line.

REACTIVE AGILITY ASSESSMENT

- Human movement – The reactive agility test used by (Gabbett et al., 2008) involves a participant starting 2m behind and in the middle of two timing gates 10m apart. Stood opposite the participant is a tester (human) who initiates the movement and begins the test. The athlete reacts to the movements of the tester by moving forward, then to the left or right in response to, and in the same direction as, the left or right movement of the tester. The timing is stopped when the athlete triggers the timing gate on either side.
- Video movement – This reactive agility test created by (Serpell et al., 2010) involved players acting as a defender and reacting to a video screen, representing an attacker. Players ran forward before reacting to one of twelve defined movements, cutting left or right and sprinting towards the timing gates.

The reactive agility test was able to distinguish between differing playing levels (Serpell et al., 2010) compared to traditional change of direction tests, which questions the validity of the latter. This research suggests such reactive agility methods may be more appropriate for assessing agility performance within rugby players and ensures the open skills and reactive element required for rugby. However, traditional change of direction tests may still provide useful agility data along with being easier to conduct in a controlled manner. The factors that were considered for speed assessment (e.g. timing gates versus handheld devices, surface and weather conditions) also need to be considered when assessing agility performance within rugby players.

## Strength

Due to the contact and collision nature of rugby and the relationship between strength and other physical characteristics (e.g. speed), high levels of muscular force are important for rugby performance. Strength has been shown to differentiate between playing levels (Baker and Newton, 2008, Gabbett and Seibold, 2013) and playing positions (Kirkpatrick and Comfort, 2013, Till et al., 2014d). Owing to the importance of strength it is strongly recommended to assess this quality within the lower and upper body of players.

The standard strength assessments used commonly within research and practice are isointerial measures. The one repetition (1–RM) max is the highest load an athlete can lift while maintaining correct technique and form.

In addition to 1–RM testing, it is also common for athletes to complete a number of repetitions (e.g. 3–RM, 5–RM), which may be used to reduce the risk of injury. It is also common to present relative strength, whereby an individual's body mass is considered in relation to the load lifted (i.e. 1–RM / body mass [kg.kg$^{-1}$]). Within rugby the most common assessments of strength for the lower and upper body are the squat and bench press exercises (Baker and Newton, 2008, Kirkpatrick and Comfort, 2013, Till et al., 2014d). However, recent studies have also started to assess pulling strength via the weighted chin up (Gabbett and Seibold, 2013) and prone row (Till et al., 2014d) exercises, which may be important to develop an equal pushing to pulling strength ratio (Baker and Newton, 2004). It is strongly recommended that a qualified strength and conditioning coach supervises all strength assessments.

Although not as common, most likely due to the reduced access to equipment, recent studies have used isometric strength testing protocols to assess the strength or maximum force output of rugby players using the squat (Comfort et al., 2011, Tillin et al., 2013) or mid-thigh pull (Fig. 2.2; (Crewther et al., 2012)) exercises. Isometric tests involve an athlete applying maximal force to an immovable object so there is no movement and the joint angle is fixed. Force is measured through the ground reaction forces via a force platform that is applied through an athletes' feet. These studies have demonstrated that isometric force is related to the dynamic actions of jumping and sprinting and is therefore an effective, and possibly safer, assessment of strength. In addition, a recent review of strength assessments (McMaster et al., 2014) demonstrated laboratory-based measures of the isometric squat and mid-thigh pull (Coefficient of variation < 2.0 per cent) are more reliable than isoinertial 1–RM strength measures of the squat and bench press exercise (Coefficient

**Fig. 2.2: Isometric mid-thigh pull assessment.**

of variation < 4.3 per cent). However, it should be noted that both isometric and isoinertial methods are both deemed highly reliable. Therefore, strength assessments can be performed via isointerial or isometric methods with the availability of expertise and equipment affecting the method to be used.

## Power

Like strength, power is also an important physical characteristic for rugby performance. Power has been shown to differentiate between playing levels (Baker and Newton, 2008, Gabbett and Seibold, 2013) and playing positions (Kirkpatrick and Comfort, 2013, Till et al., 2014d). Due to the importance of power, it is strongly recommended to assess upper and lower body power within rugby players.

The most common assessment of lower body power is the vertical jump assessment and this has been used in a wide range of research studies. The vertical jump assessment involves players squatting and then jumping vertically as high as possible and landing in the same position. Two forms of the vertical jump test can involve a squat jump (where the player starts in a paused squat position) or a countermovement jump (where the player starts standing and performs a squat before explosively jumping). The squat jump involves a concentric-only action whereby a countermovement jump involves an eccentric and concentric action, therefore assessing different power qualities. In addition to the type of jump performed, it is also important to consider the arm action during a jump (i.e. with an arm swing or with hands placed on the hips), which affects the jump height. Vertical jump assessments can be performed via jump and reach apparatus, portable jump mats or force platforms. Isoinertial assessments of the jump squat and bench press throw have typically been used to assess power output (Watts [Baker and Newton, 2008]). Such assessments use linear transducers and accelerometer devices to quantify barbell velocity and acceleration at a range of differing loads. Like strength assessments, the availability of expertise and equipment should be considered when assessing power alongside the jumping protocol.

## Aerobic Capacity and High-Intensity Running Ability

As rugby is an eighty-minute game requiring players to intersperse high-intensity running efforts with low-intensity recovery bouts, the development of both an aerobic capacity and high-intensity running ability are important considerations for performance (Johnston et al., 2014c).

Aerobic capacity is traditionally assessed via a maximal oxygen uptake assessment in the laboratory involving an incremental test performed to volitional exhaustion. However, limited research studies in rugby have assessed aerobic capacity via laboratory-based assessment, probably due to the expense and specialized equipment required to perform such assessments alongside the questionable validity of such continuous protocols for rugby players. Therefore, a plethora of research studies since the early 2000s (Gabbett, 2000) have used the multi-stage fitness test (MSFT) to report and evaluate aerobic capacity via estimated $VO_2$max or running distance during the test. The MSFT involves players running back and forth along a 20m track, keeping in time to a series of signals played from a CD player. As the test progresses, the time between signals decreases (i.e. requiring running speed to increase) until subjects reach volitional exhaustion.

Due to the high-intensity running demands of rugby, recent studies (Austin et al., 2013, Till et al., 2014d) have started to use the Yo-Yo intermittent recovery test (YYIRT) to assess high-intensity running ability. This assessment is similar to the MSFT but includes a 10–second rest interval between 2 × 20m shuttle runs and therefore does not require continuous running. The running intensity depends upon the Yo-Yo protocol used with the YYIRT Level 1 starting at lower velocities compared to the YYIRT Level 2, with most research to date using the Level 1 protocol.

In addition to the YYIRT, high speed running ability has been assessed via repeated sprint ability protocols. Protocols involving 12 × 20m (Gabbett et al., 2013), 12 × 30m (Smart et al., 2013) and 8 × 12sec (Gabbett et al., 2013) repeated efforts on a 20 or 48sec repeat have been conducted. Such assessments can include calculating the total time or distance across the number of repetitions and can include the measurement of a fatigue decrement in a specific time. Such assessments may be easier to include within the field. However, further research is required to understand the best repeated high-intensity running protocol with considerations for contact also important for both rugby league and rugby union.

# PRACTICAL APPLICATION

The above section discusses a range of fitness tests that could be used to assess physical capacities relevant to rugby. However, applying, evaluating and managing such fitness testing data to be used effectively to inform decisions and practice is the challenge for the practitioner. This section details the fitness testing protocol used within a rugby league academy, how this protocol was implemented and how fitness testing results were evaluated and used within the programme. Although arguments for the (non)inclusion of specific fitness tests can be made (and are discussed above), the testing protocol was developed to provide consistent data on a seasonal and annual basis for the monitoring and evaluation of players' fitness performance while considering the equipment and funding available to undertake such assessments on a consistent basis.

## Fitness Testing Protocol

The following fitness testing protocol was implemented with all academy players aged sixteen to twenty years:

- Anthropometry – Height, body mass, sum of four skinfolds
- Speed – 10 and 20m sprint

- Momentum – 10m momentum
- Agility – Agility 505
- Power – Countermovement jump, 4kg medicine ball chest throw, 1–RM power clean (for those players who were competent)
- Strength – 1–RM squat, bench press and prone row
- High-Intensity Running Ability – YYIRT Level 1

## Fitness Testing Schedule

Fitness testing was conducted four times per year within the academy to monitor the development and change of fitness performance. This involved testing:

- Pre-season – November
- End of pre-season – February
- Mid-season – June
- End of season – September

On all fitness testing procedures, a consistent approach was taken in ordering and planning assessments. Two separate testing sessions were used, which involved a field and gym-based testing session. All testing sessions were preceded by a standardized warm-up that involved jogging, dynamic movements and stretches followed by full instruction and demonstrations of the assessments. The field-based testing involved players performing (in the following order) 3 × 20m sprints and 2 × agility 505 change of direction tests off each foot followed by the YYIRT Level 1. Gym-based sessions involved players performing (in the following order) anthropometric measures taken before all gym sessions, power assessments (vertical jump, medicine ball chest throw, 1–RM power clean) and strength assessments (1–RM squat, bench press and prone row). For 1–RM power clean and strength assessments, players performed a warm-up protocol involving eight, five

| Table 2.2: Academy Rugby League Fitness Standards | | | | |
|---|---|---|---|---|
| | **Poor** | | **Average** | | **Excellent** |
| | 1 | 2 | 3 | 4 | 5 |
| Skinfolds (mm) | 60+ | 50 | 40 | 30 | 20 |
| 10m speed (s) | >2.05 | 1.95 | 1.85 | 1.75 | <1.65 |
| 20m speed (s) | >3.45 | 3.30 | 3.15 | 3.00 | <2.85 |
| 10m momentum (kg.s$^{-1}$) | 250 | 350 | 450 | 550 | 650 |
| Agility 505 left (s) | >2.80 | 2.65 | 2.50 | 2.35 | <2.20 |
| Agility 505 right (s) | >2.80 | 2.65 | 2.50 | 2.35 | <2.20 |
| Vertical jump (cm) | 40.0 | 47.5 | 55.0 | 62.5 | 70.0 |
| Vertical jump (PP) | 2,500 | 3,500 | 4,500 | 5,500 | 6,500 |
| Med ball throw (m) | 5.0 | 5.8 | 6.6 | 7.4 | 8.2 |
| 1–RM power clean (kg/kg) | <0.75 | 0.90 | 1.05 | 1.20 | >1.35 |
| 1–RM squat (kg/kg) | <1.00 | 1.25 | 1.50 | 1.75 | >2.00 |
| 1–RM bench press (kg/kg) | <0.80 | 0.95 | 1.10 | 1.25 | >1.40 |
| 1–RM prone row (kg/kg) | <0.75 | 0.90 | 1.05 | 1.20 | >1.35 |
| Yo-Yo IRTL1 (m) | 600 | 1,000 | 1,400 | 1,800 | 2,200 |

and three repetitions of individually selected loads before three attempts of their 1–RM with three minutes rest between assessments allowed. These exercises were all used regularly as part of the players' training programme and all players had to demonstrate competent technique on each lift before assessment was allowed on these measures. Players' strength scores were divided by body mass to provide a strength score relative to body mass.

## Evaluation of Results

Through consistent data collection over four years, a set of club academy standards were developed. Standards were developed so an individual's fitness testing score could be ranked on a one (poor) to five (excellent) scale. Such standards allowed players to be compared to a set of reference data, therefore showing individual player development alongside player's strengths and weaknesses in relation to specific fitness variables. Such standards were developed to allow all academy players (aged sixteen to twenty) to be compared and show a long-term player progression over time (i.e. an under seventeen would be expected to be lower than an under twenty player). Likewise, playing position was also considered by the coaches in interpreting the results (i.e. backs would be faster than forwards). The club academy standards are shown in Table 2.2.

## Player X - Fitness Assessment

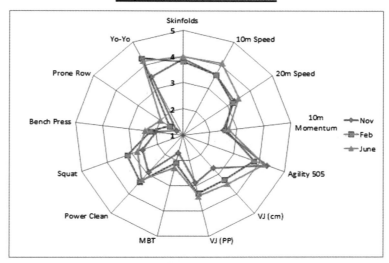

| Your Results | | | |
|---|---|---|---|
| | Nov | Feb | June |
| Body Mass (kg) | 72.0 | 74.1 | 72.5 |
| Skinfolds (mm) | 30.8 | 31.8 | 30.0 |
| 10m Speed (s) | 1.79 | 1.79 | 1.74 |
| 20m Speed (s) | 3.10 | 3.12 | 3.08 |
| 10m Momentum (kg.s$^{-1}$) | 402 | 413 | 416 |
| Agility 505 Left (s) | 2.30 | 2.41 | 2.33 |
| Agility 505 Right (s) | 2.27 | 2.36 | 2.28 |
| Vertical Jump (cm) | 52.3 | 57.6 | 59.2 |
| Vertical Jump (PP) | 4380 | 4790 | 4820 |
| Med Ball Throw (m) | 5.6 | 5.9 | 6.0 |
| 1-RM Power Clean (kg/kg) | 1.04 | 1.08 | 1.07 |
| 1-RM Squat (kg/kg) | 1.4 | 1.55 | 1.45 |
| 1-RM Bench Press (kg/kg) | 0.95 | 0.98 | 1.00 |
| 1-RM Prone Row(kg/kg) | 0.79 | 0.85 | 0.90 |
| Yo-Yo IRTL1 (m) | 1600 | 1920 | 1840 |

**Comments**

* Small improvements are generally evident in most areas across the season to date.
* Strengths are high speed running ability, acceleration and agility.
* Weaknesses are upper body strength and power. Increase upper body weights and nutrition review
* Player needs to work harder and approach conditioining sessions with greater concentration to develop the physical profile needed for progression.

**Fig. 2.3: Seasonal fitness report for an academy rugby league player.**

Such standards allowed players to be compared on an individual and long-term basis with player and coaches reports provided for each academy player. Fig. 2.3 shows a seasonal report for Player X at three time points (November, February and June). Player X is a seventeen-year-old outside back who has been within the academy for eighteen months. This report would predominantly be used to provide feedback to the player to ensure he is aware his performance and progress is being monitored. In addition, the report helps provide and develop a rationale to aid player 'buy-in' within his training programmes. The report illustrates small seasonal improvements in fitness performance with

## Player Y - Fitness Assessment

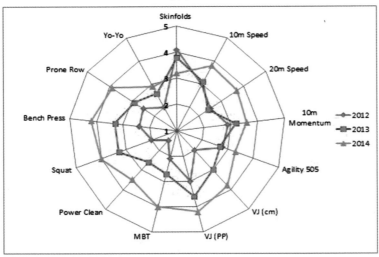

| Your Results | | | |
|---|---|---|---|
| | 2012 | 2013 | 2014 |
| Body Mass (kg) | 81.2 | 86.3 | 90.1 |
| Skinfolds (mm) | 28.8 | 32.2 | 37.6 |
| 10m Speed (s) | 1.85 | 1.84 | 1.77 |
| 20m Speed (s) | 3.22 | 3.19 | 3.06 |
| 10m Momentum (kg.s$^{-1}$) | 439 | 469 | 509 |
| Agility 505 Left (s) | 2.51 | 2.55 | 2.45 |
| Agility 505 Right (s) | 2.54 | 2.55 | 2.43 |
| Vertical Jump (cm) | 47.2 | 54.5 | 61.1 |
| Vertical Jump (PP) | 4490 | 5160 | 5735 |
| Med Ball Throw (m) | 5.9 | 6.4 | 7.5 |
| 1-RM Power Clean (kg/kg) | 0.82 | 0.98 | 1.11 |
| 1-RM Squat (kg/kg) | 1.24 | 1.57 | 1.75 |
| 1-RM Bench Press (kg/kg) | 1.01 | 1.15 | 1.28 |
| 1-RM Prone Row(kg/kg) | 0.98 | 1.04 | 1.18 |
| Yo-Yo IRTL1 (m) | 1000 | 1280 | 1360 |

**Comments**

* Improvements are evident in most attributes areas across the two year period
* Greatest improvements in strength across the 2 years
* Increase in skinfolds evident along with small increase in high speed running ability.
* Developing speed / agility and ability to repeat efforts are the developmental priorties
* Continue to develop strength into senior levels

**Fig. 2.4: Annual fitness report for an academy rugby league player.**

the player's strengths being his high-intensity running ability, acceleration and agility. The player demonstrates weaknesses in upper body strength and power alongside the need to develop body mass to improve momentum. Such findings emphasize the player's training priorities should be on resistance training alongside nutrition interventions to improve his current results.

Fig. 2.4 shows an annual report for Player Y across the end of season testing on three seasons. Player Y is a nineteen-year-old back-rower who has been with the academy for three seasons. This report would predominantly be used to provide feedback to the coach to demonstrate at what stage of development the player is at alongside demonstrating his improvement in performance across the three-year period. Such information would aid coach decisions on player retainment/progression (i.e. is he ready to become a full-time professional) alongside influencing future programme interventions. The report illustrates some development in most physical areas, especially strength over the period. Alongside continuing to develop strength, the player needs to focus upon repeated high-intensity running, speed and agility. This player did progress to become a full-time professional the following year.

## IMPLICATIONS AND RECOMMENDATIONS FOR PRACTICE

- Fitness testing can provide practitioners with objective information about a player's physical capabilities. Such data can be used to profile players' strengths and weaknesses, talent identification, evaluate and prescribe training while providing feedback to players and coaches.
- Practitioners should consider developing a fitness testing battery that includes both field and laboratory-based assessments where possible. Factors such as the availability of equipment, time and cost may affect the decisions made. However, where possible practitioners should aim to standardize conditions (e.g. surface, time of day and so on).
- Body composition should be assessed regularly via skinfolds thickness (and DXA scans where possible), to allow players to develop optimum body composition for performance and influence required training and nutritional interventions.
- Speed should be assessed at short (i.e. 5, 10m) and longer distances (i.e. 40m) via electronic timing gates where possible. Practitioners should also consider assessing momentum due to the collision aspect of rugby.
- Agility includes pre-planned changes of direction or changes of direction in response to a stimulus and the assessment of both should be considered within a fitness testing battery.

- Lower body and upper body pushing and pulling strength should be undertaken by an appropriately qualified individual using isoinertial (e.g. 1–RM) or isometric methods.
- The vertical jump assessment is the most common mode of assessment of power. Practitioners should consider the use of equipment and whether arm action is used.
- Aerobic capacity (i.e. MSFT), high speed running ability (i.e. YYIRT) and repeated sprint ability may all be considered within a fitness testing protocol for rugby, with further research required to understand the most effective protocol and consider the contact and collision element of rugby.
- Practitioners should aim to develop a consistent fitness testing protocol that can be delivered on a seasonal and annual (long-term) basis to track player development against standardized club norms.
- Seasonal and annual evaluation results and feedback to players and coaches is an important aspect of the fitness testing process. Feedback should be provided that allows comparison to norms/others, include monitoring progression over time and be presented in a format to allow player and coach education and motivation.

# CHAPTER 3

# MONITORING FATIGUE AND RECOVERY

## Ben Jones, Jamie Highton and Craig Twist

The physicality of rugby league and rugby union match play is well known and as such players will experience immediate (i.e. hours) and, sometimes prolonged (i.e. days) fatigue. Similar fatigue responses might also be caused by the demands imposed on players during training, particularly when such activities aim to mimic the demands of match play. Accordingly, monitoring fatigue appropriately and implementing suitable recovery strategies should be a paramount concern to practitioners to ensure optimal player performance and health.

The aim of this chapter is to introduce the likely causes of fatigue seen in rugby players and identify methods that can be used to monitor these responses effectively. This chapter will also detail specific recovery strategies that can be implemented by practitioners. In addition, the chapter provides a real-life case study of the application of the monitoring and recovery of fatigue within a club environment.

# RESEARCH OVERVIEW

## What is Fatigue?

Fatigue can be peripheral (i.e. muscle) or central (i.e. within the brain) in origin and it results in a player reporting symptoms of tiredness and reductions in neuromuscular performance. Symptoms of fatigue during match play or training are typically transient in nature and are the consequence of one or more contributing factors. These factors include acidosis, substrate depletion, electrolyte disturbance, dehydration, thirst or thermoregulatory disturbances. Thereafter, acute fatigue causes an unavoidable reduction in performance and/or an increase in the perception of the intensity of exercise in the days after intense training or match play. After match play and training sessions (both field and resistance-based), players will experience structural damage to skeletal-muscle tissue (Twist and Highton, 2013) accompanied by localized inflammation of the muscle (Proske and Morgan, 2001). While the role of oxidative stress is a possible contributor to fatigue after prolonged team sport activity (Andersson et al., 2010), the most likely causes here are repeated eccentric contractions from numerous decelerations and blunt force trauma from tackles or impacts (Johnston et al., 2013a). In some instances chronic fatigue can result and is considered as any prolonged (e.g. a few weeks or months) reduction in performance or increased tiredness (Coutts et al., 2007a). The occurrence of chronic fatigue

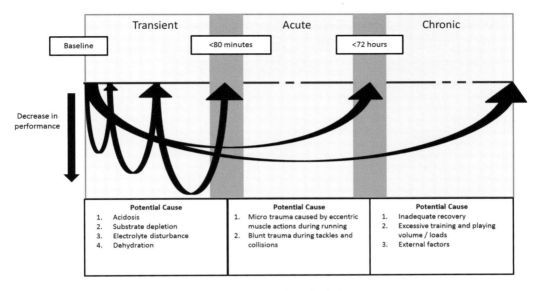

**Fig. 3.1: Potential causes of transient, acute and chronic fatigue.**

is due to inappropriate structure in training load, monotonous training, travel, poor nutritional practices and insufficient sleep (Foster, 1998, Lehmann *et al.*, 1997, Meeusen *et al.*, 2006, Meeusen *et al.*, 2013). In other sports, it has been reported that between 7 and 50 per cent of high-level athletes show signs of chronic fatigue at any given time (Naessens *et al.*, 2000, Kenttä *et al.*, 2001). Providing adequate recovery periods during a training or competition cycle is therefore essential in avoiding its development.

## Acute Fatigue after Rugby Matches

Acute fatigue after rugby match play is typically characterized by reductions in upper and lower body neuromuscular function (Johnston *et al.*, 2013b, Twist *et al.*, 2012), biochemical (e.g. creatine kinase [CK]) and hormonal (e.g. testosterone and cortisol) disturbances (West *et al.*, 2014) and a reduction in perceived well-being (Johnston *et al.*, 2013b, Twist *et al.*, 2012). The time course

of the responses varies between players and is influenced by the player's role and activity within the match (McLellan and Lovell, 2012, Duffield *et al.*, 2012). Indeed, in rugby players there is a positive association between the number of collisions and blood markers of tissue damage (Twist *et al.*, 2012, McLellan *et al.*, 2011), which are indicative of blunt trauma (i.e. increases in [CK]). Similarly, higher running loads during matches are also associated with greater muscular fatigue (Duffield *et al.*, 2012). Damage to muscle fibres as a consequence of match play causes an acute decrease in muscle function (Proske and Morgan, 2001) and increases in muscle soreness that typically co-exist for twenty-four to forty-eight hours post-match (McLean *et al.*, 2010). The varying time course of recovery for difference markers of fatigue represents the complexity of monitoring and managing fatigue and recovery. Therefore, practitioners should carefully manage the return to intense training in an attempt to avoid the development of chronic fatigue or injury.

**Table 3.1: Training Structure for Five, Seven and Nine-Day Turnaround between Rugby League Matches (McLean et al., 2010)**

| | Five-day turnaround (two training days, two recovery days) | Seven-day turnaround (four training days, four recovery days) | Nine-day turnaround (four training days, four recovery days) |
|---|---|---|---|
| **Day 0** | **Match** | **Match** | **Match** |
| **Day 1** | Recovery | Recovery | Recovery |
| **Day 2** | *Day off* | Skills, weights | *Day off* |
| **Day 3** | Skills, weights | Skills, contact, conditioning | *Day off* |
| **Day 4** | Skills | *Day off* | Skills, weights, skills |
| **Day 5** | **Match** | Speed, skills, weights | Contact, conditioning |
| **Day 6** | | Skills | *Day off* |
| **Day 7** | | **Match** | Speed, skills, weights |
| **Day 8** | | | Skills |
| **Day 9** | | | **Match** |

## Fatigue after Training

Practitioners aim to prepare players for the rigours of match play by implementing specific training programmes. Indeed, a typical training cycle will include technical, tactical, speed, strength, contact, conditioning and recovery sessions (McLean et al., 2010). The volume and intensity of training is prescribed to induce a stimulus for players to achieve the desired outcome, although this inevitably contributes to the overall fatiguing weekly load. Some training sessions will be designed to replicate match demands during field-based training (Gabbett et al., 2012b), resulting in a similar response to match play (Johnston et al., 2013a). Where appropriate, similar recovery strategies to those used after match play or periodization of training should be employed to facilitate rapid recovery. Such instances are typical during the in-season period, when coaches might be faced with short (three to five days), normal (seven days) or long (>nine days) turnaround periods between matches (McLean et al., 2010, Table 3.1). However, where training adaptation is the target of these specific conditioning sessions (specifically, pre-season), coaches should avoid aggressive recovery after such training.

Shorter turnarounds between matches (<five days) typically see lower training loads employed that result in functional and psychological recovery in advance of the next match (McLean et al., 2010). This is in contrast to longer between match periods that result in higher daily training loads than shorter periods (Fig. 3.2), which might result in under-recovery of players for the next match. These observations are probably because coaches are particularly mindful of the shorter period between

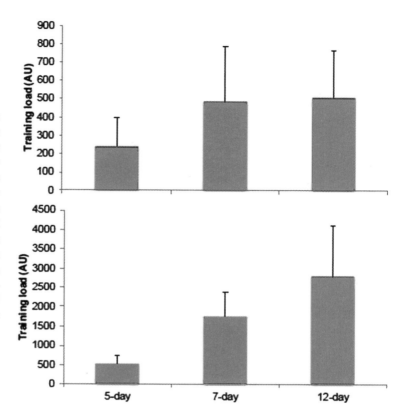

**Fig. 3.2: Session RPE data from elite rugby league players showing (a) daily training load for the different between-match microcycles; (b) total training load during the different between-match microcycles (data are mean ± SD). (Twist, personal observations)**

games and therefore adopt a more conservative approach to ensure player recovery. Longer between match periods are potentially seen as opportunities to increase training loads, and will be dependent on the results of previous matches and the coach's desire to address technical or team deficiencies. Between-match training loads should therefore be planned carefully in order to ensure players are prepared for the next match in an appropriate physical and mental state to compete. Furthermore, players with better physical qualities demonstrate faster recovery rates after match play (Johnston et al., 2014d), which means optimal conditioning earlier in the preparation (pre-season) will benefit players in the longer term.

## Measuring Player Fatigue Status

### LOWER AND UPPER BODY NEUROMUSCULAR FUNCTION

Assessments of neuromuscular function are often used to evaluate muscular fatigue in rugby players (Johnston et al., 2013a, West et al., 2014). The most common test is the countermovement jump as this provides a reliable measure of muscle function (coefficient of variation = 1.0–6.6 per cent; [Cormack et al., 2008, Twist et al., 2012]) and is unlikely to contribute additional fatigue (Twist and Highton, 2013). The countermovement jump is measured using either a jump mat or a force platform and involves players starting in an upright position, after which they flex their knees and hips to a self-selected depth, before jumping for maximal height. Players should perform three jumps, with the best flight time reported. It is important to ensure all players are accustomed to the jump procedures as part of their regular monitoring process to increase the reliability of the test (Twist et al., 2012).

The assessment of upper body fatigue is also meaningful given the high number of collisions experienced above the waist in rugby players (Twist et al., 2012). An appropriate and reliable test for upper body fatigue is a plyometric push-up on a force platform or contact mat (coefficient of variation ~5.5 per cent, Twist, personal observations). Players should start in a press-up position with their hands on the force platform or mat, with arms extended in a self-selected position. Players should then lower their body by flexing their elbows to a self-selected depth before extending the elbows as fast as possible so their hands leave the platform/mat. Studies using the plyometric press-up to monitor fatigue have had their participants perform two practice attempts before performing a single effort that was recorded (Johnston et al., 2013b).

BIOCHEMICAL AND HORMONAL MARKERS OF FATIGUE

The measurement of biochemical (e.g. [CK] C-reactive protein) and hormonal markers (e.g. testosterone, cortisol) using blood or salivary analysis allows a detailed analysis of a player's readiness to train or play (Crewther et al., 2013), as well as their health and recovery status (Twist et al., 2012, Elloumi et al., 2003). Meaningful interpretation of the data requires that individuals be compared against their respective baseline (Heisterberg et al., 2013), which is ideally identified when there is minimal accumulation of training-related stress (i.e. early pre-season). Recovery values are often compared against

pre-match concentrations, which might not be representative of an individual's actual baseline per se but more an accumulation of the training week. Day-to-day and individual variability can be influenced by non-rugby factors (e.g. external stresses) (Salvador et al., 2003), and diurnal variation means data should ideally be collected at the same time of day. Practitioners should also be aware that some biochemical disturbances possess a poor relationship with neuromuscular performance (Twist and Highton, 2013, West et al., 2014) and psychological wellbeing (Alaphilippe et al., 2012). Added to the expense and time-consuming nature of the procedures, such measures might be considered practically challenging within an applied environment (Twist and Highton, 2013). Practitioners should therefore use biochemical and hormonal measurements alongside other markers of fatigue, more specifically when confirmation of the player's health status is required.

PERCEPTUAL MEASURES OF FATIGUE

Subjective questionnaires are sensitive to changes in training stress (Coutts et al., 2007b, Halson et al., 2003) and also the recovery of rugby players after matches (Twist et al., 2012). Subjective measures of muscle soreness and perceived fatigue can also outlast neuromuscular and biochemical markers of fatigue reported by rugby players after a match (Twist et al., 2012). A range of questionnaires exist (Morgan et al., 1987, Rushall, 1990, Kellmann and Kallus, 2001, Kenttä and Hassmén, 1998) that seek to identify psychophysiological stresses such as sleep quality, muscle soreness, mood disturbance and an athlete's attitude to training (Twist and Highton, 2013). Questionnaires should be completed at the same time of the day to avoid daily and diurnal variation (Meeusen et al., 2006). Coaches might also consider the number of questions posed by the questionnaire, such that longer versions might be considered tedious by players, resulting in a reduced compliance. Shorter questionnaires have been used previously (McLean et al., 2010), although the sensitivity of shorter questionnaires has been questioned (Robson-Ansley et al., 2009).

## Recovery Strategies

Promoting recovery after rugby-related activity is important given the busy playing and training schedules for modern players. Below we discuss some of the non-nutritional approaches that might be adopted in promoting recovery of players where such strategies are deemed appropriate.

### CRYOTHERAPY

Cryotherapy is the use of cold water immersion or ice baths, which is a common recovery strategy among rugby players. Research (Venter et al., 2010) has reported the use of cryotherapy in rugby more than other team sport and players also rate ice baths among the top five most important recovery strategies available to them. In addition, international players consider their use to be more important than national or club standard players (Venter, 2014). However, despite its popularity, the evidence that cryotherapy improves recovery after exercise is equivocal.

Against control conditions, cold water immersion (~10–12°C for 10–12min) applied immediately after prolonged (~60–90min) exercise has shown positive effects on biochemical markers (e.g. [CK]), perceived soreness, muscle function and repeated sprint performance in well-trained individuals (Bailey et al., 2007, Ascensao et al., 2011, Elias et al., 2012). Cold water immersion also alleviates perceived soreness, fatigue and markers of muscle damage and inflammation when

conducted daily during tournaments in soccer (Rowsell et al., 2009) and basketball (Montgomery et al., 2008). In rugby players, cryotherapy after training and matches has resulted in better recovery of biochemical markers of tissue damage (Banfi et al., 2009, Gill et al., 2006). Pointon and Duffield (2012) have also shown that after simulated match play involving physical contact, a cold water immersion condition (compared to passive recovery) promoted recovery of muscle function and perceived soreness for up to two hours post-exercise. However, there were no differences in markers of fatigue at twenty-four hours between cold water immersion and passive recovery.

It appears cryotherapy provides some potential benefit to recovery and is well received by players. However, clarity on the most appropriate strategy to employ is made problematic by the different type, timing and duration of exposures used in the literature. Its effect on the different markers of recovery also makes interpretation of findings difficult. Readers are directed to work by Bleakley et al. (2012) and Leeder et al. (2012) for a more comprehensive overview of cryotherapy and its effects on athlete recovery.

### COMPRESSION

The use of compression garments to enhance recovery in team sports is less popular than cryotherapy (Venter et al., 2010). However, their increased commercial availability means these are becoming more popular with team sport athletes for use both during and after training or matches. Compression garments work by exerting a pressure gradient that reduces the available space for swelling to occur (MacRae et al., 2011). Wearing these garments assists in reducing oedema and haematoma formation associated with tissue damage and subsequent inflammation. Compression might also reduce muscle oscillation and provide muscle stability to reduce initial tissue damage, reduce venous pooling and enhance venous return, and thus removal of metabolic waste products and noxious stimuli (Kraemer et al., 2004).

Worn during exercise, compression garments can improve proprioception (Kraemer et al., 1998), lower perceived muscle soreness (Ali et al., 2007), increase skin temperature (Duffield et al., 2010) and improve running economy (Bringard et al., 2006). However, rugby players wearing compression garments did not improve single and repeated 20m sprint time or muscle power during intermittent activity (Duffield et al., 2010, Duffield et al., 2008). Compression garments worn after exercise has improved post-activity perceived muscle soreness (Jakeman et al., 2010, Kraemer et al., 2001, Hamlin et al., 2012, Kraemer et al., 2010) and recovery of CK (Gill et al., 2006, Hamlin et al., 2012). However, better recovery of muscle function and performance after exercise was only reported in three of these studies (Jakeman et al., 2010, Kraemer et al., 2001, Hamlin et al., 2012). Duffield et al. (2008) reported a lower body compression garment after simulated rugby activities did not improve recovery of muscle function or inflammatory markers. Wearing a full-length lower limb compression garment (~18mmHg) after matches and overnight (~18hr) during a three-day basketball tournament has also been shown to be no more effective than passive recovery for promoting recovery (Montgomery et al., 2008).

MASSAGE

Massage is also a recovery strategy used by rugby players to facilitate recovery (Venter et al., 2010) but players do not rank it among the top five recovery strategies available to them (Venter, 2014). The precise mechanism by which massage might enhance recovery is unclear. For example, massage does not increase muscle blood flow (Shoemaker et al., 1997) nor does it reduce post-exercise lactate (Hinds et al., 2004), $H^+$ accumulation (Wiltshire et al., 2010) or neutrophil count (Hilbert et al., 2003). Massage also fails to prevent losses of muscle strength or performance in the days after damaging exercise (Hemmings et al., 2000, Hilbert et al., 2003). However, despite massage offering little benefit with regard to functional recovery, it does show more favourable effects of minimizing muscle soreness after damaging exercise (Hemmings et al., 2000, Hilbert et al., 2003).

STRETCHING AND LOW-INTENSITY EXERCISE

Stretching before and/or after exercise is known to offer negligible changes in markers of fatigue twenty-four to forty-eight hours after exercise (Herbert and Gabriel, 2002, Dawson et al., 2005, Montgomery et al., 2008). Therefore, there appears to be little beneficial effect of rugby players performing pre- or post-exercise stretching with regard to recovery for rugby. Indeed, static stretching might actually impair immediate repeated-sprint and agility performance (Beckett et al., 2009), so players might wish to avoid stretching in between exercise bouts when match play is imminent (e.g. interchanges).

Low-intensity exercise performed twenty-two and forty-six hours after a soccer match had no effect on recovery of neuromuscular function, muscle soreness, or biochemical markers of inflammation (Andersson et al., 2010, Andersson et al., 2008). However, post-match low intensity cycling (Gill et al., 2006) or one-hour water-based exercise (Suzuki et al., 2004) have resulted in lower [CK] and an improved mood state in the days after a rugby match. Further work is needed to establish the benefits of low-intensity exercise for improving post-exercise recovery in rugby players.

## THE IMPORTANCE OF SLEEP HYGIENE

Sleep is an integral component of successful restoration of athletic performance (Halson, 2008), particularly given its positive association with anabolic processes that promote healing after damaging exercise (Adam and Oswald, 1984). Compared to the general population, athletes are known to experience comparable quantity but poorer quality of sleep because of thoughts about competition and nervousness (Leeder *et al.*, 2012, Juliff *et al.*, 2014). Rugby players are also likely to experience partial sleep deprivation because of evening matches, travel, social issues, caffeine and alcohol consumption, hyper-hydration or a combination of these. Sleep deprivation is therefore likely to lead to poorer recovery and cognitive function in the days after match play (Skein *et al.*, 2013). These findings reinforce that appropriate sleep hygiene (behaviours associated with the quality and quantity of sleep) is important in the recovery process and should be part of the monitoring procedures.

## ATHLETE PERCEPTIONS OF RECOVERY AND THE PLACEBO EFFECT

An athlete's perception of a strategy's effectiveness seems important to the degree of recovery actually attained (Cook and Beaven, 2013, Broatch *et al.*, 2014). For example, well-trained rugby players using cold water immersion after an intense training session reported better recovery of repeated sprint performance in the days after in those who had a more positive view of the intervention (Cook and Beaven, 2013). Such findings suggest the beneficial effects of the recovery interventions employed by rugby players are because of improved ratings of perceived fatigue that, in part, are the result of a placebo effect.

## RECOVERY STRATEGIES AND TRAINING ADAPTATION

While some strategies are likely to exert beneficial effects on post-exercise recovery for rugby players on an acute basis, little is known about the long-term effects of chronic exposure to most recovery strategies. For example, chronic exposure to cryotherapy might well blunt adaptations to training (i.e. during pre-season) by interfering with post-exercise inflammation (White and Wells, 2013). Until clearer insight is provided, it might be considered prudent to limit aggressive recovery treatments in rugby players to periods of the season when training adaptation is not a target or there is a short turnaround time between matches.

# PRACTICAL APPLICATION

During the in-season period, players will typically have five to seven days between matches. Practitioners must therefore monitor individual player recovery and manage carefully the subsequent weekly training load to ensure optimal week-to-week match performance and health status. This case study describes the between-match fatigue status and player performance in response to the internal and external loads experienced by a rugby league forward who played two games separated by five days.

## Case Presentation

The player (age: 24 years, stature: 1.86m, body mass: 95kg) had played 125 first team games and played as a hit-up forward (prop and back row). He was a regular first team player, typically used as an interchange playing two approximately twenty-minute bouts per match. Data reported here are taken from the 2011 season of the eight-day cycle surrounding round eight and nine of the domestic competition.

Training load was monitored in all matches and field-based training sessions using the same 10Hz GPS unit, which was used to quantify total distance (m), relative distance (m·min$^{-1}$), high-intensity running (>14km·h$^{-1}$), collisions (#·min$^{-1}$) and sprints (#·min$^{-1}$; >21km·h$^{-1}$). In addition, session RPE was recorded twenty minutes after all sessions to provide a measure of internal load, with individual session values summed to provide a daily total. The player's match performance was also quantified subjectively by the head coach according to his or her own opinion using the following categories: 1 = poor performance, 2 = moderate performance, 3 = good performance, 4 = very good performance, 5 = excellent performance. Measures of fatigue comprised upper and lower body neuromuscular function on a force plate using a plyometric press-up and countermovement jump, respectively. Data for jumps and press-ups are reported as a percentage of pre-season values. Players also provided ratings of perceived fatigue, muscle soreness, sleep quality, stress and mood using a five-point (1–5) Likert scale. Lower values were indicative of a positive response to the question, while higher values reflected a negative outcome. Measures were recorded every day that the player was in attendance, with all fatigue measures taken between 08:00–09:00 before any activity took place.

Table 3.2 describes the daily activity, player load (external and internal) and fatigue response for the player over an eight-day cycle. Day one and day seven report the pre-game fatigue status for the player, with data recorded before the morning game preparation session (i.e. Captain's Run). Games were played on day two (15:00) and day

eight (18:00), both of which were lost with scores of 23–20 and 30–10, respectively. Day three was a post-game recovery session that comprised fatigue measures followed by a thirty-minute swim. Days four and five were coach-led skills sessions that focused on individual and team-specific practices. Day five also included a resistance session comprising three × four sets at ~85 per cent 1RM for: hang clean, back squat, supine dumb-bell press and wide-grip chins. Day six was a rest day with players told to avoid any strenuous and rugby-related activity.

## Discussion

The demands imposed on the player in game one were higher than average values previously reported for forwards during match play (Waldron et al., 2011; Twist et al., 2012). Greater volumes of high-intensity running, sprinting and collisions during the match therefore explain the large reductions (~20 per cent) in neuromuscular function and well-being on day three. With upper and lower body neuromuscular function two per cent below baseline values and a score of 21/25 for perceptual fatigue, these data suggest that the player started game one in a fatigued state. However, despite data after the match being consistent with that observed elsewhere (e.g. Twist et al., 2012; West et al., 2013a), symptoms of fatigue appear to have remained for the eight-day period. In particular, increases in perceptual fatigue (i.e. well-being) were more prolonged than the decreases in neuromuscular function.

The coaches opted to employ extended skills session on days four and five in an attempt to address technical deficiencies that occurred in game one. However, the daily training load (measured by session RPE) on days four and five was larger than values

## Table 3.2: Player Load, Fatigue and Performance Responses of a Rugby Forward during an Eight-Day In-Season Cycle

| Activity | Day 1 | Day 2 | Day 3 | Day 4 | Day 5 | Day 6 | Day 7 | Day 8 |
|---|---|---|---|---|---|---|---|---|
| | Game preparation | Game 1 (Lost) | Recovery (Swim) | Skills | Weights (30min) Skills (95min) | Rest | Game preparation | Game 2 (Lost) |
| **Player load** | | | | | | | | |
| Total time (min) | 30 | 42 | 30 | 90 | 125 | | 65 | 45 |
| Total distance (m) | 1,995 | 5,000 | – | 3,500 | 5,900 | | 4005 | 3800 |
| Relative distance (m·min⁻¹) | 67 | 119 | – | 39 | 62 | | 62 | 84 |
| HI running (m·min⁻¹) | 9 | 16 | – | 5 | 7 | | 15 | 9 |
| Collisions (#·min⁻¹) | – | 1.8 | – | – | 0.5 | | – | 1.4 |
| Sprints (#·min⁻¹) | 0.1 | 0.6 | – | 0.2 | 0.6 | | 0.4 | 0.3 |
| Session RPE (AU) | 90 | 336 | – | 360 | 625 | | 260 | 360 |
| Coach rating | – | 4 | – | – | – | | – | 1 |
| | | | | | | | | |
| **Recovery** | | | | | | | | |
| Jump (%)* | 98 | – | 78 | 85 | 90 | | 94 | – |
| Press-up (%)* | 98 | – | 75 | 84 | 88 | | 96 | – |
| Well-being (1–5) | | | | | | | | |
| Fatigue | 5 | – | 2 | 3 | 3 | | 2 | – |
| Muscle soreness | 4 | – | 2 | 3 | 3 | | 2 | – |
| Sleep quality | 4 | – | 1 | 2 | 3 | | 3 | – |
| Stress | 4 | – | 3 | 3 | 3 | | 3 | – |
| Mood | 4 | – | 3 | 3 | 2 | | 3 | – |
| Total | 21 | – | 11 | 14 | 14 | | 13 | – |

HI = High-intensity; Coaches' rating; 1 = poor performance, 2 = moderate performance, 3 = good performance, 4 = very good performance, 5 = excellent performance; Neuromuscular function measures are presented as a percentage of Day 1 values; Well-being: 5 = Positive, 1 = Negative. * Neuromuscular fatigue data reported as a percentage of pre-season values.

previously reported for elite rugby players at this time of year (~200 AU; McLean *et al.*, 2010) and are also consistent with values previously observed in relation to intensified training (Coutts *et al.*, 2007c) and peak injury incidence (Gabbett, 2004). Furthermore, the high training loads on day seven during the game preparation session comprised a high total running distance (4,005m) and excessive high-intensity running. While it is not possible to identify the exact mechanisms, contributors to the slowed neuromuscular recovery and high perceptual fatigue are likely to be tissue damage from a high number of repeated accelerations and reduced muscle glycogen. Inappropriate management of the player's training load in the days after the intensified game one are likely to have exacerbated his fatigue status over the eight-day period. Collectively, this data indicates insufficient recovery and that the player started game two in a fatigued state that led to him underperforming (as indicated by the poor coach rating).

Given the increase in match load during the in-season and the cumulative effect of training demands, both training duration and intensity should be managed appropriately to enable further recovery, avoid the risk of injury and ensure players approach the subsequent match in a low fatigue state. Practitioners must use the training load data available from matches and training to anticipate fatigue. Thereafter, appropriate measurement tools should be employed to monitor fatigue status and, where necessary, modify the individual's training load accordingly. This case study also highlights the importance of recognizing the potential for fatigue from extended skills sessions and the need to educate coaches and players about the implications for player health status and performance. Where players are required to train but demonstrate symptoms of cumulative fatigue, practitioners should employ strategies to reduce the duration or intensity of the session for the individual. This might involve players being rotated or retracted from the session early to reduce specific movement demands.

## IMPLICATIONS AND RECOMMENDATIONS FOR PRACTICE

- Fatigue is multifactorial, consisting of neuromuscular, biochemical, hormonal and perceptual disturbances that are common following training and match play in rugby.
- The nature and time course of fatigue should be considered, which can range from transient (i.e. minutes), acute (i.e. hours – days) to chronic (i.e. months). Typically rugby players remain fatigued up to forty-eight to seventy-two hours post-match.
- Fatigue can be monitored to evaluate the overall status of a player. Tests can include neuromuscular (i.e. lower-body countermovement jump, upper-body plyometric push-up), biochemical (i.e. blood sampling to measure [CK]), hormonal (i.e. blood or saliva sampling to measure testosterone and/or cortisol) and perceptual (i.e. well-being questionnaires) assessments.

- Fatigue monitoring should consider time of day, practicalities (i.e. blood sampling), reliability of specific measures (i.e. coefficient of variation of a countermovement jump) and timing of baseline measures (i.e. pre-season or pre-match).
- Recovery strategies can include; cryotherapy, massage, compression garments, sleep and low-intensity exercise, and should be employed following match play and during periods of intensified competition.
- Cryotherapy is the most common recovery strategy used by rugby players and studies have shown cold water immersion (~10–12°C for 10–12min) improves recovery.
- Fatigue and recovery should consider daily training load, accumulative weekly training and match play load, and the daily fatigue status of a player in determining individualized weekly training schedules to optimize season-long match performance.

# CHAPTER 4

# NUTRITION AND ERGOGENIC AIDS FOR RUGBY

*Daniel Owens, Ben Jones, Warren Bradley and Graeme Close*

## INTRODUCTION

Life in the world of rugby is dictated by training on a daily basis and competition on a weekly basis. It is therefore paramount that players are able to recover optimally between training sessions and be prepared for peak performance in competitive match play at the end of the training week. To this end, sports nutrition is becoming increasingly valued as one of the most important sub-disciplines of the sports science network employed in both elite rugby union and league clubs. Despite the emphasis placed on sports nutrition, rugby players and coaching staff demonstrate a lack of understanding of the basic principles of nutrition (Walsh *et al.*, 2011, Zinn *et al.*, 2006). Sports nutritionists are therefore employed to deliver a nutrition programme that aims to educate and direct players towards a diet that will optimize health, training and performance. In order to deliver a programme that achieves these goals, it is vital it is underpinned by a sound understanding of human metabolism and the demands of rugby performance with specific reference to pertinent scientific research. This chapter will discuss such research evidence in relation to the macronutrient, micronutrient and hydration requirements for training and competition in rugby and will also discuss the use of ergogenic aids in training and performance.

## RESEARCH OVERVIEW

### Macronutrient Requirements for Rugby Training and Performance

Carbohydrates, fats and proteins constitute the major macronutrients that make up the majority of daily energy intake and are essential fuels for muscle contraction, substrates and signals for adaptive responses to exercise stimuli and for the normal functioning of all our biological systems. Each macronutrient plays specific but equally important roles and will therefore be discussed separately in relation to rugby training and performance. Note that the recommendations provided for the macronutrients are expressed herein as grams per kilogram of body mass (g.kg⁻¹) to allow intake to be tailored to expenditure and further to allow the individualized prescription of nutrient intake for different players.

## CARBOHYDRATES

Carbohydrates are classed as monosaccharides, disaccharides and polysaccharides. Simple sugars such as glucose, fructose and galactose are examples of monosaccharides. When two of these simple sugars are joined, disaccharides are formed (i.e. sucrose, lactose and maltose). Finally, starch and glycogen are types of polysaccharides in which long chains of monosaccharides are formed. In context, following a standard balanced meal, the main carbohydrate products that are available following digestion are glucose, a smaller amount of fructose and galactose (from milk). These sugars are absorbed into the bloodstream and transported to the liver, where they may be stored as liver glycogen or used for fuel in muscle, liver and adipose (fat) tissue.

As discussed, the body can store carbohydrates as glycogen in both the liver and muscle. These stores can be mobilized relatively quickly and act as main fuel source for moderate to high-intensity exercise, typical of a rugby training session or match play. However, the body's capacity for carbohydrate storage is limited (~400g and 100g for muscle and liver, respectively). It is therefore apparent that optimization of carbohydrate storage prior to match play is essential. In the applied context of rugby there is little data that demonstrates the impact of carbohydrate on performance, however carbohydrate has been investigated in other high-intensity intermittent team sports such as soccer. As a short working example, in a classical study carried out before a soccer game, glycogen was seen to be approximately 450mmol.kg⁻¹ dry weight. This value reduced to 225mmol.kg⁻¹ dry weight after the game (Krustrup et al., 2006).

The major findings from this study indicated that:

- The players started the game with what would be stated as sub-optimal muscle glycogen, probably due to an inadequate diet in the days leading into the game.
- Significant reductions in muscle glycogen were observed post-game.
- 50 per cent of the muscle fibres examined were almost empty, mainly in the Type 2 (fast) fibres, which are needed for sprinting and high-intensity work.

Given the necessity for high-intensity activity in rugby, this data demonstrates clearly an important role of carbohydrates for rugby performance.

A major consideration prior to the discussion of optimizing carbohydrate intake for training and performance is that not all carbohydrates are equal in that they produce varying responses in blood glucose. The change in blood glucose carbohydrates bring about allows us to categorize them based on glycemic index (GI). As such, carbohydrates may be grouped into the following:

- High GI (HGI; producing the most profound increase in blood sugar).
- Moderate GI (MGI; moderate change in blood glucose).
- Low GI (LGI; lowest increase in blood sugar).

Some common examples of HGI, MGI and LGI foods can be found in Table 4.1. Additionally, an extensive reference to glycemic index values for a variety of foods may be found in Atkinson et al. (2008). Consideration for the GI of carbohydrates sources allows for the manipulation of how quickly sugars are delivered into the circulation, therefore increasing availability to the muscle and liver.

## Table 4.1: Examples of Common LGI and HGI Foods

| LGI | HGI |
| --- | --- |
| Muesli | White bread |
| Milk | Cornflakes |
| Lentils | White rice |
| Greek yoghurt | Crisps |
| Porridge (rolled oats) | Soft drink/soda |
| Bran | Boiled potatoes |
| Quinoa | Baguettes |
| Baked beans | Doughnuts |
| Sweet potatoes | Jelly beans |
| Apple juice | Scones |

Due to the training demands throughout the week, it is advisable to aim for ≤3g.kg$^{-1}$ per day of carbohydrates for lighter training days and 4–5g.kg$^{-1}$ of carbohydrates per day from LGI sources for intense training days (i.e. two training sessions in one day). Such recommendations appear to be upheld in practice with reports of elite European rugby players consuming 3.3 ± 0.7 and 4.14 ± 0.4g.kg$^{-1}$ of carbohydrates on pre-season training days for forwards and backs, respectively (Bradley et al., 2015). Players who are identified as needing to lose adiposity may benefit from morning moderate intensity training (Achten and Jeukendrup, 2003) prior to carbohydrate consumption. Protein intake must be optimized if such practice is adopted in order to preserve lean mass (see protein section).

The match demands of rugby require differing strategies to training. Although lower carbohydrate intakes are beneficial in the training week for augmenting the training response and elevating fat oxidation, the day prior to and the day of match play warrant higher intakes of carbohydrates to ensure maximal exercise intensities can be sustained (i.e. players start match play with optimal muscle glycogen levels). On the day prior to match play, 6–8g.kg$^{-1}$ body mass of LGI carbohydrate is advisable. On match day, the pre-match meal should be consumed approximately three hours before kick-off and consist of 1–3g.kg$^{-1}$ body mass of carbohydrates. During the match, 30–60g.h$^{-1}$ of carbohydrate from HGI sources such as carbohydrate drinks or gels should be consumed. Following match play, there is an approximate two-hour window in which carbohydrates can be rapidly replenished through the intake of HGI carbohydrates (Jentjens and Jeukendrup, 2003). It is therefore vital that rapidly digested carbohydrate sources are made available to players immediately post-match at a rate of 1.2g.kg$^{-1}$ per hour, especially if there is a short turnaround before the next game. The day following match play (i.e. recovery day), carbohydrate intake should remain high at 4–6g.kg$^{-1}$ body mass in order to replenish fully the depleted carbohydrate stores.

### PROTEINS

Proteins have an extensive repertoire of functions and because of this are crucial for a variety of processes in the human body. It is important to consider that proteins are synthesized from amino acids and degraded to amino acids simultaneously throughout the day. Constant muscle protein turnover also allows for a mechanism of protein maintenance by recycling damaged proteins and replacing them with new proteins. In terms of exercise adaptation (i.e. muscle hypertrophy) it is necessary to accrete proteins by muscle protein synthesis (MPS) quicker than they are degraded (muscle protein breakdown; MPB) frequently throughout the day.

To achieve a net positive protein balance, MPS must be stimulated frequently throughout

**Fig. 4.1: Muscle protein balance during the waking hours of the day. The blue star represents a bout of resistance exercise and protein consumption. Green stars denote protein consumption alone. Note that resistance exercise sensitizes the muscle to protein feeding. More time spent with MPS exceeding MPB results in a net positive protein balance.**

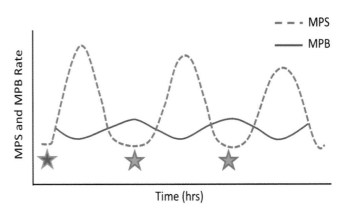

the day, as depicted in Fig. 4.1. Protein consumed in the diet or exercise can stimulate MPS. Notably, however, although resistance exercise stimulates potently MPS (Phillips et al., 1997) it is necessary to consume protein following the exercise bout to further stimulate MPS, resulting in the net positive balance in muscle proteins (Levenhagen et al., 2001). Resistance exercise sensitizes skeletal muscle to amino acids so subsequent protein feeds following the bout of exercise produce greater rates of MPS (Moore et al., 2012). This training-nutrient interaction enhances the adaptive response observed as a result of repeated training stimuli (super-compensatory effect). Such scientific background can inform applied practice as to the quantity, frequency and timing of protein ingestion to maximize training adaptation and recovery.

Regarding the quantity of protein required to maintain a protein balance, the UK Department of Health 2013 national guidelines suggest the reference nutrient intake (RNI) of protein for an average 70kg man is 0.8g. kg⁻¹ of body mass per day. Others argue this is a conservative value and suggest higher daily intakes are necessary for the athlete in the range of 1.4–1.7g.kg.day⁻¹ (Phillips, 2012). Rugby players, in particular, are likely to meet or exceed the higher end of these guidelines (Bradley et al., 2015). The absolute value per

day (i.e. g.kg.day⁻¹) can be somewhat deceptive, as the timing of protein intake and the amount of protein per serving are also very important considerations. Indeed, it is apparent that fluctuations in meal to meal MPS are extremely important in determining gain and loss of muscle mass (Breen and Churchward-Venne, 2012, Churchward-Venne et al., 2012, Phillips et al., 2009). Practically, we may therefore advise that protein intake is spread across five to six servings, approximately three hours apart especially prior to, and immediately following, exercise instead of incorporating it into three main meals during the day. This does not necessarily mean large doses of protein must be consumed at each serving as current research evidence suggests approximately 20–30g of protein is optimal for stimulating MPS (Moore et al., 2012). Rugby players may also benefit from protein ingested prior to sleep as this has been shown to be digested and absorbed effectively during the night, increasing plasma amino acid availability and stimulating post-exercise MPS during overnight sleep, thus enhancing recovery (Res et al., 2012).

In order to complete the picture of what constitutes optimal protein intake throughout the day, it is appropriate to discuss the ideal type of protein. For the athlete, the primary focus should be on obtaining whole protein from natural sources in meat, fish, nuts, grains and dairy produce since these sources contain an array of amino acids, fats and a variety of micronutrients when compared to supplemental protein. Casein (milk protein), whey protein (obtained as a by-product from cheese production) and soy protein are typical supplemental proteins used in elite rugby.

Following a bout of resistance training, rapidly digested proteins are preferable to increase plasma amino acid availability quickly to the muscle for MPS. Food sources such as white fish and chicken are digested more easily and may therefore be opted for around the time of training sessions and match play as opposed to red meats that are digested more slowly but are still capable of stimulating MPS. If supplemental protein is more practical around training sessions, whey protein ingestion results in greater MPS post-exercise compared with casein or soy-based protein (Phillips et al., 2009, Tang et al., 2009). This is likely to be as a result of the rapid appearance of amino acids in the blood following consumption of whey. Interestingly, the highest rates of MPS following exercise and whey feeding correlated with peak leucine (essential amino acid; EAA) concentration (Tang et al., 2009). This observation has been replicated in subsequent studies showing leucine plays a key role in switching on MPS, acting as a metabolic regulator (Tang et al., 2009, Pennings et al., 2011). However, we also know leucine is unlikely to maintain the anabolic signal without a range of amino acids found in whole proteins (Churchward-Venne et al., 2014, Phillips, 2004).

A common goal for many players at some point during the season is to lose unnecessary fat mass. As a result, fasted training sessions and caloric restriction are often employed. During caloric restriction an increase in MPB is likely as a mechanism to decrease metabolically active tissue in the face of less energy to fuel metabolic processes. It is therefore paramount

## Table 4.2: List of Common Protein Rich Food Sources Giving Approximately 20g of Protein

**Animal Sources**
1 x chicken / turkey fillet
1 x fish fillet (e.g. 100g standard salmon fillet)
1 x small tin of tuna
3 medium eggs
200g cottage cheese (⅔ small tub)
200g Greek yoghurt

**Non-Animal Sources**
150g quorn mince (75g is a typical portion)
400g red kidney beans (1 large tin)
300g chick peas (⅔ large tin)
100g almonds

**Liquid Sources**
Whey/caesin protein shake
1 x pint of milk

that during caloric restriction and fasted training protein intake is elevated. Research tells us daily protein intakes of 2.3–3.1g.kg$^{-1}$ fat free mass may be necessary depending on the severity of caloric restriction and leanness (Helms et al., 2014). Finally, protein feeding prior to sleep is an effective strategy for enhancing overnight recovery. Casein results in a slower appearance of amino acids in the circulation and ingested prior to sleep is shown to provide a sustained delivery of them during the overnight fast, stimulating MPS throughout the night (Res et al., 2012).

FATS
Dietary fats have received bad press in the past due to their generalized correlation with heart disease. However, this view is changing rapidly and a thorough understanding of individual fats is essential for any sports nutritionist. It is important to consider the main types of dietary fat, presented in Fig. 4.2.

**Fig. 4.2: Basic classification system and examples of common dietary fats.**

| Trans |
| --- |
| French fries |
| Pastries |
| Margarine |
| Fast food |

| Saturated |
| --- |
| Coconut oil |
| Almonds |
| Palm oil |
| Butter |
| Red Meats |

| Unsaturated |
| --- |

| Monounsaturated fatty acids (MUFA) | Polyunsaturated fatty acids |
| --- | --- |
| Avocado Cashew nuts | Essential fatty acids Omega-3 ($\omega$-3) |
| | Mackerel Tuna Salmon Herring |

Historically, saturated fats have received the worst reputation and we are often told to consume them in moderation, whereas unsaturated fats have been classed as the good fats. Saturated fats are found in many natural food sources, as listed in Fig 4.2. There is little justification for omitting saturated fat from the diet and, furthermore, research evidence suggests removing saturated fats and replacing them with refined CHO such as sugary drinks is likely to cause greater metabolic damage (Hu, 2010). It is wiser to pay careful consideration to the type of saturated fat athletes consume. As an example, coconut oil (containing lauric acid), despite containing high quantities of saturated fat, decreases the total-to-HDL cholesterol ratio, due to an increase in HDL cholesterol. From a practical perspective this means educating players on the best sources of saturated fats to include in their diet as opposed to imposing a blanket ban on dietary fat.

Trans fats also have a bad reputation. However, in contrast to saturated fat, this status is justified. Trans fats are, in fact, unsaturated fats although their structure affects the physiochemical and functional properties of the fatty acids, having adverse effects in the body. Trans fats should therefore be removed from any athlete's diet since they offer no health benefits. They increase LDL cholesterol and lower HDL, thus making them a major risk factor for cardiovascular disease.

Unsaturated fats offer clear health benefits and should be included in an athlete's diet through the intake of oily fish and nuts. Unsaturated fats can be subdivided into monounsaturated fatty acids (MUFA) and polyunsaturated fatty acids (PUFA). The essential fatty acids (EFA; $\omega$-3 and $\omega$-6) belong to PUFA and, apart from being essential for normal physiological function, reduce cardiovascular disease risk. Research evidence suggests the ratio of $\omega$-6:$\omega$-3 should be approximately 4:1, although investigations have shown western diets are more likely to be in the ratio of 16:1 (Simopoulos, 2002). In applied practice, it is uncommon to see rugby players that attain the optimal ratio of 4:1. In order to correct this ratio and move towards optimal health, players should be encouraged to consume food rich in $\omega$-3 (Fig. 4.2).

In terms of total fat intake in the rugby player's diet, it is advised that approximately $1g.kg^{-1}$ body mass of dietary fat (from healthy natural fats) should be consumed daily. This equates to about 30 per cent of total calorie intake per day. Dietary analysis of elite European rugby union players suggests they meet such guidelines. However, as mentioned

**Table 4.3: Common Minerals That Athletes (Non-Pregnant Adults) May Be Deficient in, Their Physiological Role And Typical Food Sources. Data taken from www.food.gov.uk (Minerals, 2003)**

| Mineral | Physiological Role | Food source | RNI |
|---------|-------------------|-------------|-----|
| Calcium | Important in muscle contraction and transmission of nerve impulses. Involved in developing strong bones | All dairy products including milk, cheese and yoghurt. Small fish with bones (e.g. sardines), beans and broccoli | 700mg/day |
| Iron | Important in the transport of oxygen | Red meat, liver, broccoli, spinach, fortified cereals, eggs, dried fruits, nuts and seeds | 8.7mg males 6.7mg females |
| Magnesium | Muscle contraction and transmission of nerve impulses | Meats and dairy. Vegetables and potatoes, bread and cereals, nuts (brazil, almonds and cashews), mushrooms | 300mg males 270mg females |
| Zinc | Assists immune function and is an antioxidant. Helps protein digestion, and assists in some energy pathways | Liver, kidney, red meat, seafood, poultry, milk, whole grain, leafy and root veg | 5.5–9.5mg males 4–7mg females |

earlier, attention must be paid to the ratio of ω-6:ω-3 (Bradley *et al.*, 2015).

## Micronutrient Requirements

In addition to the water, fat and protein that compose the human body, there are a number of elements that must be supplied from dietary sources to maintain normal physiological function, as the body itself does not have the capacity to manufacture them. These elements are termed minerals and given they are present in most plants and animals it is unlikely a person will be deficient in them (Table 4.3). The human body also requires vitamins for diverse biochemical functions and it is necessary we obtain small amounts of them from dietary sources since the body cannot produce sufficient quantities. In sports

where fat loss strategies are common, there is an increased risk of micronutrient deficiency since food consumption is restricted to induce a calorie deficit (Manore, 2002, Clarkson, 1991). In such cases, athletes may add supplemental vitamins and minerals to the diet. Care should be taken and adequate attention given to RNI values when supplementing with vitamins and minerals as doing so in large quantities can be toxic, particularly with minerals since there is a small margin between the RNI and a toxic dose. Moreover, supplementing with high doses of vitamins that function as antioxidants may hamper the response to training as oxidants themselves are important molecular signals (Close and Jackson, 2014). As an example, high dose vitamin C and E supplementation have been demonstrated to hamper the exercise induced adaptation to endurance training (Paulsen *et al.*, 2014).

**Table 4.4: Major Fat Soluble Vitamins, Their Physiological Role, Typical Food Sources, the Likelihood of Deficiency in Athletes and RNI for Non-Pregnant Adults. Data taken from www.food.gov.uk (Minerals, 2003)**

| Vitamin | Physiological Role | Food source | RNI |
|---|---|---|---|
| A | Antioxidant. Eye function, cell growth and division | Oily fish, liver, egg yolk, milk, butter, carrots and apricots | 700µg – males 600µg – females |
| D | Facilitates the use of calcium, cell differentiation, immunity, skin cell development and muscle function | Oily fish, eggs and fortified foods | No DRVs because of sun- related synthesis 0.01mg/day advised if confined indoors |
| E | Major fat-soluble antioxidant. Growth and development | Almonds, peanuts, shrimp, sunflower seeds and corn oil | No DRVs but 4mg for males and 3mg for females considered adequate |
| K | Essential for blood clotting and formation of some proteins | Broccoli, cabbage, liver, cauliflower and spinach | No DRVs but 1µg/kg body weight considered adequate |

Vitamin D is an exception to the rest of the vitamins since it is more structurally related to a steroid hormone than a vitamin. Furthermore, vitamin $D_3$ is synthesized in the skin from sun exposure with little available from dietary sources. A number of research investigations have found athletes who live and train indoors or reside at northerly latitudes have a high prevalence of vitamin D deficiency as a consequence of poor sunlight exposure and sunscreen application when sunlight exposure is sought.

Deficiency of vitamin D may have important consequences for the athlete as research suggests it is associated with increased infection risk, poor bone health and cardiovascular diseases. It also affects muscle function and the muscle regeneration process. Vitamin D concentrations in the blood do, however,

respond in a dose-dependent manner to supplemental forms of vitamin $D_3$ (Heaney, 2003). Vitamin $D_2$ is also available in supplemental form but has a relative potency of 9.5:1 when compared with vitamin $D_3$. Currently, a dose of 4,000IU.day$^{-1}$ is believed to be safe and is effective at elevating and maintaining serum vitamin D concentrations into the sufficient range.

## Hydration and Rugby Performance

Monitoring the hydration status of rugby players is essential to optimize performance and preserve health. Studies have shown dehydration (the process of losing water) beyond certain thresholds (usually greater than 2–5 per cent) can lead to decreases in exercise

## Table 4.5: Major Water Soluble Vitamins, their Physiological Role, Typical Food Sources, the Likelihood of Deficiency in Athletes and RNI for Non-Pregnant Adults. Data taken from www.food.gov.uk (Minerals, 2003)

| Vitamin | Physiological Role | Good Food Sources | RNI |
|---|---|---|---|
| C | Major water-soluble antioxidant. Iron absorption. Important in skin, gum and blood vessel health | Asparagus, grapefruit, limes, oranges, lemons, broccoli and sprouts | 40mg |
| $B_1$ (Thiamin) | Important in carbohydrate and amino acid metabolism (energy) | Almonds, liver, peanuts, whole grain bread and cereals, green peas | 1.4mg males 1.0mg females |
| $B_2$ (Riboflavin) | Important in carbohydrate metabolism (energy) | Asparagus, broccoli, spinach, banana, mushrooms, tuna and dairy products | No DRVs but 1.1 and 1.3mg/day for females and males prevents deficiencies |
| $B_3$ (Niacin) | Important in carbohydrate, fat and amino acid metabolism (energy) | Liver, meat and fish, milk, eggs, avocados, tomatoes, legumes and carrots | 17mg males 13mg females |
| $B_5$ (Pantothenic Acid) | Needed to synthesize co-enzyme A and important in carbohydrate, fat and amino acid metabolism (energy) | Chicken, beef, potatoes, tomatoes, liver, egg yolk, broccoli and whole grains | No DRV but 3mg considered safe |
| $B_6$ (Pyridoxine) | Haemoglobin formation and important in carbohydrate metabolism (energy) | Banana, fish, spinach, tuna, egg yolk and chicken | 1.4mg males 1.2mg females |
| $B_{12}$ (Cobalamin) | Haemoglobin formation and prevention of anaemia. Carbohydrate metabolism (energy). Plays role in nervous system | Beef, dairy products, chicken, egg yolk and tuna | 1.5µg |
| Folic acid | Cell division and important in the production of some proteins | Meat, liver, green leafy vegetables, legumes and fruit | 200µg |
| Biotin | Important in carbohydrate, fat and amino acid metabolism (energy) | Egg yolk, liver, kidney and meat | No DRV but 10–200µg considered safe and adequate |

performance (Cheuvront and Kenefick, 2014) and increases the perception of effort during exercise (Barr, 1999). The threshold associated with a decrease in exercise performance can vary dependent on the environmental condition, with warm, more humid environments causing greater decreases in exercise performance. Due to the complexity surrounding the movement and skill demands of rugby, the effects of hydration status on players' performance is difficult to delineate. For example, dehydration has not been shown to decrease sprint ability (Judelson et al., 2007), although there is evidence it reduces endurance capacity (Cheuvront and Kenefick, 2014).

Evaluating the physiological process of dehydration would infer rugby players should stay in fluid balance during the training week and also in preparation for match play. During exercise, players sweat to maintain core body temperature. The sweat loss in Super League rugby league and Premiership rugby union players is approximately 2.0 ± 0.7 (O'Hara et al., 2010) and 1.4 ± 1.0L (Jones et al., 2015) during match play. Further, Premiership rugby union players have been shown to have a fluid loss of 1.0 ± 0.4 and 0.6 ± 0.5L during field and gym training (Jones et al., 2015). When players sweat, fluid and electrolytes are lost from the extracellular (i.e. all fluid outside of cells) compartment, which is further equilibrated from intracellular (i.e. all fluid inside of cells) compartments (Baker and Jeukendrup, 2014). Large sweat losses can result in a decrease in blood volume (increase in blood viscosity), which causes an increase in cardiovascular stress (Montain and Coyle, 1992). Further, fluid imbalances (excessive losses or gains) can result in electrolyte disturbances, which can have a negative effect on muscular function (i.e. muscular cramps (Cleary et al., 2007)).

Regarding hydration status, rugby players should ensure they remain in a euhydrated state when not exercising. If this is achieved, the typical sweat losses during exercise can be tolerated and are unlikely to affect exercise performance when players can drink to thirst. If players start exercise dehydrated, this may have a negative effect on performance. During rugby league match play drinking approximately 0.9 and 0.3L in the hour prior to kick-off and at half-time, and approximately 0.2L during the first and second half has been shown to be adequate in maintaining fluid balance (body mass loss 1.3 per cent [O'Hara et al., 2010]). Within rugby union an overall fluid intake of approximately 1.0, 1.2 and 1.0L during match play, field, and gym training has been shown to maintain fluid balance (body mass loss of 1.0, 0.3 and 0.1 per cent [Jones et al., 2015]). Despite these recommendations, the environmental condition and individual variability should be a consideration for players and coaches. More fluid may be required in warmer environmental conditions to offset greater sweat loss, whereas less fluid maybe required in cooler environmental conditions.

The ideal body mass loss appears to be between 1.0 and 2.0 per cent during exercise to maintain electrolyte balance (Jones et al., 2015). A body mass loss less than this may result in a dilution of electrolytes and a body mass loss greater than this may cause a reduction in exercise workload (i.e. pacing (Edwards and Noakes, 2009)). Adjustments of fluid intake should be made to achieve the desired body mass loss.

Measuring hydration status is also a consideration for coaches and players. A common measure of hydration status is analyzing the concentration of urine, either through osmolality, refractometry, colour or specific gravity. Due to the complexity surrounding fluid balance, urine samples may not provide a precise measure of hydration status. Typically, if a player is hydrated they will likely produce dilute urine, whereas if an individual is hypohy-drated, commonly known as dehydrated, they will produce concentrated urine. This may not always be true because if a rugby player consumes a large volume of fluid, the body will produce dilute urine to protect concen-trations in different fluid compartments. The urine sample will infer the player is hydrated, whereas they may have a reduction in total body water.

A simple way of monitoring hydration status is body mass. Daily changes, greater than normal day-to-day variability ($\pm\sim$1.5 per cent) in body mass, are likely due to the change in fluid volume. Measuring body mass first thing in the morning nude is a good way of assessing the hydration status of a player. Also, measuring body mass pre- and post-exercise can help determine the level of dehydration an athlete has experienced. Body mass assessments should be performed with athletes wearing minimal clothing, ideally only underwear and being towel-dry. As with daily changes in body mass, the change during exercise is likely due to fluid balance. It should be noted other losses do occur in addition to sweat (King et al., 2008), although within the field these are hard to determine. If practitioners want to determine sweat loss, the addition of fluid intake and urine output should be accounted for. Providing players with individually labelled pre-weighed drinks containers allows the easy determination of fluid intake. Likewise, providing players with individually labelled pre-weighed jerry cans also allows easy measures of urine output.

To determine sweat loss, the following equation can be used;
Sweat loss = body mass change + fluid intake – urine output.

## Ergogenic Aids for Rugby Performance

There is a common misconception with rugby players that supplements are essential to a suc-cessful nutritional plan. However, supplements are, as the name infers, not a substitute for real food but supplemental to a good diet. Once a player's diet has been optimized and an under-standing of basic nutrition is in place, there may be some instances where a targeted supple-ment plan may be of use. Only qualified nutri-tionists should prescribe a supplementation plan, following the most recent rugby specific doping regulations. It is crucial that if a rugby player does use supplements only those from companies that have their products indepen-dently batch tested are used. A commonly used laboratory that performs such testing is the LGC group and on its website www.lgcgroup.com you can find a list of companies that rou-tinely test their products. Rugby players should also be aware that, although a product has been tested, this does not guarantee the supplement is drug free. In the author's own practice, the following questions are always asked to help decide if a supplement will be advised:

- Is there a need for the supplement (cannot get in a normal diet)?
- Is there clear scientific rationale for the use of the supplement?
- Are there no health risks associated with taking the supplement?
- Are there no banned substances in the supplement?
- Is there an independently tested version of the product available?

If the answer to all five of these questions is yes then there may be grounds to consider the use of such a supplement.

Table 4.6 lists some of the most common sports supplements reportedly used in professional sport and observed by the

## Table 4.6: Commonly Used Sports Supplements by Rugby Players

| Supplement | Ergogenic Claims | Reasons not to take | Common Dose | Further reading |
|---|---|---|---|---|
| **Creatine** | Improve speed, strength and power | Increase mass, anecdotal reports of increased cramping | 5g 4 times per day for 4–5 days, followed by 3g per day Or 3g per day for 30 days | (Birch et al., 1994, Casey and Greenhaff, 2000, Tarnopolsky, 2010) |
| **Caffeine** | Prolong endurance performance, increase lipid oxidation, increase mental alertness | Some athletes naïve to caffeine may get side effects including nausea, headache and tremors at high dose | 2–4mg/kg body mass Take 45–60min pre exercise | (Tarnopolsky and Cupido, 2000, Tarnopolsky, 2010, Tarnopolsky, 2008) |
| **Beta Alanine** | Increases muscle carnosine, which is the main intracellular buffer of hydrogen ions thus improving high-intensity exercise | Not all events require an intense sprint. Some athletes will experience skin tingling, which may cause distress | 3g per day Must be taken daily for about 4 weeks before benefits are noticed | (Sale et al., 2010, Sale et al., 2011) |
| **Branched Chain Amino Acids** | Prevent central fatigue. Increase lean mass | Little evidence to support central fatigue hypothesis. Little evidence to support increase in lean mass if consuming an appropriate diet | 5g taken 2–3 times per day | (Blomstrand, 2001, Davis, 1995, Meeusen and Watson, 2007, Williams, 1999) |
| **Green tea extract** | High in green tea catechins and epogalocatechin gallate (EGCG), which is claimed to increase fat oxidation during exercise | Contains caffeine, which may not be desired by all athletes. Most evidence so far is in animal studies | The amount in a cup of green tea is likely to be too small. 300mg taken 3 times per day used in research studies | (Maki et al., 2009, Rains et al., 2011, Venables et al., 2008, Westerterp-Plantenga, 2010) |

| Supplement | Ergogenic Claims | Reasons not to take | Common Dose | Further reading |
|---|---|---|---|---|
| **Sodium Bicarbonate** | A potent buffer preventing deleterious changes in acid-base balance and thus can delay fatigue in high intensity exercise | Only suitable for high intensity exercise. Major risk of gastro-intestinal (GI) side effects | 0.2–0.3g/kg body mass. Consume acutely 40–60min pre exercise | (Baguet et al., 2010, Bishop and Claudius, 2005, McNaughton, 1992, McNaughton et al., 2008) |
| **HMB** | A derivative of leucine that can increase muscle mass and strength through its anti-catabolic properties. Reduce post exercise muscle damage/soreness | Limited evidence of effects in trained individuals | 3g per day | (Palisin and Stacy, 2005, Slater et al., 2001, Slater and Jenkins, 2000, Zanchi et al., 2011) |
| **Vitamin D** | Correction of a deficiency is claimed to improve bone health and muscle function | High dose supplementation could result in problems such as hypercalcaemia and kidney stones | Requires individual consultation with a clinician | (Owens et al., 2014) |
| **Bovine Colostrum** | Rich in immune and growth factors. Increase lean mass, improve immune function and promote gut health | Potential for elevated IGF–1 levels and thus failed drug test | Various doses used usually between 10–20g per day | (Buckley, 2002, Buckley et al., 2002, Davison and Diment, 2010, Marchbank et al., 2011, Shing et al., 2009) |
| **Conjugated Linoleic Acid (CLA)** | CLA are essential fatty acids reported to promote loss of body fat and increase lean muscle mass | Limited studies in athletes. Most positive data is from animal studies | 1.4–6.8g/day | (Kreider et al., 2002, Schoeller et al., 2009, Terpstra, 2004) |

**Table 4.7: Example of the Training Week with Emphasis on the Carbohydrate Intake**

| | Match day | | | | | | |
|---|---|---|---|---|---|---|---|
| | −5 | −4 | −3 | −2 | −1 | GAME | +1 |
| Carb load | LOW (2–3g/kg) | | | MEDIUM (3–5g/kg) | HIGH (5–8g/kg) | MEDIUM (3–5g/kg) | |
| Reason | Body composition reasons (i.e. reduction in body fat) and enhance training adaptations | | | Start to prepare for game day | Load for game day | Top up stores and fuel the game | Recover from game day |

authors in their experience. The reported claims of the supplement, common dose and reasons not to take the supplement are also listed along with the most suitable references for further reading.

## PRACTICAL APPLICATION

*Case Study looking at typical meals for a rugby player during a week and on game day.*

So far in this chapter, we have explored the roles of macronutrients, micronutrients and hydration in rugby performance. We have also discussed the quantities and timing of ingestion for these different nutrients, so it is appropriate we put this into perspective by providing a case study example of typical dietary practices of a rugby player on a training day, pre match day and match day. It is important to emphasize this is a 'typical plan' that may not be suitable for all players and ultimately it is important diets are tailored to individual players dependent upon their specific needs. In this plan, protein and fat intake are generally kept constant whereas the carbohydrate requirements fluctuate dependent upon the training requirements and the timing in relation to match day. We have classed match day as a medium carbohydrate day for comfort reasons. If the player has eaten well the day before match day, this day is best described as a 'topping up stores' day rather than a 'loading day'.

Typically during the early part of the training week players may choose to reduce their carbohydrate intake and, as a consequence, their total calorific intake. It is important to stress this does not mean a 'no carb' or a 'ketogenic' diet (i.e. typically <50g carbohydrate), just that total intake would be about 2–3g/kg body weight. However, if players are attempting to gain body-weight or engage in high-intensity prolonged training, they would be recommended to increase their carbohydrate (and thus total calorific) intake significantly.

Given the players are relatively low in carbohydrates during the week, it is important they increase their intake towards match day significantly in an attempt to ensure maximum muscle glycogen stores. This is advisable for all players and may take some effort on the player's part to achieve these targets. In practice, we have found many players are uncomfortable trying to eat 10g.kg$^{-1}$ body mass of carbohydrate and manage very well attempting to intake 6–8g.kg$^{-1}$ body mass. Examples of a typical day's nutrition intake when loading ready for a game can be seen in Table 4.9.

## Table 4.8: Example of a Meal Plan on a Low CHO Training Day for a Typical 90kg Rugby Player

| Timing | Food | Total Macronutrient Content |
|---|---|---|
| 07:00 - Breakfast | 3 poached eggs<br>100g smoked salmon<br>2 slice (44g) wholemeal toast<br>100g Greek yoghurt<br>Green tea<br>500ml water | CHO 33g<br>Fat 29g<br>Protein 59g<br>Kcal 629 |
| 10:00 – Post weights | 30g whey protein<br>100g Greek yoghurt | CHO 10g<br>Fat 9g<br>Protein 31g<br>Kcal 246 |
| 12:30 – Lunch | Chicken (1 breast)<br>½ avocado<br>1 wholemeal wrap<br>100g diced red onion<br>red peppers<br>Kale and baby leaf salad<br>1 tbsp olive oil to dress salad<br>500ml water | CHO 47g<br>Fat 36g<br>Protein 49g<br>Kcal 708 |
| 15:00 – Post-field session | 100g Greek yoghurt<br>100g mixed berries | CHO 15 g<br>Fat 7g<br>Protein 11g<br>Kcal 168 |
| 18:00 – Dinner | 120g salmon fillet<br>200g roasted sweet potato wedges<br>100g broccoli<br>100g cauliflower<br>1 tbsp olive oil over vegetables<br>500ml water | CHO 59g<br>Fat 32g<br>Protein 30g<br>Kcal 644 |
| 22:30 – Pre-bedtime snack | 150g Cottage cheese<br>1 tbsp chives<br>Ryvita<br>250ml whole milk | CHO 30g<br>Fat 18g<br>Protein 30g<br>Kcal 400 |
| | **Daily total** | **CHO 195g**<br>**Fat 131g**<br>**Protein 210g**<br>**Kcal 2,796** |

## Table 4.9: Example of a Meal Plan on a High CHO Day (Day before a Game) for a Typical 90kg Rugby Player

| Timing | Food | Total Macronutrient Content |
|---|---|---|
| 07:00 – Breakfast | Large bowl of muesli<br>3 scrambled eggs with baked beans and 3 slices toast<br>Glass of fruit juice | CHO: 165g<br>Fat: 56g<br>Protein: 49g<br>Kcal: 1,360 |
| 10:00 – Snack | Bagel with nut butter and jam<br>Fruit and Greek yoghurt<br>500ml water | CHO: 82g<br>Fat: 9g<br>Protein: 20g<br>Kcal: 486 |
| 12:30 – Lunch | Salmon fillet (1 breast)<br>Large portion basmati rice<br>Selection of vegetables<br>Kale and baby leaf salad<br>1 tbsp olive oil to dress salad<br>Fruit salad and Greek yoghurt<br>500ml water | CHO: 99g<br>Fat: 37g<br>Protein: 50g<br>Kcal: 929 |
| 14:30 – Captain's run | 500ml sports drink during the session<br>60g carb 30g protein recovery drink post-session | CHO: 94g<br>Fat: 2g<br>Protein: 24g<br>Kcal: 491 |
| 17:30 – Dinner | Chicken (1 breast)<br>Potato wedges (1 large 369g potato)<br>Fresh vegetables and side salad<br>Rhubarb and apple crumble (homemade) with custard<br>500ml water | CHO: 147g<br>Fat: 22g<br>Protein: 61g<br>Kcal: 1,030 |
| 19:00 – Supper | Mixed berries with Greek yoghurt | CHO: 10g<br>Fat: 7g<br>Protein: 11g<br>Kcal: 147 |
| 22:30 – Pre-bedtime snack | Casein-based protein shake | CHO: 4g<br>Fat: 1g<br>Protein: 18g<br>Kcal: 96 |
| | **Daily total** | **CHO: 601g**<br>**Fat: 134g**<br>**Protein: 233g**<br>**Kcal: 4,539** |

## Table 4.10: Examples of Pre-Match Meals for a Typical 90kg Rugby Player

| Options | | Total Macronutrient Content |
|---|---|---|
| 1 | Large bowl of cereal with semi-skimmed milk + 500ml sports drink + 2 slices of wholemeal toast with peanut butter + 1 large banana | CHO: 148g <br> Fat: 40g <br> Protein: 39g <br> Kcal: 1,108 |
| 2 | Basmati rice + salmon fillet + 500ml sports drink + rice pudding | CHO: 184g <br> Fat: 19g <br> Protein: 38g <br> Kcal: 1,059 |
| 3 | Griddled chicken strips with fettuccini and a low-fat tomato-based sauce + mixed fruit and yoghurt + 500ml sports drink | CHO: 162g <br> Fat: 11g <br> Protein: 58g <br> Kcal: 979 |
| 4 | Homemade chicken burgers on a large wholegrain roll + potato wedges and side salad + 500ml sports drink | CHO: 161g <br> Fat: 7g <br> Protein: 52g <br> Kcal: 915 |

Rugby players commonly mistake the pre-match meal to be the most important meal for match day performance and this can often lead to poor practices (e.g. consuming the wrong quantity and type of foods as well as doing so too close to kick-off). Assuming players have correctly carbohydrate-loaded in the twenty-four to thirty-six hours prior to match day, the purpose of the pre-match meal is to simply *top up* carbohydrate stores and players should therefore be careful not to over eat at this time. The pre-match meal should be reasonably high in both carbohydrate (approximately $2g.kg^{-1}$ body mass) and protein content (e.g. 25–30g) and consumed about three hours pre kick-off to allow sufficient time for digestion and therefore consumption of high fibre (e.g. vegetables) and high fat foods (even those associated with protein sources such as red meat and cheese)

should be avoided given they slow down the rate of gastric emptying. Some examples of pre-game meals can be seen in Table 4.10.

Following the game it is important players refuel correctly. The goal of post-match nutrition is to replenish both muscle and liver glycogen stores as well as promoting protein synthesis to facilitate the repair of muscle tissue. Additionally, there is the obvious requirement of rehydration. The general consensus is consuming $1.2g.kg^{-1}.h^{-1}$ of carbohydrates for three to four hours is optimal to facilitate short-term glycogen re-synthesis (about 100g of carbohydrates for a typical rugby player). Importantly (and where possible), post-match feeding should begin immediately (i.e. in the changing room). These meals should also contain moderate protein intake to support post-exercise protein synthesis.

## Table 4.11: Example of Foods to be Consumed in the Changing Rooms Following a Game for a Typical 90kg Rugby Player

| Options | | Total Macronutrient Content |
|---|---|---|
| 1 | Recovery shake (3:1 CHO:PRO) | CHO: 90g<br>Fat: 2g<br>Protein: 30g<br>Kcal: 496 |
| 2 | Potato wedges (1.5 large potatoes) and chicken skewers | CHO: 94g<br>Fat: 3g<br>Protein: 44g<br>Kcal: 582 |
| 3 | Large bowl rice pudding with chopped banana and protein shake | CHO: 99g<br>Fat: 9g<br>Protein: 43g<br>Kcal: 620 |
| 4 | Two banana muffins and protein shake | CHO: 88g<br>Fat: 24g<br>Protein: 43g<br>Kcal: 741 |
| 5 | Chicken sandwich and large mixed fruit salad | CHO: 92g<br>Fat: 16.4g<br>Protein: 43g<br>Kcal: 688 |

## IMPLICATIONS AND RECOMMENDATIONS FOR PRACTICE

- LGI carbohydrate should be consumed daily and HGI carbohydrates avoided to prevent increases in fat mass. HGI carbohydrates should be consumed post-match to provide glucose rapidly to the muscle and liver as a substrate for glycogen resynthesis.

- Protein should be consumed every three hours, in close proximity to the end of a training session and before bed (0.25–0.30g.kg$^{-1}$ body mass) to build or maintain muscle mass. Total daily protein intake should be in the range of 1.4–1.6g.kg$^{-1}$ of body mass per day.

- Dietary fat should not be excluded from an athlete's diet and replacing saturated fats with refined carbohydrates is likely to be detrimental to health. Rugby players should incorporate a range of oily fish into their diet to meet omega-3 fatty acid requirements. Food sources containing trans fats should be avoided entirely.

- Eliminating food groups from diets (either due to food dislikes, allergies or moral reasons), calorie restriction, very low fat diets and lack of sunlight exposure may result in micronutrient deficiency. Mega-dosing with multi or single vitamins should be avoided. Variety in the diet will provide adequate micronutrients from a range of food sources.

- Ensuring players are hydrated prior to training or matches will mean players should not experience exercise-debilitating dehydration during exercise. Players should aim to lose 1–2 per cent of body mass during exercise to maintain electrolyte balance, which can be replaced post-exercise.

- Quality food sources should not be replaced with supplements (i.e. protein) unless it is practically difficult to meet total requirements for the day. Supplements should be taken only in consultation with a qualified nutritionist and be aware that even if a product has been tested, this does not guarantee the supplement is drug free.

# CHAPTER 5

# STRENGTH AND CONDITIONING FOR RUGBY

## *Paul Comfort*

## INTRODUCTION

Strength and conditioning refers to the preparatory training (excluding the skill-based components specific to the sporting tasks) performed in order to prepare players to not only cope with the demands of rugby but to be able to excel in these activities and therefore outperform their opponents. Strength and conditioning is generally thought of in two distinct components:

- Strength and power development (usually performed in the gym)
- Conditioning activities (predominantly performed in the field of play), which include training to enhance repeated sprint/effort ability. This also includes more skilled components such as speed and agility training; in the case of rugby this can also include wrestling skills.

Based on the importance of all components of physical development for rugby performance, the aim of this chapter is to explore appropriate methods to develop strength, power, aerobic capacity, speed and change of direction ability, all deemed important for

performance. The content will reflect the most up to date research and practices within the field. In addition, the chapter provides an example of the application of this research within a club setting.

## RESEARCH OVERVIEW

### Importance of Physical Attributes

Power is an essential component of sports performance, not just in short duration explosive activities (e.g. sprinting, jumping and throwing events) but also during decisive moments in team sports (e.g. acceleration, change of direction and jumping; [Gabbett *et al.*, 2011d]). The development of power within a rugby player's training programme is therefore essential. However, there are a variety of methods, including strength training, ballistic training, plyometrics and Olympic lifts, which are commonly used to increase power output (Cormie *et al.*, 2010), with no clear consensus regarding which methods or modes of training are optimal. What is clear is there are moderate to strong associations between power output and athletic performance in sports specific tasks (e.g. sprinting, jumping and tackling [Harris et al., 2010, Gabbett et al., 2011a, Sekulic et al., 2013, Cronin and Hansen, 2005, Cunningham et al., 2013]). Moreover, power output is one of the key determinants of tackling ability in rugby league (Gabbett et al., 2011c, Gabbett et al., 2011e) and, more importantly, both offensive and defensive performance in that code (Gabbett et al., 2011a), which is likely to be similar in rugby union.

Gabbett et al. (2011c) found lower body power and faster 10 and 40m sprint performance discriminated between match performance in terms of the number of tackles attempted, successful tackles and the number of tries scored (years of playing experience also demonstrated a positive relationship). In light of the fact that sprint performance is related to maximal strength (Comfort et al., 2012a, Wisloff et al., 2004, McBride et al., 2009) and power, along with a positive correlation between agility and hang power clean performance (Hori et al., 2008), it is imperative strength and conditioning training for rugby focuses on maximizing strength and power in the lower body. Furthermore, an increase in back squat strength has been shown to correspond to an improvement in short sprint performance (Comfort et al., 2012c, Seitz et al., 2014a).

Aerobic conditioning and repeated sprint ability are also essential within both codes of rugby due to the repeated high intensity efforts that occur throughout the game during both offensive and defensive phases (Austin et al., 2011c, Gabbett, 2012, Gabbett et al., 2011d). It is likely the performance of high intensity (90–95 per cent heart rate max for 4min) intervals (with a 3min recovery ~70 per cent heart rate max and repeated four times) twice per week, will enhance aerobic capacity even in well-trained rugby players, similar to

the protocols used in soccer (Helgerud et al., 2001, Helgerud et al., 2007, Hoff et al., 2002, McMillan et al., 2005). Such methods have recently been shown to be very effective in terms of maximizing aerobic fitness in rugby league players (Seitz et al., 2014b).

## Training for Power Development

A recent systematic review revealed upper and lower body strength and power can not only be maintained but developed during the competitive season in both codes of rugby by performing three to six sets of four to ten repetitions at 70–88 per cent 1–RM (i.e. one-repetition maximum) in a periodized programme (McMaster et al., 2013a). A longitudinal study by Baker (2013) showed strength, power and lean body mass can be increased progressively over the duration of a player's career, although larger increases are observed during the early years. This is extremely important as it demonstrates improvements in strength and power can be achieved during the long duration of the season, in both codes of rugby. Therefore, strength and conditioning coaches should focus on progressive periodized development of different physical attributes to ensure optimal performance.

### STRENGTH TRAINING

Strength training usually consists of compound (multi-joint) exercises (e.g. variations of squats, deadlifts, pull-ups and bench press) performed with relatively high loads (≥85–95 per cent of 1–RM), for four to six sets per muscle group of two to six repetitions, with a three to five minute rest between sets, two to three days per week (Baechle et al., 2008). Differences in the optimal intensity, sets, repetitions and frequency has previously been identified (Peterson et al., 2004, Peterson et al., 2005) for untrained (60 per cent 1–RM, four sets, three days per week), recreationally trained non-athletes (80 per cent 1–RM, four sets, two days per week) and trained athletes (85 per cent 1–RM, eight sets, two days per week).

Possibly the most commonly performed and extensively researched exercise for the development of lower body strength is the back squat, with a number of studies finding moderate to strong associations between maximal back squat strength and short sprint performance (McBride et al., 2009, Comfort et al., 2012a, Kirkpatrick and Comfort, 2013). In addition, Swinton et al. (2014) found relative strength (strength/body mass) was the strongest predictor of sprint, jump and change of direction performance. Research also demonstrates that as maximal back squat strength increases there is a concomitant increase in sprint performance, indicated by a decrease in sprint times over 5, 10 and 20m in well-trained rugby league players (Comfort et al., 2012c).

Greater maximal strength is also associated with greater power output (Stone et al., 2003a, Cormie et al., 2010a, Cormie et al., 2010b, Nuzzo et al., 2008, Baker, 2001c). Baker and Nance (1999) demonstrated a strong correlations between 3–RM back squat and squat jump performance, and even stronger correlations between 3–RM back squat and 1–RM hang power clean performance, in elite rugby league players. Nuzzo et al (2008) reported similarly strong correlations between 1–RM back squat and power clean performances, 1–RM back squat and vertical jump performance and 1–RM power clean and vertical jump performance. Furthermore, Stone et al. (2003a) observed stronger athletes (relative back squat 1–RM = 2.00 ± 0.24 kg/kg) generated much higher peak power during the countermovement jump and squat jump when compared to weaker athletes (1–RM = 1.21 ± 0.18kg/kg). These findings clearly demonstrate

an increase in strength results in an increase in power and athletic performance.

A commonly asked question is: 'How strong does an athlete need to be?' Maximizing strength levels has been shown to be more beneficial than high velocity power training in athletes with relatively low strength levels (those that can 1–RM squat <1.9 × body mass), whereas higher velocity power training in relatively strong athletes (those that can 1–RM squat ≥1.9 × body mass) appears to be more beneficial than focusing solely on strength development (Cormie et al., 2010a, Cormie et al., 2010b, Cormie et al., 2011, Stone et al., 2003a). Therefore, once an athlete can squat ≥1.9 × body mass a greater emphasis should be placed on power development via variations of the Olympic lifts and plyometrics, while maintaining strength levels. Variations of squatting movements (e.g. back squat and front squat) should be incorporated to provide variety, with the inclusion of some split stance (e.g. lunge and split squat variations) and unilateral (e.g. single leg squats and step-ups) exercises used to aid the development of lower limb control and transference to sport.

One issue with training power through normal strength training modes is the load has to be decelerated at the end of the range of motion, resulting in an altered force velocity profile, when compared to ballistic exercises where no deceleration is required. During traditional strength training exercises, such as the back squat, this can account for as much as 45 per cent of the entire range of motion, although this decreases as load increases (Newton et al., 1996a). Swinton et al. (2011b), however, found the inclusion of chain resistance (the chains represented 20 per cent and 40 per cent of the barbell mass) permitted force generation across a greater range of the concentric phase, with an increase in peak force and impulse.

## BALLISTIC TRAINING

Ballistic training consists usually of more dynamic versions of strength training exercises (e.g. speed squats and deadlifts), ideally with no deceleration phase during the final stages of the concentric phase. This is found in squat jumps (the athlete accelerates throughout the movement resulting in him or her leaving the ground at the end of the concentric phase) and bench press throws (the athlete accelerates the bar through the entire concentric phase and releases the bar at the end of the movement, thereby throwing the bar: to be caught on the descent, although there are obviously risks involved with catching the bar during a bench throw [Newton et al., 1996b]). Traditional recommendations include loads of 75–95 per cent 1–RM, for three to five sets of one to six repetitions, with rest periods of three to four minutes (Baechle et al., 2008). However, studies have identified the optimal loads to elicit peak power output for such exercises are substantially lower (Cormie et al., 2007a) than the loads traditionally recommended for such training, as these guidelines were based originally on performance of the Olympic lifts (Baechle et al., 2008). Multiple studies have demonstrated peak power during squat jumps is generally achieved with no or little additional external load (Cormie et al., 2007b). During squat jumps, therefore, it would be advantageous to use lighter loads (≤50 per cent 1–RM), possibly reducing load over time, to ensure maximal movement velocity and power output while maintaining maximal lower body strength with heavy load (≥85 per cent 1–RM), low volume (e.g. three sets of two to three repetitions) squats. Such training is likely to be complemented with the inclusion of some variations of the Olympic lifts.

## OLYMPIC LIFTS AND THEIR DERIVATIVES

Olympic lifts consist of the snatch and the clean and jerk, with strength and conditioning coaches incorporating numerous variations of these exercises into their players' training programmes. Olympic lifts (Fig. 5.1 and 5.2) are performed usually with the intent to move the bar as rapidly as possible for four to eight sets of one to six repetitions at loads of 75–90 per cent 1–RM, with rest periods between three to four minutes (Baechle et al., 2008). During these lifts the bar is accelerated throughout the whole of the concentric phase, removing the limitation of the deceleration phase associated with exercises such as the squat and deadlift, as highlighted previously (Newton et al., 1996).

In weightlifting competition, the snatch and clean are performed with the athlete catching the bar in a full depth squat position (i.e. thighs below parallel to the floor; see Fig. 5.3). In contrast, in rugby players' training the power snatch and power clean are used commonly as substitutes, where the athlete catches the bar in a quarter squat or alternatively in a split stance. Further variations can be seen in the starting position of the lift, where the bar can begin on the floor (as in competitive lifting), in the hang position (from just above the patella, with the athlete in what represents the mid-point of a Romanian Deadlift, with the shoulders in front of the bar (Fig. 5.1b), or from mid-thigh (bar resting mid-thigh while the athlete is in a semi-squatting position, with the shoulders directly above the bar (Fig. 5.1c). Additional variations, which eliminate the catch phase, include the mid-thigh clean pull (DeWeese et al., 2013) and the jump shrug (Suchomel et al., 2014). Variations of these Olympic lifts are used commonly to enhance power development during sports-specific movements (i.e. rapid extension of the ankles, knees and hips [Stone, 1993, Stone et al., 2003a, Stone et al., 2003b]) with performance in such lifts positively correlated with performance in athletic tasks, including sprint, jump and agility performances (Hori et al., 2008, Stone et al., 2003b).

(a)

(b)

**Fig. 5.1: Key phases of the power clean. a) start position, b) hang position, c) mid-thigh position, d) end of second pull (triple extension), e) catch position. Rapid extension of ankles, knees and hips, from the mid-thigh position (c) through to the end of the triple extension (d), generates the greatest force, RFD and peak power.**

(c)

(d)

(e)

(a)

(b)

(c)

**Fig. 5.2: Key phases of the power snatch. a) start position, b) hang position, c) hip position, d) second pull position (triple extension), e) catch position. Rapid extension of ankles, knees and hips, from the hip position (c) through the second pull (d), generates the greatest force, RFD and peak power.**

(d)

(e)

**Fig. 5.3: Catch position for the clean (a) and snatch (b).**

The optimal loads that elicit peak power output for the power clean (Comfort *et al.*, 2012b), hang power clean (Kilduff *et al.*, 2007, Kawamori *et al.*, 2005) and mid-thigh power clean (Kawamori *et al.*, 2006) have been reported to be 80 per cent, 70 per cent and 60 per cent 1–RM power clean, respectively, although these were generally not significantly different at loads ±10 per cent of the optimal load. In addition, during the mid-thigh clean pull, power and velocity are maximized at loads of 40–60 per cent 1–RM, with peak force and rate of force development occurring at loads of 120–140 per cent 1–RM power clean (Comfort *et al.*, 2012d).

The initial focus of athletic development should be on maximizing strength while developing appropriate technique during power exercises (i.e. ballistic and Olympic lifts) until athletes can be considered as being strong (parallel depth back squat ≥1.9 x body mass [Cormie *et al.*, 2007b]). Once a high relative strength level is achieved, greater emphasis should be placed on higher velocity movements, such as ballistic training, plyometrics and Olympic lifting, while maintaining or continuing to develop maximal strength levels.

Low load ballistic exercises, such as squat jumps, are likely to be most beneficial in developing speed-strength and power (Cormie *et al.*, 2008). Higher load (60–80 per cent 1–RM) ballistic exercises, such as speed deadlifts, with 20–40 per cent load from chains (Swinton *et al.*, 2011a, Swinton *et al.*, 2011b), would be useful to develop strength-speed once athletes have developed a base level of strength. Alternatively, heavy (≥100 per cent 1–RM power clean) mid-thigh clean pulls would also be advantageous for developing strength-speed (Comfort *et al.*, 2012d), with lower load (40–80 per cent 1–RM) variations of the routine being used for the development of speed-strength (Comfort *et al.*, 2012b).

PLYOMETRIC TRAINING

Plyometric exercises are characterized by a rapid eccentric muscle action followed immediately by a rapid concentric muscle action, thereby using the stretch-shorten cycle. This uses both elastic energy and neurological potentiation to increase force production and rate of force development to athletic performance. Elastic energy is from the tendons and the muscle fascia and is developed as a result of the rapid lengthening during the eccentric phase of the activity and returned during the concentric phase (Wilson and Flanagan, 2008). Simultaneously, during the eccentric phase, both the change in length and the rate of change in length is detected by the muscle spindles, which results in increased potentiation of the agonist muscles and therefore increased force production during the concentric phase (Bosco and Komi, 1979, Bosco et al., 1981).

Relatively low loads are usually used during plyometric tasks, with numerous studies highlighting that peak power occurs at body mass (no additional external load) during jumping tasks (Cormie et al., 2007a, Cormie et al., 2007c, Cormie et al., 2007d). While additional external load can be used to increase intensity of the exercise, simply performing the eccentric phase more rapidly results in an increase in force required to decelerate the body and increases the rate of lengthening of the muscles, which results in greater potentiation via stimulation of the muscle spindle. It is important to note that increasing drop height during depth jumps results in an increase in loading (force on ground contact) but this also increases ground contact time. It also appears most of the adaptations in countermovement jump performances occur during the eccentric phase, where athletes are able to perform this phase in a shorter time period and cope with the associated increase in loading (Cormie et al., 2010a, Earp et al., 2011).

General recommendations for plyometric training suggest they should be performed two to four times per week on non-consecutive days, with five- to ten-second rest between repetitions, two- to three-minute rest between sets, for 80–100 repetitions for beginners, 100–120 repetitions at intermediate level and 120–140 repetitions for advanced level athletes (Potach and Chu, 2008). If the intensity of the exercise is increased, for example progressing from a countermovement jump to a depth jump, the total volume (number of repetitions) should be reduced to accommodate the increased demands of the tasks (Potach and Chu, 2008).

Lower body plyometrics are commonly divided into long (>250ms) and short (≤250ms) contact times in an attempt to meet the demands of different sporting tasks (e.g. the longer ground contact times during the initial acceleration phase of a sprint and the low ground contact times during maximal velocity sprinting (Cross et al., 2014, Brughelli et al., 2011)). Studies identify that plyometric training enhances performance in athletic tasks (Tricoli et al., 2005), albeit generally in low load tasks such as vertical jump performance.

It is also worth noting plyometric activities can be extremely beneficial in reducing the risk of lower limb non-contact injuries, such as anterior cruciate ligament damage, especially if the focus of the activity is to ensure appropriate lower limb control/alignment during the activities but especially the landing phase (Herrington and Comfort, 2013).

## Upper Body Training

Upper body strength and power development is also essential in both codes of rugby due to the high levels of physical contact, tackling/grappling and ability to maintain possession or steal the ball. In addition, due to the level of physical contact and high incidence of shoulder injuries (thirteen injuries per 1,000 playing hours) (Usman et al., 2014), adequate levels of muscular development, strength and stability may reduce the risk of injury (Helgeson and Stoneman, 2014). However, it is worth noting inappropriate development including muscle imbalances (i.e. pushing and pulling) and reduced range of motion may predispose such athletes to an increased risk of injury (McDonough and Funk, 2014, Edouard et al.,

2009). It is important to ensure training prescription considers the volume of an exercise for each area, ensuring the relatively small pectoral muscles are not over emphasized while the posterior muscles of the upper body are left lacking appropriate training stimuli. This can be resolved by ensuring two horizontal (e.g. rowing movements) and/or vertical (e.g. pull-ups/lat pulldowns) pulling exercises are performed for each horizontal pushing exercise (e.g. bench press).

The main focus of upper body programmes should primarily be rotated between strength, maximum strength (to aid in injury prevention, tackling and wrestling) and hypertrophy to ensure adequate mass to protect the skeletal system and ensure appropriate mass to increase momentum of the athlete. Trunk strengthening exercises are also essential and, while these muscles receive a high level of training stimuli from exercises such as squats and deadlifts (Hamlyn et al., 2007) and a lower level stimuli during movement control/injury prevention sessions (e.g. planks and bridges), it is essential not to overload these muscles as with any other muscle group. Use of routines such as the Superman exercise for the spinal erectors and roll outs for the spinal flexors can easily provide such stimuli. The focus during these exercises should be to maintain a neutral spine throughout the activity. Ideally, such exercises should be incorporated at the end of the training session to ensure stability of the trunk is not compromised throughout the rest of the session.

## Field-Based Training and Conditioning

### SPEED, CHANGE OF DIRECTION AND AGILITY

In terms of the skilled aspects of athletic activities such as speed (sprint technique), change of direction and agility, these are better developed in athletes while they are young and the emphasis of all aspects of training is technical proficiency. Once movement competency is developed appropriately a greater emphasis can be placed on the development of strength, power and speed, which will further enhance athletic ability (Sheppard and Young, 2006). Swinton et al. (2014) concluded maximal strength, relative to body mass, in the squat and deadlift are associated strongly with the change of direction performance in the agility 505 test. A review by Brughelli (2008) concluded the most effective methods of enhancing change of direction performance are unilateral and bilateral jump training (i.e. horizontal, lateral and weighted vertical jumps), along with sports specific practice/rehearsal of such tasks. Importantly, Young et al. (2015) observed reactive strength and sprint acceleration was related to change of direction performance but not associated with defensive agility, concluding that sports specific skill and cognitive development should be a primary focus for defensive and reactive agility.

In young/inexperienced athletes it is essential to have specific coaching sessions relating to the development of each of these skills, albeit of short duration (30min) with quality feedback from coaches and peers as demonstrated in numerous sports (Polman et al., 2004). During change of direction tasks the athlete should lower his or her centre of mass by flexing the knees and the hips (i.e. adopting a squat position), while maintaining posture and leaning in the direction of intended travel. It is also important to maintain skill levels in such tasks but in senior athletes this can be completed within dynamic warm-ups and during coaching sessions, as long as appropriate coaching and feedback is provided.

## AEROBIC CONDITIONING AND REPEATED SPRINT ABILITY

General recommendations for aerobic conditioning are broad, usually consisting of steady state (70–90 per cent maximum heart rate, for 20–60min, 3–7 × week), or interval training (at a variety of intensities, with a range of work: rest ratios). The different volumes and intensities appear to result in different adaptive responses, with high-intensity interval training primarily resulting in central adaptation (increases in stroke volume and cardiac output) (Helgerud et al., 2007), whereas high training volumes appear primarily, although not exclusively, responsible for peripheral adaptation (increases in capillary density and mitochondrial adaptations [Bishop et al., 2013]).

What appears to be clear is that interval training is a more effective and efficient method of enhancing aerobic fitness compared with moderate and high-intensity steady state activities in team sports (Helgerud et al., 2007). Within soccer, numerous studies have identified that high-intensity training (e.g. 4 × 4min, 90–95 per cent maximum heart rate) results in significant increases in aerobic capacity in well-trained individuals (Hoff et al., 2002). While no similar studies have been performed in rugby, it is reasonable to assume a similar increase in aerobic capacity would occur in rugby players, which may also increase match performance including distance covered on the pitch and repeated sprint performances.

Small sided games have also been used within soccer (Rampinini et al., 2007b, Hill-Haas et al., 2011) and rugby (Foster et al., 2010) as a sports specific method of aerobic conditioning. The number of players, pitch size, rule manipulations and the inclusion of wrestling/contact (Gabbett et al., 2012a) can all affect the intensity of small sided games. Such methods have been shown to be an effective mode of stimulating increases in aerobic capacity and can be divided into periods of time that involve high-intensity activities (90–95 per cent maximum heart rate), interspersed with active rest periods that include skill rehearsal and coaching at lower intensities (~70 per cent maximum heart rate), mimicking the previously mentioned four × four-minute intervals. More importantly, Seitz et al. (2014b) demonstrated recently that eight weeks of small sided games performed twice per week increased aerobic and short sprint performance in academy rugby league players during the competitive season. It is worth noting that Johnston et al. (2013e) observed greatly elevated markers of fatigue and muscle damage when small sided games included contact compared to small sided games without contact, similar to findings post match play (McLellan and Lovell, 2012, McLellan et al., 2010). Such modes of exercise are important for multiple sprint sports as increases in aerobic capacity and lactate threshold have been shown to enhance repeated sprint performances by enhancing recovery between repeated efforts (Bishop et al., 2011, Girard et al., 2011, Tomlin and Wenger, 2001).

# PRACTICAL APPLICATION

The above section details a range of strength and conditioning practices that can enhance the physical capacities of rugby players, which are of utmost importance for performance. Although all these elements are important, the challenge for practitioners is the integration of each of these aspects of training into the development of a holistic training programme to enhance physical qualities and match performance. This practical application section will highlight how this can be achieved in a periodized manner to ensure a high level of development of each of these attributes.

Detailed below are examples of strength and conditioning training programmes at various parts of the season for an adult rugby league squad. The programme was aimed at developing those attributes that enhance sprint and agility/change of direction performance (including strength, power, and correct deceleration mechanics), aerobic capacity to enhance repeated sprint ability and to integrate injury prevention. Although it is acknowledged that emphasis should be placed on an individual's weaknesses, highlighted as deficient following an appropriate battery of fitness tests, the focus was on maximizing lower body strength and power while 'managing' volume during the competitive season. Examples of weekly training schedules and daily strength training programmes across the season are shown in Tables 5.1–5.8.

It is important to note this practical application is for adult players. For younger athletes, a long-term athlete development (LTAD) approach should be taken to ensure an appropriate progression, focusing on movement competency, aerobic fitness and basic strength to allow transition through to a senior squad (Lloyd *et al.*, 2013, Faigenbaum and Myer, 2010).

## Table 5.1: Example Pre-Season Weekly Training Schedule

| Day | Morning | | Afternoon | |
|---|---|---|---|---|
| **Monday** | Sprint training | Lower body strength/power | Skill-based training including wrestling | Interval training (4 × 4min, 3min active rest) |
| **Tuesday** | Agility training | Upper body strength/ hypertrophy | Skill-based training | Interval training (varying work: rest) |
| **Wednesday** | Rest day | | | |
| **Thursday** | Sprint training | Lower body strength/power | Skill-based training including wrestling | Interval training (4 × 4min, 3min active rest) |
| **Friday** | Agility training | Upper body strength/ hypertrophy | Skill-based training | Interval training (varying work: rest) |
| **Saturday** | Rest (extras for athletes that are not meeting required targets) | | | |
| **Sunday** | Rest day | | | |

## Table 5.2: Example In-Season Weekly Training Schedule

| Day | Morning | Afternoon |
|---|---|---|
| **Saturday** | **Game day** | |
| **Sunday** | Recovery session (gym- and field-based training for players who did not play) | |
| **Monday** | Rest day | |
| **Tuesday** | Lower body strength/power, Upper body strength | Skill-based training, final 28min performed as small sided games (4 × 4min) |
| **Wednesday** | Rest day | |
| **Thursday** | Lower body strength/power, Upper body strength | Skill-based training |
| **Friday** | Team preparation | |
| **Saturday** | **Game day** | |

During the season, sprint and agility drills should be incorporated into each of the pitch-based warm-ups to ensure the total training volume does not become excessive.

**Table 5.3: Example Pre-Season Lower Body Strength and Max Strength Training Programme**

| | Strength Quality/Aim | Exercise | Lower Body Strength Mesocycle | | | | Lower Body Max Strength Mesocycle | | | |
|---|---|---|---|---|---|---|---|---|---|---|
| | | | Week 1 | Week 2 | Week 3 | Week 4 | Week 1 | Week 2 | Week 3 | Week 4 |
| | | | Sets × Reps (% 1–RM) | | | | | | | |
| Day 1 | Strength | Squat variation e.g. front squat | 3 × 5 (85%) | 4 × 5 (85%) | 5 × 5 (85%) | 5 × 3 (85%) | 4 × 3 (90%) | 4 × 3 (92%) | 4 × 3 (94%) | 4 × 1 (96%) |
| | Strength speed | Clean pull variation e.g. mid-thigh | 3 × 5 (100%) | 3 × 5 (105%) | 3 × 5 (110%) | 3 × 3 (115%) | 4 × 3 (120%) | 4 × 3 (130%) | 4 × 3 (140%) | 3 × 2 (140%) |
| | Strength | RDL | 3 × 4 (85%) | 3 × 5 (85%) | 3 × 6 (85%) | 3 × 3 (85%) | 4 × 3 (90%) | 4 × 3 (92%) | 4 × 3 (94%) | 4 × 1 (96%) |
| | Strength speed/ injury prevention | Single leg CMJ (body mass) | 3 × 5 | 4 × 5 | 5 × 5 | 3 × 5 | 3 × 6 | 3 × 7 | 3 × 8 | 3 × 5 |
| Notes | | | Higher volume at the start of the week, achieved with additional sets or repetitions compared to Day 2. Week 4 used as an unloading week via a reduction in volume, achieved via a reduction in sets or repetitions not intensity. | | | | | | | |
| Day 2 | Strength | Squat variation e.g. back squat | 3 × 3 (85%) | 4 × 3 (85%) | 5 × 3 (85%) | 3 × 3 (85%) | 3 × 2 (90%) | 3 × 2 (92%) | 3 × 2 (94%) | 3 × 1 (96%) |
| | Strength speed | Clean pull variation e.g. from knee | 3 × 3 (100%) | 3 × 3 (105%) | 3 × 3 (110%) | 3 × 3 (115%) | 3 × 3 (120%) | 3 × 3 (130%) | 3 × 3 (140%) | 3 × 1 (140%) |
| | Injury prevention | Nordic curls (body mass) | 3 × 3 | 3 × 3 | 3 × 3 | 3 × 3 | 3 × 3 | 3 × 3 | 3 × 3 | 3 × 3 |
| | Strength speed/ injury prevention | Single leg depth jumps (body mass) | 3 × 5 | 4 × 5 | 5 × 5 | 3 × 5 | 3 × 6 | 4 × 6 | 5 × 6 | 3 × 4 |
| Notes | | | Reduction in total volume to ensure adequate substrate recovery and minimize neuromuscular fatigue at the end of the week to ensure optimal recovery, but intensity maintained to ensure adequate neurological stimulation. Week 4 used as an unloading week via a reduction in volume, achieved via a reduction in sets or repetitions not intensity. | | | | | | | |

## Table 5.4: Example Pre-Season Lower Body Power Training Programme

| | Strength Quality/Aim | Exercise | Week 1 | Week 2 | Week 3 | Week 4 |
|---|---|---|---|---|---|---|
| | | | Sets x Reps (% 1–RM) | | | |
| Day 1 | Power | Hang power clean | 6 × 5 (70%) | 6 × 4 (75%) | 6 × 3 (80%) | 6 × 2 (85%) |
| | Speed strength | Squat jump | 4 × 5 (40%) | 4 × 5 (30%) | 4 × 5 (20%) | 4 × 5 (body mass) |
| | Strength maintenance | Front squat | 3 × 3 (85–90%) | 3 × 3 (85–90%) | 3 × 3 (85–90%) | 3 × 3 (85–90%) |
| Notes | Higher volume at the start of the week, achieved with additional sets or repetitions compared to Day 2. Week 4 used as an unloading week via a reduction in volume, achieved via a reduction in sets or repetitions not intensity. | | | | | |
| Day 2 | Power | Mid-thigh power clean | 3 × 4 (60%) | 3 × 4 (65%) | 3 × 4 (70%) | 3 × 2 (75%) |
| | Strength speed | Clean pull variation e.g from knee | 3 × 4 (100%) | 3 × 4 (100%) | 3 × 4 (100%) | 3 × 2 (100%) |
| | Power | CMJ (body mass) | 4 × 5 | 4 × 5 | 4 × 5 | 4 × 5 |
| | Injury prevention | Nordic curls (body mass) | 3 × 3 | 3 × 3 | 3 × 3 | 3 × 3 |
| Notes | Reduction in total volume to ensure adequate substrate recovery and minimize neuromuscular fatigue at the end of the week to ensure optimal recovery but intensity maintained to ensure adequate neurological stimulation. Week 4 used as an unloading week via a reduction in volume, achieved via a reduction in sets or repetitions not intensity. | | | | | |

| | Strength Quality/Aim | Exercise | Week 1 | Week 2 | Week 3 | Week 4 |
|---|---|---|---|---|---|---|
| | | | Sets x Reps (% 1–RM) | | | |
| Day 1 | Hypertrophy/ strength | Row variation e.g. seated | 3 × 10 (66%) | 4 × 10 (68%) | 5 × 10 (70%) | 3 × 10 (72%) |
| | Hypertrophy/ strength | Bench press variation e.g. dumb-bell | 3 × 10 (66%) | 4 × 10 (68%) | 5 × 10 (70%) | 3 × 10 (72%) |
| | Hypertrophy/ strength | Pull-up variation e.g. wide grip | 2 × 10 (66%) | 3 × 10 (68%) | 4 × 10 (70%) | 2 × 10 (72%) |
| | Hypertrophy/ strength | Military press | 3 × 10 (66%) | 4 × 10 (68%) | 5 × 10 (70%) | 3 × 10 (72%) |
| | Hypertrophy (superset) | Biceps curl/ triceps extension | 3 × 10 (66%) | 4 × 10 (68%) | 5 × 10 (70%) | 3 × 10 (72%) |
| Notes | Higher volume at the start of the week, achieved with additional sets or repetitions compared to Day 2. Week 4 used as an unloading week via a reduction in volume, achieved via a reduction in sets or repetitions not volume. | | | | | |
| Day 2 | Hypertrophy/ strength | Pull-up variation e.g. close grip | 2 × 10 (66%) | 3 × 10 (68%) | 4 × 10 (70%) | 2 × 10 (72%) |
| | Hypertrophy/ strength | Dips variation e.g. rings | 2 × 10 (66%) | 3 × 10 (68%) | 4 × 10 (70%) | 2 × 10 (72%) |
| | Hypertrophy/ strength | Dumb-bell shoulder press | 2 × 10 (66%) | 3 × 10 (68%) | 4 × 10 (70%) | 2 × 10 (72%) |
| | Injury prevention | Face pulls | 2 × 10 (66%) | 3 × 10 (68%) | 4 × 10 (70%) | 2 × 10 (72%) |
| Notes | Reduction in total volume to ensure adequate substrate recovery and minimize neuromuscular fatigue at the end of the week to ensure optimal recovery but intensity maintained to ensure adequate neurological stimulation. Week 4 used as an unloading week via a reduction in volume, achieved via a reduction in sets or repetitions not volume. | | | | | |

Table 5.5: Example Pre-Season Upper Body Hypertrophy Training Programme

| | | | Week 1 | Week 2 | Week 3 | Week 4 |
|---|---|---|---|---|---|---|
| | **Strength Quality/Aim** | **Exercise** | **Sets x Reps (% 1–RM)** | | | |
| Day 1 | Strength | Row variation e.g. barbell | 3 x 5–6 (85%) | 4 x 5–6 (85%) | 5 x 5–6 (85%) | 2 x 5–6 (85%) |
| | Strength | Bench press variation | 3 x 5–6 (85%) | 4 x 5–6 (85%) | 5 x 5–6 (85%) | 2 x 5–6 (85%) |
| | Strength | Pull-up variation e.g. wide grip | 2 x 5–6 (85%) | 3 x 5–6 (85%) | 4 x 5–6 (85%) | 2 x 5–6 (85%) |
| | Strength | Military press | 3 x 5–6 (85%) | 4 x 5–6 (85%) | 5 x 5–6 (85%) | 2 x 5–6 (85%) |
| | (Superset) | Biceps curl/ triceps extension | 3 x 5–6 (85%) | 4 x 5–6 (85%) | 5 x 5–6 (85%) | 2 x 5–6 (85%) |
| Notes | Higher volume at the start of the week, achieved with additional sets or repetitions compared to Day 2. Week 4 used as an unloading week via a reduction in volume, achieved via a reduction in sets or repetitions not volume. | | | | | |
| Day 2 | Strength | Pull-up variation e.g. close grip | 3 x 5–6 (85%) | 4 x 5–6 (85%) | 5 x 5–6 (85%) | 2 x 5–6 (85%) |
| | Strength | Dips variation | 3 x 5–6 (85%) | 4 x 5–6 (85%) | 5 x 5–6 (85%) | 2 x 5–6 (85%) |
| | Strength | Dumb-bell shoulder press | 3 x 5–6 (85%) | 4 x 5–6 (85%) | 5 x 5–6 (85%) | 2 x 5–6 (85%) |
| | Injury prevention | Ring press-ups (body mass) | 3 x 10 | 4 x 10 | 5 x 10 | 3 x 10 |
| Notes | Reduction in total volume to ensure adequate substrate recovery and minimize neuromuscular fatigue at the end of the week to ensure optimal recovery but intensity maintained to ensure adequate neurological stimulation. Week 4 used as an unloading week via a reduction in volume, achieved via a reduction in sets or repetitions not volume. | | | | | |

**Table 5.6: Example Pre-Season Upper Body Strength Training Programme**

## Table 5.7: Example Pre-Season Upper Body Maximum Strength Training Programme

| | Strength Quality/Aim | Exercise | Week 1 | Week 2 | Week 3 | Week 4 |
|---|---|---|---|---|---|---|
| | | | Sets x Reps (% 1–RM) | | | |
| Day 1 | Strength | Row variation e.g. dumb-bell | 2 × 3 (90%) | 3 × 2 (92%) | 4 × 2 (94%) | 2 × 2 (96%) |
| | Strength | Bench press variation | 2 × 3 (90%) | 3 × 2 (92%) | 4 × 2 (94%) | 2 × 2 (96%) |
| | Strength | Pull-up variation e.g. wide grip | 2 × 3 (90%) | 3 × 2 (92%) | 4 × 2 (94%) | 2 × 2 (96%) |
| | Strength | Military press | 3 × 3 (90%) | 4 × 2 (92%) | 5 × 2 (94%) | 2 × 2 (96%) |
| | Strength (superset) | Biceps curl/ triceps extension | 2 × 3 (90%) | 3 × 2 (92%) | 4 × 2 (94%) | 2 × 2 (96%) |
| Notes | Higher volume at the start of the week, achieved with additional sets or repetitions compared to Day 2. Week 4 used as an unloading week via a reduction in volume, achieved via a reduction in sets or repetitions not volume. | | | | | |
| Day 2 | Strength | Pull-up variation e.g. parallel grip | 2 × 3 (90%) | 3 × 2 (92%) | 4 × 2 (94%) | 2 × 2 (96%) |
| | Strength | Dips variation | 2 × 3 (90%) | 3 × 2 (92%) | 4 × 2 (94%) | 2 × 2 (96%) |
| | Strength | Dumb-bell shoulder press | 2 × 3 (90%) | 3 × 2 (92%) | 4 × 2 (94%) | 2 × 2 (96%) |
| | Injury prevention | Face pulls | 3 × 5–6 (80%) | 4 × 5–6 (80%) | 5 × 5–6 (80%) | 2 × 5–6 (80%) |
| Notes | Reduction in total volume to ensure adequate substrate recovery and minimize neuromuscular fatigue at the end of the week to ensure optimal recovery but intensity maintained to ensure adequate neurological stimulation. Week 4 used as an unloading week via a reduction in volume, achieved via a reduction in sets or repetitions not volume. | | | | | |

## Table 5.8 Example in Season Combined Lower Body and Upper Body Strength and Power Mesocycle

| | Strength Quality/Aim | Exercise | Week 1 | Week 2 | Week 3 | Week 4 |
|---|---|---|---|---|---|---|
| | | | Sets x Reps (% 1–RM) | | | |
| Day 1 | LB power | Hang power clean | 5 × 5 (70%) | 5 × 4 (75%) | 5 × 3 (80%) | 3 × 2 (80%) |
| | LB strength maintenance | Front squat | 3 × 2 (88%) | 3 × 2 (90%) | 3 × 2 (92%) | 3 × 1 (94%) |
| | LB injury prevention | Nordic curls (body mass) | 3 × 3 | 3 × 3 | 3 × 3 | 3 × 3 |
| | UB strength | Seated row & bench press* | 2 × 5 (84%) | 2 × 4 (87%) | 2 × 3 (90%) | 2 × 2 (92%) |
| | UB strength | Pull-ups & military press* | 2 × 5 (84%) | 2 × 4 (87%) | 2 × 3 (90%) | 2 × 2 (92%) |
| | UB strength | Biceps curls & triceps extensions* | 2 × 5 (84%) | 2 × 4 (87%) | 2 × 3 (90%) | 2 × 2 (92%) |
| Notes | Higher volume at the start of the week, achieved with additional sets or repetitions compared to Day 2. Week 4 used as an unloading week via a reduction in volume, achieved by a reduction in sets or repetitions not intensity. *Superset – Alternate between exercises, with 60–90sec rest between exercises. LB = Lower Body; UB = Upper Body | | | | | |
| Day 2 | LB power | Push jerk | 3 × 6 (70%) | 3 × 5 (74%) | 3 × 4 (78%) | 3 × 2 (80%) |
| | LB strength speed | Clean pull variation e.g. from knee | 3 × 4 (100%) | 3 × 4 (100%) | 3 × 4 (100%) | 3 × 2 (100%) |
| | LB power | CMJ (body mass) | 4 × 5 | 4 × 5 | 4 × 5 | 4 × 5 |
| | UB strength | Pull-ups & dips (using rings)* | 3 × 5 (84%) | 3 × 4 (87%) | 3 × 3 (90%) | 3 × 2 (92%) |
| | UB strength | Biceps curls & triceps extensions* | 2 × 5 (84%) | 2 × 4 (87%) | 2 × 3 (90%) | 2 × 2 (92%) |
| Notes | Reduction in total volume to ensure adequate substrate recovery and minimize neuromuscular fatigue prior to game day to ensure optimal recovery but intensity maintained to ensure adequate neurological stimulation. Week 4 used as an unloading week via a reduction in volume, achieved via a reduction in sets or repetitions not intensity. *Superset – Alternate between exercises, with 60–90sec rest between exercises. LB = Lower Body; UB = Upper Body | | | | | |

## IMPLICATIONS AND RECOMMENDATIONS FOR PRACTICE

- Due to demands of rugby, strength and power are important attributes that are related to other physical qualities (i.e. speed and agility) alongside match performance indicators.
- Strength training should be the foundation for power development. It is recommended that three to six sets of four to ten repetitions at 70–88 per cent 1–RM for resistance exercises is used in a periodized program for the development of strength and power.
- Methods of developing power include ballistic exercises (i.e. jump squats), Olympic lifts and their derivatives (i.e. power clean) and plyometric exercises.
- Power training can be maintained during a strength training programme by including a power-based exercise. Strength training can also be maintained during power training programmes by including a strength-based exercise.

- For upper body strength programmes, a balance between pushing and pulling-based exercises should be considered that includes more pulling-based exercises (i.e, rows and chins).
- The use of speed and change of direction drills can be used in warm-ups.
- Increasing maximal aerobic capacity via high-intensity interval training is likely to enhance performance on the pitch. This can be achieved through the use of small sided games that consider the number of players, pitch size, rules and use of contact or wrestling.
- Daily and weekly training volumes and intensities should consider the previous and upcoming match in the development of appropriate training programmes.

# CHAPTER 6

# INJURY REHABILITATION: A PRACTICAL GUIDE

## David Joyce and Emidio Pacecca

## INTRODUCTION

Due to the high physical demands of rugby, where success is dependent upon the effective application and absorption of substantial forces (i.e. contact), the sport has a high injury risk profile. The severity of these injuries can range substantially from minor knocks and bruises to those that are potentially career threatening. It is important to appreciate there is a difference between injury incidence and injury severity. Incidence refers to how often a particular injury occurs, whereas severity refers to how much training or game time will be lost as a result of a particular injury. For example, a quadriceps contusion has a high incidence but low severity, whereas the ACL injury has a low incidence but significant severity. Due to this injury risk, professional rugby clubs employ physiotherapists and injury rehabilitation specialists to facilitate the 'return to play' of a player. During this time, practitioners will focus on rehabilitating the injured site, while attempting to maintain a player's overall fitness. Due to the range of injuries that can occur, it is important each injury and player is treated and rehabilitated on an individual basis. The aim of this chapter is to provide practical recommendations for players and practitioners, from an

interdisciplinary support team perspective, to facilitate the return to play of a player. The chapter draws on real-life examples from practitioners working within the field.

## PRACTICAL APPLICATION

### Principles of Rehabilitation

While it is beyond the scope of this chapter to detail the best rehabilitation strategies for every injury that could occur, there are critical rehabilitation principles that should be followed irrespective of the injury. It is imperative that the interdisciplinary support team is organized and ready to react as soon as an injury occurs. Ensuring the correct injury diagnosis is made in a timely manner is critical, as is the communication of the short- and long-term management plans for the player.

Whilst the tissue damage sustained in an injury will undoubtedly place restrictions upon the activity of the player, during the rehabilitation phase it is important to identify activities that a player can do, rather than those he or she cannot. Therefore, when a player becomes injured, this can be seen as an opportunity to work upon specific weaknesses (i.e specifically upper body strength when a player sustains a lower-body injury or general traits; mental or tactical skills). Accordingly, this should be the frame of reference that is presented to the player when detailing the return to performance plan for them.

It is important an appropriately qualified and experienced medical practitioner quantifies injury, including the length of time a player will miss specific activities, although this can be variable between injuries and individuals. For example, in the majority of cases, a minor hamstring strain may rule a player out of match play for three weeks. However, this amount of time should not be used as the exclusive determinant of when a player will be able to return to play. First, players need to demonstrate quantifiable measures (i.e. contractile muscle strength or range of movement) have returned to near baseline (i.e. pre-injury). Further, the player then needs to demonstrate he can cope adequately with the movement demands (i.e. high-speed running, acceleration, deceleration) reflective of the demands he will face in a match. The movement demands should also be compared to pre-injury scores. Therefore, as opposed to a rehabilitation strategy that relies on time, this approach is based on the successful completion of set performance objectives and progression from one stage to the next. These objectives become progressively more challenging as the player approaches a return to competition.

There are numerous advantages of this approach. It is a consistent and reliable strategy, used to ensure function is returned to a level considered to be high performance, as opposed to one based purely on biological healing times of the injury. Moreover, it eliminates the guesswork of determining how long a player will be out of full training and competition (i.e. a player can return to action as soon as they have demonstrated they have

passed all the exit criteria). This is the safest and most objective method to ensure a player returns to action with a reduced risk of re-injury and, indeed, that they return at a level where they can perform to a high standard (i.e. in comparison to pre-injury) during a match.

In keeping with this phased-based approach to rehabilitation planning and delivery, it is recommended a programme should follow the below stages:

- Phase One – Tissue protection
- Phase Two – Return of motion and tissue loading
- Phase Three – Strength accumulation and training integration
- Phase Four – Return to performance.

Each of the four stages is detailed below with a range of exit criteria a player must demonstrate before being able to proceed to the next rehabilitation phase and return to match play.

## REHABILITATION PHASE ONE – TISSUE PROTECTION

The tissue protection phase should commence as soon as the injury occurs and its primary objective is to provide the damaged tissue with a supportive environment in which to heal. This may mean crutches for a significant ankle injury or a sling for a fractured clavicle. Advice from an appropriately qualified medical practitioner is vital at this point and further investigations in the way of radiological scanning may be required. Following the principles of protection, rest, ice, compression and elevation will provide the basis of this phase. Anti-inflammatory medications should be avoided in the acute phase as this has been shown to delay healing. Allowing the acute injury process to settle before encouraging movement is recommended, although this will vary according to the severity of the injury.

As soon as it is safe to do so, all external support (i.e. slings, crutches, braces) should be removed and normal movement should be encouraged, as this is important for the re-establishment of appropriate movement patterns at the injured site. At this time point appropriate training activity can also commence, which may require a weight supported environment (e.g. a swimming pool) or other methods of training the body without unduly loading the injured tissue. For example, while a knee medial collateral ligament sprain may limit a player's running in the short term, he is often able to perform intervals on an arm ergometer.

The use of cross training (i.e. alternative exercise activities) should be designed to develop the areas of the player's fitness that have previously been identified as a weakness. A player may have a very good ability to perform short bursts of activity but struggle with repeated efforts, therefore developing a programme that seeks to improve their repeated effort capacity is deemed important. This is where working together as an interdisciplinary team (i.e. physiotherapists, strength and conditioning staff, sport science, coaches and so on) is very important to optimize and maximize the use of time. However, the overall needs of the athlete still need to be a consideration (i.e. excessive upper-body training may lead to shoulder pain) in developing a rehabilitation and training plan.

To allow players to progress from rehabilitation stage one, the exit criteria should be:

- Evidence of inflammatory resolution
- Substantial reduction of pain
- Return to normal everyday function (pain-free walking, etc.)
- Evidence of good muscle contractile function.

## REHABILITATION PHASE TWO – RETURN OF MOTION AND TISSUE LOADING

Phase two is focused on returning full and normal movement, while using the correct muscle recruitment patterns related to the injured site. Good quality movement is a key aspect with a focus on the form of specific exercises, which should progress through increasing repetitions, speed and resistance. However, the quality of the movement should be the main objective before progression of the exercises. As an example, the practitioner should not seek to add weight to a shoulder press until the player has demonstrated he then can perform the movement perfectly without resistance.

Strength training of injured tissue can commence once it is pain-free. On occasions, a joint compromised athlete may benefit from the use of low-intensity vascular occlusion training (LIVOT). This is where an occlusion cuff is placed around a limb and inflated to a pressure that restricts blood flow. Exercises can then be performed under these ischemic conditions that provide a muscle hypertrophy stimulus without the load usually required for an adaptation. Normally, a series of leg press exercises at 30 per cent of one-repetition maximum would be tolerable for a player with a knee injury but be insufficient to stimulate a hypertrophic response. Under LIVOT conditions seen where an occlusion cuff is placed around the thigh of the player and they perform the same drill, a marked hypertrophic and strength response is possible. However, it is recommended that LIVOT is only undertaken by suitably qualified practitioners.

Strength training, focusing on uninjured body parts, can also be programmed at this stage. Again, the injury has provided the player with an opportunity to improve his performance and as strength is a desired physical property for rugby, this should be a focus from a physical perspective. In addition, rehabilitation drills should now be incorporated to facilitate the return to rugby training. Not every rehabilitation drill needs to be recognizable as a rugby skill but the drill should aim to develop skills relevant for the sport. Running drills, such as wall accelerations and match-type drills, can be incorporated early but at a lower intensity. In this way we can retrain running before even taking a running step.

To allow players to progress from rehabilitation stage two, the exit criteria should be:

■ Successful graduation from phase one
■ No adverse reaction to loading
■ Return to low-level rugby-relevant skills (passing, jogging, running drills)
■ Full range of motion pain free
■ Full strength programme for uninjured body parts
■ Full cross training programme to enhance energy system development as required by the individual.

## REHABILITATION PHASE THREE – STRENGTH ACCUMULATION AND TRAINING INTEGRATION

Phase three focuses on increasing the player's (re)training load, so that by the end of this phase he can integrate into a full rugby training programme. This can take a number of weeks and requires the player to demonstrate objectively he is capable of returning to full training. Strength and power training are important for athletic training and the gradual increase in linear and multidirectional speed is critical. Players should demonstrate competencies in deceleration, prior to acceleration. Rugby matches require frequent and high velocity decelerations that place a large eccentric load on the player and therefore must be trained accordingly. This is especially the case when considering many injuries occur when players decelerate. When coaching deceleration, this may involve teaching correct body position when stopping (i.e. forward lean and lowering of the centre of mass) or the ability to control body load when landing on to one leg from a set height (i.e. progressions up to a 40cm box).

It is recommended that higher on-feet loads of (re)training take place with a 'day on, day off' frequency, progressing to a 'two days on, one day off, two days on, two days off' programme. This ensures players can withstand repeated loading when returning to full training. For longer term (re)training programmes, a schedule of straight line running for a number of weeks may be necessary to gain the volume of loading required for the overall musculoskeletal system. Following this, simple changes of direction that progress in speed and complexity can be introduced. A decision-making component can then be added, turning a change of direction drill into a true agility drill where reactive elements are required. This may also develop the physical qualities of a player before he returns to full training. It is also important the demands of training and matches are analyzed closely in this phase of the rehabilitation to ensure the aerobic and anaerobic requirements are being met. In rugby league, repeated efforts of 'off-the-ground' work along with 'defensive retreats' must be introduced to ensure the player is fully prepared for the demands of the game.

This is also the phase that will see ball work and skill development reintroduced. Tackle technique can also start and be progressed accordingly. This is also a good opportunity for rugby coaches to reinforce technical messages, again ensuring the player is capable when returning to the main training group.

To allow players to progress from rehabilitation stage three, the exit criteria should be:

- Successful graduation from phase two
- No adverse reaction to loading
- >85 per cent of pre-injury strength and functional tests
- Return to high-level rugby-relevant skills (contact, high-intensity running, mechanical loading through acceleration, deceleration and changes of direction).

## REHABILITATION PHASE FOUR – RETURN TO PERFORMANCE

Rehabilitation phase four is the final stage for a player. It is important that following this phase, the biological healing process is complete and the player has full confidence in the previously injured body part. Following a structured rehabilitation programme will also develop athletic competencies to allow the player to return to compete. The player should have a large amount of input during this phase to ensure all rugby attributes are at or superior to pre-injury scores. This may mean they need repeated exposure to tasks such as:

- High-intensity conditioning to ensure the player is aerobically conditioned
- Maximal speed running (i.e. repeated efforts and under fatigue conditions)
- Maximal velocity acceleration or deceleration
- Game-intensity changes of direction
- Game-intensity collisions (tackling and being tackled) in both controlled and uncontrolled contexts.

All these elements should be accounted for and compared to pre-injury status as well as those from their positional peers. Objectivity is critical here to ensure the player is competent, reducing the risk of anxiety or a lack in confidence.

To allow players to progress from rehabilitation stage four, the exit criteria should be:

- Successful graduation from phase three
- No adverse reaction to loading
- >90 per cent of pre-injury strength and functional testing results
- Demonstration of full unrestricted training loads
- Return to full sprint speed and acceleration and deceleration velocities.

At all stages, it is important to continually monitor the response of the injured tissue to the loading. This may take the form of flexibility tests, swelling observation or contractile (i.e. muscular strength) function. Following a major injury, objective testing to demonstrate the full return of function is important. Objective tests can include force plate analysis (assessing for symmetry, power and/or impulse dampening) and isokinetic dynamometry (assessing for symmetry or agonist-to-antagonist ratios).

## Case Study

A challenge for any high performance professional is to put theory into practice. For optimal injury rehabilitation and management it is necessary to read and understand current best practice, then apply it specifically to the situation. As discussed above, individualized programmes relevant to the injury and the player's strengths and weaknesses are superior to generic programmes because they are able to address specifically the issues ensuring the athlete is able to return to peak performance as quickly and safely as possible. For this case study example, the above rehabilitation principles are applied to a rugby union player who obtained a hamstring injury. The player was 189cm, weighed 95kg and played wing or fullback. Prior to injury, his maximum speed was 9.6m.sec$^{-1}$.

An informed diagnosis is imperative in planning a structured and timely rehabilitation programme. A battery of clinical tests and appropriate imaging should be undertaken to assist with prognosis and planning. In this case, the athlete has sustained a stretch-type injury while tackling at high speed. Acutely, he presents as a grade II biceps femoris strain and MRI confirms a 6cm longitudinal strain at the proximal myotendinous junction.

## PHASE ONE – TISSUE PROTECTION

- Acute principles of ice and compression
- Manual therapy of the lumbar spine and hip to improve pain-free range of motion
- Soft tissue treatment around the injured site. Distal biceps femoris, medial hamstrings, gluteals, adductors and calf are common areas that can become tight while compensating for the injured proximal biceps femoris
- Neurodynamic treatment and exercises if applicable
- Graduated exposure to low-level load to facilitate muscle repair. This commences as low-level isometric contractions through range and moving towards low-level concentric and eccentric movements.
- Low-level core and balance exercises
- Upper body weights and conditioning.

Exit Criteria

- Active Knee Extension = 75 per cent of uninjured side
- Slump = 75 per cent of uninjured side
- Pain free gait, stairs, sitting
- Pain free bodyweight squat to 90 degrees
- Double leg bridge with 5sec hold at 90/60/30 degrees.

## PHASE TWO – RETURN OF MOTION AND TISSUE LOADING

- Increased exposure to muscle contraction. Gradual progression of intensity and duration through range
- Start of straight line running program every second day. First session included 30m jog, 15m walk at 4–5 m/sec$^{-1}$. 3 sets × 6 repetitions.
- Dynamic warm-up exercises
- Gluteal muscle activation exercises
- Lumbo-pelvic disassociation exercises
- Moderate level core exercises
- Upper body weights.

Exit Criteria

- Full knee extension range of motion
- Isometric hold + 25 per cent body weight
- Single leg bridge repetitions >90 per cent of uninjured side
- Single leg squat with crossover reach
- Run 2km at 12km/h$^{-1}$.

## PHASE THREE – STRENGTH ACCUMULATION AND TRAINING INTEGRATION

- Increase running volume and pace. Incorporate rolling accelerations increasing from 6– 8m.sec$^{-1}$ over 20m. Progress up to 4 sets × 10 repetitions
- Speed technique drills
- Incorporate change of direction and agility running
- Commence punt kicking 25m stationary target
- Introduction to lower body weights including exposure to eccentric hamstring exercises (Romanian deadlifts, Nordic drops, etc).

Exit Criteria

- Repeat sprint at >8m.sec$^{-1}$ with <10 per cent decay
- Total volume of running sessions >4km with acceleration, deceleration, agility
- Maximum deceleration
- Strength tests <10 per cent difference to contralateral side with appropriate quadriceps: hamstring ration
- Symmetry of stride length, contact phase and ground reaction force
- Kick more than 45m.

PHASE FOUR – RETURN TO PERFORMANCE

- Progressing to full-speed running and acceleration
- Progress kicking to game-based scenarios over full distance
- Full, unrestricted leg weights
- Progressive contact and offloading scenarios
- Complex drills involving decision making under fatigue.

Exit Criteria

- Strength <10 per cent difference to contralateral side
- Full repeat speed and acceleration
- Training volume >5km per week
- Kicking unrestricted on run.

Once the player has fulfilled all the exit criteria he must be exposed to the load of full training gradually. It is advisable to plan a 10 per cent reduction in running volume for the initial sessions when reintegrating into team training. Generally a player should be able to demonstrate one to two weeks of training prior to exposure into a match situation. Overall the load should be managed for several weeks after returning to play in an attempt to reduce the risk of a reoccurrence of the previous injury.

## IMPLICATIONS AND RECOMMENDATIONS FOR PRACTICE

- Injuries are, unfortunately, an all too common occurrence in any form of rugby and therefore a return to play strategy, incorporating an interdisciplinary support team, needs to be developed to deal with players when injuries occur.
- When an injury occurs, this should be seen as an opportunity to work upon a player's weaknesses to turn the initial disappointment the player may feel into optimism they will return to the field in even better condition than before. This should be communicated to the player through the coach and interdisciplinary support team.
- An approach that is performance based and focused on functional exit criteria is necessary to return the player to the field in a state commensurate with not just being fit to play but fit to compete.

- The first phase concentrates on protecting the injured tissue but it is important to consider what the player can still do, not just what they cannot.
- Regaining joint range of motion and tissue extensibility is the next priority, as is the start of progressive loading of the injured tissue.
- The next phase sees the player accumulating strength and resilience in the injured tissue and integrating them into training, ideally in a drip-feed manner.
- The final phase sees the player fully fit and, having completed all aspects of his retraining, providing both the athlete and the coach with the confidence the injury has not just been fully rehabilitated but that the player is in superior condition to that prior to the injury.

# CHAPTER 7

# DECISION MAKING FOR RUGBY

## Donna O'Connor and Paul Larkin

## INTRODUCTION

Spectators marvel at players' skilled athletic performance in many dimensions of the game, including attacking (i.e. a tackle-busting run to the try line) or defensive (i.e. saving a try by holding a player up over the line) situations. Many factors contribute to the superior performance of skilled rugby players (i.e. speed, power, strength). While at the highest competition level, physiological attributes of athletes do not differentiate the successful and less successful athletes or teams (Reilly *et al.*, 2000), it is believed that perceptual-cognitive skills may be the better discriminating factor (Williams and Ford, 2013).

Evidenced by reports from elite rugby coaches, commentators and fans who lament the decision making of their teams during critical game moments, decision making is a vital component to performance in rugby. For example, in the 2014 Bledisloe Cup game won by the All Blacks 29–28, Jim Tucker writes:

> The golden punchline was ripped from them after the Wallabies had the match in their hands for all but three seconds from the end when Fekitoa crossed. The Wallabies still had their crucial brain

fades when replacement halfback Nic White gave away possession with a late kick and Bernard Foley's earlier kick-pass gifted possession when he had runners outside.

On the other side of the world, England were defeated by South Africa 31–28 with Jeremy Guscott commenting:

> …Then there was Owen Farrell, who made a poor decision in his 22. It's an easy thing to say but his choice to pass the ball to the isolated Anthony Watson, rather than belting it downfield, was a result of not being smart – it was poor decision making compounded by bad execution. Errors are bad enough but when they are unforced it is even more frustrating.

The aim of this chapter is to provide an overview of the importance of decision making for rugby performance by critiquing what decision making is, the processes that underlie decision making, how it can be assessed and the activities associated with its development. In addition, the chapter provides example strategies that coaches can use to develop decision making in their players.

# RESEARCH OVERVIEW

## What is Decision Making?

Correct decision making is a key component of match performance for rugby players, with skilled performance characterized by the consistent and efficient ability to make correct decisions (e.g. when to pass or dummy, take on a defender or when to tackle; (Gréhaigne et al., 2001)). In-game decisions are naturalistic, meaning they are made by a player who is familiar with the game situation and the decision occurs within the game environment (Johnson, 2006). Within a sport context, decision making can be defined as the process of selecting the most appropriate movement response (e.g. running an 'under's line) from a range of possible options (Abernethy, 1996), or the selection of functional actions (e.g. running the ball rather than kicking) from a range of possible actions to achieve a specific goal (Hastie, 2001). However, within a rugby context there are other possible factors that may influence the decision making process, including the technical and tactical demands (e.g. the number of players on the short side during a scrum may be influenced by the defensive capabilities of the opponents).

As such, decision making in a rugby context, can be defined as the 'case by case action choices that are made, which incorporate strategy' (MacMahon et al., 2009). Through assessing these definitions, it is clear rugby decision making is not a general process but rather in-game decision making is individualized, with the movement outcomes, such as passing, tackling or running, based upon the evolving game-play, technical attributes of the player and the need for players to understand team strategy or tactics.

In sport, the complex processing of information in the context of competition is a central and defining perceptual-cognitive skill (Mann et al., 2007). Perceptual-cognitive skills involve the cognitive processing of environmental information to inform a player's decision making (Marteniuk, 1976) and include such skills as the ability to recognize and recall patterns of play, or 'read the play' (Farrow et al., 2010); a greater sensitivity to advance cue utilization (Helsen and Starkes, 1999); and enhanced knowledge of event outcomes (Vaeyens et al., 2007). To further understand the decision making process, researchers have developed models such as the Decision Making in Sport Model (Farrow and Raab, 2008) to explain the process as it applies to athletes in game situations. The model provides an understanding of the potential processes undertaken by players during a game to make a decision. Table 7.1 lists these processes using the scenario of a ball carrier approaching the defence.

In addition to the Decision Making in Sport Model, researchers (Passos et al., 2008) have also provided an alternative view of the influences to the decision making process. Passos and colleagues (2008) proposed that decision making could be viewed from a dynamical systems approach, as rugby does not provide a stable environment in which information is consistently and uniformly available. Rather, rugby is a complex game composed of multiple components that create patterns of actions and behaviours in a constantly adapting environment (Passos et al., 2008). This constantly adapting game environment is a result of factors such as time, score, position on the field and position of teammates and opponents, all of which may constrain the decision making process. As a result, Passos and colleagues state in-game decisions are individual and context-dependent. For example, in a line-out situation, if a defending team are close to their own try line they may be less likely to contest the ball and instead concentrate on

**Table 7.1: The Seven Stages of Decision Making in Sport Model (Farrow and Raab, 2008)**

| Stage | Description | Rugby Example |
|---|---|---|
| 1 | Presentation of the problem | Defending player sprints out of the line |
| 2 | Identification of the constraints on the behaviour and the creation of goals | Ball carrier identifies the positions of his support players knowing he must pass backwards |
| 3 | Generation of possible outcomes | (a) passing the ball to a support player on his inside, (b) passing the ball to the support player on his outside who the defender rushed up on, (c) throwing a cut-out pass to the winger, (d) throwing a dummy to the outside support player and running to evade the impending defender |
| 4 | Ranking of courses of action | Options above are ranked (a) 3; (b) 4; (c) 2; (d) 1 |
| 5 | Action selection | Option ranked 1 |
| 6 | Action initiation and completion | Throws a dummy, makes a line break leading to a try |
| 7 | Evaluation of the decision | Correct decision |

their defensive structure. However, if the line-out is in the attacking half of the field they may be more likely to contest the ball to regain possession. Therefore, no decision making situation is identical. However, being attuned to the most relevant perceptual information within certain situations is the foundation for skilled decision making performance (Passos et al., 2008).

## How to Assess Decision Making in Sport

Rugby provides a unique, unpredictable environment for assessing perceptual-cognitive skills due to the ever changing sources of information, the interaction between the offence and defence, and game structure (Casanova et al., 2009). This evolving game-play provides a challenging environment for the investigation

of skilled decision making (Johnson, 2006), especially as decision making information is not gathered and processed instantaneously but instead gathered over time and then processed. Therefore, researchers have developed controlled laboratory-based methods to present game-play information to assess and monitor decision making performance (Berry et al., 2008, Larkin et al., 2013).

The main method to assess decision making in a sport-based context is the isolated decision making approach (MacMahon et al., 2009). This provides athletes with separate video-clips that are occluded (i.e. blacked out or stopped) at a key moment before a critical decision. At this point the athlete is asked to decide on a game behaviour (i.e. pass, run and so on) or movement action (i.e. move left or right). Video clips between 6 to 15 seconds in duration are used as they provide sufficient time for participants to orientate themselves in the context of play prior to the decision making situation (Berry *et al.*, 2008). The aim of this method is to design video clips that display the specific sequence of events, enabling participants to develop expectations and use situational probabilities to inform an effective decision (MacMahon *et al.*, 2009). For this method to be effective, the video scenarios should accurately represent the playing environment. Video footage from a sideline or broadcast position is appropriate as it still provides the most critical and relevant information to be identified (Berry *et al.*, 2008, Larkin *et al.*, 2013).

## Processes Underlying Decision Making in Sport

In sport, some coaches and spectators believe great players see the game differently to lesser players and attribute this to enhanced visual ability (Starkes, 1987). These generalized assumptions led to sport researchers focusing on visual abilities such as visual acuity and peripheral vision as a measure of skilled performance (Helsen and Starkes, 1999, Starkes, 1987). Results, however, indicated no significant difference between expert, intermediate or novice soccer and hockey athletes on a range of standard optometry tests. This indicates expert and novice performers are not distinguished by the physical characteristics of the visual system. However, performance differences are potentially due to cognitive involvement during perception, such as pattern recognition (i.e. ability to 'read the play'), situational probability (i.e. knowledge of event outcomes) and anticipation (i.e. predictions about future events [Starkes, 1987]).

One such perceptual-cognitive ability that differentiates between playing levels, and contributes to decision making, is situational probability. This involves the processing of in-game information to guide expectations of particular events or actions occurring during a given situation (Williams and Ford, 2013). While there is limited research within the rugby codes, investigations within other invasion sports (e.g. soccer), have found elite athletes are better than non-elite athletes at identifying the key sport-specific options and ranking those options in order from most to least threatening to the defensive team (Ward and Williams, 2003). While the majority of the research into situational probabilities has been conducted in soccer (e.g. Ward and Williams, 2003), it is believed the expert advantage when assessing the probability of certain game outcomes may exist across a range of sport contexts including rugby (Williams, 2000).

In addition to the ability to evaluate the probability of certain in-game actions, the ability to anticipate or predict the next act of play and undertake a skilled movement is fundamental to elite performance (Abernethy and Russell, 1987). Anticipation refers to the ability to make accurate predictions using contextual information (i.e. player movements, patterns of play) from the surrounding environment (e.g. a defending player intercepting the ball [Abernethy and Russell, 1987]), and is a critical perceptual-cognitive skill underlying effective decision making and motor performance (Farrow and Abernethy, 2002). However, anticipation of future actions is only possible if the athletes are attuned to the relevant task-specific information (Passos *et al.*, 2008).

In a rugby context, researchers have attempted to understand the ability to anticipate opposition movements to guide movement-based decisions (Gabbett and Benton, 2009, Gabbett *et al.*, 2008, Serpell *et al.*, 2011). Movement-based decisions, or reactive agility, is an important skill for rugby players as they need to react to offensive changes to tackle a ball carrier or identify the defensive structure to break the line. While agility is a physical change in direction movement, the process by which a player chooses to change direction involves decision making skills (Sheppard and Young, 2006). Therefore, agility has been widely defined as a 'rapid whole body movement with a change of velocity or direction in response to a stimulus' (Sheppard and Young, 2006).

Congruent with other sport expertise literature (Berry et al., 2008, Larkin et al., 2011) that has demonstrated skill-based differences for decision making skills, Gabbett and Benton (2009) found elite National Rugby League (NRL) players made faster and more accurate movement decisions than recreational players on a reactive agility test. It was then proposed reactive agility decision making tasks could provide information about player's strengths and weaknesses that may inform appropriate training strategies. In an attempt to understand potential training methods, Serpell and colleagues (2011) explored whether reactive agility decisions could be trained via a video-based programme. Participants were presented with video footage of a ball carrier coming towards them, and were asked to move in the direction to stop him. Results found that following four weeks of video training participants significantly improved their reactive agility decisions.

In addition to reactive movement-based decisions, researchers have also examined the differences in anticipation ability of high skilled (NRL), intermediate skilled (state-based competition) and low skilled (local level) rugby league players during a 'play-the-ball' situation (Gabbett and Abernethy, 2013). Participants viewed a life-sized video and at the moment of the play-the-ball the footage was occluded and the participants were required to perform the movement they would in a game (i.e. run forward, right or left). Results indicated high skilled participants had better response accuracy and quicker response times than the intermediate and low skilled participants. This further demonstrates the ability of skilled players to recognize early the relevant game-specific information to guide informed decisions.

## Decision Making Development Research

Many studies have explored the expertise effect in relation to decision making and perceptual-cognitive skills in a sporting context (Berry et al., 2008, Larkin et al., 2011). However, definitive solutions to develop decision making skills are relatively unknown (Berry et al., 2008). While talent identifiers and coaches are interested in the contributing factors to elite player development, the issues associated with early identification have limited the longitudinal methods to monitor the activities elite athletes engage in during the developmental years. Despite this limitation, researchers have used retrospective methods, such as interviews and questionnaires, to gain a greater understanding of the activities that may contribute to the development of elite level decision making skills. In a rugby context, Gabbett and Abernethy (2013) found elite rugby league players had accumulated significantly more junior games when compared to intermediate skilled and low skilled players. It was suggested this increased rugby-specific experience may facilitate the development of perceptual-cognitive skills in players. While this finding may suggest a potential influence on perceptual-cognitive skill development, the authors indicate the results do not imply a causal factor but may indicate high skilled junior players are provided with a greater opportunity to compete in matches as a result of already established perceptual-cognitive skills (Gabbett and Abernethy, 2013).

In an attempt to understand the influence of sporting engagement on the development of perceptual-cognitive skills, Berry and colleagues (2008) used retrospective interviews to ascertain the activities elite Australian Football players participated in during their development. The players, who were all participating in the elite Australian Football League competition, were categorized, based on elite coaches' opinion of their in-game decision making ability, as either expert or less skilled decision-makers. Results found a significant discriminating factor was the increased time invested within invasion sport activities during the developmental years of the experts.

While Berry and colleagues (2008) provided an indication of the hours accumulated by elite level athletes in structured and deliberate play activities, there is still limited understanding of the potential activities that assist the development of expert decision making skills. More recent research has attempted to understand the training and coaching environment. Cushion and colleagues (2012) suggested decision making and perceptual-cognitive skills may benefit more from 'playing form' (i.e. small-sided games that replicate game-related conditions) activities rather than 'training form' (i.e. individual or group activities without a game play context) activities conducted during training sessions. However, it has been reported that team sport youth coaches spend 25–35 per cent of practice in game-like activities and 65–75 per cent in fitness, grids and drills (O'Connor and Cotton, 2009). The associated benefit suggested from 'playing form' for decision making development is that the activities provide an opportunity to create links between the skills, decisions and action that are required within a game context (Ford et al., 2010).

# PRACTICAL APPLICATION

The previous section provided an overview of the scientific literature related to decision making in team sports. However, the challenge for coaches is how they develop this important but often overlooked skill in their players. This section details some examples of strategies that coaches can implement to provide increased opportunities for their players to develop decision making skills.

## Deliberate Play

Many coaches and players believe the development of skills only occurs within a structured training environment. However, time outside of structured training can also be of importance, especially for the development of skills such as decision making. It appears young players today are participating less in rugby-related play (e.g. backyard rugby [Jones, 2008]). Therefore, coaches should encourage players to participate in deliberate play activities to develop anticipation and decision making skills. This deliberate play approach would allow players to develop games where they modify the rules to suit their circumstances (e.g. skill level, available space, player numbers and so on). These informal games maximize enjoyment and experimentation by providing opportunities for players to be creative and 'play what's in front of them'. Methods to increase the opportunity for deliberate play for the youth player may be encouraging parents to allow their child to play with others at the local park. Parents may meet for a coffee and chat so they can keep an eye on young players but should not be involved in the play activities. Deliberate play can also be incorporated within a structured training session, where coaches can schedule a 'deliberate play' opportunity before or after team practice (even at the elite or professional level) so players can determine what and how they want to practice (or play).

## Athlete-Centred Coaching

Traditionally, coaching at all levels is very prescriptive, dominated by instruction with the coach in full control and telling players what to do and how to do it, with very little input from the players. This is termed a coach-centred approach in which training involves numerous repetitive skill drills (often involving little decision making) that are isolated from the context of a game. For example, structured set plays are executed either unopposed or with passive defence and when games are incorporated the coach will be yelling from the sideline on where to run, when to pass, etc. 'This form of learning... encourages athletes to be robotic in their actions and thinking (Kidman, 2010).' Alternatively, athlete-centred coaching is when the coach creates a learning environment that meets the needs of individual players, provides players with opportunities for developing tactical and decision making skills by using a games approach, and instils in their players that mistakes are a part of learning.

## Constraints-Led and Game Sense Coaching

Rugby is unpredictable in nature with players never knowing for certain what their

| Table 7.2: Constraints that can be Manipulated to Assist Skill Learning | |
|---|---|
| Player characteristics | Emotions<br>Technical skills<br>Tactical skills<br>Fitness level<br>Fatigue |
| Task characteristics | Rules<br>Field dimensions<br>Duration<br>Goal or aim of the activity<br>Number of players on each team<br>Equipment |
| Environment | Weather<br>Presence of spectators<br>Home or away<br>Ground condition |

opponents are going to do next (Passos et al., 2008). Therefore, the athlete-centred coach needs to embrace this uncertainty and unpredictable nature of rugby by using games, guided discovery and problem solving strategies to prepare players 'for the non-linear characteristics of a competitive match' (Passos et al., 2008, Davids et al., 2008). Constraints-led practice is where the coach manipulates various constraints (based on Newell's model, 1986, these are player, task and environment constraints) and the players learn by adapting to the situation through problem solving and guided discovery. Table 7.2 lists variables that can be manipulated to create a unique learning environment to enhance skill development (e.g. to encourage defenders to communicate late in the game the coach may have the players run shuttles to deliberately fatigue them, increase the width of the field, let the attacking team have the ball for four minutes regardless of whether they score or have a turn-over, etc.). Decisions made by players are in response to their interaction with other players, the environment and the task (Araujo *et al.*, 2006). For example, in rugby it has been reported 57 per cent of possession is from unstructured sources (e.g. turnovers and kicks) where there is uncertainty in attack and defence (McKay, 2012). The coach can design an activity or game with this focus where players must think quickly and respond to a constantly changing environment and adjust or self-organize to the chaotic nature of the game.

Constraints-led practice will therefore consist of activities or games that: (a) simulate aspects of a competitive match (e.g. defending your line, effective support play) while (b) challenging players to solve problems to enhance game understanding (e.g. defending an overlap when fatigued) with the coach assisting learning through the use of questions (Pill, 2014). Manipulating constraints and learning through games allows players to develop an understanding of the importance of time, space and risk.

For example, for players to gain a better understanding of the importance of shape and spatial awareness in rugby league the coach may manipulate the field dimensions (i.e. similar to a hourglass – wide at both try lines and becoming narrowest at halfway), player numbers (nine versus nine) and context (final ten minutes of the game). The coach encourages the players to respond to the constraints and determine how to 'shape' their movement patterns to progress the ball up the field and be in a position to score. The coach then provides feedback related to the aim of this activity. However, the coach must remember a player's decision cannot just be measured by the outcome as this will be influenced by their own skill level (e.g. good

decision, poor execution) and other players (e.g. good decision on when to pass, good execution in delivering the pass, however winger dropped the ball).

## Questioning

To complement constraint-led practice, questions are used to assist athletes to solve problems and reinforce correct decisions until their response becomes subconscious and automatic. Coaches should plan questions when they are devising their practice activities and can structure questions to ask about time (e.g. When should you run? When should you kick?), space (e.g. Where to run or kick to?), risk (e.g. What options are available?) or execution (e.g. What was the best type of pass to use?).

Examples of individual player questions include:

■ When was the best time to pass? Why?
■ How would the position on the field affect your decision when defending an overlap?
■ When you created a three-on-two situation, where was the space? What options did you have?

Examples of questions posed to the team include:

■ What would you do if we're up by two points with four minutes to go?
■ What strategies did you use when you had one fewer player in defence? Which ones worked well? Why?
■ What would you do differently if the opposition turned over possession on halfway rather than 5m from your try line?

Practice games need to provide players with the opportunity to interpret cues, explore options on what action to take and then execute. Through experimentation the player begins to understand what works and what doesn't. This is assisted through the use of questioning and guided discovery as the coach encourages players to consider the 'what' and 'why' of what happened, which will enhance players' learning. The coach stresses there is not 'only one way' or a 'right way' for any given situation and players need to play 'what's in front of them' by reading, reacting, adapting and responding to each scenario.

## Use of Video in Player Meetings

Coaches at all levels now use video edits in team meetings to provide visual feedback to players on recent training sessions or matches, and to scout opposition players and teams. Typically in these meetings they will be coach-led – with the coach selecting the edits to watch and highlighting critical aspects while players observe the video and listen passively to the coach.

However, with subtle changes to this scenario the coach can enhance athlete learning, particularly in relation to improving perceptual-cognitive skills. For example, rather than explicitly telling players what to do, coaches can show video of an opposition's attack and ask the players why particular plays were successful and what they will need to do defensively in those situations. Placing the players in small groups allows the players to use problem solving strategies to consider the 'what' and 'why' of each video clip, which will enhance player learning (O'Connor, 2012, Seifried, 2005).

Another example is using video to support self-reflective practice in an athlete-coach meeting where players are empowered to engage with and contribute to their technical and tactical development (Richards et al.,

2009). In this situation, players review a recent game and identify several teaching moments to discuss in a meeting with the coach. During the meeting, players present the footage and indicate why they selected the moment, what can be learned from this moment and how to implement future strategies to either promote or prevent this moment. It is proposed that providing players with the opportunity to select incidents to reflect upon and take ownership of their development means they are more likely to improve on their perceptual-cognitive skills. This strategy would generally only be used at the elite or professional level as it is very time intensive to meet each player individually for ten minutes each week considering there would be a squad of at least twenty players.

## Decision Making Video Simulation Training

Another method to develop anticipation and decision making skill is to include decision making video simulation training sessions (similar to what was previously described under 'assessing decision making skills') where video clips of rugby play are presented to players and then occluded (the screen is blacked out) at a critical point where a decision was required. Players are then asked questions such as:

- What would you do next if you were the player with the ball?
- What options are available to the ball carrier/support player/defender?
- What is the ball carrier/defender going to do next? (anticipation)
- Can you recall where players are located?

Players then watch the non-occluded video footage to see what actually happens. Each

**Fig. 7.1: Outline of the methods coaches may use to improve the decision-making ability of players.**

perceptual training session should include footage related to different aspects of the game from a defender's and attacker's perspective (e.g. defending your try line, attacking within 20m of the try line, overlap situations on different parts of the field). Using the principles of variability, the trials should be randomized. Although time consuming for the coach in preparing appropriate video clips, this is an ideal way to add decision making training without the additional physiological load.

## Game Observation

Finally, coaches may suggest to players when they are watching rugby on TV or are attending a game that they try to predict what a player will do next. This form of observational learning has been shown to potentially influence decision making ability (Pizzera and Raab, 2012), as there was a significant correlation between time watching competitive games as a spectator and decision making performance for soccer referees. Therefore, by promoting players to think about the actions and decisions players make during games they are watching, it may be possible to influence their decision making ability.

# IMPLICATIONS AND RECOMMENDATIONS FOR PRACTICE

- Decision making is the cognitive processes that informs the final action, such as a pass or movement. Correct decision making is a key component of match performance for rugby players, with skilled performance characterized by consistently and efficiently making correct in-game decisions.
- Decision making is not a singular process but, rather, incorporates numerous perceptual-cognitive skills including, pattern recognition, anticipation and situational probability to guide effective and appropriate decision making.
- The isolated decision making approach is used to assess decision making by designing video-clips that display game footage, enabling participants to develop expectations and use situational probabilities to inform an effective decision.
- Decision making skills may benefit more from 'playing form' (i.e. small-sided games that replicate game-related conditions) activities rather than 'training form' (i.e. individual or group activities without a game play context) activities. Coaches should also encourage players to engage in informal deliberate play where they can learn implicitly and trial various options in response to different scenarios.

- By manipulating the player, environment and task constraints, coaches can devise challenging and authentic game contexts to develop tactical understanding and awareness in their players.
- An athlete-centred coach uses questioning to stimulate thinking and reflection instead of always telling players what and how to play. This could include team meetings, which can be restructured from coaches solely narrating the video clips to incorporate (a) player questioning in relation to each scenario; and (b) players selecting video clips to interpret and discuss in the meeting.
- Video-simulation training sessions can supplement on-field team practice. Although preparing relevant video clips is time consuming this can provide players with further opportunity to make game related decisions as well as providing the coach with a greater understanding of what the player is likely to do in a given situation.

# CHAPTER 8

# SKILL TESTING FOR RUGBY

## *Sharief Hendricks*

## INTRODUCTION

Rugby is skill-based team sport and a prerequisite for effective participation is the ability to execute fundamental game skills such as catching and passing the ball, tackling and carrying the ball into contact (Hendricks, 2012). In addition to these general skills, position-specific skills (e.g. scrumming and jumping in the line-out in rugby union) are also required.

Furthermore, tactical proficiency, which includes visual scanning, pattern recognition, anticipatory skills, situation knowledge, adaptability and decision making in attack and defence, are all required for successful participation in rugby (Hendricks, 2012). In comparison to physical fitness testing, no standardized skill assessment for rugby league or rugby union exists to date (Hendricks *et al.*, 2015). The lack of such an assessment in rugby may be partly due to its particular requirements and the difficulty in capturing and representing the complex nature of skill demands in competition. With that said, noteworthy research in this area has been carried out that will pave the way forward for the development of a standardized skill assessment battery. The aim of this chapter is to discuss the current research in the area of skill measurement in

rugby and suggest an applied design that could be used in practice.

## RESEARCH OVERVIEW

### Importance of Testing Skill

A skill assessment should provide the coach with information with which he can monitor a player's progress and development. Further, it can aid in designing training drills to fit the needs of the player(s), establish normative and criteria data that can be used for talent identification and team selection, provide augmented feedback to the player, predict competitive performances and educate players and coaches about skill (Hendricks *et al.*, 2015).

### Skill Assessment Requirements

When designing and developing a skill assessment, a number of factors are essential for the assessment to be meaningful.

#### TECHNIQUE OR SKILL
Technique is considered to be the execution of a set of co-ordinated movement patterns,

whereas skill is the proficiency of execution of the correct actions determined by the demand of the situation (Hendricks et al., 2015). In other words, technique is the set of movements executed by the player in a relatively controlled and static environment, whereas skill is the performance of the right action at the right time in a dynamic environment. Generally speaking, good technique is a pre-determinant for good skill and the two concepts are related. For the purpose of skill assessment and measurement though, a distinction between technique and skill needs to be made. Understandably, skill will be more challenging to assess.

Whether assessing technique or skill, one will essentially be observing the execution of set movements or actions. For skill, the movements or actions will be in response to the demand of the situation. Whether or not the appropriate actions for the demand of the situation were used, the outcome of the executed skill may also be assessed. For example, in a two attackers versus one defender situation in rugby, an obvious goal for the attackers is to beat the approaching defender and ideally avoid contact. Here, the attackers' techniques of passing and receiving a ball can be observed. The ability of the ball carrier to draw the approaching defender and execute a pass to his teammate at the right time in order for him to break the defensive line without being tackled by the defender can be used as an assessment of skill in this situation. For complex skilled movements in rugby, subjective ratings are more useful than any current available 'objective' measure, because they are able to capture the true complexity of the skill (Kayes and McPherson, 2010). However, the subjective ratings should be standardized, tested for reliability and be validated to some degree.

## Reliability and Validity

Reliability concerns the repeatability or reproducibility of the assessment when the measurement is repeated. Validity of measurement indicates the degree to which the test, or instrument, measures what it is supposed to measure. It may take different forms but essentially questions the test in the following ways:

- Does it measure a relevant and important aspect of rugby performance (logical validity)?
- To what extent does the test cover adequately all the relevant aspects of the performance (content validity)?
- Does the test relate to a 'gold standard' (criterion validity)?
- How does the test relate to actual behaviour, for example, discriminate between different levels of play (construct validity)?

For a skill assessment to be credible and worthwhile, both the reliability and the validity of the assessment need to be addressed.

### REPRESENTING MATCH DEMANDS
The skill assessment should be able to capture and represent the demands of a match situation (Araujo et al., 2007, Pinder et al., 2011). Although the full complexity of match demands in the testing environment may never be achievable, the demands of specific situations within matches may be reproduced in the testing environment (e.g. one versus one attacker and defender situations). Most actions executed in team sports are the result of anticipation, which is usually based on information from the changing environment, engagement with opponents and interaction with teammates. This information the player uses to anticipate therefore needs

to be expressed in the testing environment. Researchers refer to this as 'ecological validity' (Araujo *et al.*, 2007, Pinder *et al.*, 2011). In addition to providing the cues typical of match situations, the conditions and constraints of the testing environment should represent the match so the skills and actions executed in the testing environment are transferable easily to the match performance environment (Araujo *et al.*, 2007, Pinder *et al.*, 2011).

## FEASIBILITY OF THE SKILL ASSESSMENT

The feasibility of a skill assessment can be defined as the ease in which a test can be undertaken, administered and scored or rated (Robertson *et al.*, 2014). This relates to cost, time-effectiveness, practicality, facilities and space availability to conduct the test. For rugby, the skill assessment should have the capability to test players in a team environment, in a short period and not require expensive equipment or special facilities.

# Assessment of Rugby Movements

In 1998, Pienaar, Spamer and Steyn were the first to attempt to measure skill in rugby (Pienaar *et al.*, 1998) and in a number of studies (Spamer, 2009) a range of tests were reported from handling skills (i.e. passing for distance, passing for accuracy over 4 and 7m, running and catching) to kicking skills tests (i.e. kicking for distance, kick-off distance) and air and ground abilities. However, these tests were performed in a controlled, static environment that failed to capture and represent aspects and demands of a match situation. Furthermore, the reliability and validity of the tests are questionable. Based on this, it seems this testing battery did not achieve its goal of measuring skill or technique but merely assessed an outcome of a rugby movement.

## PASSING THE BALL ON THE RUN IN REACTION TO A SIGNAL

In 2009, Pavely and colleagues set out to investigate ball-passing on the run to either side in reaction to a signal (Pavely *et al.*, 2009). Players started each trial 10m away from a 3m wide × 5m long grid marked on the ground by cones. Players were instructed to run at what they perceived to be 70 per cent of their maximum running velocity. Upon entry into the grid, players needed to react to a signal to either pass to the left or right towards a target 20m away. The signal was the raising of the hand either to the left or right by one of the researchers sitting on the opposite side of the grid (facing the player) and delivered when the player reached the first two cones. The player had to pass to the side of the raised hand of the researcher. The test was scored as follows:

- Reaction time (i.e. the time from the moment the signaller's hand moved to the moment the player initiated a movement response)
- Movement time (i.e. the time from the onset of a player response to the moment of ball release)
- Total time (i.e. from the moment the signaller's hand moved until the ball was released from the player's hands)
- Amount of head turn (i.e. players head position at the moment of ball release, scored as 0, 25, 50, 75 or 100 per cent of a 90 degree head turn that started from facing directly forward).

Also, the execution of the skill had to be legal (i.e. passes had to be thrown backwards or perpendicular to the direction of travel). The distance was also used as an outcome measure for passing. Reliability of the measurement was not reported. The player had to respond to a non-moving, non-rugby specific stimuli (i.e. a researcher sitting on the ground and raising the hand), and pass for distance to a non-moving, non-rugby specific target after entering a space marked off by cone markers. Therefore, the study did not adequately capture and represent the demands of a match situation.

## Skill Assessments

### SKILL ASSESSMENTS DURING SIMULATED MATCHES

In consultation with expert coaches, Gabbett and colleagues (2007) developed a testing battery for general skills (i.e. catching, ball carrying, basic passing and skills in the presence of fatigue), evasion skills (i.e. beating a player two versus one), tackling and defensive skills (i.e. side-on, head-on, rear tackle and defensive shape) and offensive skills (i.e. hit and spin, play the ball, pass out of tackle; [Gabbett *et al.*, 2007, Gabbett, 2008]). The execution of each skill was rated using an assessment criteria on a scale of one to five, with one representing very poor and five very good. The assessment of the skills did not take place in isolation, but was rated during a simulated match and players were unaware they were being assessed. The reliability of this assessment was good but questions regarding the use of a five-point scale to measure skill have been raised (Waldron *et al.*, 2014a).

### TACKLE TECHNIQUE

Building on from the skill assessment used during simulated matches, a standardized set of criteria to measure tackle technique was developed (Table 8.1; (Gabbett and Kelly, 2007, Gabbett, 2008)). The list of technical actions was based on cues coaches used to coach the tackle. Two players simulated a one versus one situation in a 10m grid where the defender needed to tackle the ball carrier. During

| Table 8.1: Tackle Technique Criteria (Gabbett et al., 2007) |
|---|
| **Assessment Criteria** |
| 1. Contacting the target in the centre of gravity |
| 2. Contacting the target with the shoulder |
| 3. Contacting the target with the opposite shoulder to the leading leg |
| 4. Body position square/aligned |
| 5. Arms wrapping around the target upon contact |
| 6. Leg drive upon contact |
| 7. Watching the target onto the shoulder |
| 8. Centre of gravity forward of base of support. |

contact with the ball carrier, execution of the technical actions were scored (i.e. one point was awarded for the proper execution of a technical action and no points for failure to execute the action).

This tackle technique assessment demonstrated a high degree of ecological validity and representativeness. Moreover, the tackle technique assessment was shown to be both reliable and valid. The validity of the assessment was proven by the relationship between a player's tackle technique score and defensive line speed (Gabbett and Kelly, 2007), physiological and anthropometrical characteristics (Gabbett *et al.*, 2011f), fatigue level of players (Gabbett, 2008), match performance, injury, team selection (Gabbett and Ryan, 2009) and playing level (Gabbett *et al.*, 2011d). Also, the test can be conducted in a team setting without difficulty.

### DRAW AND PASS ASSESSMENT

Using a similar approach to the tackle technique assessment, where players are awarded one point for the proper execution of a

## Table 8.2: Draw and Pass Criteria (Gabbett et al., 2011a)

**Assessment Criteria**

1. Pass on the inside shoulder of the defender
2. Small step away from the defender
3. Body position square with defender
4. Pass in opposite direction to leading leg
5. Correctly identify when to pass and when to run
6. Appropriate distance from the defender to prevent intercepted pass
7. Take the defender 'away', 'move the defender', 'create a gap', or 'open a hole'.

technical action and zero points for failure to execute the action, Gabbett, Wake and Abernethy (2011a) developed a set of criteria for the skill of drawing and passing in rugby league (Table 8.2; Gabbett, Wake and Abernethy, 2011a).

The assessment required players to execute a standardized two attackers versus one defender drill in a 10 × 5m grid. Like the tackle technique assessment, the draw and pass assessment can be considered ecologically valid and representative of match situations, as well as reliable and valid. In a separate assessment, the skill of drawing the defender and passing to a support player had to be executed while performing an additional task of recognizing and responding to a verbal tone. The addition of the secondary task was to load the attentional demands of the player, similar to those experienced in a match. Lastly, ratings on the draw and pass drill and the draw and pass drill with the additional task have been related to a player's match performance (both as a primary task and as part of a dual task assessment; [Gabbett and Abernethy, 2012]), physiological and anthropometrical

characteristics (Gabbett et al., 2011b), injury (Gabbett et al., 2012c), team selection and the effects of training on acquisition, retention and transfer of the skill (Gabbett et al., 2011a).

RUGBY LEAGUE ANTICIPATION TESTS
Across a range of sports, research has shown consistently experts are able to predict or anticipate more effectively than novices, based on observations in the sporting environment. To test anticipatory skills of rugby league players, Gabbett and Abernethy (2013) recorded several attacking match play scenarios to test the decision making of the dummy-half (i.e. player receiving the ball after a tackle is made; [Gabbett and Abernethy, 2013]). For the anticipation test, up to six defending players and a ball carrier were requested to simulate several predetermined attacking match play scenarios. The scenarios were developed in consultation with expert coaches. Scenarios included the simulation of single markers (i.e. a defender standing directly in front of the ball carrier), wide 'A' defenders (i.e. the first defender in the defensive line, closest to the markers), slow reacting defenders and fast and slow play-the-balls.

After recording the scenarios, the video footage was edited so each scenario could be replayed during testing from the moment the ball carrier approached the defensive line to the moment he played the ball with his foot. During testing, the scenarios were projected on to a wall to characterize the stature of real-life rugby league players and represent genuine match-attacking situations. The moment the player being tested had to play the ball, the video was occluded. Based on the player's initial movement into the final direction the player intended to move, response accuracy and response time were calculated.

To calculate response accuracy and response time, each test was analyzed using a high-speed camera. The anticipation test was able to demonstrate response accuracy and faster response times with an increase in age and playing level. Also, while performing the anticipation test, a secondary verbal tone recognition task can be added to load the attentional demands of the players.

MOVEMENT RECALL AND PREDICTION

As mentioned earlier, the ability to recognize useful information in a given sporting environment and anticipate the play under time constraints is a reliable discriminator for skill level (Williams, 2000). Using a similar approach to the anticipatory skill test where video footage of match scenarios are recorded and played back to players on a screen or wall to capture real match situations, studies measuring a player's ability to recall movement of players in a scenario and predict plays have also been conducted (Jackson et al., 2006). Unlike the anticipatory skill test though, players were not required to physically act but merely recall or predict the movements of players on the screen. For example, for pattern recall, players had to recall the position of all players in attack and defence at the time the video footage was occluded (Gabbett and Benton, 2009). For pattern prediction, players were required to predict the outcome of the next offensive or defensive play at the time the video footage was occluded.

Test designs of this nature are useful when attempting to measure the tactical skills of players. Also, it should be noted the players in the video acting out the scenarios should be at a similar level to the players for whom the test is intended (Jackson et al., 2006).

CARRYING THE BALL INTO CONTACT DRILL

As a result of real match analysis into attacking plays and carrying the ball into contact in rugby union, Wheeler and Sayers developed a testing drill that measured players' reactive agility and contact skill (Wheeler and Sayers, 2011). The testing drill assessed ball carrier skills, where the player had to sidestep one defender and, shortly after, engage in contact with another defender holding a padded shield. In summary, players were instructed to run with maximal effort for 7.4m, at which point the player had to react and sidestep in the opposite direction to the movements of the defender (left or right). After sidestepping the first defender, the ball carrier had to straighten the running line and, depending on the task condition, the course either terminated after 0.9m or the ball carrier made contact with a second defender holding a padded shield. Biomechanical measurements of running speed, lateral movement speed, anterior-posterior foot position and lateral foot position were measured during foot-strike and toe-off in three phases of the drill:

- sidestep (initial change of direction)
- straighten step (straightening of the running line following the sidestep)
- transition (phase between the sidestep and straighten step).

The testing drill was also conducted under different task conditions in two separate studies:

- pre-planned sidestep
- in reaction to the defender
- contacting the second defender
- fending the first defender
- contacting the second defender.

Wheeler and Sayers demonstrated how analyzing performance in real match situations could translate into the design and development of a skill assessment drill.

# PRACTICAL APPLICATION

This section outlines some practical points that need to be considered when implementing a skill assessment battery within rugby and provides specific examples for ball carrier and tackler contact skills.

## EQUIPMENT

Most of the studies outlined above made use of video to analyze skill or technique. Recording the movement and actions of players on video allows the assessor to analyze the players' technique or skill retrospectively, with the liberty to rewind, pause and slow down the footage. One does not necessarily require a high-speed video camera (although this would be ideal), and present-day smartphones may provide high enough quality for analysis. The next consideration is the placement of cameras, which is dependent on how many are accessible. Ideally, four cameras – front and back and on each side of the grid – should be used. The minimum number of cameras for analysis may be two – one on the side and one in front of the grid. All cameras should be fixed in line and facing the centre of the grid, at a distance that will capture the full grid and all players that are part of the skill assessment.

## THE DRILL

The design and number of players in the drill depends on the skill or techniques being assessed. For example, if only interested in tackle technique (and not tackler skill *per se*, which will require a slightly more demanding situation), the one versus one attacker-defender situation is appropriate. If we wanted to test tackle skill, we could create a situation with two attackers versus one defender. The two attackers versus one defender situation requires the defender to make a decision on which attacker to tackle. Here, technique will also be measured using the criteria, in addition to the outcome of the tackle.

All attempts should be made to capture and represent the match situation demands. With this in mind, instead of using cones to outline the drill, the drill should be located within a specific area on the playing field using the actual field markings as the constraints of the drill (e.g. the corners of the rugby playing field, where the touchline meets the try line). In this case, scoring a try could also be used an outcome measure of ball carrying or tackling. Also, instead of instructing the players to enter the drill directly, the drill and the assessment could take place after a phase play. This will allow players to enter the drill and contact at match-like velocities, and also afford the necessary constraints typical of rugby (e.g. sidelines). Lastly, it is recommended players perform the drill in a range of physical states (e.g. non-fatigued and fatigued).

## THE ASSESSMENT

As noted previously, a valid criteria list, similar to the tackle technique criteria or the draw and pass criteria, seems most appropriate to measure the complex skills required for rugby. As an example, technical criteria for ball carrying and both front-on and side-on tackling are provided (Tables 8.3 and 8.4). The technical criteria are based on the tackle technique assessment criteria discussed earlier, coaching literature, and consultation with coaches, sport scientists and rugby administrators. Using the recorded video of the drill, the player being analyzed is awarded either one or zero points if they achieve a particular criterion or if they fail to achieve it, respectively. There is some discussion as to whether each criterion should be scored equally, as some techniques may be more important than others for performance and safety.

## Table 8.3: Front on Tackle Proficiency Scoring Criteria for Ball Carrier and Tackler

| Ball Carrying Proficiency | Tackling Proficiency |
|---|---|
| **Pre-contact** | |
| Eyes focused on tackler | Identify/track ball carrier on to shoulder |
| Shifting the ball away from contact | Body position – upright to low (dipping) |
| Body position – upright to low body position | Straight back, centre of gravity forward support base |
| Body position – straight back | Square to ball carrier |
| Head up and forward, eyes open | Boxer stance (elbows close, hands up) |
| Shuffle or evasive manoeuvre | Head up and forward |
| | Shortening steps |
| | Approach from front/oblique |
| **Contact** | |
| Fending into contact | Explosiveness on contact |
| Side on into contact | Contact with shoulder opposite leading leg |
| Explosiveness on contact | Contact in centre of gravity |
| Body position – from a low body position up into contact | Head placement on correct side of ball carrier |
| Ball protection | |
| **Post-contact** | |
| Leg drive upon contact | Shoulder usage (drive into contact) |
| Arm and shoulder usage | Arm usage (punch forward and wrap, i.e. hit-and-stick) |
| Go to ground and present ball | Leg drive upon contact |
| | Release ball carrier and compete for possession |

## Table 8.4: Side on Tackle Proficiency Scoring Criteria for Ball Carrier (BC) and Tackler

| Ball Carrying Proficiency | Tackling Proficiency |
|---|---|
| **Pre-contact** | |
| Aware of tackler/attunement | Identify/track BC on to shoulder |
| Shifting the ball away from contact | Body position – upright to low (dipping) |
| Body position – upright to low body position | Straight back, centre of gravity forward support base |
| Body position – straight back | Head up and forward |
| Head up and forward, eyes open | Shortening steps |
| Shuffle or evasive manoeuvre | |
| **Contact** | |
| Fending away from contact | Explosiveness on contact |
| Explosiveness on contact | Contact in centre of gravity |
| Ball protection | Head placement on correct side/behind BC |
| **Post-contact** | |
| Leg drive upon contact | Shoulder usage (drive into contact) |
| Go to ground and present ball | Arm usage (punch forward and wrap i.e. hit-and-stick) |
| | Pull ball carrier with arms to ground |
| | Release ball carrier and compete for possession |

The knowledge and experience of the person evaluating the skill is an important consideration as one study has shown differences in scoring skill between novice and experts. To ensure the assessor is observing the correct actions, it is suggested he is briefed beforehand. More importantly, this may increase the intra-reliability of the individual. The proficiency scores should also be compared with another assessor (preferably of higher or similar knowledge and experience rugby skill) to test inter-reliability.

# IMPLICATIONS AND RECOMMENDATIONS FOR PRACTICE

- A skill assessment should provide the practitioner with information to monitor a player's skill progress and development, aid in designing training drills to fit the needs of the player(s), establish normative and criteria data that can be used for talent identification and team selection, provide augmented feedback to the player, predict competitive performances and educate players and coaches about skill.

- For a skill assessment to be credible and worthwhile, both the reliability and the validity of the assessment need to be addressed. Reliability concerns the repeatability or reproducibility of the assessment when the measurement is repeated. Validity of measurement indicates the degree to which the test, or instrument, measures what it is supposed to measure.

- The skill assessment should be able to capture and represent the demands of a match situation. Although the full complexity of match demands in the testing environment may never be achievable, the demands of specific situations within matches may be reproducible in the testing environment (e.g. one versus one attacker and defender situations)

- The skill assessment should not be laborious to conduct and have the capability to test players in a team environment, in a short period, and not require expensive equipment and special facilities. A knowledgeable and reliable assessor should assess technique or skill, using a standardized and valid list of criteria.

- Recording the movement and actions of players on video allows the assessor to analyze the players' technique or skill retrospectively, with the liberty to rewind, pause and slow down the footage. A minimum of two video cameras, one on the side and one in front of the testing grid, are recommended.

- Instead of using cones to outline the drill, the drill should be located within a specific area on the playing field using the actual field markings as the constraints of the drill. Also, instead of instructing the players to enter the drill directly, the drill and the assessment could take place after a phase play.

- It is recommended players perform the drill in a range of physical states (e.g. non-fatigued and fatigued state).

# CHAPTER 9

# THE YOUNG
# RUGBY PLAYER

*David Morley and Colin Sanctuary*

## INTRODUCTION

Due to the range of differences in the bio-logical, psychological and social (bio-psycho-social) characteristics of young rugby players, they cannot be viewed as mini-adults. Developmentally appropriate experiences that are directly related to their bio-psycho-social status are therefore crucial in ensuring retention in the sport from both a participation and performance perspective. Positive youth development in sport is rooted in the notion that coaches take a long-term developmental approach to coaching children that addresses the needs of the child and not the needs of the sport, team, coach or parent.

This chapter explores the idiosyncrasies that exist when considering the appropriate development of the 'young' rugby player. The first section will outline the general developmental needs of children and adolescents in sport and physical activity from a bio-psycho-social perspective and explain how these are influenced by a number of dynamic factors. The second section presents three case studies of recent practice in rugby in the Northern (England) and Southern (Australia)

Hemisphere, related to (i) competitively engineering the primary game (six to nine years), (ii) developing a 'Becoming CAYPA-BLE' qualification for children's rugby coaches (six to fourteen years), and (iii) optimizing performance of young players in a junior rugby league academy programme (thirteen to sixteen years).

### Bio-Psycho-Social Needs of Young Players

Table 9.1 outlines the key bio-psycho-social needs of young children in sport and physical activity as a guide for coaches to be able to establish their coaching practices accordingly. A note of caution: the age ranges used are typically representative of young players' development but should always be viewed in relation to individual needs, rather than chronological age development. These bio-psycho-social developmental processes should be understood when working with young players to understand how development in childhood and adolescence affects sport participation and performance.

| Table 9.1: Bio-Psycho-Social Development of Children and Young People in Sport (Adapted From (Morley *et al.*, 2011, *Muir et al.*, 2011) | | | |
|---|---|---|---|
| **Stage** | **Aspect of Development** | **Child's Development** | **Coaching Considerations** |
| Early 4–7 years | Biological | Gross motor skills | Development of gross motor skills is paramount (e.g. skipping, running, riding bike, catching, etc.) |
| | Psychological | Slow processing speeds; limited use of control processes; over-inclusion. | Keep cues short, few and simple. Use general instruction/feedback, continuous reminders of cues. Need to focus attention on task relevant stimuli |
| | Social | Development of early peer relationships; child unable to see a situation from another child's point of view | Peer relations primarily revolve around shared activities and interests. Struggles to understand different roles within the team, other than their own |
| Intermediate 8–12 years | Biological | Fine motor skills developing more rapidly; body scaling (shape variation becoming more pronounced) | Fine motor skills are developing on the gross motor skill foundation already laid. Refine and develop a 'feel' for the ball, (e.g. when carrying, catching and passing) |
| | Psychological | Increase in processing speed; uses strategies to interpret instructions and tactical demands; rehearses responses to tasks and situations as they emerge | Start using more precise instruction/feedback, shorter encoding processes means skill development is now accelerated. Less need for cue reminders but still needed occasionally. Still need to focus attention on task relevant stimuli |
| | Social | Peer group acceptance | Offer regular opportunities for players to demonstrate/develop their skills in making friends and getting along with teammates |

| Stage | Aspect of Development | Child's Development | Coaching Considerations |
|---|---|---|---|
| Later 13+ years | Biological | Puberty | Understand individual variation in maturation during this stage. Physical changes in the body require athletes to relearn some skills to accommodate for physical changes. Kinesthetic awareness and body in space are critical elements. Understand influence of fat storage and muscular development at varying levels for different players |
| | Psychological | Continued increase in processing speed; increased use and quality of control processes. May only pay attention to the areas the player feels are important for their own development | Avoid inappropriate excessive questioning, which can create anxiety and defensiveness within players, who feel as though they are being tested. Provide opportunities for deliberate practice to further refine the use of skills in sport-specific ways to increase confidence in participation. Support the establishment and achievement of clearly defined goals related to individual areas for improvement |
| | Social | Close, face-to-face communication between pairs or sub-units of players | Emphasize the importance of the individual within the collective. De-emphasize the importance of competitive outcomes and stress the importance of fun and learning with friends |

## Dynamic Factors Influencing the Young Player's Development

It is obvious young rugby players do not play under laboratory conditions and a number of influencing factors will affect their experiences within rugby. Therefore, the bio-psycho-social development of young players is facilitated or constrained by a range of dynamic factors.

These dynamic factors are:

- The capabilities, needs and wants of the *Individual* player
- The *Task* that is used to meet the needs of the Individual(s)
- The *Environment* established by the coach, predominantly determined by the behaviours the coach uses.

Dynamic systems theory (Davids et al., 2003) suggests these three aspects must be viewed simultaneously to recognize practices that are constraining a young player's development and intervene accordingly. It is evident these dynamic factors are interdependent in as much as if a task is established that fails to take account of the individual developmental needs of the young players completing the task, it is doomed to failure. Similarly, if the coach uses behaviour specifically designed to relate to the developmental stage of young players it is likely to result in increased engagement, enjoyment, skills competence and subsequent retention. The differentiation and inclusion approach to dealing with players on an individual basis highlights how the coach understands a player and how he can develop him appropriately. It must always be remembered, all players are individuals even if they are still part of a team.

# CASE STUDIES

The following case studies demonstrate three real-life examples of working with young rugby players by applying developmentally appropriate practices based on their bio-psycho-social needs and the dynamic systems theory mentioned above. The case studies are presented by explaining why the initiative was needed, the aims of the initiative, what the initiative involved and the 'take home' messages for those working with young players at specific ages and stages.

## Case Study 1: Competitive Engineering in Primary Rugby League

WHY WAS IT NEEDED?
In 2012, the National Governing Body for Rugby League in England, the Rugby Football League (RFL), instigated a review of Primary Rugby League (rugby league for 5–11 year olds). The review was prompted by growing concerns about the lack of children's meaningful experiences during matches, decreasing retention rates and a sense the game favoured the more physically developed child (RFL, 2013a, RFL, 2013b). Ensuring children's first experiences of sport are positive, child-centred and developmentally appropriate is considered vital to sustaining participation in any sport if children are going to foster a life-long love of sport and physical activity (Kirk, 2005). A range of factors influence children's participation levels in any given activity; these include their level of fun and enjoyment, being with friends and peers and having opportunities to learn new skills (Bailey et al., 2010). These early experiences should also concentrate on developing fundamental movement skills and offering opportunities for young players to interact socially with their peers in a positive way.

WHAT WERE THE AIMS OF THE INITIATIVE?
The aims of the initiative were to improve children's early experiences (e.g. social opportunities, enjoyment, physical activity levels, competence and development of fundamental movement skills) within rugby league. The initiative compared the traditional primary league game with a competitively engineered game. Competitive engineering involves modifying rules (e.g. the amount of game time or rules requiring positional rotation), the number of players, the size of equipment or the size of the pitch (Burton et al., 2011) and is designed to promote intrinsic motivation by heightening the positive experience of actually playing the sport through constructing the most appropriate form of competition to the developmental needs for certain age groups.

## Table 9.2: Variations of the 'Traditional' and 'Modified' Games

| | Traditional | Under-7s | Under-8s | Under-9s |
|---|---|---|---|---|
| Number of players | 9 v 9 | 4 v 4 | 5 v 5 | 6 v 6 |
| Pitch (m) | 60 × 40 | 20 × 12 | 20 × 15 | 25 × 18 |
| Time (min) | 2 × 15 | 8 × 5 | 8 × 5 | 8 × 6 |
| No. of tackles | 6 | 6 | 6 | 6 |
| Type of tackle | Tackle | Touch | Touch/tackle | Tackle |
| Play the ball | ✓ | ✗ | ✗ | ✓ |
| Defending team retreat (m) | 5 | 2 | 2 | 4 |
| Passive marker | ✓ | ✗ | ✗ | ✓ |
| Errors penalized | ✓ | ✗ | ✗ | ✗ |
| Coach on pitch | ✓ | ✗ | ✗ | ✗ |
| Player rotation | ✗ | ✗ | ✗ | ✓ |

WHAT DID THE INITIATIVE INVOLVE?

In response to the perceived needs of young players, a national initiative was commissioned by the RFL to explore the implications of a 'competitively engineered' modified version of primary rugby league for players aged six to nine years designed to increase skill opportunities within the game. This initiative started by deciding the changes that needed to be made from the 'traditional' to the 'modified' game. A technical group was established with RFL staff with expertise in coaching children. This group established the modifications that characterized the 'modified' game in the competitive engineered environment. Additionally, and because the appropriate age for introducing the full tackle to primary rugby league players was debated extensively within the RFL technical group, the under-8s category was engineered to explore differences between using 'full' tackles against 'touch' tackles. Therefore, both variants of tackle were piloted to assess differences in skill opportunities.

The 'traditional' primary rugby league game is a modified version of the thirteen-a-side game, with teams playing nine-a-side home and away fixtures in a non-competitive competition structure. The games are played on a modified pitch that is a minimum size of 50m x 30m to a maximum of 60m x 40m. Game rules were the same as the full international rules with the exception of no scrums, no kicking in play or at goal, no running from dummy half and a reduced defensive retreat, from 10 to 5m. Table 9.2 illustrates the changes made to the competitive engineered modified games at the under-7, 8 and 9 age categories:

The 'traditional' and 'modified' formats of rugby league were then played by 108 under-7s, 223 under-8s and 144 under-9s from twelve community rugby league clubs over a ten-week period. All games were filmed, followed by notational analysis to capture

## Table 9.3: Definition of Rugby League Skills Analyzed

| Skill | Definition |
|---|---|
| Pass | Player sends the ball towards a teammate from his hands |
| Effective pass | Player's pass arrives at the receiver between the waist and shoulder |
| Catch | Player takes initial control of the ball in his hands, following pass from teammate |
| Effective catch | Player retains control of the ball when receiving from a teammate |
| Tackle | Player attempts to stop an opponent from carrying the ball forwards |
| Effective tackle | Player's attempt at stopping an opponent carrying the ball forwards is successful; as judged by the game maker, who indicates a completed tackle |
| Kick | Player uses his foot to strike the ball |
| Knock-on | Player knocks the ball forwards (i.e. from a receive, or during a tackle) with his hand or arm and it touches either the ground or an opposing player |
| Round the world runs | Player performs a looping run (i.e. parallel with, or behind, the advantage line) to evade the opposition before running forward |
| Crossed the advantage line | Player carries the ball beyond an imaginary line drawn across the pitch where the player received the ball |
| Crossed the defensive line | Player carries the ball beyond an imaginary line drawn across the pitch where the forward most defensive player is positioned |
| Line breaks | Player evades opponents' tackles and in doing so crosses the defensive line |
| Average tackle count | The mean number of effective tackles per set |
| Completed sets | A passage of play reaching at least the fifth tackle |
| Tries scored | Player places the ball on the ground with downward pressure in the in-goal area between (and including) the goal line and up to but not including dead ball line of the opposition's half. |

the difference between skill opportunities in the 'traditional' and 'modified' versions of rugby league. Experts from the performance department at the RFL identified the most important skills that indicate meaningful participation in the game. These skills, outlined in Table 9.3, were annotated during observation of game footage.

WHAT DID THE INITIATIVE FIND?

Across every age group, there were significant advantages resulting from the 'modified' game compared with the 'traditional' game structure. This included greater overall skill opportunities, including catching, passing, running and try scoring. These differences indicated the clear superiority of the competitively engineered 'modified' game for involving players in developmentally advantageous features of match play within rugby league.

## TAKE HOME MESSAGES

It is clear from the evidence that children have more skills opportunities if the game is 'modified' to meet their developmental needs. Coaches should consider how they modify games for children (six to nine years in this case study but not exclusively for this age range) that they are coaching, in relation to the three main developmental needs of children in sport:

- Have fun – children enjoy more skills opportunities, particularly offensive action.
- Learn and refine new skills – children develop most effectively when the skills they have learned can be practised, repeated and consolidated in a wide variety of situations. Maximizing skills opportunities is key to this developmental need.
- Be with their friends – children want to interact with friends and share learning experiences. Using smaller-sided games increases this social interaction.

## Case Study 2: Becoming CAYPABLE: Designing a 'Fit for Purpose' Coaching Award for Coaching Children (6–14 years)

### WHY WAS IT NEEDED?

Recent research (Morley et al., 2011a, Morley et al., 2011b, Morley and Webb, 2009) suggested young rugby league players were not being exposed to a full range of movement competencies that would be required to produce versatile, co-ordinated athletes able to function effectively within the game. Moreover, the deficiency of movement skills being coached within rugby suggested coaching programmes failed to deliver effectively sessions relevant to the developmental needs of young players and commonly reverted to adult-based methods. Treating children like mini-adults fails to recognize their unique developmental needs and has been criticized across sports coaching in the UK (Lara-Bercial, 2012). An example of the differentiation in the development of a skill (e.g. throwing) across different ages is demonstrated in Table 9.4.

Therefore, young players need to develop movement skills such as balance, co-ordination, reaction and timing, which are the building blocks of sport and most forms of recreational physical activity (Gallahue et al., 2006). The focus on the establishment of fundamental movement skills, irrespective of their significance in terms of rugby league, is vital to a child's subsequent inclusion in any form of sport or physical activity. Using this type of environment at the correct stage of a young athlete's development can contribute to the overall pathway for him or her as they progress through certain developmental stages in relation to their capabilities.

### WHAT WERE THE AIMS OF THE INITIATIVE?

To introduce a 'movement-centred', developmentally appropriate qualification for coaching children in rugby.

### WHAT DID THE INITIATIVE INVOLVE?

The initiative involved developing a 'fit for purpose' coaching award for coaches working with children aged six to fourteen years. At the heart of the design of this coaching award was the fundamental belief that children's needs should be the focal point of any coaching award. Using the findings from the coaching deficiency analysis that had already been conducted, the design of the award was constructed around the movement needs of children at various developmental phases, according to the Lifespan Motor Development model (Gallahue et al., 2006). These movements were categorized into Stability,

## Table 9.4: A 'Throwing' Example of RFL Skills According to the Lifespan Motor Development Model (Gallahue et al., 2006) Matrix Analysis

| Areas of Skill | Current Skill Demands | Early (4–7 years) | Middle (8–12 years) | Later (13 years +) | Elite (existing skill sets) |
|---|---|---|---|---|---|
| Throwing | *Static* | Thumbs point inwards | Thumbs point upwards | Ball passes centre or side line of body | 6 o'clock |
| Ability to impart force to an object in the general direction of intent | Weighting | | | | Over the front foot |
| | Timing | Difficulty in judging | Ball is recoiled before release | offering full recoil in preparation | Ball pointed down |
| | Accuracy | Action from elbows Resembles a push | | | |
| | | Follow-through forwards and downwards | Ball does not pass centre or side of body line in preparation | Trunk, shoulders and hips fully rotate | Shoulders rotated |
| | *Moving* | | | | |
| | Weighting | | | | Wrist hands |
| | Timing | Little rotary action | Trunk and shoulders rotate towards throwing side | Able to demonstrate proficiency on both sides | Dummy half-pass |
| | Accuracy | Limited weight transfer | | | Approach |
| | | | Sideward and forwards shift of body weight | Opposite leg to throwing side acts as block to produce force | Move into sit position (step to ball) |
| | | Feet remain stationary | | | |
| | | | Opposite leg strikes ground to throwing side | Arms extend fully in direction of throw | Scans sit |

## Table 9.5: Players' Needs at the Beginner, Intermediate and Advanced Stages of Development

| Levels and stages of learning a new movement skill | Children And Young People |
|---|---|
| | Players Thinking... Individual |
| BEGINNER/NOVICE LEVEL | Player tries to form a conscious mental plan of the movement task |
| Awareness Stage | Wants to know how the body should move |
| Exploratory Stage | Knows what to do but unable to do it with consistency |
| Discovery Stage | Forms a conscious mental plan for performing the task |
| INTERMEDIATE/PRACTICE LEVEL | Player has good general understanding of the movement task |
| Combination Stage | Puts skills together with less conscious attention to their elements |
| Application Stage | Makes effort to refine skill |
| ADVANCED/FINE TUNING LEVEL | Player has a complete understanding of the movement task |
| Performance Stage | Gives little or no conscious attention to the elements of the task |
| Individualized Stage | Fine tunes performance based on personal attributes and limitations |

Object Control and Locomotion (SOL) and the sequential development of each movement was mapped into the various stages (i.e. beginner, intermediate and advanced) of a young player's development. The young player's needs within these stages of development are described in more detail in Table 9.5.

Drawing from the understanding that children's development is part of an interactive process between the individual, the task and the environment (dynamic factors related to children's development in sport and physical activity), the Becoming CAYPABLE framework was developed for coaches attending the course to understand the different processes involved in coaching children. The individual related to Children And Young People, the task related to Activity Base and the environment related to Learning Environment form the CAYPABLE acronym. This framework was the focal point of the whole course and was explored in more detail through the use of a range of coaching cards, featuring increasingly demanding exercises to enhance the SOL capabilities of young players within coaching practice. This resulted in a course, which focused around three specific bases related to dynamic factors (Individual, Task, Environment) with the 'Plan, Do, Review' (i.e. planning, delivering and reviewing a session based on these three factors).

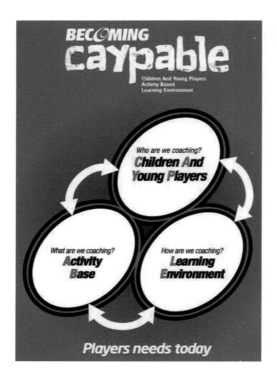

**Fig. 9.1: 'Becoming CAYPABLE' (Morley and Muir, 2012).**

of Competitive Engineering. Coaches should recognize the way in which they plan and deliver the activities they use and the environment they deliver based on the needs and wants of the children and young people they are coaching. Providing a movement-based, staged approach, to the coaching is crucial to a player's development if they are to have the requisite fundamental movement skills to participate effectively in their current playing opportunities and continue to develop in the long term.

## Case Study 3: Optimizing Performance of Young Rugby Players in a Junior Rugby League Academy Programme

This case study is based on the practical application of a junior academy programme within a club from the National Rugby League (NRL) competition in Australia. The club has a wide community and recruitment base and players are selected at respective age levels (thirteen to sixteen years) to the junior academy programme. The programme aims to develop players from a range of bio--psychosocial perspectives alongside rugby-specific skills and knowledge. This level of support is required as players come from varied backgrounds related to their development. The junior academy programme provides a development opportunity for players to progress to the high performance unit (sixteen to eighteen years). Players within the unit are those identified as having the greatest potential to progress to a professional sporting career within rugby league.

### WHAT DID THE INITIATIVE FIND?

Becoming CAYPABLE was a watershed moment for many coaches as they came to terms with player-centred coaching and the use of a movement-based approach for coaching children aged six to fourteen. The course was not without its critics, with the main concerns centred on the detraction of time spent on some 'core skills' such as tackling. Early indications are there is a need to provide ongoing mentoring for coaches who have attended the Becoming CAYPABLE course to ensure these developmentally appropriate initiatives become routine practice within coaching youth rugby league players aged six to fourteen.

### TAKE HOME MESSAGES

Becoming CAYPABLE emphasizes developmentally appropriate, player-centred practice, in a similar vein to the previous case study

Recent research (Cupples and O'Connor, 2011, Till *et al.*, 2014b) has highlighted the importance of a range of physical, cognitive, technical and tactical skills for development of junior rugby league players. Also during these ages (i.e. thirteen to sixteen years), large individual variations are apparent in the development process due to maturation (i.e. the timing and tempo of progress towards the mature adult state; see Table 9.1). In rugby league, this has resulted in early maturing players being selected to development squads, suggesting coaches focus on physical traits rather than technical, tactical and psychological characteristics (Till *et al.*, 2010a). Consequently, within the development of a junior academy programme it is important to ensure players attain appropriate levels of physical, technical/tactical and lifestyle competencies. In addition, players should be compliant with completing tasks and activities as set to help develop their understanding and application of physical preparation within the performance environment. As junior academy players are not just mini NRL or Super League players, work undertaken with such players requires a definite start point, purpose and end point (transition into an NRL/Super League Squad). Hence, it is important a systematic and progressive structure is implemented.

The junior academy programme of the club aimed to develop a range of areas within players. The main aims are detailed below with Table 9.6 providing the core development principles that the programme aimed to achieve for thirteen to sixteen year old players.

- To get players faster, fitter and stronger, within an environment of injury prevention and healthy living
- To create good attitudes, application and work ethic, not passive recipients, in developing individual physical preparation programmes

- To train regularly and consistently within a simple, progressive programme of strength and conditioning
- To provide the junior and senior academy players with the support and direction to help them achieve the standards required to reach the NRL/Super League.

Once aims and objectives, along with core development principles, were set, club staff addressed how these aspects were to be seen and presented at different levels and age groups. The key perspectives were to rationalize what level of development the player had reached and what work was to be completed through structured, planned and progressive exercise streams and sequencing of support. In addition, it was to provide appropriate and structured feedback to enhance development and learning. Alongside this, the junior academy programme considered the potential for maturation bias by providing separate thresholds/standards from a physical perspective for players based on their chronological and maturational age. Each age category was split into two (i.e. January–June and July–December) to provide more comparative thresholds for early and late birthdays within the calendar year. This allowed a more equal assessment when discussing a player's development relative to another.

Table 9.7 outlines the specific physical aspects of performance within the junior academy programme and highlights how the different aspects of physical work were broken down for strength, speed, endurance, agility, mobility and stability and movement skills. As can be seen through the style of work completed, it is firstly important to establish an appropriate 'base' of effective and efficient movement and technique. For example, aspects of work from a strength perspective highlight the importance and role of pure body weight work, which can then

## Table 9.6: Core Development Principles for Junior Academy Players

| Core Skills | Games Sense | Physical | Social | Welfare/Pastoral Support | Rugby League Specific Principles |
|---|---|---|---|---|---|
| Catch and pass | Vision | Mobility and stability | Respect | Time management | Appropriate retreat speed |
| Tackle technique | Communication | Speed/agility | Teamwork | Welfare-education/career | Footwork on turning into the defensive line |
| Play the ball | Decision making | Strength/power | Leadership | Education (school and higher ed) | Body position (leaning forward) when set in the defensive line |
| Support | Anticipation | Repeatability | Ownership | Education (rugby-related: nutrition, physical, psychological, lifestyle, tactical and technical) | Staying low in the initial explosive three steps off a defensive line |
| Ball carry | | Resilience | Life skills | | Repeatability of the defensive line speed |
| | | Movement quality | | | Strong body position in the contact area (attack and defence) |
| | | Recovery | | | Able to maintain speed/s throughout a game |
| | | Nutrition | | | Able to maintain set work rate throughout a game |
| | | | | | Speed of thought when fatigued (appropriate decision making) |
| | | | | | Effective and appropriate communication |

be progressed to thera-band and medicine ball work. It is important the basics of all the main lifts (e.g. squats, deadlifts, bench pull, bench press and the Olympic derivatives) are grounded in safe and efficient movement and technique. This principle of development can also be seen to be applied to speed, endurance, mobility and stability.

From the core development principles and physical performance matrix, specific performance benchmarks were set using a range of performance tests to monitor player development. This included a holistic approach that focused on movement (i.e. functional movement assessment), physical (i.e. height, body mass, 10 and 40m sprint, vertical jump, agility, multi stage fitness test and strength), psychological skills (i.e. mental toughness questionnaire and semi structured interview) and match and training characteristics including rugby league specific criteria, attendance and punctuality, communication, feedback and evaluation, and reflection of own perfor-

mance. Although outside the scope of the chapter to detail all the testing, this approach allowed the club to obtain information about junior players to inform player development and coaching interventions in the future.

TAKE HOME MESSAGES

Players require specific feedback and support to contextualize their performance against peers and individual expectations. Within the structure of a junior academy programme, it is important to examine all facets and not just the fact the player is, or might be, substantially larger in mass or height than his peers. However, this is where a more holistic approach is important to ensure potential players, who may be late developers, are not missed. Such players may show particular psychological traits or indicators of potential power output, which may be over looked. Therefore, it is key that appropriate case management of individual players is undertaken.

## Table 9.7: Junior Academy Movement Skills and Physical Preparation Matrix

| | Under-13s and 14s | Under-15s and 16s |
|---|---|---|
| **Movement Skills** | | |
| Aims | To further the development of gross movement skills. Players able to sustain, modify and train movement skills accordingly within the context of rugby-specific requirements | To refine and adapt the gross movement skills for rugby. Players able to sustain, modify and develop movement skills as an automatic function of rugby-specific requirements |
| Understanding and application | At least one year consistent strength and conditioning experience<br>Explains and demonstrates the essential means and methods of physical training<br>Regular engagement with strength and conditioning coach, undertakes non-dependent practice | Consistent strength and conditioning experience<br>Inputs to strength and conditioning plan as justifies and analyses strength and conditioning practice<br>Regular engagement and demonstrates 'deliberate practice' |
| Running | Intermediate technique – run in a straight line over short to long distances with increasing range, stride and forward body lean. Variable starts, accelerates, pick-ups and decelerates with control | Efficient technique for rugby-specific purposes – run with changes of direction and pace from variable starts, over variable distances, with good knee drive, faster arm/leg action |
| Turning | Intermediate turning mechanics – change from lateral to linear movement using cross-over step and cuts (one point agility). Control in backwards movement | Efficient technique for rugby specific purposes – two-three point agility with rapid change of direction using cuts and cross-overs (front and behind) |
| Jumping | Intermediate jumping mechanics – jumping for distance and height with forward and backward single foot take-off and landings. Begin movement in the air | Advanced jumping from forward or backward take-off, both single and two footed with movement in the air and on landing |
| Quickness | Responds and reacts appropriately to simple and some complex tasks with quickness of vision, feet and hands | Responds and reacts appropriately to simple, complex and random tasks with quickness of vision, feet and hands |

**Physical**

| | | |
|---|---|---|
| Aims | To promote regular exercise training to develop the fundamental physical abilities for rugby performance | To promote an understanding of the different physical requirements that are demanded by maximum rugby performance |
| Mobility and Stability | Identifies specific mobility and stability needs and implements a specific mobility and stability programme | Identifies specific mobility and stability needs and implements a specific mobility and stability programme |
| Strength | Maintains coordinated muscular control over gross movements and develops good posture. Supports own body weight. Beginning of core stability programme | Develops and maintains posture and shows refined control and coordination over complex movement skills. Beginning of strength programme |
| Style of Work | Bodyweight and stability training (e.g. bodyweight, partners, medicine ball). In phases of up to 12 weeks including 3 to 5 exercises, 3 to 5 sets per exercise, 8 to 12 reps per set | Hypertrophy/strength (e.g. medicine ball and free weights). In phases of up to 8 weeks including 3 to 5 exercises, 3 to 6 sets per exercise, 3 to 8 reps per set |
| Speed and Agility | Development of basic speed and agility patterns relevant to team sports. Timed over 10–30m | Development of speed to include agility and complex specific speed. Timed over 10–30m to meet standards |
| Style of Work | Linear and lateral speed work focusing on technique, movement and positioning of body, linear, lateral and multi-directional work. Duration of intervals 5–20 seconds | Complex speed work incorporating agility and change of direction focusing on movement and positioning of body, linear, lateral, multi-directional and chaotic speed, deceleration work into change of direction, planned agility, duration of intervals 5–20 seconds |
| Endurance | Ability to sustain efforts of varied intensity and duration and understands need for recovery | Ability to sustain efforts of varied intensity and duration and understands need for recovery |
| Style of Work | Games or skills incorporating conditioning drills | Tempo running (involves running basic intervals at approximately 75–80 per cent in a relaxed and efficient manner, using the techniques developed in speed mechanics training), conditioning games using restricted areas or skills incorporating conditioning drills |

## IMPLICATIONS AND RECOMMENDATIONS FOR PRACTICE

- Practitioners should understand and consider the differing bio-psycho-social needs of children and young people and how this impacts participation and performance within rugby.
- The bio-psycho-social development of young rugby players can be facilitated or constrained by three dynamic factors related to the capabilities, needs and wants of the *Individual* player, the *Task* that is used to meet the needs of the Individual(s) and the *Environment* that is established by the coach. Therefore practitioners need to consider these dynamic factors in the development of young rugby players.
- Practitioners should engineer games competitively to meet the developmental needs of young rugby players by offering more skills opportunities to ensure children (i) have fun, (ii) learn and refine new skills and (iii) optimize social interaction with other players. Maximizing offensive actions (i.e. scoring, breaking a defensive line) contribute more to a young player's enjoyment than other aspects of the game

- Practitioners should aim to provide a movement-based, staged approach, to coaching young rugby players that provides them with the requisite fundamental movement skills to participate effectively in their current playing opportunities and continue to develop in the long term.
- Practitioners' planning should begin with the needs of the young rugby player and then concentrate on selecting appropriate tasks and coaching behaviour to meet the player's needs. It is important as the coach you identify why are you doing what you are doing?; how are you actually going to do it?; what specifically are you going to do?; and when are you going to do it?
- Practitioners should understand the importance of an individualized and holistic approach to player development during adolescence (i.e. thirteen to sixteen years), especially considering the large differences in maturation that occur during this time.

# CHAPTER 10

# TALENT IDENTIFICATION AND DEVELOPMENT

*Kevin Till, David Morley, Stephen Cobley, Balin Cupples and Donna O'Connor*

## INTRODUCTION

Historically, Olympic nations and their sporting governing bodies have attempted to identify early athletic promise and then develop this talent to be able to perform at the highest senior elite level. This process, likely fuelled by the commercialization and professionalization of sport, has grown and intensified substantially within the last fifteen to twenty years; becoming more commonly known as Talent Identification and Development (TID). Talent identification is defined as the process of recognizing players who show potential at an early age to excel at a more advanced level while talent development refers to the provision of the most suitable learning environment for athletes to realize their potential or accelerate their development (Cobley et al., 2012). TID programmes have become progressively popular within sports and many rugby clubs now implement their own TID system to identify and develop talented rugby players into future stars of the game.

Fig 10.1 (adapted from Cobley and Cooke, 2009) provides a model of how TID programmes typically operate in UK rugby league. The community rugby playing population includes the largest number of players who participate in rugby league across all ages. Talent identification usually takes place at professional rugby league clubs at fourteen and fifteen years, whereby players (approximately twenty at under-15s and 16s) are identified to train at a professional club as part of their talent development programme. This results in enhanced quality coaching, increased playing opportunities, access to advanced facilities and additional support including strength and conditioning, physiotherapy and nutrition. From within this talent development programme, additional selection/non-selection opportunities occur between fifteen years of age and adulthood. At each stage the number of selection opportunities decreases (i.e. academy, usually eight to ten players at under-17s, 18s and 19s). The opportunities available to be selected to the subsequent TID stage decreases with only a small percentage of players successful in obtaining professional status. However, it is not always a prerequisite for players to be in the previous stage of the TID process to be selected to a subsequent stage. Players not retained within the system usually drop down a stage to a lower level, return to the community game or drop out of the sport. In addition, the Rugby Football League (RFL) will also provide international

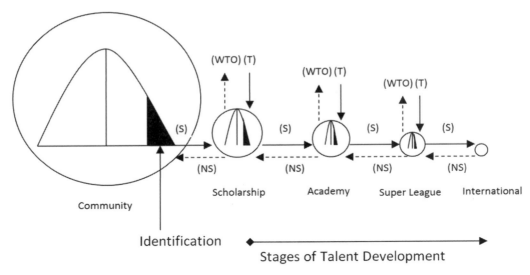

**Fig. 10.1: Conceptual diagram of talent identification and development in field-based team sports. (Adapted from Cobley and Cooke, 2009)**

opportunities at each stage (i.e. under-16s, 18s) resulting in even fewer selection opportunities from the playing population at that level.

In relation to these rugby-based TID programmes, the aim of this chapter is to provide an overview of the rugby-specific research associated with TID including highlighting some of the problems associated with talent identification in youth players and the process of talent development. In addition, the chapter provides a practically applied case study demonstrating how research and TID knowledge has been applied within a national governing body talent development programme relating to eleven- to fourteen-year-old rugby players.

# RESEARCH OVERVIEW

## Talent Identification in Rugby

One aim of talent identification research is to provide an understanding of which factors (i.e. technical, tactical, physical, psychological and so on) can differentiate between levels within junior populations that may lead to enhanced future performance. To complete this task, research studies have typically compared elite (i.e. talented) junior rugby players with non- or sub-elite counterparts. One of the first studies in this area was conducted by Pienaar and colleagues (1998), who compared the anthropometric, physical and technical skill of South African ten-year-old rugby players with a non-playing population. The findings highlighted that a range of anthropometric (e.g. stature, body mass, chest girth), physical (e.g.

| Table 10.1: Summary of Research Examining Anthropometric and Physiological Differences within Talent Identification in Rugby | |
|---|---|
| **Participants** | **Summary of Findings** |
| 11 untrained juniors, 13 trained juniors and 15 senior juniors (Baker, 2001) | Senior > trained > untrained for bench press (1–RM) strength, bench press power and jump squat performance |
| 75 elite and 76 sub-elite junior rugby League players at under-15, 16 and 17 (Gabbett and Herzig, 2004) | Vertical jump, 10m sprint, 40m sprint, agility 505 and multi stage fitness test were significantly greater in elite players than sub-elite players at the under-15, 16 and 17 age category |
| 36 elite and 28 sub-elite under 16 Australian junior rugby league players (Gabbett et al., 2009) | 10m, 20m, 40m sprint, agility 505, vertical jump and estimated $VO_2$max were significantly greater for elite than sub-elite players |
| Junior starters and non-starters at under-14 (n=53), under-16 (n=20) and under-18 (n=15) (Gabbett, 2009) | Height was greater for starters at under-14s and 16s<br>Skinfolds were lower for starters at under-16s and 18s<br>10m, 20m and 40m speed were lower for starters at under-14s, 16s and 18s<br>Agility 505 was lower for starters at under-16s<br>Vertical jump was greater for starters at under-16s<br>Estimated $VO_2$max was greater for starters at under-14s and 16s |
| 28 junior elite and 13 junior sub-elite at under-16s age category (Gabbett et al., 2011c) | Junior elite players had significantly greater tackling proficiency, height, body mass, sum of skinfolds, 10m sprint, agility 505 and vertical jump than the junior sub-elite players |
| UK Regional and National representative players at under-13s, 14s and 15s (Till et al., 2011) | Vertical jump, med ball throw, 10–60m sprint, agility 505 and estimated $VO_2$max all significantly greater in national players at under-13s and 14s but only vertical jump at under-15s |

speed, agility, endurance, strength, power) and technical skill (e.g. pass distance, pass accuracy, kick distance) indicators could be distinguished between the two groups. The authors concluded these measures might assist in selecting and developing ten-year-old rugby players. Since then, a range of investigations have compared junior rugby players at differing playing and selection levels across different ages and contexts. The majority have focused on the comparisons of anthropometric and physiological characteristics, probably due to the ease of quantifying such measures compared with skill and psychological measures.

Across these studies, findings highlighted that anthropometry, physiological characteristics and tackling proficiency (e.g. (Gabbett et al., 2011c)) can be used to discriminate between selection levels. Therefore, it can be assumed that anthropometric and physiological factors are important for the identification of youth rugby players. However, these findings do not capture the full story, especially within youth players, and TID programmes have been questioned due to their poor ability to predict future success (Vaeyens et al., 2008). In addition, numerous problems have been associated with TID programmes in youth athletes (e.g. annual-age grouping, longitudinal tracking, one-dimensional approach (Vaeyens et al., 2008)), which are discussed in the following section. This means the identification of rugby players is not as straightforward as it may seem and there are a number of considerations for the player and/or practitioner to contemplate.

## Problems in Talent Identification

### ANNUAL-AGE GROUPING

Players within junior rugby, like most other youth team sports, compete within chronological annual-age groups (i.e. under-13s, 14s, etc.). Although this process is designed to provide equal competition and developmental opportunities for all players, such an age classification provides advantages to players born nearer the selection cut-off date (i.e. 1 September in UK). This grouping process also occurs irrespective of the variations in maturation that occur between individuals during adolescence. Two concerns have been associated with the annual-age grouping process in youth rugby.

1. Relative Age Effects (RAEs) – RAEs have been defined as the short- and long-term consequences of participation and selection

within youth sport as a result of an individual's birth date relative to an annual-age group selection start date (Cobley et al., 2009). RAEs have been evidenced from rugby league's junior community participation level (Till et al., 2010b) through to professional ranks in the UK (Till et al., 2010b) and Australia (Abernethy and Farrow, 2005, Cobley et al., 2014). RAEs favour the relatively older individual (i.e. those born nearer the selection start date – Sep-Nov in the UK) and have been shown to increase with each selection level in the Rugby Football League's (RFL) TID programme for under-13 to 15 players. Approximately 85 per cent of players selected to the national squad were born between September and February (Till et al., 2010b) demonstrating greater selection advantages for relatively older players.

2. Size and maturation biases were evident for the same population (Till et al., 2010a), favouring the taller, heavier and early maturing player. Together this suggests that annual age grouping process used within rugby provides advantages to the relatively older and earlier maturing individual at junior and adolescent stages, and has an impact on identification, selection and development opportunities within youth rugby.

### LONGITUDINAL APPROACH

Current research and practical application of TID programmes use predominantly a cross-sectional approach, whereby performance is assessed at 'one-off' time points to predict success in adulthood (Vaeyens et al., 2008, Till et al., 2013). In other words, these processes take only a snapshot of performance at a specific time point and fail to consider that adolescents may not retain their performance into adulthood due to growth, maturation and training effects (Abbott and Collins, 2004). Recently, research (Till et al., 2013, Till et al., 2014a) aimed to address such concerns by investigating the longitudinal development of anthropometric and fitness characteristics in rugby players aged thirteen to sixteen. The findings illustrated firstly how maturation status can affect development and, secondly, the often unstable and non-linear nature of development in performance characteristics in adolescent athletes. For example, Till et al. (2014a) demonstrated later maturing junior rugby league players showed more progression than the early maturing players between thirteen and fifteen years of age on a range of physical tests. Therefore, tracking players longitudinally may better assess the impact of maturation and the changing perceptions of capability and future potential. For what appears to be talent at a particular time point may not be the characteristics of talent in the longer term.

A further limitation of cross-sectional studies and the research shown in Table 10.1 is that it is assumed current performance capabilities between playing levels in junior players can help predict potential success in adulthood. However, what may be more useful is to find what characteristics at junior levels are most important for future long-term career attainment. In a recent study, Till and colleagues tracked players selected to a TID programme between thirteen to fifteen years of age over an eight year period to determine whether they were successful in progressing to a professional academy (i.e. under-18s) and onward into professional (i.e. Super League) adult rugby league (Till et al., 2014b). The study found a lower sum of four skinfolds and advanced fitness performance, especially change of direction speed, differentiated between players that progressed to the academy and professional levels compared to the players that did not (i.e. amateurs). However, no differences in characteristics were found between future academy and professional players suggesting that, although anthropometric and fitness characteristics may contribute to career progression, technical skills, tactical knowledge and psycho-social development may also be important for future career progression.

ONE-DIMENSIONAL APPROACH
The majority of research to date has also adopted a one-dimensional approach to TID, focusing predominantly on the anthropometric and physiological variables as discussed above. This approach is also problematic as player ability within rugby is a complex interactive, sometimes chaotic, team event and is dependent upon a combination of individual capacities. To support this notion, Australian-based National Youth Competition (NYC) coaches were asked to identify essential position-specific indicators in youth rugby players for future performance (Cupples and O'Connor, 2011). The findings identified a number of consistent cognitive (e.g. communication, 'reading the game', mental toughness), physiological (e.g. acceleration, power) and game-related skills (e.g. ball carry, catch/pass, support play) were essential. These are summarized for three playing positions in Table 10.2, identifying highly specific skill sub-sets and attributes according to certain positions (see Cupples and O'Connor, 2011).

Despite some position specific contrasts in performance indicators, common across all positions was the need for a range of cognitive factors to be evident for future performance. The coaches' consensus on the importance of cognitive factors was further highlighted in their identification of 'initial signs of higher performance in youth players', which included the following cognitive indicators:

- Discipline (setting goals, preparation)
- Attitude (on and off the field; overcoming challenges)
- Character
- Learning ability
- Personality.

| Rank | Fullback | Halfback | Back row |
|------|----------|----------|----------|
| **Table 10.2: Position Specific Performance Indicators within Rugby League Identified by NYC Coaches** | | | |
| 1 | Support play (GS) | Communication (link between players, organize, position others) (C) | Good direct line running: lead runs, inside shoulder, into space (GS) |
| 2 | Communication: predominantly in defence, sort numbers; see threats, outside in, players inside/out (C) | Reading the game/decision making under pressure and fatigue: process information quickly, 'footy brain' (C) | Decision making in defence: knowledge of pattern own/opposition (C) |
| 3 | Reading the game: seeing/taking space, reading attack/defence, inject timing (C) | Vision, understanding and looking up (knowing when to run/pass/kick; 'game sense' (C) | Agility: good feet, change of direction, lateral movement (P) |
| 4 | Positioning: knowledge of attack/defence, on the ball (GS) | Organization (thinks ahead, game plan) (C) | Cardiovascular Endurance (P) |
| 5 | Good decisions/ability to react at speed: defence/attack, high speed/high consequence moments (C) | Catch pass (on the run) (left/right) (GS) | Mental toughness: concentrate for longer periods, less rest, increased workload (C) |

Notes: C = Cognitive, GS = Game Skills, P = Physiological

Interestingly, these cognitive factors were deemed more important than skill level, game intelligence and physical indicators (e.g. size and speed). Considered together, this study highlights the importance of a holistic assessment and evaluation for rugby performance, and that physical talent alone is unlikely to relate to long-term attainment. Notwithstanding this recognition, such factors (i.e. cognitive) are often neglected, ignored and are in part the least understood in the TID process. This may be due to the difficulty in assessing such qualities accurately, as well as the multiple and repeated observations required for valid assessment.

## Talent Development in Rugby

Based on the problems highlighted with talent identification, research recommendations have included: reducing early (de)selection policies within adolescent rugby (Till et al., 2010b, Till et al., 2014a) alongside changing coaches' philosophy and practices when working with younger players. For example, a recent study explored the collaborative perceptions of a group of Australian elite level youth coaches (NYC under-20s) who were asked to identify and rate their main coaching concerns for players at the elite under-20s level (Cupples, 2010). The most significant concern raised was the low standard of basic technical skills such as catch, pass, grip and carry; skills integral to rugby performance. Coach statements in relation to basic skills such as 'some players think they have got them and they don't actually have them' highlight this gap in youth player perception and reality. In addition, being the best player in their teams at younger ages was suggested as an indicator as to why core skills were generally poor for elite youth players. Dominating junior teams due to physical size and/or natural ability and being praised by previous coaches demonstrates how their existing core skills have not been challenged or exposed previously. This may also suggest how advanced relative age and maturity may override the need for core skills at early stages but become exposed as weaknesses in higher level competition at later (post-maturation) stages.

After basic skills, a range of cognitive factors were also identified as improvement areas by coaches (Cupples, 2010). Specifically these were: communication; vision (i.e. looking up; playing what's in front); concentration (i.e. ability to cope with increased time); and attitude to defence/defensive technique (i.e. inability to defend one versus one for extended periods). The comment 'talent isn't the most important thing, discipline and attitude are more important than anything' highlights the emphasis of cognitive aspects such as concentration and communication to performance at the NYC level. The significance of cognitive skills has also been highlighted within other team sports with expert development coaches highlighting the following as being key influential factors in individual player development (Mills et al., 2014).

- Awareness
- Resilience
- Goal-directed attributes (passion, professional attitude)

- Intelligence (sport intelligence, emotional competence)
- Sport specific attributes (e.g. coachability, competitiveness).

The above findings highlight a lack of basic skills and the importance of developing specific cognitive skills need to be reflected in talent development programmes. Initial responsibility for implementation of activities aimed at enhancing these skills falls to the coaches. At a practical level, this may mean breaking down current daily and weekly session plans to minimize and/or modify the time and type of physiological based activities to ensure the skills above are being included and targeted. Accompanying these strategies is the need to increase the players' awareness of the importance of such skills to their long-term progress. Player 'buy in' to the significance of these skills is important, with higher ranked South African youth rugby union players perceiving psychological skills training as very important (43.3 per cent versus 35 per cent) when compared to lesser ranked players (Andrew et al., 2007). Unfortunately, recent findings have identified a lack of these characteristics being taught explicitly within team-based talent development environments (Larsen et al., 2013).

## The Talent Development Environment (TDE)

The aim of talent development practice is to adapt and prepare the athlete, ultimately accelerating his or her path to becoming an elite performer (Cobley et al., 2012). The recognition of and subsequent desired optimization of the process of developing talented junior athletes into elite athletes has also led to several recent developments in the field. This includes the notion of the Talent

**Table 10.3: Summary of Research Examining Characteristics of Effective Talent Development Environments (TDEs)**

| Methods and Participants | Identified 'Effective' Environment Characteristics |
|---|---|
| Semi-structured coach interviews; 13 UK individual and team sports, including rugby (Martindale et al., 2007) | 1) Long-term aims; 2) Wide range of coherent messages/support; 3) Emphasis on development; 4) Individualized development; 5) Integrated, holistic and systematic development |
| Case studies of successful individual sport TDEs composed of interviews with coaches, managers, prospective and current elite athletes, environment observations and document analysis (Henriksen et al., 2010) | 1) Proximal role models; 2) Focus on long-term, strong organizational hierarchy; 3) Training group supportive relationships 4) Support for psycho-social development |
| Methods as per Henriksen et. al. (2010) above. In situ case study of successful Dutch football academy (Larsen et al., 2013) | 1) A culture with a strong family feeling; 2) The ethos of working hard; 3) A holistic approach to development; 4) A team first attitude |
| Semi-structured coach interviews; 10 development coaches of elite football academies (Mills et al., 2014) | 1) Importance of player welfare (understanding player world view); 2) Key stakeholder relations (trust with parents); 3) Involvement (encourage player input) |
| Delphi Poll; Coach and player perspectives from elite football academy (Morley et al., 2014) | 1) Contexts of game and training rated above social, personal and lifestyle; 2) Prioritize the role of discipline; 3) Need for target setting; 4) Importance of mental strength |

Development Environment (TDE) based on a holistic view that considers all aspects of the development situation including direct (e.g. parents, coach and peers) and indirect (e.g. policies and culture) influences (Martindale et al., 2005). The TDE perspective promotes an individual's development in a range of capacities (e.g. physical, psychological, etc.) to be examined from multiple perspectives that provide unique insights into the talent development process as a whole.

The consensus of these studies on TDEs highlight the importance of long-term aims, support for psychological skill development, the promotion of supportive relationships and managing the 'person rather than the athlete'. Overall, the path to the elite level is often non-linear and consists of many challenges that either enhance or hinder an individual's progress (Gulbin et al., 2013) involving repeat procedures of selection and de-selection (Güllich, 2013). The consistent challenges of the development pathway have been highlighted recently within elite schoolboy (under-18s) rugby in Australia with findings indicating only 12.7 per cent of Australian schoolboy players progressed to the senior national level (Barkell et al., 2013). Therefore, an athlete's ability and the TDEs processes to overcome these obstacles and transitions within a performance pathway often determine long-term success. The rugby-specific and range of TDE findings summarized above detail both the challenges and opportunities that exist within talent development.

# PRACTICAL APPLICATION

## Introduction

Research overviewed in the prior sections has discussed problems around talent identification, the need for holistic considerations in talent development and the factors that are important for effective TDEs from both athlete and coaching standpoints. However, developing and applying a TID programme within rugby that considers all these factors to create an optimal TDE and set of practices is challenging. This section provides an overview of the core content and principles of a recently introduced talent development intervention in rugby league for eleven to fourteen year olds, named Embed the Pathway.

## Embed the Pathway

Embed the Pathway was implemented at the under-14 age group as this is a key period of maturation variability for players and was a stage prior to when players were about to be formally selected on to the first exclusive segment of the RFL's talent pathway (i.e. professional club scholarship) at the under-15s age category (see Fig. 10.1). Following a review of the former RFL coaching programmes and associated resources, a number of potential problems were identified (that have been previously discussed in this chapter), including:

- RAEs, maturation and size biases were apparent
- There was a focus on physical characteristics
- There was a lack of consideration for psycho-social attributes within players
- An overriding focus on ways in which the same rugby skills were delivered and developed with players across the full spectrum of participation (six years to elite [Morley, 2011]).

The review demonstrated a need for a change in the TID processes to move away from early selection policies focusing on uni-dimensional (i.e. physical) factors. Instead, Embed the Pathway would provide delayed selection opportunities, (i.e. providing opportunities for a greater number of players to remain participating) and that selection – when it did happen (i.e. at under-15s scholarships) – would entail more holistic aspects of player development (i.e. including psycho-social, technical, tactical attributes). Therefore, based on the above rationale, Embed the Pathway was designed with the following objectives:

- To increase the quantity and quality of eleven to fourteen year old rugby league players with the ability to progress further up the talent pathway in the long term (i.e. into scholarships, academies, professional and international levels)
- To improve the connectivity between professional clubs and local community clubs and schools
- Lead to enhanced multi-dimensional talent identification processes for players entering professional clubs at scholarships at the under-15s age category
- Provide opportunities for late developers to be talent identified and remain participating in the community game.

Based on these objectives, Embed the Pathway was constructed around three core components, including the use of (1) player profiling, which was something that had not been used before with this age group, (2) coach education and (3) curriculum and resource design. Players would no longer be selected into representative squads (i.e. academy, regional, etc.) and would therefore remain in their community environments longer, playing for their local clubs. Therefore, using these three Embed the Pathway components would allow direct delivery to players in their own environments (i.e. to increase coaches' ability to develop players within community club settings) and provide a greater opportunity to influence lasting change in behaviours and skill development to a greater number of athletes.

## Player Profiling

Player profiling was the key aspect of practical change and application and it also informed the coach education and curriculum design programmes. The player profile was developed upon the RFL's previous 'six panel' player development model, which served the purposes of its entire pathway (juniors to seniors). The profile was re-formatted to a four-way player development model to reflect developmental needs of players at the under-14 stage of development and therefore became more age and stage appropriate. The development of a holistic player profile was undertaken by evaluating expert coaches' understanding of the key requirements of performance for an under-14 rugby player in terms of future performance potential and ability. This process resulted in four 'Player Development Contexts' (PDCs) and further

Player Development Features (PDFs) within each of the four contexts (Table 10.4).

The player profiling system was developed for a number of reasons including (1) maximizing player performance, aligned to the core aim of talent development; (2) identifying desirable performance characteristics in players in order to develop these characteristics further (Gould et al., 2002); (3) it is a useful method of exploring how a player perceives his or her own ability as the player is placed at the centre of the process with their perspective being viewed as fundamentally important; and (4) it creates coach-player dialogue requiring coaches and players to work together to ensure the players reach their potential and plan to develop the areas requiring more attention.

The identified PDCs and PDFs were then key aspects of the whole Embed the Pathway programme including:

- Player profiling – players and coaches were required to reflect upon the key qualities, outlined in Table 10.4, and rate themselves in terms of performance (between one and five)
- Coach education – educational opportunities were provided to support coaches in the use of a player profiling tool alongside further developing coaches understanding of the three PDCs (i.e. movement, mental and coachability) which were not as apparent in current coaching due to the focus on specific technical and tactical elements of the game
- Curriculum development – to support this coach education, a range of curriculum development opportunities and resources were developed (including an aligned eight-week training programme to support delivery).

| | **Table 10.4: Player Profile for Under-14 Rugby League Player** | |
|---|---|---|
| **PDCs** | **PDCs Statement** | **PDFs** |
| Game | 'I have good technical and tactical rugby league knowledge' | ■ Running pass 10m both ways<br>■ Dummy-half pass 5m both ways<br>■ Understand role in kick chase and escort<br>■ Proficient at line movement and retreat in defence |
| Movement | 'I have good movement skills' | ■ Hop and stick<br>■ Straight line sprint<br>■ Body weight squat<br>■ Turn off either foot<br>■ Vertical jump<br>■ Superman<br>■ Med ball throw |
| Mental | 'I have a can do attitude' | ■ I can reflect on my performance and set goals<br>■ I work hard<br>■ I can cope with physical contact<br>■ I am honest about my performance |
| Coachability | 'I am willing to listen to advice and act on it' | ■ I want to learn<br>■ I can communicate with others<br>■ I attend regularly and on time<br>■ I bring and use the correct equipment |

## Conclusion

Based on existing research and practice, Embed the Pathway was developed to create a talent development programme that reduced early identification processes, while emphasizing the importance of creating a TDE within a community environment. The emphasis on a holistic player profile consisting of rugby-specific capacities alongside physical, psychological and social aspects to inform future (i.e. at under-15s) player identification is a driver for player development through coach education. The Embed the Pathway programme will be delivered to coaches working with players aged eleven to fourteen in the future to enhance talent development practices while minimizing problems associated with TID within rugby league.

## IMPLICATIONS AND RECOMMENDATIONS FOR PRACTICE

- Talent identification is a complex, dynamic and non-linear process, especially within a multi-factorial team sport such as rugby. Practitioners should understand that what appears to be talent now may not be the characteristics of talent in the longer term.
- Annual age grouping in youth rugby can lead to relative age effects and maturational biases favouring the older, bigger and earlier maturing player. Therefore, rugby practitioners should consider relative age and maturation in their identification, selection and development programmes.
- Players should be tracked on an individual basis over a longitudinal period to analyze the changes that occur in performance instead of using assessments at one-off time points.
- Talent identification and development should be based around a holistic and multi-dimensional approach that considers and measures physiological, cognitive and skill attributes within players.

- Coaches should emphasize long-term development and player potential instead of emphasizing short-term immediate performance, especially during adolescence when a number of factors can differentiate between players.
- The key cognitive indicators for successful future performance in rugby could relate to discipline, attitude, character, learning ability and personality. TID programmes in rugby should emphasize the identification and development of these characteristics within young players.
- National Governing Bodies and professional clubs should aim to create talent development environments with long-term aims that focus on development over winning; that support bio-psycho-social development while creating a culture of discipline and attitude.
- There is no one size fits all approach to player development. Coaches need to be able to recognize areas for improvement and be able to address these across a range of player development contexts.

# CHAPTER 11

# THE SCIENCE OF RUGBY REFEREES

*Stacey Emmonds, Amy Brightmore, Stuart Cummings and John O'Hara*

## INTRODUCTION

The role of the referee is essential across both codes of rugby to enforce the rules of the game and regulate the behaviour of the players. Their decisions have the potential to influence the outcome of a game. The performance demands inherent in elite refereeing involve a number of key areas including fitness and positioning (Ghasemi *et al.*, 2011, Weston *et al.*, 2011), law knowledge and application (Schweizer *et al.*, 2011, MacMahon *et al.*, 2007a), contextual judgement and game management (Mascarenhas *et al.*, 2005a). Therefore, it is vital referees are prepared optimally for the physical, cognitive and regulatory demands of the game and the season. The generic demands of refereeing vary between and within rugby codes and competitions (i.e. one versus two refereeing system between European Super League [SL] and Australasian National Rugby League [NRL]).

In rugby league, the SL competition uses a single full-time professional referee during each fixture. They are required to officiate from February to September (not including pre-season friendlies), once a week for approximately twenty-seven rounds of the regular competition. Selected referees then officiate during the play-off system and a Grand Final during October each year. In addition there are five Challenge cup games that designated referees will officiate throughout the season. Subsequently, selected referees may also officiate international tournaments, further extending their season. The NRL has operated a two-referee system since 2009. The NRL season is similar to SL, with twenty-four rounds and four play-off rounds; however, the roles of the referees are different. In the SL, the single referee makes all the decisions and controls all aspects of the game. In contrast, in the NRL a 'lead referee' controls play from the 10m defensive line while a 'pocket referee' polices the play-the-ball area. The 'pocket referee' is unable to make decisions on stoppages or penalties but is able to communicate with the 'lead referee'. The two referees will interchange roles within the game, with the 'lead referee' changing roles presently for approximately 20 per cent of the time. Throughout a season, an NRL referee may be designated as a 'lead referee' or 'pocket referee' but will tend to dominate in one of the roles throughout the season.

Rugby union adopts a single referee system and the English season requires referees to officiate between fifteen and twenty-two games (one per round) of the twenty-two rounds of the regular competition (September to May), plus the semi-final and final, in addition to cup competitions. In the Southern Hemisphere, referees officiate in their domestic leagues as well as potentially in the Rugby Championship and Super Rugby competitions.

Regardless of code, referees are required to officiate a significant number of games throughout a season. Therefore, it is important they have optimal fitness to keep up with the pace of the game, as well as an ability to cope with the perceptual-cognitive demands, particularly the pressure to make a correct decision (Ghasemi et al., 2011). Thus, with the correct physical and psychological preparation and knowledge of the game they should be able to make the correct decisions under pressure and fatigue. Therefore, the specific aims of this chapter are to provide a review of the research on the decision making requirements and accuracy of referees, as well as the movement and physiological demands of refereeing in rugby, and how this information can be used to develop appropriate training practices.

# RESEARCH OVERVIEW

## Decision Making

The most important role of the referee is to determine whether the laws of the game have been breached by a player and, if so, apply the appropriate course of action (i.e. award a penalty). Refereeing the tackle in rugby presents a unique situation where multiple, complex and dynamic decisions are required, which may be influenced by a number of factors including the movement and physi-

ological demands of the game, positioning, viewing angle and context of the game (i.e. score and time point of the game). Furthermore, confounding this is the fact that rugby referees are much more than mere regulators of the law. A feature of refereeing rugby is the notion of advantage. For example, the referee will recognize that an offence has occurred but may choose to ignore it as an advantage has been gained or simply manage it, perhaps through communicating to the players, to balance the trade-off between game flow and control. Indeed, it is the referee's ability to allow the game to flow but also maintain the control of the players, termed contextual judgement (Mascarenhas et al., 2002), that is crucial.

Rugby referees are making decisions continuously throughout the game, with many of them classed as non-observable decisions (i.e. did the pass go backwards? Thus, the referee does not interfere with play allowing the game to continue). Therefore, quantifying overall referee decision making accuracy is difficult. To date, such accuracy has been quantified during match play by determining the accuracy of penalties awarded (Emmonds et al., 2014). Penalties only represent a small portion of the overall decision making demands, with referees reported to award on average fifteen penalties per game (Emmonds et al., 2014). This method of quantifying decision making accuracy is easy to implement, while evaluating a referee's ability in complex decision making and rule interpretation.

SL referees have been reported to award correctly penalties on 74 per cent of occasions during match play (Emmonds et al., 2014), while decision making accuracy of rugby union referees has been reported to be ~50–60 per cent using retrospective video analysis (Mascarenhas et al., 2005b). While decision making accuracy of SL referees has been quantified based on the match play decisions, accuracy of rugby union referees' decision making has only been quantified artificially by video analysis (i.e. observing a series of filmed tackle scenarios from match play). While this method is still useful and provides an insight into the decision making accuracy of rugby union referees, coaches must be aware of the limitations of this method as decision making does not occur in the context of a game, whereby accuracy may be influenced by referee positioning, physical fatigue or anxiety.

## Decision Making Training

The high volume of decisions made by referees advocates the need for highly developed perceptual-cognitive skills as a pre-requisite for successful performance. Decision making training may enhance the accuracy of decisions made by referees although the ecological validity of any training programme and transfer of skills to match play must be considered. Previously referees have mainly relied on experience to develop their perceptual-cognitive skills (Mascarenhas et al., 2005a). However, due to the limited match play exposure, it would seem developing decision making training is also important.

An effective method of developing rugby referees' decision making is video-based training in which referees are shown clips taken from games (Schweizer et al., 2011, MacMahon et al., 2007b). This method demonstrated improvements in decision making accuracy for both Premiership (4 per cent) and National League (17 per cent) rugby union referees. Furthermore, while this method is useful for training referee decision making, coaches must be aware of the limitations of using video footage taken from a stadium angle, which provides a spectator's view rather than a referee's view. Despite these inherent limitations, this training technique has its purpose

for the development of referees. In particular, the large improvement in decision making accuracy of the lower level referees indicates that this may be an effective method of training for coaches working with amateur and lower level referees to adopt.

The development of a sound rationale for decisions is important to assist in developing the accuracy of referee's decisions. MacMahon et al. (2007b) evaluated the extent of shared reasons underpinning decisions by referees through the review of video clips from pre-recorded matches. This established that referees have higher accuracy scores when all referees agreed on the rationale for the decision. This would suggest that reasons underlying decisions, as well as the actual decisions made, should be part of referee training in order to improve referee decision making (MacMahon et al., 2007b).

## Movement Demands

Rugby referees are required to keep up with play at all times in order to maintain optimal positioning when viewing decisions. Consequently, the movement demands are influenced by the movement patterns of players. In previous years, time motion analysis using video recordings has been used to quantify the movement demands (Kay and Gill, 2003). However, in recent years Global Position System (GPS) has been increasingly employed. This is an emerging data collection technique for evaluating referees within any sport and provides invaluable information to assist in the development of appropriate training. These technologies can provide information on distance, velocities and direction of movement. This information can assist the coach in developing appropriate training, which reflects the demands of the game for the referee.

**Fig. 11.1: High-intensity running demands of rugby referees.**

## DISTANCE COVERED DURING A MATCH

The total distance covered by referees during match play is 6–9km, depending upon the code of rugby and competition. Given that referees' activity patterns have been reported to be inter-related to those of the players (Martin *et al.*, 2001) it is interesting that the total distance covered by both rugby league and union referees is greater than that reported for players. A possible explanation for this is that the referee officiates the full game, while players can be interchanged during the course of a game, therefore may work at higher intensities. Further, referees also have to be close to the ball, which causes them to move laterally across the pitch, potentially increasing distance covered compared to players, who tend to be part of a defensive or attacking line and tend to move up and down the pitch.

There are likely to be large individual differences in the distance covered during match play, which needs to be considered when planning appropriate physical training (i.e. SL referees have been shown to cover between 4.2 and 9.4km during a match (Emmonds *et al.*, 2014)). Whether the differences in distance covered during match play is related to a referee's experience (i.e. better able to predict their positioning) or fitness is yet to be established. Distance covered may also be affected by the intensity of the game, as dictated by the players, as well as the competitiveness of the match, with a referee likely to be stood still more often in high scoring games. However, as well as using total distance, the intermittent nature of refereeing needs to be taken into consideration, especially the time spent at different running speeds, in particular high-intensity running.

## INTERMITTENT NATURE OF MOVEMENT DEMANDS

Rugby is a sport requiring intermittent high-intensity movement and it is important to establish the intermittent demands of refereeing. Within sport, six velocity categories (i.e. standing, walking, jogging, running, high-intensity running and sprinting (Rampinini *et al.*, 2007a)) are used typically to establish the frequency of efforts, exercise duration, distance covered and percentage time spent at different velocities. Research shows rugby refereeing is characterized by long low-intensity

## Table 11.1: Total Distance (Metres) Covered by Referees during Match Play

| Competition | Total Distance (km) | References |
|---|---|---|
| SL (2009 season). | 8.9 ± 0.8 | O'Hara et al., 2013 |
| SL (2012 season). | 7.1 ± 0.8 | Emmonds et al., 2014 |
| SL (2013 season). | 6.9 ± 0.8 | Brightmore et al., 2014 |
| NRL (1 referee system). | 6.7 ± 0.4 | Kay and Gill, 2003 |
| NRL (1 referee system). | 7.6 | Hoare, 2008 |
| NRL (2 referee system, 2013 Season). | Lead: 7.3 ± 1.2 Pocket: 7.5 ± 0.9 | Brightmore et al., 2014 |
| English Rugby Union. | 8.6 ± 0.7 | Martin et al., 2001 |
| Spanish Rugby Union (1 referee system). | 6.3 ± 0.6 | Suarez-Arrones et al., 2013 |

activity periods (i.e. standing, walking, jogging and low-intensity running) that account for 71 to 79 per cent of the total distance covered during a match. However, match play is interspersed with frequent bouts of high-intensity running and sprinting (O'Hara et al., 2013), to ensure the referee can keep up with play and obtain an optimal viewing position.

Within rugby league, the different refereeing systems appears to have some influence on the high-intensity movement demands. SL referees have been shown to perform a greater number of high-intensity efforts compared with both the NRL head and NRL pocket referees during a game (Brightmore et al., 2014). However, these data suggest the amount of high-intensity running during match play and a referee's ability to recover between high-intensity bouts may significantly influence his performance, as well as the ability to constantly change running speed.

## DIRECTIONAL NATURE OF MOVEMENT DEMANDS

Rugby refereeing is multi-directional, requiring referees to move in various directions at different phases of the game. Quantifying these directional movement demands is important for developing appropriate training protocols to ensure they reflect match demands. Research (O'Hara et al., 2013) shows SL referees cover greater distances in a forward direction (44.7 per cent) but right (18.8 per cent), left (16.9 per cent) and backwards (19.7 per cent) movements contributed substantially to the total distance covered. These data were reported using analysis of the direction of movement in four equal 90 degree quadrant planes, as per the GPS manufacturer's device settings. Following video footage analysis, it became apparent the SL referees run in a forwards direction while rotating their torso to view match play. Due to the location of the GPS device (which uses magnetometers to evaluate direction of movement) on the

## Table 11.2: Percentage Distance at Each Movement Classification for Rugby Union Referees (Suarez-Arrones et al., 2013)

| Classification | Velocity (km.h⁻¹) | % Distance |
|---|---|---|
| Walking | 0.1– 6.0 | 37.3 |
| Jogging | 6.1–12.0 | 24.1 |
| Low-intensity running | 12.1–14.0 | 10.4 |
| Medium-intensity running | 14.1–18.0 | 17.6 |
| High-intensity running | 18.1–20.0 | 5.5 |
| Sprinting | > 20.1 | 5.2 |

## Table 11.3: Percentage Distance and Frequency of Individual Efforts at Each Velocity Classification for SL Referees (O'Hara et al., 2013)

| Classification | Velocity (km.h⁻¹) | % Distance |
|---|---|---|
| Standing | < 1.8 | 3.3 |
| Walking | 1.8–7.2 | 34.0 |
| Jogging | 7.2–14.4 | 41.5 |
| Running | 14.4–19.8 | 15.5 |
| High-intensity running | 19.8–25.2 | 4.6 |
| Sprinting | >25.2 | 1.3 |

top of the torso, this movement would be classified as lateral movement, which does not reflect truly the directional movement demands. Therefore, in order to better understand the directional nature of the movement demands of SL referees, this study reduced the left and right bandwidths to 30 degrees for seven games, reporting a truer reflection of lateral movement. This analysis found the direction of movement contributions to be: 60.3 per cent 'forward', 28.1 per cent 'backwards', 5.0 per cent 'left' and 6.3 per cent 'right' of total distance covered in each direc-

tion. These findings highlight that, in order to replicate common actions during match play, referees need to include some lateral and backward movements as well as forward running with a rotation of the torso to the left and right in their training.

## Physiological Demands

To quantify the physiological demands of refereeing, downloadable heart rate monitors can be worn during a match. Based on an

| | SL | Rugby Union | SL | Rugby Union |
|---|---|---|---|---|
| | **1st Half** | | **2nd Half** | |
| Average heart rate (beats.min$^{-1}$) | 156 | 157 | 151 | 155 |
| Average heart rate (%) | 85.5 | 85.0 | 82.9 | 84.0 |
| % HRmax (61–70%) | 2.8 | 4.0 | 4.6 | 5.0 |
| % HRmax (71–80%) | 13.8 | 23.0 | 18.7 | 25.0 |
| % HRmax (81–90%) | 43.8 | 44.0 | 51.1 | 43.0 |
| % HRmax (91–100%) | 38.9 | 29.0 | 25.0 | 25.0 |

**Table 11.4: Average Heart Rate and Percentage Time in Heart Rate Zones For 1st and 2nd Halves During Match Play in Rugby League (O'Hara et al., 2013) and Union (Suarez-Arrones et al., 2013) Refereeing**

individual's maximum heart rate, the percentage of time spent in different heart rates zones can be calculated, reflecting differences in exercise intensity during match play. The average heart rate achieved by SL referees has been reported to be 154 beats per minute, which equates to approximately 84 per cent of maximal heart rate (O'Hara et al., 2013). Rugby referees spend the majority of their time exercising above 80 per cent of their maximal heart rate with a reduction in time spent above 90 per cent of maximum heart rate during the second half.

This heart rate data demonstrate that rugby refereeing is high-intensity and physiological demands are placed on both the aerobic and anaerobic energy systems during match play. Therefore, certain training sessions should aim to elicit an average heart rate of approximately 84 per cent of maximal heart rate to replicate the physiological demands of officiating. However, when comparing these physiological responses with the movement demands (i.e. 88 per cent of time is spent below 4.0 m.s$^{-1}$ [O'Hara et al., 2013]), it could

be argued that refereeing would not elicit such high heart rate responses. Therefore, it is likely that increased heart rate values may be associated with other sources of stress beyond the physiological demands of the game. It has previously been reported that heart rates measured on referees during a match may overestimate the physical intensity of matches, due to other factors (e.g. referee experience, decision making demands, personality and anxiety [Krustrup et al., 2002, Krustrup et al., 2009]). Therefore, training scenarios should take into account decision making to try to recreate as best as possible the match day experience, which seems to influence the physiological responses to refereeing.

# PRACTICAL APPLICATION

The assessment of the external (i.e. running demands) and internal (i.e. heart rate responses) load imposed during match play, in addition to quantification of decision making accuracy, is the first step preceding the design of specific conditioning programmes for rugby referees. This data can then be used to enhance training programmes for referees to ensure they are specific to the physical movement and cognitive match demands. Additionally, this data may be used to inform talent identification and talent development programmes for future referees.

## Decision Making Quantification and Training

While it is difficult to quantify every decision a referee makes within a game, referee coaches at an elite level implement retrospective analysis of matches in order to quantify referee decision making accuracy. For example, coaches review game footage in conjunction with statistical data provided by match analysis software (Opta Stats) on the number and timing of penalties awarded. Typically this would be undertaken by the organization's match officials' director and match officials' coaches, with each referee also reviewing his or her own game. Penalties can be categorized as correct, unwarranted or missed based on the agreements between staff. Unwarranted and missed penalties would then be grouped together and accounted for collectively as incorrect decisions. Penalty accuracy is then calculated as the number of correct decisions divided by the total number of penalties awarded. Each individual referee would then review their performance with one of the match officials' coaches, highlighting both positive aspects of their performance and also identify areas to improve. These methods are adopted by the majority of rugby referee organizations, although there may be some variation on the precise process. Furthermore, it would be advocated that coaches adopt these review processes with referees on a weekly basis, whereby an individual referee's accuracy and their rationale for decisions is reviewed. This may assist in referee development and will provide coaches with an opportunity to assess individual understanding and game management strategies.

The review process should also evaluate shared reasons for underpinning decisions. Thus, training that uses types of 'contentious' tackles, adjudged independently to be realistic refereeing scenarios (from stadium footage or a 'Ref Cam' as used with SL referees) may be appropriate to improve referee decision making accuracy. This may be used to speed up the process of amassing experience, bringing developing referees into line with their top flight peers and ensuring referees' decisions are not isolated but rather become common practice.

At an elite level, referee coaches are using GPS data obtained from match play to devise training sessions, which replicate the physical and movement demands of the game, shifting the focus towards training decision making under fatigue. This type of training is useful for coaches working with amateur referees as they can combine the movement and physiological demands, as well as the cognitive demands of refereeing, into the same training session, maximizing efficiency of training.

## Physical Training

If resources permit, the use of GPS tracking devices to quantify and monitor the physiological and movement demands for a referee is recommended. This will allow coaches to individualize training, monitor progress during match play, as well as optimizing physical performance. While training studies have yet to be carried out for rugby referees, incorporating high-intensity intermittent training

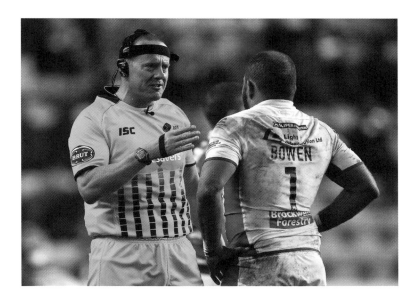

**Fig. 11.2: Rugby league referee wearing the ref cam.**

has been shown to be effective in improving soccer referees' fitness (Weston *et al.*, 2004). Further, these types of sessions have been shown to improve match performance (Krustrup and Bangsbo, 2001), specifically the ability to perform high-intensity running (Helgerud *et al.*, 2001). High-intensity intermittent training should also incorporate multi-directional movement to mimic the demands of the game. In order to improve refereeing performance, a typical training week should aim to include two to three high-intensity intermittent training sessions with each session consisting of approximately sixteen minutes of high-intensity running (Helgerud *et al.*, 2001). These types of sessions can place significant stress on the body, and without an appropriate level of aerobic fitness over-reaching (short-term reduction in performance) can occur. This type of training will enable the rugby referee to keep up with play more efficiently, potentially placing him in the optimal viewing position, especially in the second half where it has

been shown referees demonstrate a reduced ability to perform high-intensity running (O'Hara *et al.*, 2013, Suarez-Arrones *et al.*, 2013). Additionally, referees should perform training protocols that elicit an average heart rate of at least ~84 per cent maximum heart rate to replicate the physiological demands of officiating.

In conclusion, a referee's weekly training programme should have a blend of high and low-intensity aerobic sessions, as well as including training to improve running speed and the ability to perform repeated high-intensity running with incomplete recovery (speed endurance [Weston *et al.*, 2004]). Ideally, the high-intensity training sessions should also include decision making training, to ensure referees are able to maintain a high work rate during match play without affecting decision making accuracy detrimentally. It is no good improving fitness if this does not improve refereeing performance.

## IMPLICATIONS AND RECOMMENDATIONS FOR PRACTICE

- Quantifying refereeing decision making is difficult due to the multiple, complex and dynamic decisions required. These decisions may be influenced by a number of factors including the movement and physiological demands of the game, positioning, viewing angle and context of the game (i.e. score and time point of the game).
- Coaches should attempt to evaluate refereeing accuracy by quantifying penalty accuracy as a minimum.
- Coaches should aim to use video footage taken from the referee's perspective during match play to train decision making, rather than from a stadium angle. The use of video-based training methods, in which referees are shown clips of 'contentious' scenarios from match play with an expert's interpretation of the event, may be useful for training referee decision making accuracy.

- Training decision making accuracy under physical fatigue is ecologically relevant. This may be useful, as coaches can combine the movement and physiological demands, as well as the cognitive demands of refereeing into the same training session.
- Refereeing is a high-intensity intermittent activity, which includes multi-directional movement. However, there are subtle differences in the demands of refereeing between competitions, which need to be taken into account in the physical preparation of individuals. High-intensity running may provide a more sensitive measure of match intensity in comparison to total distance covered during match play.
- During match play, referees work at high heart-rates due to a combination of the physiological and psychological (i.e. pressure, crowd, experience) demands. Therefore, training should aim to replicate situations as close as possible to match play to support the preparation of referees.

# CHAPTER 12

# A FRAMEWORK FOR PLANNING YOUR PRACTICE: A COACH'S PERSPECTIVE

*Bob Muir, Kevin Till, Andy Abraham and Gareth Morgan*

## INTRODUCTION

The vision of the UK Coaching Framework is 'excellent coaching every time for everyone' (*Sports Coach UK*, 2012, p. 3). Central to the achievement of this vision is the interaction that takes place between coaches, players and other key stakeholders (e.g. club officials, support staff, parents, etc.) to generate positive outcomes in particular sporting contexts. As such, sport coaching is considered an intentional and purposeful activity through which coaches, players and other key stakeholders interact in deliberative and non-deliberative ways (Abraham and Collins, 2011a). Therefore, a key role of the rugby coach is to create meaningful learning and development experiences that bring about the guided improvement of players.

Research in player development has built a strong case for sport coaches to take a more holistic approach to coaching, one that looks beyond sport-specific technical and tactical markers of development and pays attention to the biological, psychological and social

(bio-psycho-social) needs of each individual in order to provide a platform for lifelong engagement in sport and physical activity (Bailey *et al.*, 2010). Reflecting this, policy documents (e.g. International Sport Coaching Framework, ICCE, 2014) have presented an expanded breadth and depth of coaching roles to reflect the different needs, motives and entitlements of players relative to sporting context, competitive level and domain (e.g. children, participation, performance development and high performance). As such, expert coaching is not a unitary concept; what works at one developmental stage or with one player will not necessarily be equally effective elsewhere.

Distinctions in the bio-psycho-social stage of development, goals and competitive level of players, the rule structures, strategies, techniques, performance culture and accepted practices within rugby reveals much about the construction and complexity of coaching the sport. How then do expert coaches manage such complexity? Interestingly, this question in part can be answered by examining the world of Michelin star gastronomy and amateur cookery. Have you ever wondered why people buy cookbooks? Are they trying to become the next Michelin star chef or do they simply want to have some more ideas to cook something different every now and then? We imagine more of the readers of this chapter fall into the latter of these two categories. But what has this got to do with a chapter on coaching rugby? The England men's rugby union coach Stuart Lancaster would argue quite a lot!

> The first question you need to ask is whether you are a chef or a cook. A high–performing chef has the ability to choose and combine the right ingredients then combine this with his cooking skills to make a delicious dish. If there is a problem in the creation of a recipe, he can deal with this. He innovates and discovers. (Lancaster, 2011, p. 3).

Lancaster was drawing on an article by Abraham et al. (2009) titled 'Are You a Cook or a Chef?' in which the authors used the distinction between a cook and a chef as an analogy to illustrate that high-performing chefs have an in-depth understanding of the properties of different ingredients and how to combine them using different methods to produce different blends of colour, texture and flavour. This in-depth understanding enables the chef to make continuous adjustments to the amount and type of ingredients, methods and timing to create the desired outcome. By contrast, the willing, enthusiastic, but less experienced cook follows a procedural recipe from a cookery book to recreate a dish like that of the innovative chef. However, if even a small part of the procedural recipe starts to go wrong in practice, the enthusiastic cook is soon at a loss as to what to do, since they lack the in-depth knowledge needed to solve the problem.

Furthermore, while the enthusiastic cook may be able to create a dish that on the surface looks and sometimes even tastes the same, appearances can be misleading. What we see on the surface does not always explain what the underlying causal ingredients were that generated the taste, texture and appearance of the dish. Similarly, if we observe a puzzling or troubling situation on the field during a coaching session, such as a player breaking down under pressure, what we see may not actually represent the real problem; there may be a number of underlying factors that are contributing to the player's behaviour. Without being clear about the ideas we are drawing on to make sense of what we see, we may jump to a number of inaccurate judgments (e.g. the player can't cope or is afraid of contact, etc.). Existing theories and concepts can be used as thinking tools to test our *ideas* and develop a more thorough *understanding* of the possible underlying causal problems (i.e. acute fatigue or a drop in their feelings of competence resulting from a sudden growth spurt and reduction in movement competence).

The purpose of this chapter, therefore, is to offer a conceptual framework for coach decision making in order to stimulate 'ideas' for your own practice that are grounded in an 'understanding' of more formal theories relating to the science of rugby presented within this book.

# RESEARCH OVERVIEW

## A framework for coach decision-making

Drawing on evidence generated from in-depth interviews with Coach Education Managers from nine different National Governing Bodies of sport, existing coaching and other relevant

## IDEAS AND UNDERSTANDING – A CLARIFICATION

Ideas are often about things that we can do, but where do ideas come from? They can come from other people, they can come from guesswork, or they can come about through understanding. Distinguishing where ideas come from in this manner is important because it can lead to more critical thought about why we do what we do. Such a level of critical thought led Anderson (1982) to develop a theory that identified how knowledge could be split into two broad domains – declarative knowledge and procedural knowledge. Declarative knowledge can be defined as the 'why' knowledge or the knowledge of 'understanding', while procedural knowledge is 'doing' knowledge or 'ideas' concerning how to do something. This separation is important since it explains how it is possible to have one without the other; i.e. the coach who does something (procedural) based on 'ideas' without sufficient understanding of knowing why (declarative). It also displays how if we spend more time understanding why things happen new ideas are more likely to develop.

academic and professional development literature, Abraham et al., (2010) highlighted that 'high performing' coaches are constantly seeking to maximize effectiveness through challenging personal 'practice theories' (i.e. ideas) through reference to formal 'theories of practice' (i.e. understanding [Thompson, 2000]). This professional attribute enables the 'high performing' coach to: (a) present a personal, reasoned explanation for their strategies and goals; (b) explain and provide reasons for actions taken to meet their goals; and (c) evaluate the personal and collective effectiveness of their strategies (Thompson, 2000). Thus, they concluded 'high performing' coaching practice rests on the coach's ability to draw on knowledge from several linked domains to develop optimal learning environments (Berliner, 1991); it involves a continuous process of decision-making about when and how to intervene in order to maintain momentum and progression towards the achievement of specified goals. In order to demonstrate this process, a framework for coach decision-making was proposed (Fig. 12.1).

The central premise underpinning the framework is that high performing coaches make decisions and shape their interventions and practice based on ideas about the player (the 'who'), the demands of the sport (the 'what', i.e. rugby) and principles of skill acquisition and learning (the 'how'). As such, it is suggested that a high performing coach's practice (i.e. their 'planning, delivery and reflective' practices) entails the constant integration of knowledge from the 'who', 'what' and 'how' to identify and solve problems. This process provides an environment that enables the coach's players to make progress towards their short-, medium- and long-term goals (Abraham and Collins, 2011a, Muir et al., 2011a). But, how does this process match up with the earlier innovative chef versus enthusiastic cook idea? Firstly, both can be good at their job. However, in order to be an innovative coach we suggest that the practical 'ideas' about the player (i.e. 'who'), sport (i.e. 'what') and learning (i.e. 'how') would come from in-depth 'understanding' of theories and research in each of these areas.

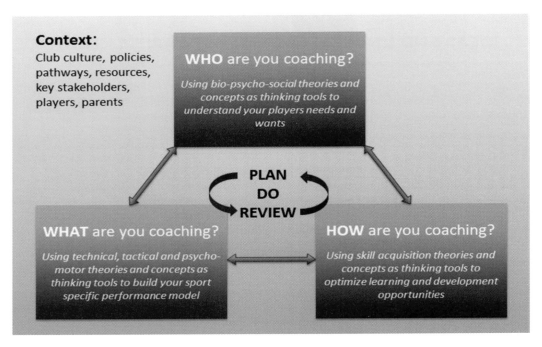

**Fig. 12.1: A conceptual framework for coaches' decision making. (Adapted from Abraham and Collins, 2011a; Muir *et al.*, 2011)**

## The player 'who'

Drawing on concepts and theories from biology, biomechanics, physiology, psychology, and sociology enables the innovative coach to develop a deeper understanding of their players. These disciplinary areas provide insights that can help explain differences between individual players and how they respond to challenges in different circumstances. Several chapters within this book offer concepts and ideas that can be used to develop a more thorough understanding of players relative to their age, stage of development, competitive level and motivation. For example, Chapters 1 and 9 highlight differences in the developmental needs and physical characteristics across the playing pathway. These ideas can also be combined with the field and laboratory based fitness assessments, skill capability assessments and decision making assessments (Chapters 2, 7 and 8 respectively) to develop a more robust understanding of individual player and team needs. In addition, Chapters 3 and 4 introduce concepts and ideas that can be used to monitor fatigue, promote recovery and enhance performance. Each of these areas of research provides different thinking tools to develop a more thorough understanding of how players are responding to the demands of training and competition.

However, the extent to which these ideas are embraced and implemented in practice should be determined in part by the age, stage of development and competitive level of the players. Drawing on contemporary research evidence from the fields of talent identification and development, Chapter 10 sets out several key implications to consider when coaching children and young academy players. Specifically, there is no 'one size fits all approach' to player development. Coaches need to be able to support players to identify personal strengths and areas for improvement in order to guide their attentional focus and mobilize effort during training and games. Moreover, 'here and now markers' of performance are not reliable indicators of potential performance in the future, as such coaches should adopt a long-term developmentally appropriate approach instead of a short-term performance mentality often driven by ambitions to 'win at the weekend'.

## The sport 'what'

An in-depth knowledge of the internal logic of rugby (i.e. the goals, rules and structures) and the tactical problems that players have to overcome enables high performing coaches to develop a technical and tactical performance model (i.e. what ideal rugby performance looks like). Using the performance model as a reference point, high performing coaches can combine observations of their players in training and competition with analytics to make decisions about 'what' to work on and in what order. Such thinking also brings into question the balance between player and performance development (these two things may or may not be complementary). Consequently a central feature of the coach's expertise is demonstrated in their ability to break their ideal performance model down into appropriate age, stage of development and competitive level stages. Like a road map, this process necessitates defining the destination in order to identify and select the most appropriate route to get there. Done well, this process can be used to:

■ Create a shared understanding between players and coaches on what target performance should look like at any stage and the

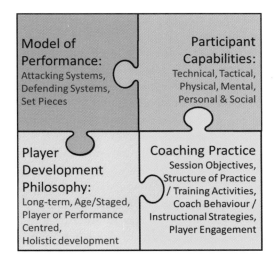

**Fig. 12.2: The components of performance planning.**

steps that need to be taken individually and collectively to achieve it.
■ Increase role clarity and recognition of the unique contribution each person will make.
■ Clarify expectations and develop a common vocabulary that is shared, understood and used by all to promote more efficient, precise and purposeful interactions between players and coaches on and off the pitch.

Muir (2012) found that the implicit performance models of national age group (NAG; i.e. England U21, U18 and U16) coaches in hockey and rugby league informed their planning process and the expectations they held of their players in training and competitive settings. Muir used video feedback with the coaches to explore the link between their implicit performance models, their players' capabilities, their philosophy on player development, and their day-to-day coaching practice (Fig. 12.2).

Working through this process challenged the coaches to consider questions such as

*'How does this camp build upon previous camps and prepare for future camps?', 'How does each session within a single camp (e.g. on pitch training, international fixture, video review session, team development session, down time) contribute to the objectives of this particular camp?'* The outcome of this process enabled coaches to generate more detailed plans to maximize the time that they had with their players within and across each annual cycle. Moreover it provoked greater dialogue between the respective NAG coaches to consider which elements of the performance model should be introduced, developed or optimized within and across each age group cycle (e.g. how does the U18s programme build on U16s and prepare players for U21s?).

While this book has not been developed to provide a review of the technical and tactical models of rugby, several concepts and ideas have been presented in relation to the movement and physiological demands (Chapter 1), fatigue and recovery (Chapter 3), nutrition (Chapter 4), strength and conditioning (Chapter 5), injury rehabilitation Chapter 6), decision-making (Chapter 7), the young rugby player (Chapter 9) and referees (Chapter 11). Each of these areas provide research evidence and examples from practice that can be used to test and adjust your existing (implicit) performance model of rugby and develop a more explicit, shared target performance that reflects the needs of the players relative to their age, stage of development and competitive level.

## The learning 'how'

Drawing on theories and concepts from learning and skill acquisition enables high-performing coaches to design and shape the constraints of learning activities (i.e. training activities on and off the pitch) and align

appropriate behavioural strategies to support player engagement, generate feedback and make sense of their progress towards the short-, medium- and long-term objectives. Indeed, all of the strategies explored in Chapter 7 for developing player's decision-making highlight specific implications for how coaches structure practice and align their behavioural strategies. Recent work of Ford et al., (2010) and Harvey et al., (2013) has used systematic observation to explore the inter-dependent relationship between the structure of the practice activities and the associated behavioural strategies employed by coaches. The results of this work have suggested that team sport coaches use a wide range of practice methods (i.e. what has the coach actually got the players doing) and communication behaviours (i.e. what verbal and non-verbal methods does the coach use and when to communicate with the players). These studies also highlighted that coaches dedicated more time to training form activities (i.e. physiological, technical or skills practices that place lower demands on player decision-making) than playing form activities (i.e. phase of play, conditioned or small sided games that place higher demands on player decision-making).

Harvey and colleagues (2013) identified that the coaches within their study made limited changes to their behavioural strategies as a function of the structure of the practice activities. Further, the work of Harvey et al., (2013) demonstrated a difference between their stated intentions (i.e. theories of practice) and their actual practice (i.e. theories in use); thus suggesting that the coaches in their study may benefit from spending more time during planning thinking about the structure of the practice activities and their associated behavioural strategies to promote specific learning returns. But what is it that coaches should think about when planning practice activities and behavioural strategies?

Perhaps the first point to make is that different practice activities and behavioural strategies do different jobs (i.e. small-sided games might be more appropriate in developing tactical skills than un-opposed technical drills). It is therefore down to the coach to judge which approach is most appropriate in meeting the needs of the players (i.e. 'who') and the challenges they need to overcome in their rugby context (i.e. 'what'). To support this judgment process coaches might consider the following principles:

■ Learning is done by the learner. While this may sound like an obvious statement, it should encourage coaches to question whether their approach is encouraging players to learn or more focused on showing the player how much the coach knows (Phillips, 1995).

■ Learning is more likely to happen when the task to be learned is meaningful to the player. Again, an obvious statement; however, experience suggests that coaches (in fact educators more broadly) assume that what is meaningful to them is also meaningful to the player (Bjork, 1993).

■ Learners have a need for self-determination that means they will generally be more motivated to engage in learning that they feel they are competent in, they feel related to, and that they have control over. This normally means that problem solving activities are useful for learners. However, if the problem becomes too much or never-ending the learner may feel controlled and hence disengage. Sometimes it is good just to give learners the (or at least part of the) answer to increase their sense of control and competence (Deci and Ryan, 2000).

■ Meaningfulness is linked to learners recognizing that a 'problem' exists and that overcoming the problem is relevant to their development. Thus over emphasizing the problem in a way that is relevant to the learner can help recognition while encouraging the player to search for a solution (Renshaw, et al., 2009).

■ Rugby is a dynamic game requiring the mastery of a variety of perceptual, decision-making and technical skills within an environment that is highly contested and often chaotic in nature. Thus, practice methods need to maintain and represent these features to ensure that the relationships between key sources of information and action for players are retained (Pinder et al., 2011).

■ Research suggests that coaches should create learning experiences that are goal focused, represent and exaggerate the key challenges of performance to shape emergent player behaviour and promote appropriate skill and game development (Renshaw et al., 2009).

■ Educating players on how to become better learners has been identified as a key mechanism for promoting self-regulated behaviours and supporting players to take responsibility for their own learning (Abbott and Collins, 2004).

■ Learners have a finite and relatively small set of mental resources to devote to learning. Consequently, learning needs to be progressive and coaching needs focus to avoid overload (Eysenck et al., 2007)

■ There is a range of practice and communication methods that support quick changes in player performance but don't actively support learning. These are related to setting the learner practice problems well within their capabilities and supporting them with solution focused feedback and instructions. There is an alternative set of methods that initially delay big changes in performance but achieve more robust long-term changes in performance. These are related to providing problems that require high levels of mental and/or per-ceptual-motor engagement from the player with little feedback and instruction which may be replaced by probing questions that prompt the player to discover relevant responses (Vickers *et al.*, 2004).

Drawing on the principles outlined above, Abraham and Collins (2011a, p. 221) devel-oped 'three golden rules' to support coaches in making judgments about how to create meaningful learning environments:

Make the content as *personally relevant* for your player as possible (e.g. does it tie in with their development plan?)

Promote player *understanding* whenever you can, especially when working towards long-term development (e.g. does the player know why they are doing what they are doing? Do you need to check understanding?)

For *rapid short-term* results make the session (mentally) easy for your player, for *long-term development* make it harder.

## The coaching 'context'

Finally, coaching doesn't take place in a vacuum; coach's practice will always be shaped and influenced by the context within which they work. This can include the club's values, accepted practices and traditions, poli-cies, pathways and resources and most of all by other people's (e.g. players, club officials, support staff, parents, etc.) beliefs, values and behaviours. For example, the playing level (e.g. adult professional club versus junior commu-nity club) significantly influences the player and development context where players have different aims, resources and abilities. There-fore, coaches can draw on a range of theories and concepts from social science to under-stand this layered context (North, 2013) and develop strategies to achieve success within

these constraints (e.g. developing a shared vision and purpose, establishing role clarity across the group, aligning behaviours that contribute to the achievement of the goals, etc.).

## The process and practice of coaching 'plan, do, review'

Given the breadth and depth of factors that the rugby coach can consider and the knowl-edge required to do this, the really innovative skill that high-performing coaches exhibit is the ability to integrate ideas from these inter-dependent areas to inform their professional judgments and decision-making when plan-ning, delivering and reflecting on their coach-ing practice. There seems little doubt that decision-making plays an important part in coaches' everyday practice and is a significant component of coaching expertise (Lyle, 2010). Consequently the decision-making behav-iours of high-performing coaches continue to attract considerable attention in research, education and professional development pro-grammes. A key feature emerging from this work is the recognition that decision-making is not a unitary concept, in other words the type of decision-making behaviour that high performing coaches exhibit is shaped and influenced by the context and the role that they are undertaking (i.e. planning, delivery or reviewing).

In a team sport such as rugby, much of the coach's decision-making in training and competition settings (i.e. delivering coaching) can be categorized as intuitive; that is, the availability of information, the uncertainty of outcomes and the time available influence the coach's desire to find the first available solution – not necessarily the most optimum (Abraham and Collins, 2011a, Harvey *et al.*, 2015). The decision-making process involved here is not a one-time per session procedure or a method for presenting clear answers. Instead, high-performing coaches are continually constructing a coherent interpretation of what is going on to search for the best available solution at that particular time and under those particular conditions (Kahneman, 2011). Given the contextual, dynamic and interactive features of the coaching environment recent literature has explored the potential of naturalistic decision-making (NDM) as a theoretical framework to explore coaches' decision-making behaviour in practice (Lyle, 2010, Harvey et al., 2015).

NDM is a research paradigm that describes how experts in their field are able to draw upon their experiences to perform in time- and information-constrained decision contexts (Klein, 1998, Lyle 2010). Explorations of military commander, aviator and firefighter decision-making in naturalistic settings has demonstrated that expert decision makers are able to identify relevant situational cues and draw upon their mental models to quickly formulate action strategies. In circumstances when they notice conflicts between their expectations and reality, uncertainty is managed by matching the features of the present context/problem with previous experiences to inform a mental simulation of possible strategies (Klein, 1998).

Drawing on the existing NDM literature, Harvey et al. (2015) developed a conceptual framework to explore coaches' decision-making behaviours across training and competition settings in basketball, hockey and volleyball. Using video-stimulated recall, 108 decision-making incidents were examined. Their findings suggested the coaches' decision-making behaviour was a serial process that involved on-going situational assessment guided by a slow, interactive script in which the coaches' tried to maintain an element of 'control' in relation to what they had

planned and drew on previous experience in order to understand what had emerged and if necessary make appropriate adjustments to 'stay on track' (Harvey et al., 2015). Their findings also revealed the coaches worked through a process of problem framing as they noticed conflicts between their expectations and reality (elsewhere this has been referred to as reflection-in-action, see Schön, 1983). These conflicts (described as 'key attractors') appeared to be critical factors in shaping the coaches' decision-making behaviour.

Whilst the NDM literature provides a helpful framework to understand coaches' decision-making behaviour in situ, concerns have been raised about humans' preference to 'do' first and 'think' later if at all (Kahneman and Klein, 2009). Indeed, coaches that solely rely on intuitive or naturalistic decisions and attribute success to 'gut feel' will eventually encounter problems of overconfidence that will lead to mistakes being ignored or attributed elsewhere (Kahneman and Klein, 2009). Such decision biases can grow through peer-group re-enforcement leading to 'accepted practices' and 'ways of working'; the danger being that 'if people fail to recognize why they became expert, expertise may be quickly lost and biases quickly established' (Abraham and Collins, 2011b, p. 375). As such the case has been made for coaches to engage in more thorough and considered decision-making (i.e. classical decision-making) during more deliberate and less time-pressured elements of the coaching process (i.e., planning and critical reflection [Abraham and Collins, 2011b, Abraham et al., 2014]). Consequently engaging in a more deliberate thoughtful planning process is a crucial element in developing coaching expertise since it encourages deep thinking, raises expectations of both coach and player and provides a template from which thoughtful reflection can occur after delivery (Abraham et al., 2014).

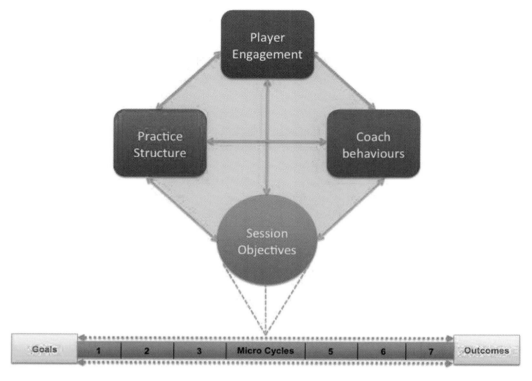

**Fig. 12.3. The coaching practice planning and reflective framework. (Muir et al., 2011)**

# CONSTRUCTIVELY ALIGNING PRACTICE FOR SUCCESSFUL LEARNING AND DEVELOPMENT

The emerging body of work on coach decision-making behaviour strengthens the case for coaches to spend more time considering their coaching goals and how they align these goals with the needs of their players, sport and learning environment in order to clarify their expectations in both training and competitive situations. This planning process should entail the constant integration and alignment of these interdependent areas. Indeed, coaches who spend time considering these factors will

be able to plan explicitly for and implement coaching that is developmentally appropriate, builds on where the player has come from and helps prepare them for where they wish to go (Muir et al., 2011a). Furthermore, a clear understanding of how each coaching interaction is nested within the long-, medium- and short-term objectives enables coaches to make more informed (appropriate) adjustments from predetermined plans based on observations, evaluations and reactions to 'goings on' (Abraham and Collins, 2011b, Jones and Wallace, 2006).

Reflecting this thinking, Muir et al., (2011b) developed the Coaching Practice Planning and Reflective Framework (Fig 12.3, CPPARF) to explore the relationship between coaches planning, delivery and reflective practice.

Combined with audio and video feedback, the CPPARF has been used to support National and Olympic coaches in hockey, rugby league and sailing to explore the relationship between their coaching objectives, the structure of their practice and learning activities, their behavioural strategies and ultimately the implications on player engagement and learning (Muir, 2012).

The CPPARF encourages coaches to begin with the question 'what do we (as coaches') want our players to be able to know and do as a result of the coaching?'. The intended learning objectives that arise from an analysis of players' needs relative to their age, stage of development and competitive level becomes the basis for designing long-, medium-, and short-term plans. This provides a key reference point from which coaches can monitor and adjust the effectiveness of their plans, delivery and reflections. In delivering their practice, coaches are essentially equipped with two key controllable 'tools': (1) the way they structure the learning experience for their players (e.g. the structure and type of training/practice activities), and (2) the behavioural strategies they employ to support players before, during and after each learning activity. How coaches use these two controllable 'tools' will either facilitate or hinder the learning experience of the player and shape their technical, tactical, physical, psychological personal and social development significantly (Muir et al., 2011b).

It is therefore suggested good coaches deliberately plan, manipulate and 'align':

- *Practice structure* (i.e. focus on single or multiple skills; opposed or unopposed practice; blocked, variable or random practice; drill, conditioned or small sided game, etc.)
- *Coach behavioural* strategies (i.e. timing and type of feedback; open or closed questioning; demonstrations; and hustles and instructional prompts, etc.)

To maximize the opportunities for:

*Players to engage*, learn and achieve the *Objectives* of the session and progress towards achieving the meso and ultimately macro goals of the programme. (Muir, et al., 2011b; Muir 2012).

The CPPARF also provides a useful framework of questions to consider when planning coaching programmes:

- What are the long-, medium-, short-term learning objectives and how can they be broken down into macro, meso, and micro cycles?
- What will players' engagement look like when the objectives have been met (e.g. different components of performance relating to technical/tactical, movement, physical, psychological and social capabilities)?
- What methods of assessment can be used to generate feedback and measure progress against the objectives?
- How will each meso-cycle build upon previous cycles and contribute to the objectives of the macro-cycle (i.e. nested planning)?
- How will each micro-cycle (e.g. training session, competition, review session) contribute to the objectives of the meso-cycle?
- What pedagogical strategies could be used to engage the players and support their progress towards the attainment of the objectives (e.g. appropriate manipulation of task constraints and adjustments to behavioural strategies employed by coach to direct attention and effort)?
- What performance data will be captured to provide feedback on the effectiveness of the programme and inform decisions regarding the focus, prioritization of time, space, and resources in relation to the different components of performance?

As such, the CPPRF can be used to guide coaches' planning and promote connections between the desired objectives and the associated coaching strategies. This process can be used to support long-, and medium-term programme planning as well as short-term individual session plans. It provokes coaches' to consider which training activities to select, how to manipulate the constraints (i.e. Space, Time, Equipment, Players, Scoring – STEPS) of those activities and align behavioural strategies to promote specific learning returns. Coaches that spend time considering these four inter-dependent areas while planning prior to their session are more likely to be attentive to the player's needs, clearer with learning task instructions, and be able to provide specific, congruent feedback. In addition, coaches that reflect during and after their coaching sessions on the alignment between these areas are more likely to enhance the learning and development experience of the players and subsequent progress towards specified goals – interestingly, a primary goal of planning!

# CONCLUSION

The aim of this chapter was to provide a framework for coach decision-making as metaphoric 'tool box' for coaches to organize and align their existing ideas about practice with more formal theories relating to the science of rugby presented within this book. Challenges associated with optimizing player development in rugby are rarely bound by specific disciplinary perspectives; indeed our experience as coaches and working with coaches suggests that more often than not coaching issues are interdisciplinary. As such, we have illustrated that effective coaching practice rests on the coach's ability to draw on knowledge from several linked domains to develop optimal learning environments;

it involves a continuous process of decision making about when and how to intervene in order to maintain momentum and progression towards the achievement of specified goals.

While there are no guarantees in player development, the range of concepts and theories from different scientific disciplines within this book provide a real opportunity for rugby coaches to develop their insights and understanding of their players, the sport and their practice. Embracing this inter-disciplinary approach, enables the high-performing coach to draw on existing theories to develop an understanding about what works for particular players, in specific circumstances and why. Embracing this way of thinking about planning and practice enables coaches to be more deliberate and purposeful in their decision-making behaviour; more specifically they can:

- Develop specific, measurable, agreed, realistic and time-phased (SMART) learning objectives based on an assessment of their players' 'needs' and 'wants' relative to their age, stage of development and competitive level
- Design and shape the constraints of different 'training and learning activities' to maximize the players' opportunities to learn by 'doing'
- Use 'behavioural strategies' that support players' 'engagement' in the training and learning activities and enable them to 'make sense' of their experience, generate 'feedback' and make progress towards the short medium and long term 'objectives'.

In other words, we suggest that 'deliberate coaching practice' is constructively aligning practice for successful learning.

# REFERENCES

Abbott, A. & Collins, D. 2004. Eliminating the Dichotomy Between Theory and Practice in Talent Identification and Development: Considering the Role of Psychology. *Journal of Sports Sciences*, 22, 395–408.

Abernethy, A. & Farrow, D. 2005. Contextual Factors influencing the Development of Expertise in Australian Athletes. In: ISSP 11th World Congress of Sport Psychology: Promoting Health and Performance for Life, 2005. *International Society of Sport Psychology*.

Abernethy, B. 1996. Training the Visual-Perceptual Skills of Athletes: Insights from the Study of Motor Expertise. *American Journal of Sports Medicine*, 24, S89–S92.

Abernethy, B. & Russell, D. G. 1987. Expert-Novice Differences in an Applied Selective Attention Task. *Journal of Sport Psychology*, 9, 326–345.

Abraham, A. & Collins, D. 2011a. Effective skill development: How should athletes' skills be developed? In Performance Psychology: A Guide for the Practitioner. D. Collins, H. Richards & A. Button (Eds.) (London: Churchill Livingstone).

Abraham, A. & Collins, D. 2011b. Taking the next step: Ways forward for coaching science. *Quest* 63, 366–384.

Abraham, A., Morgan, G., & Muir, B. 2009. Are you a cook or a chef? On the up: The official elite coaches' magazine. 5: 62–63.

Abraham, A., Muir, B., & Morgan, G. 2010. Technical Report for the United Kingdom Centre for Coaching Excellence: National & International best practice in level 4 coach development. scUK, Leeds.

Abraham, A., Saiz, S. L. J, Mckeown, S., Morgan, G., Muir, B., North, J. & Till, K. 2014. Planning your coaching A focus on youth participant development. In Practical Sports Coaching. C Nash (Eds) (London: Routledge).

Achten, J. & Jeukendrup, A. E. 2003. The Effect of Pre-Exercise Carbohydrate Feedings on the Intensity That Elicits Maximal Fat Oxidation. *Journal of Sports Science*, 21, 1017–24.

Adam, K. & Oswald, I. 1984. Sleep Helps Healing. *British Medical Journal* (Clinical Research Ed.), 289, 1400.

Alaphilippe, A., Mandigout, S., Ratel, S., Bonis, J., Courteix, D. & Duclos, M. 2012. Longitudinal Follow-Up of Biochemical Markers of Fatigue throughout a Sporting Season in Young Elite Rugby Players. *Journal of Strength & Conditioning Research*, 26, 3376–3384.

Ali, A., Caine, M. & Snow, B. 2007. Graduated Compression Stockings: Physiological and Perceptual Responses During and After Exercise. *Journal of Sports Sciences*, 25, 413–419.

Anderson, J. R. 1982 Acquisition of a cognitive skill. *Psychological Review*, 89, 369–406.

Andersson, H., Bøhn, S. K., Raastad, T., Paulsen, G., Blomhoff, R. & Kadi, F. 2010. Differences in the inflammatory Plasma Cytokine Response Following Two Elite Female Soccer Games Separated by A 72-H Recovery. *Scandinavian Journal of Medicine & Science in Sports*, 20, 740–747.

Andersson, H. M., Raastad, T., Nilsson, J., Paulsen, G., Garthe, I. & Kadi, F. 2008. Neuromuscular Fatigue and Recovery in Elite Female Soccer: Effects of Active Recovery. *Medicine and Science in Sports and Exercise*, 40, 372–380.

Andrew, M., Grobbelaar, H. W. & Potgieter, J. C. 2007. Sport Psychological Skill Levels and Related Psychosocial Factors That Distinguish between Rugby Union Players of Different Participation Levels. *South African Journal for Research in Sport Physical Education and Recreation*, 29, 1.

Appleby, B., Newton, R. U. & Cormie, P. 2012. Changes in Strength over a Two Year Period in Professional Rugby Union Players. *Journal of Strength and Conditioning Research*, 26, 2538–2546.

# REFERENCES

Araujo, D., Davids, K. & Hristovski, R. 2006. The Ecological Dynamics of Decision Making in Sport. *Psychology of Sport and Exercise*, 7, 653–676.

Araujo, D., Davids, K. & Passos, P. 2007. Ecological Validity, Representative Design, and Correspondence between Experimental Task Constraints and Behavioural Setting: Comment on Rogers, Kadar, and Costall (2005). *Ecological Psychology*, 19, 69–78.

Argus, C. K., Gill, N. D., Keogh, J. W., Hopkins, W. G. & Beaven, C. M. 2009. Changes in Strength, Power, and Steroid Hormones during A Professional Rugby Union Competition. *Journal of Strength & Conditioning Research*, 23, 1583–1592.

Argus, C. K., Gill, N., Keogh, J., Hopkins, W. G. & Beaven, C. M. 2010. Effects of a Short-Term Pre-Season Training Programme on the Body Composition and Anaerobic Performance of Professional Rugby Union Players. *Journal of Sports Sciences*, 28, 679–686.

Argus, C. K., Gill, N. D., Keogh, J. W. & Hopkins, W. G. 2011. Assessing Lower-Body Peak Power in Elite Rugby-Union Players. *Journal of Strength & Conditioning Research*, 25, 1616–1621.

Argus, C. K., Gill, N. D., Keogh, J. W., McGuigan, M. R. & Hopkins, W. G. 2012. Effects of Two Contrast Training Programs on Jump Performance in Rugby Union Players during a Competition Phase. *International Journal of Sports Physiology and Performance*, 7, 68–75.

Ascensao, A., Leite, M., Rebelo, A. N., Magalhäes, S. & Magalhäes, J. 2011. Effects of Cold Water Immersion on the Recovery of Physical Performance and Muscle Damage Following a one-off Soccer Match. *Journal of Sports Sciences*, 29, 217–225.

Atkins, S. J. 2006. Performance of the Yo-Yo intermittent Recovery Test by Elite Professional and Semi-professional Rugby League Players. *Journal of Strength & Conditioning Research*, 20, 222–225.

Atkinson, F. S., Foster-Powell, K. & Brand-Miller, J. C. 2008. International Tables of Glycaemic Index and Glycaemic Load Values: 2008. *Diabetes Care*, 31, 2281–3.

Austin, D., Gabbett, T. & Jenkins, D. 2011a. The Physical Demands of Super 14 Rugby Union. *Journal of Science and Medicine in Sport*, 14, 259–263.

Austin, D., Gabbett, T. & Jenkins, D. 2011b. Repeated High-intensity Exercise in Professional Rugby Union. *Journal of Sports Sciences*, 29, 1105–1112.

Austin, D. J., Gabbett, T. J. & Jenkins, D. 2011c. Repeated High-intensity Exercise in A Professional Rugby League. *Journal of Strength & Conditioning Research*, 25, 1898–1904.

Austin, D. J., Gabbett, T. J. & Jenkins, D. 2013. Reliability and Sensitivity of a Repeated High-intensity Exercise Performance Test for Rugby League and Rugby Union. *Journal of Strength & Conditioning Research*, 27, 1128–1135.

Austin, D. J. & Kelly, S. J. 2013. Positional Differences in Professional Rugby League Match Play Through the Use of Global Positioning Systems. *Journal of Strength & Conditioning Research*, 27, 14–19.

Austin, D. J. & Kelly, S. J. 2014. Professional Rugby League Positional Match-Play Analysis Through the Use of Global Positioning System. *Journal of Strength & Conditioning Research*, 28, 187–193.

Baechle, T. R., Earle, R. W. & Wathen, D. 2008. Resistance Training. In: Baechle, T. R., Earle, R. W (Ed.) *Essentials of Strength Training and Conditioning*. Champaign, Illinois: Human Kinetics.

Baguet, A., Koppo, K., Pottier, A. & Derave, W. 2010. Beta-Alanine Supplementation Reduces Acidosis but Not Oxygen Uptake Response during High-intensity Cycling Exercise. *European Journal of Applied Physiology*, 108, 495–503.

Bailey, D., Erith, S., Griffin, P., Dowson, A., Brewer, D., Gant, N. & Williams, C. 2007. Influence of Cold-Water Immersion on Indices of Muscle Damage Following Prolonged Intermittent Shuttle Running. *Journal of Sports Sciences*, 25, 1163–1170.

Bailey, R., Collins, D., Ford, P., McNamara, A., Toms, M. & Pearce, G. 2010. Participant Development in Sport: An Academic Review. *Sports Coach UK*, 4, 1–134.

Baker, D. 2001a. Comparison of Upper-Body Strength and Power between Professional and College-Aged Rugby League Players. *Journal of Strength & Conditioning Research*, 15, 30–35.

Baker, D. 2001b. The Effects of an in-Season of Concurrent Training on the Maintenance of Maximal Strength and Power in Professional and College-Aged Rugby League Football Players. *Journal of Strength & Conditioning Research*, 15, 172–177.

Baker, D. 2001c. A Series of Studies on the Training of High-intensity Muscle Power in Rugby League Football Players. *Journal of Strength & Conditioning Research*, 15, 198–209.

Baker, D. & Nance, S. 1999. The Relation between Strength and Power in Professional Rugby League Players. *Journal of Strength & Conditioning Research*, 13, 224–229.

Baker, D. G. 2013. 10–Year Changes in Upper Body Strength and Power in Elite Professional Rugby League Players: the Effect of Training Age, Stage, and Content. *Journal of Strength & Conditioning Research*, 27, 285–292.

Baker, D. G. & Newton, R. U. 2004. An Analysis of the Ratio and Relationship between Upper Body Pressing and Pulling Strength. *Journal of Strength & Conditioning Research*, 18, 594–598.

Baker, D. G. & Newton, R. U. 2006. Adaptations in Upper-Body Maximal Strength and Power Output Resulting From Long-Term Resistance Training in Experienced Strength-Power Athletes. *Journal of Strength & Conditioning Research*, 20, 541–546.

Baker, D. G. & Newton, R. U. 2008. Comparison of Lower Body Strength, Power, Acceleration, Speed, Agility, and Sprint Momentum To Describe and Compare Playing Rank Among Professional Rugby League Players. *Journal of Strength & Conditioning Research*, 22, 153–158.

Baker, L. B. & Jeukendrup, A. E. 2014. Optimal Composition of Fluid-Replacement Beverages. *Comprehensive Physiology*, 4, 575–620.

Banfi, G., Melegati, G., Barassi, A., Dogliotti, G., Melzi D'eril, G., Dugué, B. & Corsi, M. M. 2009. Effects of Whole-Body Cryotherapy on Serum Mediators of Inflammation and Serum Muscle Enzymes in Athletes. *Journal of Thermal Biology*, 34, 55–59.

Barkell, J., O'connor, D. & Cotton, W. 2013. An Examination of the Progression from National Schoolboy to Senior Representation in Australian Rugby Union. *University of Sydney Papers in Human Movement, Health and Coach Education*, 2, 1–16.

Barr, M., Sheppard, J., Gabbett, T. & Newton, R. 2014. Long-Term Training Induced Changes in Sprinting Speed and Sprint Momentum in Elite Rugby Union Players. *Journal of Strength & Conditioning Research*, 28, 2724–2731.

Barr, S. I. 1999. Effects of Dehydration on Exercise Performance. *Canadian Journal of Applied Physiology*, 24, 164–72.

Beckett, J., Schneiker, K., Wallman, K., Dawson, B. & Guelfi, K. 2009. Effects of Static Stretching on Repeated Sprint and Change of Direction Performance. *Medicine and Science in Sports and Exercise*, 41, 444–450.

Berliner, D. C. 1991. Educational psychology & pedagogical expertise: New findings and new opportunities for thinking about training. *Educational Psychologist*, 26, 145–155.

Berry, J., Abernethy, B. & Côté, J. 2008. The Contribution of Structured Activity and Deliberate Play to the Development of Expert Perceptual and Decision-Making Skill. *Journal of Sport & Exercise Psychology*, 30, 685–708.

Birch, R., Noble, D. & Greenhaff, P. L. 1994. The Influence of Dietary Creatine Supplementation on Performance During Repeated Bouts of Maximal Isokinetic Cycling in Man. *European Journal of Applied Physiology and Occupational Physiology*, 69, 268–276.

Bishop, D. & Claudius, B. 2005. Effects of induced Metabolic Alkalosis on Prolonged Intermittent-Sprint Performance. *Medicine and Science in Sports and Exercise*, 37, 759–767.

Bishop, D., Girard, O. & Mendez-Villanueva, A. 2011. Repeated-Sprint Ability - Part II: Recommendations for Training. *Sports Medicine*, 41, 741–756.

Bishop, D. J., Granata, C. & Eynon, N. 2013. Can We Optimise the Exercise Training Prescription To Maximise Improvements in Mitochondria Function and Content? *Biochimica Et Biophysica Acta (Bba) – General Subjects*, 1840, 1266–1275.

Bjork, R. A. 1993. Memory and metamemory considerations in the training of human beings. In J. Metcalfe & A. P. Shimamura (Eds.), *Metacognition: Knowing About Knowing*. Cambridge, MA: MIT Press.

Black, G. M. & Gabbett, T. J. 2014. Match intensity and Pacing Strategies in Rugby League: An Examination of Whole-Game and interchanged Players, and Winning and Losing Teams. *Journal of Strength & Conditioning Research*, 28, 1507–1516.

Bleakley, C., McDonough, S., Gardner, E., Baxter, D. G., Hopkins, T. J., Davison, G. W. & Costa, M. T. 2012. Cold-Water Immersion (Cryotherapy) For Preventing and Treating Muscle Soreness after Exercise. *Sao Paulo Medical Journal*, 130, 348–348.

Blomstrand, E. 2001. Amino Acids and Central Fatigue. *Amino Acids*, 20, 25–34.

Bosco, C. & Komi, P. V. 1979. Potentiation of the Mechanical Behaviour of the Human Skeletal Muscle through Prestretching. *Acta Physiologica Scandinavica*, 106, 467–472.

Bosco, C., Komi, P. V. & Ito, A. 1981. Prestretch Potentiation of Human Skeletal Muscle during Ballistic Movement. *Acta Physiologica Scandinavica*, 111, 135–140.

Bradley, W., Cavanagh, B., Douglas, W., Donovan, T. F., Morton, J. P. & Close, G. L. 2015. Quantification of Training Load, Energy Intake and Physiological Adaptations during a Rugby Pre Season: A Case Study from an Elite European Rugby Union Squad. *Journal of Strength & Conditioning Research*, 25, 534–544

Breen, L. & Churchward-Venne, T. A. 2012. Leucine: A Nutrient 'Trigger' For Muscle Anabolism, But What More? *The Journal of Physiology*, 590, 2065–2066.

Brightmore, A., O'Hara, J. P., Till, K., Cobley, S., Hubka, T., Emmonds, S. & Cooke, C. 2014. Comparison of Movement Demands in Rugby League Referees between the European Super League and Australian National Rugby League. *Journal of Sports Sciences*, 32, s44.

Bringard, A., Perrey, S. & Belluye, N. 2006. Aerobic Energy Cost and Sensation Responses during Submaximal Running Exercise: Positive Effects of Wearing Compression Tights. *International Journal of Sports Medicine*, 27, 373–378.

Broatch, J. R., Petersen, A. & Bishop, D. 2014. Post-Exercise Cold-Water Immersion Benefits Are Not Greater Than the Placebo Effect. *Medicine and Science in Sports and Exercise*, 46, 2139–2147.

Brown, T. D., Vescovi, J. D. & Vanheest, J. L. 2004. Assessment of Linear Sprinting Performance: A theoretical Paradigm. *Journal of Sports Science & Medicine*, 3, 203–210.

Brughelli, M., Cronin, J. & Chaouachi, A. 2011. Effects of Running Velocity on Running Kinetics and Kinematics. *Journal of Strength & Conditioning Research*, 25, 933–939.

Brughelli, M., Cronin, J., Levin, G. & Chaouachi, A. 2008. Understanding Change of Direction Ability in Sport. *Sports Medicine*, 38, 1045–1063.

Buckley, J. D. 2002. Bovine Colostrum: Does It Improve Athletic Performance? *Nutrition*, 18, 776–777.

Buckley, J. D., Abbott, M. J., Brinkworth, G. D. & Whyte, P. B. 2002. Bovine Colostrum Supplementation During Endurance Running Training Improves Recovery, But Not Performance. *Journal of Science and Medicine in Sport*, 5, 65–79.

Burton, D., Gillham, A. D. & Hammermeister, J. 2011. Competitive Engineering: Structural Climate Modifications to Enhance Youth Athletes' Competitive Experience. *International Journal of Sports Science and Coaching*, 6, 201–218.

Cahill, N., Lamb, K., Worsfold, P., Headey, R. & Murray, S. 2013. The Movement Characteristics of English Premiership Rugby Union Players. *Journal of Sports Sciences*, 31, 229–237.

Casanova, F., Oliveira, J., Williams, M. & Garganta, J. 2009. Expertise and Perceptual-Cognitive Performance in Soccer: A Review. *Revista Portuguesa De Ciências Do Desporto*, 9, 115–122.

Casey, A. & Greenhaff, P. L. 2000. Does Dietary Creatine Supplementation Play A Role in Skeletal Muscle Metabolism and Performance? *American Journal of Clinical Nutrition*, 72, 607s–617s.

Cheuvront, S. N. & Kenefick, R. W. 2014. Dehydration: Physiology, Assessment, and Performance Effects. *Comprehensive Physiology*, 4, 257–285.

Churchward-Venne, T. A., Breen, L., Di Donato, D. M., Hector, A. J., Mitchell, C. J., Moore, D. R., Stellingwerff, T., Breuille, D., Offord, E. A., Baker, S. K. & Phillips, S. M. 2014. Leucine Supplementation of A Low-Protein Mixed Macronutrient Beverage Enhances Myofibrillar Protein Synthesis in Young Men: A Double-Blind, Randomized Trial. *American Journal of Clinical Nutrition*, 99, 276–286.

Churchward-Venne, T. A., Burd, N. A., Mitchell, C. J., West, D. W., Philp, A., Marcotte, G. R., Baker, S. K., Baar, K. & Phillips, S. M. 2012. Supplementation of a Suboptimal Protein Dose with Leucine or Essential Amino Acids: Effects on Myofibrillar Protein Synthesis at Rest and Following Resistance Exercise in Men. *The Journal of Physiology*, 590, 2751–2765.

Clarkson, P. M. 1991. Minerals: Exercise Performance and Supplementation in Athletes. *Journal of Sports Science*, 9, 91–116.

Cleary, M., Ruiz, D., Eberman, L., Mitchell, I. & Binkley, H. 2007. Dehydration, Cramping, and Exertional Rhabdomyolysis: A Case Report with Suggestions for Recovery. *Journal of Sport Rehabilitation*, 16, 244–259.

Close, G. L. & Jackson, M. J. 2014. Antioxidants and Exercise: A Tale of the Complexities of Relating Signalling Processes to Physiological Function? *The Journal of Physiology*, 592, 1721–1722.

Cobley, S., Baker, J., Wattie, N. & McKenna, J. 2009. *Annual Age-Grouping and Athlete Development*. Sports Medicine, 39, 235–256.

Cobley, S. & Cooke, C. 2009. Talent Identification and Development: An Overview of Research and Practice. Paper Presented in the Carnegie Seminar Series, Carnegie Faculty, Leeds Metropolitan University, Leeds.

Cobley, S., Hanratty, M., O'Connor, D. & Cotton, W. 2014. First Club Location and Relative Age As Influences on Being a Professional Australian Rugby League Player. *International Journal of Sports Science and Coaching*, 9, 335–346.

Cobley, S., Schorer, J. & Baker, J. 2012. Identification and Development of Sport Talent. A Brief introduction To a Growing Field of Research and Practice. Talent Identification and Development in Sport. *International Perspectives*, 1–10.

Comfort, P., Graham-Smith, P., Matthews, M. J. & Bamber, C. 2011. Strength and Power Characteristics in English Elite Rugby League Players. *Journal of Strength & Conditioning Research*, 25, 1374–1384.

Comfort, P., Bullock, N. & Pearson, S. J. 2012a. A Comparison of Maximal Squat Strength and 5–, 10–, and 20–Meter Sprint Times in Athletes and Recreationally Trained Men. *Journal of Strength & Conditioning Research*, 26, 937–940.

Comfort, P., Fletcher, C. & Mcmahon, J. J. 2012b. Determination of Optimal Loading during the Power Clean in Collegiate Athletes. *Journal of Strength & Conditioning Research*, 26, 2970–2974.

Comfort, P., Haigh, A. & Matthews, M. J. 2012c. Are Changes in Maximal Squat Strength During Pre-season Training Reflected in Changes in Sprint Performance in Rugby League Players? *Journal of Strength & Conditioning Research*, 26, 772–776.

Comfort, P., Udall, R. & Jones, P. 2012d. The Effect of Loading on Kinematic and Kinetic Variables during the Mid-Thigh Clean Pull. *Journal of Strength & Conditioning Research*, 26, 1208–1214.

Cook, C. J. & Beaven, C. M. 2013. Individual Perception of Recovery Is Related To Subsequent Sprint Performance. *British Journal of Sports Medicine*, 47, 705–709.

Cormack, S. J., Newton, R. U., McGuigan, M. R. & Doyle, T. L. 2008. Reliability of Measures Obtained During Single and Repeated Countermovement Jumps. *International Journal of Sports Physiology and Performance*, 3, 131–144.

Cormie, P., Deane, R. & McBride, J. M. 2007a. Methodological Concerns for Determining Power Output in the Jump Squat. *Journal of Strength & Conditioning Research*, 21, 424–430.

Cormie, P., McBride, J. M. & McCaulley, G. O. 2007b. The Influence of Body Mass on Calculation of Power during Lower-Body Resistance Exercises. *Journal of Strength & Conditioning Research*, 21, 1042–1049.

Cormie, P., McBride, J. M. & McCaulley, G. O. 2007c. Validation of Power Measurement Techniques in Dynamic Lower Body Resistance Exercises. *Journal of Applied Biomechanics*, 23, 103–118.

Cormie, P., McCaulley, G. O., Triplett, N. T. & McBride, J. M. 2007e. Optimal Loading for Maximal Power Output during Lower-Body Resistance Exercises. *Medicine and Science in Sports and Exercise*, 39, 340–349.

Cormie, P., McBride, J. M. & McCaulley, G. O. 2008. Power-Time, Force-Time, and Velocity-Time Curve Analysis during the Jump Squat: Impact of Load. *Journal of Applied Biomechanics*, 24, 112–120.

Cormie, P., McGuigan, M. R. & Newton, R. U. 2010a. Adaptations in Athletic Performance after Ballistic Power versus Strength Training. *Medicine and Science in Sports and Exercise*, 42, 1582–1598.

Cormie, P., McGuigan, M. R. & Newton, R. U. 2010b. Influence of Strength on Magnitude and Mechanisms of Adaptation to Power Training. *Medicine and Science in Sports and Exercise*, 42, 1566–1581.

Cormie, P., McGuigan, M. R. & Newton, R. U. 2011. Developing Maximal Neuromuscular Power: Part 2 - Training Considerations for Improving Maximal Power Production. *Sports Medicine*, 41, 125–146

Côté, J., Young, B., North, J., and Duffy, P. (2007). Towards a definition of excellence in sport coaching. *International Journal of Coaching Science*, 1, 3–17.

Coutts, A., Reaburn, P. & Abt, G. 2003. Heart Rate, Blood Lactate Concentration and the Estimated Energy Expenditure in a Semi-Professional Rugby League Team during a Match: A Case Study. *Journal of Sports Sciences*, 21, 97–103.

Coutts, A., Reaburn, P., Piva, T. J. & Rowsell, G. J. 2007a. Monitoring For Overreaching in Rugby League Players. *European Journal of Applied Physiology*, 99, 313–333.

Coutts, A., Wallace, L. & Slattery, K. 2007b. Monitoring Changes in Performance, Physiology, Biochemistry, and Psychology during Overreaching and Recovery in Triathletes. *International Journal of Sports Medicine*, 28, 125–134.

Crewther, B., Kilduff, L., Cook, C. J., Cunningham, D., Bunce, P., Bracken, R. & Gaviglio, C. 2012. Relationships between Salivary Free Testosterone and the Expression of Force and Power in Elite Athletes. *The Journal of Sports Medicine and Physical Fitness*, 52, 221–227.

Crewther, B. T., Sanctuary, C. E., Kilduff, L. P., Carruthers, J. S., Gaviglio, C. M. & Cook, C. J. 2013. The Workout Responses of Salivary-Free Testosterone and Cortisol Concentrations and their Association with the Subsequent Competition Outcomes in Professional Rugby League. *Journal of Strength & Conditioning Research*, 27, 471–476.

Cronin, J. B. & Hansen, K. T. 2005. Strength and Power Predictors of Sports Speed. *Journal of Strength & Conditioning Research*, 19, 349–357.

Cross, M., Brughelli, M. & Cronin, J. 2014. Effects of Vest Loading on Sprint Kinetics and Kinematics. *Journal of Strength & Conditioning Research*, 28, 1867–1874.

Cunniffe, B., Proctor, W., Baker, J. S. & Davies, B. 2009a. An Evaluation of the Physiological Demands of Elite Rugby Union Using Global Positioning System Tracking Software. *Journal of Strength & Conditioning Research*, 23, 1195–1203.

Cunningham, D. J., West, D. J., Owen, N. J., Shearer, D. A., Finn, C. V., Bracken, R. M., Crewther, B. T., Scott, P., Cook, C. J. & Kilduff, L. P. 2013. Strength and Power Predictors of Sprinting Performance in Professional Rugby Players. *Journal of Sports Medicine and Physical Fitness*, 53, 105–111.

Cupples, B. 2010. The Development of Position-Specific Performance Indicators in Elite Youth Rugby League: A Coach's Perspective. Unpublished Masters Dissertation, University of Sydney.

Cupples, B. & O'Connor, D. 2011. The Development of Position-Specific Performance Indicators in Elite Youth Rugby League: A Coach's Perspective. *International Journal of Sports Science and Coaching*, 6, 125–142.

Cushion, C., Ford, P. R. & Williams, A. M. 2012. Coach Behaviours and Practice Structures in Youth Soccer: Implications for Talent Development. *Journal of Sports Sciences*, 30, 1631–1641.

Davids, K., Glazier, P., Araújo, D. & Bartlett, R. 2003. Movement Systems as Dynamical Systems. *Sports Medicine*, 33, 245–260.

Davids, K. W., Button, C. & Bennett, S. J. 2008. Dynamics of Skill Acquisition: A Constraints-Led Approach, *Human Kinetics*.

Davis, J. M. 1995. Carbohydrates, Branched-Chain Amino Acids, and Endurance: the Central Fatigue Hypothesis. *International Journal of Sports Nutrition*, 5 Suppl, S29–38.

Davison, G. & Diment, B. C. 2010. Bovine Colostrum Supplementation Attenuates the Decrease of Salivary Lysozyme and Enhances the Recovery of Neutrophil Function After Prolonged Exercise. *British Journal of Nutrition*, 103, 1425–1432.

Dawson, B., Gow, S., Modra, S., Bishop, D. & Stewart, G. 2005. Effects of Immediate Post-Game Recovery Procedures on Muscle Soreness, Power and Flexibility Levels over the Next 48 Hours. *Journal of Science and Medicine in Sport*, 8, 210–221.

Deci, E. L., & Ryan, R. M. 2000. The 'what' and 'why' of goal pursuits: Human needs and the self-determination of behaviour. *Psychological Inquiry*, 11, 227–268.

Delahunt, E., Byrne, R. B., Doolin, R. K., McInerney, R. G., Ruddock, C. T. & Green, B. S. 2013. Anthropometric Profile and Body Composition of Irish Adolescent Rugby Union Players Aged 16–18. *Journal of Strength & Conditioning Research*, 27, 3252–3258.

Deutsch, M., Maw, G., Jenkins, D. & Reaburn, P. 1998. Heart Rate, Blood Lactate and Kinematic Data of Elite Colts (Under-19) Rugby Union Players during Competition. *Journal of Sports Sciences*, 16, 561–570.

Deutsch, M. U., Kearney, G. A. & Rehrer, N. J. 2007. Time-Motion Analysis of Professional Rugby Union Players during Match-Play. *Journal of Sports Sciences*, 25, 461–471.

Deweese, B. H., Serrano, A. J., Scruggs, S. K. & Burton, J. D. 2013. The Midthigh Pull: Proper Application and Progressions of a Weightlifting Movement Derivative. *Strength & Conditioning Journal*, 35, 54–58.

Docherty, D., Wenger, H. & Neary, P. 1988. Time-Motion Analysis Related To the Physiological Demands of Rugby. *Journal of Human Movement Studies*, 14, 269–277.

Drust, B. & Gregson, W. 2013. Fitness Testing. In: Williams, M. A. (Ed.) *Science and Soccer: Developing Elite Players*. Third Edition Ed. Abingdon: Routledge.

Duffield, R., Cannon, J. & King, M. 2010. The Effects of Compression Garments on Recovery of Muscle Performance Following High-intensity Sprint and Plyometric Exercise. *Journal of Science and Medicine in Sport*, 13, 136–140.

Duffield, R., Edge, J., Merrells, R., Hawke, E., Barnes, M., Simcock, D. & Gill, N. 2008. The Effects of Compression Garments on Intermittent Exercise Performance and Recovery on Consecutive Days. *International Journal of Sports Physiology and Performance*, 3, 454–468.

Duffield, R., Murphy, A., Snape, A., Minett, G. M. & Skein, M. 2012. Post-Match Changes in Neuromuscular Function and the Relationship To Match Demands in Amateur Rugby League Matches. *Journal of Science and Medicine in Sport*, 15, 238–243.

Durandt, J., Du Toit, S., Borresen, J., Hew-Butler, T., Masimla, H., Jokoet, I. & Lambert, M. 2009. Fitness and Body Composition Profiling of Elite Junior South African Rugby Players. *South African Journal of Sports Medicine*, 18, 38–45.

Duthie, G., Pyne, D. & Hooper, S. 2003a. Applied Physiology and Game Analysis of Rugby Union. *Sports Medicine*, 33, 973–991.

Duthie, G., Pyne, D. & Hooper, S. 2003b. The Reliability of Video Based Time Motion Analysis. *Journal of Human Movement Studies*, 44, 259–271.

Duthie, G., Pyne, D. & Hooper, S. 2005. Time Motion Analysis of 2001 and 2002 Super 12 Rugby. *Journal of Sports Sciences*, 23, 523–530.

Duthie, G. M., Pyne, D. B., Marsh, D. J. & Hooper, S. L. 2006. Sprint Patterns in Rugby Union Players during Competition. *Journal of Strength and Conditioning Research*, 20, 208–214.

Earp, J. E., Kraemer, W. J., Cormie, P., Volek, J. S., Maresh, C. M., Joseph, M. & Newton, R. U. 2011. Influence of Muscle-Tendon Unit Structure on Rate of Force Development During the Squat, Countermovement, and Drop Jumps. *Journal of Strength & Conditioning Research*, 25, 340–347

Edouard, P., Frize, N., Calmels, P., Samozino, P., Garet, M. & Degache, F. 2009. Influence of Rugby Practice on Shoulder Internal and External Rotators Strength. *International Journal of Sports Medicine*, 30, 863–867.

Edwards, A. M. & Noakes, T. D. 2009. Dehydration: Cause of Fatigue or Sign of Pacing in Elite Soccer? *Sports Medicine*, 39, 1–13.

Elias, G. P., Varley, M. C., Wyckelsma, V. L., McKenna, M. J., Minahan, C. L. & Aughey, R. J. 2012. Effects of Water Immersion on Post training Recovery in Australian Footballers. *International Journal of Sports Physiology and Performance*, 7, 357–366.

Elloumi, M., Maso, F., Michaux, O., Robert, A. & Lac, G. 2003. Behaviour of Saliva Cortisol [C], Testosterone [T] and the T/C Ratio during a Rugby Match and During the Post-Competition Recovery Days. *European Journal of Applied Physiology*, 90, 23–28.

Emmonds, S., O'Hara, J., Till, K., Jones, B., Brightmore, A., & Cooke, C. 2014. Physiological and Moment Demands in Rugby League Referees; Effect on Penalty Accuracy. *Journal of Sports Sciences*, 32, s45.

Eysenck, M. W., Derakshan, N., Santos, R., & Calvo, M. G. 2007. Anxiety and cognitive performance: Attentional control theory. *Emotion*, 7, 336–353.

Faigenbaum, A. D. & Myer, G. D. 2010. Resistance Training Among Young Athletes: Safety, Efficacy and injury Prevention Effects. *British Journal of Sports Medicine*, 44, 56–63.

Farrow, D. & Abernethy, B. 2002. Can Anticipatory Skills Be Learned Through Implicit Video Based Perceptual Training? *Journal of Sports Sciences*, 20, 471–485.

Farrow, D., McCrae, J., Gross, J. & Abernethy, B. 2010. Revisiting the Relationship between Pattern Recall and Anticipatory Skill. *International Journal of Sport Psychology*, 41, 91–106.

Farrow, D. & Raab, M. 2008. A Recipe for Expert Decision-Making. In D. Farrow, J. Baker & C. MacMahon (Eds.), *Developing Sport Expertise: Researchers and Coaches Put Theory into Practice* (Pp. 137–154). New York, NY: Routledge.

Fletcher, I. M. & Jones, B. 2004. The Effect of Different Warm-Up Stretch Protocols on 20 Meter Sprint Performance in Trained Rugby Union Players. *Journal of Strength & Conditioning Research*, 18, 885–888.

# REFERENCES

Ford, P. R., Yates, I. & Williams, A. M. 2010. An Analysis of Practice Activities and Instructional Behaviours Used by Youth Soccer Coaches during Practice: Exploring the Link between Science and Application. *Journal of Sports Sciences*, 28, 483–495.

Foster, C. 1998. Monitoring Training in Athletes With Reference To Overtraining Syndrome. *Medicine and Science in Sports and Exercise*, 30, 1164–1168.

Foster, C. D., Twist, C., Lamb, K. L. & Nicholas, C. W. 2010. Heart Rate Responses to Small-Sided Games among Elite Junior Rugby League Players. *Journal of Strength & Conditioning Research*, 24, 906–911

Fuller, C. W., Brooks, J. H. M., Cancea, R., Hall, J. E. & Kemp, S. 2007. Contact Events in Rugby Union and their Prosperity to Cause injury. *British Journal of Sports Medicine*, 41, 862–867.

Gabbett, T. J. 2000. Physiological and Anthropometric Characteristics of Amateur Rugby League Players. *British Journal of Sports Medicine*, 34, 303–307.

Gabbett, T. J. 2002a. Influence of Physiological and Anthropometric Characteristics on Selection in a Semi-Professional Rugby League Team: A Case Study. *Journal of Sports Sciences*, 20, 399–405.

Gabbett, T. J. 2002b. Physiological Characteristics of Junior and Senior Rugby League Players. *British Journal of Sports Medicine*, 36, 334–342.

Gabbett, T. J. 2005. Science of Rugby League Football: A Review. *Journal of Sports Sciences*, 23, 961–967.

Gabbett, T. J. 2006. Performance Changes Following A Field Conditioning Program in Junior and Senior Rugby League Players. *Journal of Strength & Conditioning Research*, 20, 215–221.

Gabbett, T. J. 2008. Influence of Fatigue on Tackling Techniques in Rugby League Players. *Journal of Strength and Conditioning Research*, 22, 625–632.

Gabbett, T. J. 2009. Physiological and Anthropometric Characteristics of Starter and Non-Starters in Junior Rugby League Players, Aged 13–17 Years. *Journal of Sports Medicine and Physical Fitness*, 49, 233–239.

Gabbett, T. J. 2012. Sprinting Patterns of National Rugby League Competition. *Journal of Strength & Conditioning Research*, 26, 121–130.

Gabbett, T. J. 2014a. Influence of Ball-in-Play Time on the Activity Profiles of Rugby League Match-Play. *Journal of Strength and Conditioning Research*.

Gabbett, T. J. 2014b. Influence of Playing Standard on the Physical Demands of Junior Rugby League Tournament Match-Play. *Journal of Science and Medicine in Sport*, 17, 212–217.

Gabbett, T. J. & Abernethy, B. 2012. Dual-Task Assessment of A Sporting Skill: Influence of Task Complexity and Relationship with Competitive Performances. *Journal of Sports Sciences*, 30, 1735–1745.

Gabbett, T. J. & Abernethy, B. 2013. Expert–Novice Differences in the Anticipatory Skill of Rugby League Players. *Sport, Exercise, and Performance Psychology*, 2, 138.

Gabbett, T. J. & Benton, D. 2009. Reactive Agility of Rugby League Players. *Journal of Science and Medicine in Sport*, 12, 212–214.

Gabbett, T. J. & Herzig, P. 2004. Physiological Characteristics of Junior Elite and Sub-Elite Rugby League Players. *Strength and Conditioning Coach*, 12, 19–24.

Gabbett, T. J., Jenkins, D. & Abernethy, B. 2010. Physical Collisions and Injury During Professional Rugby League Skills Training. *Journal of Science and Medicine in Sport*, 13, 578–583.

Gabbett, T. J., Jenkins, D. G. & Abernethy, B. 2011a. Correlates of Tackling Ability in High-Performance Rugby League Players. *Journal of Strength & Conditioning Research*, 25, 72–79.

Gabbett, T. J., Jenkins, D. G. & Abernethy, B. 2011b. Physical Collisions and Injury in Professional Rugby League Match-Play. *Journal of Science and Medicine in Sport*, 14, 210–215.

Gabbett, T. J., Jenkins, D. G. & Abernethy, B. 2011c. Physiological and Anthropometric Correlates of Tackling Ability in Junior Elite and Sub elite Rugby League Players. *Journal of Strength & Conditioning Research*, 24, 2989–2995.

Gabbett, T. J., Jenkins, D. G. & Abernethy, B. 2011d. Relationships between Physiological, Anthropometric, and Skill Qualities and Playing Performance in Professional Rugby League Players. *Journal of Sports Sciences*, 29, 1655–1664.

Gabbett, T. J., Jenkins, D. G. & Abernethy, B. 2011e. Relative Importance of Physiological, Anthropometric and Skill Qualities to Team Selection in Professional Rugby League. *Journal of Sports Sciences*, 29, 1453–1461.

Gabbett, T. J., Jenkins, D. G. & Abernethy, B. 2012a. Influence of Wrestling on the Physiological and Skill Demands of Small-Sided Games. *Journal of Strength & Conditioning Research*, 26, 113–120.

Gabbett, T. J., Jenkins, D. G. & Abernethy, B. 2012b. Physical Demands of Professional Rugby League Training and Competition Using Microtechnology. *Journal of Science and Medicine in Sport*, 15, 80–86.

Gabbett, T. J. & Kelly, J. 2007. Does Fast Defensive Line Speed Influence Tackling Proficiency in Collision Sport Athletes? *International Journal of Sports Science and Coaching*, 2, 467–472.

Gabbett, T. J., Kelly, J. & Pezet, T. 2007a. The Relationship between Physical Fitness and Playing Ability in Rugby League Players. *Journal of Strength and Conditioning Research*, 21, 1126–1133.

Gabbett, T. J., Kelly, J. N. & Sheppard, J. M. 2008. Speed, Change of Direction Speed, and Reactive Agility of Rugby League Players. *Journal of Strength & Conditioning Research*, 22, 174–181.

# REFERENCES

Gabbett, T. J., Kelly, J., Ralph, S. & Driscoll, D. 2009. Physiological and Anthropometric Characteristics of Junior Elite and Sub-Elite Rugby League Players, With Special Reference to Starters and Non-Starters. *Journal of Science and Medicine in Sport*, 12, 215–222.

Gabbett, T. J. & Ryan, P. 2009. Tackling Technique, Injury Risk, and Playing Performance in High-Performance Collision Sport Athletes. *International Journal of Sports Science and Coaching*, 4, 521–533.

Gabbett, T. J. & Seibold, A. J. 2013. Relationship between Tests of Physical Qualities, Team Selection, and Physical Match Performance in Semi-professional Rugby League Players. *Journal of Strength & Conditioning Research*, 27, 3259–3265.

Gabbett, T. J., Stein, J. G., Kemp, J. G. & Lorenzen, C. 2013. Relationship between Tests of Physical Qualities and Physical Match Performance in Elite Rugby League Players. *Journal of Strength & Conditioning Research*, 27, 1539–1545.

Gabbett, T. J., Ullah, S., Jenkins, D. & Abernethy, B. 2012c. Skill Qualities as Risk Factors for Contact Injury in Professional Rugby League Players. *Journal of Sports Sciences*, 30, 1421–1427.

Gabbett, T. J., Wake, M. & Abernethy, B. 2011a. Use of Dual-Task Methodology for Skill Assessment and Development: Examples from Rugby League. *Journal of Sports Sciences*, 29, 7–18.

Gallahue, D. L., Ozmun, J. C. & Goodway, J. 2006. *Understanding Motor Development: Infants, Children, Adolescents, Adults*, Mcgraw-Hill Boston.

Ghasemi, A., Momeni, M., Jafarzadehpur, E., Rezaee, M. & Taheri, H. 2011. Visual Skills Involved in Decision Making by Expert Referees 1. *Perceptual and Motor Skills*, 112, 161–171.

Gill, N., Beaven, C. & Cook, C. 2006. Effectiveness of Post-Match Recovery Strategies in Rugby Players. *British Journal of Sports Medicine*, 40, 260–263.

Girard, O., Mendez-Villanueva, A. & Bishop, D. 2011. Repeated-Sprint Ability - Part I: Factors Contributing To Fatigue. *Sports Medicine*, 41, 673–94.

Gissane, C., White, J., Kerr, K. & Jennings, D. 2001. Physical Collisions in Professional Super League Rugby, the Demands on Different Player Positions. *Cleveland Medical Journal*, 4, 137–146.

Gould, D., Dieffenbach, K. & Moffett, A. 2002. Psychological Characteristics and their Development in Olympic Champions. *Journal of Applied Sport Psychology*, 14, 172–204.

Green, B. S., Blake, C. & Caulfield, B. M. 2011a. A Comparison of Cutting Technique Performance in Rugby Union Players. *Journal of Strength & Conditioning Research*, 25, 2668–2680.

Green, B. S., Blake, C. & Caulfield, B. M. 2011b. A Valid Field Test Protocol of Linear Speed and Agility in Rugby Union. *Journal of Strength & Conditioning Research*, 25, 1256–1262.

Gréhaigne, J.-F., Godbout, P. & Bouthier, D. 2001. The Teaching and Learning of Decision Making in Team Sports. *Quest*, 53, 59–76.

Gulbin, J., Weissensteiner, J., Oldenziel, K. & Gagné, F. 2013. Patterns of Performance Development in Elite Athletes. *European Journal of Sport Science*, 13, 605–614.

Güllich, A. 2013. Selection, De-Selection and Progression in German Football Talent Promotion. *European Journal of Sport Science*, 1–8.

Halson, S. L. 2008. Nutrition, Sleep and Recovery. *European Journal of Sport Science*, 8, 119–126.

Halson, S. L., Lancaster, G. I., Jeukendrup, A. E. & Gleeson, M. 2003. Immunological Responses to Overreaching in Cyclists. *Medicine and Science in Sports and Exercise*, 35, 854–861.

Hamlin, M. J., Mitchell, C. J., Ward, F. D., Draper, N., Shearman, J. P. & Kimber, N. E. 2012. Effect of Compression Garments on Short-Term Recovery of Repeated Sprint and 3–Km Running Performance in Rugby Union Players. *Journal of Strength & Conditioning Research*, 26, 2975–2982.

Hamlyn, N., Behm, D. G. & Young, W. B. 2007. Trunk Muscle Activation During Dynamic Weight-Training Exercises and Isometric instability Activities. *Journal of Strength & Conditioning Research*, 21, 1108–12.

Hansen, K. T., Cronin, J. B., Pickering, S. L. & Douglas, L. 2011a. Do Force–Time and Power-Time Measures in A Loaded Jump Squat Differentiate between Speed Performance and Playing Level in Elite and Elite Junior Rugby Union Players? *Journal of Strength & Conditioning Research*, 25, 2382–2391.

Hansen, K. T., Cronin, J. B., Pickering, S. L. & Newton, M. J. 2011b. Does Cluster Loading Enhance Lower Body Power Development in Preseason Preparation of Elite Rugby Union Players? *Journal of Strength & Conditioning Research*, 25, 2118–2126.

Harley, J. A., Hind, K. & O'Hara, J. P. 2011. Three-Compartment Body Composition Changes in Elite Rugby League Players during a Super League Season, Measured By Dual-Energy X-Ray Absorptiometry. *Journal of Strength & Conditioning Research*, 25, 1024–1029.

Harris, N. K., Cronin, J. B., Hopkins, W. G. & Hansen, K. T. 2010. Inter-Relationships between Machine Squat-Jump Strength, Force, Power and 10 M Sprint Times in Trained Sportsmen. *Journal of Sports Medicine and Physical Fitness*, 50, 37–42.

Harvey, S., Cushion, C., Cope, E. & Muir, B. 2013. A season long investigation into coaching behaviours as a function of practice state: the case of three collegiate coaches. *Sports Coaching Review*, 2, 13–32

Harvey, S., Lyle, J. & Muir, B. 2015. Naturalistic decision making in high performance team sport coaching. *International Sport Coaching Journal*. Epub

Hastie, R. 2001. Problems for Judgment and Decision Making. *Annual Review of Psychology*, 52, 653–683.

Heaney, R. P. 2003. Vitamin D, Nutritional Deficiency, and the Medical Paradigm. *Journal of Clinical Endocrinology and Metabolism*, 88, 5107–5108.

Heisterberg, M. F., Fahrenkrug, J., Krustrup, P., Storskov, A., Kjær, M. & Andersen, J. L. 2013. Extensive Monitoring Through Multiple Blood Samples in Professional Soccer Players. *Journal of Strength & Conditioning Research*, 27, 1260–1271.

Helgerud, J., Engen, L. C., Wisloff, U. & Hoff, J. 2001. Aerobic Endurance Training Improves Soccer Performance. *Medicine and Science in Sports and Exercise*, 33, 1925–1931.

Helgerud, J., Hoydal, K., Wang, E., Karlsen, T., Berg, P., Bjerkaas, M., Simonsen, T., Helgesen, C., Hjorth, N., Bach, R. & Hoff, J. 2007. Aerobic High-intensity Intervals Improve VO$_2$max More Than Moderate Training. *Medicine and Science in Sports and Exercise*, 39, 665–671.

Helgeson, K. & Stoneman, P. 2014. Shoulder Injuries in Rugby Players: Mechanisms, Examination, and Rehabilitation. *Physical therapy in Sport*, 15, 218–227.

Helms, E. R., Zinn, C., Rowlands, D. S., Naidoo, R. & Cronin, J. 2014. High-Protein Low-Fat Short-Term Diet Results in Less Stress and Fatigue Than Moderate-Protein Moderate-Fat Diet During Weight Loss in Male Weightlifters, A Pilot Study. *International Journal of Sports Nutrition and Exercise Metabolism*, 14.

Helsen, W. F. & Starkes, J. L. 1999. A Multidimensional Approach to Skilled Perception and Performance in Sport. *Applied Cognitive Psychology*, 13, 1–27.

Hemmings, B., Smith, M., Graydon, J. & Dyson, R. 2000. Effects of Massage on Physiological Restoration, Perceived Recovery, and Repeated Sports Performance. *British Journal of Sports Medicine*, 34, 109–114.

Hendricks, S. 2012. Trainability of Junior Rugby Union Players. *South African Journal of Sports Medicine*, 24, 122–125.

Hendricks, S., Lambert, M. I., Masimla, H. & J, D. 2015. Measuring Skill in Rugby Union and Rugby League as Part of the Standard Team Testing Battery. *International Journal of Sports Science and Coaching*, Accepted.

Henriksen, K., Stambulova, N. & Roessler, K. K. 2010. Successful Talent Development in Track and Field: Considering the Role of Environment. *Scandinavian Journal of Medicine & Science in Sports*, 20, 122–132.

Herbert, R. D. & Gabriel, M. 2002. Effects of Stretching Before and After Exercising on Muscle Soreness and Risk of Injury: Systematic Review. *British Medical Journal*, 325, 468.

Herrington, L. C. & Comfort, P. 2013. Training for Prevention of ACL Injury: Incorporation of Progressive Landing Skill Challenges into A Program. *Strength & Conditioning Journal*, 35, 59–65.

Hilbert, J. E., Sforzo, G. & Swensen, T. 2003. The Effects of Massage on Delayed onset Muscle Soreness. *British Journal of Sports Medicine*, 37, 72–75.

Hill-Haas, S. V., Dawson, B., Impellizzeri, F. M. & Coutts, A. J. 2011. Physiology of Small-Sided Games Training in Football: A Systematic Review. *Sports Medicine*, 41, 199–220.

Hinds, T., McEwan, I., Perkes, J., Dawson, E., Ball, D. & George, K. 2004. Effects of Massage on Limb and Skin Blood Flow after Quadriceps Exercise. *Medicine and Science in Sports and Exercise*, 36, 1308–1313.

Hoare, K. 2008. Physiological Demands of NRL Match officiating. *Journal of Australian Strength and Conditioning*, 16, 38–42.

Hoff, J., Wisløff, U., Engen, L., Kemi, O. & Helgerud, J. 2002. Soccer Specific Aerobic Endurance Training. *British Journal of Sports Medicine*, 36, 218–221.

Holway, F. E. & Garavaglia, R. 2009. Kinanthropometry of Group 1 Rugby Players in Buenos Aires, Argentina. *Journal of Sports Sciences*, 27, 1211–1220.

Hori, N., Newton, R. U., Andrews, W. A., Kawamori, N., McGuigan, M. R. & Nosaka, K. 2008. Does Performance of Hang Power Clean Differentiate Performance of Jumping, Sprinting, and Changing of Direction? *Journal of Strength & Conditioning Research*, 22, 412–418

Hu, F. B. 2010. Are Refined Carbohydrates Worse Than Saturated Fat? *American Journal of Clinical Nutrition*, 91, 1541–1542.

International Council for Coaching Excellence & the Association of Summer Olympic International Federations (2012), International Sport Coaching Framework (version 1.1), Champaign, IL: Human Kinetics.

IRB 2011. Rugby World Cup 2011 – Statistical Review and Match Analysis. International Rugby Board, 1–74.

Jackson, R. C., Warren, S. & Abernethy, B. 2006. Anticipation Skill and Susceptibility to Deceptive Movement. *Acta Psychologica*, 123, 355–371.

Jakeman, J. R., Byrne, C. & Eston, R. G. 2010. Lower Limb Compression Garment Improves Recovery From Exercise-induced Muscle Damage in Young, Active Females. *European Journal of Applied Physiology*, 109, 1137–1144.

Jarvis, S., Sullivan, L. O., Davies, B., Wiltshire, H. & Baker, J. S. 2009. Interrelationships between Measured Running Intensities and Agility Performance in Subelite Rugby Union Players. *Research in Sports Medicine*, 17, 217–230.

Jentjens, R. & Jeukendrup, A. 2003. Determinants of Post-Exercise Glycogen Synthesis during Short-Term Recovery. *Sports Medicine*, 33, 117–144.

Johnson, J. G. 2006. Cognitive Modelling of Decision-Making in Sports. *Psychology of Sport & Exercise*, 7, 631–652

Johnston, R., Gabbett, T. & Jenkins, D. 2014a. Influence of Number of Contact Efforts on Running Performance during Game-Based Activities. *International Journal of Sports Physiology and Performance*. Epub

Johnston, R., Gabbett, T., Seibold, A. & Jenkins, D. 2014b. Influence of Physical Contact on Pacing Strategies during Game-Based Activities. *International Journal of Sports Physiology and Performance*. Epub

Johnston, R. D., Gabbett, T. J. & Jenkins, D. G. 2014c. Applied Sport Science of Rugby League. *Sports Medicine*, 1–14.

Johnston, R. D., Gabbett, T. J., Jenkins, D. G. & Hulin, B. T. 2014d. Influence of Physical Qualities on Post-Match Fatigue in Rugby League Players. *Journal of Science and Medicine in Sport*. Epub.

Johnston, R. D., Gabbett, T. J., Seibold, A. J. & Jenkins, D. G. 2013a. Influence of Physical Contact on Neuromuscular Fatigue and Markers of Muscle Damage Following Small-Sided Games. *Journal of Science and Medicine in Sport*. 17, 535–540.

Johnston, R. D., Gibson, N. V., Twist, C., Gabbett, T. J., MacNay, S. A. & Macfarlane, N. G. 2013b. Physiological Responses To An Intensified Period of Rugby League Competition. *Journal of Strength & Conditioning Research*, 27, 643–654.

Jones, B. L., O'Hara, J., Till, K. & King, R. F. G. J. 2015. Dehydration and Hyponatremia in Professional Rugby Union Players; A Cohort Study Observing English Premiership Rugby Union Players During Match Play, Field and Gym Training in Cool Environmental Conditions. *Journal of Strength and Conditioning Research*. 29, 107–115.

Jones, R., & Wallace, M. 2006. The coach as 'orchestrator': more realistically managing the complex coaching context. In R. Jones (Ed.), *The Sports Coach as Educator: Reconceptualising Sports Coaching* (pp. 51–64). Abingdon: Routledge.

Jones, E. 2008. Coach's Corner: Eddie Jones. In D. Farrow, J. Baker & C. MacMahon (Eds.), *Developing Sport Expertise: Researchers and Coaches Put Theory into Practice* (Pp. 25–27). New York, NY: Routledge.

Judelson, D. A., Maresh, C. M., Anderson, J. M., Armstrong, L. E., Casa, D. J., Kraemer, W. J. & Volek, J. S. 2007. Hydration and Muscular Performance: Does Fluid Balance Affect Strength, Power and High-intensity Endurance? *Sports Medicine*, 37, 907–921.

Juliff, L. E., Halson, S. L. & Peiffer, J. J. 2014. Understanding Sleep Disturbance in Athletes Prior To Important Competitions. *Journal of Science and Medicine in Sport*. 13–18

Kawamori, N., Crum, A. J., Blumert, P. A., Kulik, J. R., Childers, J. T., Wood, J. A., Stone, M. H. & Haff, G. 2005. Influence of Different Relative intensities on Power Output during the Hang Power Clean: Identification of the Optimal Load. *Journal of Strength & Conditioning Research*, 19, 698–708.

Kahneman, D. 2011. Thinking, fast and slow. New York: Farrar, Strauss, Giroux.

Kahneman, D., & Klein, G. A. 2009. Conditions for intuitive expertise: A failure to disagree. *American Psychologist*, 64, 515–526.

Kawamori, N., Rossi, S. J., Justice, B. D., Haff, E. E., Pistilli, E. E., O'Bryant, H. S., Stone, M. H. & Haff, G. G. 2006. Peak Force and Rate of Force Development during Isometric and Dynamic Mid-Thigh Clean Pulls Performed at Various Intensities. *Journal of Strength & Conditioning Research*, 20, 483–491.

Kay, B. & Gill, N. 2003. Physical Demands of Elite Rugby League Referees: Part one—Time and Motion Analysis. *Journal of Science and Medicine in Sport*, 6, 339–342.

Kayes, N. M. & McPherson, K. M. 2010. Measuring What Matters: Does 'Objectivity' mean Good Science? *Disability & Rehabilitation*, 32, 1011–1019.

Kellmann, M. & Kallus, K. W. 2001. Recovery-Stress Questionnaire for Athletes: User Manual, Human Kinetics.

Kempton, T., Sirotic, A. C., Cameron, M. & Coutts, A. J. 2013. Match-Related Fatigue Reduces Physical and Technical Performance during Elite Rugby League Match-Play: A Case Study. *Journal of Sports Sciences*, 31, 1770–1780.

Kenttä, G. & Hassmén, P. 1998. Overtraining and Recovery. *Sports Medicine*, 26, 1–16.

Kenttä, G., Hassmén, P. & Raglin, J. 2001. Training Practices and Overtraining Syndrome in Swedish Age-Group Athletes. *International Journal of Sports Medicine*, 22, 460–465.

Kidman, L. 2010. Athlete-Centred Coaching: Developing Decision Makers, IPC Print Resources.

Kilduff, L. P., Bevan, H., Owen, N., Kingsley, M. I., Bunce, P., Bennett, M. & Cunningham, D. 2007. Optimal Loading for Peak Power Output during the Hang Power Clean in Professional Rugby Players. *International Journal of Sports Physiology and Performance*, 2, 260–269.

King, R. F., Cooke, C., Carroll, S. & O'Hara, J. 2008. Estimating Changes in Hydration Status from Changes in Body Mass: Considerations Regarding Metabolic Water and Glycogen Storage. *Journal of Sports Sciences*, 26, 1361–1363.

Kirk, D. 2005. Physical Education, Youth Sport and Lifelong Participation: the Importance of Early Learning Experiences. *European Physical Education Review*, 11, 239–255.

Kirkpatrick, J. & Comfort, P. 2013. Strength, Power, and Speed Qualities in English Junior Elite Rugby League Players. *Journal of Strength & Conditioning Research*, 27, 2414–2419.

Klein, G. 1998. *Sources of power: How people make decisions.* Cambridge, MA: MIT Press.

Kraemer, W. J., Bush, J. A., Newton, R. U., Duncan, N. D., Volek, J. S., Denegar, C. R., Canavan, P., Johnston, J., Putukian, M. & Sebastianelli, W. J. 1998. Influence of a Compression Garment on Repetitive Power Output Production before and After Different Types of Muscle Fatigue. *Research in Sports Medicine: An International Journal,* 8, 163–184.

Kraemer, W. J., Bush, J. A., Wickham, R. B., Denegar, C. R., Gomez, A. L., Gotshalk, L. A., Duncan, N. D., Volek, J. S., Newton, R. U. & Putukian, M. 2001. Continuous Compression as an Effective Therapeutic Intervention in Treating Eccentric-Exercise-induced Muscle Soreness. *Journal of Sport Rehabilitation,* 10, 11–23.

Kraemer, W. J., Flanagan, S. D., Comstock, B. A., Fragala, M. S., Earp, J. E., Dunn-Lewis, C., Ho, J.-Y., Thomas, G. A., Solomon-Hill, G. & Penwell, Z. R. 2010. Effects of a Whole Body Compression Garment on Markers of Recovery after a Heavy Resistance Workout in Men and Women. *Journal of Strength & Conditioning Research,* 24, 804–814.

Kraemer, W. J., French, D. N. & Spiering, B. A. 2004. Compression in the Treatment of Acute Muscle Injuries in Sport: Review Article. *International Sportmed Journal,* 5, 200–208.

Kreider, R. B., Ferreira, M. P., Greenwood, M., Wilson, M. & Almada, A. L. 2002. Effects of Conjugated Linoleic Acid Supplementation during Resistance Training on Body Composition, Bone Density, Strength, and Selected Haematological Markers. *Journal of Strength and Conditioning Research,* 16, 325–334.

Krustrup, P. & Bangsbo, J. 2001. Physiological Demands of Top-Class Soccer Refereeing in Relation To Physical Capacity: Effect of Intense Intermittent Exercise Training. *Journal of Sports Sciences,* 19, 881–891.

Krustrup, P., Helsen, W., Randers, M. B., Christensen, J. F., Macdonald, C., Rebelo, A. N. & Bangsbo, J. 2009. Activity Profile and Physical Demands of Football Referees and Assistant Referees in International Games. *Journal of Sports Sciences,* 27, 1167–1176.

Krustrup, P., Mohr, M. & Bangsbo, J. 2002. Activity Profile and Physiological Demands of Top-Class Soccer Assistant Refereeing in Relation To Training Status. *Journal of Sports Sciences,* 20, 861–871.

Krustrup, P., Mohr, M., Steensberg, A., Bencke, J., Kjær, M. & Bangsbo, J. 2006. Muscle and Blood Metabolites during a Soccer Game: Implications for Sprint Performance. *Medicine and Science in Sports and Exercise,* 38, 1165–1174.

Lancaster, S. 2011. Developing chefs and not cooks: How to become a coach that innovates, not a coach who follows. *International Rugby Coaching,* 2, 1–3.

Lara-Bercial, S. 2012. Quick Guide: Child Development for Coaches. Available at: Http://Sccu. Uk.Com/News/Wp-Content/Uploads/2011/07/Scuk-Child-Development-For-Coaches.Pdf. Accessed 3 Dec. 2014.

Larkin, P., Berry, J., Dawson, B. & Lay, B. 2011. Perceptual and Decision-Making Skills of Australian Football Umpires. *International Journal of Performance Analysis in Sport,* 11, 427–437.

Larkin, P., Mesagno, C., Berry, J. & Spittle, M. 2013. Development of a Valid and Reliable Video-Based Decision-Making Test for Australian Football Umpires. *Journal of Science and Medicine in Sport,* 552–555.

Larsen, C. H., Alfermann, D., Henriksen, K. & Christensen, M. K. 2013. Successful Talent Development in Soccer: The Characteristics of the Environment. *Sport, Exercise, and Performance Psychology,* 2, 190.

Leeder, J., Glaister, M., Pizzoferro, K., Dawson, J. & Pedlar, C. 2012. Sleep Duration and Quality in Elite Athletes Measured Using Wristwatch Actigraphy. *Journal of Sports Sciences,* 30, 541–545.

Lehmann, M., Lormes, W., Opitz-Gress, A., Steinacker, J., Netzer, N., Foster, C. & Gastmann, U. 1997. Training and Overtraining: An Overview and Experimental Results in Endurance Sports. *Journal of Sports Medicine and Physical Fitness,* 37, 7–17.

Levenhagen, D. K., Gresham, J. D., Carlson, M. G., Maron, D. J., Borel, M. J. & Flakoll, P. J. 2001. Post Exercise Nutrient Intake Timing in Humans Is Critical to Recovery of Leg Glucose and Protein Homeostasis. *American Journal of Physiology Endocrinology and Metabolism,* 280, E982–993.

Lloyd, R. S., Faigenbaum, A. D., Stone, M. H., Oliver, J. L., Jeffreys, I., Moody, J. A., Brewer, C., Pierce, K. C., McCambridge, T. M., Howard, R., Herrington, L., Hainline, B., Micheli, L. J., Jaques, R., Kraemer, W. J., McBride, M. G., Best, T. M., Chu, D. A., Alvar, B. A. & Myer, G. D. 2013. Position Statement on Youth Resistance Training: The 2014 International Consensus. *British Journal of Sports Medicine,* 498–505.

Lyle, J. 2010. Coaches' decision making: A Naturalisitc Decision Making analysis. In *Sport Coaching: Professionalisation & Practice.* J. Lyle & C. Cushion (Eds.) (London: Churchill Livingstone).

MacMahon, C., Helsen, W. F., Starkes, J. L. & Weston, M. 2007a. Decision-Making Skills and Deliberate Practice in Elite Association Football Referees. *Journal of Sports Sciences,* 25, 65–78.

MacMahon, C., McPherson, S. L. & Farrow, D. Year. Knowledge Base As A Mechanism For Perceptual-Cognitive Tasks: Skill Is in the Details! In: *International Journal of Sport Psychology,* 2009. Edizioni Luigi Pozzi, 565–579.

MacMahon, C., Starkes, J. & Deakin, J. 2007b. Referee Decision Making in A Video-Based infraction Detection Task: Application and Training

Considerations. *International Journal of Sports Science and Coaching*, 2, 257–265.

MacRae, M. B. A., Cotter, J. D. & Laing, R. M. 2011. Compression Garments and Exercise. *Sports Medicine*, 41, 815–843.

Maki, K. C., Reeves, M. S., Farmer, M., Yasunaga, K., Matsuo, N., Katsuragi, Y., Komikado, M., Tokimitsu, I., Wilder, D., Jones, F., Blumberg, J. B. & Cartwright, Y. 2009. Green Tea Catechin Consumption Enhances Exercise-induced Abdominal Fat Loss in Overweight and Obese Adults. *Journal of Nutrition*, 139, 264–270.

Mann, D. T., Williams, A. M., Ward, P. & Janelle, C. M. 2007. Perceptual-Cognitive Expertise in Sport: A Meta-Analysis. *Journal of Sport and Exercise Psychology*, 29, 457.

Manore, M. M. 2002. Dietary Recommendations and Athletic Menstrual Dysfunction. *Sports Medicine*, 32, 887–901.

Marchbank, T., Davison, G., Oakes, J. R., Ghatei, M. A., Patterson, M., Moyer, M. P. & Playford, R. J. 2011. The Nutriceutical Bovine Colostrum Truncates the Increase in Gut Permeability Caused by Heavy Exercise in Athletes. *American Journal of Physiology Gastrointestinal and Liver Physiology*, 300, G477–484.

Marteniuk, R. G. 1976. Information Processing in Motor Skills, Holt, Rinehart and Winston New York.

Martin, J., Smith, N. C., Tolfrey, K. & Jones, A. M. 2001. Activity Analysis of English Premiership Rugby Football Union Refereeing. *Ergonomics*, 44, 1069–1075.

Martindale, R. J., Collins, D. & Abraham, A. 2007. Effective Talent Development: the Elite Coach Perspective in UK Sport. *Journal of Applied Sport Psychology*, 19, 187–206.

Martindale, R. J., Collins, D. & Daubney, J. 2005. Talent Development: A Guide for Practice and Research within Sport. *Quest*, 57, 353–375.

Mascarenhas, D., Collins, D. & Mortimer, P. 2002. The 'Four Cornerstones' Model. Referee.

Mascarenhas, D. R., Collins, D. & Mortimer, P. 2005a. Elite Refereeing Performance: Developing a Model for Sport Science Support. *Sport Psychologist*, 19, 364–379.

Mascarenhas, D. R., Collins, D., Mortimer, P. & Morris, B. 2005b. A Naturalistic Approach to Training Accurate and Coherent Decision Making in Rugby Union Referees. *The Sport Psychologist*, 19.

McBride, J. M., Blow, D., Kirby, T. J., Haines, T. L., Dayne, A. M. & Triplett, N. T. 2009. Relationship between Maximal Squat Strength and Five, Ten, and Forty Yard Sprint Times. *Journal of Strength and Conditioning Research*, 23, 1633–1636.

McDonough, A. & Funk, L. 2014. Can Glenohumeral Joint Isokinetic Strength and Range of Movement Predict injury in Professional Rugby League? *Physical Therapy in Sport*, 15, 91–96.

McIntosh, A. S., Savage, T. N., McCrory, P., Fréchède, B. O. & Wolfe, R. 2010. Tackle Characteristics and Injury in a Cross Section of Rugby Union Football. *Medicine and Science in Sports and Exercise*, 42, 977–984.

McKay, J. 2012. Role of Unstructured Practice in Elite Rugby. Unpublished Masters Special Project. University of Sydney.

McLean, B. D., Coutts, A. J., Kelly, V., McGuigan, M. R. & Cormack, S. J. 2010. Neuromuscular, Endocrine, and Perceptual Fatigue Responses during Different Length between-Match Microcycles in Professional Rugby League Players. *International Journal of Sports Physiology and Performance*, 5, 367–383.

McLean, D. 1992. Analysis of the Physical Demands of International Rugby Union. *Journal of Sports Sciences*, 10, 285–296.

McLellan, C. P., Coad, S., Marsh, D. & Lieschke, M. 2013. Performance Analysis of Super 15 Rugby Match-Play Using Portable Micro-Technology. *Athletic Enhancement*.

McLellan, C. P. & Lovell, D. I. 2012a. Neuromuscular Responses to Impact and Collision during Elite Rugby League Match Play. *Journal of Strength & Conditioning Research*, 26, 1431–1440

McLellan, C. P., Lovell, D. I. & Gass, G. C. 2010. Creatine Kinase and Endocrine Responses of Elite Players Pre, During, and Post Rugby League Match Play. *Journal of Strength and Conditioning Research*, 24, 2908–2919.

McLellan, C. P., Lovell, D. I. & Gass, G. C. 2011. Biochemical and Endocrine Responses to Impact and Collision during Elite Rugby League Match Play. *Journal of Strength and Conditioning Research*, 25, 1553–1562

McMaster, D. T., Gill, N., Cronin, J. & McGuigan, M. 2013a. The Development, Retention and Decay Rates of Strength and Power in Elite Rugby Union, Rugby League and American Football. *Sports Medicine*, 43, 367–384.

McMaster, D. T., Gill, N., Cronin, J. & McGuigan, M. 2014. A Brief Review of Strength and Ballistic Assessment Methodologies in Sport. *Sports Medicine*, 44, 603–623.

McMaster, D. T., Gill, N. D., Cronin, J. & McGuigan, M. R. 2013b. Force-Velocity-Power Assessment in Semi-Professional Rugby Union Players. *Journal of Strength and Conditioning Research*, 8. Epub.

McMillan, K., Helgerud, J., Macdonald, R. & Hoff, J. 2005. Physiological Adaptations to Soccer Specific Endurance Training in Professional Youth Soccer Players. *British Journal of Sports Medicine*, 39, 273–277.

McNaughton, L. R. 1992. Sodium Bicarbonate Ingestion and Its Effects on Anaerobic Exercise of Various Durations. *Journal of Sports Science*, 10, 425–435.

McNaughton, L. R., Siegler, J. & Midgley, A. 2008. Ergogenic Effects of Sodium Bicarbonate. *Current Sports Medicine Reports*, 7, 230–6.

Meeusen, R., Duclos, M., Foster, C., Fry, A., Gleeson, M., Nieman, D., Raglin, J., Rietjens, G., Steinacker, J. & Urhausen, A. 2013. Prevention, Diagnosis, and Treatment of the Overtraining Syndrome: Joint Consensus Statement of the European College of Sport Science and the American College of Sports Medicine. *Medicine and Science in Sports and Exercise*, 45, 186–205.

Meeusen, R., Duclos, M., Gleeson, M., Rietjens, G., Steinacker, J. & Urhausen, A. 2006. Prevention, Diagnosis and Treatment of the Overtraining Syndrome: ECSS Position Statement 'Task Force'. *European Journal of Sport Science*, 6, 1–14.

Meeusen, R. & Watson, P. 2007. Amino Acids and the Brain: Do they Play a Role in "Central Fatigue"? *International Journal of Sports Nutrition and Exercise Metabolism*, 17 Suppl 1, S37–46.

Mills, A., Butt, J., Maynard, I. & Harwood, C. 2014. Toward An Understanding of Optimal Development Environments within Elite English Soccer Academies. *Sport Psychologist*, 28, 137–150.

Minerals, E. G. O. V. A. 2003. Safe Upper Levels for Vitamins and Minerals [online]. Available: Www.Food.Gov.Uk/Multimedia/Pdfs/Vitmin2003.Pdf [Accessed].

Montain, S. J. & Coyle, E. F. 1992. Influence of Graded Dehydration on Hyperthermia and Cardiovascular Drift during Exercise. *Journal of Applied Physiology*, 73, 1340–1350.

Montgomery, P. G., Pyne, D. B., Cox, A. J., Hopkins, W. G., Minahan, C. L. & Hunt, P. H. 2008. Muscle Damage, Inflammation, and Recovery interventions During A 3–Day Basketball Tournament. *European Journal of Sport Science*, 8, 241–250.

Moore, D. R., Areta, J., Coffey, V. G., Stellingwerff, T., Phillips, S. M., Burke, L. M., Cleroux, M., Godin, J. P. & Hawley, J. A. 2012. Daytime Pattern of Post-Exercise Protein Intake Affects Whole-Body Protein Turnover in Resistance-Trained Males. *Nutrition Metabolism (Lond)*, 9, 91.

Morgan, P. J. & Callister, R. 2011. Effects of a Preseason Intervention on Anthropometric Characteristics of Semi-professional Rugby League Players. *Journal of Strength & Conditioning Research*, 25, 432–440.

Morgan, W., Brown, D., Raglin, J., O'Connor, P. & Ellickson, K. 1987. Psychological Monitoring of Overtraining and Staleness. *British Journal of Sports Medicine*, 21, 107–114.

Morley, D., Muir, B., Morgan, E., Abraham, A. and Webb, V. 2011. A 'Fit for Purpose Strategy' For the Rugby Football League. In, A. Navin (Ed.) *Sports Coaching: A Reference Guide for Students, Coaches and Competitors*. Marlborough: Crowood Press.

Morley, D. & Muir, B. 2011. *Becoming CAYPABLE: Rugby Football League*, Coachwise, Leeds.

Morley, D., Morgan, G., McKenna, J. & Nicholls, A. R. 2014. Developmental Contexts and Features of Elite Academy Football Players: Coach and Player Perspectives. *International Journal of Sports Science and Coaching*, 9, 217–232.

Morley, D., Muir, B., & Lowe, L. 2011b. Becoming CAYPABLE: Developmentally Appropriate Approaches to Coaching Children and Young People in Rugby Football League. New Directions in Sport Coaching Conference, Leeds, 12–13 April 2011.

Morley, D. & Webb, V. 2009. A 'Fit For Purpose' Approach to Skills Development in Rugby Football League. UK Coaching Summit, Glasgow, 27–29 Apr.

Muir, B., Morgan, G., Abraham, A., & Morley, D. 2011a. Developmentally appropriate approaches to coaching children. In. I. Stafford (Eds), *Coaching Children in Sport*. London: Routledge.

Muir, B., Morgan, G., & Abraham, A. 2011b. Player learning: Implications for Structuring Practice Activities and Coach Behaviour. Football Association, London.

Muir, B. 2012. Using video & the coaching practice planning and reflective framework to facilitate high performance coaches development. In UK Sport World Class Performance Conference. Conference Presentation, Leeds, 26–28 November.

Naessens, G., Chandler, J. T., Kibler, B. W. & Driessens, M. 2000. Clinical Usefulness of Nocturnal Urinary Noradrenaline Excretion Patterns in the Follow-Up of Training Processes in High-Level Soccer Players. *Journal of Strength & Conditioning Research*, 14, 125–131.

Newell, K. M. 1986. Constraints on the Development of Coordination. Motor Development in Children: Aspects of Coordination and Control, 34, 341–360.

Newton, R. U., Kraemer, W. J., Häkkinen, K., Humphries, B. J. & Murphy, A. J. 1996. Kinematics, Kinetics, and Muscle Activation during Explosive Upper Body Movements. *Journal of Applied Biomechanics*, 12, 31–43.

North, J. 2013. A critical realist approach to theorising coaching practice. In P. Potrac, W. D. Gilbert & J. Dennison (Eds.), *The Routledge Handbook of Sports Coaching* (pp. 133–144). London: Routledge.

Nuzzo, J. L., McBride, J. M., Cormie, P. & McCaulley, G. O. 2008. Relationship between Countermovement Jump Performance and Multijoint Isometric and Dynamic Tests of Strength. *Journal of Strength and Conditioning Research*, 22, 699–707.

O'Hara, J., Brightmore, A., Till, K., Mitchell, I., Cummings, S. & Cooke, C. 2013. Evaluation of

Movement and Physiological Demands of Rugby League Referees Using Global Positioning Systems Tracking. *International Journal of Sports Medicine*, 34, 825–831.

O'Hara, J. P., Jones, B. L., Tsakirides, C., Carroll, S., Cooke, C. B. & King, R. F. 2010. Hydration Status of Rugby League Players during Home Match Play throughout the 2008 Super League Season. *Applied Physiology Nutrition and Metabolism*, 35, 790–796.

O'Connor, D. 2012. Using Technology in Coaching – Is It only For the Elite? In O'Dea (Ed). *Current Issues and Controversies in School and Community Health, Sport and Physical Education*. New York, USA: Nova Science.

O'Connor, D. & Cotton, W. 2009. Community Junior Sport Coaching: Final Report, November 2009, (Pp. 7 - 97). Canberra, Australia: Australian Sports Commission.

Owens, D. J., Fraser, W. D. & Close, G. L. 2014. Vitamin D and the Athlete: Emerging Insights. *European Journal of Sports Science*, 1–12.

Palisin, T. & Stacy, J. J. 2005. Beta-Hydroxy-Beta-Methylbutyrate and Its Use in Athletics. *Current Sports Medicine Reports*, 4, 220–223.

Passos, P., Araújo, D., Davids, K. & Shuttleworth, R. 2008. Manipulating Constraints to Train Decision Making in Rugby Union. *International Journal of Sports Science and Coaching*, 3, 125–140.

Paulsen, G., Cumming, K. T., Holden, G., Hallen, J., Ronnestad, B. R., Sveen, O., Skaug, A., Paur, I., Bastani, N. E., Ostgaard, H. N., Buer, C., Midttun, M., Freuchen, F., Wiig, H., Ulseth, E. T., Garthe, I., Blomhoff, R., Benestad, H. B. & Raastad, T. 2014. Vitamin C and E Supplementation Hampers Cellular Adaptation to Endurance Training in Humans: A Double-Blind, Randomised, Controlled Trial. *Journal of Physiology*, 592, 1887–901.

Pavely, S., Adams, R. D., Di Francesco, T., Larkham, S. & Maher, C. G. 2009. Execution and Outcome Differences between Passes to the Left and Right Made By First-Grade Rugby Union Players. *Physical Therapy in Sport*, 10, 136–141.

Pennings, B., Boirie, Y., Senden, J. M., Gijsen, A. P., Kuipers, H. & Van Loon, L. J. 2011. Whey Protein Stimulates Postprandial Muscle Protein Accretion More Effectively than do Casein and Casein Hydrolysate in Older Men. *American Journal Clinical Nutrition*, 93, 997–1005.

Peterson, M. D., Rhea, M. R. & Alvar, B. A. 2004. Maximizing Strength Development in Athletes: A Meta-Analysis to Determine the Dose-Response Relationship. *Journal of Strength and Conditioning Research*, 18, 377–382.

Peterson, M. D., Rhea, M. R. & Alvar, B. A. 2005. Applications of the Dose-Response for Muscular Strength Development: A Review of Meta-Analytic Efficacy and Reliability for Designing Training Prescription. *Journal of Strength and Conditioning Research*, 19, 950–958.

Phillips, D. C. 1995. The good, the bad, and the ugly: The many faces of constructivism. *Educational Researcher*, 24, 5–12.

Phillips, S. M. 2004. Protein Requirements and Supplementation in Strength Sports. *Nutrition*, 20, 689–695.

Phillips, S. M. 2012. Dietary Protein Requirements and Adaptive Advantages in Athletes. *British Journal of Nutrition*, 108, S158–167.

Phillips, S. M., Tang, J. E. & Moore, D. R. 2009. The Role of Milk- and Soy-Based Protein in Support of Muscle Protein Synthesis and Muscle Protein Accretion in Young and Elderly Persons. *Journal American College of Nutrition*, 28, 343–354.

Phillips, S. M., Tipton, K. D., Aarsland, A., Wolf, S. E. & Wolfe, R. R. 1997. Mixed Muscle Protein Synthesis and Breakdown after Resistance Exercise in Humans. *American Journal of Physiology*, 273, E99–107.

Pienaar, A. E., Spamer, M. J. & Steyn Jr, H. S. 1998. Identifying and Developing Rugby Talent among 10-Year-Old Boys: A Practical Model. *Journal of Sports Sciences*, 16, 691–699.

Pienaar, C. & Coetzee, B. 2013. Changes in Selected Physical, Motor Performance and Anthropometric Components of University-Level Rugby Players After one Microcycle of a Combined Rugby Conditioning and Plyometric Training Program. *Journal of Strength & Conditioning Research*, 27, 398–415.

Pill, S. 2014. Informing Game Sense Pedagogy with Constraints Led theory For Coaching in Australian Football. *Sports Coaching Review*, 1–17.

Pinder, R. A., Davids, K. W., Renshaw, I. & Araújo, D. 2011. Representative Learning Design and Functionality of Research and Practice in Sport. *Journal of Sport and Exercise Psychology*, 33, 146–155.

Pizzera, A. & Raab, M. 2012. Perceptual Judgments of Sports officials are influenced by their Motor and Visual Experience. *Journal of Applied Sport Psychology*, 24, 59–72.

Pointon, M. & Duffield, R. 2012. Cold Water Immersion Recovery after Simulated Collision Sport Exercise. *Medicine and Science in Sports and Exercise*, 44, 206–216.

Polman, R., Walsh, D., Bloomfield, J. & Nesti, M. 2004. Effective Conditioning of Female Soccer Players. *Journal of Sports Sciences*, 22, 191–203.

Potach, D. H. & Chu, D. A. 2008. Plyometric Training. In: Baechle, T. R. & Earl, J. (Eds.) *Essentials of Strength Training and Conditioning*. 3rd Ed.: Human Kinetics.

Proske, U. & Morgan, D. 2001. Muscle Damage from Eccentric Exercise: Mechanism, Mechanical Signs, Adaptation and Clinical Applications. *The Journal of Physiology*, 537, 333–345.

Pyne, D. B., Spencer, M. & Mujika, I. 2014. Improving the Value of Fitness Testing For Football. *International Journal of Sports Physiology and Performance*, 9, 511–514.

Quarrie, K., Handcock, P., Toomey, M. & Waller, A. E. 1996. The New Zealand Rugby Injury and Performance Project. Iv. Anthropometric and Physical Performance Comparisons between Positional Categories of Senior A Rugby Players. *British Journal of Sports Medicine*, 30, 53–56.

Rains, T. M., Agarwal, S. & Maki, K. C. 2011. Antiobesity Effects of Green Tea Catechins: A Mechanistic Review. *Journal of Nutrition and Biochemistry*, 22, 1–7.

Rampinini, E., Coutts, A., Castagna, C., Sassi, R. & Impellizzeri, F. 2007a. Variation in Top Level Soccer Match Performance. *International Journal of Sports Medicine*, 1018–24.

Rampinini, E., Impellizzeri, F. M., Castagna, C., Abt, G., Chamari, K., Sassi, A. & Marcora, S. M. 2007b. Factors Influencing Physiological Responses To Small-Sided Soccer Games. *Journal of Sports Sciences*, 25, 659–666.

Reilly, T., Williams, A. M., Nevill, A. & Franks, A. 2000. A Multidisciplinary Approach to Talent Identification in Soccer. *Journal of Sports Sciences*, 18, 695–702.

Renshaw, I., Davids, K., Shuttleworth, R. and Chow, J. 2009. Insights from Ecological Psychology and Dynamical Systems Theory can Underpin a Philosophy of Coaching. *International Journal of Sport Psychology*, 40, 540–602.

Res, P. T., Groen, B., Pennings, B., Beelen, M., Wallis, G. A., Gijsen, A. P., Senden, J. M. & Lj, V. A. N. L. 2012. Protein Ingestion Before Sleep Improves Post Exercise Overnight Recovery. *Medicine and Science in Sports Exercise*, 44, 1560–1569.

Richards, P., Mascarenhas, D. R. & Collins, D. 2009. Implementing Reflective Practice Approaches with Elite Team Athletes: Parameters of Success. *Reflective Practice*, 10, 353–363.

Roberts, S. P., Trewartha, G., Higgitt, R. J., El-Abd, J. & Stokes, K. A. 2008. The Physical Demands of Elite English Rugby Union. *Journal of Sports Sciences*, 26, 825–833.

Robertson, S. J., Burnett, A. F. & Cochrane, J. 2014. Tests Examining Skill Outcomes in Sport: A Systematic Review of Measurement Properties and Feasibility. *Sports Medicine*, 44, 501–518.

Robson-Ansley, P. J., Gleeson, M. & Ansley, L. 2009. Fatigue Management in the Preparation of Olympic Athletes. *Journal of Sports Sciences*, 27, 1409–1420.

Rowsell, G. J., Coutts, A. J., Reaburn, P. & Hill-Haas, S. 2009. Effects of Cold-Water Immersion on Physical Performance between Successive Matches in High-Performance Junior Male Soccer Players. *Journal of Sports Sciences*, 27, 565–573.

RFL. 2013a. Primary Rugby League Review. Leeds: RFL.

RFL. 2013b. RFL Retention and Acquisition Report. Leeds: RFL. .

Rushall, B. S. 1990. A Tool for Measuring Stress Tolerance in Elite Athletes. *Journal of Applied Sport Psychology*, 2, 51–66.

Sale, C., Saunders, B. & Harris, R. C. 2010. Effect of Beta-Alanine Supplementation on Muscle Carnosine Concentrations and Exercise Performance. *Amino Acids*, 39, 321–33.

Sale, C., Saunders, B., Hudson, S., Wise, J. A., Harris, R. C. & Sunderland, C. D. 2011. Effect of Beta-Alanine plus Sodium Bicarbonate on High-intensity Cycling Capacity. *Medicine and Science in Sports Exercise*, 43, 1972–1978.

Salvador, A., Suay, F., Gonzalez-Bono, E. & Serrano, M. 2003. Anticipatory Cortisol, Testosterone and Psychological Responses to Judo Competition in Young Men. *Psychoneuroendocrinology*, 28, 364–375.

Schoeller, D. A., Watras, A. C. & Whigham, L. D. 2009. A Meta-Analysis of the Effects of Conjugated Linoleic Acid on Fat-Free Mass in Humans. *Applied Physiology Nutrition and Metabolism*, 34, 975–8.

Schön, D. A. 1983. *The Reflective Practitioner: how professionals think in action* London: Temple Smith.

Schweizer, G., Plessner, H., Kahlert, D. & Brand, R. 2011. A Video-Based Training Method for Improving Soccer Referees' Intuitive Decision-Making Skills. *Journal of Applied Sport Psychology*, 23, 429–442.

Seifried, C. 2005. Using Videotaped Athletic Contests Within Mosston's Teaching Methods. *Journal of Physical Education, Recreation & Dance*, 76, 36–38.

Seitz, L. B., Reyes, A., Tran, T. T., De Villarreal, E. S. & Haff, G. G. 2014a. Increases in Lower-Body Strength Transfer Positively To Sprint Performance: A Systematic Review with Meta-Analysis. *Sports Medicine*, Epub.

Seitz, L. B., Riviere, M., Saez De Villarreal, E. & Haff, G. G. 2014b. The Athletic Performance of Elite Rugby League Players is Improved After an 8–Week Small-Sided Game Training Intervention. *Journal of Strength & Conditioning Research*, 28, 971–975.

Sekulic, D., Spasic, M., Mirkov, D., Cavar, M. & Sattler, T. 2013. Gender-Specific Influences of Balance, Speed, and Power on Agility Performance. *Journal of Strength & Conditioning Research*, 27, 802–11.

Serpell, B. G., Ford, M. & Young, W. B. 2010. The Development of a New Test of Agility for Rugby League. *Journal of Strength & Conditioning Research*, 24, 3270–3277.

Serpell, B. G., Young, W. B. & Ford, M. 2011. Are the Perceptual and Decision-Making Components of Agility Trainable? A Preliminary Investigation. *Journal of Strength & Conditioning Research*, 25, 1240–1248.

Sheppard, J. & Young, W. 2006. Agility Literature Review: Classifications, Training and Testing. *Journal of Sports Sciences*, 24, 919–932.

# REFERENCES

Shing, C. M., Hunter, D. C. & Stevenson, L. M. 2009. Bovine Colostrum Supplementation and Exercise Performance: Potential Mechanisms. *Sports Medicine*, 39, 1033–54.

Shoemaker, J., Tiidus, P. & Mader, R. 1997. Failure of Manual Massage to Alter Limb Blood Flow and Long-Term Post-Exercise Recovery. *Medicine and Science in Sports and Exercise*, 29, 610–614.

Simopoulos, A. P. 2002. The Importance of the Ratio of Omega-6/Omega-3 Essential Fatty Acids. *Biomedicine and Pharmacotherapy*, 56, 365–79.

Skein, M., Duffield, R., Minett, G. M., Snape, A. & Murphy, A. 2013. The Effect of Overnight Sleep Deprivation after Competitive Rugby League Matches on Post Match Physiological and Perceptual Recovery. *International Journal of Sports Physiology and Performance*, 8, 556–564.

Slater, G., Jenkins, D., Logan, P., Lee, H., Vukovich, M., Rathmacher, J. A. & Hahn, A. G. 2001. Beta-Hydroxy-Beta-Methylbutyrate (HMB) Supplementation Does Not Affect Changes in Strength Or Body Composition During Resistance Training in Trained Men. *International Journal of Sports Nutrition and Exercise Metabolism*, 11, 384–396.

Slater, G. J. & Jenkins, D. 2000. Beta-Hydroxy-Beta-Methylbutyrate (HMB) Supplementation and the Promotion of Muscle Growth and Strength. *Sports Medicine*, 30, 105–116.

Smart, D. J., Hopkins, W. G. & Gill, N. D. 2013. Differences and Changes in the Physical Characteristics of Professional and Amateur Rugby Union Players. *Journal of Strength & Conditioning Research*, 27, 3033–3044.

Spamer, E. J. 2009. Talent Identification and Development in Youth Rugby Players: A Research Review. *South African Journal for Research in Sport, Physical Education and Recreation*, 31, 109–118.

Starkes, J. L. 1987. Skill in Field Hockey: the Nature of the Cognitive Advantage. *Journal of Sport Psychology*, 9, 146–160.

Stone, M. H. 1993. Explosive Exercise and Training. *National Strength and Conditioning Association Journal* 15, 7–15.

Stone, M. H., O'Bryant, H. S., McCoy, L., Coglianese, R., Lehmkuhl, M. & Schilling, B. 2003a. Power and Maximum Strength Relationships during Performance of Dynamic and Static Weighted Jumps. *Journal of Strength & Conditioning Research*, 17, 140–147.

Stone, M. H., Sanborn, K. I. M., O'Bryant, H. S., Hartman, M., Stone, M. E., Proulx, C., Ward, B. & Hruby, J. O. E. 2003b. Maximum Strength-Power-Performance Relationships in Collegiate Throwers. *Journal of Strength & Conditioning Research*, 17, 739–745.

Suarez-Arrones, L., Calvo-Lluch, Á., Portillo, J., Sánchez, F. & Mendez-Villanueva, A. 2013. Running Demands and Heart Rate Response in Rugby Sevens Referees. *Journal of Strength & Conditioning Research*, 27, 1618–1622.

Suchomel, T. J., Wright, G. A., Kernozek, T. W. & Kline, D. E. 2014. Kinetic Comparison of the Power Development between Power Clean Variations. *Journal of Strength & Conditioning Research*, 28, 350–360.

Suzuki, M., Umeda, T., Nakaji, S., Shimoyama, T., Mashiko, T. & Sugawara, K. 2004. Effect of Incorporating Low intensity Exercise into the Recovery Period after a Rugby Match. *British Journal of Sports Medicine*, 38, 436–440.

Swinton, P. A., Lloyd, R., Keogh, J. W. L., Agouris, I. & Stewart, A. D. 2014. Regression Models of Sprint, Vertical Jump and Change of Direction Performance. *Journal of Strength & Conditioning Research*, 28, 1839–1849.

Swinton, P. A., Stewart, A., Agouris, I., Keogh, J. W. L. & Lloyd, R. 2011a. A Biomechanical Analysis of Straight and Hexagonal Barbell Deadlifts Using Submaximal Loads. *Journal of Strength & Conditioning Research*, 25, 2000–2009.

Swinton, P. A., Stewart, A. D., Keogh, J. W. L., Agouris, I. & Lloyd, R. 2011b. Kinematic and Kinetic Analysis of Maximal Velocity Deadlifts Performed With and Without the Inclusion of Chain Resistance. *Journal of Strength & Conditioning Research*, 25, 3163–3174.

Tang, J. E., Moore, D. R., Kujbida, G. W., Tarnopolsky, M. A. & Phillips, S. M. 2009. Ingestion of Whey Hydrolysate, Casein, or Soy Protein Isolate: Effects on Mixed Muscle Protein Synthesis at Rest and Following Resistance Exercise in Young Men. *Journal of Applied Physiology*, 107, 987–992.

Tarnopolsky, M. & Cupido, C. 2000. Caffeine Potentiates Low Frequency Skeletal Muscle Force in Habitual and Nonhabitual Caffeine Consumers. *Journal of Applied Physiology*, 89, 1719–1724.

Tarnopolsky, M. A. 2008. Effect of Caffeine on the Neuromuscular System-Potential as an Ergogenic Aid. *Applied Physiology Nutrition and Metabolism*, 33, 1284–1289.

Tarnopolsky, M. A. 2010. Caffeine and Creatine Use in Sport. *Annals of Nutrition and Metabolism*, 57 S2, 1–8.

Terpstra, A. H. 2004. Effect of Conjugated Linoleic Acid on Body Composition and Plasma Lipids in Humans: An Overview of the Literature. *American Journal of Clinical Nutrition*, 79, 352–361.

Thompson, N. 2000. *Theory and Practice in the Human Services*, Buckingham, Open University Press.

The Australian Rugby League: Laws of the Game and Notes on the Laws. (2011) Available: Www. Australianrugbyleague.Com.Au/Files/Arl%20international%20laws%20of%20the%20game%202010. Pdf Last Accessed on 8th Feb 2011

Till, K., Cobley, S., O'Hara, J., Cooke, C. & Chapman, C. 2014a. Considering Maturation Status and Relative Age in the Longitudinal Evaluation of Junior Rugby League Players. *Scandinavian Journal of Medicine & Science in Sports*, 24, 569–576.

Till, K., Cobley, S., O'Hara, J., Brightmore, A., Cooke, C. & Chapman, C. 2011. Using Anthropometric and Performance Characteristics to Predict Selection in Junior UK Rugby League Players. *Journal of Science and Medicine in Sport*, 14, 264–269.

Till, K., Cobley, S., O'Hara, J., Chapman, C. & Cooke, C. 2010a. Anthropometric, Physiological and Selection Characteristics in High Performance UK Junior Rugby League Players. *Talent Development and Excellence*, 2, 193–207.

Till, K., Cobley, S., O'Hara, J., Chapman, C. & Cooke, C. 2013. A Longitudinal Evaluation of Anthropometric and Fitness Characteristics in Junior Rugby League Players Considering Playing Position and Selection Level. *Journal of Science and Medicine in Sport*, 16, 438–443.

Till, K., Cobley, S., O'Hara, J., Morley, D., Chapman, C. & Cooke, C. 2014b. Retrospective Analysis of Anthropometric and Fitness Characteristics Associated With Long-Term Career Progression in Rugby League. *Journal of Science and Medicine in Sport*.

Till, K., Cobley, S., Wattie, N., O'Hara, J., Cooke, C. & Chapman, C. 2010b. The Prevalence, Influential Factors and Mechanisms of Relative Age Effects in UK Rugby League. *Scandinavian Journal of Medicine & Science in Sports*, 20, 320–329.

Till, K., Jones, B., Emmonds, S., Tester, E., Fahey, J. & Cooke, C. 2014c. Seasonal Changes in Anthropometric and Physical Characteristics Within English Academy Rugby League Players. *Journal of Strength and Conditioning Research*, 28, 2689–2696.

Till, K., Tester, E., Jones, B., Emmonds, S., Fahey, J. & Cooke, C. 2014d. Anthropometric and Physical Characteristics of English Academy Rugby League Players. *Journal of Strength & Conditioning Research*, 28, 319–327.

Tillin, N. A., Pain, M. T. G. & Folland, J. 2013. Explosive Force Production during Isometric Squats Correlates with Athletic Performance in Rugby Union Players. *Journal of Sports Sciences*, 31, 66–76.

Tobin, D. P. & Delahunt, E. 2014. The Acute Effect of a Plyometric Stimulus on Jump Performance in Professional Rugby Players. *Journal of Strength & Conditioning Research*, 28, 367–372.

Tomlin, D. L. & Wenger, H. A. 2001. The Relationship between Aerobic Fitness and Recovery from High Intensity Intermittent Exercise. *Sports Medicine*, 31, 1–11.

Tricoli, V., Lamas, L., Carnevale, R. & Ugrinowitsch, C. 2005. Short-Term Effects on Lower-Body Functional Power Development: Weightlifting vs. Vertical Jump Training Programs. *Journal of Strength & Conditioning Research*, 19, 433–437.

Twist, C. & Highton, J. 2013. Monitoring Fatigue and Recovery in Rugby League Players. *International Journal of Sports Physiology and Performance*, 8, 467–474.

Twist, C., Waldron, M., Highton, J., Burt, D. & Daniels, M. 2012. Neuromuscular, Biochemical and Perceptual Post-Match Fatigue in Professional Rugby League Forwards and Backs. *Journal of Sports Sciences*, 30, 359–367.

Usman, J., McIntosh, A. S., Quarrie, K. & Targett, S. 2014. Shoulder Injuries in Elite Rugby Union Football Matches: Epidemiology and Mechanisms. *Journal of Science and Medicine in Sport.* S1440–2440

Vaeyens, R., Lenoir, M., Williams, A. M. & Philippaerts, R. M. 2007. Mechanisms Underpinning Successful Decision Making in Skilled Youth Soccer Players: An Analysis of Visual Search Behaviours. *Journal of Motor Behaviour*, 39, 395–408.

Vaeyens, R., Lenoir, M., Williams, A. M. & Philippaerts, R. M. 2008. Talent Identification and Development Programmes in Sport. *Sports Medicine*, 38, 703–714.

Venables, M. C., Hulston, C. J., Cox, H. R. & Jeukendrup, A. E. 2008. Green Tea Extract Ingestion, Fat Oxidation, and Glucose Tolerance in Healthy Humans. *American Journal of Clinical Nutrition*, 87, 778–84.

Venter, R. E. 2014. Perceptions of Team Athletes on the Importance of Recovery Modalities. *European Journal of Sport Science*, 14, S69–S76.

Venter, R. E., Potgieter, J. R. & Barnard, J. G. 2010. The Use of Recovery Modalities by Elite South African Team Athletes. *South African Journal for Research in Sport, Physical Education and Recreation*, 32, 133–145.

Vickers, J. N., Reeves, M.-A., Chambers, K. L., & Martell, S. 2004. Decision training: Cognitive strategies for enhancing motor performance. In A. M. Williams & N. J. Hodges (Eds.), *Skill Acquisition in Sport: Research Theory & Practice* (pp. 103–120). London: Routledge.

Waldron, M., Highton, J., Daniels, M. & Twist, C. 2013. Preliminary Evidence of Transient Fatigue and Pacing During Interchanges in Rugby League. *International Journal of Sports Physiology and Performance*, 8, 157–64.

Waldron, M., Twist, C., Highton, J., Worsfold, P. & Daniels, M. 2011. Movement and Physiological Match Demands of Elite Rugby League Using Portable Global Positioning Systems. *Journal of Sports Sciences*, 29, 1223–1230.

Waldron, M., Worsfold, P., Twist, C. & Lamb, K. 2014a. The Reliability of Tests for Sport-Specific Skill amongst Elite Youth Rugby League Players. *European Journal of Sport Science*, 14, S471–S477.

# REFERENCES

Waldron, M., Worsfold, P. R., Twist, C. & Lamb, K. 2014b. The Relationship between Physical Abilities, Ball-Carrying and Tackling among Elite Youth Rugby League Players. *Journal of Sports Sciences*, 32, 542–549.

Walsh, M., Cartwright, L., Corish, C., Sugrue, S. & Wood-Martin, R. 2011. The Body Composition, Nutritional Knowledge, Attitudes, Behaviours, and Future Education Needs of Senior Schoolboy Rugby Players in Ireland. *International Journal of Sports Nutrition and Exercise Metabolism*, 21, 365–376.

Ward, P. & Williams, A. M. 2003. Perceptual and Cognitive Skill Development in Soccer: the Multidimensional Nature of Expert Performance. *Journal of Sport and Exercise Psychology*, 25, 93–111.

West, D. J., Finn, C. V., Cunningham, D. J., Shearer, D. A., Jones, M. R., Harrington, B. J., Crewther, B. T., Cook, C. J. & Kilduff, L. P. 2014. Neuromuscular Function, Hormonal, and Mood Responses to a Professional Rugby Union Match. *Journal of Strength & Conditioning Research*, 28, 194–200.

Westerterp-Plantenga, M. S. 2010. Green Tea Catechins, Caffeine and Body-Weight Regulation. *Physiology and Behaviour*, 100, 42–6.

Weston, M., Drust, B., Atkinson, G. & Gregson, W. 2011. Variability of Soccer Referees' Match Performances. *International Journal of Sports Medicine*, 32, 190–194.

Weston, M., Helsen, W., MacMahon, C. & Kirkendall, D. 2004. The Impact of Specific High-intensity Training Sessions on Football Referees' Fitness Levels. *The American Journal of Sports Medicine*, 32, 54s–61s.

Whaley, M. H., Brubaker, P. H., Otto, R. M. & Armstrong, L. E. 2006. ACSM's Guidelines for Exercise Testing and Prescription, Lippincott Williams & Wilkins.

Wheeler, K. W. & Sayers, M. G. 2011. Rugby Union Contact Skills Alter Evasive Agility Performance During Attacking Ball Carries. *International Journal of Sports Science and Coaching*, 6, 419–432.

White, G. E. & Wells, G. D. 2013. Cold-Water Immersion and Other Forms of Cryotherapy: Physiological Changes Potentially Affecting Recovery from High-intensity Exercise. *Extreme Physiology & Medicine*, 2, 26.

Williams, A. & Ford, P. 2013. Game Intelligence: Anticipation and Decision Making. Science and Soccer Iii. Routledge, London, 105–121.

Williams, A. M. 2000. Perceptual Skill in Soccer: Implications for Talent Identification and Development. *Journal of Sports Sciences*, 18, 737–750.

Williams, M. H. 1999. Facts and Fallacies of Purported Ergogenic Amino Acid Supplements. *Clinical Sports Medicine*, 18, 633–49.

Wilson, J. M. & Flanagan, E. P. 2008. The Role of Elastic Energy in Activities with High Force and Power Requirements: A Brief Review. *Journal of Strength & Conditioning Research*, 22, 1705–1715.

Wiltshire, E. V., Poitras, V., Pak, M., Hong, T., Rayner, J. & Tschakovsky, M. E. 2010. Massage Impairs Post exercise Muscle Blood Flow and Lactic Acid Removal. *Medicine and Science in Sports and Exercise*, 42, 1062–1071.

Wisloff, U., Castagna, C., Helgerud, J., Jones, R. & Hoff, J. 2004. Strong Correlation of Maximal Squat Strength with Sprint Performance and Vertical Jump Height in Elite Soccer Players. *British Journal of Sports Medicine*, 38, 285–288.

Young, W. B., Miller, I. & Talpey, S. 2015. Physical Qualities Predict Change-of-Direction Speed But Not Defensive Agility in Australian Rules Football. *Journal of Strength & Conditioning Research*, 206–212.

Zanchi, N. E., Gerlinger-Romero, F., Guimaraes-Ferreira, L., De Siqueira Filho, M. A., Felitti, V., Lira, F. S., Seelaender, M. & Lancha, A. H., Jr. 2011. HMB Supplementation: Clinical and Athletic Performance-Related Effects and Mechanisms of Action. *Amino Acids*, 40, 1015–25.

Zinn, C., Schofield, G. & Wall, C. 2006. Evaluation of Sports Nutrition Knowledge of New Zealand Premier Club Rugby Coaches. *International Journal of Sports Nutrition and Exercise Metabolism*, 16, 214–225.

# INDEX